Acknowledgments

Special thanks are due to Imogen Wilson in Shelter Publishing not only for her editing but also for her support, encouragement and understanding during the updating and rewriting of this book, especially during the times when I was ill. Her confidence that it would eventually see the light of day and meet its deadline was inspiring.

Many people have helped in providing information and in carrying out detailed checking of sections of the text. Particular thanks are due to Nik Antoniades, solicitor at Shelter for his thorough checking of the chapters relating to tenancies and for his patience in discussing some of the more thorny issues with me; to Deputy District Judge Russell Campbell, previously senior solicitor at Shelter, now Immigration Adjudicator, for allowing me to pick his brains on many different issues, especially those relating to Human Rights, as well as for checking the chapter on domestic violence; to Michael Parry, solicitor at Shelter, for updating the appendices of this book and also for his helpful checking; to Rachel Hadwen, Information Officer at Citizens Advice for her patience and thoroughness in checking and supplying detailed updated information on benefits and child support and in helping me to understand the key issues; to Joanne Harris of 2 Garden Court Chambers for checking issues relating to children and also for discussing matters with me; to Guy Skipwith of Citizens Advice Specialist Support Unit for allowing me to adapt his excellent article on the impact of the landmark case of *Royal Bank of Scotland v Etridge* on the concept of Undue Influence, and also for his input on the issue of bankruptcy and tenancies; to Tony Benjamin of Shelter for allowing me to adapt his article and useful table on the Children (Leaving Care) Act 2000; and to Frances Place and Clare Eley of Lyons Davidson, solicitors, for their input and advice on mediation as a form of alternative dispute resolution. Thanks for checking other parts of the book are due to Nancy Carlton of the University of West of England; John Gallagher, senior solicitor at Shelter; Debbie Gould of Shelter, Peter Madge of Citizens Advice Specialist Support Unit; Clare Rowsell of Albion Chambers, Bristol; and to Carol Store and Michael Parry, solicitors at Shelter. Thanks also to Sabina Bowler-Reid for putting me in contact with people who were able to help me, and to Joe Stone at Shelter for his help in checking references. Many thanks and much admiration also to Janine Roberts for the design and layout of the book, and for bearing with me in making my last minute amendments.

Special thanks are also due to Kathryn Harris who was largely responsible for the workable structure of the original edition which this one follows, as well as for researching, editing and organising the first edition. I have missed her collaboration on this edition but wish her well as a proud new mother, and in her new role within Shelter. In addition, I would like to reiterate thanks to all those who helped on the first edition which is still the main substance of this edition. Thanks are due to Anne Barlow, Kathy Barbour, Liz Barnes, Simon Baughen, Linda Cobb, Thangam Debbonaire, Ruth Frost, John Goodwin, Nigel Gosden, Nicola Harwyn, Grant Howell, Kim Joseph, Paul Kibbler, Stephen Lawson, Jan Luba, Derek McConnell, Jill Newton, Cath O'Donnell, Christine Parrish, John Smythe, Hilary Thorpe, Paul Todd, Angela Trouell and Zandra Pitt. Many thanks to everyone else who has helped me.

I should also like to give special thanks to my partner Michael Henderson and my friends who have supported and borne with me patiently over the last eighteen months.

Lesley Moroney – June 2003

Contents

RELATIONSHIP BREAKDOWN AND HOUSING

A PRACTICAL GUIDE

LESLEY MORONEY

Shelter

Published by Shelter, 88 Old Street, London EC1V 9HU.
020 7505 2000 www.shelter.org.uk/publications
Registered company number 1038133
Registered charity 263710

A Cataloguing in Publication Catalogue record for this
book is available from the British Library

ISBN 1-903595-10-x

Edited by Kat Harris and Imogen Wilson, Shelter
Design and layout by Janine Roberts, Shelter
Printed by Antony Rowe, Chippenham, Wiltshire
Distribution by Turnaround
Photography by Stephanie Hafner
Proofing by Linda Bennett, Goldleaf

Lesley Moroney is an independent housing trainer, consultant and writer with
over 20 years housing experience. In recent years she has run many training
courses on relationship breakdown and housing rights. She has been a
lecturer in housing at Bristol Polytechnic (now the University of West England)
and has also worked in both local authority and independent housing
organisations, including a Shelter Housing Aid Centre in the South West. She is
a regular contributor of articles on housing law to the Advisor magazine and
author of Homelessness: a good practice guide with John Goodwin. She lives
in Somerset and also teaches yoga.

Introduction

When I embarked upon the second edition of this book, it was with the expectation that this would be a relatively quick and easy update of the original handbook, which was published in 1997. However, I quickly became immersed in analysing the many new facets of this important area of law. In addition to new legislation, there have been significant developments in case law affecting a number of areas, with human rights issues permeating throughout. At the same time there is an increasing government emphasis on trying to reduce litigation when relationships break down, and advisers must now be aware of the need to consider mediation as a means of Alternative Dispute Resolution to settle family matters.

Legislation encompassed in this edition but not in the first includes:

- Human Fertilisation and Embryology Act 1990
- National Health Service and Community Care Act 1990
- Protection from Harassment Act 1997
- Crime and Disorder Act 1998
- Human Rights Act 1998
- Civil Procedure Rules 1998 (as amended)
- Access to Justice Act 1999
- Welfare Reform and Pensions Act 1999
- Children (Leaving Care) Act 2000
- Child Support, Pensions and Social Security Act 2000
- Homelessness Act 2002 and Priority Need Statutory Instrument
- Adoption and Children Act 2002
- Land Registration Act 2002
- Enterprise Act 2002

Changes of great significance for lesbian and gay couples are expected in the forthcoming Civil Partnership Bill, which promises to give similar rights to same sex couples as to married couples. On the housing tenure front, the Government has produced an Anti-Social Behaviour Bill, which could lead to 'demoting' of individual tenancies. The whole area of security of tenure is also currently under review with a view to wholesale reform of the complete system.

The Government has in addition, over the last five years, been active in producing in depth research, guidance and policies to help combat domestic violence. These are aimed at a wide range of organisations and bodies, including the police, the Crown Prosecution Service, the judiciary, as well as local authorities, social services departments, health professionals and education services. Just at the time of going to press the Government has also produced a consultation paper proposing the most radical changes to the law relating to domestic violence in thirty years. The proposals are designed to give those experiencing domestic violence greater confidence to come forward, and include anonymity for victims in court, a register of offenders convicted of domestic violence, criminal records for those who break non-molestation orders, and the provision of more safe houses and women's refuges. Although there will obviously be considerable debate before the proposals are firmed up, they are greatly to be welcomed.

Case law has clarified and changed certain interpretations of legislation. The House of Lords has given clear rulings on the effect of notices to quit on joint tenancies and the procedure for preventing them. At the time of writing decisions are awaited on the issues of whether there is justification for evicting a remaining partner after notice to quit has been served (*Harrow LBC v Qazi*) and confirmation of the decision in *Mendoza v Ghaidan* that discrimination against a gay partner in relation to succession rights was unlawful. Many other cases affecting matrimonial settlements, undue influence, homelessness, Children Act and community care legislation are also explored in this edition.

Aims of the book

The book is meant to be an accessible guide to the lay adviser who has to deal with the many aspects of relationship breakdown, as well as to the legal practitioner who may find it useful to have a number of issues covered in one volume. I hope it may also prove useful to housing students and both existing and potential housing officers. It does not purport to be definitive on all the areas of law it covers: I have tried to include the issues which I found myself most frequently having to deal with or explain. In summary, the book aims to:

- consider the process of giving housing advice when a relationship breaks down and to discuss important areas for good practice
- provide a clear summary of the relevant areas of the law which affect housing matters when a relationship breaks down
- highlight and explain important legal concepts and relevant case law
- give practical guidance where appropriate on steps to take to best protect a client's interests in property
- provide guidance on further reading for those dealing in more depth with specific issues, eg, bankruptcy or benefits.

Structure of the book

The chapters in the book are grouped into 7 broad areas:
- Introduction (Chapters 1-2)

- Owner-occupiers (Chapters 3-5)
- Tenants (Chapters 6-8)
- Rights of people with children (Chapters 9-10)
- Financial (Chapters 11-12)
- Emergency responses (Chapters 13-15)
- Good practice (Chapter 16)

Chapter 1: Advising on relationship breakdown
Chapter 2: The law on relationship breakdown

These are two introductory chapters: the first looks at the process of giving advice on relationship breakdown and housing and the second gives an overview of the different areas of legislation which may be relevant to housing problems. New in this edition is an overview of the implications of Human Rights legislation and a discussion of mediation as a form of Alternative Dispute Resolution. The chapter gives a general outline of which areas of legislation are applicable to which groups of people, eg, married owner-occupiers, cohabiting tenants etc.

Chapter 3: Property law
Chapter 4: Married owner-occupiers
Chapter 5: Cohabiting owner-occupiers

These chapters look at short and long-term rights to occupy owner-occupied property when a relationship breaks down. Chapter 3 gives an outline of the principles involved in property law and chapters 4 and 5 look at the legal position of married and cohabiting owners respectively, whether sole or joint owners, including the changes due to be brought in by the Land Registration Act 2002. Chapter 4 concentrates on matrimonial law and includes information on financial and pension arrangements. Chapter 5 focuses on property law, including a discussion on prospective legislation affecting lesbian and gay couples. It also examines the radical impact of the House of Lords judgment in *Royal Bank of Scotland plc v Etridge* on the concept of undue influence in transactions.

Chapter 6: Housing law
Chapter 7: Married tenants
Chapter 8: Cohabiting tenants

These chapters are a parallel to Chapters 3 – 5 looking at the short and long-term rights to occupy tenanted property and the options for settling tenancy issues when a relationship breaks down. Because the type of tenancy status affects the options available, Chapter 6 takes an overall look at different types of tenancies briefly explaining what they are and how to recognise them. It also covers the general principles of assignment and notices to quit. Chapters 7 and 8 deal in greater depth with tenancy issues relating to married and cohabiting tenants respectively, whether sole or joint tenants, in particular the effects of a tenant serving notice to quit or leaving.

New in these chapters is an outline of the Law Commission proposals to reform the system of security of tenure, and to introduce 'demoted tenancies' in certain cases of anti-social behaviour. It also brings the reader up to date on case law developments relating to rights to succeed and assign between lesbian and gay couples, service and prevention of notice to quit, and deeds of release.

Chapter 9: Children Act and property transfers
Chapter 10: Financial provision for children

These chapters cover legislation which particularly affects couples with children regardless of their matrimonial status. Chapter 9 examines the basic concepts covered by the Children Act 1989 and the powers it gives to the courts to transfer property for the benefit of children. This edition looks in greater depth at social services duties to provide services for families with children in need under the Children Act, at the Children (Leaving Care) Act 2000 provisions, and amendments made by the Adoption and Children Act 2002. It also looks at the meaning of parenthood under the Human Fertilisation and Embryology Act 1990. Chapter 10 looks at the role and powers of the Child Support Agency to order maintenance for children and situations where the courts' still have powers to order financial provision. The changes under the Child Support, Pensions and Social Security Act 2000 are explained in outline. The impact of the Child Support Act upon property and lump sum settlements is also considered.

Chapter 11: Mortgages, rents and benefits
Chapter 12: Insolvency and bankruptcy

These chapters concentrate on financial problems which may arise when a relationship has broken down. Chapter 11 focuses on rights and liabilities in respect of mortgage and rent payments, claiming benefits, dealing with arrears and negotiating with lenders over taking over mortgages. It clarifies the position on payments of benefits on two homes in cases of relationship breakdown or domestic violence. It also looks at the problem of negative equity. Chapter 12 gives a basic introduction to personal insolvency and bankruptcy and looks at the effects of bankruptcy on the non-bankrupt's share in the home and on any settlements made prior to bankruptcy. It also looks at how bankruptcy affects tenancies. It explains the changes being made to bankruptcy proceedings by the Enterprise Act 2002.

Chapter 13: Domestic violence
Chapter 14: The legal framework of homelessness and allocations
Chapter 15: Homelessness and relationship breakdown

These chapters deal with the emergency situations which occur in relationship breakdown cases where one partner may need to take action to protect her/himself from domestic violence or to find immediate housing. They deal the legislation relating to domestic violence and homelessness. Chapter 13 looks at both legal and non-legal responses to domestic violence but considers both criminal and civil remedies available to those experiencing domestic violence, in particular the Family Law Act 1996 and the Protection from Harassment Act 1997. New in this edition, it gives information on what powers the police have to arrest, and what to expect in court. It discusses case law on child contact and occupation orders. Chapter 14 looks at the framework of the homelessness legislation as amended by the Homelessness Act 2002, and local authorities' duties towards people who are homeless or threatened with homelessness and also summarises the main duties of local authorities under the new allocations legislation. It looks at ways that local authority decisions can be challenged and explains the principles by which they must act. It also gives information about the duties of social services departments which are of particular relevance to those from abroad and those who may be intentionally homeless. Chapter 15 examines the specific issues relevant to relationship breakdown and appropriate homelessness case law.

Chapter 16: Good practice

This chapter provides a discussion of the need for good practice guidelines on dealing with relationship breakdown for both voluntary organisations and housing providers. It looks at issues relevant to both types of agencies such as principles of good advice-giving, interviewing skills, awareness issues and developing an appropriate response. It examines government guidelines, policy and research on domestic violence and issues essential to developing a good practice response to domestic violence. It also looks at issues relating to housing management specifically relevant to housing providers such as rehousing prior to court action, use of notice to quit 'McGrady' procedure, policies for lesbian and gay couples, requirements for legal action, equal opportunities issues and liaison with other agencies.

Appendices

The appendices cover a summary of court procedures, hints on using case law when negotiating on homelessness and tactics in dealing with payment problems.

Lesley Moroney, May 2003

List of cases

*This is a list of all the cases mentioned in the text and refers to the paragraph
number in which a particular case can be found. For those cases only mentioned
in footnotes and not specifically in the text the paragraph number and
footnote are given, eg, 4.31n30 is in the notes to chapter 4 paragraph 31 of
the text and the number of the footnote is 30. Cases are given with their legal
references, eg, RvLB Lambeth exp Vagliviello (1990) 22 HLR 392 CA means the
case of the applicant, a Mr Vagliviello who was challenging Lambeth Borough
Council. The case was reported in 1990 in the Housing Law Reports , volume
22 and is found on page 392. The case was heard in the Court of Appeal. A list
of abbreviations used in case law reports can be found on page 44.*

Abbreviations

Statute and Regulations

These abbreviations are used throughout this book in the margin notes

ACA 02	Adoption and Children Act 2002
ACOG 02	Allocations Code of Guidance for Local Authorities 2002
CA 89	Children Act 1989
CDA 98	Crime and Disorder Act 1998
CJA 88	Criminal Justice Act 1988
CJPOA 94	Criminal Justice And Public Order Act 1994
C(LC)A 00	Children (Leaving Care) Act 2000
CLSA 90	Courts and Legal Services Act 1990
COA 79	Charging Orders Act 1979
CSDPA 70	Chronically Sick and Disabled Persons Act 1970
CLA 77	Criminal Law Act 1977
CPR	Civil Procedure Rules
CSA 91	Child Support Act 1991
CSA 93	Child Support Act 1993
CSPSSA 00	Child Support Pensions and Social Security Act 2000
DPA 98	Data Protection Act 1998
EA 02	Enterprise Act 2002
FA 88	Finance Act 1988
FLA 96	Family Law Act 1996
FLRA 87	Family Law Reform Act 1987
HA 85	Housing Act 1985
HA 88	Housing Act 1988
HA 96	Housing Act 1996 (as amended by Homelessness Act 2002)
HA 02	Homelessness Act 2002
HB Regs	Housing Benefit (General) Regulations 1987-SI 1987 No. 1971
HB & CTB Regs	Housing Benefit and Council Tax Benefit (General) Amendment Regulations 1997 SI 852
HCOG 02	Homelessness Code of Guidance for Local Authorities (England) 2002
HFE 90	Human Fertilisation and Embryology Act 1990
HOC	Home Office Circular
IA 86	Insolvency Act 1986
I & AA 99	Immigration and Asylum Act 1999
IS Regs	Income Support (General) Regulations 1987 SI 1987 No. 1967 as amended by Schedule 1 of the Social Security (Income Support and Claims and Payments) Amendment Regulations 1995
IS(AT) Regs 95	Income Support (General) Amendment and Transitional Regulations 1995 SI 1995 No. 2287
JSA Regs	Jobseekers Allowance Regulations 1996 SI 1996 No. 207
LCA 72	Land Charges Act 1972
LGA 72	Local Government Act 1972
LGA 00	Local Government Act 2000
LPA 25	Law of Property Act 1925
LRA 25	Land Registration Act 1925
LRA 86	Land Registration Act 1986

LRA 00	Land Registration Act 2000
LTA 25	Landlord and Tenant Act 1925
LTA 27	Landlord and Tenant Act 1927
LTA(C) A95	Landlord and Tenant (Covenants) Act 1995
MCA 73	Matrimonial Causes Act 1973
MFPA 84	Matrimonial and Family Proceedings Act 1984
MWPA 1882	Married Woman's Property Act 1882
NAA 48	National Assistance Act 1948
NHSCCA 90	National Health Service and Community Care Act 1990
NIAA 02	Nationality Immigration and Asylum Act 1990
OAPA 1861	Offences Against the Person Act 1861
PACE 84	Police and Criminal Evidence Act 1984
PEA 77	Protection from Eviction Act 1977
PFHA 97	Protection from Harassment Act 1997
POA 86	Public Order Act 1986
RA 77	Rent Act 1977
SCA 81	Supreme Courts Act 1981
SI	Statutory Instrument
SOA 56	Sexual Offences Act 1956
SSAA 92	Social Security Administration Act 1992
SSCBA 92	Social Security Contributions and Benefits Act 1992
SS(C&P) Regs	Social Security (Claims and Payments) Regulations
TLATA 96	Trusts of Land and Appointment of Trustees Act 1996
WA 1837	Wills Act 1837

Case law abbreviations

A & E	Adolphus & Ellis
AC	Appeal Court
All ER	All England Law Reports
CA	Court of Appeal
Ch	Chancery
ChD	Chancery Division
Cox Eq Cas	Cox's Equity Cases
EGD	Estates Gazette Directory
EGCS	Estates Gazette Case Summaries
EWCA	England and Wales Court of Appeal (neutral citation)
EWHC	England and Wales High Court (neutral citation)
Fam	Family
Fam Law	Family Law
FCR	Family Court Reports
FLR	Family Law Reports
HL	House of Lords
HLR	Housing Law Reports
KB	King's Bench
LAG	Legal Action Group
NLJ	New Law Journal
Omb	Ombudsman report
P & CR	Property and Compensation Reports
QB	Queen's Bench
SLT	Scottish Law Times
WLR	Weekly Law Reports

Glossary

This gives very brief definitions of terms which recur throughout the book and which the reader may come across in everyday work. Where specific terms are explained in some detail in the appropriate part of the text they are not repeated in the glossary, eg, the terminology for different types of tenancies is explained in chapter 6 (Housing law) rather than in the glossary. These terms can be found by referring to the index. Words in italic are defined elsewhere.

Affidavit	A sworn statement used as evidence in court proceedings.
Ancillary relief	In family law, this usually means a financial or property settlement applied for in conjunction with an application for divorce, *nullity* or *judicial separation*.
Ancillary remedy	A remedy such as an injunction which can only be applied for where other proceedings, eg, an action in tort, is being taken.
Assignment	The legal way to pass on a tenancy to another person.
Beneficial interest	An interest in land which gives a person a right to a financial share in the property. It does not come from legal ownership but is based on an agreement (or trust) between the legal owner and others.
Caution	An entry on the land register, eg, registering a beneficial interest.
Charge	A binding right formally registered against a property which any subsequent buyers or lenders must honour.
Charging order	A court order granted to a creditor securing the debt as a charge against the debtor's home.
Child of the family	Either a biological child of both parties or a child who has been treated by both parties as a child of their family (other than one who has been fostered out by a local authority or voluntary organisation). The parties must be married.
Class F charge	The registration of matrimonial home rights in respect of unregistered land.
Common Law	Unwritten judge-made law developed over many years by precedent. The ancient law of the land, not determined by statute.

Constructive notice — Where it can be held that a buyer or lender should have discovered the existence of a beneficial interest in a property if they had made proper investigations, they are held to have 'constructive notice' of that interest regardless of whether anything was written down.

Contract — A legally enforceable agreement between two or more people intending to create a legal relationship, whereby both have promised to give something of value (usually referred to as a 'consideration') as recompense for whatever benefit they are to receive.

Co-owners — Two or more people who are joint legal owners of a property.

Covenant — An implied or express contractual condition placed upon the way land or property can be used.

Decree absolute — The final decree of divorce which ends a marriage.

Decree nisi — The preliminary court order in dissolving a marriage, six weeks after which a *decree absolute* can be granted.

Estate — An estate is an *interest in land* for some particular period of time.

Estoppel — The doctrine that if one person acts to her/his detriment on another's promise or misleading behaviour, the person making the promise or behaving misleadingly is bound to honour the implicit or actual promise or action which was relied upon.

Equitable interest — An interest in land, which cannot automatically be enforced as of legal right, but which the court has discretion to recognise. Initially it may not be recorded on paper but it can be protected.

Equitable rights — As for equitable interests rights, which may not exist on paper and which are not automatically enforceable, but which may be recognised at common law, based on the principles of equity.

Equity — A body of rules which supplement the rules of common law in the interests of achieving greater justice. Where the rules of law and equity conflict, equity prevails, providing the person seeking justice has also acted fairly.

Freehold	The holding of an interest in land indefinitely (ie, until disposed of by sale or otherwise), with no-one having a superior interest.
Interest in land	An interest in land is a legally binding right which attaches to the land and automatically passes to anyone who buys or inherits it, eg, a right of way or a financial interest. It can therefore be sold, assigned or transferred.
Injunction	A court order which prohibits someone from doing something or orders them to do something, eg, an occupation order is a type of injunction, which can order a person out of the matrimonial home.
Insolvency	A state where a person's liabilities exceed her/his assets. Usually highlighted by the inability to pay debts.
Interlocutory	A pronouncement or order during the course of a legal action, before a final decision is reached by the court.
Judicial separation	A decree which does not end the marriage but enables the court to make financial and property settlements. It removes the duty of one spouse to live with another and means that if either party dies without leaving a will, the other will not inherit her/his spouse's estate.
Licence	A permission to occupy without having a tenancy or ownership.
Leasehold	Any interest in land lower than freehold (ie, a tenancy). In practice the word is generally applied to an estate for a fixed term of years where ground rent is paid to the freeholder. If no other arrangement is reached, the land reverts to the freeholder at the end of the period of the lease.
Long leaseholder	Someone with a lease which was originally for more than 21 years.
Maintenance	See periodic payments below.
Marriage	The legally recognised state of wedlock still defined in English law as 'the voluntary union for life of one man and one woman to the exclusion of all others' (*Hyde v Hyde* (1866)).
Mortgagee	The legal term for a mortgage lender.
Mortgagor	The legal term for a borrower.

Notice	An entry on the land register.
Nullity	A court order that declares a marriage was invalid from the beginning or is now invalid because, for example, it has never been consummated.
Overreaching	A procedure whereby a purchaser can buy land free of any third party interest, provided s/he pays the purchase price to two trustees.
Overriding interest	An *interest in land* which although not protected by registration gives a claimant the right to continue to occupy even where the property has been sold or is being repossessed for non-payment of a loan.
Periodic payments	Payments made at regular intervals, eg, weekly or monthly, to support the day-to-day living of a spouse and/or child. Often referred to simply as 'maintenance.'
Petitioner	The person who makes the application for a civil court action (eg, divorce) or an injunction.
Precedent	A previous case which establishes a legal principal, which must be followed in subsequent similar court cases.
Relief	Recompense in law; in matrimonial terms usually means an application to the court for property or financial settlements (see also *ancillary relief*).
Respondent	The person in civil court actions, eg, divorce, or an injunction, who is on the opposite side to the applicant (cf. *petitioner*).
Restriction	An entry on the land register.
Severance	The ending of an agreement to share the beneficial interest of a jointly-owned property.
Statutory	Something which exists by virtue of an Act of Parliament, eg, statutory rights, statutory tenancy, statutory duties.
Statutory charge	The charge made by the Legal Services Commission to recoup money from a person who has received public funding, out of finances or assets s/he has gained or held onto as a result of the legal help s/he has received.
Succession	The automatic transfer (or vesting) of a property to another person upon the death of the tenant.

Summary procedure	The power of the courts to give judgement or make an order immediately.
Surrender	The voluntary giving up of a tenancy in an unmistakable way, which is also quite unmistakably accepted by the landlord.
Survivorship	The right of surviving joint tenants to the whole tenancy upon the death of one of them.
Tied accommodation	Accommodation which is provided in connection with employment.
Title	The right to ownership of property or the facts or documents which are evidence of the right.
Tort	A civil wrong where someone does something to another person which it is considered in law that s/he should not do. An act which is an infringement or violation of the right of another person.
Trust	An arrangement whereby control over property is passed to someone (the trustee) on the understanding that's/he will deal with it in the agreed way. The trustee is then bound to act in accordance with the trust.
Undue influence	A defence whereby a person can argue that consent which s/he gave to a transaction should be set aside because of the unfair influence which the person extracting the consent had over her/him.
'Without notice' injunction	A without notice injunction is one granted after hearing one side only, ie, the person against whom the injunction is granted does not have to be present, or even served with the notice of the hearing.

1

Chapter 1: Advising on relationship breakdown

Subjects covered in this chapter include...

The advice process

Identifying what the client wants

Prioritising action and deciding tactics

Advice on relationship breakdown

Establishing the client's rights – some basic questions

Advising on possible outcomes

Sources of help or advice

Advising on relationship breakdown

Almost a quarter of a million couples separate every year.[1] This is based on a figure of heterosexual couples only, as no statistics are available for the number of lesbian or gay couples who separate. Research on heterosexual couples shows that, although many are likely to remarry or cohabit again, around a third form new separate households. Over 50,000 of these households seek housing from the public or private rented sector. Relationship breakdown is therefore generating a huge increase in demand for social and other housing and is a major factor in homelessness and housing problems.[2] In addition to solicitors, there are many different types of workers who are likely to find themselves being asked for advice on housing matters from people whose relationships have broken down. These include specialist housing advisers, social workers, counsellors, and agencies that provide support networks such as refuges, lesbian and gay centres, women's groups and groups working with asylum seekers, immigrants and ethnic minority groups.

Because of the volume of law and its apparent complexity, many workers may feel that the best course of action is to refer the client to a solicitor. This is not always the case:

- *The matrimonial solicitor, who deals regularly with divorce and associated matters, is not necessarily an expert in housing issues*

- *Whilst legal remedies may be available, many people do not wish to involve solicitors or even contemplate legal action*

- *If people are working, they may not be eligible for public funding from the legal services commission (formerly known as legal aid) or may only get partial assistance*

- *Cohabiting couples, whether lesbian, gay or heterosexual, who often have fewer rights on relationship breakdown, may consider a solicitor as an inappropriate and expensive source of advice.*

In addition, in the majority of cases an attempt at mediation will be necessary before the client can qualify for public assistance for legal help for divorce and other family matters. The client may also want legal advice prior to mediation. (see Chapter 2, Alternative dispute resolution, Section B, 2.7 – 2.11)

1. Housing Statistics Summary, Number 4, 2000, "The Effects of Divorce, Remarriage, Separation and the Formation of New Couple Households." DETR (now ODPM).

2. Housing Research Summary (No.91, 1998) DETR (now ODPM).

A   The advice process

1.1   Identifying the issues

Focusing on where to start is not always easy, but the adviser's role is to enable the client to decide which part of the problem s/he wants to work on first. A relationship breakdown may involve any or all of the following issues:

- *Financial needs* – claiming benefits and obtaining maintenance payments

- *Need for alternative accommodation* – short- and long-term

- *Children's needs* – disputes over where the child is to live and when the parents can see the child, child-minding, arrangements for change of school etc.

- *Family attitudes* – how far to involve other family members

- *Domestic violence or other abuse* – seeking support and/or legal remedies for the client and/or any children where there is, or has been, violence or mental cruelty in the home

- *Cultural and religious attitudes* – people within different cultures have widely differing views about roles within relationships (women who are beaten by their husbands may be held to be bringing shame upon their families for even complaining, especially if they involve outsiders – action to get out of a relationship may involve loss of a total family network)

- *Possible reconciliation with the partner* – need for counselling

- *Conciliation over practical issues* – seeking a mediation service

- *Legal proceedings* – against the partner, and possibly to resolve issues about the children

- *Establishing and protecting legal rights to the home*

- *Establishing the extent of the partner's liabilities and how they might affect the home.*

Whilst some of these issues, such as advising on family involvement and counselling on reconciliation, may not be directly within an adviser's brief (depending upon the service or agency concerned), it is important to help clients check whether this is what they want. This should always be done sensitively, to ensure clients do not feel that they ought to follow a certain course of action. Equally, an adviser should not rush people into taking practical steps that they may find difficult to revoke, if they have not yet fully made up their minds.

1.2   Identifying what the client wants

Identifying possible goals with clients may help them decide what they really want or need. Once the problems have been identified, advisers can help clients see the range of possible outcomes and assist them with clarifying priorities. For example, obtaining an injunction might or might not help where there has been domestic violence. A person may want to address how to become independent and find long-term accommodation, but finding a bed and breakfast or a women's refuge might be what a person needs immediately. Alternatively, although s/he may want to be out of the situation immediately, s/he may not, in fact, want the relationship to end.

Possible general goals for the sort of problems listed above could include:

• obtaining a regular income

• staying put

• finding temporary accommodation

• being rehoused

• resolving relationship problems

• protection against the partner

• separating from the partner

• remaining in the home without the partner.

This is not intended to be an exhaustive list, and there may be a number of other goals advisers could identify with the client.

It is important for advisers to realise that their clients may lack the confidence to go through with certain types of action. They may be suffering from low self-esteem as a result of their experiences. Advisers need to be sensitive to this. They should try to give clients the support and encouragement they need to follow the course of action which is most appropriate to their needs and preferences. Clients should not be pushed into following the course of action that the adviser prefers. Once the client has given an indication of the sort of outcome s/he is looking to achieve, then the adviser can start to prioritise actions with the client.

1.3   Identifying and prioritising courses of actions

It is impossible to address all the issues at once, so advisers need a systematic approach to help the client prioritise. A suggested approach could include the following:

- List the issues which need to be addressed

- Agree the issues which are the most important to the client in the short-term and in the long-term

- Consider the feasibility of achieving the desired outcome, eg, permanent rehousing may be the most desirable outcome, but is unlikely to be achieved in the short-term. It may therefore be necessary to discuss interim options, such as seeking a place in a refuge or other temporary accommodation, together with protecting legal interests in the home. The provision of advice to the client on her/his legal rights will almost certainly be necessary during this process.

1.4　Deciding tactics

- Agree with the client which issues should be tackled first

- Decide with the client who will do what. It may be appropriate to make investigations and/or act as an advocate on behalf of the client, but the client should be made aware of exactly what is being done for her/him. In relationship breakdown, it is very easy for a person to feel confused and disempowered. It is important the adviser does not add to this

- Give the client a copy of the list of problems you have identified together, marking down what has been agreed

- Make sure the client is clear about which aspects s/he is going to cover; write down appropriate names and addresses (if safe to do so) and make appointments if helpful

- If the client has asked for advice, but does not want the adviser directly involved, it is important to 'leave the door open' so that s/he will feel at ease about returning if further help is needed

- If appropriate, make another appointment to review progress or agree when further contact will be made. In certain situations, it is important to decide what form further contact should take, as a client may not want to be called or written to at home, for confidentiality, and possibly safety, reasons.

The above points may seem obvious, but it is often the case that the more experienced an adviser is, the easier it becomes to cut corners. Pressure in a busy office may make it seem more efficient to simply say to the client "I'll make some phone calls for you," or "The best thing for you to do is..." Whilst this may be acceptable in certain situations, it is rarely the right approach for relationship breakdown.

The important thing to bear in mind is that good advice-giving takes time, sensitivity and understanding.

B   Advice on relationship breakdown

It is not always easy to see how complex legal information relates to a practical problem. The adviser needs to know:

• what information is necessary

• how to interpret the information and apply it to the practical problem.

1.5   Establishing rights on relationship breakdown – basic questions

When dealing with relationship breakdown problems, there are certain fundamental questions that must be answered before any advice can be given. The questions listed below should help an adviser to get started with a relationship breakdown case, but they are not designed to be an exhaustive list. Many other related issues may arise, which advisers will need to pursue further, for example, those related to the client's financial position or their immigration status.

• *Is the person in a heterosexual or lesbian/gay relationship?*

A person may simply refer to 'my partner.' Not only is it insensitive to assume this must always mean a heterosexual partner, it is essential to clarify the nature of the relationship, since the rights of heterosexual and lesbian or gay couples vary significantly.

• *If it is a man and a woman, are the couple legally married, or have they been married to each other?*

It is easy to assume people are married; they may call themselves Mr and Mrs, even if they are unmarried. Equally, people who are married may refer to their husband or wife as their 'partner.' Since the rights of married and unmarried couples vary considerably, it is essential to be sure of marital status. In addition certain rights under the Family Law Act 1996 apply to former spouses.

• *Are they taking legal proceeding for divorce, judicial separation or nullity?*

The courts have specific powers to transfer finances and property in conjunction with divorce, judicial separation or nullity proceedings.

• *Have they shared a home with someone in the past as either a married or cohabiting couple?*

The Family Law Act 1996 gives rights to the ex-spouse and ex-cohabitant in some situations.

• *Are they owner-occupiers or tenants?*

If they are tenants, clarify exactly what type of tenancy it is, since rights vary depending on tenancy type. They may even be licensees, for example, having only permission to stay in someone else's home.

• *Are they joint owners, or joint tenants, or is ownership or the tenancy in one name only?*
This is crucial, especially in the case of cohabiting couples.

• *Are there children?*
Whilst some rights exist whether or not there are children, responsibility for children can be very relevant in terms of the courts' powers to transfer property.

• *If there are children, whose children are they?*
It is also important to know whether the children are the natural offspring of both parties, since this also affects certain rights.

1.6   Interpreting the information

The following chapters look at each of the main situations of occupiers and the area of law that is likely to be most relevant. With the answers to the questions above, the adviser should be able to use the reference sections to analyse the problem, find the relevant information and apply it.

Advising on possible outcomes

A person who seeks housing advice when a relationship breaks down may want to:

• remain in the home

• leave immediately

• be rehoused in the longer term.

Even if someone does not particularly want to remain, it may nevertheless be in her/his interests to protect any rights s/he may have in the home. In other cases, it may be vital to health and safety to leave. These issues are addressed in detail throughout this book.

The following are key pointers to steps which can be of crucial importance to the person seeking advice, and refer the reader to the appropriate sections of the book.

1.7   Remaining in the home

Where the person has expressed a wish to remain in the home, the following points may be relevant:

Tenancies

Four main situations arise which can threaten the existence of a tenancy and/or the client's right to remain in the home:

Heterosexual cohabiting or divorced couples where the tenancy is in one name only

If the tenant leaves, this can jeopardise the status or existence of the tenancy, eg, a secure tenancy is no longer secure if the tenant is not living in it as her/his only or principal home (see 8.10 – 8.16).

Steps to take:
It is crucial to take action to preserve the security of tenure of the tenancy. The non-tenant (divorced or cohabiting, provided the relationship is heterosexual) may be able to obtain an occupation order, under the Family Law Act 1996, to extend the right to occupy and protect the status of the tenancy. An application for an order should, if possible, be made before the tenant leaves, or as soon as possible afterwards (see 8.3 and Chapter 13, section C). However, an occupation order will not prevent the tenant from serving notice to quit, and therefore applications for occupation orders should include injunctions to prevent a tenant serving such notice (see next section below). In the longer term, the tenant may be prepared to voluntarily assign the tenancy, and if so, this should also be done before the tenant leaves (see 6.13 – 6.28). Alternatively, if there are children, a transfer could be applied for under the Children Act 1989 (see 9.13 – 9.15 and 9.17 – 9.21).

Joint or sole tenants where one tenant gives valid notice to quit

In most cases this will bring the tenancy to an end (see 6.29 onwards, 7.10 – 7.17, 7.29 – 37 and 8.6 – 8.9).

Steps to take:
There are some possible ways of preventing a notice to quit taking effect. It may be possible to get an injunction preventing a notice to quit from being served (see 7.38 – 7.42 and 8.17). Advisers should ensure, wherever possible, that steps are taken in advance to prevent a notice to quit being served.

Rent arrears

The landlord may refuse rent from a non-tenant or arrears may accrue because the tenant is no longer paying.

Steps to take:
1. Non-tenants who are married have the right to pay rent (see 11.24) – as does anyone with an occupation order in force under the Family Law Act 1996.

2. Housing benefit may also be claimed, even by non-tenants, and can be backdated in certain circumstances (see 11.25 onwards). Advisers should check that benefit is being claimed.

3. Non-tenants may also be able to intervene in possession proceedings (see 11.31).

Eviction of non-tenant cohabitant or ex-spouse
The tenant may evict the non-tenant.

Steps to take:
Under the Family Law Act 1996, it may be possible to get an occupation order in this situation (see Chapter 13, Section C). although such an order is essentially a short-term measure and a transfer of tenancy may need to be sought (see Chapter 8, Section D 8.18 – 8.20). Where a transfer is being sought under the Children Act 1989 it may be possible to seek an injunction to remain (see 8.1 – 8.4). If neither of these actions is appropriate, and there is reason to believe that the client may be in priority need, then a homelessness application should be made (see 14.11).

Owner-occupiers

Problems for owner-occupiers can also sometimes be avoided by early advice.

Preventing the sole owner from taking out a second mortgage or selling the property
Where ownership is in one name only, the partner may want to prevent further loans being raised on the property or the property being sold.

Steps to take
Differing preventative steps can be taken. These depend upon whether the person is married or has a financial stake in the home. This involves registering a charge or interest (see 4.11 and Chapter 5, Section C). Advisers should check that the charge or interest has been registered, where it is possible to do so.

Eviction of non-owner cohabitant or ex-spouse
The owner may evict the non-owner.

Steps to take:
It may be possible to obtain an interim injunction to remain if proceedings are being taken under the Children Act (5.8). See also the possibilities set out at 5.3 – 5.7. Under the Family Law Act, it may be possible to get an occupation order (see Chapter 13, Section C), although such an order is only a short-term measure and a long-term settlement of property may need to be sought (See Chapter 4, Section F and Chapter 5, Section B and 5.48).

Bankruptcy
Financial problems often accompany relationship breakdown. A partner may want to try to safeguard her/his interest in the home.

Steps to take
Although solutions are limited, there is protection for certain

pre-bankruptcy settlements of property. Also, a declaration of the non-bankrupt person's financial interest in a property can be obtained. This share will not normally be included in the bankrupt's assets (see 12.9 – 12.10). In some cases it may be possible for the non-bankrupt owner to increase her/his share in the proceeds of a sale (see 12.10). Advisers may wish to refer to a specialist if bankruptcy seems a possibility.

Inheritance problems for joint owners

A partner may want to prevent a separated spouse or partner from inheriting her/his share of the property if s/he dies.

Steps to take:
Steps can be taken to enable a joint owner to will her/his share of a property to another person, eg, a new partner (see 5.33 – 5.34). Advisers should explain the implications of joint ownership on inheritance.

Disputes over financial shares

Disputes may arise over who contributed what to the property.

Steps to take:
The court can decide and declare who owns what share (see Chapter 5, Section B). Advisers should give preliminary advice on whether an interest could be established, and may wish to refer the client on for legal representation.

Mortgage arrears

The lender may refuse mortgage payments from a non-owner or arrears may accrue because the owner is no longer paying.

Steps to take:
1. Non-owners who are married and anyone with an occupation order in force under the Family Law Act have the right to pay the mortgage (see 11.1 and 13.34).

2. Income Support or Jobseeker's Allowance may also be claimed in respect of the interest on the mortgage, even by non-owners, and can be backdated in certain circumstances.

3. Advisers should check to see if benefit is being claimed and if the lender has been contacted.

4. Other steps can be taken to prevent repossession (see 11.20).

1.8 Leaving the home and long-term rehousing

Although there are steps which can be taken to help a person stay in the home, these should not be insisted upon where the person wishes to leave, especially if there is any risk of violence, or it is not reasonable to expect her/him to remain there (see 15.5 – 15.9).

Homelessness

Where someone is in need of immediate assistance under the homelessness legislation, advisers should check the following points:

Has the person been accepted as homeless or has s/he only been considered under the local authority's allocations scheme?

Steps to take:

1. Check whether s/he falls within the legal definition of being owed a duty as a homeless person (see 14.16 – 14.18).

2. Check whether the applicant has been given formal written notification of the local authority's decision on homelessness (see 14.16 – 14.18 and 15.34).

3. Check whether the situation has any parallels in established case law (see Chapter 15).

4. If the applicant has been refused immediate assistance, check whether there is any basis for challenging the local authority's decision and, if so, whether it is appropriate to request a review (see Chapter 14, Section C). Advisers must be aware of the time limits allowed for requesting reviews (see 14.26). There may also be some occasions where the authority refuses to accept an application at all, and it may then be necessary to consider an application for judicial review (see 14.30 – 14.32).

5. If long-term housing is needed, check whether the applicant has also been accepted for consideration under the allocation scheme and awarded appropriate preference under statutory provisions, in accordance with the terms of the authority's allocation policy (see Chapter 14, Section D).

Has the person been told by the local authority homelessness section to obtain an injunction or use legal rights or remedies to remain?

Steps to take:

1. If there has been violence, or threats of violence, which are likely to be carried out, refer to the statutory provisions in the Housing Act 1996, and to case law which has held such advice to be unlawful[3] (see 14.6 and 15.5 – 15.6).

2. Check whether it is otherwise reasonable for the person to remain in the home, for example, is maintaining the home an affordable option? (see 15.8 – 15.9 and 16.27).

3. Refer to the code of guidance (see 15.1 and 16.27).

4. Decide whether the local authority is acting reasonably.

---

3. Bond v Leicester CC [2001] EWCA Civ 1544, [2002] HLR 6 CA.

5. Negotiate with the local authority, but also be aware of the time limits for requesting reviews or taking other actions (see Appendix 4 and Chapter 14, Section C).

Has the person been told that s/he is not eligible for assistance?
Steps to take:
1. Check the person's immigration status.

2. If s/he is an asylum seeker, check whether s/he applied for asylum inside the country or upon entering and check whether the date of the application was before 3 April 2000 (see 14.10).

3. Check if the immigration status is likely to change in the near future, ie, whether s/he is about to be accepted as a refugee, is likely to pass the habitual residence test, or is a sponsored person who will soon have been in the country for five years (see 14.7 – 14.9).

4. If there is no eligibility under the homelessness legislation and the person has a child or children under 18, check whether s/he was asked to consent to a referral to social services.[4] People without children who have a special need for help as a result of old age, health problems or disability should also be referred to social services with their consent (see Chapter 14, Section F and Chapter 15, Section B, and 14.17).

NB. Advisers should act sensitively when ascertaining a person's immigration status and also should be careful not to make assumptions about their client's status.

Has the person been told s/he is not in priority need because the child only lives with her/him some of the time?
Steps to take:
1. Check whether the child is dependent upon the person in question (see 15.17).

2. Check whether the child could be said to reside with the applicant (15.18). If the child does not normally reside with the applicant, check whether it would be reasonable to expect the child to reside with the applicant.

3. Use case law to negotiate with the local authority (see Appendix 4).

4. Offer assistance to the applicant with requesting a review, and appealing to the county court, if appropriate (see Chapter 14, Section C).

Has the person been refused help for any other reason?
Steps to take:
1. Check if there has been a written notification letter (see 14.16 – 14.18).

---

4. s.213A Housing Act 1996 as amended by the Homelessness Act 2002.

2. Check the reason for the refusal and check relevant sections of legislation and case law.

3. If appropriate, offer assistance with requesting a review and appealing to the county court (see Chapter 14, Section C).

Does the applicant have a child and could the child be deemed to be a 'child in need?'

Steps to take:

1. Check whether there is likely to be a duty on social services (see 9.7 onwards).

2. Check whether there is a duty upon housing and social services to co-operate and if they have done so (see 9.10).

3. Where appropriate, assist the applicant in an approach to social services under the provisions of the Children Act (see Chapter 9, Section C).

1.9 Sources of help or advice

Organisations should ensure that advisers are aware of all relevant sources of help and advice in the area. This could be made available in leaflet form and in appropriate languages. Any leaflet should give addresses and/or contacts and information on the services offered. References to advice available on the Internet may also be helpful. A leaflet could therefore include:

• information about the local women's refuge and how to contact it
• Women's Aid Federation
• counselling services – eg, Relate, women's groups, violence support networks, abusers' therapy groups
• law centres, solicitors funded by the Legal Services Commission
• Citizens' advice bureaux
• independent housing aid centres
• money advice/debt counselling
• social services
• probation service
• health centres/visitors
• police
• Department of Work and Pensions
• Housing Benefit department
• local housing authority

- registered social landlords, such as housing associations
- hostels
- victims support scheme
- useful websites (such as www.womensaid.org.uk, www.shelternet.org.uk).

A list of useful national bodies is included at the back of this book.

2

Chapter 2: The law on relationship breakdown

Subjects covered in this chapter include...

Implications of the Human Rights Act

How to recognise and challenge a breach of Human Rights

Alternative Dispute Resolution in family matters

When and how mediation may be appropriate

The difference between matrimonial/family law, child law and property or housing law

How to decide which area of law can be used in differing situations

What powers the courts have to decide who gets the family home

Areas of law affecting rights when a relationship breaks down

An overview of matrimonial, family, property and child law

Establishing rights to Property

How rights can be established for people who are married or cohabiting, have or do not have children

The law on relationship breakdown

This chapter looks at the different areas of law that are relevant to those giving advice on relationship breakdown and housing, and aims to help an adviser understand which areas are appropriate to a particular client's situation.

Underlying any interpretation of the law, there must also be a recognition and understanding of an individual's human rights, as granted by the Articles of the European Convention of Human Rights. In addition, if someone wants help with legal costs from public funding, s/he will normally have to turn to Alternative Dispute Resolution (ADR), before qualifying for such financial help. This chapter therefore also includes an overview of the implications of the Human Rights Act 1998, and of the process of Alternative Dispute Resolution.

A   Implications of Human Rights Act 1998

The Human Rights Act 1998 came into force on 2nd October 2000 and incorporates the provisions of the European Convention on Human Rights within all UK law.

From a family law and relationship perspective, there are already a number of issues which have come before the European court (European Court of Human Rights [ECHR]), and an increasing number of significant cases have been heard in the domestic courts in England and Wales. One of the most significant housing-related developments has been the Court of Appeal's judgment that there can be no justification for discriminating between a lesbian or gay couple living together as husband and wife and a heterosexual couple living in the same type of relationship. This was in the context of succession rights to a tenancy in the Court of Appeal hearing of the case of *Mendoza v Ghaidan*.[1] At the time of writing, an appeal to the House of Lords on this case was awaited. Since the *Mendoza* case, the government has announced its intention to introduce legislation to give lesbian and gay couples legal rights which at present are enjoyed only by husbands and wives (see introduction to Chapter 5 and 2.12). The long-established procedure for evicting an ex-joint tenant after service of a notice to quit is also currently under scrutiny for interference with human rights (see 2.6 and 7.42).

Other issues have been raised with the European Court, notably issues about contact with children, and the rights of gay men and transsexuals in connection with Article 8, the right to respect for private and family life. Because relationship breakdown so often leads to homelessness, or the need for social housing, other articles are also likely to come into play. Areas which have been challenged or may prove challengeable are outlined below.

1.   Mendoza v Ghaidan [2002] EWCA Civ 1533 CA.

2.1   Challenging a breach of human rights

Individuals are not bound by the provisions of the European Convention on Human Rights and the Human Rights Act 1998, and so cannot challenge each other in court for alleged breaches. However, the state is the guardian of all its citizens' human rights, and therefore if an individual believes her/his convention rights have been infringed where the state ought to have protected those rights, s/he can rely on her/his rights as a basis of a claim or defence, or alternatively seek judicial review (see 14. 28, 14.30 and 14.32 for further information on judicial review). There might also be cases where the infringement of rights may give rise to a claim for damages for breach of those rights.[2]

The Human Rights Act 1998 imposes obligations only on 'public
s6(3) HRA98   authorities.' In the housing context the obvious authorities include:

- the ODPM (Office of the Deputy Prime Minister, formerly DTLR)

- local housing authorities

- social service authorities

- Housing Corporation

- Housing Inspectorate (Audit Commission)

- Local Government Ombudsman

- Independent Housing Ombudsman.

'Public authorities' also includes courts and tribunals, family, civil and criminal courts, rent assessment committees, the Lands Tribunal and the Leasehold Valuation tribunal. In addition, it has been held that the actions of Registered Social Landlords (RSLs), such as housing associations, come within the remit of the Human Rights Act when their functions are 'of a public nature'[3] or they are acting in a 'public capacity'.

2.2   Public authorities must act compatibly with the Convention

Any decisions made or actions taken by public authorities such as those listed above must be compatible with the Human Rights Act 1998 and the articles of the European Convention on Human Rights. A useful practical approach which has been suggested[4] when using Convention rights is to apply three stages of analysis:

- Is any Convention right applicable?

- Has there been an interference with, or denial or limitation of, that right?

- Can the interference, denial or limitation be justified, where this is permissible?

2.   Eg, R (Bernard) v Enfield LBC [2002] EWHC 2282 Admin Crt., where damages were claimed for breach of Article 8 rights.
3.   Poplar Housing and Regeneration Community Association v Donoghue [2001] EWCA Civ 995 CA. [2001] 33 HLR 73 CA. The Court of Appeal held that the housing association was a public authority on these particular facts.
4.   'Housing and Human rights Law' Baker C, Carter D, and Hunter C p.8, Legal Action Group, 2001.

In most cases, Convention rights are not 'absolute,' that is, there may be some qualification or limitation which means that an interference with the right may be permissible by law in certain specified circumstances. However, some articles, such as Article 3 (see 2.6) confer an absolute right which cannot be interfered with.

2.3   Applicability of Convention rights

To establish whether there has been a breach of human rights, it is necessary to see whether the matter complained of relates to one of the Articles covered by the Human Rights Act 1998. Matters related to home and family life will normally come within the scope of Article 8, the right to respect for private and family life. It is also certainly arguable that a number of human rights come into play when domestic violence occurs or is threatened (for example, Articles 2 and 3), and the State therefore has a duty to protect its citizens from infringement of those rights. Lesbian or gay couples have a right not to be discriminated against in matters affecting their human rights (Article 14) and the government has already recognised this by signalling that it intends to introduce legal rights for same sex couples which will allow access to similar rights to married couples (see introduction to Chapter 5). See below for references to these and other Human Rights' Articles.

2.4   Can interference with a human right be justified?

Except in cases where rights are absolute, some degree of interference with a human right may be justifiable by the state. A fair balance of interests must be reached. Where Article 8 is concerned, however, interference with an individual's right to respect for home and family life can only be permitted if it is:

• in accordance with the law, eg, is not discriminatory

• pursues a legitimate aim, and

• is necessary in a democratic society.

Interference with a right must be in reasonable proportion to the end it is seeking to achieve, for example, refusing a parent contact with a child could be a proportionate response if it were necessary to protect the partner's right to be protected from violence, threats to life or limb, or abusive treatment (Articles 2 and 3). The interference must not be excessive in relation to the end it seeks to achieve. If a less drastic alternative exists, it should be taken, eg, ordering indirect or supervised contact, but if the alternative breaches another person's rights, the rights of all parties must be taken into account and carefully balanced.

2.5   Law interpreted in the light of the Convention

All legislation must, if possible, be interpreted so as to be compatible with the Convention. This means that domestic courts must strive to give a meaning to the legislation that is both consistent with the intentions of parliament and the wording of legislation, and also fully compatible with Convention rights. In some cases, this can be dealt with by the courts ordering that the legislation be interpreted in a way that is compatible with Convention rights, for example, by stating that where legislation reads 'as his or her wife or husband,' the words should be read to mean '*as if they were* his or her wife or husband.'[5]

Declaration of incompatibility

Where it is simply not possible to interpret legislation so as to be compatible with the Convention, the courts have no power to strike it down. However, the House of Lords, the Judicial Committee of the Privy Council, the Court of Appeal and the High Court have power to make a 'declaration of incompatibility' which (in theory) should prompt government action.

The case of *Mendoza v Ghaidan* referred to above raises the interesting question of whether the provisions of the Family Law Act 1996 itself, which defines '*cohabitants*' as '*a man and a woman who, although not married to each other, are living together as husband and wife*' and therefore limits certain remedies which can grant rights to remain in the home to heterosexual couples only, could be held to be discriminatory and therefore incompatible with Convention rights. The government's announcement in December 2002, less than a month after the Court of Appeal's ruling, that it intends to introduce legislation to grant certain relationship rights to lesbian and gay couples, suggests that it is aware of the need for action in this context.

s62(1)(a) FLA96

2.6   Human Rights Articles relevant to relationship breakdown and family matters

The following are the Articles under the Human Rights Act 1998 that are most likely to be directly relevant to relationship breakdown:

- *Article 2 gives the Right to Life*: Article 2(1) states that 'Everyone's right to life shall be protected by law'

- *Article 3 grants freedom from torture or inhuman or degrading treatment*: 'No-one may be subjected to torture, or to inhuman or degrading treatment or punishment.' Unlike some of the other Articles, this is an absolute prohibition, so that it is meant to be an absolute guarantee of freedom, with no room to argue a

5.   Mendoza v Ghaidan, para 35, see 1 above.

lessening of its scope. This clearly has relevance in the context of chastisement of children, or violence or cruelty towards partners or children

• *Article 8(1) – right to respect for an individual's private and family life, home and correspondence*: 'Family life' includes not just partners or parents and children, but also connections with close relatives. Contact of parents with children, or the right of a child to be protected from contact would fall under Article 8 (see 9.2 and 13.6).

Right to respect for a home is clearly at issue when a local authority proposes to evict someone. A local authority must consider whether its actions amount to an interference with an individual's human rights, and whether that interference can be justified. Eviction is clearly an interference under article 8(1), so that where such an interference occurs, the human right will have been violated unless it can be justified by the state (see 2.4 for an explanation of when an interference can be justified). However, the courts have held that the provisions made by Parliament in statutory schemes like the assured shorthold regime and introductory tenancies are not incompatible with an individual's rights under Article 8, or Article 6 (right to a fair hearing).[6]

At the time of writing, a judgment in the case of *Qazi v Harrow LBC*[7] was awaited concerning the justification of evicting a remaining partner after one joint tenant has served a notice to quit (see 7.42). This procedure has been used for many years as a management tool in cases of relationship breakdown, particularly if domestic violence is involved (see 6.34 and 7.31). The outcome of this case is therefore of major significance.

• *Article 12 – the right of men and women of marriageable age to marry and found a family*: The European Court has not yet recognised a stable relationship between lesbian and gay couples as constituting 'family life'[8] although a transsexual couple with a child were held to constitute a family unit.[9] For the purposes of Article 12, the right to marry, the Court has affirmed the heterosexual nature of marriage, and refused to treat lesbian, gay or transsexual couples as the same as heterosexual couples. However, the Court of Appeal in England and Wales held that same-sex partners must be treated 'as if they were [the partner's] wife or husband'[10] (see below under Article 14). Despite the government's announced intentions to grant rights to lesbian/gay couples to register a recognised civil partnership, they will still not have the right to a legal marriage.

• *Article 14 – the right to the enjoyment of convention rights and freedoms without discrimination on any ground such as sex, race,*

6. Poplar Housing and Regeneration Community Association v Donoghue, see above. R (McLellan) v Bracknell Forest BC; Reigate and Banstead BC v Benfield and Forrest [2001] 33 HLR 989 CA; Sheffield CC v Smart [2002] EWCA Civ 4 CA.

7. Harrow LBC v Qazi [2001] EWCA Civ 1834; [2002] HLR 14 CA.
8. Grant v South West Trains Ltd. (1998) 3 B.H.R.C. 578, 594 European Court of Justice.
9. XYZ v United Kingdom (1997) 24 E.H.R.R. 143 ECJ.
10. Mendoza v Ghaidan, see 1 above.

colour, language, religion, political or other opinion, national or social origin, association with a national minority, property, birth or other status: To establish discrimination, it is necessary to be able to show a difference between the treatment of the individual making the complaint, and the treatment of another in an analogous situation, in respect of a convention right. If such a difference in treatment is shown, the state then has to consider whether the difference has an objective and reasonable justification, ie, does it:
– pursue a legitimate aim and
– is the differential treatment reasonably proportionate to the aim sought to be achieved?

Succession rights to tenancies and the security of tenure which a successor inherits have been held to be covered within the ambit of 'Right to respect for a home.'[11] In this context, the Court of Appeal has held that there can be no justification for discrimination between the rights of lesbian/gay couples and heterosexual couples. In 1999, the House of Lords held by a majority that a gay man had the right to succeed to a Rent Act 1977 tenancy as a 'member of [his partner's] family,'[12] but this was not based specifically on human rights considerations (see 6.17). The issue was revisited in *Mendoza v Ghaidan,* where the law on succession of tenancies was held to be an impermissible ground for discrimination under Article 14. At the time of writing, an appeal to the House of Lords was awaited.

• *Article 1 of the First Protocol – the Right to property and peaceful enjoyment of possessions*: This includes all interests in land and matrimonial assets, so that matrimonial settlements and orders excluding someone from their family home all fall within this Article.

B   Alternative Dispute Resolution in family matters

Although many people who separate or divorce have to resort to the law to settle disputes over finances, property and children, family mediation provides a constructive alternative approach. It is now supported and encouraged by the government and attracts public funding. Even if the client does not want, or is not eligible for public funding, going to court can be costly, stressful and time-consuming. The outcome can also be unpredictable. All solicitors practising family law should advise clients about family mediation.

Following the *Woolf* report,[13] there is a growing trend for the Courts to consider that parties should be attempting to sort out their dispute or to reduce the breadth of issues to be dealt with either before coming

11. Mendoza v Ghaidan, see 1 above.
12. Fitzpatrick v Sterling Housing Association Ltd (2000) 32 HLR 178 HL.
13. 'Access to Justice – Final Report' Lord Woolf, July 1996. Available at www.lcd.gov.uk/civl/finalfr.htm or, www.law.warwick.ac.uk/woolf/report/contents.html

to court or alongside the proceedings. In the recent case of *Dunnett v Railtrack*,[14] the judge set the precedent which penalised a party on costs where no reasonable attempt was made to consider mediation. It is therefore well worth suggesting to parties in dispute that they try mediation for a wide range of issues, including divorce/separation, housing and neighbour disputes. In addition, if public funding is necessary, there is a requirement to assess the suitability of mediation (see 2.9).

2.7   Scope of mediation

Mediation (formerly termed conciliation) should not be confused with reconciliation. The aim of mediation is to help a couple make joint decisions about how to move forward separately. It is, of course, possible for a couple to decide to reconcile during mediation, but in such cases they would end their mediation and perhaps be referred to a suitable counselling service.

The purpose of mediation is to help couples settle such matters as:

• Arrangements for the children

• Accommodation

• Dividing up property

• Financial arrangements

• Any other practical issues arising from the breakdown of the relationship.

The approach is intended to empower people to resolve their own disputes constructively, making well-informed, joint decisions. The mediator focuses on what is in the best interests of both parties and their children and encourages give and take. As a neutral third party, the mediator can give general information about the law and the way the legal system works, but cannot give advice about legal rights. The client may still, therefore, require independent legal advice.

At the end of mediation, the clients will usually be given a written summary of the decisions they have made. This can include complete disclosure of all their finances, ie, assets, liabilities, income and expenditure – the information on which their budgets and decisions were based. This is generally a cost effective way of providing formal disclosure. The parties may leave the agreement as totally informal, or they may wish to take their proposals to their solicitors to convert it into an enforceable agreement.

---

14.   Dunnett v Railtrack 22 February 2002 CA.

2.8   Confidentiality

On the whole, mediation is confidential – agreements or discussions which occur cannot be used later in court. However, factual information disclosed about income or property can be used in any later court proceedings and passed to lawyers. Also, where it appears that a party associated with the mediation, particularly if a child is at risk or has suffered a serious assault, the mediator is obliged to inform the appropriate statutory authorities, ie, police, social services, NSPCC.

2.9   Public funding requirement to assess suitability mediation

When a person wishes to apply for Community Legal Service Public Funding to be represented by a solicitor in family proceedings, with some exceptions, s/he must first be referred to a mediation service to assess the suitability of mediation. Assessment (or intake) meetings can be attended alone or by both parties together.

Following referral the applicant for funding may request that the mediation service finds out first whether the other party will attend a meeting before attending her/himself. If the other party refuses then the applicant need not attend an assessment meeting and the mediation service will supply a form to the applicant's solicitor showing that mediation has been considered. The requirement to attend an assessment meeting can also be waived by the solicitor in cases where mediation is obviously unsuitable, such as when it is unreasonably difficult to access a service or where the applicant has a reasonable fear of domestic abuse from a potential party to the mediation and is in fear of participating with them.

Accessing mediation

There are a number of organisations which offer mediators (see Useful Organisations at the end of this book). Advisers should check to see whether the organisations are eligible to receive public funding from the Legal Services Commission if the client is likely to need financial assistance. Mediation services are also listed in Yellow Pages, and clients can generally refer themselves. Any third party can, with the client's permission, make a referral to mediation.

Mediation will not commence until the case has been assessed as suitable. This involves both parties attending an assessment meeting either separately or together, as explained above. Mediation is voluntary, and no pressure will be placed on either party to proceed if they do not feel able to meet jointly. Even where a client does not go on to mediation, the meeting can be a helpful opportunity to discuss the issues with a neutral third party whose aim is the adoption of a conciliatory approach.

If both parties decide to proceed, mediation is then arranged involving one or several sessions with the mediator(s), depending on the issues being covered and the complexity of the case. Occasionally, the parties will attend mediation in separate rooms, and the mediator 'shuttles' back and forth between them. Any special arrangement for mediation like this, or co-mediation (using two mediators), is usually agreed at the intake stage (ie, the assessment meetings).

2.10   Cost of Mediation

At the assessment meeting, which is often free, each client will be assessed to see if they are eligible for free mediation. It may be that one person qualifies but not the other. Anyone who does not qualify should be given an estimate for the cost of mediation in their particular case with that service. They can then decide whether or not they wish to proceed. Costs compare favourably with that of resolving matters through the courts. Costs are generally between £150 to £500, compared to possible costs of using solicitors, particularly when all issues are disputed, in excess of £5,000.

When a person qualifies for free mediation, it is exactly that. There is nothing to pay, either then or in the future. They also qualify for a limited amount of free help and advice from a family solicitor who has a Legal Services Commission contract. The funding for both mediation and the solicitor's 'Help with Mediation' contrast with Legal Help or Representation from a solicitor, which are basically loans that have to be repaid through the Statutory Charge, when a financial settlement of more than £3,000 is ultimately achieved. The Statutory Charge does not apply to mediation or 'Help with Mediation.' See 4.40 for more information on the Statutory Charge.

2.11   Outcome of mediation

Mediation can lead to full agreement on all the issues raised and full implementation of the agreement. However, as mediation is voluntary, the parties can withdraw at any time. Indeed, they may do so because they find that one session is all that is required to start them off in working out the issues for themselves, without help.

Sometimes the parties decide that they cannot continue, and as a result no agreement can be reached. In such circumstances, mediation is said to have broken down. When this happens, the parties may return to the traditional approach and use solicitors, and perhaps the courts, to resolve matters on their behalf.

The breakdown of mediation may occur after some issues have been resolved, and the mediator will, if appropriate, supply the parties with a document showing what has been agreed. This, at least, can then be implemented and ratified by the solicitors if the parties wish. Outstanding issues can be dealt with as above, in the traditional way.

The Courts know that mediation is 'privileged,' and do not expect any reports to be sent concerning the discussions. They can incorporate agreements reached into a consent order.

C   The difference between matrimonial/family law, child law and property or housing law

Much confusion arises in advisers' minds about the factors which decide who will end up with the lion's share of what was the family home. Some will say whoever has the children will get the home; others say it depends on who paid what towards the home. The reason for this confusion is that the outcome can be different depending upon which of the main branches of law, explained below, is used in reaching a settlement.

In both *matrimonial/family* and *child law* the courts have wide powers to override actual ownership of property and literally take it from one party and give it to another. The courts can actually adjust ownership of property, and a common term used for such orders is therefore 'property adjustment (or transfer) orders.' There are fixed factors which the courts must consider when deciding on this, and they are explained at 4.32, but the amount of money put into a property is not directly relevant. These powers can be used to transfer owner-occupied or tenanted property.

In *property law*, on the other hand, the courts have no power to adjust or transfer ownership of property rights, although it may sometimes seem as if that is what is happening. The courts can adjudicate where there is a dispute over who owns what proportion of the property and declare what they deem, on the face of the evidence, to be the parties' respective shares. They cannot take it upon themselves to simply order a transfer, for example, because of the needs of children. Whilst there is nothing to stop a married couple using both areas of law, an order for a transfer of property under matrimonial law would override rights established in property law (see Chapters 3 and 5).

Housing law contains no powers to allow the courts to transfer tenancies, although in certain circumstances the law allows one tenant to voluntarily assign a tenancy to a partner. Special statutory provisions allow all tenancies to be transferred by the court under matrimonial/family law, but child law powers are not so wide. Whether the court can order a transfer of tenancy under the Children Act depends upon rules relating to assignment (see 9.17). The different areas of law are therefore interdependent (see Chapters 6 – 8).

D   Areas of law affecting rights when a relationship breaks down

There can be said to be four tiers of legal rights in relation to property which are relevant to those giving advice on relationship breakdown and housing. They are granted by:

• Matrimonial/family law

• Child law

• Property law

• Housing law.

These different types of law give different rights on relationship breakdown. The main points are outlined below and explained in detail in the relevant chapters of this book.

2.12   Overview of matrimonial/family law

Married couples

For many years, married couples have received special treatment in the eyes of the law in terms of establishing rights to property, whether owner-occupied or tenanted. Although cohabitation has more than doubled since the early 1980s, the law has traditionally been reluctant to accept that such a relationship should give any special rights to property.

Heterosexual cohabitants

The Family Law Act 1996[15] redressed the balance to some degree, by granting additional rights to heterosexual cohabitants. It grants the court powers to make orders affecting short-term rights to occupy the family home and allows for transfer of tenancies between the parties. The law relating to protection from domestic violence and exclusion from the family home is also contained within the Family Law Act 1996. It allows for short-term exclusion of one or other party in a heterosexual relationship, and in certain circumstances for those in lesbian or gay relationships. It also covers other people in close relationships known as 'associated persons'(see 13.20). These orders can override rights to occupy, but do not in themselves affect long-term property settlement. There are no powers within the Family Law Act 1996 to transfer owner-occupied property.

Lesbian/gay cohabitants

For lesbian or gay cohabitants, there is no special provision in relation to property settlement, nor is there any legal method for transfer of tenancies under the Family Law Act 1996. At the time of writing, the government

---

15. Based on the recommendations of the Law Commission Report Family Law Domestic Violence and Occupation of the Family Home (1992).

finally appears to be about to address this obvious discrimination, and has announced its intention to bring forward legislation to grant property and inheritance rights to lesbian and gay couples who have registered their partnership. Registration would be permissible after a couple have lived together for a certain period, possibly six months or a year.

A consultation paper on the proposals is expected to be published in summer 2003. It is unlikely that draft legislation will be produced before late 2003 or 2004, possibly later (see also the introduction to Chapter 5).

2.13   Legal rights under matrimonial/family law

Married couples only

Matrimonial law gives the court wide powers to decide who gets what in the long term in financial[16] and property terms. The court can order a transfer of owner-occupied or most tenanted property from one spouse to another, regardless of who owns what. These powers are granted by the Matrimonial Causes Act 1973.[17] The matrimonial powers to adjust property rights may be used only in conjunction with proceedings for divorce and judicial separation, or nullity. (For an explanation of these terms, see the glossary at the front of this book). Financial provision orders, as well as property transfer orders, may also be made together with an order of Judicial Separation. Applications for property transfer orders and/or financial provision are normally made in the county court (or High Court, in exceptional circumstances). Financial provision can also be made by the magistrates' court, but the maximum amounts which can be awarded in lump sums are more limited, and in practice the magistrates court is seldom used.

The Family Law Act 1996 grants further rights to married couples:

s30(2)(a) FLA96
- Automatic rights to occupy the family home, regardless of ownership/tenancy rights (see 4.1 and 7.1)

s40(1)(a) FLA96
- When making an order regarding occupation, the court can order a transfer of liabilities and obligations in respect of a family home owned or rented solely by one of the spouses (see 13.23)

s53 & Sch7 FLA96
- The court can order a transfer of tenancy from one spouse to the other (see 7.43 onwards).

Heterosexual cohabitants, ex-spouses and former heterosexual cohabitants

The Family Law Act 1996 gives similar rights to heterosexual cohabitants, former heterosexual cohabitants and ex-spouses as exist for married couples:

---

16. The provisions of the Child Support Act 1991 as amended by the Child Support, Pensions and Social Security Act 2000 mean that the powers of the court to order financial provision are limited. See Chapter 10.

17. As amended by the Matrimonial and Family Proceedings Act 1984.

s35(2)-(4) &
s36(2)-(4) FLA96
• The right to apply to the courts for an occupation order giving rights to occupy the home (see Chapter 13, Section C)

s40(1)(a) FLA96
• When making an occupation order, the court can order a transfer of liabilities and obligations in respect of a family home (see 13.23)

s53 & Sch7 FLA96
• The court can order a transfer of tenancy from one partner to the other (see 8.19 and 7.43 onwards).

Lesbian/gay cohabitants

At the time of writing, under the Family Law Act 1996, only lesbian or gay cohabitants who already have some legal right in the home, such as joint owners or joint tenants, have the following rights:

s33(1)(3)(6)-(10)
FLA96
• The right to apply to the courts for an occupation order to enforce rights to occupy or to exclude the partner from all or part of the shared home (see Chapter 13, Section C)

s40(1)(a) FLA96
• When making an occupation order, the court can order a transfer of liabilities and obligations in respect of a family home (see 13.23)

• There is currently no power under the Family Law Act for the court to order a transfer of tenancy between lesbian/gay cohabitants.

2.14　An overview of child law

There have been legal powers for many years to order maintenance for children of a relationship. Within the last twenty years, the law also recognised the need for special legislation[18] to give rights to property for the benefit of the children of a relationship, regardless of the marital status of the parents. Nevertheless, such transfers of rights to property are usually between either married parents or step-parents, or unmarried parents who are also natural biological parents. These rights will not usually extend to lesbian or gay couples who may have brought up a child together (but see next section and 9.14), nor to unmarried couples who do not have children.

2.15　Legal rights under Child Law

Applications for transfers of property under Child law, ie, the Children Act 1989, may be made to the court by a parent or guardian of a child, or by anyone in whose favour a residence order is in force with respect to a child, but property or finance can only be transferred from a natural parent, or married parents where the child is a 'child of the family.' This was confirmed in the case of *In Re J* Family Division, November 1992.[19] A lesbian or gay partner would only be able to apply to the court if s/he had a residence order in relation to her/his partner's child, and wanted to apply for support or a property transfer from the biological parent for

18. Firstly under the Family Law Reform Act 1987, later
consolidated in Schedule 1 of the Children Act 1989.　　19. In Re J (A Minor: Property Transfer) 1993 2 FLR 55.0

the benefit of the child (see 9.3 for a list of who may apply for residence orders and 9.13 onwards for more information on property transfers).

Under the Children Act 1989, an application may be made to the courts for financial provision, eg, lump sums of money and transfer of property, provided it is for the benefit of the children. This could include owner-occupied property and certain tenancies (see 8.18 and Chapter 9, Section D).

The powers may be used at any time, as long as it can be shown to be for the benefit of the children. Applications for a transfer of property and/or financial provision may be made in the county court (or, exceptionally, the High Court). Applications for financial provision may also be made in the magistrates' court, but, as for matrimonial cases, its power to order lump sums is limited. Child maintenance will usually be dealt with by the Child Support Agency (see Chapter 10).

Social services duties under the Children Act 1989

The Children Act lays duties on social services departments to provide a range of services for 'children in need' and their parents. These services can, and in some cases must, include the provision of accommodation for children, although not necessarily together with parents.[20] The case of *R(G) v Barnet LBC*[21] (see 9.9), which addressed this issue of accommodating parents with children, was due to be heard by the House of Lords at the time of writing. These social services' powers can be of considerable significance in cases of homelessness (see 9.7 – 9.9).

The Children (Leaving Care) Act 2000 amends the Children Act 1989 and lays further duties on social services to provide support and accommodation in relation to certain children who have been in care (see 9.12).

2.16   An overview of property law

Regardless of relationships or children, the law has always been prepared to intervene in general disputes about owner-occupied property. Those who have no special rights to property because of their relationship may therefore still find some assistance from the law, although of a much more restricted nature. It is used solely in relation to owner-occupied property, including long leasehold.

2.17   Legal rights under property law

Property law applies equally to heterosexual, lesbian, gay, or married couples, or any other people sharing owner-occupied property, regardless of their relationship.

---

20. R (G) v Barnet LBC [2001] 33 HLR 59 CA.   21. R (G) v Barnet LBC ibid.

- It establishes the legal position of joint or sole owners in relation to their financial shares (or interest) in the home

- It gives the court power to 'declare' respective interests in property, ie, to decide who owns what, but it cannot transfer that ownership. It also allows the court to make any order requiring the owner to deal with the property in a certain way, which could include ordering or postponing a sale of the property, as it sees fit (see 5.48 – 5.49).

s14 TLATA 1996

Rights under property law stem mainly from statutes such as the Law of Property Act 1925 and the Trusts of Land and Appointment of Trustees Act 1996, and from the common law, eg, the 'doctrine of trusts.' Property law can be used at any time when rights to property are in dispute, and is not directly dependent on the nature of the relationship between the people concerned. Applications should be made in the county court unless the value of the claim is very high.

s17 MWPA 1882

In addition, there is a special procedure available under the Married Women's Property Act 1882 which allows the court to declare the shares in property of:

- People who are married

- Those whose marriage was dissolved less than three years before the application

- Those whose engagement ended less than three years before the application.

The principles used by the court to decide on a couple's respective shares are covered in more detail in Chapter 5. Those who are, or were, married are more likely to take advantage of the wider matrimonial powers of the court to redistribute property, unless remarriage has already taken place.

Some of the principles of property law are explained in Chapter 3.

2.18   Overview of housing law

There is also a whole body of law which governs the position and rights of tenants. This applies regardless of the nature of the relationship of the parties involved.

Housing law can be said to be an amalgamation of the old common law principles relating to the relationship between landlords and tenants (landlord and tenant law) and the rights and obligations which have been created by statute, such as the various rent and housing acts.

In general, the principles of housing law apply equally to any people occupying rented property, married or cohabiting, heterosexual, lesbian or gay. However, certain statutory rules relating to succession are limited to spouses, cohabitants or members of the family, depending upon the type of tenancy, and these can also affect the right to assign a tenancy.

2.19   Legal rights under housing law

The important aspects of housing law in cases of relationship breakdown are as follows:

- Housing law explains the status of occupiers in relation to the shared home and determines the rights to occupy. Note that matrimonial/family rights to occupy can take precedence over housing law principles

- It lays down rules relating to assignment and termination of tenancies

- It gives certain rights to be protected from eviction without the correct procedure being followed

- It contains rules determining liability for rent and any arrears.

These rights and rules are found mainly in the Rent Act 1977, the Housing Act 1985, the Housing Act 1988, the Housing Act 1996, the Protection from Eviction Act 1977 and the various Landlord and Tenant Acts. Some of the principles of housing law are explained in Chapter 6.

E   Establishing rights to property

When a relationship breaks down, there are two main issues which are likely to need resolving:

- Who has the right to remain in the matrimonial/family home in the short-term?

- Who will get the home in the long-term?

Short-term rights to occupy are dealt with in detail in Chapter 13. This section gives a summary of which areas of law can be used by people in different situations, in order to reach a final settlement about who gets the shared home.

2.20   Married couples

Most disputes over property between married couples are resolved through matrimonial/family law because of the wide discretion available to the court. Property law principles are now normally relied on by married couples only when matrimonial law cannot apply, for example where there is no divorce or judicial separation, or one party has remarried without any property settlement being made.

Married couples with children

Long-term property rights may be settled either by:

- *Matrimonial/family law (for owner-occupiers and tenants)*
  Note that long-term transfers of owner-occupied and tenanted
  property between married couples can only be ordered when there
  are legal proceedings being taken for divorce, or judicial separation,
  or nullity, and will not take effect until the order is finalised.
  Applications for transfers can be made at the same time as a decree,
  or at any time after (but before remarriage).

- *Child law (for owner-occupiers and certain tenants)*
  Children Act 1989 proceedings do not need to be taken in conjunction
  with any other legal proceedings. The Children Act is a useful option
  for non-divorcing couples.

- *Property law (for owner-occupiers only)*
  This can be used at any time, but cannot transfer property rights: it
  may only decide who actually owns what. Section 17 of the Married
  Women's Property Act offers the speedier 'summary' proceedings in
  certain limited circumstances.

- *Housing law (for tenants)*
  This can be used at any time, and may be used to assign a tenancy,
  or bring it to an end. Its principles need to be considered in
  conjunction with matrimonial/family and child law.

Married couples without children

Long-term property rights may be settled either by:

- Matrimonial/family law (owners or tenants)

- Property law, including use of section 17 of Married Women's
  Property Act (owners)

- Housing law (tenants).

2.21 Cohabitants

At present, there are no special legal provisions concerning disputes
over long-term settlement of owner-occupied property between those
who have lived together without marrying, but the Government is
considering giving lesbian/gay cohabiting couples a legal right to apply
for a property transfer (see 2.12 and introduction to Chapter 5). These
proposals do not extend to heterosexual cohabitants, who are seen as
already having a choice to marry if they wish to acquire such rights.
The implementation of the Family Law Act 1996 did not affect long-term

rights to owner-occupied property, which includes long leasehold, but allows for the transfer of tenancies between heterosexual cohabitants

The answers to questions about final settlement of owner-occupied property for cohabitants must still, therefore, be found in either child law or property law. When considering the use of the Children Act 1989, a distinction must be made between couples who have a child born of their relationship and those who have not, since property may only be transferred from a biological parent.

The Family Law Act extends some matrimonial/family law rights to heterosexual cohabitants and former heterosexual cohabitants, in particular in respect of rights to occupy the family home.

Heterosexual cohabitants with children of the relationship

Long-term property rights may be settled either by:

• family law (tenants)

• child law (owners or certain tenants)

• property law (owners)

• housing law (tenants).

Heterosexual cohabitants without children

Long-term property rights may be settled either by:

• family law (tenants)

• property law (owners)

• housing law (tenants).

Lesbian or gay couples

Matrimonial/family and child law does not usually apply to lesbian or gay cohabitants (but see 2.15 and 9.14), except to protect existing rights to occupy under the Family Law Act. There are no specific legal rights stemming from a lesbian/gay relationship which allow a non-owner or non-tenant to occupy the shared home when a relationship breaks down. Neither are there any specific powers granted to the courts to transfer property or make orders for financial provision between lesbian or gay cohabitants.

Long-term property rights must be settled in accordance with:

• property law (owners)

• housing law (tenants).

What the adviser needs to know

In order to help a client decide which is the most appropriate form of law and course of action, the adviser therefore needs to know:

- *are the parties in a heterosexual or lesbian/gay relationship?*

- *are the parties legally married or have they been married to each other?*

- *are they taking legal proceedings for divorce, judicial separation or nullity?*

- *are they or have they in the past lived together or intended to live together?*

- *are they owner-occupiers or tenants?*

- *is the ownership or tenancy in one name or in joint names?*

- *do they have any children?*

- *are the children the natural biological children of both parties?*

See 1.5 for information on the implications of these questions.

Chapter 3: Property law

Subjects covered in this chapter include...

Ownership

What is meant by legal ownership

What the difference is between freehold, leasehold and commonhold ownership

How someone can have rights to property without being a legal owner

What beneficial ownership and beneficial interest means

Interests in land

What it means to have an 'interest' in land

What the difference is between a legal and equitable interest

What is meant by a 'trust'

Property law

This chapter explains the underlying principles of property law which determine shares in owner-occupied property. These can apply both where property is in one name or in joint names. Property law does not deal with tenancies, unless they are let on a long lease (see 3.2 below). The law relating to tenancies is governed by landlord and tenant law. See Chapter 6 for more information.

To understand the way property law works, it is crucial to have a basic understanding of the principles and terms. These often put people off, as the terminology seems strange and sometimes archaic but, once understood, it is much easier to advise people of their rights.

A   Ownership

An adviser needs to know who owns the property in order to give advice on the client's legal rights to the home. But what exactly is meant by ownership?

3.1   Establishing ownership

To find out who is the legal owner of a property, it is necessary to establish whose name is on the title deed or land registry certificate. Even if a person does not contribute to the mortgage, or has not paid towards the purchase, s/he will still be a legal owner if her/his name appears on the title deed or the certificate. For example, council tenants exercising the right to buy can add the names of family members living with them, and they will all become joint legal owners. There is a legal maximum of four co-owners in any purchase of property.

Registered or unregistered land

Chapters 4 and 5 explain how rights relating to property are protected, depending upon whether land is registered or unregistered.

If land is registered, the information on ownership will be included in the land or charge certificate. In order to find out who is the legal owner, it will be necessary to get up-to-date copies of the certificate from the Land Registry.

If land is unregistered, information on ownership will be on the title deeds. Approximately 80% of land in England and Wales is now registered at a centralised Land Registry. The Land Registration Act 2002, which is due to come into force in October 2003, aims to extend registration to all land as soon as is practicable. For more information on the Land Registration Act, see 5.15 – 5.16.

3.2   Legal ownership – freehold, leasehold or commonhold

Legal ownership of a property may be freehold or leasehold, or, once the relevant provisions of the Commonhold and Leasehold Reform Act 2002 come into force, commonhold. The Commonhold and Leasehold Reform Act 2002 received Royal Assent in May 2002, and provisions relating to collective enfranchisements for tenants of flats and enhancement of rights to acquire a new lease came into force on 26 July 2002. At the time of writing, an implementation date for the commonhold and other provisions of the Act was not known.

Freehold ownership is unlimited in time, whilst leasehold properties are let on a long lease (tenancy) for a fixed term, which must originally have been of at least 21 years. Originally, leasehold properties would have reverted to the owner of the freehold at the end of the fixed term, but more recently most leaseholders have been given rights either to purchase (enfranchise) the freehold or to extend the lease. The Commonhold and Leasehold Reform Act 2002 introduces the right to manage for leaseholders of flats, and makes it easier for leaseholders to either extend their leases or, for leaseholders of houses, buy the freehold, as well as strengthening other leaseholder rights. These rights were not fully in force at the time of writing.

Commonhold will be a new form of tenure that will enable flats and other buildings with shared services or common parts to be owned on a virtual freehold basis. Each separate property will be called a unit, so that the owner will be a 'unit' holder. There will also be a commonhold association made up of all the unit-holders, and this association, which will be a private company, will own and manage the common parts and facilities of the whole development. Commonhold will be available for new developments and conversion of existing leasehold properties, but in the latter case only where all the leaseholders agree to participate and buy out any other interests involved. It is beyond the scope of this book to go into further detail, but readers may wish to read further on the subject.[1]

Legal ownership gives the right to manage and dispose of property, in other words to maintain and repair it, to sell it or to transfer ownership. It does not necessarily mean that the legal owner, the person who has the title to the property on paper, has the right to the whole or even part of the proceeds of a sale or to the financial value of the home. The right to the whole or part of the proceeds of the sale of the home is known as a beneficial or equitable interest. Legal ownership is what is referred to throughout this book when the word 'ownership' is used.

---

1   For the government's factsheet on the Commonhold and Leasehold Reform Act 2002, see www.housing.odpm.gov.uk/information/leaseholdreform/factsheets/pdf/clra.pdf and for the explanatory notes of the CLR Act 2002, see www.hmso.gov.uk/acts/en/2002en15.htm. For a brief and simple explanation, see www.rics.org.uk/downloads/static/residential_news_april.pdf.

3.3   Beneficial ownership[2]

Legal ownership does not affect who is entitled to the proceeds of a sale. This entitlement is known as beneficial (or equitable) ownership. The terms 'equitable' and 'beneficial' ownership are often used interchangeably, although, strictly speaking, beneficial ownership is just one form of equitable ownership. Beneficial ownership normally gives the right to live in and use the property and the right to share in the proceeds of any sale. A beneficial owner is said to have a 'beneficial interest' in the property, which is a type of equitable interest (see 3. 6 below). For simplicity, this book will use the term 'beneficial interest' in subsequent chapters.

Beneficial interest

Although the legal owner will in most cases also be a beneficial owner (ie, someone with a financial interest in the property), there may be other people who are not on the title deeds who have contributed in some way. The court may decide that such a person has a beneficial interest, even if that person is not named on the title. This kind of entitlement is based on the principle that, whilst the law should be followed, if it results in injustice the principles of 'equity' (see below) should take precedence to achieve a fair result. The applicant would need to establish that s/he has a right to a share in the property (see Chapter 5, Section B).

B   Interests in land

3.4   Owner-occupiers as tenants

Although we normally talk about people owning houses or flats, what they actually have is an 'estate'. An estate is an interest in land for some particular period of time. Technically, all land in England and Wales belongs to the Crown, and for this reason 'owners' are known legally as tenants, since they are deemed to 'hold the land' from the Crown.[3] This stems from feudal times.

In practice, use of the term 'tenant' in respect of freeholders is usually confined to joint owners. Joint owners of the legal estate will be either beneficial joint tenants or tenants in common. This relates to the way the beneficial or equitable interest is shared between them and is explained more fully in 5.31 – 5.32.

Legal rights or a legal interest in land (ie, legal proprietary rights) will almost always be recorded on the Land Registry certificate, where the land is registered, or on the title deeds of property on unregistered land. It will therefore be clear-cut as to who has them.

---

2   For a more detailed but clear and straightforward explanation of the types of property ownership, see 'Factsheet: Joint ownership of property' at www.thompsons.law.co.uk/ltext/fsfam004.htm

3   Scotland and Northern Ireland have different systems of tenure and different laws.

Legal rights in land may be:

- **Estates**

    1. Freehold interest – unlimited in time.

    2. Leasehold interest – limited in time, eg. 99 or 999 years, or

    3. Commonhold – unlimited in time (due to come into force spring 2004).

- **Interests or charges**

    1. An easement or right over land, eg, a right of way.

    2. A mortgage or legal charge.

3.5   Meaning of interest in land

An 'interest' in land gives rights which are not merely personal or contractual; they attach to the land itself and automatically pass to anyone who buys or inherits it.

An interest can therefore be sold, assigned or transferred (eg, rights of way, or a freehold or leasehold interest in the property). Where a transaction is between two people and nobody else's rights are involved, the situation is straightforward. But in some cases there may be more than one person who believes s/he has an interest in the property, for example, a partner living in the home. The partner may not have a legal interest as s/he may not be named as a legal owner, but s/he may have, for example, contributed to the purchase of the home in such a way as to have a beneficial (equitable) interest (see 5.9 onwards for how to establish a beneficial interest).

Whether a purchaser or person to whom the land is transferred, or someone who lends money on the security of a property, is required to honour an interest depends, in the first instance, upon whether the interest is a 'legal' or 'equitable' interest and, if it is equitable, then upon whether s/he can be held to have known or had 'notice' of the interest. For a full discussion of the subject of what constitutes 'notice' see 5.21.

3.6   Legal and equitable interests

In medieval times, there were 'Courts of Law,' which dealt with strictly legal matters. However, this sometimes gave rise to injustice and therefore 'Courts of Equity' were established. These courts would give a ruling on the basis of principles of fairness and natural justice, rather than strict legal rules. Where the application of the law would lead to an injustice, then the principles of 'equity' were meant to take precedence.

The principle is simply explained as follows:

> *'The courts of law recognised various estates and interests in land and would enforce the rights of a legal owner; the courts of equity might override this in favour of a person with, in its view, a stronger right to the land. The owner of the legal interest was deemed by equity to hold it on behalf of the person who had the better right. Even today there may be one owner of a legal interest and another person recognised as holding an equitable interest in the same house.'* [4]

This notion of holding land on behalf of someone else is the fundamental principle of what is known as the 'equitable doctrine of trusts.'

The Courts of Law and Equity were not finally amalgamated until the late nineteenth century.[5] It was then enacted that in cases of conflict between the rules of law and equity, the rules of equity should prevail.[6] Nevertheless, the distinction between legal and equitable rights is still extremely important.

3.7   Trusts

The origin of the 'trust' goes back hundreds of years, and arose because of feudal law restraints upon owners of land. These restraints meant that landowners could not leave their land to family members because of the rights of the feudal lord. A doctrine therefore arose regarding the 'use' of land: the landowner conveyed land to friends on the basis that they would hold it, ie, take charge of it, but allow the landowner to use it for her/his lifetime and then hold it for the use of, for example, the landowner's family. This prevented the land from reverting to the feudal lord.

From this idea of 'use' came the doctrine of 'trusts.' Essentially, the main feature of a trust is that the legal title to property is vested in a nominee (or 'trustee') whose duty is to ensure that the benefit of the property (eg, its value and/or use) devolves in accordance with the wishes of the creator of the trust. The property is therefore 'entrusted' to the trustee who must faithfully observe the conditions upon which the trust property was transferred to her/him. The person who benefits from the trust (the beneficiary) can apply for a court order directing the trustee to act according to the terms of the trust, or to recover damages in respect of any breach of trust which has already occurred.

In theory a trust should be written down as a formal legal document or 'deed' but, as will be seen later in this book, the courts will often find that a trust is 'implied' by, 'results' from or can be 'construed' from a person's actions without the need for such formalities. Hence we now have the doctrines of implied, resulting and constructive trusts (5.9 onwards).

4   K.Green 'Land Law' (Macmillan, 1989).
5   Supreme Court of Judicature Acts of 1873 – 1875.   6   S.25(ii) Supreme Court of Judicature Act 1873.

> **Example**
>
> *Margaret and Jane decide to buy a house and Jane contributes £20,000 from the sale of her previous home, on the understanding that she will have a financial share in the home. However, the property is conveyed into Margaret's name only. The relationship breaks down and Jane wants her money back.*
>
> *Margaret is the sole legal owner, since only her name is on the title. However, since it would be unjust for Jane to have simply lost her £20,000, she would be held to have an equitable interest in the house because of her contribution to the purchase and their expressed common intention that she should have a share in the property. Margaret and Jane therefore share the beneficial interest, ie, each has a right to benefit from a proportion of the value of the house. In effect, Margaret is holding Jane's money 'on trust' for her and will therefore be obliged to repay her out of any proceeds of a sale.*
>
> *The expressed common intention is a very important factor in Jane's claim. This is discussed at greater length at 5.11.*
>
> *If they cannot agree on their respective shares, Jane can apply to the court, under the Trusts of Land and Appointment of Trustees Act 1996, for the court to make a declaration as to the division of the beneficial interest and an order for sale.*

3.8   The differences between legal and equitable interests

The main differences between legal and equitable rights or interests are:

Legal interests

1. Legal interests are enforceable as of right; the courts can only apply the law.

2. Legal rights survive a transfer of ownership and remain valid and enforceable against any new owner, ie, legal rights are binding upon everyone.

Equitable interests

1. Equitable interests depend on the court's discretion as a 'court of conscience' and will normally take account of whether the claimant has acted fairly.

2. Equitable rights may not be recorded on the legal title and are therefore less secure. Nevertheless, equitable rights will be binding on all third parties, such as purchasers or lenders on the security of

the property, provided the purchaser or lender has notice of those rights. Ways of protecting equitable/beneficial interests are explained at Chapter 5, Section C.

Note that, unlike in matrimonial law, the courts cannot alter a person's property rights using property law and the principles of equity. They can only declare the interests that each person can be deemed to hold already.

Chapter 4: Married owner-occupiers

Subjects covered in this chapter include...

Sole legal owner

What rights a non-owner spouse has to stay in the matrimonial home

What rights a non-owner spouse has to deal with the mortgage

How a spouse can be made to leave

How matrimonial rights to the home can be protected

How to prevent a spouse selling the home or disposing of property

Joint legal owner

What rights joint owners have in the matrimonial home

How joint owners can exclude each other

How a joint owner can prevent a spouse from selling the home or disposing of property

Sole and joint legal owner

How the court can transfer property from one spouse to the other

How to deal with inheritance problems if a spouse dies

What powers the courts have to order financial support for a spouse

How property can be transferred if the couple are not divorcing

Married owner-occupiers

The areas of law available to married couples in owner-occupied property to settle rights to property are:

Matrimonial/family law

Part 4 of the Family Law Act 1996 deals with short-term rights to occupy the home. Long-term settlement of property is dealt with by the Matrimonial Causes Act 1973. This chapter deals with these areas of law.

Property law

This is available to all owner-occupiers whether married or cohabiting. The basic principles of property law are dealt with in Chapter 3 and the position on relationship breakdown is covered in more detail in Chapter 5.

Child law

This is only available to couples with children. Transferring property under the Children Act 1989 is in Chapter 9.

Domestic violence

This is covered in Chapter 13.

Sole legal owner

A   Rights in respect of the matrimonial home

The following information applies to married couples where one partner's name only appears on the title deeds.

4.1   The right to live in the matrimonial home

The Family Law Act 1996 gives a non-owning spouse 'matrimonial home rights.' These are rights to occupy the home and to prevent the owner-spouse from evicting or excluding the non-owner spouse during the

s30(2)(a) FLA96   marriage without a court order. When there is a matrimonial dispute or estrangement and the court is making one of these orders, it can also make an order which states that matrimonial home rights will not be brought to an end either by the death of the other spouse or by the

s33(5) FLA96   termination of the marriage.

In most cases, therefore, both parties will have a right to remain living in the matrimonial home for as long as the marriage continues and as long as the owning spouse has a legal right to occupy the home. Where matrimonial home rights have been registered in the Land Registry or

s31(2) &
s31(9) FLA96   the Land Charges Register the non-owning spouse will have the right to continue to occupy, even when the owning spouse surrenders her/his interest or sells the property (see 4.9).

A non-owning spouse has a number of other rights relating to the matrimonial home, listed below.

4.2   Other matrimonial rights of the non-owning spouse

The Family Law Act gives a spouse who is not the owner the following rights whilst the marriage is still in existence.

Occupation of the home

s30(2)(a) FLA96

1. To occupy the matrimonial home and not to be excluded, except by court order, as explained above.

s30(2)(b) FLA96

2. If not occupying the home, to obtain a court order to gain entry and to live there.

Payment and liabilities

s30(3) FLA96

s30(5) FLA96

3. To pay the mortgage or other outgoings which are to be treated as if paid by the owner. Such payments could still count towards establishing a beneficial interest in the property. Note that this is a right to have mortgage payments accepted and does not mean that the non-owning spouse can be held legally liable for the owner's arrears, unless an order has been made transferring liability in conjunction with an order regarding rights to occupy (an 'occupation order' under the Family Law Act). Even if such an order has been made there can be problems enforcing payment if the order is disregarded (see 11.17).

s40(1)(a) FLA96

Possession action

4. The right to apply to the court to be a party to the action in any mortgage possession proceedings taken against the spouse if the court sees no special reason against it and the applicant is likely to be able to contribute to the payments.

s55 FLA96

5. The right to be notified by the lender of any mortgage possession action, provided that matrimonial home rights have been registered.

s56 FLA96

The important point to recognise about matrimonial home rights is that the non-owning spouse occupies as if s/he were the owner *without* having the actual status of an owner.

Matrimonial home rights are a charge on the property but need to be registered to be binding on third parties such as lenders or purchasers (see 4.8-9).

s31 FLA96

4.3   The matrimonial home

Matrimonial home rights apply only to a home which has been lived in jointly by both parties as their matrimonial home or which was intended by the spouses to be a matrimonial home. If a couple buy a house with the intention of moving into it together, but the relationship breaks down before they can move in, both will therefore have matrimonial home rights.

s30(7) FLA96 Where one spouse obtains a new home for her/himself alone, the other spouse will not however have the right to occupy it.

4.4   Occupation orders under the Family Law Act 1996

Occupation orders were brought in by the Family Law Act 1996 and replaced previous legislation on regulation of occupation of the home in cases of relationship breakdown. They allow the court to decide who should be allowed to live in the home and whether either party should be excluded. Occupation orders are discussed in depth in Chapter 13, Section C.

Because occupation orders have a dual function – both declaring, extending and conferring rights to occupy and also restricting or controlling existing rights to occupy – they can, in theory, be used not only in cases of violence but also in cases where there is a 'dispute about living arrangements during a marital breakdown in which there is no molestation but relations have become intolerably strained.'[1] In these latter cases the court has a power, rather than a duty, to make an order, on the basis of specified criteria. In practice, it is still rare for a spouse to be excluded where there is no significant harm, but in the case of *S v F* (see box) an order was granted allowing the ex-husband to occupy the ex-matrimonial home which neither party were occupying at the time.

S v F (Occupation order) (No violence involved)[2]

An ex-husband, together with his new wife and family, was granted an occupation order to occupy the family home in London where his 17 year old son was living. The ex-wife had decided to move to Somerset and wanted to sell the house.

The judge found that the father's financial position was weaker than the mother's and the well-being of the son and the father's children by the second marriage required the occupation order to be made. The mother's conduct in abandoning the son and moving without warning were also taken into account.

The order was for six months or until property proceedings were resolved – the marriage had ended five years previously but no settlement had been reached.

---

1. Family law, domestic violence and occupation of the family home. Law Commission Report No. 207, para 4.20(ii).

2. S v F (Occupation order) (2000) 1 FLR 255 (No violence involved).

Orders

Under the Family Law Act a distinction is drawn between those who are 'entitled' to be in the home and those with no entitlement to occupy the home. An entitled person is someone who has an existing legal right to occupy a dwelling because of a legal interest, beneficial interest or other contract or statute, or who has matrimonial home rights. Spouses who are legal owners and non-owning spouses both therefore come under the heading of 'entitled applicants.'

s33(1) FLA96

The orders available to non-owning spouses which deal with rights to remain in occupation are:

s33(3)(a) FLA96 & s33(4) FLA96
• to declare that someone has matrimonial home rights and enforce those rights

s33(3)(b) FLA96
• to grant orders that they should be allowed back in and allowed to remain, if they have been excluded

s33(5) FLA96
• where an application is made during marriage, to extend the matrimonial home rights beyond death or divorce

s33(3)(f) FLA96
• to exclude the owning spouse from all or part of the home

s33(3)(g) FLA96
• to exclude the owning spouse from a defined area around the home.

The owning spouse can, of course, also seek an order against the non-owning spouse, and the court will decide what order to make on the basis of the relevant criteria (see below and also Chapter 13).

The court can also attach provisions which can oblige either party to repair and maintain the home and meet mortgage liability and other outgoings (but see 11.17 for details of the limitations on the courts' powers to enforce such financial orders). In addition it can make orders granting one partner the use of furniture and contents and ensuring that a partner in the home takes reasonable care of such furniture and contents and the home itself.

4.5   Criteria for occupation orders

The criteria which the court must take into account are:

• housing needs and resources

• financial resources

• the likely effect of any order or of not making an order on the health, safety or well-being of the parties and of any child involved

• the conduct of the parties in relation to each other and in general.

Housing resources include, for example, the likelihood of either party qualifying for rehousing under the homelessness legislation.[3]

3.   Akintola v Akintola [2002] 1 FLR 701, B v B (Occupation Order) (1999) 1 FLR 715.

This means that in theory it is now possible for a non-owning spouse to obtain an order excluding the owning spouse on the basis that it is necessary for the well-being of the children. Violence or misconduct by the other partner is not essential, nor does violence by one party automatically lead to her/his exclusion, since the needs of the children may be the deciding factor.[4] The courts have however reiterated the pre-Family Law Act attitude that *'An order to vacate the matrimonial home is a draconian one and should be restricted to exceptional cases under the 1996 Act, as was recognised in previous case law under the DVMPA 1976.'* In the case of *Chalmers v Johns*,[5] the court held that the facts of the case came nowhere near that category. *'The disharmony between the parties would have been perfectly capable of control by injunctive order.'* In addition the parties were encouraged to take advantage of mediation facilities to resolve their dispute.

In non-violent situations therefore, whilst the courts have a power to make occupation orders excluding one of the parties, they seem reluctant to do so. In contrast, where there is a likelihood of significant harm, a 'balance of harm' test (see 13.29) must be applied and the court is s33(7) FLA96 under a duty to make an order.

Duration of orders

s33(10) FLA96 Occupation orders for non-owning spouses may be made either for a specified period, until a specific event occurs (eg, divorce) or until further order, at the court's discretion. The usual period is between 3 and 6 months.

4.6 Matrimonial rights after divorce

Matrimonial rights relating to occupation normally cease on termination of marriage by death or final decree of divorce (decree absolute). An application must be made to the court for an extension of the rights beyond divorce if it looks as if a property settlement will not have been reached by that time and the non-owner wants to remain in the s33(5) FLA96 matrimonial home.

s35 FLA96 Under the Family Law Act it is possible for an ex-spouse who is not an owner to apply for an occupation order. However, the court does not have as much discretion when giving occupation orders to ex-spouses (see 13.32) and so it is still preferable to apply before the end of the marriage. Nevertheless, in one case an ex-husband was granted an order to occupy the home which his ex-wife wanted to sell[6] (see box above).

---

4. B v B (Occupation Order) (1999) 1 FLR 715 CA.
5. Chalmers v Johns, (1999) 1 FLR CA.
6. S v F (Occupation Order) (2000) 1 FLR 255 (No violence involved).

4.7   The non-owning spouse's rights where the owner is declared bankrupt

s34(1)(b) FLA96   Provided that matrimonial rights of occupation are registered as a charge on the property, they continue to hold good against the spouse's trustee in bankruptcy. The trustee therefore has to apply for an order under section 33 of the Family Law Act to terminate the matrimonial rights to occupy. In practice, there is likely to be a 'breathing space' of 12 months,

s335A IA86   after which the spouse will normally have to leave the home (see 12.12).

B   Protecting non-owning spouse's matrimonial home rights and other rights

Note: the implications of the Land Registration Act 2002, which will come into force on 13th October 2003, are explained in Chapter 5 as these affect the registration of beneficial interests. The following information is correct at the time of writing and the registration of matrimonial home rights is not expected to be affected by the implementation of the Act, although the forms to be used may change after 13 October 2003.

For the latest information on the Act and the rules which will give details of how the Act will work see www.legislation.landreg.gov.uk

4.8   Protecting matrimonial home rights

Matrimonial home rights must be formally registered, otherwise they cannot help in preventing a sale or remortgage of the matrimonial home. A non-owning spouse with the matrimonial home rights explained in section 4.2 above can register the rights as a charge on the matrimonial home. S/he can do this, even if s/he is not living in it at that point in time, although s/he must have lived there with the owning spouse at some point.

4.9   Matrimonial home rights as a registered charge

What is a charge?

Placing a charge on a property is a way of indicating to a prospective buyer or lender that someone other than the owner has an interest or right in or over a property. The charge will be binding upon third parties, ie, if the property were sold or remortgaged it would still be subject to that registered charge and the new owner or lender is obliged to honour it. The existence of a charge on a property is therefore very important to anyone wishing to buy a house or who is considering lending money on its security.

Charges can include loans on property, a financial interest in the property or, as in the case under discussion, a right to occupy.

If the land is registered land (as most land in towns and cities now is) charges are registered in accordance with the Land Registration Act 1925, as amended by various Land Registration Acts in the 1980s and 1990s, and the Land Charges Act 1971. If the land is unregistered charges are registered in accordance with the Land Charges Act 1972. The Land Registry publishes useful leaflets, Explanatory Leaflet No.4 'Protecting Matrimonial Home rights under the Family Law Act 1996' and Explanatory Leaflet No.9 which contains a list of areas and the district land registries which deal with them. These and the necessary forms for registration can be downloaded from the Land Registry website at www.landreg.gov.uk or obtained from any of the Land Registry offices or Citizens Advice Bureaux.

The effect of registering a matrimonial charge

Matrimonial home rights are statutory rights granted on a purely personal basis to a spouse protecting her/his right to live in the matrimonial home. The spouse can continue occupying the home but this right does not give any financial stake (beneficial interest) in the home. Registering the matrimonial home rights means that the non-owner's right to occupy is binding upon any subsequent purchaser or lender on the property. It also requires a lender to notify the non-owning spouse of any possession proceedings (see 4.2).

s56 FLA96

If the owning spouse tries to sell the home without her/his spouse's knowledge the registered right to occupy will show up in the searches made by the prospective buyer. A prospective buyer is not likely to want to buy a house with a recalcitrant husband or wife sitting tight in it. There is further legal protection in that when a house is sold with vacant possession, it is a term of the contract that the seller will obtain cancellation of registration of a spouse's matrimonial home rights.

Example

A husband exchanges contracts to sell the matrimonial home thinking he will be able to persuade his wife to move out. She has registered her matrimonial home rights and refuses to cancel them. The husband is then in breach of contract and may have to pay substantial damages for failing to complete as agreed.

The registration therefore effectively prevents an owning spouse from selling without the non-owner's agreement.

4.10   How to register a matrimonial charge

This can be done quite simply without a solicitor. The procedure differs depending on whether the land is registered or unregistered.

Finding out if land is registered or unregistered

• Buy Land Registry form No. 96 from a law stationer (these should be listed in yellow pages)

• Fill in the form and write across the top: 'This search is being made solely for the purposes of the Family Law Act 1996. Please reveal details of any registered lease'

• Send it to the appropriate District Land Registry Office. At the present time, the service is free.[7]

This search will tell if the land is registered or unregistered.

Registered land

Matrimonial home rights can be registered with the Land Registry (totally distinct and separate from the Land Charges Register used for unregistered land).

s31(10)(a) FLA96   They must be registered as a notice under the Land Registration Act 1925.

A 'notice' is registered in the charges register and recorded on the land certificate and will be binding on everyone. The registered owner does not have to consent but will be notified of the registration.

• Obtain and complete Land Registry form MH1.[8] Charges are made against the land, not the owner

• Send to the District Land Registry Office which deals with the area in which the house is situated. There is no fee

• A letter will be sent notifying the applicant that the notice has been registered within approximately two weeks

• A notice will always be sent to the spouse advising her/him that an application has been made.

Unregistered land

The charge to be registered is known as a Class F land charge and is registered on the Land Charges Register.

• Obtain and complete Land Charges form K2. All charges made in the Land Charges register are registered against the name of the land owner and not against the land itself. It is essential that the name is exactly correct, ie, the full name of the owner as recorded on the title

---

7.   The Central Land Registry at The Information Centre, Lincoln's Inn Fields, London WC2A 3PH, Tel. 020 7917 8888, Fax 020 7955 0110 publishes addresses of District Land Registry offices. At the time of writing the service was free.

8.   MH1 and other Land Registry can be freely downloaded from http://www.landreg.gov.uk. Check for information on new forms after 13/10/03.

deeds. Failure to use the correct name, eg, by omitting a middle name, could result in the charge being totally ineffective

• Send the form with the fee, currently £1, to the Land Charges Department.[9] This registers the charge on the property and the applicant should be notified in writing of the registration within a day or two. The spouse is not notified of the registration although any subsequent searches will of course reveal the charge.

4.11 Registering other rights

In addition to matrimonial rights to occupy, the non-owning spouse may have additional rights to remain in occupation if s/he has a beneficial (or financial) interest and is living in the property concerned. The same procedures for protecting the rights based on a beneficial interest apply to both married couples and cohabitants and are explained in detail at Chapter 5, Section C.

C   Preventing disposal of the solely-owned matrimonial home

Where the home is in a sole name disposal can be prevented or remedied in a number of ways.

4.12 The right to sell the matrimonial home

Technically, only the legal owner's consent is required to sell the property. In practice a non-owning spouse can effectively prevent a sale of the home by registering her/his matrimonial home rights as a charge on the property as explained above.

4.13 Raising a loan on the matrimonial home

Technically, only the legal owner's consent is required to secure a loan on the family home, but in recent years lenders have considerably tightened up their procedures when deciding whether or not to grant a loan or second mortgage. Lenders now normally insist on obtaining written consent to the loan from anyone living in the home regardless of whether or not they appear on the title deeds. The Family Law Act provides for a non-owning spouse to agree in writing that another

para 6 Sch4 FLA96   charge will rank in priority over her/his matrimonial rights of occupation.

This is sometimes referred to as 'waiving' rights.

In practice, therefore, a non-owning spouse living in the home may be able to refuse consent and thereby prevent the raising of a loan on the security of the property.

---

9.   At the time of writing the fee was £1.00 and the address was Land Charges Department, Plumer House, Tailyour Road, Crownhill, Plymouth PL6 5HY. Tel. 01752 636666.

4.14   Rights of a non-owning spouse to remain in the matrimonial home despite the claims of a lender or new owner

The matrimonial home rights are registered as a charge

If the charge is registered then the non-owning spouse will have the right to remain in the home unless the rights have been waived.

If the non-owner waived her/his rights before the loan was taken out or the property sold then s/he will have no rights to remain in the property. However, any transaction which can be shown to have been carried out as the result of 'undue influence' (eg, emotional pressure) or misrepresentation may be declared void in law (see Chapter 5, section H, 5.37 – 5.43).

No charge is registered

s31(10)(b) FLA96   The matrimonial home rights to occupy are not binding if they are not registered. Even if a purchaser or lender actually knows that the non-owner wishes to remain there and has done nothing to gain consent, the right to occupy becomes void. In other words, without registration, the non-owning spouse would have no matrimonial right to remain if the property were sold or a lender wished to repossess because of an unpaid loan.

This differs from other rights to occupy which may arise as a result of a beneficial interest and be enforceable even without registration (eg, an 'overriding interest' – see 5.24).

Transfers for no money

All existing interests, including rights of occupation hold good, even if they are not registered, if the property is transferred without 'valuable consideration,' ie, a reasonable amount of money or money's worth. Thus, if the owner of the family home gave it away, for example by transferring it into a relative's name whilst the non-owning spouse was still in occupation, the non-owner's right to occupy would still hold good against the new owner. In other words, s/he could not be evicted.

In some cases, people have tried to avoid this effect by requiring nominal payments; the courts have held that this is not sufficient where the amount is clearly not representative of the value, for example £1.[10] However, a transfer at a substantially reduced price, but not a ridiculous level, could qualify as a 'disposal for value' and the wife's interest would then only be protected if it were registered.

---

10.   Peffer v Rigg (1977) 1 WLR 285.

> ### Example: Rights to remain in the home
> *Frank Roberts has a mortgage of £95,000 with the Goodlife Building Society. He took out the mortgage to buy the home he shares with his wife Wendy, who is not a legal owner of the property. He raises a second mortgage of £40,000 with Shark Investments to help his business through a bad patch. However, the business fails, the loan repayments fall into arrears and Shark Investments seek possession.*
>
> ### If the charge is registered
> *Wendy has matrimonial home rights to occupy which she registered as a charge on the property. Her rights to remain in the home will take precedence over Shark Investments' interest, provided they were registered before Frank took out the loan, thus giving Shark Investments notice of her rights. They will not be able to enforce payment of the loan against her and they cannot repossess. The loan will be enforceable against Frank's equitable share only and it is unlikely that any court would order possession on that basis.*
>
> ### If the charge is not registered
> *If Wendy's rights were not registered before the loan was taken out she will have effectively lost her right to remain.*
>
> ### Wendy agreed to waive her rights
> *In practice nowadays, Shark Investments are almost certain to have asked Frank to obtain Wendy's signature saying she agrees that their right to repossess if payments are not made will take precedence over her registered rights to occupy. If she has signed such a document, the only other possibility is to argue that she was under undue influence (explained at 5.37 – 5.43) from her husband to sign.*

OTHER WAYS OF PREVENTING DISPOSAL

4.15 Registering a pending land action where a property adjustment order is being sought.

Under matrimonial law it is possible for the court to 'adjust' the ownership of property as part of a divorce, for example, by transferring the property from one person to the other (see 4.28). An application for a property adjustment order constitutes a 'pending land action' and as such can be registered as a charge in the Land Register if the land is unregistered or s17 LCA72 by notice or caution in the Land Registry if the land is registered (see 5.23). This effectively gives notice of the action to any purchaser or lender.

> **Perez-Adamson**[11]
>
> *The wife registered her application for a property adjustment order and the husband subsequently obtained a £60,000 bank loan on the security of the house saying that it was for the divorce settlement. In fact he sent the money abroad. The bank did not make a search of the land charges register and so, it was held, the wife's claim took priority.*

4.16   Using section 37 of the Matrimonial Causes Act 1973

Section 37 of the Matrimonial Causes Act grants the court two important powers:

• To grant an injunction to prevent a sale or disposal of property

• To grant an order setting aside such a disposal after it has happened.

Preventing disposal

Section 37 injunctions can be applied for only during divorce, judicial separation or nullity proceedings when there is also an application for a financial settlement and/or property adjustment order.

The court has power to grant an injunction to stop either party from disposing of or transferring any property, if the intention is to defeat the spouse's claim for finance or property belonging to the other. The court can also make whatever order it thinks fit to protect the other partner's claim.

s37(2)(a) MCA73

A section 37 injunction can be sought where there is evidence that the spouse:

• is about to dispose of her/his property

• is about to transfer it out of the country

• is about to deal with it in any other way.

In effect, it 'freezes' property. 'Property' can include 'real' property (ie, dwellings or buildings) or personal property (cars, jewellery or assets) and even property which has not yet been received such as expected redundancy payments or anticipated damages claims.

> **Example: Using section 37 of the Matrimonial Causes Act to prevent disposal**
>
> *If Mr X is intending to transfer all his property, including cars and valuables, as well as a house, to his new partner, or to a relative, so that his wife will not be able to claim any of it in their divorce proceedings, an injunction can be sought to prevent this.*

---

11. Perez-Adamson v Perez Rivas (1987) 2 FLR 472; (1987) 3 All ER 20; (1987) NLJ 409 CA.

Reversing a sale or transfer

The courts have powers to undo steps taken to defeat a spouse's claim. A sale or gift of property, or a loan or second mortgage raised on a property can be set aside by order of the court and it may order that the property be transferred back and that any purchase money be repaid.

s37(2)(b) & (c) MCA73

Section 37 orders to set aside transactions are not routine measures and are only made in exceptional circumstances, where it can be shown that the spouse has deliberately disposed of the property to avoid the other spouse's claim and the person to whom it was disposed was aware of this. Where it seems that one partner may be trying to outwit the other by getting rid of property it is best to seek an injunction to prevent this in advance.

s37(4) MCA73

Section 37 orders to set aside transactions cannot be granted where the buyer or lender acted in good faith and did not know, nor could reasonably be expected to know, that the seller was trying to defeat her/his spouse's claim. This is known as having 'constructive notice' (see 5.21). This highlights once again the importance of registration of rights. If an interest is registered it will be held that the buyer should have known about it and therefore a section 37 order may be obtainable.

Procedure for applying for section 37 orders

These orders must be made in conjunction with matrimonial proceedings under the Matrimonial Causes Act 1973. The hearing is generally before the district judge in the divorce county court and must, if practical, take place at the same time as any connected application for financial provision.

4.17 Orders to protect property under the inherent jurisdiction of the court

s37 SCA81 & s3 CLSAct90

If a husband or wife fears that the partner may abscond with money or goods but has no specific evidence, ie, nothing has been said or done to indicate such an intention, it may still be possible to prevent sale or disposal. There is an inherent jurisdiction in the court, as well as a power provided for in the court rules, which allows the court to make an order for the detention, custody or preservation of any property which is the subject of a disputed claim. This is not however a well-used power.

4.18 Freezing injunctions

Freezing injunctions[12] are more frequently used in commercial situations since the powers under the Matrimonial Causes Act 1973 are adequate for most matrimonial situations.

---

12. ss 2 and 3 County Court Remedies Regulations 1991 (SI 1991 No. 1222 as amended by SI 1995 No. 206).

They are a similar but more draconian power which can be used to prevent disposal of assets anywhere in the world which could be the subject of legal proceedings. Freezing injunctions can apply even where the person is living abroad and would normally be out of the jurisdiction of British legislation although success will depend upon which country is involved. In addition orders can be made requiring a person to provide information about the location of relevant property or assets or to provide information about relevant property or assets which are or may be the subject of an application for a freezing injunction.

CPR 25.1(f)
s37(3) SCA81

CPR 25.1(g)

4.19   Search orders

A search order is again a draconian measure which allows the court to make an order requiring a person to admit another person to premises for preserving evidence or inspecting or copying documents and other possessions. This might, in extreme cases, be used to obtain evidence about disposal of assets. However it is not normally used in family proceedings.

CPR 25.1(h)

Joint legal owners

This is where both partners' names appear on the title deeds.

D   Rights in respect of the matrimonial home

4.20   The right to live in the matrimonial home

If a couple are joint legal owners, property law entitles both parties to live there. Neither can legally exclude the other except by court order.

4.21   Rights to occupy under the Family Law Act 1996

Joint legal owners do not have matrimonial home rights granted by the Family Law Act. It was considered unnecessary to grant joint owners the same statutory rights to occupy as a non-owning spouse because as joint owners they have existing rights to occupy by virtue of property law.

4.22   Occupation orders under the Family Law Act 1996

The only specific right under the Family Law Act given to joint owners is for one owner to apply for an occupation order in exactly the same way as a non-owning spouse with matrimonial home rights. S/he would be an 'entitled' applicant with pre-existing rights to occupy and so in the same position as a sole owner (see 4.5 above).

s33 FLA96

A joint owner can therefore apply for orders declaring or enforcing her/his rights to occupy or to regain entry if necessary. S/he can also apply to exclude the other spouse or restrict her/his right to occupy the matrimonial home. The criteria for making such orders is exactly the same as for non-owning spouses.

4.23 Occupation orders and 'occupation rent'

s40(1)(b) FLA96   The court may also attach additional provisions to an occupation order imposing obligations to pay an 'occupation rent' to the other 'entitled' spouse or ex-spouse, ie, a compensatory payment to the spouse who has been excluded from occupation of the home. It may also make orders regarding who should make mortgage payments and other outgoings

s40(1)(a) FLA96   and carry out repairs and maintenance (but see 11.17).

E Preventing disposal of the jointly owned matrimonial home

4.24 The right to sell the matrimonial home

The consent and signatures of both owners is required for a sale to be valid. If there is no consent, a sale may be ordered by the court under

s17 MWPA,   either property or matrimonial law compelling the owner to comply
s14 TLATA
& s24A MCA73   (see also 4.33 and 5.48 – 49).

4.25 Raising a loan on the matrimonial home

Raising a loan involves giving the lender a charge on the property. If there is already a mortgage in existence a subsequent loan is usually referred to as a second mortgage. If the loan is not repaid the lender can call in the debt which frequently results in an order for possession of the property.

Where a property is owned jointly, the consent and signature of both parties is required, but in some cases, such consents can be held to be invalid, if it can be shown that the partner signing did so under undue influence (emotional pressure) or misrepresentation from her/his partner (see 5.37 – 5.43).

4.26 Preventing disposal of property

Since both are legal owners, there could be no valid disposal of the jointly owned property without the consent and signatures of both parties except by order of the court. Disposal of other types of property, eg, cars, belongings, money, can be prevented in a number of ways, listed above (4.15-9).

Sole and joint legal owners

The following sections apply equally to sole and joint owner-occupiers.

F Matrimonial courts' powers to transfer property

It is often assumed that 'whoever has the children gets the house.' Since the Children Act 1989 came into force there is far more scope for voluntary agreements between parents to share responsibility for the children and the situation may not be that clear-cut. Indeed it never has been, since the courts have to consider a wide variety of factors as well as giving first consideration to the needs of the children.

In practice, nowadays, lawyers, mediators and Citizens' Advice will advise a Consent Order wherever possible (see 4.27 below). The following sections aim to explain the courts' powers and the criteria they must use in reaching a decision. The Children Act and the Child Support Act are discussed in Chapters 9 and 10.

4.27   Consent Orders

In recent years the emphasis has shifted to reaching agreement about matrimonial finances and assets without going to court. This is usually done by negotiation through the parties' respective solicitors, or sometimes, though less often, by mediation (see 2.7 – 2.11). The Family Proceedings Rules 1999 added impetus by aiming to enable parties to reach agreement. If a couple voluntarily reach an agreement, it will normally be drawn up as a draft court order, which is then presented to the court for ratification as a 'consent order.' The court will check to see, for example, that one spouse has not unwittingly accepted less than s/he could reasonably be entitled to, and has the power to amend the terms of an agreement. However, if both parties have been advised independently and the terms of the order seem reasonable, the court will not normally interfere. If the agreement is not subject to a consent order, there is a strong presumption that it should still be enforced by the court.[13] Nevertheless, this is a matter of discretion for the court to decide.

In reaching a negotiated settlement, the spouses should be aware of the factors which the court would consider, in order to agree terms which are fair to both parties. The courts' powers and the statutory considerations are therefore examined below.

4.28   The courts' powers in respect of property

It is very important to understand that the matrimonial courts' powers to deal with property on the breakdown of a marriage differ fundamentally from the powers based on property law. Under matrimonial law, the courts can actually reallocate or transfer ownership of property regardless of legal ownership or beneficial interests. In other words, the court's decision as to who gets what need not reflect whose name the property is held in, how it was acquired or who paid what. The court

13.   Xydhias v Xydhias (1999) 1 FLR 683 CA.

is empowered to adjust property rights, hence the term used for these sorts of orders is property adjustment orders. In addition to these powers the court can order the sale of the property.

s24 MCA73
s24A MCA73

There are specific criteria which the court must consider when reaching a decision as to what type of order to make.

4.29   Court order to transfer ownership

s24 MCA73

- Applications for a property adjustment order can only be made in conjunction with a divorce petition or application for nullity or judicial separation. If a couple have simply separated, the matrimonial court has no jurisdiction to make an order. If no legal proceedings to formalise the end of the marriage are contemplated, it would be necessary to consider other courses of action to deal with property (using either the Children Act or property law, see 9.13 – 9.16 and 5.48)

s24(1)(a)
& s29 MCA73

- Property can be transferred to either spouse, any 'child of the family' (although where the child is 18 years old or over, the property can only be transferred in limited circumstances) or to a specified person for the benefit of a child. The term 'child of the family' is explained at 9.4

- The courts can order a settlement of property for the benefit of the other spouse or any children of the family. The courts can vary any ante- or post-nuptial settlement, eg, property left to one party in a will

- When filing the divorce petition, the person presenting it has to indicate if at some stage s/he intends to apply for finance or property to be made over to her/him from the other spouse. This is usually referred to as applying for financial or ancillary relief. If s/he does, this must be followed up by a separate application. If no notice is given at this time but subsequently the spouse decides to make a claim, then it will be necessary to get permission from the court to make the application

s26 MCA73

- Applications for a property adjustment order can be made before or after the decree absolute or at any subsequent time until remarriage. The court may make an order after remarriage, provided the application was lodged before the remarriage.[14]

4.30   When the property adjustment order takes effect

- If the petition is for divorce or nullity, the property adjustment order cannot take effect until decree absolute has been pronounced

- If the petition is for judicial separation, the property adjustment order may take effect once the decree has been pronounced

14. Jackson v Jackson (1973) Fam 99.

For those advising people on homelessness applications, it is important to remember that proceedings may be long and drawn out (eg, divorce by mutual consent requires two years' separation) and if the petition is based on two years' separation by consent, then the parties have to live in separate 'households' under the same roof. If one or the other refuses to move out, it may therefore be necessary to argue that it is not reasonable to expect the parties to remain under the same roof until the decree is made absolute.

4.31   Property that can be transferred under a property adjustment order

The courts may order a transfer of any property to which a spouse is entitled. 'Property' includes houses, cars, a business, the contents of the home, some tenancies and any other assets of either party.

4.32   Deciding on what order to make – the court's criteria

s25 MCA73   The legislation sets out the criteria which the court must use for deciding what orders are made, but the court is given wide discretion on how to interpret them and it has been accepted that different judges could come to different conclusions in any particular case.[15] The court may also take additional factors into account and whilst there is no one statutory objective specified in the legislation, the House of Lords in the landmark decision of *White v White*[16] has held that:

> *'Implicitly, the objective must be to achieve a fair outcome. The purpose of these powers is to enable the court to make fair financial arrangements... the powers must always be exercised with this objective in view, giving first consideration to the welfare of the children.'*

White v White is a case involving 'big money' – total assets of £4.5 million. In cases such as this, it was held that previous court decisions which had treated a spouse's 'reasonable requirements' as the determining factor in deciding how to divide up property and assets were incorrect. The judge's views should always be measured against the 'yardstick of equality of division,' but this principle may be departed from, for example, where contributions to the welfare of the family plus other factors justified a higher proportion of total assets being awarded to one spouse. The House of Lords has firmly reminded the lower courts that financial needs are only one part of the equation in reaching a fair solution. However, in many cases, where the total resources are small, financial needs and requirements are still bound to be highly influential.

Note that property rights and financial payments towards the acquisition of the home do not figure as such, except in so far as they come under

---

15. Piglowska v Piglowski (1999) 2 FLR 763 HL.   16. White v White (2000) 2 FLR 981; [2001] 1 All ER 1 HL.

contributions to the welfare of the family. The court must have regard to the following matters:

- *In general, all the circumstances of the case, with first consideration being given to the welfare of any child of the family under 18*
  Note that the interests of the children are of first but not paramount consideration, in that they do not override the court's duty to try to achieve a 'financial result which is just as between husband and wife.'[17] Case law has also shown that the courts are entitled to consider local authority rehousing obligations to either spouse[18]

- *Income, earning capacity, property and financial resources of the parties now and in the foreseeable future, including any increase in earning capacity which the court considers it reasonable for either party to take steps to acquire*
  The income of a second spouse or cohabitant is not treated as part of the first spouse's income for distribution on marriage settlement,[19] but it may be taken into account in so far as it may be considered to relieve one spouse from some part of the duty of maintaining the other.[20] The capacity of a spouse to get work will be taken into account. What might appear to be deliberate unemployment (ie, an avoidance of work so as not to have to pay anything to an ex-spouse) will not prevent the court from assuming an appropriate earning potential. However, the courts have held that it was not reasonable to expect a 45-year-old woman to seek full-time employment or set up her own business, despite the fact that she had an engineering degree. The outcome may well have been different had she not devoted many years to childcare, or if she had been younger[21]

- *Financial needs, obligations and responsibilities each party has or is likely to have in the future*
  Again first consideration of 'needs' will be given to children's needs. In most cases it is accepted that the most important need is for the provision of a home. The ability of either spouse to obtain a mortgage will be taken into account when the court makes its decision

- *Standard of living during the marriage*
  Awards should reflect the style of life lived by the spouses, eg, orders should not be made merely to subsistence level if there was substantial income and capital. This is why spouses of wealthy people are often awarded far more than they could be said to 'need!'[22] Since the case of *White v White*, even the fact that a large sum of money may seem more than enough for someone's 'reasonable requirements' will not necessarily stop the court from awarding a larger amount. The approach taken by the House of Lords was that if the spouses have contributed

---

17. Suter v Suter and Jones (1987) 2 All ER 336; (1987) Fam 111.
18. Jones v Jones (1996) Fam Law 787 CA.
19. B v B (Periodical Payments: Transitional Provisions) (1995) 1 FLR 459.
20. Atkinson v Atkinson (1995) 2 FLR 356.
21. A v A (Financial Provision) (1998) 2 FLR 180.
22. see for example F v F (Ancillary Relief: Substantial Assets) (1995) 2 FLR 45.

equally in the marriage to the welfare of the family, and all other matters seem equal, why should each spouse not be entitled to enjoy half of any 'excess' assets? Or, as Lord Nicholls put it *'why should the surplus belong solely to the husband?'*[23]

- *Age of parties and duration of marriage*
  The older the parties and the longer the marriage, one might think that the greater the settlement is likely to be to compensate for 'lost opportunities,' likelihood of regaining employment, obtaining a mortgage etc. However, in one case, despite a marriage of 20 years which followed 40 years cohabiting, it was not deemed appropriate to give a half and half share. The wife's age (78) meant that her reasonable needs could be met by a smaller amount.[24] Until *White v White*, a spouse's needs were sometimes based on a so-called 'Duxbury calculation,' leading to *'the well known paradox that the longer the marriage and hence the older the wife, the less the capital sum required for a Duxbury type fund.'* [25] A Duxbury calculation involves assessing a spouse's annual financial needs and multiplying it by the number of remaining years of life expectancy. This is a complicated calculation and is not now used much in practice. The approach must now certainly be treated with caution since Lord Nicholls' words in *White v White* in the House of Lords:

  > *'As I have been at pains to emphasise, financial needs are only one of the factors to be taken into account in arriving at the amount of an award. The amount of capital required to provide for an older wife's financial needs may well be less than the amount required to provide for a younger wife's financial needs. It by no means follows that, in a case where resources exceed the parties' financial needs, the older wife's award will be less than the younger wife's. Indeed, the older wife's award may be substantially larger.'*

- *Physical and mental disabilities of either party*
  Adaptations which have been made to the home and ability to find suitable alternative accommodation are likely to be taken into account, as well as the financial implications of any disability. A serious disability could result in all the assets being awarded to the person with the disability even if it left the other spouse dependent upon social security benefits.[26]

- *Any contributions (and likely future contributions)*
  to the welfare of the family
  Unlike property law rules, this can include looking after the home or caring for the family and does not have to reflect contributions in monetary terms. Changing attitudes to the roles within the family have been reflected in court decisions. The court will not accept, for

23. White v White (2000) 2 FLR 981; [2001] 1 All ER 1 HL.
24. W v W (1995) 2 FLR 259.
25. White v White in the judgment by Holman J. (see above).
26. C v C (Financial Provision: Personal Damages) (1995) 2 FLR 171.

example, that a wife's award should be reduced simply because she has not brought any money into the household[27]

- *Conduct, if inequitable to disregard it*
  Violent physical conduct by one spouse has affected the court's financial awards although it must be very severe to be taken into account.[28] In *H v H (Financial provision: conduct)*[29] the husband had been sentenced to three and a half years imprisonment for assault and attempted rape on his wife. He had lost his salaried job of £27,000 and its pension rights and had thereby destroyed the wife's material security, reducing them both to income support. He was ordered to transfer his share in the former matrimonial home. 'Very unreasonable' non-violent conduct may also be taken into account.

In *Kyte v Kyte*,[30] the wife behaved callously when the husband, a manic depressive, made two suicide attempts. On the first, she was present and only called assistance at the last moment. On the second she encouraged him, giving him the tablets and alcohol with which to kill himself and jeering at him when he failed to carry out his intention. The court found as a fact that the wife wanted the husband dead so that she could inherit his money and share it with her lover. Her award was reduced from £14,000 which she would have received to £5000.

In another case, *Whiston v Whiston*,[31] a wife's bigamy through a 15 year 'marriage' was held to be misconduct which, whilst not totally extinguishing her right to financial provision, should reduce her entitlement. This has now been overruled in the case of *Rampal v Rampal* where the court held that where the marriage itself is bigamous and therefore a crime, there can be no award.[32] Where one party has squandered or been devious with monies the court may also be persuaded to take a harder line. Good conduct may be rewarded, as in a case where the wife studied for a degree and started a new career, whilst the husband gave up his job and made no attempt to work.[33]

- *Benefits lost on divorce, such as pension.*
  Where one spouse has a pension which would have benefited both spouses then this can be taken into account as part of the divorce settlement. The Pensions Act 1995 allows for a proportion of the pension to be 'earmarked' for the other spouse. The Welfare Reform and Pensions Act 1999 gave the court power, from November 2000, to split a spouse's pension into two portions upon divorce. For further information see 4.44.

27. A v A (Financial Provision) (1998) 2 FLR 180; White v White see above.
28. Bateman (1979) Fam 25, (1978) Fam Law 86; M v M (Financial Provision; Conduct) (1982) 3 FLR 83; S v S (1982) 12 Fam Law 183;Evans v Evans (1989) 1 FLR 351; A v A (Financial Provision: Conduct) (1995) 1 FLR 345.
29. H v H (Financial Provision: Conduct) (1994) 2 FLR 801; (1994) Fam Law 672.
30. Kyte v Kyte (1990) 2FLR 225.
31. Whiston v Whiston (1994) 2 FLR 906; (1994) Fam Law 620.
32. Rampal v Rampal (2000) 2 FLR 763.
33. A v A (Financial Provision: Conduct) (1995) 1 FLR 345.

4.33 Types of orders

s24 & s24A MCA73 The courts have a great deal of discretion as to how they use their powers to adjust ownership of property, make orders for lump sum payments and order the sale of property and have developed a wide variety of orders for different circumstances. The different types of orders that are commonly made are set out below under three broad headings. In many cases it is not stated in the order under which of the court's powers the order was made and in practice the distinction between the types of order is of little importance unless one of the parties wishes to apply for a variation at a later date (see 4.35).

Transfer from one party to another

This may be in the form of one partner buying out the other or by placing a charge on the property for a specified share of the proceeds, which will be repaid when the property is sold, usually not before a specific time or event, for example, when the children reach 18. This has the advantage that one party is the outright owner and they do not have to deal with each other at a later date to agree the sale.

Deferred interest orders

This is where the interest is not transferred, but one party is given the right to occupy the property and it is held on a 'trust for sale,' with the parties having specified shares. The sale is postponed again until some future event such as when the children or wife/husband no longer needs it as a home. The courts may make orders deciding who should pay the outgoings depending upon the respective financial positions of the couple. They can only order payment to cover certain outgoings rather than a specific debt.

The courts have developed even further variations within this theme, with certain solutions losing popularity as difficulties became apparent in executing them. The cases referred to below relate to situations where the wife had been bringing up the children and so it was she who was given the right to occupy the home. The same principles may also be applied if it is the man who is the child-rearer, but it should be noted that in the cases below much weight was given to the earning capacity of the child-rearer and the courts may consider that a man has a higher earning potential than a woman and therefore this might bring about a different result.

Mesher[34] or Martin[35] orders

These are orders where the property is transferred to the wife subject to the mortgage with a 'second' charge being granted to the husband. Depending on the type of order, the sale is not enforced until the

---

34. Mesher v Mesher and Hall (1980) 1 All ER 126.   35. Martin (BH) v Martin (D) (1977) 3 All ER 762 at 768.

youngest child reaches 17 or ceases full time secondary education ('*Mesher*' orders), or upon the wife's death, remarriage, or cohabitation with a man for a period of more than six months ('*Martin*' orders).

It can also be written into the terms of the order that if the wife wishes to move house during the duration of the charge to the husband, she can transfer the charge onto a new property. It may also be written into the terms of the order that if the wife remarries or cohabits for more than 6 months during the children's minority and the wife does not consent to the realisation of the charge, permission of the court is required before the charge can be enforced.

The problem with a *Mesher* order was that it frequently put a wife onto the property market at an age when she would find it difficult to obtain a mortgage, thus rendering her homeless, and consequently such orders are now much less common. *Martin*-style orders are therefore favoured and do not hinge upon children.

Under both these orders the mortgage usually remains in joint names unless the occupying spouse's income is sufficient for the lender to transfer the obligation into her/his sole name. If it remains in joint names, the occupying spouse will give an indemnity to the other spouse for any costs or claims arising under the mortgage after the transfer into her/his sole name.

There may be other variations on the theme include adjusting the shares in the proceeds, or stipulating sale if some other 'trigger event' occurs. There is no case law clarifying the position if the wife enters a lesbian relationship but it would probably depend on the actual wording of the order.

The sale of the home and the division of its net proceeds
A sale may be voluntarily agreed between the spouses. If both parties agree as part of their divorce settlement that they will sell the property, this agreement can be ratified by the court and is usually referred to as a 'consent order.'

If there is no agreement, the court can determine the shares to be held in the property and make an order for sale. Ordering a sale is normally only favoured if it will not render the children or either of the parties unnecessarily homeless; or the marriage has been short and childless and it is deemed unfair that either party should not be able to realise their asset by the sale of the home. Much depends on how much equity there is in the property, and whether the party who cares for the children can be adequately rehoused.

4.34   Homelessness and orders for sale

If an order for the sale of property is made by the court then it would usually be very difficult for a local authority to come to a finding of intentional homelessness (see 14.12) if a homelessness application is subsequently made. However, this is not the case if the spouse consents to a sale.

4.35   Varying an order

Although in exceptional circumstances, the court does have the power to vary orders for sale, a property adjustment order, once made, cannot usually be varied. Great care must therefore be taken to ensure that the best order is made at the initial hearing. Case law has shown that where, as in many cases of this kind, the order made is a property adjustment order with order for sale attached then the courts' power to vary the order is limited to minor matters of implementation, enforcement and procedure and it will not be possible to obtain a variation of the substance of the order.[36]

In certain limited circumstances, the court may be prepared to make a further order, provided it does not contradict the spirit of the original order, eg, an order for sale, before the fruition of a *Mesher* order.[37]

If no variation order can be made then the only other option would be to get the original order set aside. This is unlikely to be successful unless there has been an intervening event which invalidates a fundamental assumption of the original order.[38]

4.36   Clean break orders

Since the Matrimonial Causes Act 1973 was amended in 1984[39] the emphasis has been on both parties doing everything possible to become self-sufficient. It was suggested that wives should not expect 'a meal ticket for life' and that divorced parties should not have to live with the uncertainty of not knowing how much they might have to pay to their ex-partners at some unexpected time in the future. The courts were given powers to decide whether it was reasonable to expect someone to increase her/his earning capacity and adjust any financial orders accordingly. The Act now contains three provisions which require the courts to consider whether it is appropriate to make what has become known as a 'clean break order.'

s25A MCA73

- The court must consider whether it is appropriate to make an order which will terminate the financial obligations of each party towards the other as soon as possible after the divorce

- More specifically, if the court makes a periodical payments order

36. Omielan v Omielan (1996) 26 Fam Law 608 CA.
37. Thompson v Thompson (1985) FLR 863 CA.
38. Barder v Caluori (1987) 2 WLR 1350 HL.
39. Matrimonial and Family Proceedings Act 1984.

(maintenance) it must consider whether it should make it only for so long as to allow the partner to adjust without undue hardship. Note that this applies to spouse, not child, maintenance. An application to vary the amount is always possible whilst a maintenance order is in existence

• If a party applies for a maintenance order the court may dismiss the application and rule that no further applications can be made. This was envisaged in order to free a spouse from any future claim for financial support in years to come.

However, the following points should be noted:

• 'Clean break order' considerations only apply in respect of spousal maintenance, not child maintenance. Whilst it is very unusual for a spouse on benefits to be ordered to pay maintenance, a nominal order may be made to enable a variation to be applied for if the spouse subsequently obtains work

• Where a spouse has continuing charge of very young children it is not normally considered appropriate to cut off spousal maintenance. Responsibility for child maintenance will also continue but is now normally dealt with under the child support legislation (see Chapter 10).

4.37 When clean break orders are made

'Clean break' orders were and still are most likely to be made in situations:

• where the couple is childless

• the marriage is of comparatively short duration between a husband and wife who both have income or earning capacity or

• where there was an adequate amount of capital for division in longer marriages

• where there is parity of income between the parties

Although the court has never abdicated its powers to intervene at a future date in cases where there are still children to bring up, it was quite possible for spouses to make a 'maintenance agreement' ratified by the courts as a 'consent order.' However the courts held that adults cannot conclusively bargain away their children's rights to support.[40]

Social security legislation provides that where a husband or wife claims income support or income-based jobseeker's allowance for her/himself and any children, the Secretary of State for Work and Pensions has a power to complain to a magistrate's court and the court could order the other spouse to pay spouse maintenance equivalent to the amount of her/his personal allowance. Courts have this power even where a

40. Minton v Minton (1979) AC 593.

Part V SSAA92 'clean break' settlement has been accepted. This is known as the 'liable relative' procedure, and in practice the power is now rarely used, but nevertheless still exists.

The clean break provisions in so far as they affect child maintenance have now largely been superseded by the Child Support Act 1991 as amended by the Child Support, Pensions and Social Security Act 2000. The Act provides that where a person is in receipt of benefit, the Child Support Agency can override any amount agreed to and impose its own formula for the amount of child maintenance to be paid. The parties may however have agreed an amount for child maintenance. It is usual nowadays for a clause to be drafted in a matrimonial settlement that states that the amount of maintenance ordered to be paid will be reduced pound for pound by any subsequent child support agency assessment.

4.38   Effect of child support on property adjustment orders

The introduction of child support means that even where a parent has made over an interest in the home with little or no financial payment in return for an agreement not to apply for any further child maintenance, such an arrangement cannot override the powers of the Child Support Agency. If the parent with care who has agreed to such an arrangement subsequently had to claim benefit, the Child Support Agency can still apply the maintenance formula to the non-resident parent (including an amount deemed to cover spousal maintenance) even if a house and substantial sum have already been made over.

The potential for unfairness in such situations gave rise to public outcry and in early 1995, the Government agreed to make some concessions where clean break settlements had been reached prior to the implementation of the Child Support Act, ie, April 1993. The value of the clean break settlement is assessed and a proportionate amount of income is treated as being paid, thus reducing the amount of child support payable. No allowance is made for settlements reached after April 1993, which are assumed to be entered into with full knowledge of the system and its powers.

For more information on child support see Chapter 10.

4.39   Inheritance problems

After divorce a former spouse will be treated for the purposes of any will as if s/he had already died. Therefore even if a deceased former spouse has failed to amend her/his will the surviving former spouse will not ss18-18A WA1837 benefit from it. The same applies if there has been a decree of nullity. However, it is possible to specifically include an ex-spouse in a will if so desired.

New relationship where no divorce

Where a relationship breaks down, but there has been no divorce and a husband/wife leaves everything to a new partner, the surviving spouse can make a claim under the Inheritance (Provision for Family and Dependents) Act 1975 that some part of the estate be given for her/his benefit. The basis for such an application is that the deceased's estate has not made reasonable financial provision for the surviving spouse. The court can weigh up the moral versus the legal obligation.

Where a husband/wife dies intestate both her/his cohabitant and the spouse can apply for financial provision. For cohabitants the Act only gives provision for amounts 'required for maintenance' and this concept has been restrictively interpreted.[41] The spouse, on the other hand, might get provision of a similar amount to a divorce settlement. A cohabitant for this purpose is someone who lived with the deceased as husband and wife for the two years immediately before the date of the death. The requirement that the cohabitant must have been maintained either wholly or partially by the deceased at the time of death in order to make a claim was removed by the Law Reform (Succession) Act 1995.

Divorced spouse

The position of a divorced spouse is more complicated. A divorced spouse (not remarried) may also claim if s/he can prove lack of reasonable financial provision. In most cases finances and property will have been dealt with in conjunction with divorce. If the proceedings have been handled by lawyers, an order will normally have been applied for in conjunction with the divorce, nullity or judicial separation, which will include a standard clause stating that the divorced spouse shall not be entitled to apply for financial provision from the deceased's estate. The court will only make such an order if it considers it just.

4.40 Community Legal Services Funding and matrimonial proceedings – the Law Society's statutory charge

Matrimonial proceedings can often be long and drawn-out, with each party unwilling to agree with the other about who gets what. There may be considerable bitterness and a determination not to give in to the ex-partner. Despite current emphasis on conciliation to help clients reach an amicable out of court agreement, in some cases clients may be determined to 'fight on' for a better deal.

In some situations, clients will be able to get assistance with legal costs through the Legal Help scheme (See appendix A3). Even if a client is legally assisted, the public funding is required to be repaid out of any settlement over £3,000,[42] whether in property or a lump sum.

---

41. Re. Jennings (deceased), Harlow v National Westminster Bank plc (1994) 1 FLR 536 CA.

42. The Statutory Charge disregard was increased from £2,500 to £3,000 as from 3.12.01.

Payment must normally be made at once if the settlement is a lump sum, unless it is to be used towards the purchase of a new home for the legally assisted party or her/his dependents. In that case it must be used for that purpose within a year of the order or agreement. Where the settlement is property, a sale of matrimonial property will not be forced but the statutory charge will be registered as a charge against the property and will accrue interest at a specified rate.[43] If a sale is deferred for many years, this can become a substantial sum to be paid when the equity is finally released.

G   Matrimonial courts' powers to order financial provision for spouses on divorce, nullity or judicial separation

4.41   Court orders for financial provision for a spouse

s23 MCA73

s25A MCA73

The court may order periodical payments (maintenance) from one spouse to another. The payments can be for whatever amount the court sees fit, according to the same criteria as for property transfers listed above (4.32) and also for however long the court sees fit, subject to the 'clean break' considerations (see 4.36 – 4.37). If an order for maintenance has been made, it is possible to return to the court for a variation of the order, unless the court has ordered otherwise. In considering whether to vary an order the court must consider any changes to matters previously considered by the court, and variation will usually only be ordered where there has been a significant change in circumstances. Maintenance automatically comes to an end if the person receiving it remarries, but not if s/he cohabits, although if the cohabiting partner is being supported and hence her/his needs are less, this may give grounds for a reduction in the amount of maintenance being paid. There can also be

s28(1)(A) MCA73

a bar imposed on the seeking of maintenance after a specified period.

> ***Hedges v Hedges***[44]
>
> *A couple had been married for four and a half years. The marriage broke down and the husband stayed in the accommodation which was tied to his job. The wife moved to rented accommodation. There were no children, she was working and both were in middle age. Interim maintenance had been set at £200 per month.*
>
> *After separation the husband bought a house as an investment on a 90 per cent mortgage. He had assets of £5,000 and a pension. The wife had a lower income and could not meet all her*

---

44. Hedges v Hedges (1990) 21 Fam Law 267.

> *living expenses. She argued that she should be able to buy too.*
> *She was awarded £2,500 and £200 per month for 18 months.*
>
> *At the wife's appeal the court held that section 25A of the*
> *Matrimonial Causes Act 1973 discouraged 'meal tickets for life'*
> *in marriages of short duration. The award she had been given*
> *would be enough to allow the wife to adjust and aid a clean break.*

4.42 Court orders for transfers of capital in the form of lump sums

s23(1)(c) & (f) MCA73

In addition to or instead of an order for maintenance for a spouse, the court may order payment of a lump sum or sums as it sees fit and subject to the criteria laid down by the Act. A spouse may agree to pay a lump sum in return for being relieved of future requirements to pay maintenance for a spouse.

4.43 Variation of orders

s31 MCA73

It is possible to apply to vary maintenance but not lump sum orders.

4.44 Powers of court relating to pensions

Under the Matrimonial Causes Act 1973 the court has always been required to take loss of pension rights into account when reaching a financial settlement and offset them by redistributing assets. The Pensions Act 1995 introduced powers to 'earmark' pensions which meant the court could require occupational pension schemes to pay maintenance from a member's pension to her/his ex-spouse. The court could also order part or all of a lump sum which is payable on death or retirement to be directed to the ex-spouse. These provisions have not been widely used because of the following limitations of the Act:

- The ex-spouse has to wait for the pension-holder to retire before being entitled to receive the earmarked pension and has to wait if s/he decides to postpone retirement

- The pension may be lost if the pension-holder dies before retirement (although any earmarked death grant will be payable)

- The pension income may be lost if the pension-holder remarries, (although any earmarked lump sum is not lost unless the Order states otherwise)

- The intended retirement income is delayed if the pension-holder delays retirement

- The orders are expensive to implement for the pension funds.

To overcome these problems, the Welfare Reform and Pensions Act 1999 gave the court power to order 'pension sharing.' The provisions are not compulsory but are an alternative to the method of 'offsetting' pension rights against assets and/or earmarking pensions. Pension sharing is not available on judicial separation, so that only offset or earmarking may be used.

s21A(1) MCA73   A pension sharing order means that a fixed percentage of one spouse's shareable pension rights is transferred to the other. The pension-holder therefore loses that proportion and the other spouse is credited with the fixed amount thereby giving her/him a pension fund of her/his own.

Pension sharing is likely to be the best option for many spouses without a pension of their own, since only those with considerable assets can normally afford to make an immediate settlement which would compensate for loss of pension rights.

4.45   Financial provision before divorce

A divorce may take two or more years to be finalised, and a spouse may need financial support but either not be eligible for benefit or not wish to claim it. Financial provision can also be awarded when a couple separate, even if divorce proceedings have not been started or are not being considered.

Financial orders on separation

Where the couple are not divorcing but one spouse wants financial support from the other, there are a number of options which do not affect the status of the marriage itself. In practice, the first three below are now not often used as most people who consult a solicitor will normally be contemplating divorce proceedings, or may resolve the matter by mediation:

- *Domestic Proceedings and Magistrates Court Act 1978* – heard in the Magistrates Court. Different sections allow for applications on the basis of failure to provide reasonable maintenance, by consent order, or on the 'voluntary separation' ground

- *Section 27 Matrimonial Causes Act 1973 (as amended by section 63 of the Matrimonial and Family Proceedings Act 1978)* – heard in the County Court. Again applied for on the basis that the other spouse has failed to provide reasonable maintenance

- *Separation and Maintenance Agreements* – In most cases, a mediated arrangement or a consent order would now take the place of these agreements

- *Section 15 and Schedule 1 of the Children Act 1989* – this provides for the grant of a range of financial orders for the benefit of a child. The applicant must be the parent or guardian of the child and the orders can be made only against a parent. It must be stressed that the availability of these orders is not dependent upon the parties to the application being married to one another – it is dependent upon parenthood. Nevertheless, married parents may wish to make use of the Children Act, which is a provision whereby the court can grant lump sum financial payments without the necessity of the parties first issuing decree proceedings.

For further details see of Chapter 10, Section B.

s22 MCA73 *Financial orders pending divorce proceedings*

Where divorce proceedings are in progress and a final settlement has not been reached or taken effect the court has power to make an order requiring either spouse to make to the other such maintenance as the court thinks reasonable. This is often referred to as 'maintenance pending suit'.

H   Property transfers for non-divorcing couples

4.46   When can property be transferred if no divorce?

The property transfers referred to above can only be ordered by the courts between married couples who are divorcing, or seeking a decree of nullity or judicial separation. If a couple separate, but take no legal action, these provisions do not apply. The ideal situation is for the couple to agree matters between themselves, thus saving lengthy and often costly legal proceedings. However, there are other possibilities at law, if agreement cannot be reached. These will be considered separately in later chapters.

- The Children Act 1989 can be used for the benefit of children of the family. This is available to non-divorcing married couples with children, including step-children (see 9.13 onwards)

- Property law provisions which can be used are (see 5.48):

    - Married Women's Property Act 1882 which is available to married non-divorcing couples and engaged couples and

    - Trusts of Land and Appointment of Trustees Act 1996 which is available to anyone with an interest in the property.

5

Chapter 5: Cohabiting owner-occupiers

Subjects covered in this chapter include...

Sole legal owner

What rights a non-owning cohabitant has to occupy the family home

How a non-owner can establish a stake (beneficial interest) in the home

What kinds of beneficial interest there are

How to protect the right to occupy and other interests in property

How to prevent a partner from disposing of the family home

Joint legal owners

What rights joint owning cohabitants have in the home

How to establish a joint owner's share in the home

What the difference is between beneficial joint tenants and tenants in common

What the effect is of one joint owner dying

How to sever a joint interest in the home

Sole and joint legal owners

How consent to a loan may be set aside by the defence of undue influence or misrepresentation

How financial shares are quantified

How to apply for an order to sell the home

Cohabiting owner-occupiers

Chapter 2 explained that the areas of law available to cohabitants in owner-occupied property to settle rights to property were either

* *child law*

or

* *property law.*

Child law is available to cohabitants who have a child born of the relationship, as well as to non-divorcing married couples and allows either party to apply to the county court or the High Court for an order to have property transferred to the other for the benefit of the child. It can also be used by a guardian of a child, or someone with a residence order, to apply for a transfer of property from the biological parent for the benefit of the child. This process is explained in more detail in Chapter 9, Section D. Child law may also be used by parents who have a child, even if they have never actually lived together.

Property law (as explained in Chapter 2), applies to people sharing owner-occupied property or those who have an interest in the property, regardless of their relationship. It is therefore very important to unmarried heterosexual couples without children or to lesbian or gay couples. Whilst it can be used by married couples to establish interests in the home, an order under matrimonial law could still override and transfer those interests from one party to the other (see Chapter 4).

As well as the long-term rights set out in this chapter, certain cohabitants may have short-term rights to occupy or exclude their partner from the family home. These are discussed in Chapter 13. This chapter concentrates mainly on issues relating to property law. Readers who are not familiar with the basic principles and terminology of property law may find it helpful to read Chapter 2 before using this chapter.

Prospective changes in legislation for unmarried couples

Towards the end of 2001, a new Bill, the Civil Partnership Bill, was laid before Parliament by Lord Lester of Herne Hill. Its proposals were radical and far-reaching, introducing rights for cohabiting couples, whether heterosexual or lesbian or gay. These rights related, amongst other things, to the settlement of finances and property akin to those for married couples, provided the couple had registered a 'civil partnership,' which could be done after six months' cohabitation. As a result of comments made in the House of Lords and a promise that the government would seriously consider the whole area of law relating to cohabiting couples, Lord Lester withdrew the Bill in February 2002.

In December 2002 the government announced its proposals to bring forward legislation to give civil partnership rights to lesbian or gay couples. It was suggested that a Bill could be expected some time in 2003. The Bill would allow the registration of civil partnerships giving next-of-kin entitlements to lesbian or gay couples on inheritance tax, pensions and property that are currently only available to married couples. However, it was made clear that the government did not intend to extend the proposals to heterosexual cohabiting couples, and it was suggested by the media that this would almost certainly be challenged. At the time of writing no further proposals had been announced.

At present therefore the following rights are those which are available to unmarried couples.

Sole legal owner

A   Rights to occupy the family home

Most discussions in text books about property law centre financial interests in the home, such as how much money each party is entitled to get out of the shared property. In practice, people who seek housing advice are often far more concerned with their rights to remain living in the home, rather than how much, if any, money they could get out of it.

5.1   The right to live in the family home

A non-owning cohabitant does not have an automatic right to occupy the family home. If the home is in one name only, non-owning cohabiting partners, whether heterosexual, lesbian or gay, are usually in a very tenuous position. They are not legal owners, and unless they are able to establish a financial interest in the property, their legal status will normally be that of a bare licensee. This means, broadly, that they have the right to remain only for as long as the licensor, in this case the owning partner, gives them permission to do so.

It is therefore important to be aware of other ways in which it may be possible to remain in occupation of the home. These are explained in sections 5.2 – 5.8 below.

5.2   Occupation orders

Some cohabitants are able to apply for occupation orders under the Family Law Act 1996 giving temporary rights to remain. Eligibility for occupation orders, the different orders available, the criteria which must be used and their duration are explained from 13.22 onwards. The following is an outline of the provisions.

Entitled applicants and those with no entitlement to remain

The Family Law Act 1996 gives rights to certain cohabitants to apply for occupation orders. The type of occupation order obtained depends upon whether the applicant is 'entitled' to remain in the home. Entitled applicants are those with a legal or beneficial interest in the property, or matrimonial homes rights (the latter obviously not being applicable to cohabitants).

The Act also says that a person is 'entitled' if they have a right to occupy by virtue of contract, or a right to remain by virtue of any statute. This would therefore include anyone who has protection against eviction without a court order under the Protection from Eviction Act 1977, such as a licensee with basic protection (see 6.10). In practice, cohabitants, former spouses and former cohabitants without an existing right to occupy based on a legal or beneficial interest in the property, are unlikely to come within this definition, so these groups will only be able to obtain orders in more limited circumstances. The definition of a 'cohabitant,' contained in section 62 of the Act, only covers:

> *'a man and a woman who, although not married to each other, are living together as husband and wife.'*

This means that whereas heterosexual cohabitants may apply to be granted a right to occupy the home even when they are non-owners, lesbian or gay cohabitants may only apply if they already have an existing right to occupy. In the latter case, the main purpose of applying would probably be to exclude the other partner. Whether the obvious discrimination underlying this definition will be challenged in terms of the European Convention on Human Rights remains to be seen (see 2.5).

Where a cohabitant is not registered as a legal owner of a property, establishing that s/he has a beneficial interest in a property can be a complicated process (see 5.9) and, if it has not yet been established, it will not be possible to decide whether an applicant is entitled or non-entitled. The Act allows for this by giving heterosexual cohabitants or former spouses the option of applying for an occupation order under sections 35 or 36 as if there is no entitlement to occupy, whilst still retaining the right to apply as an entitled applicant under section 33, if a beneficial interest can be established.

s35(11)-(12) FLA96 & s36 (11)-(12) FLA96

Effect of occupation orders for non-entitled cohabitants

Apart from giving the applicant the right to live in the home, an occupation order also gives a non-owning cohabitant similar rights to those of a non-owning spouse whilst the occupation order is in force:

s35(13) & s36(13) FLA96

s30(3) &
s30(5) FLA96

- the right to have rent or mortgage payments accepted, as if they were paid by the owning partner (and this may then entitle the non-owner to claim a beneficial interest)

s55 FLA96

- the right to be heard in possession proceedings, if the court sees no special reason against it, and the non-owner may be able to make contributions which would affect the outcome of the proceedings.

The length of the occupation order that can be obtained depends upon whether the applicant is a former spouse or cohabitant/former cohabitant.

OTHER OPTIONS TO REMAIN

This section looks at possible options where the non-owning cohabitant cannot get one of the orders mentioned above. In most cases, however, the cohabitant will be an excluded licensee with very few rights to remain (see 5.3). A right to occupy will not necessarily also give the cohabitant a financial interest in the property. This section does not cover long-term financial interests in property, nor how to protect them. For these see sections B and C of this chapter.

5.3   Non-owning cohabitant is an excluded licensee

s3A PEA77

A non-owning cohabitant will usually be sharing accommodation with the owning partner. In terms of residential status, this makes the cohabitant an excluded licensee within the meaning of the Protection from Eviction Act 1977 (see 6.11). This means that the excluded licensee is not protected by sections 3 (no eviction without a court order) or 5 (validity of notice to quit) of the Protection from Eviction Act 1977, and can therefore be legally evicted without a court order. However physical force must not be used. No formal notice to quit is required to be given to an excluded licensee, but s/he must be given reasonable notice. Unfortunately, there is no legal definition of what constitutes 'reasonable' notice; in practice, if the owning partner changes the locks and puts the cohabitant's belongings out, there is very little the cohabitant can do about it, unless a claim for damages could be brought under an action for trespass to belongings (see 13.50). Such an action would not, however, result in reinstatement in the property.

5.4   Non-owning cohabitant has a beneficial interest

Section 3.3 gives a definition of 'beneficial interest.'

Section 12 of the Trusts of Land and Appointment of Trustees Act 1996 makes it clear that someone with a beneficial interest has a right to occupy, provided that the initial understanding was that s/he would be entitled to live in the property. However, this only applies once the beneficial interest has been established.

If the non-owning cohabitant wants to try and establish a beneficial interest in the home, s/he should start proceedings either in the county court or the High Court under section 14 of the Trusts of Land and Appointment of Trustees Act. Heterosexual couples who have been engaged in the last three years can also use section 17 of the Married Woman's Property Act 1882 which can be a quicker procedure.

Where there is a dispute over land and a court action is pending, the court has power to grant an injunction to prevent sale of the property until the case is heard. For more information on orders for sale, see section J of this chapter.

This will protect the financial interest and it may then be possible for the court to grant an interim injunction giving a non-owning cohabitant the right to continue to occupy until the court hearing.

s12 TLATA96

5.5 Non-owning cohabitant has a contractual licence

As explained in 5.3, non-owning cohabitants will often be in the position of being excluded licensees of their partners, and thus entitled only to reasonable notice before having to leave. However, the court may decide that the non-owning cohabitant has a contractual licence, which cannot be ended until a particular event occurs that ends the contract. A contractual licence of this type would also make an illegal eviction a criminal offence.

s1 PEA77

Such a decision was reached in 1975 in *Tanner v Tanner*,[1] where a woman gave up her rent-controlled flat to move into a house, which the father of her children, who was already married, had purchased for her and their twin daughters. The man's argument, that she was a bare licensee, was defeated on the basis that the terms of the licence were that she was entitled to occupy the house so long as the children were of school age, or unless some other circumstances arose which made it unreasonable for her to retain possession. In addition, by giving up her rent-controlled flat, she had provided consideration for the licence, thereby making it a contractual licence. Although it was not necessary in this particular case, because the woman was rehoused by the council, the court indicated that it would otherwise have been possible to obtain an injunction to restrain the man from revoking the licence.

In subsequent cases[2] the courts have been less willing to find this type of contractual licence; and in most cases a contract will not be inferred unless there is good evidence that there was such agreement.

---

1.   Tanner v Tanner (1975)1 WLR 1346 CA.

2.   Horrocks v Forray (1976) 1 WLR 230 CA; Coombes v Smith (1986) 1 WLR 808.

5.6 Non-owning cohabitant has an equitable licence

For an equitable licence to exist, it is necessary to demonstrate that the cohabitant had acted to her/his detriment, eg, by giving up a job or a home, to live with the owner of the home in question.

In one case, *Ungurian v Lesnoff*,[3] a woman had given up a promising academic career and her home in another country. Her partner bought a house for both of them to live in, together with her two sons and his son. When he claimed possession four years later, the court held that she had an equitable right to reside in the house for life and that her consent would be necessary before any sale could take place. It should be stressed that this is also quite an unusual case and in similar situations now it would probably be decided on 'estoppel' principles.[4]

5.7 Non-owning cohabitant has a licence by estoppel

This is similar to a contractual licence, except that there has been no clear agreement. Instead the legal owner has led the cohabitant to believe that s/he will have a right to live in the property on a long-term basis and s/he has acted to her/his detriment in relying on that belief. The right to occupy cannot then be revoked.

5.8 Non-owning cohabitant is applying for a transfer under the Children Act

Where a cohabiting couple have a child of their relationship, the court has powers similar to those of the matrimonial court to order a transfer of property from one partner to the other for the benefit of the child (see 9.13 – 9.15). Whilst this provision, which came into force in 1989, still does not appear to be widely used, it is theoretically possible for the court to award either an outright transfer of interest in property or, alternatively, it might decide to grant occupation rights to the non-owning spouse with care of the child, until a specified time in the future (comparable to *Mesher* and *Martin* orders – 4.33).

The Children Act does not give any automatic right to occupy. However, if a non-owning cohabitant commences proceedings under the Children Act for a transfer of property, the court would also have jurisdiction to grant an injunction for that cohabitant and the child to remain in the home, in the interests of the child, pending the outcome of the hearing (see 5.23).

B Establishing a non-owner's interest in the family home

Establishing who has a right to a share in the proceeds of a sale of the home is not as simple as knowing in whose name the property was

---

3.   Ungurian v Lesnoff (1990) 3 WLR 840.

4.   'Cohabitants and the law' Barlow A. 2001, Butterworths 3rd edition, pp. 322-323.

bought (see 3.3). The property may be in one name only, but the non-owner may still be able to claim some or even all of the financial value of the property. How such an interest may be established in the case of sole ownership is explained in the sections below.

Problems relating to quantifying shares in jointly-owned property are discussed at section I of this chapter.

5.9 Establishing a non-owner's interest in the home

When a property is in one name only and there is a written, signed declaration or statement or a formal trust deed[5] spelling out the parties' intentions about who should have what, this express statement will always take effect, except in the case of fraud or mistake.

Unfortunately, few people think of making such formal written statements when they enter a relationship, even when considerable sums of money may have been invested in property. The courts have warned solicitors that express statements of interest should be a routine part of conveyancing[6] and this should now be common practice. Failure to find out and declare beneficial interests is now held to be a failure of professional duty. Unfortunately, problems still arise in cases where property was bought before this became standard practice, or, more commonly nowadays, where one partner moves in with another after the property was bought.

Where there is no express written declaration as to interests, it may still be possible for the non-owning partner to establish that s/he has a beneficial interest in the property. This may also allow her/him to continue to occupy the property until any financial dispute is settled (see 5.4). Applications can be made to the county court or the High Court for a declaration of beneficial interests, in conjunction with either an application for an order directing, preventing or postponing sale under section 14 of the Trusts of Land and Appointment of Trustees Act, or with section 17 proceedings under the Married Woman's Property Act 1882 (for previously engaged couples only) (see 5.48-9).

An interest may be established by either:

• resulting or implied trust

• constructive trust

• proprietary estoppel.

Although the courts have tended to blur the distinctions in the past, more recently the Court of Appeal has held[7] that it is important to distinguish between a resulting and a constructive trust, since in the

5. The formalities required for creating a legally binding trust are laid down in section 53(1)(b) of the Law of Property Act 1925. They are not necessary for the creation of a resulting, implied or constructive trust.

6. Goodman v Gallant (1986) Fam 106 CA; Springette v Defoe (1992) 2 FLR 388; (1992) 24 HLR 552 CA.
7. Drake v Whipp (1996) 1 FLR 826 CA.

latter, the court has discretion in deciding what share would be fair, whereas in the former, the shares are determined in proportion to the original contribution. In other cases the courts have held that there is an overlap between the law relating to constructive trusts and the law of proprietary estoppel.[8]

The following sections explain the principles for establishing a beneficial interest. Quantifying financial shares is covered in section I.

5.10   Resulting or implied trust – who has contributed towards the purchase?

Two things are necessary to establish a resulting trust:

- The person who is not the legal owner has made financial contributions to the acquisition of the property, and

- There was a common intention that the person claiming is to have an interest.

A common intention is normally inferred by the courts if money is provided, so that even if nothing has been said, there will be what is known as a 'presumption of resulting trust,' provided that there is no evidence to indicate that the parties intended otherwise. It is then assumed that the legal owner holds the money on trust for the other.

Tinsley v Milligan[9]

The property was bought jointly but registered only in the name of Ms Tinsley, in order to allow Ms Milligan to make a false claim to the Department of Social Security. Even though there was an unlawful purpose, Ms Milligan was held to have an interest in the property under a resulting trust.

Arguments against the existence of a resulting trust

If it can be argued that a payment of, for example, a lump sum, was in fact a loan or a gift and not intended to lead to the contributor gaining an interest in the home, a claim of resulting trust might fail. This is particularly likely to occur in certain relationships where contributions may be presumed to be a gift unless there is evidence to the contrary. This is based on the principle of 'advancement.'

Where there is a 'presumption of advancement' in a relationship, it will be assumed that any payments made to the other person are intended as a gift and no beneficial interest will be created. Transactions between husband to wife *(but not wife to husband)* and between parent to child

---

8.   Gillett v Holt (2000) 3 WLR 815 CA; Yaxley v Gotts (1999) 3 WLR 1217 CA

9.   Tinsley v Milligan (1994) 24 Fam Law 18; (1993) 2 FLR 963 HL.

are subject to this presumption, but those between cohabitants are not. The principle is, however, now rarely applied, and the courts are likely to hold that the presumption has been rebutted if it can be shown that the intention of the couple was different.[10]

Payments which count as financial contributions

Resulting trusts are relatively straightforward, in that money has been paid or agreed at the outset, although there may be difficulties in quantifying the amounts contributed where a person has undertaken a mortgage liability.

Financial contributions can include payments towards a deposit, capital repayments on the outstanding mortgage debt, or contributions towards the monthly payments, provided the payments are regular and substantial. They should be directly attributable to the purchasing of the property, whether at the initial purchase or later on.

Indirect contributions remain problematic. If a person had contributed to bills or the household expenses, these payments would not establish a resulting trust. However, they may be evidence of conduct, which could contribute to establishing a constructive trust (see below).

Burns v Burns[11]

The court held that housekeeping duties and bringing up children were not factors which could be taken into account in establishing a trust. The cohabitant had made no substantial contribution to the purchase price. A distinction was drawn between this and where, through a pooling of income, direct or indirect contributions had been made to mortgage payments.

Resulting trusts and Midland Bank v Cooke[12]

The case of *Midland Bank v Cooke* affected the outcome where the conditions for a resulting trust are met. In some cases the courts may decide to infer that in fact the true position was that of a constructive trust (see below and 5.45 – 5.46). This means that the court then has discretion to decide on the amount of shares to which each party is entitled.

5.11   Constructive trust

In the leading case of *Lloyds Bank plc v Rosset*,[13] three things were held to be normally necessary to establish a constructive trust:

- There must have been a common intention that the claimant gain a beneficial interest in the property

---

10. Tribe v Tribe (1995) 2 FLR 966 CA; McGrath v Wallis (1995) 2 FLR 114 CA.
11. Burns v Burns (1984) 2 WLR 582 CA.
12. Midland Bank v Cooke (1995) 27 HLR 733; 2 WLR 915 CA.
13. Lloyds Bank plc v Rosset (1990) 2 FLR 155 (1990) 1 A11 ER 1111, (1991) AC 107, HL.

- There must be evidence of express discussion giving rise to the common intention (but see below)

- The claimant must have acted to her/his detriment by relying on the intention that they would both have beneficial interest.

This means that even if there is no legal ownership and the non-owner has not contributed in financial or equivalent terms to the purchase, s/he may still have a beneficial interest. However, it must be possible to show that it was intended or implied that the non-owner should have a share and that the non-owner had acted to her/his own disadvantage, on the understanding that s/he would be entitled to a share in the property. Again, the principle is that the law should not lead to injustice.

Establishing common intent by express agreement or discussions

A constructive trust will normally only be inferred where there has been express discussion, arrangement or agreement giving rise to an understanding that the property is to be shared beneficially between a couple. This means that there must be evidence of an actual conversation which took place, and in which it was agreed that the parties would share actual ownership and not just jointly occupy the property. The court has held that accounts of the express discussions should be provided in the *'greatest detail, both as to language and as to circumstance.'*[14] Obviously firm proof of a spoken conversation is not always easy to establish, but affidavit evidence can be introduced and the judge must decide on balance which party is to be believed.

Simply planning to 'do up' a house together would not on its own be enough to establish a common intention, since the House of Lords has held that:

> *'neither a common intention by spouses that a house is to be renovated as a 'joint venture' nor a common intention that the house is to be shared by parents and children as the family home throw any light on their intentions with respect to the beneficial ownership of the property.'*[15]

Lloyds Bank v Rosset[16]

It was held that:

'The finding of an agreement or arrangement to share... can only...be based on evidence of express discussion between the partners, however imperfectly remembered and however imprecise their terms may have been.'

---

14. Hammond v Mitchell (1992) 1 FLR 229 at 243.

15. Lloyds Bank v Rosset, see 13 above.
16. Lloyds Bank v Rosset ibid.

> ### *Hammond v Mitchell (H v M)*[17]
>
> *The same point was confirmed. It was crucial to discover whether, prior to the acquisition of the property, there had been any discussions leading to any agreement, understanding or arrangement that the property was to be shared beneficially. In this case the judge believed the woman's recollection of the man's words which were:*
>
> *'I'll have to put the house in my name because I have tax problems... and if I could prove my money had gone back into a property I'd be safe-guarded. ...Don't worry about the future because when we're married it will be half yours anyway and I'll always look after you and the boy.'*
>
> *It has been commented that this was not so much an expression of common intention as an intention to mislead Ms Mitchell and therefore an alternative argument could have been proprietary estoppel (see 5.12 – 5.13).*

It is unclear when the agreement to share must have taken place. In *Lloyds Bank plc v Rosset*, the judge suggested that it must be when the property was bought and only 'exceptionally' at a later date. Later cases have been more ready to rely on agreements made many years after purchase, which is of considerable significance to those who move in with their partners when the partner is already the sole owner of the property.[18]

Establishing common intent in cases where there is no express agreement

If there has been no express discussion, the problem has always hinged upon whether it is possible to infer the common intention even before considering detriment. In the landmark case of *Lloyds Bank plc v Rosset* (see above), it was clearly established that where there has been no evidence of an express agreement, the court will only infer the necessary common intention if the claimant has made direct contributions to the purchase, either initially or by mortgage payments. The court was not prepared to infer a common intention where the claimant has assumed responsibility for household expenses so that the property owner can afford to repay the mortgage, since the contributions must be direct, but such action might be sufficient to constitute acting to one's detriment, once common intention has been proved.

Direct contributions which might be enough to infer a common intention have been held in certain cases to be contributions to the

---

17. Hammond v Mitchell (H v M), see 14 above (Property: beneficial interest) (1992) Fam Law 437; (1992) 1 FLR 229 at 233. 18. Hammond v Mitchell, ibid.

purchase price by way of:

- payments by relatives[19]
- mortgage payments[20]
- contribution of tenant with right to buy discount[21] although there is no rule that such a contribution must give rise to a beneficial interest[22]
- capital injections to buy out co-owner or repay mortgage.[23]

In the important case of *Midland Bank v Cooke*,[24] the man's parents gave the couple £1,000 towards the deposit on a £8,500 house as a wedding gift. This was held to be sufficient to establish a beneficial interest for the wife, as half of the £1,000 was deemed to be a direct contribution from her.

Once a trust has been established from contributions, it remains to establish the exact shares. The situation has been significantly affected by *Midland Bank v Cooke* (see 5.45 – 5.46).[25]

Indirect contributions to family assets, for example working in a partner's business or meeting expenses which enable the other to make mortgage payments, will not by themselves earn a beneficial interest.[26] They would need to be coupled with an agreement, arrangement or understanding to establish the common intention. However, once the common intention is established, such contributions may be sufficient to establish that the person has acted to her/his detriment.

Acting to one's detriment

Once the common intention has been established by evidence of express discussion or agreement or direct contributions, it is only necessary for the claimant to show that she had acted to her/his detriment. What constitutes detriment has been shown to cover a wide range of financial and other contributions, which may be measurable in money terms but could generally be said to involve giving something up, forgoing an opportunity, doing some work or making some payment or contribution which, if there had not been a common understanding between the parties, the partner would not have made.

Case law shows that the court is willing to extend this concept of detriment considerably. In the case of *Hammond v Mitchell* (see above), the couple lived together for 13 years. Ms M looked after the children and helped Mr H in running a business venture in Spain. She was held to have acted 'to her detriment' even though she was supporting her partner in a successful venture, which she might have been expected to do even if she had not been going to receive a beneficial interest in the property.

19. McHardy and Sons v Warren (1994) 2 FLR 338 CA; Midland Bank v Cooke see 12 above; Halifax Building Society v Brown (1996) 1 FLR 103 CA
20. Harwood v Harwood (1991) 2 FLR 274; Huntingford v Hobbs (1993) 1 FLR 736 CA; Marsh v von Sternberg (1986) 1 FLR 526.
21. Marsh v von Sternberg ibid. Springette v Defoe, see 6 above, Savill v Goodall (1993) 1 FLR 755 CA.
22. Ashe v Mumford [2001] BPIR 1 CA.
23. Risch v McFee (1991) 1 FLR 105, Stokes v Anderson (1991) 1 FLR 391 CA.
24. Midland Bank v Cooke, see 12 above.

In the past differing judgements in the Court of Appeal have defined detriment as:

- conduct which a person could not reasonably be expected to embark upon unless they were to have an interest in the house (see *Grant v Edwards* below) or alternatively

- '*any act done by (a person) to (that person's) detriment relating to the joint lives of the parties... The acts do not have to be inherently referable to the house...*'[27]

In *Grant v Edwards*,[28] the judge accepted that Ms Grant did pay some of the mortgage installments as part of general household expenses, but held that they were not substantial enough to give her a beneficial interest by way of resulting trust. She therefore had to establish a constructive trust, ie, a common intention that she should have a beneficial interest which had been acted upon by her. Mr Edwards had told Ms Grant that her name would have been on the title deeds but for her divorce proceedings with her husband, as it might operate to prejudice the proceedings. The court accepted this was sufficient to establish that there was a common intention that she should have an interest in the house, but it then had to look for conduct demonstrating reliance on that intention. The assurances from Mr Edwards were held to be sufficient to establish the common intention and the court held that:

> '*The making of substantial indirect contributions to the mortgage installments was sufficient to constitute conduct upon which she could not reasonably be expected to embark unless she was to have a beneficial interest in the house...*'

However, in the same case the opinion was expressed that:

> '*In many cases of the present sort it was impossible to say whether or not the claimant would have done the acts relied on even if she thought she had no interest in the house.*
>
> *Setting up house together, having a baby, making payments to general housekeeping expenses (not strictly necessary to enable the mortgage to be paid) might all be referable to the mutual love and affection of the parties and not specifically referable to expectation of an interest in the house.*'

The fact that Ms Grant's contributions enabled Mr Edwards to pay the mortgage, which he would not otherwise have been able to do, proved conclusively in her favour.

Unfortunately, this still leaves open the question of whether having children and foregoing work opportunities can be seen to be sufficient

---

25. Midland Bank v Cooke, see 12 above.
26. McFarlane v McFarlane (1972) NILR 59,67,74, Ivin v Blake (1995) 1 FLR 70 CA, and Lloyds Bank v Rosset, see 13 above.

27. Grant v Edwards (1986) Ch.638; (1987) 1 FLR 87 CA.
28. Grant v Edwards, ibid.

detriment. Although recent cases indicate a willingness on the court's part to take a wide view of this concept, there has still been a reluctance in the courts to accept that committing oneself to a relationship and thereby giving up the chance to earn one's own living is sufficient on its own (see *Burns v Burns* at 5.10).

Establishing an interest by home improvements

For a cohabitant, spending money on a property does not necessarily mean that s/he acquires a beneficial interest, as explained above. In *Thomas v Fuller-Brown*,[29] where the partner had expended considerable physical labour on building works to his partner's house, he got nothing. The judge said:

> '...under English law, the mere fact that A expends money or labour on B's property does not by itself entitle A to an interest in the property. 'In the absence of express agreement or a common intention to be inferred from all the circumstances or any question of estoppel, A will normally have no claim whatever on the property in such circumstances.'

Thus, the court must be able to find or infer an intention, or find an estoppel, in order for home improvements to constitute the basis of a beneficial interest.

The situation is quite different, however, if the couple are married. Section 37 of the Matrimonial Proceedings and Property Act 1970 makes special provision that where a spouse makes a substantial contribution in money or monies worth to the improvement of any property then, subject to any agreement to the contrary, s/he is treated as acquiring a share in the property. The Court makes a declaration as to the shares in these circumstances. The same provision applies to engaged couples, provided an application is made within three years of termination of the engagement.

s2(1) LR(MP)A
1970

5.12   Proprietary estoppel

Where the partner has no evidence of express discussion on which to establish a constructive trust, it may still be possible to establish an interest by what is known as proprietary estoppel. This has been explained by the courts in the following way:

> 'Where one person A has acted to his detriment on the faith of a belief which was known to and encouraged by another person B, that he either has or is going to be given a right in or over B's property, B cannot insist on his strict legal rights if to do so would be inconsistent with A's belief.'[30]

---

29. Thomas v Fuller-Brown (1988) 1 FLR 237 at 240 CA.

30. Re Basham (Deceased) (1987) 2 FLR 264. Also Wayling v Jones (1995) 2 FLR 1029 CA. Gillett v Holt, see 8 above.

Certain criteria must be fulfilled:

• That the claimant was misled by the owner into believing that s/he would acquire a beneficial interest, and

• That s/he had acted to her/his detriment in reliance on that belief

• the owner must be aware of her/his own interests in the property and must have known and encouraged the claimant's belief.

'Encouragement' can be in words or in conduct, and can also be in the future, for example, *'One day all this will be yours'* or *'I'll leave it to you in my will.'* Obviously, a person can renege on such a promise, but what makes it irrevocable is if the person claiming the interest can also show that s/he has acted to her/his detriment in reliance on the promise or implied promise. Sufficient actions to establish detriment might be expenditure, works of improvement, or a detrimental change of position. Simply moving into someone else's house would not on its own be enough, although giving up a secure home to do so might be. It need not be financial detriment, as long as it is something substantial and there is a link between the detriment and the promise.[31]

The Court of Appeal has also said that the key principle underlying proprietary estoppel is one of conscionability, or fairness. In the case of *Wayling v Jones,*[32] it was held that:

> *'For a claim in proprietary estoppel to succeed it had to be shown that one party had made promises to the other in reliance on which that other had acted to his detriment. There had to be a sufficient link between the promises relied upon and the conduct which constituted the detriment.*
>
> *The promises relied upon did not have to be the sole inducement for the conduct.'*

In this case, two men had lived together since 1971. The deceased man said he would leave the other a house and business, and made a will to that effect. When they moved he failed to change the will, but the claimant helped him run his businesses, and acted as his chauffeur and companion for little more than pocket money. This was held to be sufficient conduct from which to infer his reliance upon the deceased's clear promises.[33]

A more in-depth discussion of the problematic aspects of proprietary estoppel can be found in other text books.[34]

5.13 The difference between proprietary estoppel and constructive trusts

Although the courts often seem to blur the distinction between common intention constructive trusts and proprietary estoppel, the differences can be summarised as follows:

---

31. Gillett v Holt, see 8 above.
32. Wayling v Jones, see 30 above.

33. Wayling v Jones, ibid.
34. Eg, Family Law, Herring, J. 2001. Longman, p.131-133

Proprietary estoppel

- Requires only unilateral conduct by legal owner plus detriment

- Does not always generate a proprietary interest – court need only give the minimum necessary to prevent detriment following conduct – it could grant only a personal right to occupy the home

- Operates only from the date the court confers the remedy on the non-legal owner.

Constructive trust

- Based upon bilateral agreement/arrangement/ understanding plus detriment

- Interest is a proprietary interest – a beneficial interest in the home

- Creates equitable rights capable of binding third parties from the moment of detriment not the date the court makes its declaration.

C Protecting rights to occupy and other interests in property

Although a non-owning cohabitant may not always have a right to occupy which is enforceable against the owning cohabitant, s/he may have rights to occupy which are enforceable against third parties. S/he may also be able to obtain injunctions to remain in the home and/or prevent a sale, pending the hearing of any proceedings about the home. It is also important that any financial interest in the home is protected.

5.14 Rights in property

Rights in property can arise in three main ways:

- As a legal owner named on the conveyance

- As a non-owning spouse with matrimonial home rights, or

- As a person with a financial (ie, beneficial) interest in the property.

In addition, a person with a potential interest on behalf of a child stemming from the Children Act, may issue court proceedings and apply for an order or agreement that s/he may continue to occupy pending the hearing of a case concerning the disposition of the property (see 5.8).

In the case of a legal owner, no further action is necessary to protect rights; but in the other cases, steps need to be taken to protect these rights.

Chapter 4 looked at protecting matrimonial home rights by way of registering a charge. This chapter looks at protecting rights arising from having a financial stake (beneficial interest) in the property. It also looks at protecting financial interests against third parties (lenders or purchasers).

Significant changes are due to come into force under the Land Registration Act 2002 on 13 October 2003, and these are explained in the following sections.

5.15   Land Registration Act 2002

The Land Registration Act 2002 received Royal Assent on 26th February 2002, and will come into force on 13 October 2003. The overriding aim of the Act is to modernise the system of land registration and create the necessary legal framework in which the sale and transfer of all registered land will be able to be carried out electronically. This means that the land register must be a complete and accurate reflection of who owns land and any rights or restrictions attached to it, so that investigations can be carried out on-line, with the minimum of additional inquiries and inspections.

At present, approximately 80% of all land is registered with records held by the Land Registry, so that charges can be dealt with centrally. The remaining 20% of land is unregistered, ie, the proof of ownership is found in a bundle of deeds, usually deposited in a bank or building society. Although there is a central Land Charges Register, quite separate from the Land Registry, for unregistered land, not all types of interests in land are capable of being registered on it, and uncertainty can arise, as explained below. The deeds must normally be inspected and searches carried out and inspections made of the land, to ensure that the seller has the right to sell the land (see 5.18 – 5.21).

Voluntary registration

Since land registration was introduced in the 1860s, voluntary registration has been possible. The Land Registration Act 1925 gradually extended compulsory registration across the country; since the Land Registration Act of 1990, registration of unregistered land becomes compulsory if the property is sold, or a long lease is assigned.

An objective of the Land Registration Act is therefore to encourage the registration of all land, although it does not go so far as to make it compulsory to register, and the position will remain much as it is at present, with the addition of compulsory registration when properties change hands in any way (see next section).

Registering and protecting interests and rights over land

Another important objective of the Act is to simplify and clarify the protection of interests or charges. The key prospective changes which are relevant to relationship breakdown are summarised below.

5.16   Changes under the Land Registration Act 2002

Registration of unregistered land

One of the key aims of the Act is to complete registration, so that, in time, all land will become registered. From 13 October 2003, where an unregistered freehold property, or leasehold with more than 7 years left to run, is transferred, whether by sale, gift, court order, assignment or agreement, it will be compulsory to register the land. There will also be compulsory first registration after the creation of a first legal mortgage. Registration may also be voluntary, at a reduced cost.

Overriding interests

These are interests that bind the registered owner, although not noted on the register. Generally, overriding interests will have to be revealed on certain applications for registration and will be noted on the register, thereby losing their overriding status. However, where someone is in actual occupation of the land, s/he may still have the benefit of overriding status (see 5.24).

Cautions against registered land to go

From 13 October 2003 there is a new system for protection of third party rights. At present, third parties with a claim against registered land can protect themselves in one of four ways:

• By caution against dealings

• By notice

• By restriction

• By inhibition.

The Act abolishes inhibitions and cautions against dealings. Existing cautions against dealings will remain on the register and the old law will apply to them, but it will not be possible to register new cautions against registered land. The Act provides for two new types of notice. So third parties will in future protect their interests by notice on the register or restriction.

Details of other changes under the Land Registration Act 2002 are available in a series of leaflets on the Land Registry website.[35]

---

35. www.landregistry.gov.uk/lract2002

5.17   **Non-owner's rights arising from a beneficial interest**

If a non-owner (married or not) has an equitable interest which gives her/him a financial (beneficial) stake in property in which s/he is living, case law has now established that the interest performs two functions:

• It entitles the holder of the interest to a percentage share in the proceeds of sale, and

• It entitles the holder to assert rights of occupation against a third party lender or purchaser in certain circumstances. This is not the same as being able to assert rights of occupation against the owner.

In addition, once a beneficial interest is established, s/he will have a right to occupy the home and the owner would have to apply to the court under section 13 of the Trusts of Land and Appointment of Trustees Act to exclude her/him or restrict the right to occupy. This is not to be confused with the court's powers to make occupation. When deciding on this, the court must have regard to the intentions behind the trust.

Resisting claims from third parties

Where a non-owner has a beneficial interest in property, s/he may be able to resist the claims of a third party, unless s/he has agreed that the lender's right will take precedence (see 5.18 *'Waiving rights'*).

5.18   **Protecting non-owner's right to occupy and financial interest in the home**

In order to ensure that the non-owner can prevent actions by a lender or buyer of property, there are certain steps that can be taken to protect her/his rights. The procedure to protect a cohabitant's interest is the same as that for any people sharing property, regardless of their relationship. It depends firstly upon whether land is registered or unregistered.

The nature of a charge and the difference between registered and unregistered land is explained in 4.9, and the procedure for finding out if the land is registered or not is at 4.10.

Waiving rights

Lenders often ask non-owners to sign a document agreeing that the lenders' rights will take precedence over their own. In most cases, this will result in the non-owner being unable to resist claims by lenders, but in some cases it may be possible for the non-owner to use the defence of undue influence. For more information, see Section H.

UNREGISTERED LAND: PROCEDURES FOR PROTECTING NON-OWNERS' INTERESTS

There are five separate registers under the Land Charges Act 1972 for unregistered land. For the purposes of this book, the first two are of significance: the Land Charges Register and the register of Pending Land Actions. Matrimonial home rights of occupation can be registered as a Class F land charge on the Land Charges Register (see 4.10), but do not apply to cohabitants. The other classes of land charge do not normally affect couples in a relationship, whether married or cohabiting.[36]

5.19 Protecting a beneficial interest in unregistered land

The problem with beneficial interests in unregistered land is that they cannot be registered. Beneficial interests will survive a transfer of property where no money or valuable consideration changes hands (see 4.14), but if a property is sold or a loan is raised against it, those interests will be lost unless it can be shown that the buyer or lender had 'notice' of their existence when the transaction took place. This principle goes back to the medieval principles of equity, which held that if someone had bought property in good faith, not knowing there were any equitable interests attached to the land and there was no way the buyer could reasonably have been expected to know of those interests, then the buyer could not be made to honour the interests.

Giving notice

How someone with a beneficial interest in unregistered land could ensure that any buyer would know of the existence of that interest (ie, how they could give them that crucial notice) has been a thorny problem throughout the centuries. The system of Land Registration provides much easier solutions to the problem, as interests can be noted on the register.

Two legal concepts – *'overreaching'* and the *'doctrine of notice'* – are supposed to afford adequate protection where the land is unregistered, but it will be seen that this is not always the case.

5.20 Overreaching

Apart from the matrimonial Class F charge available to married couples, all the other registrable interests in unregistered land are 'commercial' rather than 'family.' This means that beneficial interests cannot be registered, since it is assumed that these interests will be 'overreached.'

Overreaching means that a buyer buys land free of any interests, provided the money is paid to two trustees. A 'trustee' is someone who is strictly the legal owner of property or money, but holds it on behalf of and for the benefit of someone else. The beneficial interest is converted from a right of occupation and a financial interest into hard cash. This is the normal situation where property is jointly owned and cannot be sold without the consent of both parties.

---

36. Although note the case of Lloyds Bank v Carrick (1996) The Times 13 March CA in which there was found to be an estate contract.

Therefore, if a property is legally owned by one partner only, and the other partner has a beneficial interest, theoretically the buyer should pay the purchase price to two trustees in order to take over the property free of the non-owning partner's beneficial interest. However, in practice, the buyer may not know that anyone else has, for example, paid a deposit or contributed towards mortgage payments, and is likely to pay the money simply into the hands of the one legal owner and not two trustees. In this case, there will have been no overreaching and whether the non-legal owner's beneficial interest is protected depends upon the 'doctrine of notice.' Where overreaching has occurred or the non-owner with a beneficial interest will have no rights to remain in the property, but may be able to get her/his money back by pursuing the trustees.

Under section 14 of the Trusts of Land and Appointment of Trustees Act 1996, it may be possible to get an order preventing such a sale (see 5.48-9).

5.21 Doctrine of notice

Someone who buys or lends on a property (note that financial consideration must change hands – see above) is only bound to honour equitable, ie, beneficial interests, of which s/he had 'actual, imputed or constructive' notice. Problems arise from what is deemed to be 'constructive notice.' The rule is that a buyer or lender is bound by any interest which s/he would have discovered if s/he had 'prudently' inspected the title deeds and the land itself, making such enquiries and inspection as s/he ought reasonably to have made.

s199(1) LPA25

Constructive notice

Case law shows a dramatic change in emphasis since the 1960s: the rights of a wife or partner in occupation were deemed to be nothing more than living in the man's shadow, and the fact that a wife was living in the property in question was held not to be sufficient to constitute notice of a beneficial interest to a lender.[37] This is no longer the situation.

If the person with the beneficial interest is living in the property and inspection of the property could have been expected to reveal that s/he was living there, it will almost certainly be held that a buyer or lender should be deemed to be aware of any rights such an occupier might have.[38] Recent cases suggest a stringent requirement on banks and finance companies to make enquiries.

Lending institution practice now normally includes asking a borrower if anyone else is living in the property being used as security; this may be done simply by a question on a form. However, it would appear that this could be insufficient, since the fact that an owner has lied on a

38. Williams and Glyn's Bank v Boland, (1981) AC 487, HL; Kingsnorth Finance Co v Tizard (1986) 1 WLR 783. For a further discussion of the requirements for inquiries and inspection, see Parry, M.L. The Law Relating to Cohabitation (1993), third edition, Sweet and Maxwell, pp.36.

37. Caunce v Caunce (1969) 1 WLR 286.

form is not necessarily enough to protect a lender's interest. If there is any basis for saying that the lender should have known that a non-owner might be occupying the home used as security, eg, a partner had been to meetings at the lenders with the owning partner or been at the original interviews for the mortgage, it may be possible to argue that the lender had constructive notice of a potential interest and should have made further enquiries.

Constructive notice is of considerable importance, since it means that, even if the lender wanted to repossess the property on the basis of the unpaid second mortgage, the partner's right to live there based on her/his prior beneficial interest would take precedence.

5.22 Recording the interests on the title deeds

A beneficial interest can be recorded on the title deeds, but as it would require the agreement of the legal owner, this is not likely to be of much help in most relationship breakdown situations.

5.23 Pending land actions – property adjustment orders, Children Act applications, order for sale

s17(1) LCA72 Any court action started but not yet resolved can be registered as a pending land action under the Land Charges Act 1972. This would apply when a property transfer order or a Children Act transfer is being sought, or where there is an application for an order for sale, or declaration of beneficial interest, under the Trusts of Land and Appointment of Trustees Act. An application for a property adjustment order also constitutes a pending land action under this Act (see 4.15).

Registering a pending land action

Advisers should obtain form K3 from the Land Charges Department in Plymouth and return it with full details of the action being taken and a fee.[39] This will give notice to any buyer or lender of the rights of the non-owner with a beneficial interest and the buyer/lender should then make sure that the action is discharged before completing any transaction.

It should be possible to get an injunction to prevent any dealing with the home, pending the outcome of proceedings. Whether the court would grant an injunction to continue to occupy the home would depend on the circumstances of the case (see 5.4 and 5.8). This is not

s37 SCA81 & s3 CLSA90 a routine procedure, but would appear to be within the interlocutory powers of the court.

---

39. At the time of writing, this fee was £1, but this should be confirmed with the Land Charges Department, Plumer House, Tailyour Road, Crownhill, Plymouth PL6 5HY. Tel. 01752 636666.

REGISTERED LAND: PROCEDURES FOR PROTECTING NON-OWNERS' INTERESTS

5.24 Protecting a beneficial interest

There are two ways in which a beneficial interest in registered land may be protected.

Registration

Until 13 October 2003

Unlike unregistered land, it is possible to protect a beneficial interest by an entry of a restriction, inhibition, notice or caution on the land register. Under the Land Registration Act 2002, which is due to come into force on 13 October 2003, inhibitions and cautions will be abolished but existing inhibitions and cautions will remain. Details of the basis for claiming a beneficial interest need to be sent to the Land Registry, which will then decide if the claim is sufficient to be registered. It is not necessary to have had the interest declared in court prior to registration.

A *restriction* prevents disposal without the consent of the person with the registered interest and notice of is binding upon purchasers. Both restrictions and notices usually require production of the land certificate, and therefore the cooperation of the named owner. This is not needed for a caution, as it is seen as a 'hostile action.' The Land Registry will notify the owner once the action has been registered.

The most common way for a beneficial interest to be protected has been by registering a *caution*, obtaining/completing Form CT2 from the Land Registry and return with the fee.[40] From 13 October 2003 this will no longer be possible and will be replaced by notices or restrictions (see below).

Cautions can in certain circumstances be overridden. However, once registered, the person with the beneficial interest (the cautioner) would then be notified of any proposed disposal, and could therefore seek an injunction to prevent it.[41]

Registration is of paramount importance if the non-owner is not in occupation, since the interest will not be protected if it is not registered.

After 13 October 2003

Inhibitions are replaced by restrictions and cautions are replaced (depending on the type of interest) by notices or restrictions.

Restrictions

Although at the time of writing the Land Registration Rules had not been published with finalised details, restrictions rather than notices must be

40. This is currently £40, but should be checked with the Land Registry.

41. Waller v Waller (1967) 1 WLR 451.

used where an equitable interest is capable of being overreached, ie, where there are two or more owners or trustees. A restriction would therefore have to be used, for example, where a property is jointly owned, perhaps by a partner and her/his first spouse or partner, but a third party, such as a new partner, wishes to protect her/his beneficial interest.

Notices

A non-owning partner who wishes to protect a beneficial interest will normally do this by way of applying to register a notice. As with old cautions, the new type of notice can be applied for without the owner's consent, but the owner will be notified, and can object. An Adjudicator is to be appointed who will hold hearings to resolve disputes.

s107 LRA02

A notice under the Land Registration Act 2002 differs from a caution in that, although the act of registering the notice does not in itself make the interest claimed a valid one (since this may have to be decided by the court under the Trusts of Land and Appointment of Trustees Act 1996) the notice will confer priority upon any interest that is proved valid. This means that it would protect the interest should the property be sold or re-mortgaged. A caution did not do this but merely meant that, if there was any attempt to deal with the property, notice was served on the cautioner giving her/him the choice of objecting or having the caution cancelled. If s/he failed to respond, the caution would be cancelled. Once a unilateral notice has been entered on the register, it will remain there until either the applicant applies for it to be removed, or the registered owner applies for it to be cancelled. The only time notice will be served on the applicant will be on an application for cancellation.

Overriding interests

Until 13 October 2003

If the interest is not protected by registration, but the non-owner is in occupation, s/he may have an 'overriding interest.' If someone has an overriding interest, it is binding upon a buyer or lender whether they knew about the interest or not.

To establish an overriding interest, the claimant must prove three things:

- That s/he has a right 'subsisting in reference to land.' A matrimonial right of occupation or a bare licence to occupy is not enough. Contributions towards the purchase price or mortgage payments, ie, a beneficial interest, would qualify

- That s/he was in 'actual occupation' at the moment the buyer or lender registered her/his title to the property[42]

- That no enquiry was made of the person in occupation.

---

42. Abbey National Building Society v Cann (1990) 2 WLR 832 HL.

This means that a non-owner, in occupation, with a beneficial interest, who has not registered that interest, may still be able to hold out and retain the right to occupy against, for example, a bank calling in a second charge taken out by the sole owning spouse or partner.[43]

The turning point in the law was the House of Lords case of *Williams and Glyn's Bank v Boland*[44] in the early 1980s. In this case, the wife had a beneficial interest in the family home, as she had contributed substantially to the purchase price. She was in actual occupation at a time when, unknown to her, her husband, the sole owner, mortgaged the property to the bank for business purposes. The court held that she could resist the lender's claim for possession on the grounds that she had an overriding interest over the lender's charge.

The reasoning behind this was the lender had not made adequate enquiries about equitable interests in the property offered as security, and had not obtained a release of her interest from the wife.

The result was that lenders tightened up on procedures for obtaining consents from those either in occupation, or likely to be in occupation, but not on the legal title.

Thus, those not on the legal title, but who are in occupation and who have a beneficial interest, effectively have to be consulted about dealings with the property.[45]

After 13 October 2003

Unregistered interests with overriding status are binding on the registered owner, or someone buying from her/him without their existence being apparent from the register. One aim of the Land Registration Act is to make the register more comprehensive by noting certain overriding interests, and thereby reducing the scope and number of these interests which can complicate transfers of land.

The Act reduces the importance of overriding interests, and allows for many types of interests to be noted on the register. Only the person who is in actual occupation of the land will in future have the benefit of overriding status. For the majority of partners, this means that the position remains the same, *provided they are still in occupation.* If s/he has moved out, or if it is not obvious, on a reasonably careful inspection of the property, that the person claiming an interest is occupying it, then her/his interest is not protected. The onus is on that person to protect the interest by registration of a notice or restriction, as appropriate. *Advisers should ensure that clients take advice to protect their interests if they have moved out, or are considering moving out, of a house in which they consider they have a beneficial interest.*

43. Williams and Glyn's Bank v Boland, see 38 above.
44. William and Glyn's Bank v Boland, ibid.
45. Bull v Bull (1995) 1 QB 234; Williams and Glyn's Bank Ltd v Boland ibid.; Barclay v Barclay (1970) 2 QB 677.

Enquiries by the lender

Stringent requirements on lenders to make enquiries are required, as for unregistered land (see 5.21). It is now normal practice for lenders to ask anyone living on premises at the time a loan is agreed to sign a document giving the lender's rights precedence over her/his own (see Section H for information about possible defences). The aim of the Land Registration Act is to simplify dealings with properties, and the registered owner will therefore, from 13 October 2003, be obliged to disclose any overriding interests when dealing with the property in any way, eg, sale or raising a loan.

5.25 Children Act transfers or other land actions

Until 13 October 2003

These may also be registered as a caution, and are similar to pending land actions for unregistered land.

After 13 October 2003

These must be registered either as a restriction or notice.

D Preventing disposal of the solely-owned family home

5.26 Selling the family home

s11 TLATA96

In theory, only the consent of the legal owner is required to sell a property. However, the Trusts of Land and Appointment of Trustees Act has improved the position for those occupying the home with a beneficial interest, who are now entitled to be consulted if there is an express trust. Unlike a married partner, a cohabitant has no matrimonial home rights which can be registered. Non-owning cohabitants have a potential power to prevent a sale only if they can establish that they have an interest in the home which will hold against the purchaser (see Section C above). This may be in terms of a beneficial interest, or as a result of a right to apply for a transfer of property under the Children Act for the benefit of a child of the relationship (see 9.13).

5.27 Raising a loan on the family home

Once again, technically only the legal owner's consent is required, but, as with registered matrimonial home rights, beneficial interests may also be binding upon lenders and override their rights. For this reason, the stringent requirements for consent from anyone living in the property which is to be used as security apply equally to cohabitants and other family members as to married partners (see 4.13 and 5.21 and 5.24).

5.28 Preventing disposal of property if the non-owner has no beneficial interest

This is an area in which the cohabitant is at a distinct disadvantage compared with a married counterpart, since the law offers cohabitants no automatic rights to occupy which can be registered:

- *Court's inherent jurisdiction:* The court has an inherent jurisdiction to prevent disposal of any property which is the subject matter of a case; it should therefore be possible to obtain an injunction to prevent sale or disposal before a court hearing to decide who gets the property, eg, where a Children Act transfer is pending[46]

- *Transfer for no money:* If a property is given away 'without valuable consideration,' any existing interest remains enforceable

CPR 25.1(f)
- *Freezing injunctions:*[47] These replaced 'Mareva' injunctions. They are normally used in commercial proceedings, and enable the court to prevent disposal of any asset which could be the subject of legal proceedings. They could now be used in Children Act property transfer cases, since there is no other equivalent to section 37 of the Matrimonial Causes Act 1973 (to prevent a deliberate depletion of assets) (see 4.18)

CPR 25.1(h)
- *Search orders:*[48] These were formerly 'Anton Piller' orders. A draconian measure normally used in business contexts (see 4.19).

Joint legal owners

E Rights to occupy the family home

5.29 The right to live in the family home

If a couple (heterosexual, lesbian or gay) are joint legal owners, property law entitles both parties to live there. Neither can legally exclude the other without a court order.

5.30 Occupation orders under the Family Law Act 1996

Joint legal owners are 'entitled' applicants for the purpose of obtaining occupation orders under the Family Law Act. This means that both heterosexual and lesbian or gay cohabitants are entitled to apply for occupation orders enforcing their rights to occupy in the same way as married couples with matrimonial home rights. They can also apply to exclude the other partner (see 13.30).

---

46. S37 Supreme Court Act 1981 and by virtue of Statute s3 Courts and Legal Services Act 1990, the county court has the same power.

47. s2 & 3 County Court Remedies Regulations 1991, (SI 1991 No. 1222 as amended by SI 1995 No. 206).
48. Ibid.

F   Establishing the joint owner's interest in the family home

Establishing shares in the proceeds of a sale of the home is not as simple as knowing in whose name the property was bought. A couple may be joint legal owners, but may have different financial shares in a property. How such interests in cases of joint ownership may be established is explained in the sections below.

5.31   The nature of joint ownership

A confusing feature of property law is that where there is shared ownership of a property, the co-owners are often referred to as 'joint tenants' of the property they own. This has nothing whatsoever to do with rented property.

If both partners' names appear on the title deeds, they will be known as 'joint tenants at law.' This means that they are each entitled to possession of the whole land and the right to occupy it. In law they hold the property as trustees under a 'trust of land.' There is now no primary duty on the trustees to sell, and it is implied in every trust for sale of land that the trustees can postpone the sale. They can do this for as long as they wish, and problems only arise when one joint owner/trustee decides s/he wishes to sell and the other does not, in which case it is necessary to apply for an order for sale (see 5.48). The courts' powers regarding orders which can be made were widened by the Trusts of Land and Appointment of Trustees Act 1996, and they can direct not only that the property be sold, but can also prevent or postpone a sale.

s36 LPA25
s4 TLATA96

5.32   Deciding the interests of joint owners

Beneficial joint tenants and tenants in common

Joint tenants at law can be:

- *'Beneficial joint tenants' (or 'joint tenants in equity')*: This would mean that they would both be equally entitled to the whole net financial value of the house

- *'Tenants in common' (or 'equitable' or 'beneficial' tenants in common)*: this means that they hold distinct shares in the property, even though the property has not yet been divided up physically. Where the contributions (and hence the shares) are unequal, it will normally be presumed that it is a tenancy in common, although it is also quite possible to have a tenancy in common where the owners have equal shares.

In determining the share of a beneficial interest, it will be necessary to establish whether there is a resulting or constructive trust, as is the case for establishing a beneficial interest for sole owners (see 5.9 onwards).

The situation may best be understood by looking at an example: Rashida and Owen have bought a house and put it in their joint names. Although this means that they are both legal owners, it does not necessarily mean that they are each entitled to half the proceeds of sale. This situation can vary, depending upon the understanding between them:

1. Rashida has contributed £10,000 as the deposit and they share the mortgage payments. No further statement about their rights in the property has been made.

2. Rashida has contributed £10,000 as the deposit, they share the mortgage payments and they stated expressly in a trust deed when they bought the property that they intended to hold the property jointly on trust for themselves as joint tenants beneficially.

3. Rashida has contributed £10,000 as the deposit and they share the mortgage payments. When she put down the money, she said she wanted Owen to consider the money his just as much as hers.

1. Resulting trust

In the first instance a 'resulting trust' arises, in the same way as for sole owners (see 5.10). As both partners' names appear on the title deeds, they will be known as joint tenants at law. They are not, however, beneficial joint tenants, which would mean that they would both be equally entitled to the financial value of the house. In this case, because they have not contributed to the purchase equally, they are tenants in common, meaning that they hold the property in distinct shares, even though the property has not yet been divided up physically.

In other words, Rashida's beneficial interest in the property will be greater than Owen's in proportion to the amount of her contribution. However, because nothing was written at the time, if there is a dispute, it would be necessary to show a common intention that Rashida was to hold a greater beneficial interest. In the absence of an express statement and any evidence of a contrary intention, the unequal contribution itself would be sufficient evidence of the common intention that Rashida should have the greater beneficial interest.

> 'If two (or more) persons purchased property in their joint names and there had been no declaration of trusts on which they were to hold the property, they would, as a matter of law in the absence of evidence to the contrary, hold the property on a resulting trust for

the persons who provided the purchase money in the proportions in which they provided it.'[49]

2. Express declaration of interests

Although the situation appears the same, Rashida and Owen have made an express declaration of how they intended to share the property. This means that the courts will assume that they hold the property equally, and will therefore be entitled to share the proceeds of sale equally, despite the fact that Rashida contributed substantially more. An express declaration of joint beneficial interests will be conclusive in the absence of fraud or mistake.[50] They will be beneficial joint tenants.

3. Common intention constructive trust

As with sole owners, the court will look to see if there was any express agreement which gave evidence of a common intention to hold in any other proportions than those in which they had contributed. In this case, as in 1 above, because nothing was written at the time the courts would have to consider what the parties' intentions were as to their beneficial interests. Despite their unequal contributions, Owen may be able to argue that Rashida's statement to him was sufficient to give rise to a constructive trust under which he will have an equal beneficial interest.[51] Alternatively he may be able to claim proprietory estoppel. In order to be successful in his argument Owen would also need to show that he had acted to his detriment (see 5.12).

5.33 Effect of one joint owner dying

If land is jointly owned as beneficial joint tenants and one partner dies, the other automatically becomes the owner of the whole property. If the home is jointly owned as tenants in common when one partner dies, her/his share goes to her/his estate, ie, s/he can will the proportion s/he owns to someone else. The inheritor would then be able to apply to the court for an order for sale under the Trusts of Land and Appointment of Trustees Act 1996 (see 5.48-9).

Ending beneficial joint ownership (ie, a beneficial joint tenancy)

When a relationship breaks down, it may take some time to settle what happens to the property, and the parties may wish to prevent their partners from inheriting their share if they should die before settlement. Equally, if one party wishes to leave her/his share in the property to someone else, this can only be done by 'severing' the joint tenancy and becoming tenants in common. This can be a very important issue for cohabitants where one party is still married (although separated).

---

49. Springett v Defoe, see 6 above; see also Dyer v Dyer
   (1788) 2 Cox Eq Cas 92; Walker v Hall (1984) FLR 126.
50. Goodman v Gallant, see 6 above.   51. Savill v Goodall (1992) 25 HLR 588 CA.

McDowell v Hirschfield Lipson and Rumney and Smith[52]

A married couple jointly bought a house as beneficial joint tenants. The husband left in 1982 and set up home with another partner, by whom he had two children. The wife remained in the matrimonial home. The husband began divorce proceedings twice, and the sale of the matrimonial home was discussed by solicitors, but nothing was settled. The husband died in 1988, two months after he filed for divorce the second time.

If the joint tenancy had been severed, the husband's half share in the matrimonial home would have gone to his partner, who was the sole beneficiary of his will, and the wife would have had to give up half the original home. As the tenancy was held not to have been severed, the whole of the ownership of the former home went to the wife.

The husband's solicitors tried to argue that they had brought about severance by virtue of their correspondence with the wife's solicitors. However, the court held that divorce did not call for severance. The Matrimonial Causes Act 1973 allowed the court to adjust property rights, regardless of joint tenancies or tenancies in common, and there was no evidence it had been their intention to sever the joint tenancy. The wife therefore became the sole owner by survivorship.

NB. See also the case of Hunter v Babbage below.

A beneficial joint tenancy can be severed with or without the agreement of both parties. To avoid dispute, it is best if this is done by:

s36(2) LPA25

- giving written notice to the other joint tenant.[53]

However, it may be possible to bring about severance in other ways:

- By agreement
- By one joint tenant dealing with her/his share, for example, by selling it
- By some kind of dealing between the joint tenants which shows an intention that property should be held in common and not jointly.

Once a notice of severance has been served, it can be entered as a restriction on registered land through the Land Registry. However, the Land Registry will no longer accept the post office receipt of posting (registered or recorded) as proof that a notice of Severance of Joint Tenancy has been served on the other party. To accompany the notice, there should therefore be a certificate signed by the person serving the notice that it has been served on the other party.

---

52. McDowell v Hirschfield Lipson Rummey and Smith October (1992) Fam Law QBD.

53. Section 36(2) of the Law of Property Act 1925; a memorandum should be endorsed on the conveyance if the land is unregistered and a restriction entered if the land is registered.

Severance does not have to have been formalised to be held to have taken place (see also 12.11 for the effect of bankruptcy and insolvency on severance of joint tenancies and the case of *Hunter v Babbage*). It is also easy to make a mistake, and severance cannot simply be withdrawn; therefore legal advice is always advisable before any attempt is made to sever a joint tenancy (see *Kinch v Bullard* in box).

Hunter v Babbage[54]

A couple divorced in 1988, and in December 1989, during property adjustment proceedings, a draft agreement was prepared stating that the property was to be sold and the proceeds divided. The husband died before the agreement was finalised. The wife appealed against the decision that the joint tenancy had been severed, which meant that the husband's share went to his estate and not automatically to her, as it would have done if the joint tenancy could be hold still to exist. The court held that it did not matter whether the agreement was enforceable: the significance of an agreement was not that it bound the parties, but that it served as an indication of a common intention to sever.

Kinch v Bullard[55]

A terminally ill wife successfully severed a joint tenancy she held with her husband, even though she tried to stop this from happening after realising her husband was also terminally ill. After retrieving her letter giving notice of the severance from the property where her husband had lived, the husband's executors brought an action against the wife to claim the joint tenancy had been severed. The court subsequently agreed with the executors in finding the joint tenancy had been severed, even though the deceased husband had not even been aware of the wife's letter. Consequently, the wife was not entitled to the entire property as the surviving owner.

G   Preventing disposal of the jointly-owned family home

5.34   Selling the jointly-owned family home

The consent and signatures of both legal owners are needed for a sale to be valid. If there is no consent or one joint owner has disappeared, application may be made to the court for an order for sale under either section 14 of the Trusts of Land and Appointment of Trustees Act 1996,

---

54. Hunter v Babbage (1994) EGCS 8 ChD.   55. Kinch v Bullard (1998) 4 A11 ER 650; (1999) 1 FLR 66 Ch.D.

or section 17 of the Married Woman's Property Act 1882 for those engaged in the last 3 years (see 5.48-9). If a sale is ordered, the share of a missing owner would have to be held in trust. Although there does not appear to be any authoritative case law on the matter, it is probable that where one owner has disappeared, the court would have discretion to appoint an additional trustee, with the trustees then being 'trustees of a trust of proceeds of sale for land.'

s17 TLATA96

5.35   Raising a loan on the jointly-owned family home

If the property is jointly owned, the consent and signature of both parties are required. The only possibility of having such a consent set aside is if the partner signing can be shown to have signed under undue influence from the other (see below).

5.36   Preventing disposal of jointly-owned property

Where both are legal owners, there can be no valid disposal of jointly owned property without the consent and signature of both parties, except as in 5.34 above. Disposal of other types of property such as cars, jewellery or family assets, can be prevented, regardless of ownership rights, as for sole owners (see 5.28).

Sole and joint legal owners

Sections H-J apply equally to both sole and joint ownership of property.

H   Undue influence and misrepresentation in obtaining consent to a loan

It is expected that institutions such as banks or other lenders must make thorough enquiries to discover whether there could be any undisclosed beneficial interest in both registered and unregistered land (see 5.21 and 5.24).

The result of this is that a lender will require anyone living in a house to agree that the mortgage will come before her/his interest, if any. This is to protect the lender from being subject to a spouse's matrimonial home rights, or a spouse/partner's beneficial interest which could override the lender's own claim. It also means that a partner is in effect agreeing that, if repayments are not met, her/his right to occupy and/or financial share in the home could be lost or overridden.

If the lender has taken all the necessary precautions to discover any undisclosed beneficial interests, and a signature giving consent has been obtained from the spouse/partner with such an interest, there will normally be no protection of the interest if the lender later has grounds to call in the loan and/or repossess. The same principle applies if a joint owner gives consent to the raising of the loan. However, there may be a possible defence, which relates to the concepts of 'undue influence' and misrepresentation.

5.37 The defences of undue influence and misrepresentation

It may seem that if a wife or partner (or indeed any family member who has a beneficial interest in the property) has signed an official document agreeing to the loan, with the consequent effect of waiving of rights to occupy, then s/he would have no hope of holding out against the lender. A number of cases since the mid 1980s have shown that this is not necessarily the case, and that lenders are required to take even further precautions if they wish to protect their interest beyond any possible challenge.

One possible defence is if a partner (or family member) can successfully argue that the consent was obtained as a result of 'undue influence' from the person who had obtained the loan, and that the lender had notice of this. Alternatively, if the partner was deceived by the other partner, about something that may have led her/him to come to a different decision about giving consent, this 'material' misrepresentation may also be a defence, if the lender had 'notice' of the misrepresentation.

In a landmark decision in 1984, the House of Lords held in *Barclays Bank v O'Brien* that where a wife is led to agree to be party to a mortgage of jointly held property as security for her husband's debt by his undue influence or misrepresentation, she has a right not only to have that agreement set aside as against her husband, but also against a third party lender who has actual or constructive notice of the undue influence or misrepresentation. This means that she can resist the lender's claim for possession.

In 2001, the House of Lords revisited this issue in a series of cases reported collectively as *Royal Bank of Scotland plc v Etridge (No.2)*[56]. This case completely reassesses situations which might involve undue influence, and replaces the judgment in *O'Brien*.

The guidance laid down by it is now authoritative. The interpretation of the case which follows is based on an article by Guy Skipwith,[57] and readers advising in this area are recommended to read the full text of the article, which also contains a useful flowchart. It is a complex area, and if possible undue influence is identified, the client should be referred for expert legal advice.

---

56. Royal Bank of Scotland v Etridge (No. 2) [2001] UKHL 44 [2002] HLR. 4.

57. 'Banks, solicitors, husbands and wives' by Guy Skipwith. Adviser magazine 95. Jan/Feb 2003 p.40.

5.38 What is 'undue influence?'

The House of Lords in *Etridge* defined undue influence as the misuse of influence, including inaccurate explanations of a proposed transaction and, in a relationship of trust and confidence, where a husband puts his own interests before his wife's and makes a choice for both of them on that basis.

Who can claim undue influence?

Although the seven cases in *Etridge* alleged undue influence on wives, the principles outlined by the case apply to all relationships that are non-commercial, whether or not a sexual relationship exists. Lesbian or gay couples are therefore included, as are family members. In the explanation of this case, reference is made to the 'wife' since it was wives who were the claimants in this instance.

5.39 Whether undue influence can be presumed or must be proved

It is well-established that certain categories of relationship will of themselves give rise to a presumption that undue influence was involved, although evidence to the contrary could overturn such a presumption. Examples of such relationships are parent and child, doctor and patient and those involving a religious superior. However, in Etridge it was held that the relationship of husband and wife does not ordinarily give rise to a presumption of undue influence, although it might possibly do so in husband and wife (or presumably cohabitants') cases, where it can be shown that:

• there is a relationship involving the dominance of one person over the other or a relationship involving trust and confidence, and

• there is a transaction of sufficient disadvantage to the wife to require explanation.

'Sufficient disadvantage' to a wife was not defined, although one Law Lord speculated that charges known as 'all monies' charges and unlimited guarantees may come within this definition.[58]

If there is such a presumption of undue influence, it can be overturned by the lender showing that the wife was properly advised about the transaction by the lender or an independent solicitor (see below), or that there was in fact no undue influence or misrepresentation. In practice, therefore, it will almost always be necessary for evidence of actual undue influence or misrepresentation to be proved instead of it being assumed, as was often the case in the past.

---

58. Barclays Bank v O'Brien (1993) 26 HLR 75 HL; 4 All ER 417; Royal Bank of Scotland v Etridge (No. 2).

5.40 Constructive notice – putting a lender 'on inquiry'

O'Brien introduced into English law the idea that, in certain situations the lender ought to have known that there was a possibility of undue influence or misrepresentation by her husband. In such cases, the lender is deemed to have 'constructive notice' of any undue influence that is exerted by a husband.

Etridge held that lenders are deemed to have 'constructive notice,' and thus be put 'on inquiry,' in all cases where they know of the husband/wife relationship or that the relationship between the debtor and person giving security (the surety) is non-commercial.

Where an advance is made to a husband and wife jointly, the lender will not be deemed to have constructive notice unless it is known that the loan is in fact for the husband's sole benefit.

Lenders will, however, be fixed with constructive notice and be put on inquiry of undue influence where a wife gives security for the debts of a company in which she and her husband are both the share holders, even where she is a director, shareholder or company secretary.[59]

5.41 What a lender must do to avoid being fixed with constructive notice of possible undue influence

Etridge made a distinction between transactions entered into on or before 11.10.01 ('past transactions'), and those entered into on or after 12.10.01, the date of the judgment ('future transactions'[60]).

Safeguards before 11.10.01

The safeguards before 11.10.01 include taking 'reasonable steps' to ensure that a wife understands the nature, effect, risk and practical implications of the transaction being entered into. Knowledge that a solicitor is acting for a wife is not enough in itself for the lender to assume that the wife has been adequately advised. Usually a lender will be able to rely on an independent solicitor's certificate stating that the wife has been advised appropriately, but not if the lender should have known that this was not the case, for example, where the solicitor did not speak the claimant's language.[61]

Safeguards after 11.10.01

The House of Lords in *Etridge* laid down detailed and stringent responsibilities upon lenders if they are to avoid being fixed with constructive notice. These include checking directly with a wife as to the name of a solicitor she wishes to act for her, and direct communication with the wife informing her that it will require written confirmation from

59. See 56 above, para 49.
60. ibid. para 50.
61. National Westminster Bank v Amin [2002] 28.02.02 HL.

the solicitor that the transaction has been fully explained. The lender must also inform her that the purpose of the solicitor's certification is to make the transaction legally binding, with the result that she will be unable to challenge it. The overall aim is to give greater protection to vulnerable members of the public. Fuller details of the requirements are to be found in the article referred to in 5.37.[62]

5.42 The role of solicitors

Although the scope of the duties imposed on solicitors advising people who agree to give security has been narrowed, in that they do not have to satisfy themselves that the person is free from undue influence, nor advise her/him not to enter into a transaction or veto it, the detailed requirements (the 'core minimum') as to how and what they must advise have been extended considerably.[63]

5.43 Proving undue influence where lender fixed with constructive notice

If the lender has failed to comply with the requirements laid down in Etridge, then it is open to the claimant to claim the defence of undue influence. It is important to realise that this will still have to be proved, and will not simply be assumed because of the nature of the relationship. If the lender has followed the necessary procedures, no claim of undue influence can validly be brought.

Increased protection against undue influence

The judgment in *Etridge* is a welcome one. It should ensure that better protection is provided for potentially vulnerable wives, and other people in non-commercial situations, who are asked to provide security for a husband's or another's debts, because lenders are now required to make contact directly with them to emphasise the importance of independent legal advice.

I Quantifying financial shares

Where one partner has successfully established a beneficial interest, the next step is to quantify the share each party is entitled to and when the entitlement should start. This can apply to both sole and joint ownership of the home. It is particularly relevant where the parties have separated, with one partner remaining in the home and possibly paying the whole of the mortgage, and there is a significant time lapse before an application is made to the court.

---

62. Banks, solicitors, husbands and wives, by Guy Skipwith, see 57 above.

63. See Guy Skipwith's article 57 above for further details.

5.44 Date when partner's shares should be valued

In the 1980s, case law established that the value of the respective parties' shares in a property should be decided at the time of sale or when one party buys the other out, and not at the time when the couple ceased to live together.[64] This means that when a couple separate and do nothing about settling their financial interest for some time, the partner who left may still benefit by an increase in value of the property between the time of leaving and the time of settlement. Equally, of course, if the property drops in value, the amount will decrease.

If one partner has remained in the property and spent money which has improved the value of the property for some time after separation, this may be taken into account, in what is often referred to as 'equitable accounting,' to decide the amounts each party should get.

5.45 Quantifying the proportions of the shares

The guidelines for quantifying a beneficial interest were significantly affected by the important case of *Midland Bank v Cooke*[65] in 1995 (see 5.46 below).

As with establishing the existence of a beneficial interest, the court will look to see whether there was an express declaration concerning the shares in the property. If there is no express declaration, the court will look for evidence of a common intention regarding the shares.

In *Savill v Goodall*,[66] an unmarried couple bought a council house in joint names. The woman had the tenancy transferred to her from her ex-husband, and hence had a 42 per cent right to buy discount. The remainder was bought with a 100 per cent mortgage, which it was agreed the man would repay. He made the payments for one year, but then left the household, never to return.

The woman tried to argue that she should be entitled to a 42 per cent interest before the rest of the value was distributed.

Her appeal was dismissed. The court held that the couple had bought the property with the common intention that they should hold it in equal shares. However, since it had been agreed that the man would pay the mortgage, the outstanding amount of mortgage should be repaid from his share of the proceeds. The woman had repaid the mortgage interest since the man had left and this was deemed to be an 'occupation rent,' ie, it did not affect the settlement: the woman had had the benefit of occupying the property and the man had not. Such payments are therefore held to be 'cancelled out' and do not affect valuation (see below).

64. Walker v Hall; Turton v Turton (1987) 3 WLR 622 CA
    (1984) FLR 126, (1984) Family Law 21, CA.
65. Midland Bank v Cooke, see 12 above.   66. Savill v Goodall, see 51 above.

However, in *Springette v Defoe*,[67] a couple also bought a council house in joint names under the right to buy. The woman was entitled to a 41 per cent discount. In the first instance the court held that the beneficial interest was in equal shares, but this was overturned by the Court of Appeal, which accepted that the woman was entitled to 75 per cent of the proceeds. This was because there had been no shared common intention communicated between the couple regarding the shares. Where there are no express discussions of common intention, the property will be deemed to be held on a resulting trust[68] in proportion to the shares of the purchase money which they had provided. The right-to-buy discount was held to be the equivalent to a direct contribution of the full amount of the discount. The fact that they paid the mortgage in equal shares after the purchase was not evidence that they intended to share the beneficial interest equally.

The key difference between these two cases is that in the first there had been express discussions about how the couple would share the property, thereby giving rise to a constructive trust, whilst in the second there had not been any such communication, and the court dealt with the case as a straight resulting trust. Following *Midland Bank v Cooke*, the courts may now decide to infer an intention to share when none has been expressed, once a resulting trust is established, since the court may infer a constructive trust (see 5.46).

The court may well construe different outcomes, depending on its view of the facts. For example, where one person has taken on mortgage liability, the court may decide that the person should be credited with the full value of the amount of the mortgage, but that the amount still outstanding on the mortgage should be deducted from that person's share; or they could be credited simply with the amount of mortgage payments made; or where the parties have agreed to share the mortgage payments, they may be treated as contributing half the amount each. The position remains unclear.[69] In *Drake v Whipp*,[70] the woman provided 19.4% of the purchase price, but was held to be entitled to one-third of the house's value. It has been commented that this shows how hard it can be to predict the court's response, and that the proportion that should be awarded may perhaps be an issue for the judge's individual discretion.

5.46 The position after *Cooke*

Once a foothold has been obtained by way of contributions to the home, if the court can infer a constructive trust, even without express discussions, then it is not bound to decide the proportion of the interest strictly on the basis of the cash contribution. Despite the lack of express discussion,

67. Springette v Defoe, see 6 above
68. See also Huntingford v Hobbs, see 20 above; J. Hayes, 'Quantifying beneficial interests in residential property' Solicitors Journal, 15.1.93.
69. See Huntingford v Hobbs, see 20 above; (1994) 24 HLR 652 CA; P. Wylie, Mortgages and Ownership of the Family Home, Fam Law (1993) 176; E. Cooke, Equitable Accounting Between Co-owners Family Law (1993) 695.
70. Drake v Whipp (1996) 1 FLR 826 CA.

the court may still decide to attribute an intention to the parties to share the beneficial interest in some different proportion. However, if there is no direct contribution and no express discussions, then the court still has no alternative but to find that there is no beneficial interest by way of either resulting or constructive trust.

Whether the court decides to infer an agreement when the couple explicitly said that there was none will be up to the court's discretion. In *Cooke*, the judge adopted a 'common sense' approach:

> *'When people, especially young people, agree to share their lives in joint homes, they do so on a basis of mutual trust and in the expectation that their relationship will endure... There will inevitably be numerous couples, married or unmarried, who have no discussion about ownership... It would be anomalous... to create a range of home buyers who were beyond the pale of equity's assistance in formulating a fair presumed basis for sharing of the beneficial interest, simply because they had been honest enough to admit that they never gave ownership a thought or reached any agreement about it.'*[71]

In order to come to this decision, the judge had to distinguish between this case and that of *Springette v Defoe* (above) in which the opposite finding was made. The judge made the distinction on the somewhat tenuous basis that the earlier case looked at the position of a mature couple who could have been expected to have reached an agreement about shares, whilst in *Cooke* the couple were younger and so entitled to be less formal. It seems unlikely that this approach would now be followed.

In reaching a decision about the share in which the property was held, the judge drew on the case of *Gissing v Gissing*,[72] in which one of the judges (Lord Diplock) clarified the approach to be used in deciding on shares once a beneficial interest had been established by way of direct contributions by the non-owner:

> *'...the court must first do its best to discover from the conduct of the spouses whether any inference can be drawn as to the probable common understanding about the amount of the share of the contributing spouse upon which each must have acted in doing what each did, even though that understanding was never expressly stated by one spouse to the other or even consciously formulated in words by either of them independently.'*

The judge in *Cooke* held that the court should

> *'...undertake a survey of the whole course of dealing between the parties relevant to their ownership and occupation of the property and their sharing of its burdens and advantages. That scrutiny will*

---

71. Midland Bank v Cooke, see 12 above, p747.   72. Gissing v Gissing (1971) AC 886.

*not confine itself to the limited range of acts of direct contributions
of the sort that are needed to found a beneficial interest in the first
place. It will take into consideration all conduct which throws light
on the question of what shares are intended.'*

Midland Bank v Cooke[73]

*The matrimonial home was owned in Mr Cooke's sole name. It
was purchased before the marriage for £8,500 with a mortgage
of £6,540. The deposit was paid using a £1,000 wedding gift
from Mr Cooke's parents and the rest was made up from Mr
Cooke's savings.*

*Mrs Cooke made no direct payments to the mortgage, but from
her wages paid for the household expenses, redecoration,
alterations and improvements. The property was subsequently
remortgaged, and Mrs Cooke agreed that the mortgage lender's
charge would take precedence over her own rights.*

*The mortgage company took proceedings for possession of the
property, and Mrs Cooke argued that she had signed the
consent under undue influence, and that she had a beneficial
interest in the property. The court found that she had been
acting under undue influence, of which the bank was aware,
and that the consent was void. It also found that she had a
beneficial interest by resulting trust due to the contribution of
half the value of the wedding present giving her a 6.47 per cent
interest. Mrs Cooke appealed against this quantification.*

*The court found that the gift from Mr Cooke's parents had been
to both of them and therefore gave Mrs Cooke an interest in the
property. The court was not bound to find a resulting trust but
was free to attribute a different intention. The evidence that the
position was never discussed did not prevent the courts from
inferring an intention on general equitable principles. Taking
into account the nature of their relationship and their sharing of
the burdens and advantages of the property, the court held that
the property was held in equal shares.*

5.47 Occupation rents

If one co-owner is excluded from the property by the other, the party
out of possession can claim an 'occupation rent' from the other
partner. S/he cannot normally do this if s/he stays out of possession
voluntarily. Starting divorce proceedings will normally signal a refusal

---

73. Midland Bank v Cooke, see 12 above, p745.

to take the other party back, and thereby justify payment of an occupation rent.[74]

The co-owner who remains in occupation is entitled to claim credit for that proportion of the mortgage repayments made by her/him, which should have been paid by the absent partner to cover her/his share of the property. This is on the basis that by paying the mortgage on the absent spouse's share of the property a 'benefit' is conferred on her/him.

A common practice is to treat the interest element of the mortgage repayment as being the equivalent of the occupation rent and set one against the other, so that credit is only given for the appropriate proportion of the capital repayment or contribution to the endowment policy.

J   Applying for an order for sale

5.48   Orders for sale

Where there is no agreement between a couple about whether the home should be sold or not, and the property is either jointly owned or solely owned with the non-owner claiming a beneficial interest, an application can be made to the court for a declaration of interest and an order directing, preventing or postponing sale. Such an application by cohabitants has to be made in the county court or the High Court under section 14 of the Trusts of Land and Appointment of Trustees Act 1996.

Married couples and cohabitants who have been engaged within the last three years can also use the Married Woman's Property Act 1882.

Although the Married Woman's Property Act provides a summary (or quick) procedure for the court to make orders concerning disputed property 'as the judge sees fit,' the principles on which the judge bases the decision are still the principles of property law. The advantages are mainly procedural, but can be significant in terms of costs and speed and ease of proceedings. In particular, there is exemption from the statutory charge if the Married Women's Property Act is used, but not where the Trusts of Land and Appointment of Trustees Act is used. The statutory charge is explained in Appendix A3.

5.49   The court's criteria in ordering a sale

Whichever proceedings are used, the court may order a sale. Under the TLATA the court has power to prevent a sale, order an immediate sale or postpone a sale. This discretion is given to the court by virtue of the s14 TLATA96   wording of the Act, which says that the *'court may make such order as*

74. Re Pavlou (1993) 1 WLR 1046.

it thinks fit.' This is not the same as the test of *'what is reasonable.'*[75] In exercising this power, the court can give one party the opportunity to buy out the other.[76]

s15 TLATA96

When deciding whether to make an order under the TLATA, the court must consider:

1. The intentions of the person(s) who created the trust.

2. The purpose for which the property is held.

3. The welfare of any minor (ie, child under 18) who occupies or might reasonably be expected to occupy the accommodation as her/his home.

4. The interests of any secured creditor, eg, a lender.

Case law under the legislation[77] which TLATA has replaced has shown that when considering the purpose of the trust, the court must consider the underlying purpose of the 'trust for sale.' In the case of *Re Evers's Trust*,[78] the house was bought and conveyed to the couple on trust for sale as joint tenants. The woman remained in the home with three children and the man sought an order for sale. The court held that the underlying purpose of the trust for sale was to provide a family home for both the parents and the children 'for the indefinite future.' The interests of the children were a circumstance to be considered, the man had no great need to realise his investment, having a secure home elsewhere, the woman was prepared to accept full responsibility for the mortgage liability, and would have found it very hard to rehouse herself if the house had been sold. The court therefore postponed any question of sale. Sale might become appropriate at some time in the future if circumstances changed.

A sale is also likely to be refused even if there are no children, but the underlying purpose exists and it would be unfair to order a sale, as in the case of *Abbey National v Moss*,[79] where a mother transferred the property into the joint names of herself and her daughter on condition that she continue to live there during her lifetime. The underlying purpose was providing occupation for the mother.

Whether the original purpose for which the home was bought still exists must therefore be considered, although since the TLATA came into force other factors may be relevant to the court in exercising its discretion, and earlier cases under the Law of Property Act 1925 should be treated with caution.

75. Jones v Challenger (1961) 1 QB 177.
76. Bernard v Josephs (1982) CH391 CA, Huntingford v Hobbs, see 20 above.
77. Section 30 Law of Property Act 1925.
78. Re Ever's Trust (1980) 3 All ER 399.
79. Abbey National v Moss (1994) 1 FLR 307, Jones v Challenger (1961) 1 QB 176.

6

Chapter 6: Housing law

Subjects covered in this chapter include...

General terms

The different terminology that applies to tenancies and licences

Types of tenancy

How to recognise different types of tenancies or licences

Long-term disposal of sole and joint tenancies

How tenancies can be passed from one partner to another

How to assign a tenancy

Who is responsible for arrears after assignment

What happens when a tenant serves notice to quit

What steps a landlord must take to remove a remaining spouse or cohabitant

When acceptance of rent may imply a new tenancy

Housing Law

This chapter explains some of the basic principles which an adviser needs to understand in order to advise on tenancy rights when a relationship breaks down. It then considers aspects of housing law which are of particular relevance in assigning and terminating tenancies when a relationship has broken down.

The scope of this book does not allow for a detailed explanation of housing status, and other references should be consulted if an adviser is in doubt.[1] Sections A and B of this chapter give a brief explanation of the main types of tenancy/occupation status referred to in this book.

Giving housing advice to tenants on relationship breakdown

In order to be able to advise married or cohabiting tenants on the options available to them, it is necessary to have a grasp of certain basic principles:

- To understand and recognise the different types of tenancy

- To know the legal rights to remain which attach to different types of tenancies

- To recognise which tenancies can be assigned and under what conditions

- To know the procedures for a tenant who wishes to give a valid notice to quit

- To know the procedures a landlord must follow to gain possession.

Changes in housing law

Law commission proposals: In April 2002, the Law Commission published a consultative paper 162 'Renting Homes 1: Status and Security.'[2] This proposed radical reform to the whole system of security of tenure has the dual aims of achieving simplicity and increasing flexibility. Criticisms of the current system are largely based on the complexity created by layers of legislation piling on top of one another, and the many special cases, or exceptions, to rules arising from the legislation. The proposals are basically that all housing agreements should be in writing and be of one of two main types, one being modelled on the existing secure tenancy, with a high degree of security, and a second type modelled on the current assured shorthold tenancy, with a reduced level of security. A second consultation paper 168 'Renting Homes 2: Co-occupation, Transfer and Succession,' relating to succession, assignment and subletting, was published in August 2002. The aim is to produce a report and draft Bill by the summer of 2003.

1. A. Arden, Manual of Housing Law, 7th edition
(Sweet and Maxwell, 2002), Evans and Smith: The Law
of Landlord and Tenant 6th edition (Butterworth, 2002);   2. Both consultation papers are available at
J.E. Martin, Residential Security (Sweet and Maxwell, 1989);   www.lawcom.gov.uk. Summaries are also available at
A. Alder and C.R. Handy, Housing Associations Law and   www.ardenchambers.com/lawcom.doc and
Practice 4th edition (Sweet and Maxwell, 2003).   www.cch-uk.org/docus/single_tenancy.

Historically, effecting change as a result of Law Commission Reports is not an overnight process, and so it can be expected that the current system will be in force for some time yet. However, radical changes at some time in the future seem likely.

Current legislation: On 15 January 1989, the Housing Act 1988 brought into effect three major types of occupancy: assured and assured shorthold tenancies and excluded tenancies/licences. Most private and RSL (Registered Social Landlord) tenancies are now governed by this Act, which has since been amended by the Housing Act 1996.

Assured shorthold tenancies under Housing Act 1996
The Housing Act 1996 changed the criteria for creating assured and assured shorthold tenancies from 18 February 1997. The position before February 1997 was that, provided the basic requirements for an assured tenancy were satisfied, a tenancy was assured unless the landlord served notice that it was to be an assured shorthold. This position is now reversed. Any tenancies created since 18 February 1997 which fulfil the requirements of the Housing Act 1988 are now automatically assured shorthold tenancies, unless certain specific criteria are met or the landlord specifically opts to make the tenancy assured and serves a notice to that effect.

Introductory tenancies
The Housing Act 1996 also created the option for local authorities to opt to use 'introductory' tenancies for the first year of all new tenancies. Introductory tenants have fewer rights than secure tenants and possession orders can be obtained against them very easily. Many local authorities now operate these introductory tenancy schemes. See also 6.5 for information on the unsuccessful challenge against introductory tenancies on human rights grounds. In April 2002 the ODPM (then DTLR) published a consultation paper, 'Tackling Anti-Social Behaviour,' proposing permanent 'introductory' status for tenants engaged in anti-social behaviour. Alternatively, it was suggested that tenants could be demoted from secure to introductory-type tenancies.

This latter proposal has now been incorporated in the Anti-Social Behaviour Bill which was published in March 2003. It allows a landlord to apply to the county court on the ground of anti-social behaviour for a 'demotion order' which terminates the secure tenancy and creates a 'demoted tenancy.' If the landlord does not seek possession within twelve months, the tenancy will become secure again. The court would have to consider it reasonable to make such an order. There are similar powers proposed to allow Registered Social Landlords to apply to convert an assured tenancy into a 'demoted assured shorthold tenancy.'

Rent Act 1977 and Housing Act 1985 tenancies

Privately rented tenancies granted before 15 January 1989 are still governed by the Rent Act 1977. All secure council tenancies and those RSL tenancies which were granted before 15 January 1989 are governed by the Housing Act 1985.

Rent Act 1977 and Housing Act 1985 tenants, in general, have greater security to remain in their homes and greater rights to rent control than Housing Act 1988 tenants. It is easier for landlords to obtain possession against assured and, in particular, assured shorthold tenants. Rents are set at 'market rent' level, as opposed to 'fair rents' for Rent Act tenants, with a limited right to independent rent assessment.

A   General terms

6.1   Periodic/fixed term

All tenancies can be either 'periodic' or 'fixed-term.'

- A periodic tenancy is a tenancy which simply runs from week to week or month to month and there is no agreement that it will last for a fixed length of time. For example, most council tenancies are periodic. In situations where a landlord simply agrees to rent out a property and asks for the rent weekly or monthly, the tenancy will be periodic

- A fixed-term tenancy is created where it is stipulated at the start that the tenancy is for a set length of time, eg, six months, two years etc. Once the agreement expires, if the tenant remains, the landlord continues to accept rent, and there is no further fixed term granted, the tenancy normally becomes periodic. This happens either because of statutory protection (see below), or in some cases a new periodic tenancy may be held to have been created (see 6.38).

6.2   Contractual/statutory

All tenancies start as contractual, but they may become statutory at a later date.

Contractual

In order for there to be a binding contract, there must be an agreement which involves the exchange of 'consideration.' For example, Errol agrees to rent out a room in return for Jim paying rent. This will result in a contractual tenancy or licence.

If there is no element of 'consideration,' there can be no contract. For example, if Errol allows Jim to stay at his house because he feels sorry for him or because he likes Jim, it will result in a 'bare licence' being given, ie, bare permission to occupy for as long as Errol wishes. There is no contract.

A contractual tenancy does not have to be in writing. It can be verbal or written. A contractual tenancy is capable of being brought to an end either:

- by natural passage of time, eg, if it was originally for one year only, the contract will end at the end of the year

- by notice being given by either party. The nature of the contract itself may impose limitations upon when such notice can validly be given

  or

- by formal notice of increase of rent (in the case of protected tenants only). Such a notice does not bring the tenancy to an end, but a valid notice will convert a contractual to a statutory tenancy.[3]

Statutory

Statutes such as the Rent Act 1977 and the Housing Acts 1988 and 1985 have given extra rights to tenants. Without them an occupier would have no legal right to remain once a contract ends. These Acts grant certain rights to most tenants and some licensees, and allow their tenancies to continue even though the agreed contract has ended. These are known as statutory rights and can give rise to 'statutory' tenancies. Although various tenancies may become statutory periodic (see below), the actual term 'statutory tenancy' is normally reserved for Rent Act tenancies which were originally protected contractual tenancies but for which the contract has now expired.

6.3   Tenancy/licence

The distinction between a tenancy and a licence is very important in housing law. This is mainly because licences are outside the protection of both the Housing Act 1988, as amended by the Housing Act 1996, and the Rent Act 1977, and therefore licensees in the private sector enjoy considerably less security than do many tenants. Distinguishing between a tenancy and a licence can be very difficult, particularly as some landlords may try to disguise a tenancy as a licence to avoid their obligations. However, any arrangement which has the hallmarks of a tenancy will be a tenancy, no matter what it is described as. The distinguishing features are:

- that there should be exclusive possession
- that the arrangement is for a defined period, eg, for a month at a time (periodic) or for a fixed term
- there should be an intention to create a legal relationship

---

3.   s.49 Rent Act 1977.

• there should be identifiable premises and

• there should be identifiable parties to the agreement.

There has been a great deal of case law on the subject, most notably the case of *Street v Mountford*.[4] The topic has been covered in depth in many housing law text books, and it is not within the scope of this book to go into detail.[5]

B Types of tenancy

The section below gives basic information about the major types of tenancy and licence. Information about assignment of tenancies and other ways of dealing with tenancies is in section C.

6.4 Secure tenancies and licences

Unlike the other types of protection covered below, the security offered by the Housing Act 1985 applies equally to tenants and licensees. All references in this book to secure tenants therefore apply equally to secure licensees.

• Most secure tenancies are local authority tenancies. Also, RSL tenancies which started before 15 January 1989 will normally be secure tenancies

s81 HA85

• In order for a tenancy to remain secure, the tenant, or at least one of the joint tenants, must continue to occupy the dwelling as her/his 'only or principal home'

Sch 1 HA85

• There are some exceptions to having the status of a secure tenant,[6] even if being housed by a local authority, most notably:

1. If the council is housing a homeless person under its homelessness duties, and

2. Private sector leasing, ie, where a local authority leases property from a private landlord or RSL for use as temporary housing accommodation, and agrees to return it with vacant possession when the landlord needs it

s84 & Sch 2 HA85

• Possession can be granted against secure tenants only for specific reasons. The landlord must prove in court one of a list of specified grounds for possession against the tenant. A secure tenancy cannot be ended simply because the landlord authority wishes to transfer it to someone else.

6.5 Introductory tenancies

Introductory tenancies can be granted to new tenants of local authorities and housing action trusts. They cannot be granted by RSLs.

4.   Street v Mountford (1985) 17 HLR 402 HL.
5.   J.E. Martin, see 1 above, Chapter 2 'Licences'; P. Walker
     and J.Harris, Claims to the Possession of Land, 4th   6.   Note that Schedule 1 Housing Act 1985 has been
     edition (Tolley, 1998); Evans and Smith, see 1 above.   amended by para 3 Schedule 17 Housing Act 1996.

An introductory tenancy covers the first year of the tenancy. After this period the tenancy will become secure. It is an optional scheme and is not adopted by all local authorities. If the local authority chooses to operate the scheme, it applies to all new tenancies, except where the new tenant is already a secure tenant in another council property or an assured tenant of an RSL. It cannot be used selectively for certain tenants (but see the introduction to this chapter for the government proposals to introduce 'demoted' tenancies). The provisions apply equally to tenants and licensees.

s126 HA96

- As for secure tenancies, it is a requirement that the tenant, or at least one of the joint tenants, must continue to occupy the dwelling as her/his 'only or principal home'

s81 HA85
& s124(2) HA96

- The same exceptions apply to introductory tenancies as to secure tenancies

s124(2) HA96

- Possession can be granted against introductory tenants without the landlord having to prove any ground for possession. However, correct notice must still be served, and the tenant can ask the landlord to review its decision to take possession; the landlord must give reasons if the decision is not changed. The landlord must then get a court order before evicting the tenant. Provided the correct procedures have been followed, the court has no option but to grant possession.

s127-129 HA96

Appeals to the Court of Appeal[7] arguing that the introductory tenancy regime was incompatible with Articles 6 and 8 of the European Convention on Human Rights were dismissed. The court held that the right to a fair and independent hearing (enshrined in Article 6) was satisfied by the availability of judicial review, 'intensified so as to ensure that the tenant's rights are protected' to correct any irregularity in the conduct of a review. An introductory tenant's right to respect for her/his home (Article 8) was sufficiently recognised by the fact that the county court judge has power to adjourn a possession claim pending an application for judicial review.

6.6   Assured tenancies

- Assured tenancies can be granted either by private non-resident landlords or RSLs. The tenancy must have started on or after 15 January 1989

- In order for a tenancy to remain assured, it is necessary for the tenant or one of the joint tenants to continue to occupy the dwelling as her/his only or principal home

s1(1)(b) HA88

- Some tenancies cannot be assured, even if there is a non-resident private landlord or an RSL landlord, eg, if the authority has enlisted

---

7.   R. (McLellan) v Bracknell Forest BC; Reigate and Banstead BC v Benfield and Forrest [2001] 33 HLR 989 CA;
     Sheffield CC v Smart [2002] EWCA Civ 4 CA.

the help of the landlord to house a homeless person under one of its interim duties,[8] then the tenancy cannot be assured for twelve months unless the landlord notifies the tenant that the tenancy is to be regarded as either an assured or assured shorthold tenancy. Before the Homelessness Act 2002 came into force on 31 July 2002, RSLs could only offer assured shorthold tenancies and could not convert the tenancy to an assured tenancy unless it was allocated to the tenant under Part 6 of the Housing Act 1996. This restriction has now been lifted. If the landlord does not choose to offer an assured or assured shorthold tenancy, the tenancy will be a tenancy with basic protection only for the first twelve months

s209 HA96
as amended by
HA02

- For tenancies which began after 28 February 1997, landlords wishing to create an assured tenancy must serve notice on the tenant, stating that the tenancy is not to be an assured shorthold tenancy agreement to the same effect

s9A & Sch 2A HA88

- Possession can be granted against assured tenants only for specific reasons, ie, if the landlord can prove in court one of a list of specified grounds for possession. During a fixed term, only a limited number of grounds can be used, mainly those where the tenant is 'at fault', eg, rent arrears, nuisance etc.

6.7 Assured shorthold tenancies

- Assured shorthold tenancies are a type of assured tenancy and therefore the same pre-conditions apply as for assured tenancies, ie, they must be granted by private non-resident landlords or registered social landlords on or after 15 January 1989

- For the tenancy to remain an assured shorthold, it is necessary for the tenant or one of the joint tenants to continue to occupy the dwelling as her/his only or principal home.

s1(b) HA88

Tenancies commencing before 28 February 1997

- For tenancies granted before 28 February 1997, an assured shorthold must in the first instance be a fixed-term tenancy for a minimum of six months. Any subsequent arrangement between the same landlord and the same tenant will be an assured shorthold tenancy, regardless of its length or whether it is a periodic arrangement, unless the landlord serves a notice saying that it will be assured

s20(4) & (5) HA88

- There must be no provision for the landlord to end the tenancy during the first six months, other than by forfeiture, ie, for breach of tenancy conditions, eg, non-payment of rent

s20(1)(b) HA88
s45(4) HA88

- A notice in a prescribed form, stating that the tenancy is an assured shorthold tenancy, must be served before the tenancy is entered into.

8. Interim duties under s.188, 190, 200 or 204(4) HA 1996 which are pending inquiries, providing accommodation for intentionally homeless applicants, pending a local connection referral or if accommodation is provided pending a county court appeal.

s20(1)-(2) HA88

If the correct notice is not served, the tenancy will be assured by default. However, the Court of Appeal has held that the correct test of the validity of a section 20 notice is whether, when the notice was read in context, it was sufficiently clear to leave a reasonable recipient in no reasonable doubt as to the terms of the notice and its purpose. It followed that mis-stating the start or end date of a tenancy or departing from the precise terms of the prescribed form did not necessarily make a section 20 notice invalid[9]

s21 HA88

s21(1) & Sch 2 HA88

- During the fixed term, the landlord can regain possession on limited grounds only, as for assured tenancies. After the fixed term ends, the landlord does not need to prove any specific ground for possession, but merely follow the correct notice and court procedure. In addition to this special 'automatic' right to recover possession, the usual grounds for possession against assured tenants can also be used, although in practice they are rarely needed.

Tenancies commencing on or after 28 February 1997

s19A &
Sch 2A HA88

- All new assured tenancies granted from 28 February 1997 are assured shorthold tenancies, except in certain prescribed circumstances. There is no need for a pre-tenancy notice or a fixed term, and break clauses are allowable

s21(5) HA88
s8 & Sch 2 HA88

- A possession order under the assured shorthold ground cannot take effect until after the first six months of the original tenancy. During the initial six months the landlord can, however, use any of the grounds which would be available to evict an assured tenant

6.8   Protected contractual tenancies

- A protected tenancy is a tenancy let by a private non-resident landlord and created before 15 January 1989. It is one of the Rent Act 1977 tenancies

s4-16A RA77

- There are some specific exceptions where tenancies could not be protected, eg, tenancies granted by a resident landlord, those with board or attendance included, holiday lettings, those with very high or low rents

- Protected tenancies can be either contractual or statutory. All start off as contractual agreements, even if there is nothing in writing. A contract is created when consideration is exchanged, eg, rent is paid in return for the right to live in the dwelling

- The tenancy will continue as contractual until:

1. The end of a fixed-term contract

---

9.   Ravenseft Properties Ltd. v Hall; White v Chubb; Kasseer v Freeman [2001] EWCA Civ 2034; [2002] HLR 33 CA.

2. The landlord or tenant services notice to quit, bringing a periodic contract to an end, or

3. The landlord serves a valid notice of increase of rent, giving the minimum notice required for a notice to quit. Once the contract has ended, the tenancy becomes statutory (see below).

- It is not necessary for the tenant or even one joint tenant actually to live in the home in order to maintain a protected contractual tenancy. Unlike assured and secure tenancies, the contract is sufficient to keep the protected status

- Possession can be granted against protected tenants only for specific reasons, ie, if the landlord can prove in court one of a list of specified grounds for possession against the tenant.

s98 & Sch 15 RA77

6.9 (Protected) statutory tenancies

- A (protected) statutory tenancy is one which automatically arises when a protected contractual tenancy comes to an end. The same initial conditions apply, eg, the private landlord must be non-resident at the start of the contractual tenancy. It is governed by the Rent Act 1977

- Unlike protected contractual tenancies, a statutory tenancy is a personal right to remain. In order to maintain a statutory tenancy, the tenant must occupy the dwelling 'as her/his residence'

s2(1)(a) RA77

- Possession can be granted against statutory tenants only for specific reasons, ie, if the landlord can prove in court one of a list of specified grounds for possession against the tenant, as for protected contractual tenancies.

s98 & Sch15 RA77

6.10 Tenancies and licences with basic protection

These include:

- tenancies which were assured or secure, but the tenant is no longer occupying the dwelling as an only or principal home

- tenants with resident landlords, where the tenant does not share accommodation with the landlord or a member of the landlord's family (unless the property is a purpose built block of flats, in which case they will normally be assured)

Sch 1 HA88,
Sch 1 HA85
& Sch 15 RA77

- tenants who for some other specific reason are excluded from the statutory protection of the Rent Act or Housing Acts

- all licences except secure licences.

But not:

s3A PEA77
• tenancies/licences which are excluded from virtually all protection by the Protection from Eviction Act 1977 as explained below (6.11).

These tenancies and licences are sometimes referred to as 'unprotected,' because it is not necessary to have a specific reason, ie, to prove a ground for possession, in order to obtain a possession order against a tenant or licensee with basic protection, but a notice to quit (for periodic tenants) and a court order (for fixed-term and periodic tenants) are required before the tenant or remaining occupier can
s3 PEA77
be evicted legally.

6.11 Excluded occupancies (tenancies or licences)

This is the only form of licence or tenancy for which it is not legally necessary to get a court order when evicting because they are excluded from the protection granted by the Protection from Eviction
s3A PEA 77
Act 1977. Excluded occupiers are:

• occupiers under contracts granted on or after 15 January 1989, where the landlord is resident and the occupier shares accommodation, other than stairs or hallway, with the landlord or a member of the landlord's family (this covers most people living at home with their parents)

• people in holiday lets

• people in public sector hostels, owned by local authorities or RSLs, where the accommodation is not separate and self-contained and
s622 HA85
food or communal facilities for food are provided

• people granted licences as a temporary expedient after entering without permission (squatters)

• people who pay no rent or money's worth, for example, occupiers of tied accommodation, whose rent is paid by lower wages, would not be excluded occupiers, because the work would be treated as money's worth.

It is not necessary to have a specific reason nor even a court order to evict an excluded occupier (but see 6.35). The occupier will normally have a right at least to 'reasonable notice,' but this does not have to be in writing. If there is a contract (verbal or written), then any notice period agreed there will apply. If the occupier is a tenant, as opposed to a licensee, then the common law rule relating to notice to quit will apply (see 6.31).

Bare licensees

'Bare licensee' is the term used to describe a particular type of excluded licensee. Bare licensees include people staying at a friend's house or the common situation of someone who shares, rent free, all the accommodation with a partner who is the owner or tenant of the accommodation. In housing law, a bare licensee has no rights to remain in the accommodation once the person who had given permission for them to be there withdraws that permission (but a cohabitant may be able to obtain an occupation order to remain in her/his partner's home for up to twelve months, see Chapter 13, Section C). Because there is no contractual relationship between them, rights to notice are extremely limited.

6.12 Long leaseholders

These are generally classed as a form of owner-occupation rather than a normal tenancy. Hence the information in Chapters 3, 4 and 5 of this book, covering owner-occupation, should be consulted on a relationship breakdown. However, some of the general rules of tenancies concerning issues such as assignment and forfeiture apply.

- A long leaseholder is someone who owns the leasehold of a house or flat on a lease which was originally for a fixed term of at least 21 years

- A lease is the length of time the leaseholder may stay in the property; it is also the name given to the contractual agreement between the leaseholder and the freeholder

- The lease will contain obligations or covenants which will be binding on both leaseholder and freeholder.

C   Long-term disposal of sole and joint tenancies

When a relationship breakdown first occurs, the short-term concern is likely to be what rights the respective parties have to continue living in the home. However, having the right to live in the same house as the person you want to separate from is obviously not the ideal long-term solution! Unlike owner-occupation, there is usually no cash value in a tenancy (excluding considerations of right-to-buy discounts) and so the issue is who should ultimately have the sole right to occupy the shared home.

Matrimonial law gives the courts power to transfer tenancies in conjunction with divorce, judicial separation and nullity proceedings (see Chapter 7, Section F) and child law gives similar powers to transfer certain tenancies where children are involved (see Chapter 9, Section D). Since October 1997, the court also has powers under the Family Law Act 1996 to transfer tenancies between heterosexual cohabitants (see Chapter 8, Section D). However, in many cases people either may not want to, or cannot, invoke those court powers, eg, lesbian or gay couples and non-divorcing married couples without children.

It is therefore necessary to be aware of the different methods if one or other of the partners wishes to dispose of the tenancy, either by termination or transfer, without recourse to the courts. These are:

• voluntary assignment

• notice or surrender by the tenant.

As with any breakdown, amicable agreement is the ideal solution. Unfortunately, this is not always possible. Even if a couple agrees between themselves as to who should have the tenancy, the rules of landlord and tenant law may prevent this. The following chapters look at the rules which apply specifically to married and cohabiting couples with sole and joint tenancies. The rest of this chapter looks at general points which apply to sole and joint tenancies, whether the couples are married or not.

6.13 Definition of assignment

'Assignment' is the process of legal transfer of a tenancy by which a tenant passes on a tenancy during her/his lifetime. It is, of course, of particular significance in cases of relationship breakdown, where one partner wishes to leave and the other to remain.

Assignment should not be confused with 'succession,' which is the term used where a tenancy is passed on automatically when a tenant dies. However, for some types of tenancy, the conditions for assignment and succession are closely linked.

6.14 How to assign a sole or joint tenancy

Stating that you want someone else, such as a partner, to take over your tenancy is not enough to bring about the transfer of that tenancy. Many people also make the mistake of thinking that merely to write to a landlord asking for an assignment of the tenancy is sufficient. This has been held not to be the case.[10] Under section 52 of the Law of Property Act 1925, assignment must be carried out formally in writing, by signed and witnessed deed, in order to be legally binding.

---

10. *Crago v Julian* (1991) 24 HLR 306 CA.

Crago v Julian[11]

The husband made an undertaking in divorce proceedings to transfer the tenancy from his sole name to that of his wife. The wording of the undertaking was:

'within 14 days of the granting of the Decree Absolute herein to do all acts and things as may be necessary to transfer to the Petitioner the tenancy of the flat...'

Neither party was aware that anything further had to be done to give effect to the transfer. Mrs Julian continued paying rent to the agents, who were unaware of the change until she asked them to change the name on the rent book. They then refused further rent and served notice to quit.

The court held that the tenancy had not been assigned and the Court of Appeal upheld the decision: an assignment of tenancy is the disposal of an interest in land and therefore comes within section 53(1)(a) Law of Property Act 1925, which states that a tenancy cannot be created or assigned except by writing, by will or by operation of law. Since there had been no assignment in writing, the tenancy had not been legally assigned.

LB Croydon v Buston and Triance[12]

The son of a secure tenant who left to remarry tried to argue that the tenancy had been assigned to him because there had been an agreement to assign. The judge held that because at that stage there was no actual assignment, then it was not possible to argue the assignment had happened. All that had happened was that his mother wished to assign to him and that enquiries were being made to the authority. This emphasises the need to ensure an assignment is carried out by deed.

Deed of Release

It may also be possible to effectively transfer a joint tenancy into a sole name by means of a Deed of Release, which relinquishes one tenant's interest to the remaining joint tenant(s). This method is expressly permitted by s.36(2) of the Law of Property Act 1925, but cannot be used in respect of a joint secure tenancy, except possibly by order of the court following a matrimonial or Children Act order (see 6.15 and 6.18).

---

11. Crago v Julian, ibid.

12. Croydon LB v Buston and Triance (1991) 24 HLR 36 CA.

6.15 Distinction between assignment and creating a new tenancy

This is an area which gives rise to considerable confusion. Local authorities or RSLs often say 'we transferred the tenancy.' In fact a landlord of a secure, assured or protected tenant has no power to 'transfer' a tenancy. *If there has been no court order, the tenancy must either have been assigned, or the old tenancy must have been brought to an end*, either by the landlord or the tenant, and a new tenancy granted. Different practices are examined below.

Sole tenancies

In many cases, landlords and tenants believe that an assignment has taken place when in fact it has not. In some cases, instead of an assignment, a new tenancy may have been inadvertently created. As explained above, the only way to assign a tenancy is by deed.

Common examples of this are in local authority tenancies:

- A tenant may write saying s/he wishes to assign a tenancy to a partner and do no more

- The person to whom the tenant wishes to assign may continue to live in the premises and pay the rent, in the belief that the assignment has occurred; the local authority may take no action or simply change the name on the tenancy.

It would appear from case law[13] that an assignment has not in such circumstances taken place: what may in fact have happened is that the tenant has surrendered the original tenancy and the authority has implicitly agreed to the surrender and granted a new tenancy to the partner. There will be a new implied contract between the putative assignee and the landlord and s/he will be liable for rent from the time the new tenancy was granted. This may actually be a good outcome for the tenant, because the number of assignments/successions is limited in some tenancies and s/he will therefore get a new tenancy with these rights intact. Conversely, where a new tenancy cannot be deemed to have been granted, any security of tenure conferred by the tenancy may be lost.

Case law has now confirmed that where a local authority accepts rent payments without protest from a new occupier, clearly knowing that the original tenants have left, a new tenancy will have been created.[14] This issue is, however, not without complications (see 6.38).

Joint tenancies

Many problems occur in the public sector: since the House of Lords case of *Burton v Camden*, assignment of joint secure tenancies now appears not to be possible, unless an assignment is ordered by the court in

---

13. Crago v Julian see 10 above; see also Bassetlaw DC v Renshaw and Renshaw (1991) 23 HLR 603 CA.   14. Tower Hamlets LBC v Ayinde (1994) 26 HLR 631 CA.

matrimonial or Children Act proceedings to one of the secure joint tenants (see 6.18). However, a joint tenant often writes to the landlord stating that s/he wishes to give up or surrender her/his 'half' of the tenancy. The practice of a number of organisations to respond by simply removing one tenant's name from the tenancy is not legally correct. The significance of this normally only arises in connection with rights to succession, as in the case of *Bassetlaw DC v Renshaw* (see box). Either the joint tenancy must be held still to exist, or the original tenancy must have been ended and a new one granted, possibly with new succession rights.

Bassetlaw DC v Renshaw[15]

In this case, the couple were joint secure tenants. In March 1989, the husband gave notice 'terminating' his part of the agreement on 1 May 1989. On that day, a new agreement was entered into between the council and Mrs Renshaw. Mrs Renshaw died on 6 July 1989 and her son then claimed the right to succeed. On first hearing, the court found Mrs Renshaw to be a successor who was a joint tenant and had become a sole tenant, and that no further succession was possible. The Court of Appeal overturned this, finding that the whole tenancy had been terminated and the council had granted Mrs Renshaw a new sole tenancy, albeit of the same house, and there had not therefore been a succession. The son was entitled to succeed.

It is not possible for one joint secure tenant to simply 'surrender' her/his half of the tenancy. One joint tenant cannot unilaterally surrender a joint tenancy. Therefore, if both tenants do not agree to the surrender of the joint tenancy, it remains a joint tenancy. However, if notice to quit is served by either tenant, this will end the tenancy for both tenants. For a fuller explanation about terminating joint tenancies, see 6.34.

'Surrender' as a legal concept is not the same as notice to quit; it requires the agreement and unequivocal action of both parties and unequivocal acceptance by the landlord (see 6.29). If both tenants are in fact saying they wish the tenancy to be changed from joint names to one only, acceptance by a landlord of such a request could be treated as a surrender of the old tenancy, and a new one could then be created, thus granting the new tenant a new right of succession (as for sole tenants above).

s81 HA85   Occupation by one joint tenant is sufficient to preserve the secure tenancy conditions, so that if a joint tenant wishes to end liability for

---

15.   Bassetlaw DC v Renshaw and Renshaw, see 13 above.

the tenancy, either s/he must agree with the other tenant to surrender the tenancy and obtain the landlord's acceptance of the surrender, or give notice to quit, as described in section 6.31. Valid notice to quit ends the whole tenancy, in which case the landlord needs to be persuaded to grant a new tenancy to the remaining occupier. See 6.32 onwards for more information on termination and notice to quit, and Chapters 7 and 8 for information about the position on relationship breakdown. If the landlord continues to accept rent from the remaining partner after notice to quit, then it may be possible to argue that a new tenancy has been granted, as discussed above for sole tenants.

6.16 The right to assign

Whether a tenant has the right to assign a tenancy varies, depending upon:

- whether there is sufficient legal interest in property to be passed on

- what is said in the tenancy agreement about assignment or, if there is nothing in the contract, ie, contractual rights or conditions, what was agreed verbally at the start of the tenancy, and

- the tenancy type, ie, whether statute has amended the general position in particular situations (see 6.17 onwards).

The basic position on assignment at common law is that all tenancies (but not licences) can be assigned without the consent of the landlord. However, it is also necessary to look at the contract agreed at the start of the tenancy, to see if there is any term which prohibits assignment. The tenancy agreement may:

- *prohibit assignment absolutely*
  This means that the tenancy has a clause which says, for example, 'the tenant agrees not to assign the tenancy,' or 'assignment is forbidden.' In this situation, any assignment will be a breach of the contract, unless a variation of the agreement can be agreed with the landlord.

- *prohibit assignment without the landlord's consent*
  The tenancy agreement may say, for example, 'the tenant agrees not to assign without the consent of the landlord' or 'assignment is allowed only with the landlord's consent.' In the situation where there is such a qualified prohibition on assignment without the landlord's consent, the contractual law position has been modified by statute. As a result of this, it is implied in the contract that the landlord must not withhold her/his consent unreasonably.

s19 LTA27
s1 & 3 LTA 88

- *allow assignment*
  For example, the agreement may say 'the landlord agrees that the tenant may assign.' Where the agreement allows assignment without

conditions, then assignment can take place without consent, ie, the common law position.

- *not mention assignment*
In this situation, the common law position will apply, ie, that assignment is allowed without consent.

Where an assignment is carried out in breach of a prohibition or without required consent, the assignment will still have taken place (provided it has been properly executed by deed), but the breach of agreement may give the landlord a ground for seeking possession. The landlord may also be able to sue for damages. Alternatively, the landlord could 'waive' the clause in the agreement prohibiting assignment and take no action.

Assignment of particular types of tenancy

Once the common law and contractual positions on assignment have been established, it is then necessary to look at the position of individual types of tenancy. Acts of Parliament amend or complement the common law and contractual position for certain types of tenancy. In particular, note the statutory exception to assignment of secure tenancies at 6.17.

The position on each type of tenancy is set out below, and is summarised on the table on page 156.

Assignment by lesbian, gay and heterosexual couples

Whether a couple are married or lesbian, gay or heterosexual cohabitants should now make no difference to the legal right to assign. See 6.17 for an explanation of how human rights legislation has changed the position for lesbian and gay couples where there is a sole secure tenancy.

6.17 Sole secure tenancies – assignment

A secure tenancy or licence is not capable of being assigned unless it falls under one of three exceptions.

s91(1) HA85

These exceptions are listed in section 91(3) of the Housing Act 1985 as follows:

1. Assignment by way of mutual exchange.

2. Assignment following a property adjustment order made in matrimonial proceedings, ie, divorce, judicial separation or nullity, under section 24 of the Matrimonial Causes Act 1973, or an order under Schedule 1 of the Children Act.

3. Assignment 'to a person who would be qualified to succeed the tenant if the tenant died immediately before the assignment.'

A person qualifies under 3 if s/he is:

- a spouse living with the tenant at the time of the assignment
  – temporary absence from home would not jeopardise this right

- a member of the tenant's family occupying the dwelling as her/his only or principal home at the time of assignment, who has resided with the tenant throughout the twelve month period ending with the assignment

s87 HA85

- s/he is a 'member of the tenant's family'
  A person is defined as a member of another person's family if *"s/he is the spouse of the tenant or s/he and that person live together as husband and wife or s/he is that person's parent, grandparent, child, grandchild, brother, sister, uncle, aunt, nephew or niece (including stepchildren and 'illegitimate' children)."*

s113 HA85

In this context, the law has traditionally discriminated against lesbian and gay couples, in that the courts held that they could not be treated as 'living together as husband and wife.' However, in November 2002, in the landmark case of *Mendoza v Ghaidan*,[16] a case involving succession rights of a same sex partner to a deceased Rent Act statutory tenant, the Court of Appeal held that the words *"as his husband or wife"* had to be read to mean *"as if s/he was her or his husband or wife;"* otherwise a same sex partner would be discriminated against under Article 14 of the European Convention on Human Rights, and sexual orientation is an impermissible ground for discrimination. This would therefore appear to mean that lesbian or gay partners have to be allowed to succeed to secure and assured tenancies as well as Rent Act tenancies, in the same way as heterosexual couples. At the time of writing, permission had been granted to appeal to the House of Lords in summer 2003. The commentary below is based on the assumption that the judgment will be upheld.

Mendoza v Ghaidan[17] – lesbian and gay couples

The case of *Mendoza* now effectively reverses the decision in *Harrogate Borough Council v Simpson*,[18] in which the surviving member of a lesbian couple failed in her claim to succeed to the secure tenancy on the basis that she had lived with the tenant as 'husband and wife.' Application for leave to appeal to the House of Lords against the decision in *Harrogate BC v Simpson* was at the time dismissed with the following comment:

> *"It seems to me that you are fighting for a social revolution, but that is more than the courts can do. It is a matter for Parliament. I do not accept that when Parliament passed the Housing Act 1980 (now the Act of 1985) they meant a homosexual couple to be treated as husband and wife."*

---

16. Mendoza v Ghaidan [2002] 4 All ER 1162 CA.
17. Mendoza v Ghaidan ibid.
18. Harrogate Borough Council v Simpson (1985) 17 HLR 205 CA.

Clearly, now that the courts are obliged to reach decisions which are consistent with human rights, they can no longer 'sit on the fence' in this way. *Mendoza* goes a significant step further than the 1999 House of Lords case of *Fitzpatrick v Sterling Housing Association,*[19] in which it was held that a gay man was entitled to succeed to his partner's tenancy under the Rent Act 1977, as he was held to be a 'member of the family' of his partner, but could not be held to be a spouse or someone living as *'husband or wife,'* since, it was argued, Parliament clearly intended those terms to mean a man and a woman. In addition, because s.113 of the Housing Act 1985 gives a strict definition of 'member of the family' which refers to people *'living together as husband and wife,'* *Fitzpatrick* could not be held to apply to secure tenancies.

Although *Mendoza* also concerned a Rent Act tenancy, the issue raised once again was whether a same sex couple could in fact be treated as living together *'as husband and wife,'* and so the arguments therefore would seem to apply equally to secure tenancies. The court identified four questions which had to be asked:

1. Did the facts of the case fall within the ambit of one or more of the European Convention on Human Rights provisions; in this case, the applicant's right to respect for his home (Article 8 of the European convention)?

2. If they did, was there different treatment between the applicant's rights and that of other people put forward as being in a comparable position (the 'chosen comparators')?

3. Were those chosen comparators in a similar situation to the applicant?

4. If so, was there an objective and reasonable justification for the difference in treatment? In other words, did it pursue a legitimate aim and was the difference in treatment proportionate to the end it sought to achieve?

The point at issue was that a surviving partner in a same sex relationship, Mr Mendoza, could succeed only to an assured tenancy. Had he been a heterosexual cohabitant, he would have succeeded to a statutory Rent Act tenancy. The court held that the security which a tenant enjoyed in her/his home fell within the scope of Article 8 (right to respect for home) and that a heterosexual surviving partner was in an analogous situation to that of a same sex surviving cohabitant, yet would have been treated differently as a result of the wording of the Rent Act schedule, which referred to living together 'as his or her husband or wife.' Article 14 (the enjoyment of convention rights without discrimination) was therefore applicable. The court then had to decide whether there was any

19. Fitzpatrick v Sterling Housing Association (2000) 32 HLR 178 HL.

objective or reasonable justification for such discrimination. It decided that, as parliament had already *"swallowed the camel of including unmarried partners within the protection given to married couples"* it was not for the court to *"strain at the gnat of including such partners who are of the same sex as each other."*

The matter of extending succession rights by statute is considered in the Law Commission's consultation paper 'Renting Homes No 2: Co-occupation, Transfer and Succession.' The proposals include granting specific rights of succession to same sex couples; rights to assignment would be linked to the right to succeed.

In the meantime, on the basis of *Mendoza*, a same sex partner can succeed to a secure tenancy, provided s/he has lived with the tenant for 12 months before death. If a succession would be permissible, then an assignment is equally permissible, provided the residence requirement is satisfied.

S/he has been living with the tenant for 12 months

For assignment to be permitted, a cohabitant or member of the family (but not a spouse) must establish twelve months' residence with the secure tenant. A House of Lords case has established that this does not mean twelve months' residence at the same tenancy, but simply twelve months' residence with the tenant in any property or combination of properties (not necessarily subject to secure tenancies for the whole period) for the one year ending with the date of death.[20]

Temporary absences should not be taken into account. An absence of 10 weeks was held not to break the period of one year, if there was sufficient physical manifestation of the would-be successor's occupation during the absent period.[21] Where a couple have separated and been living apart for some time, it may be difficult to argue that the residence requirement is fulfilled. However, it may be possible to argue an intention to return still existed, provided some physical signs of occupation remain in the home, such as furniture and possessions.

Crawley BC v Sawyer[22]

The Court of Appeal held, in a case where a secure tenant left to live with his girlfriend for over a year but finally returned, that a tenant need not be physically present and that two houses can be occupied as a home at the same time. The judge was entitled to form the view that the tenant was only occupying his girlfriend's home on a temporary basis, and that his own home remained his principal home throughout.

---

20. Waltham Forest LBC v Thomas (1992) 24 HLR
    622 HL.

21. Camden LBC v Goldenberg (1996) 28 HLR 727 CA.
22. Crawley BC v Sawyer (1988) 20 HLR 98 CA.

Permission to assign a secure tenancy

Provided the assignment falls into one of the permitted exceptions (see above) under the Housing Act 1985, the local authority's agreement is not necessary for assignment by deed to be validly executed. However, many tenancy agreements contain a prohibition on assignment without the landlord's consent. If there is such a prohibition, the tenancy can still have been validly assigned, but the landlord may then attempt to use the breach of the tenancy agreement as a ground for possession.[23] However, the court has discretion to decide whether it is reasonable to grant possession, and the facts ought to be put to the court, with a request for discretion to be exercised in favour of the person to whom the tenancy was assigned.

Assignment as a succession

s88 HA85

The main disadvantage to assignment in the public sector is that if a voluntary assignment has taken place, the right to succession will have been used up, because a voluntary assignment counts as a succession. For example:

> Mr Brown assigns the tenancy to Mrs Brown, who lives in the home with her 18-year-old daughter. Mrs Brown then dies; Miss Brown is not entitled to succeed to the tenancy, since only one succession is allowed, and that has taken place by way of assignment.

Transfer of tenancy through the courts under matrimonial or child law does not, however, count as succession, nor does assignment by mutual exchange.

6.18 Joint secure tenancies – assignment

s91(3)(c) HA85
s91(3)(c) HA85

As explained above, assignment is generally only permitted in three situations. The first two – mutual exchange and following a matrimonial or Children Act court order – apply equally to joint tenants. The third – assignment to *'a person who would be qualified to succeed the tenant if the tenant died immediately before the assignment'* was generally held to allow a joint tenant to assign her/his interest to the other tenant spouse or partner, but this is no longer deemed to be legally possible. The precise wording of this subsection of the Housing Act 1985 had for some time thrown the technical correctness of this procedure into doubt and the matter was raised in the case of *Burton v Camden LBC*, which was a case primarily concerning the validity of a Deed of Release as a means of transferring a joint secure tenancy.[24]

It was held in the Court of Appeal that on a strict interpretation, assignment to a potential successor as referred to under s.91(3)(c) could not apply to joint secure tenancies:

---

23. Peabody Donation Fund Governors v Higgins (1983) 10 HLR 82 CA.

24. Burton v Camden LBC (2000) 17 February HL.

"Section 91(3)(c) is clearly inapplicable to a joint tenancy; even if the expression 'the tenant' is read as including joint tenants, it cannot be predicated of 'the tenant' that 'the tenant died immediately before the assignment.'"[25]

The tenancy could not therefore be assigned to a potential successor, but could the same result be achieved by a Deed of Release? The Court of Appeal thought so, but the House of Lords disagreed. The issue before the Lords was whether the prohibition against assignment in s.91 also extended to Deeds of Release. It was held that a release in these circumstances was in essence the same as an assignment. Even though the two 'modes of conveyancing' were different in property law, four of the five Law Lords agreed that s.91 could not have been meant to forbid one type of transfer of interest but allow another. If the tenancy was non-assignable, then a Deed of Release could not take effect either.

Lesbian/gay joint secure tenants

Outside marriage, assignment of a joint secure tenancy is only possible following a matrimonial or Children Act order, or by way of mutual exchange. Lesbian and gay couples will therefore not normally be able to assign a joint interest. There is no legal provision allowing assignment of an interest in a joint secure tenancy from one same sex partner to another; nor may the landlord body permit it, even if it so wishes.

If a joint tenant wishes to end liability for the tenancy, the only way to do so is by serving a notice to quit which ends the whole tenancy (see 7.31). This is obviously a fairly drastic step, and even where a relationship has broken down very badly, one partner may not want to be held responsible for making the other homeless. Once the notice to quit has expired, the remaining partner is then at the mercy of the landlord, who may or may not decide to grant a new sole tenancy. The case of *Harrow LBC v Qazi*[26] raises the issue of whether the person remaining after a notice to quit has any defence against possession by a local authority under Article 8 of the European Convention on Human Rights (right to respect for home and family life). This case is, at the time of writing, due to be heard by the House of Lords. The outcome could be of immense significance if it results in a decision ratifying this procedure or judging it unlawful. See 7.42 for a further discussion of this issue.

Some local authorities and housing associations have policies in relation to service of notice to quit by one joint tenant, and advisers should check if this is the case, and whether the landlord body is prepared to rehouse one or both partners.

---

25. Burton v Camden LBC (1997) 5 November CA.   26. Harrow LBC v Qazi [2001] EWCA Civ 1834; HLR 14 CA.

The Code of Guidance on Allocation of Accommodation states that where a joint tenant serves a notice to quit, housing authorities have a discretion to grant a sole tenancy to the remaining tenant. It states that, in exercising this discretion, they should ensure that there are not adverse implications for the good use of their housing stock and their ability to meet housing need. If an authority wishes to use its discretion to grant new tenancies in such circumstances, it must have allowed for this within its allocation scheme.[27]

RSL tenants

s35(4)(d) HA88

For RSL tenants, the possible loss of rights is even more significant. If the original joint tenancy was secure, ie, granted before 15 January 1989, and the tenancy is then terminated by one partner, any new tenancy granted by the RSL can only be secure if it is granted immediately following the expiry of the notice to quit. If the tenancy lapses and a new tenancy is granted after an interval of time, the tenancy will be assured. Assured tenancies in general are subject to higher rent levels and fewer statutory rights.

Effect of assignment on succession

s88 HA85

Where one joint tenant dies, the remaining tenant becomes the sole tenant by survivorship. This counts as succession. Where the court orders an assignment of a joint secure tenancy to one of the partners under matrimonial or child law, this does not count as a succession.

6.19 Introductory tenancies – assignment

s134 HA96

The provisions for assignment of introductory tenancies are similar to those for secure tenants, except that mutual exchange is not permitted.

6.20 Joint and sole assured and assured shorthold tenancies – assignment

Unlike secure tenancies, above, there are no legal restrictions on whom an assured tenancy may be assigned to, and therefore the position is the same for all couples.

Fixed-term joint and sole tenancies

s19 LTA27 s1 & 3 LTA88

The common-law position described in section 6.16 applies. Whether assignment is allowed will depend upon the terms of the contract. If assignment is expressly prohibited except with the landlord's consent, ie, a conditional prohibition, then that consent cannot be withheld unreasonably. If there is nothing in the agreement concerning assignment, then assignment is presumed to be allowed.

---

27. Para 3.9 Allocation of Accommodation, Code of Guidance for Local Authorities, ODPM November 2002.

Periodic joint and sole tenancies

Under section 15 of the Housing Act 1988, an underlying term of any assured periodic tenancy (including assured shorthold periodic tenancies) is that the tenant may not usually assign without the landlord's consent. Unless there is a term in the contract allowing assignment, it is presumed that assignment is forbidden unless the landlord gives consent, ie, the reverse of the common law position. This is not the same as secure tenancies, which are actually incapable of assignment except in the permitted exceptional cases. A valid assignment of an assured periodic tenancy could therefore be made without the landlord's consent, but would always give rise to a breach of tenancy conditions.

s15(2) HA88

The landlord may withhold consent without any good reason, as the Housing Act 1988 expressly excludes assured periodic tenancies from the implied right that the landlord should act reasonably.

The only exceptions are:

• where assignment is conditionally prohibited in an agreement, ie, it is subject to the landlord's consent or

s15(3) HA88

• where a premium is payable for the granting or renewal of the tenancy.

s19 LTA27,
s1 & 3 LTA88

In these two cases the landlord may not withhold consent unreasonably. These exceptions only apply during the contractual period, and do not apply to statutory periodic assured tenancies, ie, periodic tenancies which have arisen after the expiry of a fixed term.

Assignment of assured tenancies does not count as succession.

Joint tenancies

If consent is not given for assignment or Deed of Release, the only way to end liability (apart from court powers) is to give notice to quit (see 6.34).

6.21 Joint and sole protected contractual tenancies – assignment

Joint and sole tenants

The common law position described above applies (6.16). Unless an agreement specifically forbids assignment, it is presumed that assignment of protected contractual tenancies is allowed. In theory, if nothing is said in the tenancy agreement, then no consent is required from the landlord. However, as there is a discretionary ground for possession if the landlord's consent is not gained, consent is, in effect, needed in all circumstances. It should not be unreasonably withheld. No specific residence criteria have to be met.

Case 6 Sch 15 RA77

s19 LTA27

Assignment of protected tenancies does not count as succession.

Joint tenants

In addition to the above:

- If there is a prohibition on assignment, a joint contractual tenant could serve notice to quit, thereby converting the tenancy into a sole statutory tenancy for the other spouse

Case 5 Sch 15 RA77
- However, this could give rise to a landlord's ground for possession if the landlord re-lets or sells the property on the basis of the notice. The landlord should therefore be notified that the remaining tenant does not intend to leave.

6.22 (Protected) statutory tenancies – assignment

Joint and sole tenants

para 13 Sch 1 RA77
Statutory tenancies cannot be assigned, as a statutory tenancy is a solely personal right to occupy. However, the Rent Act allows a 'change' in the statutory tenant where the landlord is in agreement. As this is not strictly an assignment, the Landlord and Tenant Act 1927 does not apply, and the landlord does not have to be reasonable about withholding consent. This practice is extremely rare.

Joint tenants

Although the above principles apply, assignment is not necessary for joint tenants, since a statutory tenancy depends on the tenant remaining in occupation. Once one tenant ceases to occupy the home 'as a residence,' the tenancy automatically becomes a sole statutory tenancy.

Statutory tenancies differ from secure tenancies, because there is no parallel provision in the Rent Act which says that occupation by one joint tenant sustains the joint tenancy.

6.23 Tenancies with basic protection and excluded tenancies – assignment

If a tenancy has basic protection or is excluded it can theoretically be assigned and the common law position stated at 6.16 applies. The position will depend upon the terms of the agreement or, if nothing has been stated, the general principle that assignment is allowed without consent.

In practice, the security of an excluded tenancy is so limited that it is unlikely to be worth assigning. However, a periodic tenancy with basic protection must be ended by service of a notice to quit and a court order before eviction can take place, so there may be some value in the exercise, which may also lead to negotiations with the landlord.

6.24   Licences – assignment

A licence is simply a personal permission to occupy. It cannot therefore be assigned. This includes licensees in tied accommodation. Joint licensees would need to terminate the licence and ask the licensor to grant a new sole licence. Secure licences are covered by the statutory provisions at 6.17 (sole) and 6.18 (joint).

RIGHTS TO ASSIGNMENT

Local authority secure and introductory tenancies	Can only be assigned by 1. Mutual exchange. 2. Matrimonial proceedings or Children Act order. 3. To someone entitled to succeed.
Registered Social Landlord secure tenancies	As for local authority secure tenants
Assured tenancies periodic, ie, weekly or monthly etc. (RSLs or private landlords)	1. Normally, assumed to be prohibited. Landlords can usually withhold consent without reasonable grounds. 2. For contractual tenants, if agreement states assignment allowed with landlord's consent, then agreement cannot be withheld unreasonably. 3. For contractual tenants, if premium paid for grant or renewal of tenancy, landlord cannot withhold consent unreasonably.
Assured tenancies fixed-term, eg, six months, one year (RSLs or private landlords)	1. If nothing in agreement, assignment presumed to be allowed. 2. If agreement stated assignment only with landlord's consent, agreement cannot be withheld unreasonably.
Assured shorthold tenancies	As for assured fixed-term tenancies during fixed-term. After fixed-term expires, as for assured periodic.
Protected contractual tenancies	1. Unless agreement expressly forbids assignment, presumed to be allowed. 2. If consent required, cannot be withheld unreasonably.

(Protected) statutory tenancies	Technically cannot be 'assigned.' Tenancy could be 'transferred' if landlord agrees. Consent can be withheld without reason.
Tenancies with basic protection and excluded tenancies	1. If nothing in agreement, assignment presumed to be allowed. No consent needed. 2. If agreement stated assignment only with landlord's consent or if no agreement, assignment permitted.
Licences	A personal permission to occupy which cannot be assigned.

6.25 Arrears and assignment

The law governing liability on assignment of leases (which includes tenancies) was radically reformed by the Landlord and Tenant (Covenants) Act 1995, which came into force on 1 January 1996.

Under the old law, it was possible for the original tenant to be held liable for subsequent arrears, and indemnities were required to safeguard the assignor from having to pay arrears which accrued after the assignment. The main purpose of the Act was to abolish the liability of the original tenant for arrears or breaches of covenants which take place after the assignment.

The main provisions of the Landlord and Tenant (Covenants) Act apply only to tenancies which were created on or after the commencement date. Some of its provisions also modify and improve the position for tenants prior to January 1996. The position for tenancies granted before and after 1 January 1996 are considered separately below.

Special statutory provisions have been made to allow for transfer of liabilities when a court orders a transfer of tenancy by vesting under the Family Law Act 1996 (see Chapter 7, Section F).

6.26 Arrears and assignment – tenancies starting before 1 January 1996

Arrears accrued before assignment

- The position in contract law is that the person to whom a tenancy is assigned (the assignee) is not legally liable to meet the contractual terms of the original tenant's agreement with the landlord which arose before the assignment, eg, arrears existing at the time of assignment

- This is because, in contractual terms, there is no direct relationship between the landlord and the assignee

- The assignee becomes responsible from the date of assignment for those covenants which 'touch and concern' the land, eg, the payment of rent from the time of assignment

- Also, in many deeds of assignment, there is a written term that the assignor has complied with all the terms of the tenancy, ie, there is a promise that any previous arrears will have been paid. This used to be an implied term in all deeds of assignment, but from 1 July 1995 it must be actually written on the deed.[28]

s76 & Part II
Sch 2 LPA25

As the breach occurred before the assignment, the original tenant is the only person who can legally be sued for those arrears.[29]

In practice, some local authorities require the assignee to agree to clear any existing arrears. If the assignee has promised to do so, s/he might be considered legally liable for the arrears, although the legal status of such a promise, which could be deemed to constitute an illegal premium, must be in some doubt and enforceability would be by no means certain (see 11.33).

Arrears accruing after assignment

If the new tenant (ie, the assignee) runs up arrears after the assignment, the landlord is in the fortunate position of being able to take action against either the new tenant, under the terms of the tenancy agreement, or, if the arrears are not recovered, against the original tenant (assignor). The new Act modifies the possible damage in such cases by stating that a landlord will not be able to recover any fixed charge (rent or service charges) unless, within six months of the charge becoming due, s/he serves upon the assignor a prescribed form of notice giving details of the amounts due.

In order to protect her/himself, the original tenant would have to rely on an indemnity against the assignee, ie, if s/he is held liable for the assignee's arrears, s/he can sue to reclaim them. This indemnity is implied by statute, but it is good practice to include it expressly in the deed of assignment and avoid any possible future dispute. It also means that the parties are made aware of their respective liabilities.

s77 & Parts VII, VIII,
IX of Sch 2 LPA25

- If the assignee fails to pay rent after the assignment, the landlord can take possession proceedings against her/him and obtain an order for payment of the new arrears

- If s/he then fails to pay the arrears, the landlord could reapply to the court to join the original tenant in the money proceedings and enforce payment of the new arrears by that original tenant, subject to the six months' notification rule

---

28 s.76 Law of Property Act 1925 was repealed by the Law of Property (Miscellaneous Amendments) Act 1994.

29. Parry v Robinson-Wyllie (1987) 54 P&CR 187 and Tickner v Clifton (1929) 1 KB 207.

- However, as stated above, an indemnity is implied which protects the original tenant from liability for arrears after the assignment; and so the original tenant can sue to reclaim the money.

6.27 Arrears and assignment
– tenancies granted after 1 January 1996

Arrears accrued before assignment

The Landlord and Tenant (Covenants) Act 1995 does not alter the position on tenant's arrears accrued before assignment. The assignor remains liable (see above).

Arrears accruing after assignment

Section 5 of the Act abolishes the original tenant's liability for any future obligations of the tenancy, eg, rent which may become due after the assignment. Only the assignee can be held liable for rent after assignment unless:

Section 5 does not apply
This is where the assignment is in breach of covenant, ie, there is a prohibition against assignment or the landlord's consent should have been obtained. In these cases, the original tenant could still be held liable for arrears after assignment, as under the old law (see above).

The landlord has obtained a guarantee from the original tenant
In addition, section 16 of the Act allows a landlord in certain circumstances to require the tenant who wishes to assign to act as a guarantor of the new assignee. This kind of guarantee can be imposed:

- If there is an absolute prohibition against assignment – always

- Where the tenant may assign with the landlord's consent
  – where it is reasonable to do so but not

- Where the tenant is free to assign without the landlord's consent.

If the assignee assigns the tenancy, the guarantee will no longer bind the original tenant (unless it was in breach of covenant).

6.28 Arrears and assignment – possession proceedings for former tenants' arrears

The law received welcome clarification in 1999 in the case of *Notting Hill Housing Trust v Jones* (see box overleaf). In this case, the court confirmed that an assignee was not liable for assignor's arrears, and therefore possession could not be sought on that basis.

> ### Notting Hill Housing Trust v Jones
>
> In *Notting Hill Housing Trust v Jones*,[30] *Mrs Jones obtained an order for the transfer of her husband's sole secure tenancy in divorce proceedings and the tenancy was assigned to her in January 1997. The husband's rent account had been in arrears and in February 1997 Mrs Jones made a written agreement to discharge those arrears. After this, she paid sufficient to cover her own rent, but the Trust obtained a suspended possession order based on the £400 rent arrears still outstanding.*
>
> *The court held:*
>
> - *that possession ground 'rent lawfully due from the tenant has not been paid or an obligation of the tenancy has been broken or not performed' was not made out.*
>
> - *an assignee is not liable for an assignor tenant's arrears and therefore the rent was not 'lawfully due' from Mrs Jones*
>
> - *nor was there a breach of obligation of the tenancy, since the agreement she had made in February 1997 was not part of the tenancy and was at most a personal obligation 'of the tenant'*
>
> - *the money claim could not be sustained because the agreement relied on had been made after the assignment and thus there was no 'consideration' – therefore there was no contract and it was unenforceable.*
>
> - *the whole action for possession and money was dismissed.*

In practice, some local authorities require the assignee to agree to clear any existing arrears. Even if the assignee has promised to do so in return for the landlord's consent to the assignment, ie, for a 'consideration,' the legal status of such a promise, which could be deemed to constitute an illegal premium, must be in some doubt and enforceability would be by no means certain (see 11.33).

TERMINATION

This section looks at actions by a tenant which terminate a tenancy. This is the basic position in housing law and does not cover any additional rights that tenants may have to prevent disposal under matrimonial or child law. Therefore, before advising tenants on relationship breakdown, advisers should also check the relevant chapter on married and cohabiting tenants' rights (Chapters 7 and 8).

---

30. Notting Hill Housing Trust v Jones (1999) 1L and TR 397 CA.

6.29 Ending a tenancy

Fixed-term tenants

Fixed term tenancies can end in three ways:

The fixed term ends

At the end of the fixed term the tenancy will end. However, in some cases the landlord may allow the tenant to remain as a periodic tenant or grant a new fixed term. Assured, contractual protected and secure tenants have the right to stay on because, if they remain, a statutory tenancy arises at the end of the fixed term.

Where there is a break clause in the agreement

A fixed-term tenancy cannot be ended by notice before the end of the fixed term, unless there is a breach of the tenancy or an express statement in the agreement to the contrary. A clause allowing notice during a fixed term is known as a 'break clause.' In many tenancy agreements, there is such a break clause. The agreement should state whether the landlord or tenant (or either) can operate the clause and how this can be done. Notice served in accordance with a break clause effectively brings the fixed term to an early end. If it is a joint tenancy, both tenants must agree to serve the notice. Whether a statutory periodic tenancy then arises depends upon the type of tenancy and whether the tenant remains in occupation.

Surrender

An express surrender is where the tenant and the landlord agree to end the arrangement before the expiry of the fixed term, without the service of a notice to quit. It can be done at any time, but all parties must agree, (see 6.34 for the court's comments on surrender in the cases of *Hounslow LBC v Pilling* and *Greenwich LBC v McGrady*). Express surrender must be made by deed, but if there is no deed, then surrender might be deemed to have happened by 'operation of law.'

For a surrender by operation of law to occur, it would be necessary to show that both the tenant and the landlord clearly acted in a way that was inconsistent with the tenancy still being in existence. It is a contractual step. The tenant/s offer to surrender the tenancy. The landlord accepts. The exchange of consideration is that the tenant agrees to give up the tenancy and the landlord agrees to release the tenant from her/his obligations under the tenancy. However, case law has established that a sole tenant can surrender a tenancy, despite the spouse remaining in possession. The fact that the spouse had matrimonial homes rights did not affect the wife's right to surrender her sole tenancy.[31] However, another case has suggested that it may be possible to get a court order to set aside a surrender, but not a notice to quit (see 7.40).

---

31. Sanctuary Housing Association v Campbell (2000) 32 HLR 100 CA.

> ### Camden LBC v Alexandrou[32]
>
> *A sole tenant can surrender even without giving vacant possession.*
>
> *The tenancy was a sole secure tenancy. When the relationship broke down, the husband wrote to the council:*
>
> *"The above flat is no longer my responsibility, as I am unable to pay for the upkeep. My wife wishes to keep the said flat and pay the rent, to which I agree."*
>
> *The council treated the tenancy as having been assigned to the wife. She later gave NTQ and the council took possession proceedings against Mr A (who had moved back in). The council decided that the wife had become the sole tenant, the notice to quit was valid and Mr A was now a trespasser. He argued that there was no assignment, as there was no deed and no evidence of a surrender.*
>
> *The Court of Appeal held that there was no deed and therefore no assignment, but that a surrender by operation of law had been made out, even though the tenant had not given vacant possession at the date of the letter or thereafter.*

Periodic tenants

Periodic tenancies can be ended in two ways:

Notice to quit

A notice to quit must be valid, or deemed valid by agreement between the landlord and sole tenant, as in *Snowden v Hackney LBC* (see 6.31). It can be served either by the landlord or the tenant. It must comply with the common law, the contract and the terms of the Protection from Eviction Act 1977, where appropriate. For some types of tenancy, the position for landlords is different, and a different notice must be served. For example, a local authority would have to serve a 'notice seeking possession' on a secure tenant and the tenancy would not actually end until there is a court order, whereas a secure tenant need only serve a valid notice to quit.

Surrender

See above under fixed term.

6.30 Notices to quit

The effect of a notice to quit (or notice determining a licence) can vary depending upon:

• the type of tenancy or licence

---

32. Camden LBC v Alexandrou (1998) 30 HLR 534 CA.

- whether the tenancy or licence is fixed-term or periodic

- whether it is joint or sole tenancy

- whether the couple are married, divorced or cohabiting, heterosexual or same sex couples.

The position for individual tenancy types is dealt with in Chapters 7 and 8 under headings of sole and joint occupancy. However, the general conditions for notices to be valid are explained below.

6.31 Requirements for a tenant's notice to quit to be valid

Sole tenants notice to quit

Case law has established that a landlord and a sole tenant may agree short notice.[33]

Snowden v Hackney LBC

The wife who was the sole tenant signed a notice to quit, to take effect 3 days later. She vacated and was permanently rehoused and paid no more rent. The husband moved into the property and requested that the tenancy be transferred to him. The council refused. The husband counterclaimed for a declaration that he was the tenant and asserted that the notice to quit was invalid, as it did not comply with s.5(1) of the Protection from Eviction Act 1977.

The court held that the notice to quit was valid. If there was agreement between the landlord and the sole tenant that the notice would take effect according to its terms, even before the notice was given, the agreement would be effective.

Joint tenant's notice to quit

Many tenants are unaware that they, as well as their landlords, are bound by legal rules regarding notice to quit. This is, no doubt, because landlords do not usually enforce notice conditions. In many cases, the validity of notice to quit governs whether the tenancy still exists or not. In cases of relationship breakdown, this is obviously of great significance to the other spouse or partner, since it affects her/his right to remain. In addition, disputes may arise over liability for rent if one partner has tried to end the tenancy.

The requirements for a valid notice to quit vary depending on the nature of the tenancy, but are based on the common law principles on notice s5 PEA77   which have been extended by the Protection from Eviction Act.

---

33. Snowden v Hackney LBC [2001] 33 HLR 554 CA.

Common law and contractual provisions on notice to quit

A notice to quit must expire on either the first or the last day of the period of a tenancy, eg, where the tenancy runs from week to week and started on a Monday, notice must expire on a Sunday or a Monday. The notice must be equal in length to the period of the tenancy, eg, a monthly tenancy requires a month's notice.[34] If the contract allows a different period or timing of the notice, this will override the common law provisions.

These common law provisions do not apply to licensees who are only entitled to 'reasonable' notice under common law. Licensees must therefore rely on the provisions of their contract and the Protection from Eviction Act where appropriate.

The Protection from Eviction Act 1977

The Protection from Eviction Act applies alongside the common law and contractual rules. In situations where the contract or common law conflicts with the Act, then the rules set down in the Act will take precedence. The Act states that no notice to quit by either a landlord or a tenant will be valid unless it complies with two minimum rules:

• It must be in writing and (only for the landlord) contain certain information

• It must be given not less than 4 weeks before the date on which it is to take effect.

Notice requirements under the Protection from Eviction Act do not apply to excluded tenants or licensees (see 6.11) but do apply to licensees with basic protection.

6.32 **Notice to quit for the different types of tenancy**

The above sections explaining the common law and contractual and statutory position about notice to quit apply to nearly all types of tenancy and licence. Only protected statutory tenants, excluded licences and tenancies have rules which amend this position.

• *Protected (statutory) tenancies*: If there was a term in the contractual tenancy which stated how much notice was required, then this will apply (subject, of course, to common law provisions on timing and section 5 of the Protection from Eviction Act). However, if there was nothing in the contractual agreement about notice the tenant must give three months' notice. This requirement is frequently overlooked

• *Excluded tenants and licences*: Neither excluded tenancies nor excluded licences are covered by section 5 of the Protection from Eviction Act. Licences are also not subject to the same common law rules as tenancies. Excluded tenants must therefore give notice

---

34. See also Arden, Carter and Dymond, *Quiet Enjoyment*, 6th edition (Legal Action Group, 2002), pp 39-40.

equal to the period of the tenancy, unless the contract says otherwise. Excluded licensees must only give reasonable notice, unless the contract says otherwise. There is no requirement that either notice should be in writing, unless the contract specifically requires this.

For more information about how the procedures work in practice and for information about how to prevent a notice to quit, see Chapters 7 and 8.

6.33 Invalid notice to quit

It is very common for a notice to quit to be invalid. Where this is the case, the landlord or tenant is entitled to hold that it is ineffective and continue with the tenancy until a valid notice is served. However, in many situations landlords and tenants are happy to treat the notice as if it were valid. Case law has held that this approach is acceptable, as indicated in 6.31 above.[35] However, the position is complicated where there are joint tenants, as both tenants must agree to treat the defective notice as valid.

6.34 Ending the tenancy – the position of joint tenants

Periodic tenancies

A valid notice to quit by one joint tenant will effectively terminate all joint periodic tenancies (with the exception of Rent Act protected or statutory tenancies, see 7.33 – 7.34).

This means that the landlord will easily be able to obtain possession since anyone remaining in occupation has no legal status in the property and is technically a trespasser. However the Court of Appeal[36] has held that the property can still be the 'home' of the person who remains there as a 'trespasser' and therefore Article 8 of the European Convention on Human rights (right to respect for home) must be considered. A landlord must be able to show that interference with Article 8 rights is a proportionate and justifiable response when seeking possession. At the time of writing, Harrow Borough Council had appealed to the House of Lords on this issue, and a decision is awaited on the legality of the procedure (see 7.42 for further discussion on human rights in this context.) Advisers should check on the outcome of this important case before advising on this procedure. For information on possible steps to take to prevent service of a notice to quit, see 7.38 – 7.42 and 8.17.

If the tenancy is periodic, the joint tenants are only bound to the tenancy for each period, eg, from month to month or week to week, and so either can choose not to renew at the end of any period, by giving notice to quit.

> 'A periodic tenancy continues from period to period unless the notice agreed or implied by law is given. ... A periodic tenancy renews itself unless either side brings it to an end.'[37]

35. Snowden v Hackney LBC, see 33 above, and Elsden v Pick (1980) 1 WLR 898 CA.
36. Harrow LBC v Qazi [2002] HLR 14 CA.
37. Moorlands Building Society (1952) 2 All ER at p495.

Donaldson MR summed up the principle in the important case of *Greenwich v McGrady*:

> '*In my judgement, it is clear law that, if there is to be a surrender of a joint tenancy – that is, a surrender before its natural termination – then all must agree to the surrender. If there is to be a renewal, which is the position at the end of each period of periodic tenancy, then again, all must concur. In this case, Mrs McGrady made it quite clear by her notice to quit that she was not content to renew the joint tenancy... That left Mr McGrady without any tenancy at all, although it was faintly argued... [that] the joint tenant who did not concur was left with a sole tenancy. That cannot be the law and no authority has been cited in support of it.*'

As a result of this case, the procedure whereby one tenant brings a tenancy to an end without the other's agreement (as often happens in cases of domestic violence) has become known as the 'McGrady' procedure.[38]

Greenwich LBC v McGrady[39]

Mr and Mrs McGrady were joint periodic tenants of a LB Greenwich flat for four years. One year after divorce proceedings were finalised, Mrs McGrady served notice to quit on the landlord and Mr McGrady refused to leave.

The local authority tried to obtain a possession order against Mr McGrady and the county court found in his favour. On appeal, however, the decision was reversed in favour of Greenwich. The appeal decision determined that notice to quit given by one party to a joint tenancy effectively ends the secure tenancy and thereby the security of the other party.

The decision effectively provided local authorities with a 'device' with which to resolve tenancy disputes arising from relationship breakdown. This enables one partner, whether married or unmarried, to terminate a tenancy on the agreement of the landlord authority to provide her/him with a new tenancy.

The remaining partner may or may not be rehoused, dependent upon the local authority's policy. The procedure applies equally to assured tenancies, and can therefore be used by RSLs and other landlords of assured tenants.

---

38. The principle was subsequently confirmed in Hammersmith and Fulham v Monk & Barnet LBC v Smith (1990) 23 HLR 114 CA (affirmed in the House of Lords at 24 HLR 206 HL).

39. Greenwich LBC v McGrady (1982) 6 HLR 36 CA.

However, if there is to be a surrender, or notice is served to operate a break clause in a fixed-term agreement, all joint tenants must agree. These principles have been extended by case law[40] to confirm that, for one joint tenant successfully to end a periodic tenancy, the minimum four weeks' notice and all the other formalities of a valid notice to quit must be complied with. Where a landlord accepts less than valid notice from one joint tenant, the tenancy will continue to exist, and any attempt to exclude the other joint tenant would amount to illegal eviction, and could lay the landlord open to substantial damages.[41]

Hounslow LBC v Pilling[42]

The local authority had a domestic violence policy whereby it undertook to rehouse any tenant who was a victim of violence, provided that the person who had experienced the violence surrendered her or his tenancy. Miss Doubtfire, a joint council tenant, wrote to Hounslow stating "I wish to terminate my tenancy held on the above mentioned property with immediate effect." This was held to be invalid notice to quit, since it did not comply with the common law rules. It was argued that she was operating a break clause written in the agreement which allowed the tenant to give less than four weeks' notice and that the landlord could accept less than the required notice. The court held that "a single joint tenant cannot exercise a break clause in a lease..." and that, in any case, it is not possible to override the Protection from Eviction Act requirement of at least four weeks' notice. (Note, however, that an invalid or short notice could be treated as valid after the event if it was served by a sole tenant or both joint tenants as long as the tenant(s) and the landlord agree.)

In addition it could not be deemed to be a surrender, since a surrender of a joint tenancy requires the agreement of both tenants. A surrender must either be in writing from both tenants, or by operation of law through unequivocal acts (see 6.29). The fact that one tenant remained in possession meant that it could not be a surrender by operation of law. Accordingly, the tenancy continued to exist.

Osei-Bonsu v Wandsworth LBC[43]
Ignorance of the law on valid notices is no defence

This was a case involving a joint tenancy where the wife had been subject to domestic violence from her husband. The wife

continued overleaf

---

40. LB Hounslow v Pilling (1993) 25 HLR 305 CA.
41. Osei-Bonsu v Wandsworth LBC (1999) 1 All ER 265; (1999) 1 FLR 276 CA.
42. LB Hounslow v Pilling see 40 above.
43. Osei-Bonsu v Wandsworth LBC, see 41 above.

> was rehoused by the council and gave 14 days' notice to quit, not the required 28 days.
>
> The council refused to allow the husband back in. The county court held that the husband was still the tenant – shortness of notice could not be waived by the landlord and only one joint tenant.
>
> The husband claimed damages for unlawful eviction. He was awarded £30,000 damages, later reduced by the Court of Appeal to £10,000, since it was Mr Osei-Bonsu's violence which broke up the family and started a chain of events which culminated in his unlawful eviction. Nevertheless, the fact that the landlords believed the notice to be valid in law was no defence, and there was no reasonable cause for such a belief.

Fixed-term tenancies

A valid notice to quit by one joint tenant will not end a joint fixed-term tenancy unless the notice to quit ends on or after the date of termination of the fixed term. In fact, a notice to quit by the tenant has no relevance during a fixed-term, since the only ways a tenant can bring the tenancy to an early end are by operating a break clause or offering a surrender which is accepted by the landlord (see 6.29).

The chief distinction between the fixed-term and the periodic joint tenancy lies in the length of the period which tenants have contracted to be bound to, and when they are entitled to opt out of the agreement. In a fixed-term tenancy, both tenants have contracted to take on and be liable for the tenancy for the agreed fixed term. It is not possible for one party to end the contract on behalf of the other party. S/he must wait until it is time to renew the fixed term and can choose not to do so, thus ending the joint agreement. For this reason, a break clause in a fixed-term tenancy cannot be operated by only one joint tenant.

> 'It is common ground that under the general law a notice taking advantage of a "break" clause during the currency of the fixed term of a lease has to be given by both tenants if it is to be effective.' [44]

Breach of trust and notice to quit

For some time, it had been suggested that if a joint tenant unilaterally gave notice to quit, thereby ending the tenancy without the other tenant's consent, such an action could constitute a breach of trust. The Court of Appeal decision in *Crawley BC v Ure* has now clarified that this is not the case. The court later held also that service of a notice to quit was

---

not an exercise by a trustee of a power or duty, nor was it a function within the meaning of s.11 of the Trusts of Land and Appointment of Trustees Act 1996, and therefore there was no duty to consult. A notice to quit was merely an indication by the joint tenant that s/he did not consent to the tenancy continuing beyond the end of the notice period.[45]

> ### Crawley BC v Ure[46]
>
> *A husband and wife were joint council tenants. The wife left and applied as homeless. The council suggested she should give notice to quit to terminate the tenancy. She did so, but the husband refused to leave. When the council obtained a possession order against him, he appealed, arguing that his wife's action was a breach of trust and that the council had been guilty of the tort (ie, civil wrong) of procuring a breach of trust.*
>
> *His argument failed. Section 26(3) of the Law of Property Act 1925 required one trustee to consult the others on 'the exercise of any statutory or other power vested in the trustees for sale.' This meant that consultation was required before a 'positive act.' The court held that the giving of a notice to quit in these circumstances was not a positive act within the section. The husband's appeal therefore failed.*

6.35 Landlord's legal procedures to remove a cohabitant or former spouse after a valid notice to quit by a joint or sole tenant

Most housing advisers are aware that, except for excluded tenants or licensees, a landlord cannot legally evict a tenant or licensee without a court order. These statutory rights stem either from the relevant Housing or Rent Act or from the Protection from Eviction Act 1977 (see below).

Unfortunately the situation becomes more complicated where the tenant has ended the tenancy by serving a valid notice to quit. After the notice has expired, the landlord will normally have to obtain a court order before the non-tenant partner can be legally evicted. In some cases however a court order is not required even though the occupation is not within the definition of an excluded occupation. How these anomalies arise is explained below.

Protection from Eviction Act 1977

Section 3 of the Protection from Eviction Act 1977 states that when most tenancies or licences come to an end neither the tenant/licensee nor anyone lawfully residing in the dwelling at the time the tenancy/licence

45. Notting Hill Housing Trust v Brackley [2001] EWCA Civ 601 CA.

46. Crawley BC v Ure (1995) 27 HLR 524 CA.

came to an end can be evicted without a court order. This means that, even if the tenant/licensee has ended the tenancy/licence by notice to quit, the landlord would still in most cases have to obtain a court order to evict the tenant and/or remaining occupier.

Section 3 does not apply where the tenancy was let as a dwelling under a tenancy which is one of the following:

• Assured and assured shorthold tenancies which are covered by section 5 of the Housing Act 1988 (see below); assured agricultural occupancies

• Protected contractual tenancies (but statutory tenancies are covered)

• Protected occupancy or statutory tenancies as defined under the Rent (Agriculture) Act 1976

• Excluded tenants and licensees.

s8(1) PEA77 Certain other less common types of tenancy are also included. In the case of assured, assured shorthold and protected contractual tenancies there are provisions written into the relevant statutes which mean that the landlord cannot gain possession without going through court procedures. Section 5 of the Housing Act 1988 states that an assured tenancy (including assured shortholds) cannot be brought to an end by a landlord except by obtaining an order of the court. If a landlord serves notice to quit on a protected contractual tenancy, it automatically becomes a statutory tenancy and is then covered by section 3 of the Protection from Eviction Act (unlawful to recover possession other than by court proceedings).

However, these provisions refer to situations where the *landlord* is taking action to end the tenancy and not to situations where the *tenant* has brought the tenancy to an end her/himself. This means that when assured, assured shorthold and protected contractual (but not statutory) tenants serve a notice to quit, technically there may not be a legal entitlement to a court order if they or their partners remain, and they will therefore be in the same position as an excluded occupier. However, physical force must not be used and so it is always advisable for a landlord to obtain a court order to avoid any possible offence under the Criminal Law Act 1977, or claim for damages for trespass to goods if belongings are lost or damaged in the process of eviction.

The detailed requirements for landlord procedures when a tenant leaves or gives notice to quit in respect of individual tenancies are explained fully in the next two chapters.

6.36 Landlord's legal procedures to remove a cohabitant or former spouse if the sole tenant leaves

Where the tenant has left and the non-tenant does not have occupation rights under the Family Law Act 1996, or they have ended (see 7.7), occupancy by the ex-spouse or cohabitant will no longer fulfil the tenant condition. Therefore, (protected) statutory tenancies will end, and secure and assured tenancies will become tenancies with basic protection (sometimes referred to as 'non-secure' or 'non-assured'), unless there can be deemed to have been a surrender, in which latter case they too will end (see 6.29). This does not mean that the landlord is entitled to evict the remaining occupier without any further action.

Where the tenancy has become a tenancy with basic protection only, or was never secure or assured in the first place – as is the case with tenancies granted to homeless persons under Part 7 of the Housing Act 1996 – the landlord will have to terminate the occupancy by serving notice. The appropriate notice to terminate such a tenancy is a notice to quit. It is therefore crucial that social landlords have a clause in their tenancy agreements allowing for service of NTQ at the premises, otherwise they may not be able to prove good service of a notice at all (see 6.37 onwards). In addition, where the tenancy is not secure or assured, there is no provision for Notices seeking Possession.

6.37 Service of landlord's NTQ on tenants with basic protection

s196(5) LPA 1925 Service of notice to quit at the tenant's premises when the tenant is known to have left, is only allowed if there is express provision for this method in the tenancy agreement.[47] The Court of Appeal clarified this requirement further in the case of *Enfield LBC v Devenish*,[48] where service through a letterbox knowing the tenant was no longer there was held not to be proper service.

The solution is either to serve notices personally or to insert a clause in the tenancy agreement allowing for notice to be served at the premises. For personal service to be effective, it must be served on the tenant or the tenant's spouse. Service on a cohabitant when the authority knew the tenant was not at the property has been held not to be sufficient.[49] If a notice is inserted in the tenancy agreement, this would then comply with the Law of Property Act requirements. However, if a tenancy agreement is to be amended, a notice of variation of a secure tenancy
s103 HA85 agreement must itself be 'served on the tenant.'

If there is no provision in the tenancy agreement for serving notice, the only remaining possibilities are:

a) If a surrender by operation of law can be made out or

---

47. Wandsworth LBC v Atwell (1995) EGCS 68 CA.

48. Enfield LBC v Devenish and Sutton (1997) 29 HLR 691 CA.
49. Enfield LBC v Devenish and Sutton ibid.

b) To use the lengthy procedures of the Landlord and Tenant Act 1954 as follows:

Where

- surrender by operation of law cannot be made out, and
- there is no provision in the tenancy agreement for service of notice to quit at the premises, and
- the landlord is not a local authority, and therefore cannot rely on the provisions of the Local Government Act for service of a statutory notice seeking possession (see below)

Then, section 54 of the Landlord and Tenant Act 1954 allows for an application to be made to the county court to bring to an end a tenancy where:

- the tenant has been absent for at least six months; and
- no rent has been paid during that time; and
- the landlord has taken all reasonable steps to communicate with the tenant and failed.

There is also an archaic provision under s. 16 of the Distress for Rent Act 1737 which enables an application to be made to a Magistrates, Court where at least six months rent is owing, but this is very rarely used.

Not surprisingly, very few landlords use these cumbersome procedures since they do not usually wish to lose six months' rent or leave a property empty for so long. Technically, however, they may in certain situations be the only legal route open.

Service of Notice Seeking Possession

Notices seeking possession are used for assured and secure tenancies. They tell the tenant that the landlord intends to seek possession, but do not actually terminate the tenancy. The tenancy can only be terminated by an order of the court.

A landlord may only serve notice at the premises when the tenant is no longer there, if the tenancy agreement permits such service. Most social landlords (local authorities and registered social landlords) now have such clauses in their agreements.

In practice, local authorities may, and often do, serve both a notice to quit and a Notice Seeking Possession without prejudice to each other (ie, service of a Notice Seeking Possession is not admitting that the tenancy is in fact still secure or assured). This covers the eventuality of the tenant reappearing, taking up residence and arguing that they had intended to return, in which case the security of the tenancy could be revived.[50] This in turn would mean that the notice to quit would be ineffective.

---

50. Hussey v Camden LBC (1995) 27 HLR 5 CA; Crawley BC v Sawyer (1988) 20 HLR 98 CA.

6.38 Acceptance of rent implying creation of a new tenancy

It is commonly believed that the acceptance of rent by a landlord will lead to a new tenancy being created. Although this may be the case, the position is complicated. It is, however, highly relevant to relationship breakdown. For example, when a tenancy ends after a statutory tenant leaves or notice to quit has been served, the remaining partner may be able to argue that s/he has acquired a new tenancy based on the actions of the landlord.

The courts have shown considerable reluctance to accept this kind of argument, and the test is whether it is right and proper, taking into account all the circumstances, including any payments made, to infer that the parties concerned had actually agreed upon a new tenancy.[51]

In order for a tenancy to be implied, it must be demonstrated that the landlord and the tenant had an 'intention to create a legal relationship.' Where a landlord accepts payments from an occupier after the tenancy has ended or where the tenant has left, and the landlord is fully aware of this, it may be possible to argue that a new tenancy has been granted. However it will be difficult to imply that a new tenancy has been created in certain situations:

- Where the landlord is unaware that the tenant has left
- Where the landlord is aware of the position and refuses to accept rent
- Where the landlord writes and says that s/he will accept payments but that they do not constitute rent nor indicate an intention to create a tenancy
- Where the tenant had some statutory right to remain, such as matrimonial home rights, and payments were accepted as if from the tenant and do not show that the landlord wanted to enter a new contract of tenancy
- Where rent was paid following a computer-generated demand.[52]

Accepting rent for only one or two months is unlikely to be construed as a new tenancy, but it will depend on all the facts of the case.

> ### *Westminster CC v Basson*[53]
>
> *Westminster granted a secure tenancy to Mr and Mrs Simpson in 1977. Mrs Simpson moved out and Miss Basson moved in as Mr Simpson's partner in 1984. The relationship broke down and Mr Simpson left. When Westminster found out that Miss Basson*
>
> *continued overleaf*

51. Longrigg, Burrough and Trounson v Smith (1979) EGD 472 CA.

52. Dreamgate v Arnot (1970) EGCS 121.
53. Westminster CC v Basson (1990) 23 HLR 225 CA.

was there alone, they told her that she had no right to remain and wrote to her in September 1985 asking her to pay a 'use and occupation charge,' and said that legal proceedings were being commenced. They stated in the letter that:

"In making the payments as Use and Occupation Charges this arrangement is not intended as the creation of a tenancy or a Licence akin to a tenancy in any way whatsoever."

In November 1986, possession proceedings were started. In spring 1987 a rent book was issued. At the hearing, the county court judge found that no tenancy had been created and ordered possession. Miss Basson appealed. The Court of Appeal dismissed the appeal, as the letter of September 1985 was entirely inconsistent with the proposition that occupation was with the council's consent. The issue of a rent book and various references to rent by the housing benefit section did not demonstrate that the letter did not mean what it said or that there had been a change in Miss Basson's circumstances.

Tower Hamlets v Ayinde[54]

The court distinguished between this case and the Basson case. In this case, the council had accepted rent from Mrs Ayinde for over two years, in full knowledge that she was living there and paying the rent, and had taken no action. Mrs Ayinde had gone to the council numerous times requesting the tenancy be transferred to her, and also written stating she was the tenant. At the possession hearing, the judge found that a tenancy had been granted to Mrs Ayinde.

54. Tower Hamlets LBC v Ayinde (1994) 26 HLR 631 CA.

7

Chapter 7: Married tenants

Subjects covered in this chapter include...

Sole tenancies

What short-term rights a married non-tenant has in the matrimonial home

How sole tenancies may be dealt with in the long-term

What effect a notice to quit or surrender has on a sole tenancy

What happens if a sole tenant leaves

Joint tenancies

How joint tenancies may be dealt with in the long-term

What effect a notice to quit or surrender has on a joint tenancy

What happens if a joint tenant leaves

Sole and joint tenancies

How to prevent a tenant serving notice to quit

What powers the courts have to transfer tenancies between divorcing couples

What happens to rent arrears and liability after a court transfer

Married tenants

When a marriage breaks down, the tenancy situation will have to be resolved in one of the following ways:

Married couples divorcing or seeking a decree of nullity or judicial separation

Under matrimonial/family law, the court can order a transfer of tenancy from one party to the other (see Section F, 7.43 onwards). Tenancies can also be transferred under the Children Act 1989 (see 9.17).

Non-divorcing married couples without children

The power to transfer tenancies between married couples can only be exercised in conjunction with proceedings for divorce, nullity or judicial separation. If a married couple is not taking matrimonial proceedings, the situation will have to be resolved using housing law as it would be used between any two sharers (including lesbian and gay cohabitants – see Chapter 8).

Non-divorcing married couples with children

If a married couple is not divorcing but have children, they have the same rights to use housing law as anyone else; but, in addition, it may be possible to have the tenancy transferred for the benefit of a child under the Children Act 1989. However, this does not necessarily apply to all tenancies (see 9.18 – 9.21).

The position after divorce

After divorce, if the situation regarding property has not been resolved, the ex-spouse will be in the same position as a cohabitant or former cohabitant. The position is explained in Chapter 8.

Sole tenancies

A   Establishing the short-term right to occupy the home

One of the first questions which presents itself when a marriage breaks down is: who has the right to stay in the matrimonial home? Will the person seeking advice have to leave or can s/he stay?

7.1   The right to live in the matrimonial home

s30 FLA96   Matrimonial home rights under the Family Law Act 1996 apply equally to owner-occupiers and to tenants. Where the married couple is in tenanted property and the tenancy is in one name only, both parties to the marriage have legal rights to remain in occupation of the matrimonial home, regardless of who is the tenant.

This right exists automatically provided that:

• the marriage continues and

s30(1) FLA96 • the tenant has a legal right to remain by virtue of contract or statute and

• the non-tenant has not been excluded by a court order.

The tenant's spouse has the right to occupy the home as if s/he were the tenant. This applies to all types of tenancies.

Provided the tenancy continues (eg, it has not been ended by the tenant), then even if the tenant leaves, the landlord cannot evict the spouse unless s/he has the right to claim possession against the tenant. This may involve proving specific grounds for possession, eg, rent arrears. Similarly, the tenant cannot exclude her/his spouse without a court order.

7.2 Rights to occupy of excluded occupiers

Matrimonial home rights apply only where one spouse has a contractual or statutory right to remain. Where both spouses are bare licensees (see 6.11), such as those living with family or friends, they do not have matrimonial home rights under the Family Law Act 1996 in respect of the dwelling which they are occupying or staying in, since neither is an owner or tenant. Nevertheless, the dwelling is still treated as the matrimonial home for the purpose of obtaining occupation orders
s37 FLA96 (see below).

Excluded occupiers, including bare licensees, have the right to apply for occupation orders against each other. This means that if one spouse had excluded the other, the excluded spouse could apply for an order to re-enter. S/he could also apply for an order to exclude the other spouse from all or part of the place where they were staying which was at that time the matrimonial home (see Chapter 13, Section C). This would not prevent a third party, eg, the friend or relative with whom they were staying, from giving either or both of them reasonable notice to leave.

7.3 Rights to occupy of those in tied accommodation

It is necessary to distinguish between people who occupy accommodation provided by the employer in the following ways:

• Where the occupation is not related to the work or necessary for its better performance, eg, local authorities who offer council accommodation to employees as part of a package of benefits with the job

- Where the occupier/employee is required to occupy the accommodation in order better to carry out the job, eg, caretakers, housekeepers, companions.

Service tenants

Ground 16 Sch 2
HA88 & case 8
Sch 15 RA77

The former are service tenants and could be assured, protected or secure tenants if the conditions are fulfilled (see Chapter 6, Section B). The relevant possession ground will have to be established, depending on the type of tenancy. However, where the landlord is seeking possession on the basis that employment has ceased, the court has discretion and must consider whether it is reasonable to grant possession. Service tenants also have statutory protection from illegal eviction and the right to a valid notice (if appropriate to the type of tenancy), court hearing and court order.

Service occupants

s8(2) PEA775

The latter are service occupants, occupying normally under a contractual licence, ie, the accommodation is provided in return for carrying out the job. They also have statutory protection, but of a more limited kind.

- The Protection from Eviction Act 1977 gives service occupiers the right not to be evicted without a court order (unless they are excluded occupiers)

- Where the licence is a periodic licence, notice to quit for a minimum of four weeks is also required before possession proceedings can be started

- Such notice is not required if the licence was indeterminate, eg, for the duration of employment[1]

- No possession ground needs to be proved and possession is therefore mandatory.

Provided there can be shown to be a contract, ie, a consideration being provided in return for the accommodation, the spouse of the employed person would have matrimonial home rights.

Employee leaves the home

If, as may happen in a relationship breakdown, a service tenant leaves the home but continues in the employment, the tenancy continues and the non-tenant spouse has the right to occupy.

If a service occupant leaves the home but continues in the employment, what happens will depend upon whether it was a condition of the contract of employment for the service occupant to remain living there. If there is a breach of contract because of the employee leaving, the

---

1. Norris v Checksfield (1991) 23 HLR 425 CA.

landlord will be able to seek possession, but the non-tenant spouse as a lawful occupier still has protection under the Protection from Eviction Act and the right to remain until ordered to leave by a court.

7.4 Other matrimonial rights of the non-tenant spouse

Basically, the same rights apply as for owner-occupiers (see 4.2). Those relevant to tenants are:

Occupation of the home

The right:

s30(2)(a) FLA96

1. To occupy the matrimonial home and not to be excluded, except by court order

s30(2)(b) FLA96

2. If not occupying the home, to obtain a court order to regain entry and to live there

s30(4) FLA96

3. To occupy the home as if s/he were the tenant.

s1 RA77

- If it is a tenancy under the Rent Act 1977 or the Rent (Agriculture) Act 1976, which requires the tenant to 'occupy the property as a residence,' occupation as a residence by the non-tenant spouse will be treated as satisfying this condition

s81 HA85
s1 HA88

- If it is a tenancy under the Housing Act 1985 (secure) or the Housing Act 1988 (assured), which requires the tenant to 'occupy the dwelling as her/his only or principal home,' occupation as an only or principal home by the non-tenant spouse will be treated as satisfying this condition.

Payment and liabilities

s30(3) FLA96

4. To pay rent or other outgoings which are to be treated as if paid by the tenant (see 11.24). Note: this is a right to have payments accepted by the landlord as rent, and does not mean that the non-tenant spouse can be held legally liable for the tenant's arrears, unless an order has been made transferring liability, either with an occupation order or upon transfer of the tenancy (see 7.6 and 7.52).

Possession action

s85(5) HA85,
s100(4A) RA77
& s9(5) HA88

5. The special right to intervene in possession proceedings and apply for suspension or postponement, even after the order has already been made terminating the tenancy, but not after the order has been enforced and possession lawfully obtained by the landlord.

The important point to recognise about matrimonial home rights is that the non-tenant spouse occupies as if s/he were the tenant without having the actual status of a tenant.

7.5 The matrimonial home

Matrimonial home rights under the Family Law Act 1996 apply only to a dwelling which has been lived in by both parties as the matrimonial home, or was intended to be lived in as the matrimonial home. Merely allowing a separated spouse to stay on occasions would not necessarily give her/him matrimonial rights to occupy.

s30(7) FLA96

7.6 Occupation orders under the Family Law Act 1996

Occupation orders are also covered in depth in Chapter 13, Section C and the position of married couples is summarised at 4.5.

A non-tenant spouse has exactly the same rights as a non-owning spouse to apply under the Family Law Act for an occupation order, falling under the same category of 'entitled applicants.' The orders may declare or extend rights to occupy whilst the other spouse remains in the home as well, or they may restrict either spouse's rights to occupy all or part of the home.

s33 FLA96

When the court makes an occupation order, it may include certain provisions. These include:

s40(1)(a) FLA96

• imposing obligations on either spouse to repair or maintain the home or to take responsibility for its rent and other outgoings (this could end the owning spouse's liability for rent and order that the non-owning spouse take on that liability). However, enforcement by the courts of such an order imposing liability can be difficult, as there is no ultimate sanction of imprisonment if the person ignores the order (see 11.17)

s40(1)(b) FLA96

• obliging the spouse who remains in occupation to pay an occupation rent to the other spouse who has been excluded from all or part of the home

s40(1)(c)-(e) FLA96

• making orders granting use of furniture and contents, and orders to take reasonable care of furniture, contents and the home generally (see 13.23).

s33(10) FLA96

The court has discretion to make occupation orders for non-tenant spouses either until a further order is made or for a specific period, or until a specific event occurs, such as divorce.

7.7 Matrimonial rights after divorce

Matrimonial rights relating to occupation normally cease on termination of marriage by death or decree absolute. An application must be made to the court for an extension of the rights beyond divorce if it looks as if a property settlement will not have been reached by that time, and the non-tenant wants to remain in the matrimonial home.

s33(5) FLA96

Once matrimonial home rights cease, the non-tenant normally becomes an excluded licensee and is only able to remain if the ex-spouse allows it.

Under the Family Law Act 1996, it is possible for a former spouse who is not a tenant to apply for an occupation order, even after s/he has left the ex-matrimonial home (see 4.6). However, the court does not have as much discretion when giving occupation orders to former spouses (see 13.32), and so it is still preferable to apply before the end of the marriage.

s35 FLA96

7.8 The non-tenant's rights where the owner is declared bankrupt

This is covered in Chapter 12.

B Long-term settlement of tenancies

In the short-term, a client may have established the right to stay in the home and even to get her/his spouse out. But this does not transfer the tenancy from one spouse to another. In most cases, once it is clear that the relationship has definitely ended, people want to settle things for good.

7.9 Reallocation of tenancy on marriage breakdown

The options for sorting out what happens to the tenancy in the long term vary, depending upon marital status, type of tenancy or licence, sole or joint tenancy and whether legal proceedings are being taken. As explained at the start of this chapter, the courts have powers to transfer certain tenancies between married and divorcing couples and between non-divorcing couples who have children. However, many people do not wish to get involved in court proceedings.

The matrimonial home rights can usually only be terminated permanently by death or termination of the marriage, ie, on decree absolute. In addition they will terminate if the court so orders, or where the other spouse no longer has the right to occupy because the tenancy has ended. In relationship breakdown, there are three common ways of altering the tenancy position without involving the courts, which are based on housing law principles:

s30(8) FLA96

1. *Assignment*: the tenancy may be able to be assigned voluntarily

2. *Notice or surrender*: the tenant can give notice that s/he wishes to terminate the tenancy or simply surrender it to the landlord

3. *Leaving*: the tenant may leave or simply disappear.

Certain general principles apply to all assignments, regardless of whether they are between married couples or lesbian, gay or heterosexual cohabitants. The following general information is found in Chapter 6 and applies to cohabitants and married couples:

• How a sole tenancy is assigned (6.14)

• Distinguishing between assignment or new tenancy (6.15)

• What happens to arrears when the tenancy is assigned voluntarily (6.25 onwards)

• The requirements for the sole or joint tenant's notice to quit to be valid (6.31–6.33)

• Rights to assign sole and joint tenancies (6.16–24).

The effects of notice to quit or surrender and of the tenant leaving are examined separately below, in relation to differing types of tenancy.

NOTICE TO QUIT OR SURRENDER BY THE SOLE MARRIED TENANT

When a marriage breaks down, one party may decide to give notice to quit to end the tenancy and its liabilities. The other party will obviously want to know whether anything can be done to prevent the tenant serving notice to quit, or, if it has been served, whether the notice to quit actually brings the tenancy to an end. If the tenancy is ended, the remaining partner will also need to know what rights s/he has to remain in the home.

For information on preventing a tenant from serving notice to quit, see Section E 7.38 – 7.42. In order to know whether the notice will end the tenancy, two main points need to be grasped. Matrimonial home rights give a non-tenant spouse the right to occupy as if s/he were the tenant provided that:

• the marriage still exists, (ie, there has been no decree absolute, nor death of the tenant), or the rights have been extended by the court after marriage, and

• the tenancy still exists, ie, it has not been brought to an end by a valid notice to quit or court order.

In addition, if the tenant has served notice to quit and brought the tenancy to an end, it is necessary to know what steps the landlord has to take to remove the non-tenant spouse, and whether a court order will be required. The non-tenant will want to know whether s/he can defend her/his right to remain, and the local authority's homelessness section may try to insist that the non-tenant remain as long as possible. For these reasons, an adviser needs to be clear as to whether the non-tenant spouse has any rights defendable in law.

The law offers different types of protection to different types of occupiers. The situation is complicated and for this reason each type of tenancy is considered separately below.

7.10 Validity of notice to quit

In order for a notice to quit to take effect, it must normally be valid (see 6.31–6.33). In many cases, however, the stringent requirements for validity are not met. Case law has held that a landlord and a sole tenant are free to agree to terminate a tenancy on short notice (see case of *Snowden v Hackney LBC* below). If there is such an agreement, the position will be the same as if a valid notice to quit had been served (see below).

> ### *Snowden v Hackney LBC*[2]
>
> *A sole secure tenant gave 3 days' notice of termination of tenancy in August 1991, on a form produced by the council, who then rehoused her. Her husband tried to argue that the notice was invalid, and that as a notice seeking possession was served in November 1991 and a new rent book for 1992/3 was issued, the council had treated the tenancy as continuing. The court did not agree: the council had voided the rent account after August 1991, had not sought any further rent, and had rehoused the tenant.*
>
> *The court held that failure to comply with the rules on notice to quit (s.5 Protection from Eviction Act 1977) had been waived by the council, and the notice was therefore valid, since the parties to a sole tenancy are free to terminate a tenancy on short notice (Elsdon v Pick).[3]*

7.11 Surrender

If the tenancy is ended by surrender, then the position for sole tenants will be the same as if a valid notice to quit had been served (see below). Case law has established that neither matrimonial home rights, nor the fact that a spouse remains in occupation, prevents a sole tenant from surrendering her/his tenancy. A landlord may, however, refuse to accept a surrender, whereas notice to quit, provided it is valid, will automatically bring the tenancy to an end (see also 6.29 and 6.34 for more detail on surrender).

7.12 Secure and introductory tenancies – sole tenant's notice to quit

- Valid notice to quit by the sole tenant ends a periodic secure or introductory tenancy. (Fixed-term tenancies are very rare but there

2. Snowden v Hackney LBC [2001] 33 HLR 554 CA.   3. Elsdon v Pick (1980) 1 WLR 899.

would have to be a break clause, or the tenant would have to wait for the end of the term)

- The remaining spouse has no legal status, but because secure and introductory tenancies are covered by section 3 of the Protection from Eviction Act 1977, the landlord must obtain a court order to recover possession. No grounds for possession need to be proved.

7.13 Assured and assured shorthold tenancies – sole tenant's notice to quit

Fixed-term

- Whether a tenant can end the tenancy within the fixed term will depend upon the terms of the contract, ie, whether there is a break clause

- If there is no break clause allowing for a tenant to give notice, then any notice served will have no effect and the tenancy will continue until the end of the fixed term. A statutory periodic assured tenancy will still arise at the end of the fixed term. If there is a break clause, notice will end the fixed term tenancy and no statutory periodic assured tenancy will arise

s5(2) HA88

- There is no right not to be evicted without a court order once the tenancy has ended (see 'periodic' below).

Periodic

- Valid notice to quit by the sole tenant ends the tenancy

- The remaining spouse has no legal status. Assured tenancies are not covered by section 3 of the Protection from Eviction Act and protection from the Housing Act 1988 will have ceased. Therefore, the landlord is not legally obliged to get a court order to recover possession. It would, however, not normally be considered good practice for a registered social landlord to evict without a court order.

Physical force to evict constitutes a criminal offence, so that if the non-tenant spouse remains on the premises, the landlord should obtain a court order for possession to avoid the commission of an offence. The claim is a possession claim against trespassers.

7.14 Protected contractual tenancy – sole tenant's notice to quit

- Valid notice to quit by the sole tenant ends the contractual tenancy

s2 RA77

- Provided the tenant remains in residence, a statutory tenancy arises. Even if the tenant has left, matrimonial home rights mean that the non-tenant spouse occupies as if s/he were the tenant (see 7.4), and therefore residence by the non-tenant spouse will 'keep alive' the statutory tenancy whilst the marriage exists. After divorce, the non-tenant former spouse is in exactly the same position as a non-tenant former cohabitant (see 8.8).

Sch 15 RA77
• It may be possible to use case 5 to obtain a possession order against the remaining spouse if the landlord has contracted to re-let or sell the property on the basis of the notice. Therefore, where possible, the spouse should inform the landlord of her/his intention to remain. Otherwise, the landlord would have to seek possession by using one of the other specific Rent Act cases (as for statutory tenancies, below).

7.15 (Protected) statutory tenancy – sole tenant's notice to quit

• Where the statutory tenant gives notice and either does not leave or the non-tenant spouse remains, the statutory tenancy is preserved (because the requirement for residence is fulfilled)

Sch 15 RA77
• The landlord would have to seek possession by using one of the specific Rent Act cases. As for protected contractual tenants, if the spouse does not inform the landlord of her/his intention to remain, then the landlord may be able to use case 5 if s/he has contracted to re-let or sell the property on the basis of the notice. However, this is a discretionary ground and the court must consider it reasonable to award possession

para 7.16
s3 PEA77
• A landlord is not required to serve notice to quit on a statutory tenant and can therefore apply directly to the court claiming possession. A possession order will only be granted if the court is satisfied that one of the cases for possession applies, and, if it is a discretionary case, that it is reasonable to make the order. This means that the non-tenant spouse is likely to be able to remain whilst the marriage is in existence. After divorce, the non-tenant former spouse is in exactly the same position as a non-tenant former cohabitant (see 8.9).

7.16 Tenancies/licences with basic protection – sole tenant/licensee's notice to quit

• Notice to quit by the tenant/licensee will normally end a tenancy or licence with basic protection (except for a fixed-term tenancy/licence where it is necessary for there to be a break clause in the agreement). The remaining spouse will have no legal status

s3 PEA77
• Tenancies or licences with basic protection are covered by the Protection from Eviction Act; therefore the landlord must obtain a court order for possession to evict the spouse. No grounds need to be proved.

7.17 Excluded occupancies – sole tenant/licensee's notice to quit

- Notice will normally end an excluded tenancy or licence unless there is a fixed-term contract, in which case a break clause is needed

- Excluded tenancies or licences are not covered by the Protection from Eviction Act, and therefore the landlord is not legally obliged to get a court order to recover possession.

s3A PEA77

Physical force to evict may still constitute an offence so that if the occupier remains constantly on the premises, the landlord must obtain a court order for possession.[4] The claim is a possession claim against trespassers.

s6 CLA77

CPR 55.1(b)

THE SOLE TENANT LEAVES OR DISAPPEARS

When a marriage breaks down, a tenant may simply leave or disappear and give no indication of what s/he intends to do about the tenancy. The act of leaving cannot of itself be deemed to be a surrender of a tenancy: an unequivocal act by the tenant is necessary and there must be an intention to end the tenancy (see 6.29).

Leaving does not therefore necessarily end the tenancy and the non-tenant spouse will normally have a right to continue to occupy by virtue of matrimonial home rights, where s/he occupies as if s/he were the tenant. This must not be confused with the situation where the tenant gives notice to quit (see above).

The following information applies as long as the matrimonial home rights last, ie, for as long as the marriage is in existence (unless extended by the courts). For the non-tenant's position after divorce, see Chapter 8.

7.18 Secure and introductory tenancies – sole tenant leaves

Non-tenant spouse has a right to remain – the tenancy continues.
If the sole tenant has left, matrimonial home rights mean that occupation by the spouse fulfils the tenancy condition of occupying as the only or principal home, and the secure or introductory tenancy continues whilst the marriage exists.

> ### *Lambeth LBC v Moseley*[5]
>
> *The tenant left after matrimonial breakdown, leaving her husband in possession. The council served a notice to quit, addressed to the tenant, and brought an originating application for possession under CCR Order 24 (now CPR 55).*
>
> *continued overleaf*

---

4. Bristol Corporation v Persons Unknown (1974) 1 All ER 593.

5. Lambeth LBC v Moseley (1996) 1 August Lambeth County Court.

> The case was dismissed – occupation by the spouse fulfils the
> condition to occupy and the tenancy therefore remained secure.
> A landlord's notice to quit could not terminate the tenancy.

The landlord would have to go through the usual possession procedure of
serving a notice seeking possession and proving a ground for possession
in order to obtain a possession order, after which s/he should apply for a
warrant, which must be enforced by a bailiff if the occupier has not left.

7.19 Assured tenancy – sole tenant leaves

Fixed-term tenancies

Non-tenant spouse has a right to remain – the assured tenancy continues
If the sole assured tenant has left, matrimonial home rights mean that
occupation by the spouse fulfils the assured tenancy condition of
occupying as the only or principal home, and the assured tenancy
continues whilst the marriage exists.

s7(6) & Sch 2
HA88

The landlord would have to serve notice seeking possession on the
tenant and, as it is still within the fixed term, the landlord can use only
a limited number of possession grounds to claim possession, mainly,
but not exclusively, those where the tenant is in some way at fault, eg,
arrears or breach of tenancy. There would also need to be a clause in
the agreement allowing for action to be taken during the fixed term.

Periodic tenancies

Non-tenant spouse has a right to remain – the assured tenancy continues
As for the fixed-term assured above, if the sole assured tenant has left,
matrimonial home rights mean that occupation by the spouse fulfils
the assured tenancy condition, and the assured tenancy continues
whilst the marriage exists.

s7(1) & Sch 2
HA88

The landlord would have to serve notice seeking possession on the
tenant and would need to prove one of the specified grounds for
possession in order to obtain a possession order and follow the
procedure as in 7.18

7.20 Assured shorthold tenancies – sole tenant leaves

Fixed term

The position is the same as for assured fixed term tenants.

Periodic

Although the tenancy continues, as for assured tenants, because of the
limited security of an assured shorthold periodic tenant, it is relatively

easy for a landlord to gain possession and evict the partner once any fixed term ends. All s/he need do is serve the correct notice on the tenant (a minimum of two months' which must end on the last day of the period of the tenancy) and obtain a court order. No grounds for possession need be proved. The accelerated possession procedure means that a possession order could be made without a hearing. The usual possession procedure must be followed (see 7.18).

s21(4)(a) HA88

For tenancies which started on or after 28 February 1997, it is not necessary for the initial tenancy to be fixed term, but possession cannot be ordered under the assured shorthold ground until six months have elapsed since the commencement of the initial tenancy.

CPR 55 Part II
s21 HA88

7.21 Protected contractual tenancies – sole tenant leaves

Non-tenant spouse has a right to remain – the protected tenancy continues
Protected contractual tenancies continue as long as the contract is in existence, regardless of whether the tenant is living in the dwelling or not. If the tenant leaves, the non-tenant spouse has a right to continue to occupy both by virtue of the contract still being in existence and also by virtue of matrimonial home rights.

A contract may be written or verbal, and can be ended either by expiry of a fixed-term contract or exercise of a break clause, or, where the tenancy is periodic, by the landlord or tenant serving notice to quit, or a notice of increase of rent being served which would meet the notice requirements for a notice to quit (see 6.31).

Even if the contractual tenancy is brought to an end, the tenancy itself does not end, but simply becomes a statutory tenancy (see below), so that the non-tenant spouse still has a right to continue to occupy by virtue of matrimonial home rights whilst the marriage exists.

s49(5) RA77

7.22 (Protected) statutory tenancies – sole tenant leaves

Non-tenant spouse has a right to remain – the statutory tenancy continues
A statutory tenancy is a personal right to remain which arises after a protected contractual tenancy has ended. If the sole statutory tenant has left, matrimonial home rights mean that occupation by the spouse fulfils the requirement that the tenant occupies the dwelling as her/his residence, and the statutory tenancy continues whilst the marriage exists.

Although the landlord does not have to serve notice to quit on a statutory tenant, s/he would need to prove one of the specified cases (or grounds) for possession in order to obtain a possession order and follow the usual possession procedure (see 7.18).

s3(4) RA77

Sch 15 RA77

7.23 Tenancies or licences with basic protection

Fixed-term tenancy/licence

Non-tenant/licensee has a right to remain
– the tenancy/licence continues

If the sole tenant/licensee leaves, the remaining partner, whether still married or not, has a right to remain during the fixed term. Unless there is a break clause, the landlord would have to show that there had been a breach of the tenancy conditions, or wait until the fixed term expired to recover possession. No notice to quit is required at the end of a fixed term.

As a tenancy/licence with basic protection is covered by the Protection from Eviction Act, the landlord would have to obtain a court order for s3 PEA77 possession, but no grounds for possession are needed. The usual possession procedure must be followed (see 7.18).

Periodic tenancy/licence

Non-tenant licensee can remain whilst the tenancy/licence continues

If the sole tenant/licensee leaves, the remaining spouse can stay whilst the tenancy/licence continues. The landlord/licensor would have to serve notice to quit on the original tenant/licensee and, because an occupancy with basic protection is covered by the Protection from Eviction Act, the landlord would have to obtain a court order for s3 PEA77 possession. No grounds for possession are required. The usual possession procedure must be followed (see 7.18).

7.24 Excluded occupancies – sole tenant/licensee leaves

Contractual tenancy/licence

Non-tenant/licensee spouse can remain whilst the
tenancy/licence is in existence

Where there is a contract, eg, the occupier pays rent or other 'consideration' to the owner/licensor in return for permission to occupy and the sole tenant/licensee leaves, the spouse has matrimonial home rights to remain as long as the contract still exists.

For periodic tenants, the landlord would have to give notice equal in length to the period of tenancy. This could vary from as little as one day where rent is paid a day at a time to a month or longer. 'Reasonable notice' is all that is required for an excluded licence. If there is a clause in the contract referring to notice, then for both tenants and licensees it will be necessary to comply with this (see 6.31 and 6.32 for more information on notice to quit and determining licences).

If there were a fixed-term contract, then this would continue until the end of the term, unless there is a break clause.

Excluded tenancies or licences are not covered by section 3 of the Protection from Eviction Act, and therefore the landlord is not legally obliged to get a court order to recover possession. Once the contract has been ended, the only protection is under the Criminal Law Act 1977 which makes it an offence to use physical force to gain entry to property against the wishes of someone inside. If the occupier remains constantly on the premises, the landlord would have to obtain a court order for possession to avoid the commission of an offence.

s6 CLA77

Non-contractual (bare) licensees

Non-licensee spouse can remain until the licence is brought to an end

Matrimonial home rights to occupy apply only to licences which are contractual. A bare licence will continue until the licensor ends it.

Reasonable notice must be given, although in some cases this will only be a few days. As for contractual occupancies above, there is no legal obligation upon the landlord to obtain a court order to recover possession, but use of physical force constitutes a criminal offence and may give rise to a claim for damages.

Joint tenancies

C   Rights of occupation

7.25   The right to live in the matrimonial home

If a couple are joint tenants, both parties are entitled to live in the home. Neither can legally exclude the other except by court order.

7.26   Rights to occupy of joint tenants

The rights of joint tenants to occupy stem from their legal rights in landlord and tenant law. For this reason no special matrimonial home rights are needed under the Family Law Act 1996 for married couples who both have a legal interest in the home. Both are jointly and separately liable for the full amount of the rent, regardless of who is occupying the home.

7.27   Occupation orders under the Family Law Act 1996

Occupation orders are covered at Chapter 13, Section C.

Joint tenants have the same rights as sole married tenants, sole married owners, joint owners and joint tenant cohabitants to apply for occupation orders. They all qualify as 'entitled persons.'

s33 FLA96

Joint tenants are therefore able to apply for orders declaring or enforcing rights to occupy or to regain entry, if necessary, and also to exclude the other spouse or restrict her/his right to occupy the matrimonial home.

The court may also make provision for payment of an 'occupation rent' to a spouse who is ordered out of the home and they may also make orders imposing liability for repairs, maintenance, rent and other outgoings (see 11.17). It can also make orders granting use of furniture and contents, and orders to take reasonable care of furniture, contents and the home generally (see 13.23).

s40(1)(a) & (b) FLA96
s40(1)(c)-(e) FLA96

D   Long-term settlement of tenancies

7.28 Re-allocation of joint tenancies on relationship breakdown

Both joint tenants have a legal right to occupy the home whilst they remain joint tenants. If legal proceedings are not being taken, it will be necessary to use one of the following methods to either terminate or transfer the tenancy, and with it long-term rent liability:

• Voluntary assignment

• Notice by tenant.

Certain general principles apply to all assignments, regardless of whether they are between married couples or lesbian, gay or heterosexual cohabitants. The following general information is found in Chapter 6 and applies to cohabitants and married couples:

• When a joint tenancy may be assigned (6.15 – 6.14)

• Distinguishing between assignment or new tenancy (6.15)

• What happens to arrears when the tenancy is assigned voluntarily (6.25 onwards)

• The requirements for the sole or joint tenant's notice to quit to be valid (6.31 – 6.33)

• Rights to assign sole and joint tenancies (6.16-24).

NOTICE TO QUIT OR SURRENDER BY ONE JOINT MARRIED TENANT

When a marriage breaks down, one party may decide to give notice to quit to end the tenancy and its liabilities. The other party will obviously want to know whether anything can be done to prevent the tenant serving notice to quit, or, if it has been served, whether the notice to quit actually brings the tenancy to an end. If the tenancy is ended, the remaining partner will also need to know what rights s/he has to remain in the home, and whether s/he has any defence to a possession action (see 7.42).

For information on preventing a tenant from serving notice to quit, see Section E 7.38 – 7.42. The outcome of service of notice to quit differs depending on the type of tenancy. The following sections on notices to quit apply equally to married and cohabiting couples, whether heterosexual or same sex.

7.29 Valid notice to quit

In order for a notice to quit to take effect, it must be valid (see 6.31 – 6.33). It does not need to be served by both joint tenants. In many cases however the stringent requirements for validity are not met, and in this situation the notice will not take effect unless the landlord and all of the joint tenants agree to treat it as valid. Unless this happens the tenancy would continue.

7.30 Surrender

One joint tenant cannot surrender a tenancy (see 6.34). Therefore, unless the landlord and all the joint tenants agree to a surrender, the tenancy will continue.

7.31 Secure and introductory tenancies – one joint tenant's notice to quit

- It is now well established in case law that one joint tenant may end a joint periodic tenancy (ie, one that runs from week to week or month to month, rather than for a fixed term, eg, six months) by unilaterally giving notice to quit. This can be done without the other tenant's knowledge or agreement. See Section E for information on preventing a tenant's notice to quit

- In practice virtually all secure and introductory tenancies are periodic. The practice of encouraging notice to quit from one tenant has become known as the *McGrady* procedure, following the case of the same name.[6] It has been confirmed as a valid legal procedure by a subsequent House of Lords case.[7] However, it has also been established that the procedure is only valid if the tenant has given the correct legal notice (see 6.31 and 6.34)

- If the joint tenancy has been ended by valid notice, the remaining tenant has no legal status and becomes a trespasser. However, the Protection from Eviction Act 1977 means that s/he can only be evicted by court order. In addition, a remaining occupier may have a defence to possession by the landlord under Article 8 of the European Convention on Human Rights (see 7.42).

s3 PEA77

---

6. Greenwich LBC v McGrady (1983) 6 HLR 36 CA.

7. Hammersmith and Fulham LBC v Monk (1992) 24 HLR 206 HL; Barnet LBC v Smith (1990) 23 HLR 114 CA.

- This notice procedure can be used when the couple cannot agree about who should have the tenancy and one party wishes to remove the other. This device is often used in cases involving domestic violence.

Despite the fact that the Family Law Act 1996 now gives cohabitants and divorcees rights to apply for a transfer of tenancy, court proceedings can be costly and the notice to quit procedure offers a cheap, quick and relatively easy solution. Nevertheless, it is a potentially disastrous situation for the partner who wants to remain in occupation, and advisers should take care to advise clients to take early action to prevent a notice to quit, if there is a possibility that the other tenant may serve notice to quit, whether to end her/his own liability, or possibly out of spite (see 7.41)

There are still no court powers to transfer tenancies between non-divorcing couples without children (unless judicial separation is applied for), nor for lesbian or gay couples, who may therefore also need to make use of the '*McGrady*' procedure (see 6.34)

- It is not possible for one joint tenant to unilaterally end a joint tenancy during a fixed term.

The following points about the *McGrady* procedure should, however, be noted:

- Whilst this procedure is now common practice in many local authorities, it is crucial that the tenant serving notice gains an assurance in writing from the local authority that it will rehouse or re-grant the tenancy to her/him in her/his sole name; if this is not done, the tenant could run the risk of becoming homeless and possibly being deemed 'intentionally homeless' (see 14.12). Some local authorities also have relationship breakdown policies, which may mean their allocation policies are framed to allow them to grant a smaller unit of accommodation to the other party as well (see 16.25)

- There have been findings of maladministration against local authorities who have complied with this procedure without informing the tenant who is to be dispossessed[8] (see 16.28)

- The landlord must consider whether there is justification for interfering with the remaining partner's Article 8 human rights (right to respect for a home) before seeking possession (see 7.42).

A deserted joint tenant is very vulnerable since the departed tenant could end the tenancy, even if the partner wishes to stay. There are some options available to prevent notice to quit being served, (see 7.41), but if notice has already been served and the tenancy ended, then the only possibility is to try to persuade the landlord authority to grant a new tenancy.

8. Complaint against Hackney LBC Omb 88/A/979.

7.32 Assured and assured shorthold tenancies – one joint tenant's notice to quit

Fixed-term tenancies

- Notice by one joint tenant is insufficient to operate a break clause to end a fixed-term assured tenancy (see 6.34). The joint tenant can therefore remain.

Periodic tenancies

- The tenancy ends (as discussed under secure tenancies above)

- The remaining spouse has no legal status. Because assured tenancies are not covered by section 3 of the Protection from Eviction Act 1977, the landlord is not legally obliged to get a court order to recover possession

s6 CLA77

CPR 55.1(b)

- Physical force to evict will constitute a criminal offence, so that if the occupier remains constantly on the premises, the landlord would have to obtain a court order for possession to avoid the commission of an offence. The claim is a possession claim against trespassers

- Joint assured tenants are therefore extremely vulnerable and dependent upon the landlord's goodwill if the partner serves a valid notice to quit.

7.33 Protected contractual tenancies – one joint tenant's notice to quit

Fixed-term tenancies

- The principle is as for assured tenancies above – both joint tenants must give notice during a fixed term, but they cannot require the landlord to agree to end the tenancy before the end of the fixed term, except in accordance with a break clause.

Periodic tenancies

s2(1)(a) RA77

- If one joint tenant gives notice, this ends the contractual tenancy and that tenant's liability for rent; the remaining tenant becomes the sole statutory tenant. One tenant cannot in effect terminate the other joint tenant's right to occupy.

Case 5 Sch 15 RA77

- The landlord should be alerted to the tenant's intention to remain, since a tenant's service of notice to quit may lead to a ground for possession against a protected tenant. This is a discretionary ground and the court would have to consider it reasonable to grant an order (see 7.14).

7.34 (Protected) statutory tenancies – one joint tenant's notice to quit

- Valid notice to quit by one joint tenant converts a joint statutory tenancy into a sole statutory tenancy and the other tenant will be able to remain

- As for protected contractual tenancies, notice can give rise to a ground for possession, and the landlord should therefore be informed of the tenant's intention to remain (see 7.15).

Case 5 Sch 15 RA77

7.35 Tenancies/licences with basic protection – one joint tenant/licensee's notice

- Notice to quit by one tenant/licensee will normally end a periodic tenancy or licence with basic protection. The remaining spouse/partner will have no legal status

- Tenancies or licences with basic protection are covered by section 3 of the Protection from Eviction Act therefore the landlord must obtain a court order for possession to evict the spouse/partner but no possession ground need be proved

- Fixed-term tenancies can only be ended during the fixed term if there is a break clause. Therefore notice by one joint tenant will not end the tenancy. A break clause can only be operated by all the joint tenants.

7.36 Excluded occupancies – one joint tenant/licensee's notice

- Notice by one joint occupier will normally end an excluded tenancy or licence, unless it is during a fixed-term contract. In this case a break clause will be needed (which can only be operated by both tenants)

- Excluded tenancies or licences are not covered by section 3 of the Protection from Eviction Act, and therefore the landlord is not legally obliged to get a court order to recover possession

- Physical force to evict will constitute a criminal offence, so that if the occupier remains constantly on the premises, the landlord would have to obtain a court order for possession to avoid the commission of an offence. The procedure is possession against a trespasser.

s6 CLA77
CPR 55.1(b)

ONE JOINT TENANT LEAVES OR DISAPPEARS

This section applies equally to married and cohabiting joint tenants (heterosexual or same sex couples).

7.37 Joint tenant leaves or disappears – the position for different tenants

- *Secure tenancies*: the tenancy remains a joint secure tenancy, since only one of the joint tenants has to occupy in order to satisfy the tenant condition

s81 HA85

s1(1)(b) HA88
- *Assured and assured shorthold tenancies*: as for secure tenancies

- *Protected contractual tenancies*: residence is not necessary to sustain a protected contractual tenancy; therefore it remains a joint protected contractual tenancy

s1 RA77

- *Statutory tenancy*: if one joint tenant ceases to reside in the home and has no intention of returning, it automatically becomes a sole statutory tenancy

s2(1)(a) RA77

- *Tenancies/licences with basic protection*: tenancies/licences with basic protection will continue until they are ended by notice, as there are no residence requirements on the tenant

- *Excluded tenancies/licences*: as for tenancies/licences with basic protection.

Sole and joint tenancies

E Preventing a tenant's notice to quit

7.38 Setting aside dispositions of property

Married couples who are divorcing or seeking a decree of judicial separation or nullity can apply to the court under section 37 of the Matrimonial Causes Act 1973 to 'set aside,' or declare null and void, a 'disposition' of matrimonial assets. An order to set aside transactions for disposal of property can only be granted where it is shown that the third party involved was aware that the disposal was intended to frustrate the spouse's claim to the property in question.

Until the late 1990s, it was thought that this provision could be used to set aside a tenant's notice to quit. A series of important cases have unfortunately ruled that this is not possible. A notice to quit cannot be set aside after it has taken effect (see 7.41). Preventative steps may, however, be possible to forestall the actual service of a tenant spouse's or partner's notice to quit, although the mere existence of a matrimonial injunction, such as an occupation order, will not in itself prevent a notice to quit being served (see 7.41).

7.39 Notice to quit cannot be set aside

In 1998, in the case of *Newlon Housing Trust v Al-Sulaimen,*[9] the House of Lords confirmed that a notice to quit is *not* a disposition and therefore could not be set aside. As the joint tenancy had been terminated by the wife's notice to quit, it could not be revived. The question of whether an order could have been obtained to restrain the ex-wife from giving a notice to quit was left open, but has now been clarified and is discussed below in 7.41

Newlon Housing Trust v Al-Sulaimen and another[10]

The case involved a married couple who were joint periodic assured tenants. The relationship broke down, the wife left and gave notice to quit ending the tenancy. The housing trust brought possession proceedings against the husband, who remained in occupation. He applied for an adjournment because he wished to apply for the tenancy to be transferred to him in matrimonial proceedings.

The House of Lords held that the husband's application could only succeed if the tenancy could be revived, since it had ended six months before, when the notice to quit expired. The court could only revive the tenancy if termination by notice to quit was a 'disposition' of property falling under s.37 MCA 1973. Disposition could include a surrender of a proprietary interest which would cause a tenancy to merge in reversion or remainder. However, when a tenancy terminated by the passage of time (ie, the period of the tenancy reached an end) there was no 'disposition' of the tenant's interest. The tenancy ceased to exist and the landlord became entitled to possession by virtue of his own interest and not by acquiring the tenant's interest. This applied to both fixed-term and periodic tenancies.

The notice indicated that the tenant was not willing to consent to the continuation of the tenancy beyond the date when it would otherwise expire by passage of time. The tenancy having expired, it could not be revived, and Mr Al-Sulaimen had no defence to the claim for possession.

7.40 Setting aside a surrender

Although notices to quit cannot be set aside, can a non-tenant spouse do anything if the tenant spouse simply surrenders the tenancy to the landlord? (see 6.29). In the case of *Newlon Housing Trust v Al-Sulaimen* (see above) the key words spoken by the judge are:

---

9. Newlon Housing Trust v Al-Sulaimen and another (1998) Times 20 August HL.

10. Newlon Housing Trust v Al-Sulaimen, see 9 above.

'The court could only revive the tenancy if termination by notice to quit was a 'disposition' of property falling under s.37 MCA 1973. Disposition could include a surrender of a proprietary interest which would cause a tenancy to merge in reversion or remainder.'

This suggests that in a case where, for example, a sole tenant has simply given the keys back to the landlord to spite the spouse who remains there, saying s/he no longer wants the tenancy, it should be possible to apply for an order under section 37 to set aside the surrender and revive the tenancy, provided it could be shown that the surrender had been done with the intention of preventing the non-tenant making any claim to the tenancy, and that the landlord was aware of this. This has not yet been tested in the courts.

Also, where the landlord is a local authority or RSL, the remaining spouse may be able to argue that seeking possession would be a breach of Article 8 of the European Convention on Human Rights (right to respect for a home) See 7.42.

7.41   Preventing service of a notice to quit

Once a notice to quit has expired, the tenancy cannot be revived (see 7.39). Since a notice to quit cannot be cured, prevention is usually advisable.

In 1997, in the House of Lords' case of *Harrow LBC v Johnstone,*[11] it was held that a matrimonial injunction (now an occupation order) preventing the wife from excluding the husband did not prevent the wife from serving a valid notice to quit. The court also cast doubt on the suggestion that section 37 could be used to set aside a notice to quit, since its power is limited to setting aside a 'disposition' and a notice to quit was unlikely to be held to be a 'disposition.' In *Newlon Housing Trust v Al-Sulaimen,* the House of Lords confirmed that notice to quit was not a disposition and therefore could not be set aside after expiry (see 7.39).

Harrow LBC v Johnstone[12]

Mr and Mrs Johnstone were joint secure (council) tenants. They separated and the husband obtained an order under the Domestic Violence and Matrimonial Proceedings Act 1976 (the current equivalent would be an order under the Family Law Act 1996) that his wife must not 'exclude or attempt to exclude (him) from the (house).' She subsequently gave notice to quit and was rehoused by the council. The council sought possession against the husband. Although the Court of Appeal dismissed the council's claim, the House of Lords found in favour of the Council.

continued overleaf

---

11. Harrow LBC Johnstone (1997) 29 HLR 475;
     1 All ER 929 HL.   12. Harrow LBC v Johnstone ibid.

> The wife had not been in contempt of the earlier order when she gave notice. The earlier order was not made in connection with an application for property relief. It was concerned with the husband's rights of occupancy under the tenancy, not with future continuance of the tenancy itself. The question raised was: 'Did the requirement that the wife should not 'exclude or attempt to exclude' the husband from the house prohibit her from notifying the council that the tenancy would not be renewed?' Lord Mustill said:
>
> 'It is in my view absolutely plain that the prohibition against excluding the husband was not intended to be a mandatory order requiring the wife to co-operate in maintaining in force the rights created by the joint tenancy pending the adjustment of those rights on a future date in proceedings not yet started. The application was made at a time of crisis when the husband had been locked out of the house and wanted to get back in. His concern was that his wife had excluded him from the exercise of the rights of occupation which he undoubtedly possessed under the joint tenancy. There is no sign in the documents of an apprehension on his part that the rights themselves were under threat and would require protection by an order requiring the wife to keep the tenancy in being. If the court was to grant something on the lines of a mandatory Mareva-like injunction (now a 'freezing order') the first step was to ask for one. This the husband did not do. Instead he invited the court to make an order designed to ensure that the molestation of which she was accused did not happen again. The Domestic Violence and Matrimonial Proceedings Act 1976 was the right vehicle for such an order... As such it was concerned with the exercise of rights under the tenancy and not with the continued existence of the rights themselves.'

However, if divorce or other relevant proceedings are under way, an injunction may be sought *before service of notice to quit* to preserve the integrity of the proceedings: eg, to prevent the tenancy being terminated before the court can decide whether to transfer it or not. Section 37 of s37(2) (a) MCA73 the Matrimonial Causes Act 1973 allows the court to make injunctions when the respondent is about to 'deal with' any property. In the important Court of Appeal case of *Bater v Greenwich LBC*,[13] the judge suggested that in dealing with relationship breakdown cases, advisers should take early steps to guard against notices to quit by seeking to obtain an injunction under section 37 (if divorcing) or under the inherent jurisdiction of the court in family proceedings. For unmarried couples with children, injunctions could be obtained under the Children Act 1989 or wardship jurisdiction.

13. Bater v Greenwich LBC (1999) 4 All ER 944; EGCS 111 CA.

Although the judge did not suggest it, there seems no reason why a court could not also grant an injunction to preserve the integrity of proceedings, together with an application for a transfer of tenancy under the Family Law Act 1996 (see 7.47 – 7.49). Advisers must be aware of the need to act promptly to obtain an injunction.

Summary of action to prevent notice to quit

It may be possible to obtain an injunction to prevent a tenant serving a notice to quit by seeking an injunction either:

- under s.37 of the Matrimonial Causes Act 1973 in divorce, nullity or judicial separation proceedings. It is necessary to show that the spouse has an intention to deal with a property to frustrate the other spouse's claim to it, or

- together with some form of family proceedings under the Children Act 1989, or

- under the jurisdiction of the court in wardship proceedings, or

- possibly (but not yet confirmed) together with an application for a transfer of tenancy under the Family Law Act 1996.

Bater v Greenwich LBC[14]

A notice to terminate a joint tenancy cannot be set aside by a court under s37 of the Matrimonial Causes Act 1973 even where it is served unilaterally and extinguishes the other party's right to buy.

The husband and wife occupied the matrimonial property under a joint tenancy. After the couple agreed to buy the matrimonial property from the local authority under the right to buy provisions, but before the purchase was completed, the wife terminated the joint tenancy of the matrimonial property. The husband sought to set aside the termination of the joint tenancy on the basis that it was a reviewable disposition of property. The judge ruled that the right to buy was not property, and that service of notice was not a disposition of property and therefore the court had no jurisdiction to set it aside. The tenancy had come to an end and could not be revived.

However, it was possible for a court, acting either under the powers given by the Matrimonial Causes Act 1973 or its inherent jurisdiction, to restrain a spouse from unilaterally terminating a tenancy in these circumstances. If joint tenants were not married but had children, the powers contained in the Children Act 1989 or inherent in the wardship jurisdiction could be used.

continued overleaf

---

14. Bater v Greenwich LBC (1999), see 13 above.

> *The judge warned practitioners of the need to protect a joint tenancy from unilateral termination between the date of separation and the date of determination of the application for transfer, whether or not there were children and whether or not a right to buy was involved. In any situation where the unilateral act of one was capable in law of destroying the interests of both, steps should be taken to protect the interest of the joint tenant who would be prejudiced by the service of notice to terminate.*

After service but before expiry of notice to quit

If a notice to quit has been served but has not yet expired, it is unclear whether an injunction could be sought to prevent it taking effect. It seems unlikely since case law has established that a notice to quit, once served, operates automatically and cannot be withdrawn. Neither can the landlord and tenant revoke or waive it, even if they are prepared to agree to do so. All they can do is create a new tenancy on the old terms.[15]

7.42   Human rights after notice to quit

If a notice to quit has been served by one joint secure or assured tenant, the tenancy will come to an end, and the landlord can seek possession against the remaining occupier (see 7.31 – 7.32). In *Harrow LBC v Qazi*,[16] the Court of Appeal was asked to consider whether the person remaining had any defence under Article 8(1) of the European Convention on Human Rights, ie, right to respect for her/his private and family life, home and correspondence. Even though the occupier had no legal or equitable interest in the house which he had occupied for 7 years prior to the notice to quit, the Court of Appeal said that the relevant question was whether the property in question was a residence with which the occupier had sufficient and continuing links, and in this case, in answer to the question, this was plainly his home. It was therefore necessary for the court to decide whether the council was justified in seeking possession in accordance with Article 8(2).

Article 8(2) sets out the conditions upon which the State may interfere with the right to a home. These are based on the assumption that there will be no interference with the right except as:

• is in accordance with the law, and

• is necessary in a democratic society, based on either it being:

• in the interests of national security, public safety or the economic well-being of the country, or

15. Clarke v Grant (1950) 1 KB 104.   16. Harrow LBC v Qazi [2001] EWCA Civ 1834 CA.

- for the prevention of crime and disorder, or

- for the protection of health or morals, or

- for the protection of the rights and freedoms of others.

At the time of writing, the case was due to be heard in the House of Lords. In other cases,[17] compliance with rules laid down by statutory schemes such as the Housing Acts and the Protection from Eviction Act 1977 which allow the landlord to recover possession with a court order, has been held not to breach Article 8 provided that the landlord has acted fairly and reasonably in conformity with the scheme. In *Royal Borough of Kensington and Chelsea v O'Sullivan*[18] the judge implied that where possession proceedings were taken in accordance with the law, the court would only be required to consider Article 8(2) if there were 'exceptional circumstances.' However, this was a case concerning a notice to quit by a sole tenant, and it is possible that different issues may be raised in *Harrow LBC v Qazi*.[19] Advisors should check the outcome of this important case and in the meantime, it would be advisable to consider assisting clients to seek an injunction to prevent a notice to quit, (see 7.41) where appropriate, rather than rely on Article 8 rights as a defence to possession after notice to quit has been served.

F   The courts' powers to transfer tenancies

7.43   The courts' powers to transfer sole and joint tenancies between married couples

If assignment is not possible or the couple cannot agree, the court can decide who should have the tenancy, in conjunction with proceedings for divorce, judicial separation or nullity.

7.44   Transferring a tenancy under the Matrimonial Causes Act 1973

This can be done by applying for a property adjustment order in conjunction with divorce, nullity or judicial separation proceedings, exactly as for owner-occupied property (see Chapter 4, Section F). This procedure applies to any tenancy which counts as 'property.'

The same considerations as for owner-occupiers (see 4.32) must be taken into account by the courts when deciding who gets the tenancy. The matter is, therefore, far from straightforward, and although it frequently turns out to be the case, one should not assume that a woman with children will automatically be granted the tenancy.

17. Sheffield City Council v Smart [2002] HLR 639 CA; Michalak v LB Wandsworth [2002] 4 All ER 1136; R v Bracknell Forest BC ex parte McLellan [2001] 33 HLR 36 CA.

18. Royal Borough of Kensington and Chelsea v O'Sullivan [2003] EWCA Civ 371 CA.

19. Harrow LBC v Qazi, see 16 above.

7.45 Procedure for transferring a tenancy under the Matrimonial Causes Act 1973

The courts can order the transfer of any property (see below). The tenant is ordered to transfer the tenancy to the other spouse by way of a deed of assignment after the court order. Under the Matrimonial Causes Act, the court's order does not bring about the assignment. The tenants themselves must ensure that a deed of assignment is executed or the tenancy will not be legally assigned (see 6.14).[20]

A prohibition against assignment does not prevent the court from ordering one, since an assignment can still be effected, but it may create a breach of tenancy conditions. In such cases, the court is likely to take such a prohibition into consideration and may be reluctant to make an order where it would constitute a clear breach of the terms of the tenancy.

Chapter 6 explains which tenancies can be assigned and, if there is a right to assign, whether it is qualified or unconditional.

7.46 Tenancies which count as property

A tenancy constitutes property if it is a legal interest in land capable of assignment.[21] This means that virtually all tenancies count, except statutory (protected) tenancies, which cannot be assigned. Licences do not count.

7.47 Using the Family Law Act to transfer non-assignable tenancies

Since statutory tenancies are not capable of assignment, they cannot be transferred under the Matrimonial Causes Act. Other tenancies may have prohibitions against assignment which can complicate matters. The provisions of the Family Law Act grant the court additional powers to circumvent this problem.

s53 & Sch 7 FLA96

The Act allows the courts, during divorce, nullity or judicial separation proceedings and until remarriage, to vest 'relevant' tenancies (see below) in one of the partners, rather than ordering the tenant to transfer it. 'Vesting' differs from assignment in that the order of the court effectively brings about the transfer of the tenancy from one spouse to another, as if it were a conveyance. No deed of assignment is necessary when the court orders the tenancy to be vested in the other spouse.

para 4 Sch 7 FLA96

The provisions on transfer apply only to a tenancy of property which actually was the matrimonial home and not to a tenancy of property which was only intended to be the matrimonial home.

There are specific criteria as to who gets the tenancy. These differ from

20. Crago v Julian (1991) 24 HLR 306 CA.

21. Hale v Hale (1975) 1 WLR 931; Thompson v Thompson (1976) Fam 25, (1975) 2 WLR 868.

those laid down by the Matrimonial Causes Act. The court also has power to award compensation where a tenancy is transferred. Which proceedings are the most appropriate should therefore be carefully considered in cases where there is clearly a choice (ie, secure and protected contractual tenancies).

7.48 Tenancies which the court may transfer under the Family Law Act 1996

Sch 7 Pt 1, para 1 FLA96 Only 'relevant' tenancies may be transferred by the court. These are tenancies which are:

- secure under the Housing Act 1985
- protected or statutory Rent Act 1977
- statutory under the Rent (Agriculture) Act 1976
- assured or assured agricultural occupancies under the Housing Act 1988.

7.49 The courts' criteria for transferring (vesting) tenancies under the Family Law Act

The court must consider all the circumstances, including:

- the circumstances in which the tenancy was granted to one or both of the parties (how they became tenants)
- respective housing needs and housing resources
- respective financial resources
- likely effect on health, safety and well-being of the two parties and of any child

para 5 Sch 7 FLA96 • the respective suitability of the parties as tenants.

Additional criteria apply for cohabitants (see 8.19).

Since the court must consider the circumstances in which the tenancy was granted, it is clearly relevant if one person was the original tenant and had lived there for some time before her/his spouse, eg, as a result of having succeeded to the tenancy. The ability of each spouse to afford alternative accommodation and whether s/he would qualify for full housing benefit will also be taken into consideration (see the case of *B v M* at 8.19).

Compensation

As mentioned above, the Act also allows the court to order the spouse or cohabitant to whom the tenancy is transferred to pay compensation

para 10 Sch 7
FLA96

to the other. If the court decides to award compensation, it may also direct that:

- payment of the compensation be deferred until a specific date or until some specific event occurs (eg, remarriage, cohabitation, moving home etc.) or

- the compensation be paid in instalments.

The court must not use these provisions unless immediate payment would cause the person who has to make the payment, ie, the new tenant, greater financial hardship than the other party would suffer by having the payment deferred or paid in instalments. The directions can be varied at a later date by application to the court.

When deciding on compensation, the court must have regard to all the circumstances, including:

- the financial loss that would be suffered by the person losing the tenancy

- the financial needs and resources of the parties

- the financial obligations which the parties have or are likely to have in the foreseeable future, including financial obligations to each other and any children.

7.50 Landlord's objections to a transfer of tenancy

para 14(1)
Sch 7 FLA96

If the court is considering ordering a transfer of tenancy under the Family Law Act, it must give the landlord an opportunity to be heard. This does not appear to mean that the landlord has the right to veto the transfer, although presumably the court will take the landlord's view into consideration when deciding whether to order a transfer of tenancy.

7.51 When transfers can be effected

For spouses, the courts technically have power to either order a transfer or vest the tenancy (when proceedings for divorce, nullity or judicial separation are taken) at any time up to remarriage, using either the Matrimonial Causes Act 1973 or the Family Law Act 1996, as appropriate. The order cannot take effect before the decree absolute or the decree of nullity or judicial separation is granted. Under the Family Law Act, at the time of the order, the tenancy must be a relevant tenancy, ie, secure, assured, protected, statutory, or a statutory agricultural tenancy or assured agricultural occupancy (see 7.48).

However, for most tenancies it is advisable that the matter is dealt with before decree absolute, and for protected tenancies it is likely to be crucial. As explained in Chapter 6, sole secure and assured tenancies will become tenancies with basic protection if the tenant does not remain in occupation of the dwelling to fulfil the tenant condition, and Rent Act statutory tenancies will cease. Whilst the marriage exists, the non-tenant spouse can fulfil the tenant condition, as s/he occupies as if s/he were the tenant. After decree absolute, the matrimonial home rights given by the Family Law Act no longer exist, unless specifically extended beyond decree absolute by the court.

Applications for orders extending rights should wherever possible be made before decree absolute, in order to maintain the status of the tenancy. Without such extension rights, if the sole tenant is no longer using the dwelling as a main home, secure and assured tenancies become tenancies with basic protection and statutory tenancies cease to exist (see *Lewis v Lewis*).

Lewis v Lewis[22]

Mr and Mrs Lewis lived in private rented accommodation where Mr Lewis was the sole tenant. The five year lease had expired and the contractual tenancy became a statutory tenancy. Mr Lewis left and Mrs Lewis remained in occupation, paying the rent. Three years later they were divorced, but no application for a tenancy transfer was made in conjunction with proceedings.

After a further three years, the landlords discovered Mr Lewis's departure and took proceedings for possession, claiming Mrs Lewis was not the tenant. Mrs Lewis applied for and was granted an order under the Matrimonial Homes Act 1983 (now the Family Law Act 1996), transferring the tenancy to her.

The landlords appealed and the Court of Appeal held that the Matrimonial Homes Act did not have retrospective effect, ie, to win back possession from the landlord, and even if it did have retrospective effect, the statutory tenancy must subsist at the date of application of transfer.

Mrs Lewis appealed to the House of Lords which dismissed the appeal because a statutory tenancy must exist at the date when application is made for a transfer. The House of Lords did not consider whether Mrs Lewis's continued occupation and payment of rent after decree absolute should have entitled her to the statutory tenancy.

The position with secure and assured tenancies is different from Rent Act 1977 statutory tenancies, and the court has held[23] that it is possible

22. Lewis v Lewis (1985) 17 HLR 459 HL (1985) 2 All ER 449.   23. Gay v Enfield LBC (1999) 31 HLR 1126 CA.

for a non-tenant cohabitant or former spouse to apply for an occupation order effectively to 'revive' the secure or assured status of the tenancy, therefore making it possible also to apply for a transfer of the tenancy, provided the tenancy has not been brought to an end by the tenant or landlord's notice to quit. See 8.3 for a discussion of this procedure and the case of *Gay v Enfield LBC*.

7.52 Arrears, rent liability and possession orders when a transfer is ordered under the Family Law Act 1996

Where a transfer is made under the Family Law Act, the statute gives the court powers to make directions about liabilities and obligations of the tenancy.

The Act states that:

para 7(1)(a) Sch 7 FLA96
- all the rights of the tenancy are transferred, but subject to all covenants, obligations and liabilities

para 7(1)(b) Sch 7 FLA96
- if the tenancy had been assigned to the outgoing spouse, the new sole tenant takes on the same liabilities and is bound by any covenant to indemnify the assignor

para 7(2) SCH 7 FLA96
- the outgoing tenant cannot have any obligation or liability of the tenancy due on or after the date of transfer enforced against her/him. In other words, the outgoing tenant could not be held responsible for any arrears which accrue after the tenancy has been transferred.

para 11 Sch 7 FLA96
The court may also make an order directing that both spouses are jointly responsibly for any arrears or other liabilities existing at the date of the order, although it could alternatively order that one partner indemnifies the other against any such payment of liabilities.

Transfers of property subject to a possession order

Where there is a possession order in existence at the time of a transfer under the Family Law Act the tenancy will remain subject to the order even after the transfer.[24] However, if the tenancy is a sole tenancy it will not be possible to enforce the order against the new tenant, as it will not be in her/his name, and so the landlord will need to start new possession proceedings against the new tenant in order to repossess on breach of the existing order.

If the tenant has difficulties keeping to the terms of the suspended order it is always possible to apply to the courts for a variation.

7.53 Arrears on assignment under Matrimonial Causes Act 1973

This is covered in 6.25 onwards

---

24. Church Commissioners for England v Al-Emarah (1996) EGCS 88 CA.

7.54   Courts' powers to transfer tenancies under the Children Act

The courts' general powers to order transfer of property between non-divorcing couples with children are explained in Chapter 9 and see also 8.18.

Chapter 8: Cohabiting tenants

Subjects covered in this chapter include...

Sole tenancies

What short-term rights cohabiting tenants and non-tenants have to live in the family home

How to apply for an occupation order to preserve tenancy status

What effect a tenant's notice to quit or surrender has on the tenancy

What happens if a tenant leaves or disappears

Joint tenancies

Points to note when applying for an occupation order

Sole and joint tenancies

How to prevent a tenant serving notice to quit

What powers the courts have to transfer tenancies

Cohabiting tenants

This chapter concentrates on the rights of cohabiting tenants when their relationship breaks down. Short-term rights to occupy the shared home are covered by the Family Law Act 1996, although lesbian or gay partners who have no legal rights in the home cannot make use of the provisions (see 8.2).

Cohabiting couples, whether lesbian, gay or heterosexual, will have to resolve the long-term tenancy situation in one of the following ways:

Heterosexual cohabitants with a child of the relationship

Either by housing law or court order for transfer of the tenancy for the benefit of the child under the provisions of the Children Act 1989 (see Chapter 9) or by transfer of tenancy under the Family Law Act 1996.

Heterosexual cohabitants with no children or no children of the relationship

Housing law or by transfer of tenancy under the Family Law Act 1996.

Lesbian and gay couples

The only avenue open is to use housing law, as between any two sharers, although in exceptional cases where a child is involved, the provisions of the Children Act 1989 may be relevant (see 9.14).

The different types of tenancy are described in Chapter 6.

Sole tenancies

A   Establishing the short-term right to occupy the home

Before October 1997, the rights of cohabiting couples to occupy the shared home stemmed largely from the principles of housing law, ie, whether it is a joint or sole tenancy or licence and what type of tenancy or licence it is. Since October 1997, the Family Law Act 1996 allows some cohabitants to apply for an occupation order granting or enforcing rights to occupy. However, there is still no automatic right to occupy for a non-tenant, since occupation orders are always subject to the court's discretion.

This section looks at the position for the non-tenant cohabitant in rented property or property occupied under licence only.

8.1   The right to live in the family home

Cohabitants have no special automatic rights to occupy by virtue of their relationship: this is true of lesbian and gay couples as well as heterosexual couples. If the partner is the tenant, status is normally that of a bare licensee, ie, s/he is entitled to remain there only as long as the tenant gives permission. If the tenant wishes the partner to leave, all that is legally required is 'reasonable notice.' Once the notice expires, the non-tenant cohabitant becomes a trespasser.

8.2 Occupation orders for cohabitants, former cohabitants and former spouses

The Family Law Act 1996 gives cohabitants in certain circumstances the right to apply for occupation orders. Chapter 13, Section C covers occupation orders in detail.

The Family Law Act distinguishes between 'entitled' persons and those who have no entitlement to occupy the home. To be 'entitled,' it is necessary to have either:

- a legal (or beneficial) interest in the property in question (ie, to be a tenant or joint tenant), or

- matrimonial home rights in respect of the property in question, or

- a contractual or statutory right to remain, eg, rights not to be evicted without a court order under the Protection from Eviction Act 1977.

s33 FLA96 An entitled person may apply for an occupation order against any 'associated person,' which includes relatives and sharers (see 13.20 for a definition of 'associated persons'). Same sex partners who are joint tenants are 'entitled persons' and may therefore apply for occupation orders against their partners.

Neither a non-tenant cohabitant nor a divorced non-tenant will normally be 'entitled' within the meaning of the Family Law Act, since s/he will normally be sharing accommodation with the partner and will therefore be an excluded occupier. Exceptions would be:

1. In the case of a divorced person, where her/his matrimonial home rights have been extended by court order beyond divorce, s/he would retain matrimonial home rights for the duration of the order and would therefore remain an entitled person, or

2. Where the person has reached a contractual arrangement with a sole tenant ex-partner to remain in what was the shared home, but s/he no longer shares any accommodation with the tenant. In this case s/he could be a tenant or licensee with basic protection (see 6.10) and hence an entitled person.

However, a heterosexual cohabitant or former spouse who has none of the above legal rights is a non-entitled person and may only apply for an occupation order as against her/his heterosexual partner or former ss35-36 FLA96 spouse. Same sex partners, with no entitlement to occupy, are excluded because the Act defines 'cohabitants' as:

s62(1)(a) FLA96 *'a man and a woman who, although not married to each other are living together as husband and wife'*

As the law stands, same sex couples do not therefore qualify as 'cohabitants' within the definition of the Act, and a non-tenant lesbian or gay partner has no right to apply for an occupation order. In the light of the case of *Mendoza v Ghaidan* (see 2.4), however, there would appear to be no justification for such discrimination, and hopefully the law will be amended to comply with Human Rights before too long.

Nature of the orders available

s35 & s36 FLA96 Occupation orders can grant the right to occupy, or to re-enter if excluded. They can also exclude the other party.

Duration of the order

The length of the occupation order which the court can grant depends upon whether the applicant is a cohabitant, former cohabitant or former spouse and whether s/he has an entitlement to occupy.

s35(10) FLA96 An occupation order for a non-tenant former spouse can only be made for a maximum of six months, but is initially renewable for further periods of six months.

s36(10) FLA96 An occupation order for a non-tenant, heterosexual cohabitant, or former cohabitant, can only be made for a maximum of six months, and is initially renewable once only for a further period of up to six months.

The effect of an occupation order

Whilst the occupation order is in force, the non-tenant cohabitant will have the equivalent of matrimonial home rights in respect of the home s35(13) & (see 7.4):
s36(13) FLA96

- The right to have payments accepted by the landlord as rent (but not the liability for rent unless the court orders it)
- The right for her/his occupation to be treated as occupation by the tenant, thus fulfilling the tenancy conditions for statutory, secure and assured tenancies
- The right to intervene in possession proceedings.

In order to be sure of 'keeping a tenancy alive' once the tenant has left (ie, by fulfilling the tenancy conditions relating to occupation), the non-tenant will need to obtain an occupation order. However, this is a costly procedure if the person is not eligible for public funding. Where there is a possibility that the partner might return, and the regulation of the occupation of the dwelling served a practical purpose, the courts have held[1] that there could be no objection to a non-entitled cohabitant obtaining an occupation order for the purpose of seeking a transfer of tenancy (see 8.3 below). Community legal service funding should therefore be granted if the applicant is eligible (see Appendix A3).

8.3 Applying for an occupation order to preserve tenancy status

A difficulty is met where the non-tenant has no warning that the tenant is going to leave. Can s/he apply for an occupation order after the tenant has left? The court held in the case of *Gay v Enfield LBC*[2] that it was possible to do so. The judge first clarified that it was possible to make a retrospective order to transfer a tenancy:

> *"It cannot be right that only at the very moment of the cesser of cohabitation can the court make a Part II (transfer of tenancy)order... There is no impediment in the lapse of time since cohabitation ceased to Miss Gay applying for a transfer order."*[3]

A number of important points were also clarified:

• Under the Family Law Act, the courts can only order a transfer of a relevant tenancy, ie, an assured, secure or protected tenancy, (see 7.48) for a dwelling which the tenant must still be occupying as an only or principal home or residence

• As the tenant had left, the tenancy was no longer secure, but the tenancy had not been terminated

• In this case Enfield had served a notice to quit at the premises but it was not validly served because personal service had not been achieved (see 6.37)

• The court accepted that if the tenant resumed occupation the tenancy would become secure again. Similarly, if the cohabitant obtained an occupation order, the tenancy regained its secure status and the courts could in principle order a transfer of the tenancy

• An occupation order is therefore a prerequisite to any claim to transfer a tenancy where the tenancy has lost its security

• A transfer of a part interest of a joint tenancy cannot be made to a third party

• An application can only be made where the tenancy has not been ended by either the landlord or the tenant:

> *"What is obvious is the real risk that such a person [non-entitled cohabitant] could be deprived of the opportunity to obtain either order (occupation order or tenancy transfer) by the termination of*

---

1.   Gay v Enfield LBC (1999) 31 HLR 1126, at 1139 CA.
2.   Gay v Enfield LBC, see footnote 1.   3.   Gay v Enfield LBC, see footnote 1 at 1137.

*the tenancy either by the entitled cohabitant or by the landlord at
any time prior to the occupation order being obtained."*[4]

It would therefore seem highly advisable that an injunction to prevent
a notice to quit (see 7.41) should be applied for as soon as possible,
together with an application for an occupation order and a transfer of
the tenancy.

Gay v Enfield LBC[5]

*The court held that a cohabitant cannot apply for a transfer of
tenancy unless it is secure – an occupation order is needed first.*

*A and B were partners and joint tenants. B left and C moved in
to live with A. A then left and C applied for a transfer of A's
interest in the joint tenancy to her.*

The court held

a) *that the tenancy could only be vested under the Family Law Act
if it was secure at the time the transfer was applied for or at
the date the order was to be made. As neither joint tenant was
in occupation and C had not obtained an 'occupation order' to
fulfil the tenancy condition, the tenancy was not secure: ie, to
obtain a transfer once the tenant had left, the cohabitant would
need to obtain an occupation order first. There was no reason
why an order should not be obtained for this purpose.*

Also

b) *even if, in this case, C obtained an occupation order, there is
no power to order a transfer of a part interest in a joint secure
tenancy unless the only joint tenants were the applicant and
the respondent – in this case C was a third party.*

8.4   Circumstances in which the non-tenant cohabitant can be evicted

Eviction by the landlord

If the tenant has left or given notice to quit, the non-tenant cohabitant
may have protection from being evicted by the landlord without a court
order, even where no occupation order is in place (see Section B below).
The degree of protection will depend upon the tenant's residential status.

Eviction by the tenant

In the majority of cases, the non-tenant cohabitant will be sharing
accommodation with the tenant. S/he will therefore be an excluded

---

4.   Gay v Enfield, see footnote 1 at 1136.   5.   Gay v Enfield LBC, see footnote 1

licensee and so not entitled to a court order before eviction. In practice, there is nothing to stop a tenant from removing a partner's belongings and changing the locks.

A heterosexual cohabitant is able to apply for an occupation order, as explained above, which, if granted, would prevent a tenant partner from excluding her/him without a court order, or could reinstate her /him in the home in which they had lived together or intended to live

s36(1-3) FLA96   together. The court could also exclude the tenant partner if appropriate
s36(5) FLA96   (see Chapter 13, Section C).

B   Long-term settlement of tenancies

8.5   Reallocation of tenancy on relationship breakdown

The Family Law Act 1996 gives the court powers to transfer tenancies between heterosexual cohabitants with or without children or between divorcing couples. These powers do not apply in relation to lesbian and gay couples. In any case, the cohabitants may not wish to be involved in court proceedings. It is therefore important to establish certain facts when advising on long-term settlement of tenancies:

• What type of tenancy is it?

• Is the tenancy assignable?

There are three avenues which may alter the tenancy position without resort to the courts, and these are based on housing law principles:

1. *Assignment*: the tenancy may be able to be assigned voluntarily.

2. *Notice or surrender*: the tenant or one of the joint tenants may give notice that s/he wishes to terminate the tenancy, or simply surrender it to the landlord.

3. *Leaving*: the tenant may leave or simply disappear.

Certain general principles apply to all assignments, regardless of whether they are between married couples or lesbian, gay or heterosexual cohabitants. The following general information is found in Chapter 6 and applies to cohabitants and married couples:

• How a tenancy is assigned (6.14)

• Distinguishing between assignment or new tenancy (6.15)

• What happens to arrears when the tenancy is assigned voluntarily (6.25 onwards)

• The requirements for the sole or joint tenant's notice to quit to be valid (6.31 – 6.33)

• Rights to assign, sole and joint tenancies (6.16 – 16.24).

The effects of notice to quit and the tenant leaving in relation to differing types of tenancy are examined separately below.

NOTICE TO QUIT OR SURRENDER BY SOLE COHABITING TENANT

8.6 Notice to quit or surrender – effect on non-tenant

Whilst the tenancy exists and the tenant remains in occupation, the landlord has no right of action against the cohabiting licensee, ie, only the tenant can give the licensee notice. The cohabitant becomes vulnerable once this situation changes.

8.7 Sole cohabiting tenant gives notice to quit or surrenders the tenancy

The situation varies depending on the tenancy. Following the judgment in *Harrow LBC v Johnstone*[6] an occupation order is not enough to prevent a notice to quit (see 7.41). There are no rights to have a notice to quit set aside, nor even a surrender as there may be for married tenants (see 7.40) although an injunction may be obtainable (see 7.41) together with other family proceedings (see 7.41, eg, with an application for the transfer of tenancy under the Children Act (see 9.10), or an application for a transfer of tenancy under the Family Law Act. Such an injunction would make a subsequent notice to quit from the tenant unlawful, as it would be in breach of a court order.

Once a valid notice to quit has been served or a surrender accepted, then, depending on the tenancy, the landlord may be legally obliged to obtain a court order before evicting the cohabiting partner. The position for all tenancies except protected (statutory and contractual) is the same as that for married non-tenants (see 7.12 – 13 and 7.16 – 7.17).

8.8 Protected contractual tenancies – sole tenant's notice to quit

- Tenant's notice to quit ends the contractual tenancy
- If the tenant remains in occupation, the tenancy would continue as a statutory tenancy, depending upon the tenant residing in the home
- If the tenant has gone, no statutory tenancy arises. This is because, unlike the case with married couples, occupation by the non-tenant cohabitant does not count as occupation by the tenant, unless an occupation order is in force
- If a non-tenant cohabitant (heterosexual only) or former spouse obtains an occupation order before a notice to quit is served, s/he gains the right to occupy as if s/he were the tenant. This keeps a statutory tenancy 'alive' as long as the occupation order lasts. This option is not open to lesbian or gay cohabitants

---

6.   Harrow LBC v Johnstone (1997) 29 HLR 475; 1 All ER 929 HL.

- Where there is no occupation order, no court order is legally required to evict the cohabitant, since protected tenancies are not covered by the Protection from Eviction Act 1977; but the Criminal Law Act prevents the use of violence to evict, and therefore a court order should be obtained to avoid a possible criminal offence.

s6 CLA77

8.9 (Protected) statutory tenancies – tenant's notice to quit

- If a statutory tenant gives notice and leaves, the cohabitant will have no right to remain unless an occupation order can be obtained
- If no occupation order is obtained, the landlord would have to obtain a court order to recover possession, as a statutory tenancy is covered by section 3 of the Protection from Eviction Act 1977.

THE SOLE TENANT LEAVES OR DISAPPEARS

8.10 The tenant leaves or disappears

If there is no formal notice or surrender, and the tenant simply disappears leaving the cohabitant in occupation, the situation will vary depending on the type of tenancy. Cohabitants and former spouses do not have an automatic right to occupy so in most cases, they will have no long-term right to remain. If an occupation order is obtained, the situation is the same as for married tenants as long as the order lasts. The non-tenant will occupy as if s/he were the tenant. If an occupation order has not been obtained or it expires, the position is as follows:

s81 HA85, s1 HA88
s1 RA77

- Where the tenancy depends upon the tenant occupying the dwelling 'as her/his only or principal home' (as in the case of a secure or assured tenancy) or, 'as a residence' (in the case of statutory tenancies) then, if the tenant has left permanently, the tenancy will no longer be secure or assured or statutory, as the case may be

- The non-tenant ex-spouse or cohabitant will usually have no rights to the original tenancy (ie, secure, assured, statutory, etc.). However, it may be possible to argue that a new agreement has been entered into with the landlord after the divorce or since the tenant left, or, that by accepting rent from the non-tenant, knowing that the tenant had left, the landlord has entered a new contract with the partner, thereby creating a new tenancy. Proving that a new tenancy has been created is not easy (see 6.38), and it is therefore crucial that, if possible, an occupation order is obtained quickly to keep the original tenancy alive before a notice to quit is served, either by the landlord or the tenant. As an occupation order for a non-tenant cohabitant can only last for a maximum of twelve months, an application for transfer of tenancy should also be made as soon as possible if the non-tenant wishes to try to retain the tenancy (see also 8.3 for a discussion on applying for occupation orders after a tenancy has become non-secure or non-assured).

The position where the tenant leaves and there is no occupation order is set out for each tenancy type below.

8.11   Secure and introductory tenancies – sole tenant leaves

- If the sole tenant has left, the tenancy ceases to be secure or introductory and becomes a tenancy with basic protection.

In order to avoid this, it would have to be shown that the tenant had a real intention to return. This may of course be difficult in cases of relationship breakdown, where the cohabitant may not know what the tenant's intentions are. In practice, if the tenant has left personal belongings or continues to receive mail at the address and is not known to have taken up permanent residence elsewhere, it should be possible to persuade a local authority or housing association that the secure tenant condition is still fulfilled.

> ### *Amoah v Barking and Dagenham LBC*[7]
>
> *A secure tenant was sentenced to 12 years' imprisonment. He left items of furniture in the property and appointed a relative to act as 'caretaker' in his absence. The council served a notice to quit and obtained a county court possession order on the basis that he had lost his status as a secure tenant. He appealed.*
>
> *The Court of Appeal allowed his appeal and held that he had retained his secure status. While there was some doubt about the actual evidence of the resident 'caretaker,' other factors provided evidence of an intention to return.*
>
> *The following principles could be drawn from the case law:*
>
> - *Absence of a tenant might be sufficiently prolonged to raise a presumption that the tenant was no longer occupying – whether or not that was the case was a matter of fact and degree*
> - *Assuming an absence of this length, the onus was then on the tenant to rebut the presumption*
> - *In order to rebut the presumption, the tenant had to establish:*
>   - *A real (de facto) intent to return*
>   - *A practical possibility of the fulfilment of that intention within a reasonable time; and that*
>   - *The intent had some formal outward and visible sign, which was sufficiently substantial and permanent.*

7.   Amoah v Barking and Dagenham LBC [2001] 23 ChD.

> ### *Notting Hill Housing Trust v Etoria*[8]
>
> *A man sentenced to life imprisonment, but hoping for review by a parole board in 9 years' time was held to have a real and practical intention to return, as he regarded the flat as his home, his belongings remained there and his brother lived there as a caretaker.*

s5 PEA77
- To evict a tenant with basic protection, the landlord must serve notice to quit on the original tenant to end the tenancy. (Notice of seeking possession should not be used since the tenancy is no longer secure)

- The ex-spouse or cohabitant will still have been a lawful licensee when the secure tenancy ended, and so would be covered by the Protection from Eviction Act. The landlord must therefore obtain a court order to recover possession. No
s3 & s8 PEA77   grounds for possession are needed.

8.12   Assured and assured shorthold tenancies – sole tenant leaves

- If the sole tenant has left, the tenancy ceases to be assured and becomes a tenancy with basic protection

- In order to avoid this, it would have to be shown that the tenant had a real intention to return, as described for secure tenants above.

Fixed-term tenancies

- The tenancy is still subject to the fixed-term contract, and, unless there is a break clause, the landlord would have to rely on any forfeiture clause which may be in the agreement, or wait until the fixed term had expired, to recover possession. No notice to quit is
s7(6) HA88   required at the end of a fixed term

- As a tenancy with basic protection is covered by section 3 of the Protection from Eviction Act, the landlord would have to obtain a court order to recover possession. No grounds for possession are needed.

Periodic tenancies

- Notice to quit must be served on the original tenant to end the tenancy

- As a tenancy with basic protection is covered by section 3 of the Protection from Eviction Act, the landlord would have to obtain a court order to recover possession. No grounds for possession are needed.

8.   Notting Hill Housing Trust v Etoria (1989) April Legal Action 22, Bloomsbury County Court.

8.13 Protected contractual tenancies – sole tenant leaves

- If the sole tenant has left, the contractual tenancy continues, with the partner being allowed to remain until the contract ends

- The contract can be ended either by:

  1. Expiry of a fixed term.

  2. Exercise of a break clause in a fixed term.

  3. Notice to quit served by landlord or tenant where the tenancy is periodic.

  4. Notice of increase of rent served by the landlord, giving notice equal to the length of time needed for a notice to quit.

- Once the contract is ended, the protected tenancy ends and no statutory tenancy will arise, since the tenant no longer uses the home as a 'residence' and the non-tenant has no matrimonial home rights (unless s/he has obtained an occupation order). The remaining non-tenant partner has no legal status

- An anomaly now arises: because protected tenancies are not covered by section 3 of the Protection from Eviction Act (see 6.35), the landlord is not legally obliged to get a court order to recover possession. This creates the strange result of putting the partners of those with less security, eg, Rent Act statutory tenants or even tenants with basic protection, in a better position than those of fully protected tenants

s6 CLA77
- Physical force to evict will still constitute an offence, so that if the occupier remains constantly on the premises, the landlord would have to obtain a court order for possession to avoid the commission of an offence.

8.14 (Protected) statutory tenancies – sole tenant leaves

s2 RA77
- If the sole tenant has left, the statutory tenancy ceases to exist

- The tenant maintains a statutory tenancy 'if and so long as he occupies the dwelling-house as his residence.' This is different from the secure and assured tenancy conditions. The length of absence has been held to be significant, and whether it is sufficiently long to infer that the person no longer occupies the dwelling is a matter of fact and degree.[9] It is possible for someone to live elsewhere and yet still maintain a statutory tenancy, although the premises must be occupied sufficiently 'as a home' in order for the claim to succeed.[10] Case law has established that there must be both an intention to return and some visible state of affairs indicating that intention to return.[11] However,

9. Brown v Brash and Ambrose (1984) 2 KB 247 at p.254.
10. Regalian Securities Ltd v Scheuer (1984) 5 HLR 38 CA; and Brickfield Properties Ltd v Hughes (1988) 20 HLR 108 CA, where the statutory tenancy of a flat was retained despite long absence because of moving to a cottage inherited by the tenant's wife. A 'pied-a-terre' or holiday home will not suffice: Walker v Ogilvy (1974) 28 P & CR 288. For further discussion of 'occupying as residence' see, J.E. Martin, Residential Security (Sweet and Maxwell, 1989) pp. 80-87.
11. Richards v Green (1983) 11 HLR 1, (1983) 268 EG 443; Brown v Brash and Ambrose ibid.

occupation by a tenant's cohabitant is not in itself sufficient to maintain a statutory tenancy, and if the tenant clearly no longer intends to live there, the landlord will be able to obtain possession

- No further tenancy arises when the statutory tenancy ends. Therefore no notice is required

- Statutory tenancies are covered by section 3 of the Protection from Eviction Act, and the landlord must therefore obtain a court order to recover possession. No grounds for possession are needed.

> ### *Richards v Green*[12]
>
> *The tenant left his flat to look after his parents and subsequently inherited their house and remained there to sell it. He left his possessions in the flat, to which he intended to return. Despite an absence of two and a half years, still continuing at the time of the hearing, the statutory tenancy was held to still exist.*

8.15 Tenancies and licences with basic protection – sole tenant/licensee leaves

Fixed-term

- If the sole tenant/licensee leaves, the remaining partner, whether still married or divorced, has a right to remain during the fixed term. Unless there is a break clause, the landlord would have to show that there had been a breach of the tenancy conditions (forfeiture, if there is a forfeiture clause in the tenancy agreement) or wait until the fixed term had expired to recover possession

- No notice to quit is required at the end of a fixed term, although if the landlord continues to accept rent after the end of the fixed term, a periodic tenancy or licence would arise, which would then require service of a notice to quit

- A tenancy/licence with basic protection is covered by section 3 of the Protection from Eviction Act, the landlord would have to obtain a court order to recover possession. No grounds for possession are needed.

Periodic

- If the sole tenant/licensee leaves, the landlord/licensor would have to serve notice to quit on her/him

- An occupancy with basic protection is covered by section 3 of the Protection from Eviction Act, the landlord would have to obtain a court order to recover possession. No grounds for possession are required.

---

12. Richards v Green, see footnote 11.

8.16 Excluded occupancies – sole tenant/licensee leaves

Contractual occupiers

- Where there is a contract, eg, the occupier pays rent or other 'consideration' to the owner in return for permission to occupy, the partner has rights to remain as long as the contract still exists

- The landlord/licensor must therefore terminate the contract either by giving notice as specified in the contract or, if it is not specified:

  1. If it is a tenancy, the landlord must give a notice to quit equivalent to the period of the tenancy[13]

  2. If it is a licence, the licensor must give 'reasonable notice' which does not have to be in writing

- The landlord/licensor is not legally required to obtain a court order to recover possession.

Non-contractual (bare) licensees

Where there is no contract, the licensor need only give reasonable notice.

Joint tenancies

The points made for married couples apply equally to joint tenant cohabitants (whether heterosexual, lesbian or gay), since the rights of joint tenants to occupy stem from landlord and tenant law, and not by virtue of their relationship. Readers are referred to Chapter 7, Sections C and D.

Joint tenants are also able to apply for occupation orders in exactly the same way as married couples, whether heterosexual or lesbian or gay. This is because, unlike cohabiting non-tenants, each joint tenant will be an 'entitled person' by virtue of her/his interest in the tenancy.

s33 FLA96

The following important points should be noted:

- Both tenants have rights to occupy and both are jointly and severally liable for the whole of the rent regardless of whether they are in occupation or not. The courts are able to make orders transferring liabilities when making occupation orders (but see 11.17 for problems of enforcement)

- A joint secure tenant cannot assign her/his interest in the tenancy except under a matrimonial or Children Act order. This means that lesbian and gay joint tenants cannot assign an interest in a joint tenancy at all (see 6.18).

---

13. Because it is an excluded tenancy, section 5 of the Protection from Eviction Act 1977, which states that notice must be for a minimum of four weeks, does not apply.

Sole and joint tenancies

C Preventing a tenant's notice to quit

8.17 Preventing a notice to quit

Where an order is applied for under the Children Act or wardship proceedings, it is possible to apply for an injunction forbidding the tenant from serving a notice to quit. This would prevent the tenant from ending the tenancy by notice to quit (see 7.41). This procedure is normally only available to heterosexual couples with children. It is also possible to apply for an injunction if applying for a transfer of tenancy under the Family Law Act 1996. As the law stands, this procedure is also only available to heterosexual couples.

Lesbian and gay cohabitants

There appears to be no remedy available for lesbian or gay partners to prevent each other from serving notice to quit to end the tenancy. However, as the dwelling constitutes the home, there may be a defence against possession under Article 8 of the European Convention on Human Rights. At the time of writing, the House of Lords' hearing of the case of *Harrow v Qazi* on this issue was awaited (see 7.42).

D The courts' powers to transfer tenancies

8.18 The courts' powers to transfer tenancies under the Children Act 1989.

Cohabitants with children of the relationship may use either the Children Act 1989, or the Family Law Act 1996 to seek a transfer of a tenancy. The Children Act can be used even if the couple never lived together, and provides for the transfer of a tenancy for the benefit of a child. However, for cohabitants the provisions are normally only available to the natural biological parents. They cannot therefore be used between lesbian and gay couples, even where they have children living with them, unless the non-biological partner has a residence order or is the guardian of the biological parent's child[14] (see 9.14).

s15 & Sch 1 para 2(e) CA 89

Unlike the Family Law Act, the court may order a transfer of any tenancy which constitutes property, which could include a tenancy with basic protection (eg, a non-secure tenancy)[15]. For more information on Children Act transfers, see Chapter 9, Section D.

---

14. In Re J (1992) Sol Jo Bol 136 no 46 pp 136 LB-137 LB, also known as J V J (A minor: property transfer) (1993) 2 FLR 56.

15. R v Hammersmith and Fulham LBC ex parte Quigley (1999), LTL 21/4/99 ex. tempore (unreported elsewhere) QBD.

> **R v Hammersmith and Fulham LBC ex parte Qulgley**[16]
>
> *The sole secure tenant left, leaving his cohabitant and child living in the house. The council served a notice to quit on the basis that the tenancy had ceased to be secure. The cohabitant applied for judicial review and succeeded in getting the council's notice to quit quashed – she argued that the council's notice had deprived her of the right to apply for a transfer of the non-secure tenancy under the Children Act, for the benefit of the child and the council had failed to have regard to that important consequence in taking its decision.*

8.19 The courts' powers to transfer tenancies under the Family Law Act 1996

s53 & Sch 7 FLA96 As for married couples, the Family Law Act gives the courts powers to vest a secure, protected, statutory or assured tenancy or an agricultural tenancy in one of the partners. There is no power to order a transfer of a part interest of a joint secure tenancy, unless the joint tenants were the applicant and partner. In other words, a third party who lives with one of the joint tenants after the other joint tenant has left cannot apply for a transfer of her/his partner's part interest – if it were possible, this would result in, eg, a new cohabitant being a joint tenant with her husband's spouse![17] (see 8.3).

The Act extended the right to apply for a transfer of tenancy to heterosexual cohabitants, whether sole or joint tenants, when or after cohabitation ends. Unlike the Children Act, an order can only be made in respect of a dwelling in which the cohabitants lived together as man and wife. For more information on transferring tenancies under the

ara 4(b) Sch 7 FLA96 Family Law Act see 7.47 –7.49.

The criteria for transferring a tenancy are the same as for divorcing couples, with the addition that if the parties are cohabitants and it is a sole tenancy, the court must also consider:

• the nature of the relationship

• the length of the cohabitation

• whether there are any children

ara 5(b) Sch 7 FLA96 • how long it is since cohabitation ended.

When considering the nature of the relationship, the courts must have 'regard to the fact that they have not given each other the commitment

s41 FLA96 involved in marriage.'

16. R v Hammersmith and Fulham LBC ex parte Quigley ibid.   17. Gay v Enfield, see footnote 1 .

The outcome is not always what might be expected. The needs of the children are not necessarily the first consideration. The first person to hold the tenancy will be at an advantage, and the ability of either party to afford alternative accommodation with or without access to benefit will also be relevant (see case of *B v M* in box).

The court may also award compensation in the same way as for divorcing couples (see 7.49).

B v M[18]

Two heterosexual cohabitants had a joint secure tenancy of a one-bedroomed council flat. They had qualified for the flat because the woman had been a child of council tenants and she had therefore met the conditions for the council's 'family quota' scheme.

When the relationship broke down, an application was made for a transfer of tenancy from the joint names into the name of one partner. The judge transferred the tenancy to the woman.

Factors identified included:

- *it was because she qualified for the council's scheme that the tenancy had first been granted*
- *she was working and could not afford alternative accommodation*
- *the man was unemployed and claiming housing benefit, which would enable him to pay the rent of other premises.*

The woman was ordered to pay the man £1500 compensation.

8.20 Options for lesbian and gay couples and heterosexual couples without children

As there are no court powers available to transfer tenancies between lesbian and gay couples, the only options which are available are notice to quit and voluntary assignment. These are discussed earlier in this chapter and in Chapter 6.

18. B v M (1999) FD Fam Law 72.

Chapter 9: The Children Act and property transfers

Subjects covered in this chapter include:

Basic principles of the Children Act 1989

What is parental responsibility for a child and who has it

How the courts decide on matters concerning the child's upbringing

Who can apply for a residence or contact order in respect of a child

Protecting children in the home

How children can be protected in the home

Social Services' duties to children in need

When social services must provide help or accommodation to children in need

What social services must do for care leavers

Transfers of property

Who can apply for a transfer of property for a child's benefit, including when a lesbian or gay partner could apply for a transfer of property

How the court decides whether property should be transferred

How the court can transfer property

Which tenancies can be transferred

The Children Act and property transfers

The Children Act 1989, which came into force in full from October 1991, was a fundamental review of all areas of child law, public and private, with the exception of financial provision for children, which is now largely contained in the Child Support Act 1991 (as amended by the subsequent Child Support Acts). This chapter summarises the main implications relating to housing. Readers involved in issues relating to child residence, contact, protection, etc., will need to consult specialist literature.[1] Useful, easy to understand information and explanations can be found on the Compactlaw website.[2]

Financial provision relating to children is covered in Chapter 10.

A   Basic principles of the Children Act 1989

The Children Act contains certain key concepts:

- The fundamental principle is that the welfare of the child is paramount

- The rights of parents and guardians in relation to 'parental responsibility' are clearly defined and given greater emphasis than before, and

- The Act seeks to protect families from unwarranted state interference.

9.1   Parental responsibility

s12 CA89   Parental responsibility means all the rights, duties, powers, responsibilities and authority which a parent has in relation to the child.

Who has parental responsibility?

- Married fathers and all natural/birth mothers, whether married or unmarried, automatically have parental responsibility

s4 CA89
- Unmarried fathers may acquire parental responsibility by court order or written agreement with the mother in the prescribed form. In deciding whether to grant a Parental Responsibility Order, the court will consider:

  – the degree of *commitment* the father has shown to the child

  – the degree of *attachment* which exists between him and child

  – the father's *motive* for applying for the order.[3]

s111 ACA 2002 amending s4 CA 1989   Unmarried fathers, who become registered as the child's father, will automatically acquire parental responsibility once the amendment to the Children Act, brought in by the Adoption and Children Act 2002, comes into force. At the time of writing, the provision was not expected to come into force until 2004. It will apply only from that date, so that only those who become registered as fathers after that date will acquire parental responsibility, ie, it is not retrospective.

---

1. Child Support Handbook 2003/2004, 11th edition, CPAG (available from July 2003).
2. www.compactlaw.co.uk/child.html.
3. Re: G (A Minor) (Parental Responsibility Order) (1994) 1 FLR 504.

s4 & s12(1) CA89

When a father is granted a residence order, the court must also grant a Parental Responsibility Order in his favour. This gives him full rights in respect of the child, and parental responsibility cannot then normally be brought to an end even if the residence order is terminated; eg, *Bill is the natural father of Jack and successfully applies for a residence order. The court must also grant him a parental responsibility order for Jack together with the residence order. Jack's mother later successfully applies to have the residence order brought to an end. Bill will still nevertheless retain parental responsibility, even though he no longer has a residence order in respect of Jack*

s12(3) CA89

- Others may also acquire parental responsibility. For example, a residence order granted in favour of any person who is not a parent or guardian also confers parental responsibility on that person for the duration of the order. They are not, however, permitted to have a say in any adoption proceedings, or the appointment of a guardian. Once the residence order comes to an end, parental responsibility also ceases, eg, *grandmother obtains residence order for a grandchild and is also given parental responsibility. When the residence order ends, grandmother no longer has parental responsibility.*

What does having parental responsibility mean?

A person with parental responsibility is empowered to make important decisions regarding the child's life, eg, about education, religion, giving consent to medical treatment, etc. S/he may act independently of another person with parental responsibility, unless that action is in breach of a court order or the law.

S/he only loses that responsibility if the child is adopted. Parental responsibility is not removed if the parents separate, divorce, or if the child lives elsewhere, or someone else also acquires parental responsibility, eg, by obtaining a residence order.

Re J (Parental Responsibility)[4]

J, aged 11, had never lived in a household with the father, but did have some contact with him, which was not obstructed by the mother. When the mother was sentenced to a term of imprisonment, the father applied for a residence order, a contact order and an order conferring parental responsibility. After the mother's release from prison, the residence application was discontinued, and the father discontinued the contact application after J informed the court welfare officer that she did not wish

---

4. Re J (Parental Responsibility) (1999) FD 1 FLR 784.

> *to see the father, although the parties agreed on monthly indirect contact.*
>
> *The magistrates refused the parental responsibility order, on the basis that the father had shown insufficient commitment to J. The making of the application did not show sufficient commitment in the absence of regular contact during J's lifetime. The father was almost a stranger to J, and there was insufficient attachment between father and child.*
>
> *The justices' conclusions were supported entirely by their findings regarding the limited contact between father and child, and the child identifying the father as a stranger.*

9.2 Children Act 1989 orders relating to upbringing of children

Court orders under section 8 of the Children Act 1989

The Children Act abolished orders for custody, legal custody, care and control, joint custody and access. They were replaced by orders known as residence, contact, prohibited steps and specific issues orders, known collectively as section 8 orders. These orders must only be made subject to the principle which underlies the whole Act, ie, that the child's welfare is paramount.

In any proceedings regarding the child's upbringing (but not in relation to financial support – see below), it is a fundamental principle that:

s1(5) CA89
> *'Where a court is considering whether or not to make one or more orders under this Act with respect to a child, it shall not make the order or any of the orders unless it considers that doing so would be better for the child than making no order at all.'*

Where the court decides to make an order, it must take into account all the matters in the welfare checklist.

s(1)(3) CA89
Welfare Checklist

• The ascertainable wishes and feelings of the child concerned (considered in the light of her/his age and understanding)

• Her/his physical, emotional and educational needs

• The likely effect on her/him of any change in her/his circumstances

• His age, sex, background and any characteristics of hers/his which the Court considers relevant

- Any harm which s/he has suffered or is at risk of suffering

- How capable each of her/his parents, and any other person in relation to whom the court considers the question to be relevant, is of meeting her/his needs

- The range of powers available to the court under this Act in the proceedings in question.

This is not an exhaustive list, and is intended as guidance. Courts are encouraged to consider what is best for the overall psychological development of the child, so ability to provide better for a child materially, eg, by having a bigger or different kind of house, or more money, should not outweigh other factors which would affect the child's happiness and wellbeing.

The principle of the child's welfare being the paramount consideration does not, however, apply when the court is making orders relating to financial support or property transfers. When making such orders, the court must have regard to all the circumstances of the case (see Section D below).

Effect of homelessness

If there is no accommodation at all available for the child, then the court cannot order that a child reside with that parent, and therefore applications whilst homeless remain problematical. Although a housing authority is obliged to consider whether it is reasonable for a child to live with a person who has presented as homeless, even if s/he is not living with her/him at the time of application (see 15.3, 15.17 – 15.18 and 16.26), sometimes there may be reluctance to provide accommodation for someone who has not obtained a residence order. Equally, the court will not grant a residence order if the person has nowhere for the child to live. However, if the parent can put forward proposals, perhaps backed up by a written assurance from the housing authority that housing will be provided if residence is granted, then the court can consider making a residence order. Advisers need to be aware that this situation can present difficulties.

Residence orders

- Residence orders settle the arrangements as to the person with whom the child is to live. Anyone obtaining a residence order also obtains parental responsibility whilst the order remains in force, if they do not already otherwise have parental responsibility (see 9.1 above). In deciding on residence orders, the court is not entitled to depart from the recommendation of an experienced court welfare officer without at least giving reasons for the departure.[5]

---

5.   Re W (Residence Order) (1999) 1 FLR 869

The principle that orders should only be made where it is better for the child than making no order at all means that residence orders are now only made in exceptional cases, such as where there is serious dispute. Residence orders are not made routinely on divorce. Local authorities should therefore not insist on the equivalent of custody orders before making decisions on homelessness and priority need. If parents agree that they will share residency of the child, eg, one parent has the child during the week, the other at weekends, the court will not normally intervene. This is despite the fact that the courts have not traditionally favoured shared residence because of the disruption to the child, (see 15.17 – 15.18 and 16.26 for a discussion of problems relating to shared residence and homelessness).

Re K (Residence order: Securing contact)[6]

The judge made a residence order in the father's favour, permitting the two-year-old son to remain with the father, having concluded that if he made a residence order in the mother's favour, there would be a serious risk that the child would be deprived of contact with the father. The mother appealed, arguing that even if there had been any rational basis for fearing loss of contact, the court's powers could have been used to secure compliance with a contact order.

In view of the judge's finding that the mother, unlike the father, was unreliable and untrustworthy, and that she was likely to end contact with the father if she were granted a residence order, the judge had been entitled to grant residence to the father. Cazalet J. commented that 'fathers are much better equipped to look after children nowadays than they were some 10 years ago.'

Contact orders

• Contact orders may require the person with whom the child lives to allow the child to visit or stay with the person named in the order, or for the person and the child to have contact with each other. They replace 'access orders.'

Serious problems have arisen when a perpetrator of violence applies for a contact order, since in many cases the courts insist that the address of the parent with the child be released, even when s/he may still be at risk of violence. The judgment in four Court of Appeal cases in 2000 has given guidance to the courts about the factors to weigh up when there has been domestic violence.[7] See 13.6 for further details.

6.   Re K (Residence Order: Securing Contact) (1999) CA 1 FLR 583.

7.   Re L (Contact: Domestic Violence); Re V (Contact: Domestic Violence); Re M (Contact: Domestic Violence); Re H (Contact: Domestic violence) (2000) CA 2 FLR 334 CA.

Despite these judgments, and the Good Practice Guidelines produced by the Lord Chancellor's department,[8] contact may still be awarded at the discretion of the court. For further comment on the problems of confidentiality when contact orders are made against a background of domestic violence, see 13.6.

Types of contact

The court has discretion to award contact on different bases. Contact may therefore be indirect, direct, supervised, unsupervised, or the order may be for no contact at all.

The most usual type of contact that is ordered is direct and unsupervised, which simply means face to face, without any other person present. Sometimes, however, one parent is hostile to the other having contact for various reasons. Perhaps there is a history of domestic violence that has been witnessed by the children, and they themselves are against contact. Courts will try to encourage contact, as it is felt that any relationship with the absent parent is better than no relationship (but see the contact cases referred to in 13.6).

Where there is hostility between the parents, it is most likely that supervised contact will be granted, usually at a contact centre where there are volunteers in attendance. However, places are limited and there is often a waiting list. In more extreme cases, contact is limited so that it is indirect, whereby the absent parent is permitted to telephone the child and/or send cards and letters.

In very serious cases, where the child does not want contact and is considered old enough and with sufficient understanding to make that decision, the courts will not force contact and will, reluctantly, dismiss the application. Orders stating that no contact should take place are rare. This is because a 'no contact' order remains in place until the order is discharged, and such an order is made after having found that contact is detrimental. Therefore, the more usual situation is to make no order at all, bearing in mind the principle that the court should make no order unless it is positively in the child's best interests to do so (see 9.2).

Prohibited steps orders

- Prohibited steps orders are orders which prevent someone from taking certain action or actions. No action specified in the order which could be taken by a parent for a child may be taken by any person, without the consent of the court whilst the order is in force. This bears a resemblance to wardship,[9] where the High Court takes on responsibility for a child when the child may be in serious danger or at risk, and 'no important step' may be taken without the consent of the court. Prohibited steps orders differ in that the areas prohibited must be

8.   Good Practice Guidelines on Contact Between Children and Violent Parents, available at http://www.lcd.gov.uk/family/abfla/cvpsec3.htm.   9.   see www.compactlaw.co.uk/childf18.html.

specified. As the Children Act allows the courts to make orders relating to children, wardship proceedings where the child becomes a 'ward of court' are now only used in very rare circumstances.

Specific issues orders

• Specific issues orders give directions to determine a specific question, which has arisen or may arise, in connection with any aspect of parental responsibility for a child. This might be necessary where there was more than one person with parental responsibility and agreement could not be reached, eg, regarding education or religion, holidays, changes of names, circumcision of boys.

9.3 The right to apply for a residence or contact order under the Children Act

Residence or contact orders can be applied for by:

• any parent or guardian of the child

• any party to a marriage (whether the marriage still exists or not) of which the child is a 'child of the family' (ie, step-parent)

• any person with whom the child has lived for at least three years

• any person who has the consent of either:
  – people with a residence order in respect of the child
  – the local authority
  s10 CA89 – every person with parental responsibility for the child.

Parents or guardians, or anyone with a residence order may apply to the court for any section 8 order in respect of a child, without specific permission from the court. Others must seek permission from the court to make an application.

These provisions may be of help to people in lesbian or gay relationships, who wish to retain contact with a child whose upbringing they have shared. Orders can be made on separate application or by the courts during any family proceedings.

9.4 Definition of 'child of the family'

The definition 'child of the family' relates only to children of married couples. A child is a child of the family in relation to a couple where:

• s/he is the child of both of them, or

s105(1) CA89 • s/he has been treated by both of them as if s/he were their child.

A child will not be a 'child of the family' of a couple if s/he was placed with that couple as their foster child by a local authority or voluntary s52(1) MCA73 organisation.

This definition is the same as that used under the Matrimonial Causes Act 1973. Under that legislation, the meaning of 'treated' has been the subject of debate, and there is a great deal of case law on the subject.[10]

B Protecting children in the home

9.5 Non-molestation orders

s42(6) FLA96 Non-molestation orders can be obtained under the Family Law Act 1996 to protect a 'relevant child' not only from violent behaviour, but also from harassing and pestering. The court must have regard to all the circumstances of the situation, including the need to secure the health, safety and well-being of the child concerned (see 13.19 for details of non-molestation orders).

9.6 Emergency exclusion orders

Occupation orders, which can include a provision to exclude someone from the home, are also obtainable under the Family Law Act 1996. When deciding whether to make an order, the court must consider factors affecting children (Chapter 13, Section C). This type of order is made in response to an application by an individual applicant, who has been living in the family home.

In addition to these orders, the Family Law Act granted the court a much needed power which allows it to include an exclusion requirement when making either an interim care order or an emergency protection order, in response to an application by a social services department.

The exclusion order may be made where:

s38 ACA89
> 'there is reasonable cause to believe that, if a person is excluded from a dwelling-house in which the child lives, the child will cease to suffer or cease to be likely to suffer, significant harm...'[11]

and, where there is someone living with the child who is able and willing to give the child appropriate care and that person consents to an exclusion requirement being included in the order. The court may also attach a power of arrest to the exclusion requirement.

'*Significant harm*' must be sufficient to justify public intervention. Harm means ill-treatment or impairment of health or development. The Adoption and Children Act 2002 amends the definition of 'harm' to make it clear that harm includes any impairment of the child's health or development as a result of witnessing the ill-treatment of another person. At the time of writing, this amendment was not yet in force. Ill-treatment includes sexual abuse and emotional abuse. Development

---

10. Eg, M v M (Child of the Family) (1981) 2 FLR 39; Teeling v Teeling (1984) FLR 808; D v D (Child of the Family) (1981) 2 FLR 93; Carron v Carron (1984) FLR805.

11. Section 52 and Schedule 6 Family Law Act 1996 amending the Children Act 1989.

s31(9) CA96 means physical, intellectual, emotional, social or behavioural development, and health is defined as physical or mental health.[12]

C   Social services' duties to children in need

9.7   Duty to assess whether children are in need

Sch 2 Pt 1
para 1 CA89
The social services department of the local authority is under a duty to take reasonable steps to identify the extent to which there are children in need within its area. Unfortunately, other than this general duty, there is no specific statutory trigger for assessing whether a child is in need. However, if another agency contacts a social services department expressing concern about a young person, it would seem that the 'reasonable step' would then be for social services to carry out an assessment of whether the child is in need. The Department of Health provides detailed guidance to social services departments on carrying out assessments of need, and advisers may find it useful to refer to it.[13] Where the authority refuses to carry out an assessment of need, the procedure is to make an application for permission for judicial review for breach of statutory duty (see 14.28–32 for information on judicial review). The application includes an interim injunction for an assessment and a final injunction for the services identified to be provided. There is no one authority on this point, but the practice is frequently used.

9.8   General duty to assist 'children in need'

s17(1) CA89
s17(6) CA89
s17(10) CA89
Social services have a general duty under section 17 of the Children Act to 'safeguard and promote the welfare of children... in need.' This includes power to provide accommodation, help in kind or in cash. 'Children in need' are defined as those whose mental or physical health or development is at risk, or who are disabled. They also have a duty to try to enable children to be brought up by their parents, provided it is not against the child's interests, eg, if the child were at risk in the family.

s17(7)-(9) CA89
Social services may also provide these services to the child's family if it promotes the child's welfare and helps to keep the family together. This could cover helping a separated parent to be with her/his child. Examples of help might be money for deposits, fuel bills, furniture, rent in advance, money towards travel costs to visit children or payments towards arrears. Social services can ask for repayment of the money, but not whilst the person is on income support. Following two differing judgments in the Court of Appeal,[14] the court held that social services may, if they see fit, provide accommodation under s.17, but there is no duty upon them to do so. In addition, the Adoption and Children Act

12. F v Suffolk CC (1981) 2 FLR 208.
13. Framework for Assessment of Children in Need and their Families, Department of Health www.doh.gov.uk/. Children Act 1989 Guidance and Regulations Volume 2, Family Support, Day Care and Educational Provision for Young Children; Volume 6, Children with Disabilities.
14. R(A) v Lambeth LBC [2002] HLR 57 CA and R (W) v Lambeth LBC [2002] EWCA Civ 613; [2002] HLR 41; [2002] All ER 901 CA.

2002 addressed this situation by specifically permitting local authorities to provide housing for children in need and their families, under s.17 of the Children Act 1989. The provision came into force on 8 November 2002, when the Act was given Royal Assent. Nevertheless, it still does not impose a duty to provide accommodation.

In *R (A) v Lambeth LBC*,[15] the Court of Appeal held that section 17 (the general duty to promote the child's welfare) was no more than a 'target' duty, and there was no specifically enforceable duty owed to any particular child. It did not amount to a specific duty to provide accommodation for an individual child and its family. This was distinguishable from section 20 (see below), which gave rise to a specific duty to accommodate children in narrowly defined circumstances, where the parents were unable to provide accommodation for the children. The court implied here that section 20 was purely about accommodating children alone and not with their families.

> 'In a case where the child's needs indicate a requirement for accommodation of a particular kind or having particular characteristics, and the child remains in a family unit with parent or parents (so that CA s.20 is not engaged), Parliament has in my judgment vouchsafed that provision is generally to be made through the housing legislation... (Otherwise) the local authority would be obliged to provide housing under CA s.17... quite outside the four corners of their duties as housing authorities... this rubs against the provisions of Part VII relieving the authority of their duty where an applicant for housing is intentionally homeless; more generally it allows a family with a child, or children whose assessed needs point to a requirement of accommodation of a particular size of kind not merely to jump the queue, but to turn it into a rabble.'

At the time of writing, an appeal to the House of Lords on this case was awaited.

The limitations imposed by this judgment and its implications for human rights were subsequently addressed in the case of *R(J) v Enfield LBC*,[16] (see box) where a mother and child who were ineligible for homelessness assistance (see 14.10) faced being separated purely because of lack of accommodation; it was agreed that her right to respect for family life (Article 8 of the Convention on Human Rights) would be breached. It was held in this case that the council had a wide-ranging power under

s2(1) LGA2000

the Local Government Act 2000 to 'do anything' to promote or improve the 'social well-being' of its area, and that included a power to 'give financial assistance to any person.' The financial assistance could be used to secure accommodation, in order to prevent an infringement of a person's Convention rights under Article 8.

15. See 14 above.

16. R(J) v Enfield LBC [2002] EWHC 432, [2002] HLR 38.

Local authority can provide accommodation to prevent breach of human rights under s2 Local Government Act 2000

R(J) v Enfield LBC

An overstayer and her daughter were ineligible for assistance under the homelessness legislation, and asked for a community care assessment from social services. They decided that the applicant was not sufficiently at risk to require them to provide accommodation under the National Assistance Act 1948, and that as a result of the decision in R(A) v Lambeth LBC, neither money nor accommodation could be provided under s.17 of the Children Act.

This meant that Article 8 (right to respect for family life) of the Convention on Human Rights came into play, since the family faced being separated by the child being taken into care. The council agreed that accommodation problems were not sufficient justification for taking the child into care, and that the applicant's Convention rights would be infringed.

The judge confirmed that section 2(1) of the Local Government Act 2000 allowed the council to provide financial assistance to secure accommodation, thereby preventing an infringement of the applicant's human rights.

A further case, *R (W) v Lambeth LBC*,[17] heard in the Court of Appeal, modified the judgment in *R(A) v Lambeth LBC*, and effectively reinstated the power to accommodate under section 17. The applicant had been declared intentionally homeless, and applied for help with the provision of accommodation under section 17 of the Children Act 1989. The Court of Appeal held that, although section 17 did not impose a *duty* to accommodate a parent and child in need, it did nevertheless provide a *power* to assist with accommodation, and to that extent *R(A) v Lambeth LBC* had been incorrectly decided. However, in this case the authority had considered exercising its discretion but decided against it, and that decision could not be held to be flawed.

9.9 Social services' duty to provide accommodation for children in need

Unlike section 17, which is a general duty that cannot be strictly enforced by an individual, section 20 of the Children Act says that social services must provide accommodation for any child in need where:

---

17. R (W) v Lambeth LBC [2002] see 14 above.

- no-one has parental responsibility for the child (eg, a child is orphaned), or

- the child is lost or abandoned, or

- the parent is unable to provide suitable accommodation or care, whether permanently or not, for whatever reason.

s20(1) CA89   For some time, it was thought that this section had to be read in the light of the general duty to keep families together. If the only reason a parent and child were apart was because of lack of accommodation, it was argued that accommodation would have to be provided not only for the child, but also for the parent or parents concerned. However, the Court of Appeal in *R(G) v Barnet LBC* (see box) has held that this is not so.

R(G) v Barnet LBC[18]

In R(G) v Barnet LBC the applicant was a young homeless Dutch national with a young child. She was not habitually resident and therefore not eligible for assistance, nor able to claim benefits. She applied to Barnet social services, which provided temporary accommodation whilst a Children Act assessment was made. The assessment concluded that the child's needs would be best met by returning with the mother to Holland. They offered to pay travelling expenses, and if the offer were refused, to accommodate the child alone. The mother refused to return to Holland or be separated from her child.

The Court of Appeal held that nothing in the Children Act imposed a duty on social services to provide accommodation for every child in need together with its own parent. If it were so, it would make the provisions of intentional homelessness virtually irrelevant where the homeless person is a parent with young children.

'S.20... imposes a duty on an authority to provide accommodation for a child in need, but not for the parent of such a child; the authority's duty under section 23(6) is to make arrangements to enable the child to live with... his parent, not to provide accommodation which the parent cannot provide; the authority were therefore entitled to make arrangements for the claimant's child to live with the claimant on condition that she accepted their offer of assistance to return to Holland.'

However, separating a family purely because they lack accommodation may be held to be a breach of an individual's Human Right to respect for family life (Article 8) (see *R (J) v Enfield LBC* above). It would,

---

18.   R (G) v Barnet LBC [2001] 33 HLR 59 CA.

however, seem that if another option is offered, for example, assistance for the parent and child to be together but not necessarily where the parent wishes to be, there is unlikely to be a breach of human rights. The local authority has discretion to decide how best to ensure that a breach of human rights does not occur, just as it has discretion as to how it carries out its general duty to safeguard the welfare of children in need under section 17. The only method of challenge would be by challenging the reasonableness of the authority's actions, by means of judicial review. The test is known as 'Wednesbury unreasonableness,' and requires an action to be so unreasonable as to be virtually absurd. It can therefore be very difficult to prove that an authority has acted in such a way (see 14.28).

All three cases, *A*, *W*, and *G*, have permission to appeal to the House of Lords and it is expected that all three will be heard together in 2003.

Duties towards 16 and 17-year-olds

s20(3) CA89   Social services are also under a specific duty to provide accommodation for any 16 or 17-year-old who is in need and whose welfare will be seriously prejudiced without the provision of that accommodation. If this duty is owed, the young person will not be in priority need as homeless (see 14.11), but will be the responsibility of social services.

9.10   Co-operation between housing and social services authorities

Power under Children Act 1989

s27 CA89   Under section 27 of the Children Act 1989, social services may ask for another local housing authority's help in dealing with cases where it owes duties to children in need, for example, by providing accommodation, helping families who have been declared intentionally homeless, or transferring someone from unsuitable accommodation. The housing authority is then bound to respond, unless it can argue that to do so unduly prejudices its work. However, the Act refers to 'another... authority,' and the duty therefore cannot be invoked by unitary authorities, eg, a London local authority's social services department cannot make a referral to its own housing authority – it must rely on internal co-operation.[19]

In the case of *R v Northavon DC ex parte Smith*,[20] the House of Lords held that section 27 of the Children Act imposes only a limited duty of co-operation between authorities, and does not amend the powers or duties of those authorities under other statutes. The housing authority had refused to provide accommodation for a family it had already

20. R v Northavon DC ex parte Smith (1994)
     26 HLR 659 HL.

19. R v Tower Hamlets LBC ex parte Byas (1993) 25 HLR 105.

declared intentionally homeless, saying that this would break the rules that applied to people on the waiting list, and would therefore unduly prejudice the discharge of its functions. For this reason, it was entitled to decline to provide accommodation.

If the housing authority refuses to help, the duty remains with social services to ensure that the child's needs are met in an appropriate way. This might include assistance with providing accommodation, as explained in the sections above.

Duty under Housing Act 1996

s213A HA96 As a result of the cases of *A v Lambeth LBC* and *R(G) v Barnet LBC* (see above), the Government added an amendment to the Homelessness Act 2002, which in turn amended the Housing Act 1996, requiring housing authorities to refer to social services (with the applicant's consent) any applicants with children under 18 who either are, or may be, declared intentionally homeless, or ineligible for assistance. Once the social services authority is aware of the facts, the department should carry out an assessment of whether the child is a child in need, and have regard to their general duty of promoting the upbringing of families by their parents (s.17 CA 1989).

The code states that *'where the child is a child in need solely as a result of family homelessness, the authority may wish to consider whether the best way of meeting his or her needs would be by assisting the family to obtain accommodation, possibly by providing temporary accommodation or a rent deposit under section 17 of the 1989 Act.'*

para 10.6

If social services then request advice and assistance from the housing authority, the latter must offer 'such advice and assistance as is reasonable in the circumstances, which might mean help in identifying suitable accommodation, but does not amount to a duty to on the housing department to provide accommodation for a family'[21] (for further information on this homelessness duty, see 14.17). The duty to co-operate is separate from, and additional to, the power social services has under section 27 of the Children Act.

The same duty applies if the housing authority and the social services authority are one and the same authority (a 'unitary authority').

9.11 Social services' duties to accommodate people without children

If there are no children involved, the provisions of the Children Act cannot apply. However, help may be available for people over 18 under Community Care legislation, if they need help for reasons other than solely being

---

21. Para 10.7, Homelessness Code of Guidance for Local Authorities July 2002.

destitute, for example, because of age, illness, disability or other particular circumstances. See 14.41 – 14.44 for an explanation of social services duties to provide accommodation under community care legislation.

9.12 Children (Leaving Care) Act 2000

There are many reasons why children end up in some form of local authority care. Sadly, children are often the casualties of a relationship breakdown, and it may be that children have had to go into care whilst their parents try to sort their relationship out. Difficulties with step-parents, violence, or abuse within the family, are other reasons why children may find themselves in care. In the past, the so-called 'safety nets' of the homelessness legislation and the Children Act have notoriously failed many young care-leavers, who often found themselves on the streets after leaving care. In an attempt to tackle this problem, in 2001 the Government brought in the Children (Leaving Care) Act 2000:

> *'The Act's main purpose is to help young people who have been looked after by a local authority move from care into living independently in as stable a fashion as possible.'*[22]

This Act came into force in October 2001. It amends the parts of the Children Act 1989 relating to provisions in respect of children being looked after by local authorities; ie, it lays down new duties towards 16 and 17-year-olds in particular who have been in care.

Pt II Sch 2 CA89

Terminology

Certain terms are used within the Act:

- 'Eligible children' are those aged 16 or 17 who have been looked after for a total of at least 13 weeks from the age of 14[23]

s19(2) CA89 as amended by s1C (CL)A2000

- 'Relevant children' are those aged 16 or 17 no longer being looked after, but who had been looked after for a total of at least 13 weeks from age 14, some of which time was when they were 16 or 17.

s23A CA89 as amended by s2 C (CL)A 2000

For the purposes of the Children Act, 'looked after' by a local authority means a young person who is:

s22 CA89 as amended by Adoption and Children Act 2002

- in the care of the local authority, or

- provided with accommodation under any of its functions (particularly under the Children Act), apart from functions under:

  - s.17 of the Children Act[24]

  - s.23B, ie, duties towards relevant children, or

  - s.24B, ie, powers to give help to those under 24 who were looked after between the ages of 16 and 21.

---

22. Explanatory note to Children (Leaving Care) Act 2000 www.hmso.gov.uk/acts/en/2000en35.htm.

23. s19B(2) Children Act 1989 (as amended by Children (Leaving Care) Act 2000).

24. Amendment inserted in s.22 of CA 89 by s.116 Adoption and Children Act 2002.

In turn, the definition of 'looked after, accommodated or fostered' used within the extension of priority need groups for homelessness purposes, means:

SI 2002 No. 2051

- looked after by a local authority (as defined above)

- accommodated by or on behalf of a voluntary organisation, or

- accommodated in a private children's home, or

- privately fostered

or who at the time s/he reached the age of 16:

- was detained[25] or in hospital, and immediately before that detention or hospitalisation has been looked after for a period or periods of 13 weeks in all, since the age of 14.

Some housing authorities report that social services authorities deny that young people are 'relevant children' because they accommodated them under s.17 and not s.20. This would appear to be a misunderstanding of the definition of 'looked after.' The duty to accommodate a child in need under s.20 arises whenever a child is homeless, or where the child's welfare would be seriously prejudiced without the provision of accommodation. Where a child has been taken into care alone, s/he will therefore normally be accommodated under s.20 (general powers and duties to accommodate children in need) or s.21 (remand or police protection). Section 17 would normally be used to provide accommodation to children with their families, eg, those not eligible for assistance, or intentionally homeless. The intention in excluding children accommodated under this provision was, presumably, because it would be inappropriate to consider children who had remained with their families to be in need of the in-depth 'after-care' offered to 'relevant children' under the Children (Leaving Care) Act provisions.

Duties of responsible local authority

The responsible authority is defined as the one which last looked after the child, and that authority has a duty to keep in touch with relevant

s23B(1) CA89

children, wherever they choose to live.

The responsible local authority (social services department) will be under a duty to:

- carry out an assessment of each child's needs to establish what advice, assistance and support the child will need during and after

s23B(5) & (6)

leaving care

- 'keep in touch' with all its care leavers who qualify for the new support arrangements, including those aged 18–21 and beyond in some cases

25. 'Detained' means detained in a remand centre, a young offenders' institution or a secure training centre, or any other institution under a court order. Para 1(4)(a), SI No. 2874 Children (Leaving Care) (England) Regulations 2001.

s23B(3)

- prepare a 'pathway plan' for the child which will take over from the existing care plan and will run at least until they are 21, covering education, training, career plans and support needed, for example, to move into supported lodgings. A needs assessment will be carried out in the context of the duty to safeguard and promote the child's welfare

- provide each 'eligible' child with a personal adviser who is responsible for keeping in touch and ensuring they receive the advice and support to which they are entitled

- assist with vacation accommodation where needed

- assist with costs associated with employment to the extent that the child's welfare needs it

- assist with the costs of education and training up to the end of the agreed programme, even if it is beyond 21, if required

s23B(9)

- give general assistance to the extent that her/his welfare requires it, either in kind, or, exceptionally, in cash.

Financial Support and claiming benefits

s23B(8)

Prior to the Children (Leaving Care) Act, young people leaving care could claim welfare benefits, eg, Income Support, Housing Benefit, or income-based Job-Seeker's Allowance. The Act removed entitlement to these benefits in most cases, and placed a statutory duty on local authorities to support these care-leavers. The idea is to *'ensure that young people leaving care are suitably accommodated, supported and advised according to their needs, rather than simply given money and obliged to fend for themselves.'*

Most 16 – 17-year-old care leavers are therefore no longer able to claim income-based Job Seeker's Allowance (JSA) or Income Support. As a consequence, they do not qualify for other associated benefits, such as a Social Fund community care grant, free prescriptions, eye tests etc. For as long as a young person is a relevant child (ie, up to the age of 18) the responsible local authority is her/his primary source of income.[26] A young person who is a lone parent, or who is unable to work because of illness or disability, is exempt from the rules and can still claim Income Support or income-based JSA. This applies whether they are still in care or have left care. They would still be eligible for the rest of the 'package' of support provided under the Children (Leaving) Care Act.

Government regulations and guidance state that the financial support provided includes the cost of accommodation, food and domestic bills, pocket money, transport costs for education and training, clothing and childcare costs.[27]

26. s23B(8) Children Act 1989 as amended by s3 Children (Leaving Care) Act 2000.

27. Chapter 9 para 7 of The Children (Leaving Care) Act 2000 Regulations and Guidance available at www.doh.gov.uk/qualityprotects/work_pro/projects 5.htm.

There is no prescribed standard for calculating a weekly allowance level for a young person who is a relevant child. Each local authority must develop a mechanism for calculation of weekly allowances, but no one should receive less than they would have received had they been entitled to claim benefits. This does not mean that each young person must receive cash to that amount. The type of support and how it is delivered will vary from young person to young person. The support provided will be co-ordinated by the personal adviser.

Those who leave care at 18 will still be entitled to the same benefits as previously. Their personal adviser should ensure that those entitled to claim benefits receive their full entitlement. Any payments they receive from social services under the amended Children Act[28] are to be disregarded when calculating entitlement to income support, housing benefit, council tax benefit, or working families tax credit.

Accommodation for care leavers

The Children (Leaving Care) Act requires that 16 – 17-year-old relevant children are provided with, or maintained in, suitable accommodation, unless the local authority is satisfied that their welfare does not require it.[29] To be suitable, accommodation must be reasonably practicable for the young person, given her/his needs, and the local authority must be satisfied as to the suitability of any landlord.[30] Generally, it would not be appropriate for 16 – 17-year-olds to be given the responsibility of sustaining their own tenancy without appropriate support, nor would bed and breakfast be appropriate, except as an emergency measure. It is envisaged that local authorities will make use of a range of accommodation options, such as hostels, self contained accommodation and specialist accommodation, as well as newer projects such as 'foyers,' often run by housing associations, which offer safe, high-quality, reasonably priced accommodation together with a package for training and personal development for young people aged between 16 and 25.

There is no duty for social services to provide accommodation to a care leaver once s/he reaches 18 unless s/he is in full time higher or residential further education. In the latter case, social services must provide accommodation during the vacations, or pay the young person enough to secure accommodation for her/himself, if the term time accommodation is not available.[31] The young person is then termed a 'relevant student.' This duty is to encourage care leavers to stay in higher education when they do not have a family home to return to during the vacations. The duty remains until the care leaver's 24th birthday. Once the care-leaver is 18, and whilst s/he is under 21, if homeless and *not* a 'relevant student,' s/he must be automatically accepted as in priority need under the amended homelessness legislation (see 14.11).

28. Refers to payments made under ss 23C,24A or 24B of Children Act 1989 as amended by Children(Leaving Care) Act 2000.

29. s23B(8) and s.23c (4) Children Act 1989 as amended by s2 Children (Leaving Care) Act 2000.

30. SI 2001 No. 2874 para 11(2) Children (Leaving Care) (England) Regulations 2001.

31. s24B(5) Children Act 1989 as amended by s2 Children (Leaving Care) Act 2000.

Department of Health guidance states that local authorities should develop strategies in partnership with housing providers to meet the housing needs of care leavers. Where possible, housing needs should be addressed before the young person leaves care as part of their pathway plan. Joint protocols should be in place to ensure that both housing and social services play a full role in providing support. The aim of the Children (Leaving Care) Act 2000 and the priority need changes to the homelessness legislation, which were brought in on 31 July 2002, were to ensure that the majority of careleavers who became homeless before the age of 21 would have to be found accommodation.

Complaints

Every local authority is required to establish a complaints procedure, and regulations have been made to allow for an informal resolution stage. For all complaints, a fortnight is allowed for the young person and the local authority to reach a satisfactory conclusion before invoking the formal complaints procedure under the Children Act.

s24D CA89

s26 CA89

Duties to those 'looked after' by local authority

Before Leaving Care Act	Leaving Care Act
16 – 17-year-olds:	**16 – 17-year-olds:**
• Duty to advise	• Duty to assess and meet needs
• Duty to befriend	• Duty to ensure a pathway plan is in place
• Power to provide assistance	
	• Duty to provide financial support
	• Duty to provide personal adviser
	• Duty to ensure accommodation
18 – 20-year-olds:	**18 – 20-year-olds:**
• Duty to advise	• Duty to maintain contact and to provide support through the personal adviser
• Duty to befriend	
• Power to provide assistance	• Duty to assist with costs of education, employment and training
21+ years-old	**21+ years-old**
• Power to assist with education and training if the course commenced before the age of 21	• Duties to 18 – 20-year-olds continue if still in education or training
	• Vacation accommodation for higher education

The general duties to children in need and those who have not been in care, or do not fall under the new Act, remain as before under the Children Act, eg, duties to promote and safeguard the child's welfare under s.17 and s.20.

D   Transfers of property

9.13   Transfer of property under the Children Act 1989

Until the late 1980s, court orders for transfers of property (including tenancies) could be applied for only by those who were or had been married, and in conjunction with an application for divorce, nullity or judicial separation. This avenue was not therefore open to cohabitants, whether heterosexual, lesbian or gay, or to married couples not making such an application.

The only remedy therefore was to use the provisions of property law by making an application to the court, under the Law of Property Act 1925 (now replaced by the Trusts of Land and Appointment of Trustees Act 1996) for owner-occupied property (see 5.48 – 5.49), or to rely on rights under housing law if a tenancy was at stake (see Chapter 7).

s15 & Sch 1 CA89

Under the Children Act, the court may order the transfer of property (including certain tenancies) from one parent to another, or to the guardian of a child, or someone who has a residence order in respect of the child, provided it is for the benefit of a child (or children). The general purpose of these provisions was to remove the discrimination between children born inside and outside marriage, and they mirror the powers given to the courts under the Matrimonial Causes Act 1973 to order transfers of property (see Chapter 4, Section F).

Cohabitants or ex-cohabitants, whether heterosexual, lesbian or gay, who do not have children and who are in owner-occupied property, must still use property law to reach a settlement.

Cohabitants in tenanted property can apply for a transfer of tenancy under the Family Law Act 1996 (see 8.19). However, the Family Law Act defines cohabitants as:

s62 FLA96

> *'a man and a woman who, although not married to each other, are living together as husband and wife.'*

Because of the specific reference to 'a man and a woman,' lesbian and gay partners cannot use the Family Law Act to obtain a transfer of tenancy and it remains to be seen whether, in the light of developing caselaw on Human Rights,[32] the legislation will be held to be discriminatory in affecting rights to a home (Articles 14 and 8), and therefore incompatible with the Convention on Human Rights (see 2,4).

---

32. Mendoza v Ghaidan [2002] EWCA Civ 1533.

9.14 Applications for transfers of property under the Children Act

Applications for property transfer orders may be made to the court by a parent or guardian of a child, or by anyone in whose favour a residence order is in force with respect to a child.

It has been established in the courts that, if the parents are not married, the courts have the power to order property transfers from unmarried fathers or mothers but not other cohabitants, even if they have been bringing the child up as their own.[33] If the parents are married, an order can be made against a step-parent if the child is a 'child of the family' (see 9.4).[34]

Lesbian/gay couples

People in lesbian or gay relationships, and heterosexual cohabitants where one party has a child from a previous relationship, will not usually be able to take advantage of the Children Act provisions, and their options regarding transfers of property are extremely limited. The Family Law Act can only be used to transfer tenancies between heterosexual couples. The only option available, if the property is owner-occupied, is to use property law (see Chapters 3 and 5). If it is a tenancy, the options are either assigning the tenancy (subject to certain restrictions (see 6.16 onwards), or terminating it by notice to quit and persuading the landlord to grant a new tenancy (see 6.3, 7.3 onwards and 8.5 onwards).

The only circumstances in which a lesbian or gay couple would be able to use the Children Act for a property transfer would be if the child is living with a non-biological parent who either has guardianship or a residence order in respect of the child. S/he may then, in theory, seek provision from the biological parent. However, it seems very unlikely that the courts would transfer residence from a biological parent to a non-biological parent in the first place, except in cases where it is alleged that the biological parent may cause harm to the child. It would be more likely that a non-biological parent would be granted contact, or possibly a shared residence order. The courts cannot order transfers of property from a non-biological parent to a parent or guardian, even if they have jointly brought up a child.

Artificial insemination – definition of parents

It is not uncommon for lesbian couples to have a child by artificial insemination. The Human Fertilisation and Embryology Act 1990 lays down who is to be treated in law as the mother or father of the child for all purposes.

ss27-29
HFE Act 1990

- A woman who carries a child as a result of having either an embryo or sperm and eggs placed in her is treated as the mother of the child

---

33. In Re J (A Minor: Property Transfer) (1993) 2 FLR 55.

34. Para 16(2) Schedule 1 Children Act 1989 gives the definition of parent for the purposes of the schedule.

- If the woman was married at the time of the insemination, the other party to the marriage is treated as the father of the child, unless he did not consent to the insemination

- If the woman was not married at the time of the insemination, but the embryo or sperm and eggs were placed in the woman during treatment for the woman and a man together, that man is treated as the father

- Unless the donor of the sperm falls into one of the above categories, he is not treated as the father.

A lesbian partner who carried a child would therefore be the lawful mother, but, until the law is changed, the partner still has no legal status. It is not uncommon in such cases for successful applications for joint residence orders to be made. This has the advantage of giving the other partner parental responsibility for the child, in the event of anything happening to her partner.

9.15 Factors which decide property transfers

As for matrimonial transfers of property, there are certain considerations which the court must take into account when deciding what order to make. They are similar but more limited than those for married and divorcing couples. The factors are:

- income, earning capacity, property and other financial resources of both parties now, and in the foreseeable future

- financial needs, obligations and responsibilities of both parties now, and in the foreseeable future

- income, earning capacity (if any), property and financial resources of the child

- any physical or mental disability of the child

- the manner in which the child was being, or was expected to be, educated or trained.

para4 Sch 1 CA89

In divorce settlements, the child's welfare must be the court's first consideration. This is not the case under the Children Act, nor is the child's welfare the paramount consideration when the courts are considering financial and property arrangements.[35]

s25 MCA73

Matters which specifically relate to the relationship between the parents, such as conduct, age, length of relationship, must not be taken into consideration in the court's decision. This is because the transfer is not meant to be for the benefit of either partner, but solely for the benefit of the child.

---

35. J v C (Child Financial Provision) (1999) 1 FLR 152.

9.16 The court's use of powers to transfer property under the Children Act

The court may order that property should be transferred to a child or to the parent, guardian, or person with residence order caring for the child, for that child's benefit. This can include transfers of certain tenancies (see 9.17).

Although this provision does not seem to be very widely used,[36] the courts have a wide discretion as to the type of orders they can make, as with matrimonial law (see 4.33). Property may be settled for the benefit of the child, eg, the family home may be retained for one partner's use until the children are 18, when the property would be sold and the proceeds of sale would revert to the owning cohabitant, if appropriate; or it could become the child's property.[37] The court may also order that property should be transferred to a child, or to the parent caring for the child, for that child's benefit.[38]

K v K (Minors Property Transfer) [39]

The Court of Appeal held that the court had the power to order an unmarried father to transfer his interest in the family home (a joint tenancy) to the mother for the benefit of their children.

Pearson v Franklin[40]

The Court of Appeal held that an appropriate remedy for an unmarried mother was to apply under Section 15 of the Children Act 1989 for a transfer from the father of his interest in the joint tenancy. This case is also authority for the proposition that you can get an order excluding one party from the property within those same proceedings.

Bater v London Borough of Greenwich[41]

This case dealt with service of notice to quit by one joint tenant and is authority for the proposition that an application for an injunction to prevent such service can be made within proceedings under the Children Act 1989 (see also 7.41).

Some solicitors also report using it as a 'lever' to trade off with. By threatening proceedings, better settlements have been reached voluntarily.

Since the settlement is meant to be for the benefit of the child and not the partner, the courts may sometimes be reluctant to order outright

36. 'Property Rights on Family Breakdown' article by Lord
    Justice Thorpe in 'Family Law' December 2002.
37. A v A (A Minor) (Financial Provision) (1994) 1 FLR 657.
38. J v J (A Minor: Property Transfer) (1993) 2 FLR.

39. K v K (Minors Property Transfer) (1992) 2 FLR 220 CA.
40. Pearson v Franklin (19940 1 FLR 246 CA.
41. Bater v London Borough of Greenwich (1999) 2 FLR 993 CA.

transfers of valuable property from one parent to another, where this might result in a disproportionate benefit to the partner. In such cases, orders granting rights to occupy the home until a child reaches a certain age will be more likely to be favoured by the courts. This is similar to '*Mesher*' and '*Martin*' type orders (see 4.33).

> ### J v C (Child: Financial Provision) [42]
>
> *The court ordered a transfer of capital from the father's lottery winnings to provide a home and furnish it for the mother and the child, but the same was to be transferred back to the transferor when the child reached 18.*

9.17   Transfer of tenancies under the Children Act

There are some obstacles in obtaining a transfer of tenancy under the Children Act. The Family Law Act 1996 gives the courts powers to vest tenancies, thus allowing them effectively to transfer tenancies, even where an agreement prohibits assignment (see 7.47 – 7.48). There is as yet no equivalent power that extends to transfers under the Children Act. This means that whether the court can order a transfer will depend upon whether the tenancy can be considered 'property,' which in turn is affected by whether it can be assigned.

If a tenancy is not capable of assignment (eg, a Rent Act statutory tenancy), it may not qualify as property, and could not therefore be transferred under the Children Act powers. If it may be assigned, but the landlord's consent is required, whether that consent is likely to be given will no doubt affect the court's decision. Where an order to assign would be a clear breach of a tenancy agreement, a court may be reluctant to make such an order (see 6.16 onwards for a discussion of conditions for assignment of different tenancy types).

The use of the Children Act to transfer tenancies is of lesser significance, since it has been possible to apply for transfers of tenancies between heterosexual cohabitants or former cohabitants under the Family Law Act 1996. However, because the criteria under the Children Act differ from those under the Family Law Act, a different result might be obtained, depending upon which legislation was used (see 8.19). There is no authoritative case law to indicate how the courts would decide, but advisers may want to consider the merits of advising careful consideration as to which legislation to use. A suggested scenario is given below:

---

42. J v C (Child: Financial Provision) see 35 above.42. J v C (Child: Financial Provision) see 35 above.

> *A woman moves into her partner's council flat. He has lived in the council flat all his life and succeeded to the tenancy when his mother died. They have a child. A year later the relationship breaks down. If s/he applies under the Children Act, will the interests of the child carry more weight than his if s/he cross-applies under the Family Law Act, when the fact of his succession to the tenancy (how the tenancy was acquired) weighs in his favour? Or would the needs and resources of either – say her right to housing as homeless, and his non-priority, carry it in his favour anyway?*
>
> *There are no definitive answers to such a situation, but the respective legal merits of the applications should be carefully weighed up.*

In addition, married couples may still only use the Family Law Act provisions in conjunction with divorce, nullity or judicial separation proceedings. Non-divorcing couples may still, therefore, find themselves forced to resort to the powers of the Children Act to obtain an order to transfer a tenancy.

The tenancies to which these provisions can be applied, and a brief summary of the position on assignment, are listed below.

9.18 Secure and introductory tenancies

The Housing Act 1996[43] amended the cases where assignment of a secure tenancy is permitted to include orders made under the Children Act. Spouses and cohabitants who are secure, or introductory tenants, may therefore apply for a transfer without having to fulfil one of the other criteria for assignment to be allowed. Same-sex partners would only be able to use these provisions in the situations outlined above in 9.14.

9.19 Assured tenancies

For periodic tenants the landlord's agreement to assignment is normally required. Whether the courts will order assured tenancies to be transferred under the Children Act is a matter for the court's discretion, taking into account the co-operation of the landlord.

Assignment rules can differ between fixed-term and periodic tenancies, and depend on the terms of the contract. This is explained at 6.20.

9.20 Assured shorthold tenancies

Assured shorthold tenancies are simply a form of assured tenancies with an extra mandatory right to possession in certain circumstances.

---

43. Para 12. Part III Sch 18 Housing Act 1996.

They are therefore capable of assignment, subject to the same provisos as assured tenancies. The value of obtaining a transfer may be limited, given the lack of long-term security.

9.21 Protected contractual and statutory tenancies

Assignment is normally allowed for contractual tenancies unless expressly forbidden, and the landlord cannot unreasonably withhold consent. The courts should therefore be prepared to order a Children Act transfer unless there is a reasonable objection from the landlord.

It is generally considered not possible to transfer a Rent Act statutory tenancy under the Children Act, as it is a personal right of occupation, which is not assignable (see 6.22). However, if a landlord were willing to agree to such a transfer, the courts might be prepared to do so. There is no authoritative case law on the matter.

Chapter 10: Financial provision for children

Subjects covered in this chapter include:

Powers to order financial provision – family court and child support agency

How to apply for financial support for children

How child support legislation has changed since 3 March 2003

When to use the Child Support Agency and when to use the family court

How the Child Support Agency can enforce payment

Who can apply for financial support for children

Powers to order financial provision under the Children Act 1989

What powers the courts have to make financial orders under the Children Act 1989

Financial provision for children

A Powers to order financial provision – family court and child support agency

Jurisdiction

In general, the family court no longer has an automatic right to make orders for child maintenance, which is now normally dealt with by the Child Support Agency (CSA), except where the CSA does not have jurisdiction and in certain limited circumstances (see 10.7–10.8). If the parent with care of a child cannot persuade the other partner to make a financial contribution, s/he may therefore be able to turn to the CSA. However, where the parent with care is not on benefit there are still also ways of using the courts, depending on the circumstances (see 10.8–10.9). Certain limited types of provision are still not normally dealt with by child support, and remain the sole jurisdiction of the family courts (see 10.8). The child support legislation does not apply to financial provision for spouses.

Child support legislation

Child support legislation first came into force in April 1993 under the Child Support Act 1991. The purpose was to transfer the family court's powers to order maintenance for children to the Child Support Agency (CSA), with the aim of increasing state powers to enforce payment of child maintenance.

Due to public pressure and problems with the system, the Child Support Act 1995 was passed to amend the previous Act, ostensibly to create more flexibility, but in practice adding further complications to an already complex system. There were still many problems, and numerous amending sets of regulations have been issued. The Child Support, Pensions and Social Security Act 2000 (CSPSSA 2000) was passed in July 2000, to further amend the Child Support Act 1991. Although certain provisions, including changes in terminology, came into force in 2000 and 2001, the main provisions came into force on 3 March 2003.

Aim of the Child Support, Pensions and Social Security Act 2000

The aim of the CSPSSA 2000 is to reform completely the scheme for child support *'to ensure that maintenance is more effectively collected and delivered to children'*.[1] The key objective is generally acknowledged to be administrative ease, and the end result is therefore a massively simplified system which is relatively easy to calculate, but which nevertheless creates certain anomalies.

---

1. 'Changes to Child Support' Child Support Agency, part of the Department for Work and Pensions www.csa.gov.uk.

To whom the CSPSSA 2000 rules apply

Most of the new provisions currently apply only to new clients applying on or after 3 March 2003, although some clients from before that date may be converted to the new scheme if they have a link with a new application. Other cases in existence on 3 March 2003 will transfer to the new scheme, at a date which was yet to be announced at the time of writing. For them, the old rules remain in force.

This chapter gives information about child support applications after 3 March 2003, and highlights some key differences between the new and the old scheme. It explains the position for people who are on benefit, and also explains when those not on benefit may apply to the CSA and when they may apply to the family courts. It then looks at the financial orders which the court may make under the Children Act 1989. Orders for financial provision made during divorce, nullity or judicial separation are dealt with in Chapter 4.

It is beyond the scope of this book to go into further detail and information can be found elsewhere.[2] Advisers should always check that rates and specific amounts, which are subject to change, are up-to-date. The CSA's website provides comprehensive information and links for cases before and after 3 March 2003.

10.1 Child support terminology

Certain terms are now used throughout the child support system regardless of whether the case is pre-March 2003 or not:

Non-resident parent (NRP)

Sch 3 para 11(2)
CSPSSA00

A non-resident parent (before 31 January 2001 referred to as an 'absent parent') means a parent who is not the main provider of day-to-day care for the qualifying child(ren). If the child stays with both parents, the non-resident parent is the one who provides fewer nights of care than the other parent.

Parent with care (PWC)

A parent with care means a parent who is the main provider of day-to-day care of the qualifying child(ren).

Person with care (PeWC)

This term is used for people other than parents, for example grandparents, who provide the main day-to-day care of the children for whom maintenance is applied.

---

2. CPAG Child Support Handbook 2002/2003 is an essential guide for those advising on Child Support. Detailed information is also available at www.csa.gov.uk. The 2003/2004 edition is due to be published in July 2003.

Qualifying child (QC)

A qualifying child means a child who does not live with the non-resident parent, and for whom the non-resident parent is liable to pay maintenance under the Child Support Act 1991.

10.2 The role of the Child Support Agency

The Child Support Agency (CSA), an executive body of the Department for Work and Pensions, assesses, collects and enforces child maintenance for those cases to which the child support legislation applies.

10.3 Key changes in Child Support from 3 March 2003

The main features of the new scheme, which at present relate mainly to applications on or after 3 March 2003, are:

- the calculation of child maintenance has been simplified

- for non-resident parents, elimination of the protected income calculation, which has been replaced mainly by standard maintenance rates

- 'departures' are renamed 'variations' and some grounds for applying have changed

- those receiving benefit will automatically be treated as having applied unless they *specifically request* the CSA not to do so, whereas previously an application form had to be signed to authorise the CSA to act

- the Child Maintenance Bonus for coming off benefit and returning to work will not be payable to new cases, but a child maintenance premium is payable

- changes to when people with court maintenance orders may apply to the CSA

- new severe powers to deal with non-payment, including possible imprisonment or disqualification from driving.

These changes are explained below.

10.4 Child maintenance calculations

The old scheme applied a complex fixed formula, with discretion to make 'departures' in certain cases. The new scheme has removed these complexities, and consists of a basic rate, a flat rate, a reduced rate and a nil rate. The rate used depends on the non-resident parent's income. Income taken into account is net salary, overtime, bonus/commission, tax credits and income from a personal or occupational pension. Other income, for example, from savings, maintenance or renting out property, is ignored. If the parent with care thinks her/his ex-partner could afford more, s/he can ask for a 'variation.' A non-resident parent can also ask for a variation in certain circumstances, for example, if s/he has extra costs due to the disability of a child living with her/him.

Change for non-resident parents

Since 3 March, the 'protected income calculation' has been abolished for non-resident parents. In cases before 3 March 2003, the actual financial circumstances of each non-resident parent were automatically examined to ensure that the amount of maintenance was reduced if there were special circumstances such as disability, high housing costs or a large second family. This has been replaced by a series of what are basically fixed rates (eg, even if there are more than 3 children in the second family, the net income is still only treated as reduced by 25%, as for second families with 3 children – see below). The non-resident parent may be able to apply for a variation of the calculation as explained above. However, the non-resident parent's housing costs and travel to work costs no longer affect the maintenance liability, and so are not available under the new rules as grounds for variation.

Rates from 3 March 2003

Basic rate

The basic rate is based on a percentage of the non-resident parent's net weekly income, when it is £200 or more. The percentages are:

- 15% if there is one child
- 20% for two children
- 25% for three or more children.

However, if the non-resident parent has a new family living with her/him, eg, step-children, the CSA will treat the net weekly income as reduced (before the basic rate percentage is applied) for each child in the new family by:

- 15% if there is one child
- 20% for two children
- 25% for three or more children.

Reduced rate

Non-resident parents with a weekly income of more than £100, but less than £200, will pay a reduced rate of maintenance. This rate is £5 plus a percentage of the net weekly income in excess of £100. The percentage is based on the number of qualifying children and the number of other children who live with the non-resident parent.

Flat rate

The flat rate is £5 per week for any number of children, and applies to anyone who has a net income of less than £100 per week, or who is in receipt of a wide range of benefits, for example, Income Support, Jobseeker's Allowance, War Pension or a contributory benefit. Note that for pre-3 March 2003 cases, where someone in receipt of Income Support or income-based Jobseeker's Allowance has children in a second family, no child maintenance is payable. Applicants under the new rules will now usually have to pay a minimum of £5.

Nil rate

A small number of non-resident parents do not have to pay maintenance, for example, full-time students and prisoners.

Shared residence

Where residence is shared between parents, the amount of child maintenance payable is reduced. The reduction depends on the number of children with shared care arrangements, the number of nights they spend with each parent, and the rate of maintenance to which the shared care calculation is applied. In some cases, for example, maintenance liability may be reduced by half or more, or the flat rate can be reduced to nil, by the effect of the shared care calculation.

Variations

There are also a number of circumstances in which the calculation can be varied. This replaces 'Departures' under the old scheme, and allows for account to be taken of, for example, pre-1993 property transfers, exceptional costs for disability of other children, and paying boarding school fees for the qualifying child.

It is beyond the scope of this book to go into further detail, and information can be found in the CPAG Child Support Handbook.[3]

10.5 Applying for child support – parent with care in receipt of benefit *('benefit' means Income Support and income-based Jobseeker's Allowance.)*

From 3 March 2003, where the parent who cares for the child is receiving Income Support or income-based Jobseeker's Allowance, or starts to receive either benefit, the CSA will automatically treat her/him as if s/he has applied, unless s/he specifically asks the Agency not to act. This differs from the old scheme, where the CSA could not proceed with a case unless they had the signature of the parent with care on the maintenance application form. This effectively gave her/him a chance to consider whether an application could put her/him or any children at risk. Under the new scheme, the CSA may not act if the parent with

s6 CSA91

3. CPAG Child Support Handbook 2003/2004.

s6 (5) CSA91 care has made a specific request that it should not do so, and such a request does not need to be in writing. It is important for advisers to note that if someone is afraid of violence, or other harm from a partner, and s/he does not wish them to be contacted, *s/he must now take the step of requesting the CSA not to act.* This will however trigger an inquiry into whether there is good cause for such a request. 'Good cause' is defined as:

• there being reasonable grounds for believing that there is a risk of harm or undue distress to the parent with care, or any children living with her/him, if the CSA calculate and collect maintenance.

If the CSA deems that there is no good cause, then benefit may be reduced. If the parent does not ask the CSA not to act, they will make an assessment irrespective of whether there is already a maintenance agreement or order in force, and regardless of whether the order was made before or after the implementation of the 2000 Act. If the parent with care is no longer in receipt of benefit, she may ask the CSA to stop
s6(9) CSA91 claiming child support from the non-resident parent.

10.6 Child maintenance bonuses and premiums

Applications before 3 March 2003
Parents with care in receipt of Income Support, or income-based Jobseeker's Allowance, who applied before 3 March 2003, are eligible for a 'Child Maintenance Bonus.' This is a one-off payment of up to £1,000 (depending how long the person has been in receipt of benefit) when the person comes off benefit and goes back to work.

Applications on or after 3 March 2003
The child maintenance bonus explained above is not payable to new cases. However, a parent with care of a child, who is on Income Support or income-based Jobseeker's Allowance, is allowed to keep up to £10 per week as a 'child maintenance premium.' This will either be paid to the parent by the CSA by an indirect adjustment to Income Support or income-based Jobseeker's Allowance (if they are collecting maintenance); or, if the parent gets maintenance direct from the other parent, up to £10 a week will be ignored when calculating her/his benefit.

10.7 Applications by parent with care not in receipt of benefit

The aim of the child support legislation is gradually to phase out the right of the court to make maintenance orders, and the original intention was to replace them within four years of the CSPSSA coming into force. At the time of writing, the situation was under review. The situation remains complicated, and in every case one has to consider whether the CSA has jurisdiction. If the CSA has jurisdiction to calculate maintenance liability, the court has no jurisdiction to make a maintenance order for a child, unless the order is by consent (see 10.9). Once a consent order has been made, the court may vary it and, prior to 3 March 2003, unless the parent with care went onto benefit, an application could not be made to the CSA. For applications made on or after 3 March 2003, the rules have changed somewhat – see under 'Maintenance order in force' below.

s8(3) CSA91
s8(5) CSA91

s4(10) &
s8(3A) CSA91

No maintenance order

Where the parent with care is:

• not in receipt of any type of benefit, and

• no court order for maintenance has been made

s/he may apply to the CSA for a maintenance calculation and collection of that maintenance. However, this is voluntary and s/he could instead have a voluntary agreement or convert a written maintenance agreement to a consent order.

People in receipt of working tax credit (for people who are working, whether or not they have children) and child tax credit (for people with children, whether or not they are working) are not treated as being on 'benefit,' and therefore will not automatically be treated as applying (see above), but it is likely to be in their interests to do so, as child support maintenance is fully disregarded for these benefits, and therefore will provide extra real income for the applicants.

Maintenance order in force

In some cases, where a maintenance order is in force, the parent cannot apply to the CSA and must still use the courts if s/he wishes to vary or revoke an order or increase the amount of an agreement.

Cases where the parent cannot apply to the CSA

The parent cannot apply to the CSA where there is:

• a written agreement between the parents, made before 5 April 1993, for the non-resident parent to pay regular child maintenance, or

• a court order requiring the non-resident parent to pay regular maintenance made before 3 March 2003 (but if a court has no power to vary or enforce the order, a CSA application is possible), or

• a court order requiring the non-resident parent to pay regular maintenance made after 3 March 2003, but which has been in force less than a year.

A parent who cannot apply to the CSA could ask the courts for a variation of the order, requesting the court to take into account the likely contribution which would have been made by the other partner if an application to the CSA had been made,[4] or, if s/he has a written agreement from before 5 April 1993, could see if the non-resident parent will end it or break it so it is not in force.

If none of the above applies, then the parent can apply to the CSA, but this is not mandatory. S/he could instead make a voluntary maintenance agreement, or apply to court for a consent order if s/he has an existing written agreement.

10.8   Additional cases outside the jurisdiction of the CSA

In addition to the situations listed in 10.7 above ('Cases where parent cannot apply to the CSA'), the CSA has no power to calculate maintenance liability in the following cases; therefore application must be made to the courts for child maintenance and enforcement:

- For stepchildren or children of the family who are not biological children of the non-resident parent

- Against the parent with care (although caution is necessary, since it is not uncommon for a parent to be classified as both a 'parent with care' and a 'non-resident parent,' for example where care is shared equally)

s5 CSA91

- For children aged 16 or 17 and not in full-time education; or aged over 18

- Where there is an existing maintenance order made in the UK on behalf of a UK resident, and that person wants the order registered and enforced by courts or other authorities in other countries against people resident there[5]

- Where there is a maintenance order made in another country by an individual abroad, and that person wants the order registered and enforced by UK courts against UK residents of another country[6]

- Where the non-resident parent or parent with care is not habitually resident in the UK (although some parents working abroad may be liable for child support, for example if they are working for the UK government, the armed forces or another employer based in the UK).

10.9   Cases where the court can make orders where the CSA also has jurisdiction

It is possible for the court to make a consent order (as opposed to imposing a maintenance order), even where the CSA could have jurisdiction, when parents are divorcing and want to convert a written agreement. A 'consent order' is an order made by the court with the

4. E v C (Child Maintenance) (1996) 1FLR 472.
5. This process is known as Reciprocal Enforcement of Maintenance Orders (REMO). See www.csa.gov.uk/newcsaweb/remo.htm.   6. ibid.

written consent of both parties, which is legally binding and can be enforced like any other court order, and cannot be changed by one party without the court's permission.[7] Provided the parent with care is not in receipt of benefit, this has in the past effectively prevented a future application to the CSA. Where a court order is made after 3 March 2003 and has been in force for a year or over, application may be made to the CSA.

s4 (10)(aa) CSA 91 as amended by CSPSSA00

The court can also make orders in addition to the CSA assessment in the following cases:

- Orders for expenses for the education of the child or children, ie, school, further or higher education fees

- Orders for the expenses relating to the disability of a child who is receiving Disability Living Allowance or is blind, deaf or dumb, or is substantially or permanently handicapped (routine maintenance for the child will be dealt with by the CSA)

- Higher level awards where the maximum child support maintenance is payable (usually referred to as top-up awards in cases where the non-resident parent is wealthy)

- Lump sum and property adjustment orders, as long as these are for an identifiable purpose and not in lieu of periodical maintenance payments (see *Phillips v Pearce*).[8]

Phillips v Pearce

The father was a self employed businessman with a house worth £2.6 million and cars worth £190,000. He was assessed by the CSA as having no liability to support his child because he was drawing no salary at the time of the assessment.(NB. Under the post March 2003 rules, he would have had to pay at least the flat rate of £5, even if assessed as having no income). The mother applied under the Children Act 1989 for a lump sum for the child's benefit. The court thought that, although it could not use its residual jurisdiction under Schedule 1 of the Children Act to order a lump sum to provide regular support for the child, it could order a lump sum for a particular item of capital expenditure, for example, to provide a home for the child. The court ordered a lump sum payment of £90,000 for the purchase of a home and £24,500 for furniture and other items for the child.

---

7. See pp 34–35 CPAG Child Support Handbook 2002/2003.

8. Phillips v Pearce (1996) 2 FCR 237 and also V v V (Child Maintenance) [2001] 2 FLR 799.

10.10 Enforcement of child maintenance payments by the CSA

Where application was made to the CSA before 3 March 2003, the CSA may enforce payment by:

- direct deductions from wages, if the non-resident parent is employed, or

- by taking court action to enforce payment as a debt. This can include sending in bailiffs or securing court orders against property or deposit accounts, or

- by deduction from Income Support/income-based Jobseeker's Allowance, if the person is in receipt of either benefit.

Where an application is made on or after 3 March 2003, the CSA has additional powers, which could result in a non-resident parent who does not pay being either imprisoned or disqualified from driving.

10.11 Amounts of child maintenance ordered by the court

Whereas the CSA assesses amounts payable according to a fixed formula (explained in 10.4), the court has considerable discretion in deciding on how much maintenance to award (see 4.32).[9] Where the court (as opposed to the agency) retains jurisdiction, it may make orders concerning financial provision, but only in conjunction with divorce, nullity or judicial separation proceedings. The powers listed below apply.

Maintenance

s23 MCA73   The court may order maintenance from one spouse to another for the benefit of a child of the family. The payments can be for whatever amount the court sees fit, according to the same criteria which are used for orders transferring property (see 4.31). They may also last for however long the court sees fit, subject to the 'clean break'
s25A MCA73   considerations explained at 4.36 – 4.37.

Lump sums

The court may also order payment of a lump sum for the benefit of a child. Such an award would not affect liability for child maintenance under the Child Support Act, and this is therefore likely to be a disincentive to a parent who might previously have been prepared to make over a substantial lump sum in return for reduced maintenance payments.

10.12 The effect of child support on financial provision orders

The introduction of child support inevitably has a 'knock-on' effect upon the types of lump sum payments to which parents are likely to agree.

---

9. 'At a Glance: Essential Court Tables for Ancillary Relief' Nicholas Mostyn QC, published by Family Law Bar Association, is extremely useful, and distributed to all judges by the Lord Chancellor's Department.

Payment of lump sums will not necessarily protect a parent from further payments, and indeed never has done with respect to child maintenance (see 4.37). If the parent who cares for the child subsequently has to claim Income Support or income-based Jobseeker's Allowance, the CSA will still apply the maintenance calculation to the 'non-resident parent,' even if a substantial sum has already been made over.

However, certain transfers of property from before April 1993 can be taken into account to vary the maintenance calculation, if the non-resident parent applies for such a variation. No allowance is made for transfers made after April 1993.

B   Powers to order financial provision under the Children Act 1989

10.13 Financial orders which can be made under the Children Act 1989

In addition to providing for the transfer or settlement of property for the benefit of children, the Children Act consolidated previous court powers relating to financial provision for children. These powers allow the court to order maintenance for the benefit of a child, and the payment of a lump sum either to the applicant for the benefit of the child, or directly to the child.

s15 & Sch 1
para 1 CA89

Either parent can apply for maintenance or a lump sum payment for the benefit of a child of the relationship. In addition, application for an order for the child's benefit can also be made by a guardian or by anyone who has been granted a residence order in respect of the child. Payments can only be enforced against a biological parent. These powers have now largely been taken over by the Child Support Agency, as explained above. They will still be applicable in certain cases, such as married couples where there is a stepchild and the couple are not divorcing or taking other matrimonial proceedings. They are also still available as a means of applying for lump sums.

10.14 People eligible to apply for financial provision under the Children Act 1989

para 1(2)(a)-(c)
Sch1 CA89

As for property transfers, applications for financial provision may be made by either parent, a guardian of a child, or anybody to whom a residence order for the child has been granted. However, payment can only be required from one or both parents of the child in question.

This means that it would be possible for a lesbian or gay partner to seek financial provision, or a property transfer, from a child's parent provided s/he had either guardianship of the child, or a residence order in respect of the child. Transfers of finance or property must be for the child's benefit (see 9.15).

'Parent' is defined as including any party to a marriage (whether or not the marriage still exists) where the child concerned is a 'child of the family' (see 9.4) of that person. In some cases, a child may have more than one 'set' of parents, eg, where there have been remarriages, there may be two parents and two step-parents. The Act provides that payment could then be required from any or all of those parents, as long as the child had been a child of both families. Parents may of course also be unmarried.

para 16(2) Sch1 CA89

S1 FLRA 1987 & S2(3) CA 89.

10.15 Factors that determine orders for financial provision under the Children Act

These factors are exactly the same as those for property transfers under the Children Act (see 9.15).

10.16 Courts that may hear applications for financial provision under the Children Act

Applications may be made to the magistrates' court, the county court, or the High Court. However, the maximum lump sum which can be awarded in the magistrates' court is £1,000. If a higher sum is hoped for, the county court or the High Court should be chosen for proceedings.

Chapter 11: Mortgages, rent and benefits

Subjects covered in this chapter include...

Mortgages

Who is entitled to make mortgage payments

Who is actually liable for the mortgage payments

How to get help to pay the mortgage

How to deal with arrears and possession proceedings

Taking over the mortgage

Rent

Who is entitled to pay rent

Who is actually liable to pay the rent

How to get help with paying the rent

How to deal with arrears and possession proceedings

How to safeguard the tenancy for the future

Mortgages, rent and benefits

Whilst this chapter covers broad aspects of the benefit system relating to payments for the home after a relationship breakdown, a detailed examination of the Income Support/Jobseekers Allowance/Housing Benefit system is not within the remit of this book. Advisers should refer to one of the many books on the subject before giving advice.[1]

Mortgages

Mortgage difficulties form an increasing proportion of housing advisers' work. When combined with the breakdown of a relationship, problems may arise over:

- who has the right to make mortgage payments
- who is actually liable for the mortgage payments
- getting help to pay the mortgage
- dealing with arrears and possession proceedings
- taking over the mortgage.

A   The right to pay the mortgage

Married couples and cohabitants have differing rights relating to payments of mortgages where a property is in one name only. In most other aspects, married couples and cohabitants, whether heterosexual, lesbian or gay, are in virtually the same position.

11.1   Right to pay where the mortgage is in one name

Married couples

Only the person named on the mortgage deed is legally liable for the payments on a mortgage loan. However, a non-owning spouse

s30(3) FLA96   automatically has the right to make payments towards the mortgage loan for the matrimonial home. Both the married owner and the non-owning spouse are therefore entitled to make mortgage loan repayments, and the lender cannot legally refuse them from either party. However, the non-owner will only be liable for mortgage payments

s40(1)(a) FLA96   where the court makes a Family Law Act order (see Chapter 13, Section C), which includes a provision imposing obligations to meet mortgage loan payments.

This could transfer liability from one spouse to another (but see 11.17 for problems enforcing such liability).

---

1.   See, for example, Child Poverty Action Group's Welfare Benefits and Tax Credits Handbook, published each year.

Either spouse is entitled to claim Income Support or Jobseeker's Allowance towards mortgage loan payments if s/he meets the general criteria for a claim (see 11.3 below).

Cohabitants

Unlike married couples, non-owning cohabitants have no automatic legal right to pay the mortgage loan, even if they wish to do so, to avoid repossession. There is no legal obligation on a lender to accept such payments. In practice, however, if payments are made, the lender will not necessarily refuse them, although it may refuse to provide information to the cohabitant about amounts due.

If a heterosexual cohabitant has been able to obtain an occupation order in respect of the property concerned, s/he will acquire matrimonial home rights for the duration of the order, including the same right as a married non-owner to pay the mortgage loan but not the liability for it, unless the court makes provisions transferring liability. Lesbian and gay non-owners have no right to apply for occupation orders and cannot therefore acquire the right to pay the mortgage loan.

However, cohabitants who are not legal owners may be entitled to claim Income Support or Jobseeker's Allowance towards mortgage loan payments if they can be treated as liable (see 11.6 below).

11.2   Right to pay where the mortgage is in joint names

Where a mortgage loan is in joint names, the position is relatively straightforward, regardless of whether a couple are married. Both parties are jointly or separately liable for the whole amount. If one disappears, the lender is entitled to require payments from the remaining borrower to cover all (not half) the loan.

Either partner can make payments and either is entitled, if eligible, to claim income support or income-based jobseeker's allowance towards mortgage loan payments.

B   Income Support and income-based Jobseeker's Allowance

This section does not aim to be a comprehensive guide to Income Support (IS) and income-based Jobseeker's Allowance (JSA), but aims to highlight areas which are likely to be of particular relevance to people whose relationship has broken down. A more detailed explanation of the IS/JSA system is not within the remit of this book. Advisers should refer to one of the many books on the subject before giving advice.[2]

---

2.   See footnote 1.

11.3   Who can claim Income Support and Jobseeker's Allowance

Income Support is for people who do not have to be available for work. Jobseeker's Allowance is for people who are available for work and entitlement is based on either national insurance contributions or income. However, housing costs are only included in income-based JSA. In the remainder of this chapter, references to JSA mean income-based JSA.

Income Support eligibility

The main regulations relating to IS are the Income Support (General) Regulations 1987 (IS Regs)[3] and the entitlement conditions are found in the Social Security Contributions and Benefits Act 1992(s.124). Income Support is available to applicants who:

1. Are over 18 (or 16 in special circumstances. The rules relating to young people are complicated and specialist advice should be sought when dealing with under 18-year-olds).

2. Have income less than the applicable amount.

3. Have capital below certain specified limits.[4]

4. Are not engaged in work of 16 hours or more per week (and if there is a heterosexual partner s/he is not engaged in work), and usually not studying full-time.

5. Are not getting any Jobseeker's Allowance (and any heterosexual partner is not entitled to any income-based Jobseekers Allowance).

6. Have passed the habitual residence test.

7. Fall within a 'prescribed category' of people who do not have to be available for work.

There are many prescribed categories, which mainly relate to age, health or disability. The main groups are:

• lone parents with a child under 16

• pregnant women who are incapable of work or who are within 11 weeks before the expected date of delivery or seven weeks after the birth

• a person who is temporarily looking after a child under 16 because the person who normally looks after the child is ill, absent from home, or looking after a family member

• a person who is a regular carer for a disabled person

• a person who is considered to be incapable of work

• a person who is 60 or over.

If the applicant is under 18 or a student, then special rules apply.

---

3. Income Support (General) Regulations S1 1987 No.1967.

4. At date of writing, capital of £8,000 or less, or £12,000 or less if claimant or partner is 60 or over, £16,000 if in residential care.

Jobseeker's Allowance eligibility

The main regulations relating to JSA are the Jobseeker's Allowance Regulations 1996 (JSA Regs).[5] Jobseeker's allowance is available to applicants who satisfy all of the following conditions:

1. Are unemployed or working less than 16 hours each week. If there is any heterosexual partner s/he is unemployed or working less than 24 hours a week.

2. Are not in full-time education (with certain exceptions). The rules relating to students are complex and specialist advice should be sought.

3. Are capable, available for and actively seeking work and have a jobseeker's agreement.

4. Are below state pensionable age. This effectively means that a man over 60, but under 65, can choose whether to apply for Income Support or JSA.

5. Have passed the habitual residence test.

6. Is not getting income support.

In addition the applicant must either:

• pass the means test (i.e. income and capital as above) for income-based JSA, which provides help with mortgage costs

or

• have been on JSA for less than six months and have sufficient National Insurance contributions for contribution-based JSA. This form of JSA does not provide help with mortgage costs.

It is possible to qualify for both types of JSA if you have sufficient National Insurance contributions and have been on JSA for less than 6 months, but also pass the means test for your circumstances. The income-based element is then paid as a 'top-up' to the contribution-based amount.

If the applicant is under 18 or a student, then special rules apply.

11.4 Definition of a couple or partner

For IS and JSA a 'couple' or 'partner' refers only to those in heterosexual relationships, who are cohabiting together.

11.5 Help with mortgage payments

Help with housing costs is available to people who qualify for IS and to people who qualify for income-based JSA because they have passed the means test. The rules relating to housing costs for the two benefits

5. Jobseeker's Allowance Regulations S1 1996 No.207

are the same. If someone is only in receipt of contributions-based JSA, they are not eligible for help with their housing costs.

It is quite common for people to assume that because they are not legally liable for the mortgage, they will not therefore be entitled to claim benefit to help with the payments. This is not the case (see 11.6).

Even if a married or cohabiting partner is not named on the mortgage deed, and therefore not legally liable to pay the mortgage, s/he may still be eligible for benefit to help meet the mortgage interest loan payments. Some service charges and some loans for repairs and improvements, plus ground rent on long leaseholds can also be included as housing costs, which are eligible for benefit (see 11.8 – 11.9). The help available for mortgage interest repayments covers loans up to a certain limit. This help can make all the difference between a person keeping the home or losing it.

Most people making a new claim have a waiting period before they can receive help with housing costs, and the proportion of the costs they receive rises over time (see 11.12). People who have had a continuous claim since 2 October 1995 (when the rules changed) may get more generous help, and people who took their loan out before this date may have a shorter waiting period.

11.6 Responsibility for mortgage costs

In addition to those who are legally liable to make mortgage loan payments, an IS/JSA claimant will be deemed to be responsible for mortgage payments if:

• her/his partner is liable

or

• s/he shares the cost with other household members (but not close relatives), at least one of whom is liable for the costs, and it is reasonable to treat her/him as jointly liable. Where there is joint liability, or the claimant is treated as jointly liable, s/he gets help with her/his share of the costs, unless the liability is shared with her/his heterosexual partner only and s/he (the partner) is making the IS/JSA claim as a couple

or

para 2 Sch 2 JSA Regs 1996

• the liable person (eg, the ex-partner) is not making payments and the IS/JSA claimant must make the payments in order to continue to live in the home. It must be reasonable to treat her/him as liable.

para 2 Sch 3 IS Regs 95 as amended by Sch 1 of IS Regs

If either partner is liable, IS/JSA will not give help if the payments are due to a member of the same household.

11.7   Payment of IS/JSA on two homes in cases of domestic violence and relationship breakdown

Payment on two homes where no intention to return

IS/JSA is not usually payable on two homes. However, when a relationship breaks down and the claimant leaves the home because of violence, it is possible to claim IS/JSA for two dwellings, provided that:

- the claimant is liable (or treated as liable, as above) to make payments in respect of both dwellings

- s/he is treated as occupying both dwellings as her/his home because s/he has left and remains absent through fear of violence, and

- it is reasonable that housing costs should be met on both the former and the present dwelling. For example, there must not be anyone else who is paying or could be made to pay.

para 3(6)(a) Sch 2
JSA Regs
& para 3(6)(a)
Sch 3 IS Regs

There is no specified limit on the length of time for which two sets of payment can be made in cases where absence is because of violence, or fear of violence, in the home or by a former member of her/his family. As long as absence began and continues because of violence, it does not matter if there is any additional reason why the person is absent from the home. Nor does this part of the regulation require that the claimant is intending to return home, for example, s/he may have left because of violence and be intending to sell the home. However, the Department of Work and Pensions (DWP) has discretion in deciding on whether it is reasonable to meet both housing costs and, in some cases, two payments may be refused. Payment is likely to be refused if the claimant does not intend to return home and no steps are being taken to deal with the property. Housing providers should be aware that this can give rise to unavoidable arrears.

Payment on two homes during temporary absence

Payment on two homes should be made for up to fifty-two weeks in cases where:

- the claimant has left through fear of violence in the home or by a person who was formerly a member of her/his family, and

- s/he intends to return to occupy the dwelling as her/his home, and

- the part which s/he normally occupies has not been let or sublet. and

- the period of absence is unlikely to exceed fifty-two weeks or unlikely to substantially exceed that period.

There are also a number of other specified circumstances where payments on two homes should be made during temporary absence, including where a person is required to reside in a bail hostel or is hospitalised, on a training course or undertaking care of a child whose parent or guardian is absent because s/he is receiving medical treatment. The regulations should be consulted for the full list of those who qualify. The payment is for up to fifty-two weeks.

paras 3(11) & (12) Sch 2 JSA Regs paras 3(11) & (12) Sch 3 IS Regs

If the person does not fall into one of these specified groups, for example, if s/he has left home to stay with friends or relatives temporarily due to a separation, but there is no fear of violence, payments on two homes will be made for up to thirteen weeks, provided the period of absence is unlikely to exceed thirteen weeks.

para 3(10) Sch 2 JSA Regs para 3(10) Sch 3 IS Regs

Payment on two homes where claimant has moved into a new home

Where the claimant has moved into a new home permanently and the liability for payments on two dwellings is unavoidable, payments should be made for both dwellings for not more than four weeks.

para 3(6)(c) Sch 2 JSA Regs para 3(6)(c) Sch 3 IS Regs

11.8 Housing costs which qualify for Income Support/ Jobseeker's Allowance

Assistance can be given towards:

- mortgage interest payments

- interest on some loans for repairs and improvements, or loans to meet a service charge for major repairs and improvements

- most service charges, for example cleaning of communal areas

- ground rent on long leaseholds.

The rules, which exclude service charges, are the same as for Housing Benefit; broadly, some supported accommodation charges will not be eligible, for example, charges for food, laundry and other charges not connected with the 'provision of adequate accommodation' are not eligible.

No help will be given towards:

- endowment premiums

- capital repayments

- buildings insurance.

paras 14-16 Sch 2 JSA Regs & paras 15-17 Sch 3 IS Regs

Not all loans which are secured on the home will therefore qualify for assistance.

'Supporting People'

In addition, from April 2003 when the 'Supporting People' provisions came into force, certain other charges are no longer eligible for Income Support or income-based Jobseeker's Allowance (or Housing Benefit), but will be funded via the 'supporting people' scheme. These are, in particular, service charges for:

- general counselling and support

- cleaning of customer's own room and windows where s/he is not able to do so

- emergency alarm systems where the customer lives in accommodation occupied by the elderly, sick or disabled persons and certain conditions are satisfied.

Further information is available on the 'Supporting People' website.[6]

11.9 Loans qualifying for Income Support/Jobseeker's Allowance

Help will only be given towards the interest payments due on certain types of loan. The loan must be for the property in which the claimant is living (see 11.7 for exceptions), and include:

- loans taken out to buy a home

- loans taken out to acquire an interest in a home, including buying out a partner's interest in the home on relationship breakdown (but see 11.14)

- loans taken out to pay for repairs or improvements which are necessary to maintain the property's fitness for occupation, or to meet a service charge for major repairs and improvements

- loans taken out to repay a loan which had originally been obtained to buy a home or to carry out necessary improvements or repairs, ie, remortgaging the original house purchase loan.

These are the only loans which qualify if the claim started after 2 October 1995. The rules prior to 2 October 1995 were more generous in terms of the definition of qualifying repairs and improvements. Many claimants who qualified before 2 October 1995 should be assessed under the old rules. See 11.11 for other help available to people who were receiving IS on 1 October 1995.

Not normally covered by Income Support/Jobseeker's Allowance:

- Loans taken out for non-housing purposes, eg, business loans secured upon the home (but see 11.11)

6. www.spkweb.org.uk/files/drftISJSABulletin1003_1.doc

- Loans taken out to enlarge a home where this was not deemed necessary under the regulations

- Where an additional loan results in housing costs which are considered excessive.

There are also limits on how much of a loan can be covered.

11.10 Date of claim

People in receipt of IS on or before 1 October 1995 continue to be eligible for help with housing costs under the old rules, which were more generous. It is therefore important to establish the date of claim and check that the person is receiving her/his full entitlement.

Claims treated as starting before 2 October 1995

para 13(1)c)
Sch 2 JSA Regs
para 14(1)(c)
Sch 3 IS Regs

Where a relationship breaks down, it may be that the claim has been made in the other partner's name. The IS/JSA regulations provide that a former heterosexual cohabitant/spouse will be treated as having been in receipt of IS/JSA from the date of her/his former partner's claim, or from the date s/he was treated as having claimed. In other words, if a couple have been receiving IS (and/or JSA if appropriate) in the other person's name continuously since before 2 October 1995 and the relationship breaks down, the other partner can make a claim, but still be treated under the old rules.

In some cases there may be a gap between the relationship breaking down and the separated partner making a fresh claim. Provided this is not more than 12 weeks, any break in the claim will be ignored and the claim will be treated as continuous. The applicant should not delay in claiming IS/JSA because if s/he does s/he will be subject to the new rules, including new waiting periods (see 11.12). In some cases, however, the gap can be up to 52 weeks, if the gap is due to going into work or training, or becoming a 'welfare to work beneficiary.' This applies to some people who take up work or training after previously being incapable of work.

11.11 Extra help for claims commencing prior to 2 October 1995

Under the old rules, extra help was available in certain specific situations. This extra help is available only if the claim commenced or is treated as commencing before 2 October 1995 (see above).

Deserted partner rule

If someone had housing costs covered by benefit on 1 October 1995 that cannot be covered under the current rules, s/he will continue to receive help with these costs as long as the claim is treated as continuous. This includes some loans which no longer qualify, eg, business loans and second mortgages taken out for non-housing purposes during a relationship, where the partner who was solely or jointly liable subsequently left.

Interest on arrears

For claims starting before 2 October 1995, the Department of Works and Pensions (DWP) will meet the extra interest that was payable on interest, which had been deferred under the terms of a deferred interest mortgage, for at least two years.

11.12 Waiting periods for claims made on or after 2 October 1995

Unfortunately, even if a claimant and the loan meet all the appropriate criteria, IS/JSA payments to help meet the costs will not be payable immediately. There is a 'waiting period,' which means that most claimants must wait a fixed period after making the claim before all eligible housing costs will be paid. These waiting periods have been dramatically increased since 2 October 1995. How long a claimant must wait varies, depending upon:

• individual circumstances

• whether the loan was taken out before or after 2 October 1995.

Waiting periods will be one of the following:

• No waiting period

• 26 weeks (but for 18 of these, half of the eligible costs are payable)

• 39 weeks.

No waiting period

para 8 Sch 2 JSA Regs & para 9 Sch 3 IS Regs

The only people who do not have to wait before receiving assistance with mortgage costs are those aged 60 or over. If a claimant (or her/his current partner) is aged 60 or over, s/he will receive the full amount of the 'eligible' interest from the start of the claim.

26 week rule

paras 1(2) & 6 Sch 2 JSA Regs paras 1(2) & 6 Sch 3 IS Regs

This rule applies for 'existing housing costs.' These are costs arising from a mortgage or loan which started before 2 October 1995. The rule applies to everyone who took on a loan before 2 October 1995, except those over 60, who are subject to no waiting period.

para 7(3)-(6)
Sch 2 JSA Regs
& para 8(2) & (3)
Sch 3 IS Regs In addition, certain groups who took on loans after 2 October 1995 are also treated as having 'existing housing costs.' In the context of relationship breakdown, the most significant of these groups are people who are not required to sign on for work because they are a carer, or deserted partners caring for a dependent child. The other special groups are prisoners on remand or awaiting sentencing, and certain people whose claims on insurance protection policies have been turned down because the claim is due to a pre-existing medical condition or because of HIV infection.

Claimants who qualify under the 26 week rule are entitled to the following amounts towards mortgage costs:

• First 8 weeks – nothing

• Next 18 weeks – half the eligible interest

• From week 27 – the full amount of eligible interest.

39 week rule

para 1(2) & 7 Sch 2
JSA Regs &
paras 1(2) & 8
Sch 3 IS Regs This rule applies to 'new housing costs' which are those arising from a mortgage or loan agreed on or after 2 October 1995. Anyone who is not covered by one of the situations above (no waiting period or 26 weeks waiting period) will fall within this rule.

People in this category will receive the following amounts towards mortgage costs:

• First nine months (39 weeks) – nothing

• From week 40 – the full amount of eligible interest.

11.13 Payment of mortgage interest

Reg 34A & para 2
Sch 9A SS
(C&P)Regs As most lenders now participate in the mortgage interest direct scheme, the majority of claimants will have their interest paid directly to the mortgage lender. If interest is being paid directly, or would have been paid directly if the lender had not opted out of the scheme, deductions from benefit for arrears cannot also be made. Other claimants may have deductions made from benefit and paid direct to the lender because of arrears, but only in certain circumstances:

• The claimant must have missed at least 8 weeks of interest payments
or
• It must be in the overriding interests of her/his family for the deductions to be made.

Reg 35 and Sch 9
(C&P)Regs The calculations of the amount which may be deducted is complicated, and the regulations and further guidance should be consulted.[7]

7.   CPAG Welfare Benefits and Tax Credits Handbook 2003/2004, p.1049.

11.14 Restrictions on increases in housing costs

When a relationship breaks down, the family home is often sold and a separated partner may have to buy another property, involving an increase in mortgage costs. If housing costs are increased through new borrowing whilst receiving IS/JSA, or during a period of 26 weeks or less between claims, the amount of IS/ISA payable towards them will usually be restricted.

para 4 Sch 2
JSA Regs & para 4
Sch 3 IS Regs

There are some exceptions to these restrictions. A restriction will not be applied if the increase is due to additional borrowing for:

• necessary repairs or improvements, or

• adaptations for a disabled person or in order to provide separate bedrooms for children of different sexes aged 10 or over, or

• financing a move to alternative accommodation

which:

1. Provides separate bedrooms for children of different sexes aged 10 or over, or

2. Better meets the needs of a disabled person.

There are also restrictions on the size of the loan which will be met, even if it qualifies.

Buying out a partner's interest

A common arrangement on relationship breakdown is for one partner to obtain an additional loan to finance buying out the other partner's interest. If this results in an increase in housing costs, as will normally be the case, the increase will only be met if it is more than 26 weeks since the claimant or the claimant's former partner received IS/JSA and the new loan is obtained before a fresh claim is made.

In any other circumstances, no IS/JSA will be payable on increased interest payments for buying out a partner.

Restrictions based on high costs

Restrictions on the amount of interest payable may also be limited in certain other circumstances, eg:

• if the total loan is more than £100,000, or

• the property is deemed too big for the claimant, or

• the area is deemed too expensive, or

para 12 Sch 2
JSA Regs

• eligible housing costs are greater than other suitable accommodation in the area.

11.15 Housing costs calculation

Under the pre-October 1995 rules, the interest payable under IS was based on the amount of interest that was actually payable by the individual claimant. Unless the claim is transitionally protected from that date (see 11.10) the DWP calculates the 'eligible interest' on the basis of what is known as its 'standard rate.' The standard rate is arrived at by taking an average of the rates of interest charged by the main building societies. The claimant's actual interest rate is used only if it is less than 5% per annum. Otherwise the standard rate is used, whether it is less or more than the actual rate.

para 11 Sch 2 JSA Regs & para 12 Sch 3 IS Regs

11.16 Underpayments

As a result of the complexity of the benefits system, mistakes continue to be made in the calculation of housing costs. It is essential that advisers check that claimants are receiving their full entitlement. Even then, it is likely that there will be a shortfall between help from benefit and the actual interest due.

C   Arrears and possession proceedings

11.17 Liability for mortgage arrears

A person will normally only be held liable for mortgage arrears if s/he is named on the mortgage or has acted as a guarantor. S/he will not normally be liable for the mortgage if it is in someone else's name, even if s/he is married to that person. If the mortgage is in joint names, each borrower is deemed to be jointly and severally liable for the mortgage debt. This means that they can each be pursued by the lender for the whole of the mortgage debt, not just half of it.

Short-term liability

If an occupation order is obtained by a married, cohabiting or former couple granting or declaring occupation rights or excluding one party, the court may also attach a provision imposing on either party (whether sole or joint owners) obligations to discharge outgoings during the period the occupation order is in force (see 13.23). This could include making payments towards arrears.

s40 FLA96

Unfortunately, a recent case has shown that the courts have limited power to enforce payments ordered in this way. In *Nwogbe v Nwogbe*,[8] the court made a non-molestation order and occupation order, and under the terms of the occupation order, Mr N was ordered to make payments of rent and other outgoings concerning the property. When he did not

---

8.   Nwogbe v Nwogbe (2000) 2 FLR 744.

comply with the order, Mrs N applied to the county court to commit him to prison for non-compliance with the order. The court held that it did have power to enforce the order since s.40 of the Family Law Act 1996:

- Did not fall under the exceptions in s.4 of the Debtors Act 1869 (which had abolished imprisonment for debtors except in certain circumstances)

- Fell outside the scope of s.1 of the Attachment of Earnings Act 1971 and Schedule 8 of the Administration Act 1970, which the court held did not contain any reference to sums payable under s.40 of the Act.

The court held that it was disturbing that s.40 orders might be unenforcable and of no value to the spouse or cohabitant remaining in occupation. However, until the legislation is repealed or amended by Parliament, the courts have no ultimate sanction to enforce money orders under s.40 of the Family Law Act 1996.

Long-term liability

Even if the court attaches provisions to an order under the Family Law Act 1996, as above, the person or persons named on the mortgage deed remain technically liable for any mortgage arrears, unless released from the liability by the lender. Such a release is only likely to be granted if the other partner is both willing to take on the liability and can show sufficient financial viability to meet both current payments and arrears. It may then be possible to negotiate a solution to payment problems.

11.18 Tactics in dealing with payment problems

The degree of involvement in dealing with payment problems will vary from agency to agency, depending on its role. In many cases it may be helpful to refer to a specialist money adviser. However, for those in areas where there is no specialist support available, or for those who wish to help in negotiations on arrears, it may be useful to contact one of the national organisations listed in the appendices.

11.19 Possession proceedings – the right to be notified

Mortgage in sole name

Married couples
If the property is in one name only, the non-owning spouse must be notified of the possession action by the lender, provided that her/his matrimonial home rights are registered as a charge or notice or caution, as appropriate (see 4.10). If the rights are not registered, then see cohabiting couples below.

Cohabiting couples

CPR 55.10   Under the Civil Procedure Rules, lenders are under an obligation to send notification of a possession hearing to the premises at least 14 days before the hearing. The notification should be addressed to 'the occupier' and should give details of the place and date of the hearing

CPR 55.10 para (3)   and of the names of the parties.

Mortgage in joint names

In all instances where a mortgage is in joint names (irrespective of whether or not the couple are married or cohabiting), both borrowers must be notified separately of the possession proceedings.

11.20   Right to be heard in court

Mortgage in sole name

Married couples

If the couple are married, regardless of whether rights of occupation have been registered or not, a non-owning spouse has the right to be

s55 FLA96   made a party to a repossession action, provided that:

s30(3) FLA96   1. S/he is entitled to pay the mortgage by virtue of matrimonial home rights.

2. The court does not see any special reason against it, and the court is satisfied that the non-owning spouse may be able to affect the outcome of the proceedings by making payments or coming to some satisfactory arrangement.

Cohabitants

A non-owning cohabitant has no right to be heard in court unless s/he can acquire the same rights as the married non-owner, above, by obtaining an occupation order, which grants the equivalent of

6(13) & s30(3) FLA96   matrimonial home rights, including the right to be a party to a possession action and therefore to be heard in court (see 13.22).

Non-owning lesbian and gay cohabitants are not able to obtain occupation orders and so have no legal right to appear in court.

Mortgage in joint names

In all instances where a mortgage is in joint names (irrespective of whether or not the couple is married or cohabiting), both borrowers have the right to be heard in court.

D   Taking over the mortgage

When a relationship has irrevocably broken down, people usually wish to make arrangements that will make them as independent of each other as possible. This frequently involves transfer of ownership of the family home from one party to another. The person who has transferred her/his interest may want to take out a new mortgage to finance her/his own purchase of a new home. If s/he is still liable for the original mortgage, it may prove difficult to obtain a further mortgage. Tax relief problems also arise. For these reasons, both parties may wish the mortgage to be taken over by the person remaining in the home.

Unfortunately, problems may arise where parties wish to transfer a sole interest in the home to the other partner or a joint interest to one partner only. The following sections therefore apply equally where the mortgage has been in either sole or joint names.

11.21 Reasons why the lender might refuse to approve the transfer

A couple may have agreed, or been ordered by the court, to transfer a property from one to another and may also wish to transfer liability for the mortgage.

A mortgage deed routinely contains covenants stating the liabilities of the borrower(s), in particular to repay the loan. Although the court may adjust the legal ownership or beneficial interests of the property and make orders as to who must make payments to the lender, it cannot affect the actual liabilities of the parties to the mortgage lender or actually transfer the mortgage into someone else's name, unless the mortgage lender agrees.

There may be a number of reasons why the lender is reluctant to agree to a transfer of the mortgage loan:

Existence of mortgage arrears

If there are already mortgage arrears, the lender is unlikely to give up its rights to pursue an employed person who is liable for the debt. It is only likely to do so if it feels that the new sole borrower is a good security risk and is likely to be able to pay off the arrears. Even so, particularly in the case of joint borrowers, it is likely to prefer to have two people to pursue than one.

Concern about security

The lender is most likely to agree a release from the mortgage covenants where there is a high proportion of equity to loan. This will mean that the loan is safely secured, even if the partner now solely liable is unable to meet the mortgage repayments in the future.

Reluctance to allow mortgage payments to be maintained on the basis of Income Support/Jobseeker's Allowance

In many cases, the remaining partner will be reliant on IS/JSA and the lender will be aware that not only will there be a period when no or partial payments may be made (see 11.12), but that they will at best cover interest only, with the capital debt remaining untouched. Where there is equity in the property, this should not be a major cause for concern, although the debt may increase due to arrears incurred because of various benefit restrictions. If the mortgage loan is greater than the value of the home (ie, there is negative equity), the lender may also be concerned that there is no prospect of full repayment of the loan.

11.22 Tactics

Dealing with arrears and methods of repayment

For more information on negotiating with lenders, readers should contact one of the organisations listed in the appendices.

Transferring the property

If the mortgage lender will not agree to release one party and transfer a mortgage to the other, then the original joint or sole borrowers remain liable. To get around this problem, the court may require an undertaking from one party to indemnify the other against the mortgage repayments. The mortgage therefore remains in joint names, with the sole owner agreeing to indemnify the other borrower.

> **Example: agreement to indemnify one party against mortgage repayments**
>
> *Jane and Steve have a joint mortgage; Jane wants the property transferred into her sole name; the building society will not release Steve from the mortgage liability. The court therefore orders the transfer of the property on condition that Jane gives an undertaking to pay the mortgage payments. If she fails to meet them, and Steve thus becomes technically liable, she agrees to indemnify him. If she fails to do so, he can sue her in a third party action. In practice, this may of course be of little help if Jane has no money.*

11.23 Problems that can result if there is negative equity

In terms of court orders for transfers of property, negative equity can complicate settlement considerably. Where there is positive equity in the home, one party may be willing to undertake to indemnify the other (as indicated above) in return for a transfer of the partner's interest, since the interest will obviously be a financial asset.

Where there is negative equity, a property transfer would in fact mean a transfer of the debt along with ownership. There is therefore little incentive for the person in occupation to agree any undertakings which would release the other partner from her/his liabilities. Any property transfer would therefore have to be accompanied by a carefully worded undertaking. This could offer indemnity against liability for future mortgage payments to the partner not in occupation, but would ensure that both parties (if the property had been jointly owned) remained jointly responsible for any debt outstanding on the property if it were sold.

If the mortgage is in one name only and the non-owning partner wishes to remain in occupation, an order giving the right to occupy, rather than a transfer of the legal interest, might be preferred (i.e. a *Martin* or *Mesher* style order, see 4.33).

Rent

As with mortgage difficulties, rent problems frequently accompany relationship breakdown. There may be problems over:

- who is entitled to pay the rent

- help with paying rent

- who is liable for rent and/or arrears

- whether a non-tenant spouse should agree to take on arrears to preserve the tenancy in future.

E   The right to pay rent

Married couples and cohabitants have differing rights relating to payment of rent where a tenancy is in one name only. The rights of non-tenants mirror those of non-owners. In most other aspects relating to rent payment, married couples and cohabitants, heterosexual, lesbian or gay, are in virtually the same position.

11.24   Rights of sole and joint tenants to pay the rent

Sole tenancy

Married couples
s30(3) FLA96   Both the married tenant and the non-tenant spouse have a right to pay rent. The landlord is obliged to accept payments from the non-tenant as if they were from the tenant.

Cohabitants

Unlike married couples, non-tenant cohabitants have no automatic right to pay rent and the landlord can therefore refuse payment. However heterosexual non-tenant cohabitants can apply for occupation orders and acquire the right to pay rent (see 13.23 and 13.33).

If there is no occupation order and rent is refused, this may of course lead to arrears, which will give the landlord a right to possession. If the landlord accepts rent from the cohabitant, knowing that the tenant has gone, this may be a basis for arguing that the landlord has entered into a new contract for a new tenancy with the cohabitant (6.38).

Joint tenancy

Both joint tenants, married or not, are entitled to pay rent and are jointly and severally liable for the whole of the rent.

F   Housing benefit

For the purposes of the housing benefit regulations, a 'couple' or 'partner' refers only to heterosexual relationships.

11.25 Help with rent payments

A person who is not legally liable for rent payments may be entitled to housing benefit towards rent in the same way as a non-owner can be eligible for IS/JSA to help meet mortgage costs. There is often confusion over this, since people do not realise a claimant may be 'treated as liable' for housing costs. There are a number of situations where people may be treated as liable, and the most relevant to relationship breakdown are where:

• s/he is liable

• s/he is the partner of the liable person, or

• s/he is the former partner of the liable person, who is not paying the rent, and it is necessary for her/him to make the payments in order to remain living in the accommodation, or

• s/he has taken over paying the rent but is *not* the former partner of the liable person and the local authority considers it reasonable to treat her/him as liable. The local authority has discretion to decide whether to pay where the claimant is not a heterosexual former partner, for example, if the couple were lesbian or gay.

Reg 6(1) HB Regs

A non-tenant heterosexual partner will be treated as liable if the partner who was liable is not now making rent payments and the non-tenant needs to make payments in order to remain living in the home. It does not require the landlord to be about to evict the non-tenant, nor does it matter whether or not the landlord is prepared to agree to a transfer of tenancy (by the courts or assignment).

Reg 6(1)(3)(i) HB Regs

11.26 Treated as not liable for Housing Benefit purposes

Since January 1999, Regulation 7 of the Housing Benefit Regulations specifically excludes a person who rents a former joint home from their ex-partner, or where the landlord is the ex-partner of the claimant's partner and it is their former joint home.

Other examples of situations where the claimant will be treated as not liable are:

- where the claimant or partner is responsible for her/his landlord's child

- where the agreement is not on a commercial basis

- where the accommodation is a condition of employment.

This is not an exhaustive list of exclusions and advisers should be sure to check the regulations and seek further guidance.[9]

11.27 Payment of housing benefit on two homes in cases of domestic violence and relationship breakdown

Payment of housing benefit on two homes where no intention to return

Housing benefit is usually only payable on the dwelling that the claimant normally occupies as her/his home

Reg 5(1) HB Regs No. 1971

However, s/he can be treated as occupying two homes so that housing benefit may be paid on both where:

- the claimant is liable or treated as liable (as above) to make payments in respect of both dwellings and

- the claimant has left the former dwelling and remains absent through fear of violence there or by a former member of her/his family, and

Reg 5.5(a) HB Regs

- it is reasonable that housing benefit should be paid in respect of both the former and the present dwelling.

Under this regulation, in cases where absence is because of fear of violence, there is no specified limit on the length of time for which two sets of payment may be made . Nor is there a requirement that the claimant is intending to return home, for example, s/he may be

9. See 'Who's being abused' by Kate Smith, article in Advisor magazine 92, July/August 2002, p.19.

waiting to be rehoused by the local authority. However, the local authority's housing benefit department has discretion in deciding on whether it is reasonable to meet both sets of payments, and, where the claimant does not intend to return home, two payments may well be refused. This can cause problems where the tenancy is a joint tenancy and the claimant does not want to return to the home, but does not want, or is afraid, to make her/his partner homeless by serving notice to quit to end the tenancy and her/his rent liability. In such cases, advisers need to argue that it is reasonable to make the payments in the circumstances. Housing providers should be aware that unavoidable arrears may arise.

Payment of Housing Benefit during temporary absence and intention to return

Payment of Housing Benefit on two homes must be paid for up to fifty-two weeks where:

- the claimant intends to return to occupy the dwelling as her/his home, and

- the part which s/he normally occupies has not been let or sublet, and

- the period of absence is unlikely to exceed fifty-two weeks, or unlikely to substantially exceed that period.

This might occur, for example, during a separation when someone has moved out and is staying with friends or relatives. Unlike JSA/IS claims, no specific reason for the absence has to be shown, eg, fear of violence does not have to be shown. Payment is not at the discretion of the local authority, so that advisers can insist that payment should be made.

Reg 5(8) HB Regs

Payment of Housing Benefit on two homes where claimant has moved into a new home

Payment of Housing Benefit may also be made on two homes for an overlapping period of four weeks, if rental payments on the old home could not reasonably be avoided.

Reg 5.5(d) HB Regs

11.28 Rent restrictions

There are restrictions on how much rent can be covered by Housing Benefit. Rent restrictions are complicated, and further guidance should be sought before giving advice. Broadly, the Rent Officer identifies:

- a 'local reference rent'

- a 'claim-related rent', and

- a 'single room rent' if applicable (see below).

The lowest of these is then used to decide the maximum eligible rent. However, some people with older claims, from before 5 October 1997. may have some limited protection from the restrictions imposed by the introduction of 'claim-related rents.'

If a person has been claiming HB for the same property since 5 October 1997 (with some breaks for certain tenants with disabilities ignored), there is transitional protection to the local reference rent plus half the difference between the local reference rent and the claim-related rent.

The local reference rent is fixed at the mid-point of a range of rents for similar accommodation in the locality. Market rents are not the main determining factor for assessing maximum eligible rents for Housing Benefit.

A claim-related rent is affected by size of accommodation in relation to the household, and whether the rent is deemed significantly higher than similar tenancies in the vicinity, or exceptionally high generally.

11.29 Single room rent for under 25-year-olds

Reg 11(3A) & (4)
HB Regs & Reg
4(2A) HB & CTB Regs

The single room rent is the level for a single person who is under 25 and is generally fixed at the rate of a room in shared accommodation, although some care leavers, young people with disabilities and other special groups are exempt from the single room rent.[10]

Not all tenancies are subject to these restrictions: for example, protected tenancies are excluded because the rent is set by the rent officer. In addition, some claimants are exempt because of transitional protection,[11] ie, their claim is linked or continuous since 1 January 1996 or earlier. This can apply where someone claims Housing Benefit:

- because her/his former partner, who was an exempt claimant, leaves, and

- they are no longer a couple, and

- the claim is for the same property and

CPAG pps 234-235
& 239-240

- the claim is made within 4 weeks of the partner's departure.

It is beyond the scope of this book to go into further details on rent restrictions about this area; advisers should check one of the many books on housing benefit and welfare rights.[12]

10. Housing Benefit (General) Amendment Regulations 1996, SI 1996 No. 965.
11. Reg 10 HB (General) Amendment Regs 1996 SI 965 for transitional protection and old Reg 11 HB Regs prior to January 1996.
12. J. Zebedee & M. Ward, Guide to Housing Benefit and Council Tax Benefit 2002-03 (Shelter/Chartered Institute of Housing, 2002); 'Housing Benefit for Housing Managers in the Social Sector,' (Chris Smith 2002).

11.30 Non-dependent deductions

A non-dependent deduction is made for people who live with the claimant and are over 18, if they are not responsible for paying the rent but could be expected to make a contribution.This might include:

• adult children

• relatives

• friends

• a lesbian or gay partner.

The deduction will be made whether or not the claimant actually receives money from the non-dependent to pay the rent. The amount that is taken off varies depending on the income of the non-dependent. The claimant will therefore need to give evidence of the person's income.

G   Rent arrears and possession proceedings

11.31 Liability for rent and/or arrears if the sole tenant leaves

Married couples: the legal position

• The tenant remains liable for the rent and any arrears as long as the tenancy continues

• A sole tenant can normally end her/his rent liability by giving valid notice to quit (see 6.33)

• However, if a married Rent Act 1977 protected or statutory tenant wishes to end her/his liability for rent on a tenancy, s/he should apply through the Courts for an order under the Family Law Act 1996, with attached provisions to transfer rent obligations. This is because a statutory tenancy continues to exist, even after notice to quit, if the tenant or tenant's spouse remains living there. If such an order is not obtained s/he may be held liable for rent even after giving notice (see *Griffiths v Renfree* in box on next page), apart from where:

 – the court has ordered a transfer of liability as above: a non-tenant spouse cannot be held liable for rent or arrears despite having a right to occupy (see also 11.17)

 – the tenancy has been transferred from one spouse to another: the position differs depending upon whether this is by assignment (see 6.25 – 6.28), either voluntarily or under the Matrimonial Causes Act 1973 (see 6.25) or by vesting under a Family Law Act 1996 order (see 7.52 – 7.53).

> ### Griffiths v Renfree[13]
>
> *A protected shorthold[14] tenant moved out after marriage breakdown, leaving his wife in occupation. The tenant gave notice terminating the tenancy, but did not deliver the keys and his wife remained in possession. The landlord subsequently sought possession and rent arrears from the tenant. The Court of Appeal held that the notice turned the shorthold into a statutory tenancy and that the tenant remained liable because the spouse's occupation was treated as possession by the tenant for the purposes of Rent Act 1977. The court held that a tenant does not effectively divest himself of a tenancy by notice, so long as his wife remains in occupation. A court order transferring liability should have been applied for.*

s33 & s40(1)(a) FLA96

Married couples: the practical position

- In practice, although the non-tenant spouse is not liable, if the tenant fails to pay any arrears accrued, a landlord may seek possession

- Where the tenancy is secure or protected, the court has discretion as to whether to award possession on the basis of rent arrears, and will only do so if it considers it reasonable. If the current rent is being paid, the court may well refuse possession and suggest that the landlord pursue the tenant, not the spouse, for the arrears

ground 8 Sch 2 HA88

- If the tenancy is assured and the landlord is seeking possession on the ground that the arrears are more than eight weeks or two months, the court will have no choice but to award possession, since this is a mandatory ground. If the arrears are reduced to less than two months by the date of the hearing, the landlord may still have a ground for possession, but the court will have discretion as to whether to award possession

ground 10 & 11 Sch 2 HA88

- If the spouse wishes to remain in the property, it will therefore normally be wise for her/him to start paying current rent if possible (Housing Benefit may be available), but to repay or offer to repay arrears only if it appears essential to prevent possession being granted

- The Family Law Act 1996 gives a non-tenant spouse the right to pay rent and therefore the landlord cannot legally refuse it. If a landlord refuses to take the money, the tenant should be advised to put the offer of rent in writing to the landlord (keeping a copy) and to set the money aside, eg, deposit it in a savings account, so that it is available should the landlord try to allege rent arrears as a ground for possession.

14. This is a type of protected tenancy which is now very rare as most protected shorthold tenancies have become assured shorthold tenancies by virtue of s.34 (3) Housing Act 1988.

13. Griffiths v Renfree (1989) 21 HLR 338 CA.

Cohabiting couples

- A cohabiting non-tenant does not have any legal responsibility to pay the rent to the landlord

- A heterosexual non-tenant cohabitant may be able to obtain an occupation order, which also gives her/him the right, but not the liability, to pay rent. Liability can only arise if the court has attached provisions to an occupation order that impose obligations regarding rent payments on either party

s40(1)(a) FLA96

- In the absence of a Family Law Act order, a non-tenant cohabitant is not responsible for the tenant's arrears; however, some local authorities will require the cohabitant to agree to repay arrears as a condition of granting her/him the tenancy. There is no legal basis for this and there have been ombudsman decisions against local authorities who try to make the new tenant responsible (see 11.33). A cohabitant should be wary of agreeing to enter any contractual arrangement to clear arrears

- The court may order a transfer of tenancy between heterosexual former cohabitants and make orders regarding rent and arrears as for married couples (see 7.52 – 7.53 and 8.19).

11.32 Liability for rent and/or arrears if one joint tenant leaves

The legal position

Where the tenancy is in joint names, whether the partners are married or not, both partners are liable for the rent both jointly and independently of the other joint tenant, and regardless of whether they are in occupation. This means that either or both tenants can be held responsible for the whole rent, and it is not possible to argue that a tenant is only liable for a particular share, such as half the rent each. This is known as 'joint and several liability.'

The practical position

If one joint tenant fails to pay anything towards the rent, then it will be necessary for the other to pay the rent to prevent the landlord taking possession proceedings. It would then be necessary for the tenant who has paid to take a third party civil action against the other tenant to reclaim her/his share of the rent. This must be done by the tenant – it is not the landlord's concern. In practice, of course, it may be very difficult to recoup money from a vanished spouse or partner.

Ending liability for rent

It may be possible to end rent liability by voluntary assignment, notice to quit or by court order. Which of the first two avenues are open depends upon the type of tenancy (see Chapter 6, Section C). The court also has powers to transfer liabilities for married couples and for some cohabitants when making orders and transferring tenancies under the Family Law Act.

11.33 Paying arrears to take over the tenancy

Illegal premiums

- Arrears should not be paid out of fear of not being granted a tenancy. Many local authorities charge what, in effect, may be an illegal premium by demanding that a new tenant pays the former tenant's arrears before 'taking over' the tenancy.

Complaint against *Wellingborough BC*[15]

In an ombudsman investigation, Wellingborough BC were found guilty of maladministration as a result of a policy which allowed officers to allocate tenancies in certain circumstances if the new tenant paid the former tenant's arrears. This led one man to pay £400 towards his ex-wife's rent arrears. The ombudsman found maladministration on the basis that 'the way in which this policy works suggests that, if prospective tenants provide an inducement, their chances of obtaining an allocation improved.'

- There are legal options available to both married and cohabiting couples which mean that a tenancy may be able to be transferred even without the landlord's consent. These are explained in full in Chapters 7, 8 and 9.

11.34 The right to appear in court

Sole tenancy

Married couples

s85(5) HA85, s9(5) HA88 & s100(4B) RA77

For assured, secure and protected tenants, a non-tenant spouse has a special right to intervene in possession proceedings and apply for a suspension or postponement, even after the order has already been made terminating the tenancy.

Cohabitants

A non-tenant cohabitant has no right to intervene in possession proceedings, unless an occupation order has been obtained. Where an occupation order has been obtained, the right to be heard is the same as for married couples. Note that lesbian and gay non-tenant

---

cohabitants cannot obtain occupation orders and therefore have no right to intervene in possession proceedings.

Joint tenancy

Where the tenancy is in joint names, regardless of whether the couple are married or cohabiting, both must be notified of possession proceedings and can be heard in court.

Chapter 12: Insolvency and bankruptcy

Subjects covered in this chapter include...

Debt and insolvency

What it means to be insolvent or bankrupt

When an Individual Voluntary Arrangement may be appropriate

What a charging order does

Bankruptcy and owner-occupiers

What happens when a bankruptcy order is made

What effect a bankruptcy order has on the non-bankrupt partner's share of the home

What rights a partner has to occupy after a bankruptcy order

How the property may be sold and when a sale may be postponed

What effect bankruptcy has on transfers of property

Bankruptcy and tenancies

What effect bankruptcy has on tenancies

What happens to rent arrears after bankruptcy

Whether a landlord can seek possession after a bankruptcy order

Bankruptcy and family proceedings

What effect bankruptcy has on maintenance or lump sum orders

Insolvency and bankruptcy

*Debt problems leading to insolvency and bankruptcy are an increasingly
significant factor which has to be dealt with on relationship breakdown. The
number of creditors' bankruptcy petitions more than tripled from 7,717 in the
late 1980s to 28,468 in the early 1990s. Since then the figure has dropped to
17,496 in 1999, but this is still more than double the 1980s figures.[1] Financial
difficulties can obviously be an important factor in the breakdown of a
relationship. The rights of a spouse, or a cohabitant, to the family home may
be jeopardised and it is therefore very important that the correct advice is given.*

*The law on insolvency and bankruptcy is complex and this book cannot hope
to go into any depth on the subject. What it aims to do is to explain some very
basic principles and signpost potential 'danger zones' which an adviser should
be aware of, and upon which a client may need to be advised to seek further
expert advice. Reference books are available for those advisers who find
insolvency to be a significant proportion of their work.[2]*

A   Debt and insolvency

The law on insolvency is covered by the Insolvency Act 1986 for all cases
which commenced after 29 December 1986. Changes to both insolvency
and individual bankruptcy are made by the Enterprise Act 2002, which
received Royal Assent on 7th November 2002. The main provisions are
coming into force from June 2003 to early 2004. One of the aims of the
Enterprise Act is to help people who have become bankrupt through no
fault of their own.

12.1   Enterprise Act 2002

The key changes for individual bankrupts are:

- those made bankrupt will generally be discharged one year after
  the date of the bankruptcy order, instead of the previous three years

- where the court considers the bankruptcy is as a result of irresponsible
  or reckless conduct, it will have power to impose a Bankruptcy
  Restriction Order (BRO). A BRO generally imposes restrictions that
  apply after a bankrupt has been discharged. These restrictions apply
  for a period of between 2 and 15 years

- there is a limit of three years on the period during which the trustee
  in bankruptcy (the person appointed by the courts to manage the
  bankrupt persons finances) can deal with a bankrupt's interest in a
  dwelling, which is the sole or principal home of:

1. Company Winding Up and Bankruptcy Petition Statistics
    2nd Quarter 2000, Lord Chancellor's Department,
    available at www.insolvency.co.uk/news/08040lcd.htm.

2. See for example G. Howell, Family Breakdown and
    Insolvency (Butterworth, 1993); S. A. Frieze, Personal
    Insolvency Law – in Practice, (Sweet and Maxwell,
    publication due July 2003); S. Lawson, Individual
    Voluntary Arrangements (Jordan, 1996).

- the bankrupt

- the bankrupt's spouse, or

- the bankrupt's former spouse

After the three years, the home will revert back to the bankrupt (ie, it will no longer form part of the bankrupt's estate) unless the trustee, during the three year period has:

- realised the interest in the home

- applied for an order for sale or possession in respect of the home

- applied for a charging order over the home in respect of the value of the interest or

- has entered into an agreement with the bankrupt regarding the interest

• there is a new fast-track regime for Individual Voluntary Arrangements after bankruptcy (IVAs – see 12.4), where the Official Receiver is the proposed nominee. The IVA annuls the bankruptcy

• Income Payments Orders (IPOs) will last for three years from the date of the IPO. An alternative to an IPO, which is made by the court, will be to make an Income Payments Agreement (IPA), which is a written agreement between the bankrupt and the Official Receiver or Trustee that requires the bankrupt to make specified payments to the trustee for a specified period. An IPA will be enforceable as if it were an IPO made by the court. It cannot last for more than three years after the date of the IPA.

For more information on the Enterprise Act 2002, see the government website.[3]

12.2 Insolvency

An individual is insolvent if:

• s/he is unable to pay her/his debts when they fall due and

s341(3) IA86
• her/his liabilities, both existing and prospective, exceed the value of her/his assets.

Obviously, many of us are insolvent at various times in our lives, but the issue often only comes to a head when creditors are no longer prepared to wait. A person who is insolvent will not necessarily go bankrupt. It can, however, be very important to know whether a spouse is insolvent at the time when a matrimonial property transfer is made, since it can put that transfer at risk at a later date.

COURT ACTION AFFECTING THE HOME

12.3 Bankruptcy

People quite frequently say they are bankrupt when they mean they are insolvent. A person is not actually bankrupt until a bankruptcy order has been made by the court, but it is important to bear in mind that if a bankruptcy order is made, then any property disposed of after the bankruptcy petition was presented (including matrimonial transfers) is at risk (see 12.15 for the effect of bankruptcy upon prior property transfers).

s284 IA86

A bankruptcy order can be made following an application (called a bankruptcy petition) which can be presented either:

- by a creditor

- by the debtor her/himself, or

- where there has been default under a 'voluntary arrangement' (see below).

A bankruptcy order signifies that the individual concerned is unable to pay her/his debts, and that the assets are to be administered for the benefit of creditors. This means that the bankrupt is no longer entitled to dispose of them. The appointment of the trustee in bankruptcy actually deprives the bankrupt of her/his assets, apart from certain essential personal belongings and essential tools of the bankrupt's trade. An Income Payments Order may also be made where the bankrupt's income exceeds her/his reasonable needs. Any excess income is paid directly to the trustee in bankruptcy. Such orders are relatively uncommon.

Where advising on rights to the family home, it may be advisable to carry out a bankruptcy search. This can be done where the land is registered or unregistered, through the Land Charges Department in Plymouth.[4] This search may reveal entries which shed light on the state of proceedings:

- PA(B) – this means that a bankruptcy petition has been presented

- WO(B) – this means that a bankruptcy order has been made.[5]

Debts covered by bankruptcy – the effect on the home

Bankruptcy applies only to unsecured debts, such as credit card debts, rent arrears, fuel and water rate arrears. Secured debts such as mortgages and other loans, where a charge has been registered on the home, are not covered. This means that owner-occupiers who go bankrupt may still be pursued by their lender for possession if they are in mortgage arrears, regardless of whether they are bankrupt, or have had their other debts discharged after bankruptcy. Any equity in the home will

---

4. Land Charges Department, Burrington Way, Plymouth, PL5 3LP. Tel. 01752 635 600. The fee was £1.00 at the time of writing.

5. For more information see L. Ayrton, 'Preserving the Family Home in the Face of Bankruptcy' (1993) 23 Fam Law 180.

still go to the trustee in bankruptcy, ie, if there is money left after all secured loans have been paid off, this amount will be kept by the trustee. This issue is covered in detail in Section B below.

12.4 Individual voluntary arrangements

In certain cases, it may be better for the debtor to enter into an Individual Voluntary Arrangement (IVA).[6] This concept was introduced by the Insolvency Act 1986 as an alternative to bankruptcy. It enables the debtor and a licensed insolvency practitioner to formulate proposals together for agreement with the creditors. An interim order can be made to protect the assets whilst the proposal is being put together and considered. Once the arrangement is agreed, it is binding on the creditors. As explained above for bankruptcy, secured loans are not covered by Individual Voluntary Arrangements and it will be necessary to deal with the lender separately.

Most IVAs are initiated by the debtor but, where a bankruptcy petition is presented, the court can appoint an insolvency practitioner to deal with the bankrupt's affairs in situations where:

- the total bankruptcy debts would be below the small bankruptcies level (currently £20,000)[7]

- the assets exceed the minimum amount (currently £2,000)

- there has been no other bankruptcy or scheme of arrangement of affairs within the previous five years, and

- it appears appropriate to the court.

An IVA may include income payments to creditors as well as realisation of assets.

An Individual Voluntary Arrangement is obviously far less restrictive than bankruptcy, leaving the debtor with some control and possibly the right to keep the home or even to remortgage it, if appropriate. However, the debtor will still have to account to creditors for her/his assets. If the debtor has a viable business, the right to trade is also usually retained. In an IVA, the debtor and creditors can agree whether or not assets are to be included or excluded, but in a bankruptcy they cannot. The 'stigma' of bankruptcy is also avoided and the overall costs of an IVA are normally less than those of a bankruptcy.

IVAs post-bankruptcy

s264 EA2002   Under the changes made by the Enterprise Act 2002, it will also be possible to enter a 'fast-track' IVA after bankruptcy by agreement with the Official Receiver. Once the proposal is agreed with the receiver, it

---

6.   For a fuller explanation of IVAs see G. Sharma, 'Individual Voluntary Arrangements' Adviser 40 (November/December, 1993), p.38.

7.   Insolvency Proceedings (Monetary Limits) Order 1986, SI 1986 No. 1996.

will be filed with the court. No meeting of the creditors will be called, and it will not be possible to modify the proposal. The Official Receiver will send out the proposal to the creditors on a 'take it or leave it' basis, and the creditors will either agree or disagree with the proposal by correspondence. If the IVA is approved, the Official Receiver becomes the supervisor and will notify the court, which can then annul the bankruptcy order.

12.5 Charging orders

The charging order has become an increasingly popular procedure with creditors in order to obtain security for a debt.[8] Over 30,000 a year were granted in the late 1980s, a trebling over earlier years. The numbers dropped in the 1990s, but in 2000 the number of applications for charging orders was 16,357, a fifth more than in 1999.

s1 COA79 Under the Charging Orders Act 1979, where a creditor has obtained a court judgment ordering payment of the debt against a debtor and the debtor has defaulted on the terms of the order (ie, she/he is in arrears), the creditor can apply to the court to obtain a charge against the debtor's property. This makes him/her a secured creditor. The county court has jurisdiction in all cases, regardless of the amount of the judgment, or whether it is a High Court or county court judgment that is being enforced. The High Court only has jurisdiction if the judgment is for more than £5,000.

s2 COA79 A charge can be placed not only on property where the debtor is a legal owner, but also on a beneficial interest in property which the debtor may have. If the property is jointly owned, the charge is only on the debtor's beneficial interest, and not the whole property.

When a charging order is applied for, the court must consider all the circumstances of the case, and, in particular, any evidence before it as to:

• the personal circumstances of the debtors, and

s1(5) COA79 • whether any other creditor of the debtor would be likely to be unduly prejudiced by the making of the order.

In the context of insolvency, the court may refuse to make a charging order absolute under section 1(5)(b) where, by doing so, the particular creditor concerned would be given priority over other unsecured creditors of the debtor. In *Rainbow v Moorgate Properties Ltd*,[9] it was held that, in cases of multiple debt, the court should not exercise its discretion in such a way that it places the creditor applying for the order at an advantage over the creditors, and for this reason it is unlikely that an order will be granted.

8. See S. Oyebitan and RJ. Wilson 'Where now?' an article on charging orders in Adviser 97 (May/June 2003) p.44.

9. Rainbow v Moorgate Properties Ltd; Same v Same (1975) 2 All ER 821, CA.

In the case of *Harman v Glencross,*[10] it was held that a wife who was a joint owner and in occupation of the matrimonial home was an interested party, within the meaning of the Charging Orders Act, and was therefore s3(5) COA79 entitled to apply for an order discharging or varying the charging order. The wife had filed a divorce petition and was applying for her husband's interest in property to be transferred to her. She was not notified of the charging order, but subsequently applied successfully to have the order varied and the property transferred to her. The Court of Appeal upheld this decision, although it stressed that this was exceptional and hinged largely upon the fact that the wife's divorce application had been made before the charging order application. In such a case both claims should be heard together in the Family Division of the court. Where the charging order comes first, the order would normally be made absolute (subject to the comments made in the paragraph above), and therefore take precedence over a matrimonial claim.

Enforcing a charging order

Once a charging order has been made, the creditor can either content her/himself with the security, or apply for sale of the property. Where the property is solely owned, or where it is jointly owned but both owners are jointly liable for the debt, application for sale must be made under the Charging Orders Act. Where the property is jointly owned but the debt is that of one joint owner only, the creditor must apply under section 14 of the Trusts of Land and Appointment of Trustees Act 1996 for an order for sale (see 5.48). The creditor is 'a person interested' in the property, and hence has the right to apply for sale and settlement of the debt.

In deciding whether to make an order for sale, the courts must have regard to the criteria laid down in section 15 of the Trusts of Land and Appointment of Trustees Act (see 5.49). In the case of *Mortgage Corporation v Shaire,*[11] Ms Shaire's partner, who was entitled to 25% of the beneficial interest in the home, died insolvent and his creditors applied for an order for sale. The court held that under section 15, a secured creditor had no necessary priority, unlike the trustee in bankruptcy. Where one of the co-owners is bankrupt, the creditors' interests outweigh all other considerations. However, where one of the co-owners has charged her/his interest, the interest of the creditor was given the same importance as the interests of the children residing in the house. Nothing in the code laid down by the Trusts of Land and Appointment of Trustees Act 1996 supported the presumption that the court should order a sale. The judge contrasted this with the earlier position under the Law of Property Act 1925, where there was a presumption that the court should order a sale. The judge concluded that it might be right to refuse a sale,

10. Harman v Glencross (1986) Fam 81; (1986) 1 All ER 545.

11. Mortgage Corporation v Shaire (2000) 80 P&CR 280 Ch.D. See also Bank of Ireland v Bell (2000) EGCS 151 CA.

provided that the person who was occupying the property was able to service the loan, which was secured on the beneficial interest. This was because it would be unfair to leave a secured creditor locked into a trust of land without being able to obtain the return of her/his money.

If the court decides that it is appropriate to order a sale, there will be no twelve month period of grace as there is for a bankrupt, since section 335A of the Insolvency Act does not apply to charging orders (see 12.12).

Effect of charging order on joint beneficial tenancy

Once a charging order is made absolute, a joint beneficial tenancy is severed, making the owners tenants in common (see 5.32 – 5.34).

12.6 Voluntary charges

A lender who has given an unsecured loan may invite a debtor to agree to a voluntary charge over the property. This could be in return for an extension of the loan, or what appear to be more favourable terms. If the property is jointly owned, the partner must agree to the charge and if s/he does, s/he accepts liability. This then puts the lender in the position of a mortgagee with a right to possession and sale if the debtor defaults.

A voluntary charge differs from a charging order. In the case of charging orders, the judge has some discretion as to whether to order a sale, but for voluntary charges, s/he has not. Voluntary charges should, therefore, be treated with great caution, and only be agreed to if the other terms are very advantageous (eg, freezing of interest from the date of charge, stopping of instalments and a promise not to apply for sale while certain circumstances exist), and there is no likelihood of the agreement being broken. It is important to make sure the debtor is not at risk of losing the home as a result of not being able to pay.

12.7 Money advice

All of the above are fairly drastic actions, to be taken once a financial situation has got out of hand. There are, of course, alternatives which may be reached by negotiation, especially with the help of experienced money advisers. Money advice should always be undertaken to try to forestall any of the above courses of action, unless it is to the debtor's advantage to go bankrupt.

The field of money advice is beyond the scope of this book, but other literature is available to guide the reader.[12] In addition, readers could contact one of the specialist organisations listed at the end of this book.

---

12. For example M. Wolfe, *Debt Advice Handbook*, fifth edition (CPAG, 2002).

B   Bankruptcy and owner-occupiers

With charges or voluntary arrangements, there is still a possibility of keeping the family home intact. This cannot normally be said of bankruptcy, and special consideration is therefore given to the way bankruptcy affects those in owner-occupied property.

The adviser needs to know:

• how the bankruptcy will affect a partner's share in the home

• whether the partner is likely to be able to remain in occupation of the home, and if so, for how long

• whether a transfer of property that has taken place prior to bankruptcy is affected.

As explained at 12.3, bankruptcy does not actually deal with secured debts, therefore, in addition to the claims of the trustee in bankruptcy to any equity in the home, there may also be claims of repossession from the mortgage lender, or any other creditor who has a charge on the property.

12.8   What happens when a bankruptcy order is made

When a bankruptcy order is made, the matter is initially dealt with by the official receiver. Then, if there are sufficient assets, a trustee in bankruptcy will subsequently be appointed. If there are not sufficient assets, the official receiver will carry on. Once the order has been made, all the bankrupt's assets (except for certain essential personal belongings and tools of her/his trade) are automatically taken over by the trustee in bankruptcy. This is technically referred to as assets 'vesting in' the trustee. In this situation, it is obviously important to look at what proportion of the value of the home the non-bankrupt partner is entitled to. This will depend on whether the property is jointly or solely owned, and on whether any of the debts were secured on the home.

12.9   Effect of a bankruptcy on non-bankrupt partner's share of the home – where no debts secured

Where there is no debt or mortgage secured on the property, the position is relatively straightforward. A spouse or partner is entitled to keep her/his own share in the matrimonial home, since this share will not vest in the trustee in bankruptcy. Problems may arise where the shares are not clearly defined.

Property owned jointly

Where the property is in joint names and the owners are beneficial joint tenants, the bankrupt's partner will normally be entitled to half the value of the property (see 5.31 – 5.32). Section 12.11 below discusses the effect of bankruptcy on a joint tenancy.

Where the property is in joint names and the owners are joint tenants in common, the bankrupt's partner will be entitled to whatever share was agreed when the property was purchased (see 5.32).

If there is any doubt about the shares, a partner should be advised to take the initiative by seeking a declaration of her/his property rights, by applying to the court under section 15 of the Trusts of Land and Appointment of Trustees Act 1996 (see 5.48). It has been suggested[13] that it is better for the spouse to 'go on the attack' to try to establish a greater share, rather than wait for the trustee to apply for an order for sale.

Property in sole ownership

If a property is owned in the bankrupt partner's sole name but both parties have a beneficial interest, the bankrupt's partner still has a right to retain her/his beneficial interest in the home, ie, it does not vest in the trustee. The trustee in bankruptcy will, of course, wish to realise all the assets of the bankrupt's home in order to meet the claims of the creditors, and may therefore try to contest a partner's claims to a beneficial interest. In the same way, if the bankrupt does not own the home, but has a beneficial interest in it, the trustee will take over that beneficial interest.

In both these situations the trustee will be an 'interested party' under the Trusts of Land and Appointment of Trustees Act 1996, and is therefore entitled to apply to the court for an order for sale of property, even if the non-bankrupt partner does not want to sell. However, the trustee will bear in mind the economics of realising assets and will be open to suggestions if they are likely to improve the position of the creditors.

At the same time as making an order for sale, the court can make a declaration as to the respective beneficial interests of the partners, if these have not been spelt out by the conveyance.

In the absence of an express signed declaration, the court may find a beneficial interest as a result of a:

• resulting trust

• constructive trust, or

• proprietary estoppel.

The distinction between these is explained in some detail at 5.9 – 5.12.

Although it has been said that the distinction between trusts and proprietary estoppel is becoming increasingly blurred, bankruptcy is one area in which it is crucial to distinguish between them:

---

13.   G. Howell, see 2 above, p.131.

- *Proprietary estoppel* takes effect only from the date when declared by the court. If the court decides that there is a beneficial interest based on proprietary estoppel and that decision is made after the bankruptcy order, it can have no effect, since the property will already be vested in the trustee in bankruptcy

- *A constructive or resulting trust*, on the other hand, takes effect from the date of the relevant act(s) which is/are deemed to lead to the creation of the trust (see Chapter 5 for what actions and intentions are necessary for the creation of a trust). It is therefore likely to predate the bankruptcy order, and means that the partner's share in the proceeds, ie, her/his beneficial interest, is protected.

It is therefore in the partner's interest to try to establish a beneficial interest by way of resulting or constructive trust.

12.10 Effect of bankruptcy on non-bankrupt partner's share – where some debts are secured

Where there is a secured debt on the property, the non-bankrupt partner should have been consulted at the time it was taken out because:

- joint owners must both agree to a loan which is secured on the property (see 5.35)

- non-owners are usually asked to sign a waiver of their rights when a loan is taken out (see 5.18).

Because the non-bankrupt spouse has agreed to the loan taking precedence over her/his own rights, her/his share in the property can be used to pay off these loans. In this situation, the non-bankrupt spouse will be entitled to her/his share of whatever is left over once the loan has been paid back.

Example: interests in property on bankruptcy

Jill and John are joint tenants in common, with shares of 70 per cent and 30 per cent respectively. They own a house worth £100,000 which has an £80,000 mortgage. Jill is declared bankrupt. As they both agreed to the mortgage, the debt must be paid back by them both in proportion to their respective shares in the property. This means that, of the £20,000 left after paying off the debt, John will receive £6,000 and the trustee in bankruptcy £14,000.

However, it may be possible for the non-bankrupt owner to obtain a greater share of the proceeds of sale by invoking what is known as the 'equitable doctrine of exoneration'[14] which is linked to the concept of 'marshalling'. This means that the particular debt applies first to the bankrupt's share with only the unsatisfied balance being taken from the partner's share, provided it can be shown that the partner did not benefit in any way from the debt. For example, a home is owned jointly by beneficial joint tenants. It is worth £150,000, with an original joint mortgage of £50,000, ie, an equity of £50,000 each. If a second mortgage for £60,000 has been taken out for family purposes, it will also be deducted equally from the partners' equity. This leaves an equity of £20,000 each: £20,000 goes to the non-bankrupt partner and £20,000 to the trustee in bankruptcy.

However, if the second mortgage is a business loan taken out for the benefit of the bankrupt, the second mortgage can first be offset against the bankrupt's share. In this example, the loan is for more than the bankrupt's share in the equity, and, therefore after the bankrupt's £50,000 has been used up, only £10,000 of the partner's equity must be used to pay off the debt. The non-bankrupt partner therefore receives £40,000. The overdraft secured for a business can be 'marshalled' against the bankrupt's share of the home, and the partner will only have to pay any unsatisfied balance out of her/his share. This doctrine can make a significant difference to the financial outcome for the non-bankrupt owner and specialist advice should be sought to advance arguments on 'exoneration,' if at all appropriate.[15] It applies in the same way to joint tenants in common, beneficial joint tenants and to beneficial interest in solely-owned property.

12.11 Effect of bankruptcy upon beneficial joint tenants

Where a property is legally owned in joint names and where the partners are beneficial joint tenants (see 5.32), a bankruptcy order automatically severs the joint tenancy. The bankrupt's share vests in the trustee in bankruptcy, whilst the other partner retains her/his share of the beneficial interest. It might seem that there is therefore no need for any action on behalf of the partner, but the case of *Re Dennis (A bankrupt)*[16] showed that this is not the case.

A married couple owned the property as beneficial joint tenants. A bankruptcy petition was presented in December 1982 and the husband was adjudicated bankrupt in November 1983. Unfortunately, the wife had died in the interim, in February 1983, leaving her property to the two children of their marriage. The issue arose as to when the joint tenancy was severed.

14. Pittortou (A Bankrupt), Re (1985) 1 All ER 285.
15. Pittortou, Re, ibid. For a useful discussion of this case and 'marshalling' in general, see G. Howell, above, Chapter 15.
16. Dennis (A Bankrupt) Re (1993) Fam Law 195.

- If the joint tenancy was severed before the wife's death, on the presentation of the bankruptcy petition, thereby becoming a joint tenancy in common, the children would be entitled to inherit her share in the property and the trustee in bankruptcy could claim only the husband's share

- If the tenancy was not severed until the bankruptcy order had been made, the wife's share of the property would have devolved to the husband upon her death, and therefore the whole property would be vested in the trustee in bankruptcy; the children would receive nothing.

The court held that the latter was the case; severance only occurred when the bankruptcy order was made. The trustee took the whole of the property.

Since this case, the Insolvency Act 1986 has clarified the point further; section 306 states that the bankrupt is divested of her/his estate as soon as the trustee in bankruptcy is appointed.

To summarise: A beneficial joint tenancy must be severed as soon as possible when bankruptcy is considered, otherwise if the other party dies before the trustee's appointment, that share will be claimable by the trustee. In cases of relationship breakdown, it is likely that one ex-partner will not know that bankruptcy is being considered, and in this situation it may be sensible to sever the tenancy in any case (see 5.34).

12.12 Partner's rights to occupy after a bankruptcy order.

Married partners

Once a bankruptcy order has been made, the bankrupt's share of any property is in the hands of the trustee in bankruptcy. A spouse's registered matrimonial home rights hold good against the trustee and

s34(1)(b) FLA96

the trustee must apply to the court dealing with the bankruptcy for a termination of matrimonial home rights, under S33 of the Family Law

s335A IA86

Act 1996. In virtually all cases, the trustee is likely to succeed, since the interests of the creditors are normally deemed to take priority. Where the property is jointly owned, immediate application for a sale could be made by the trustee under the Trusts of Land and Appointment of Trustees Act (see 5.48).

In practice, however, for both sole and joint married owners a twelve month breathing space is usually allowed before the trustee will apply for a sale. This breathing space is not a right as such, but stems from section 335A of the Insolvency Act, which lays down the factors the court must consider when deciding on termination of matrimonial home rights, or an application for sale of the matrimonial home by the trustee.

These are:

- the interests of the bankrupt's creditors
- the conduct of the spouse or former spouse, so far as it contributed to the bankruptcy
- the needs and financial resources of the spouse or former spouse
- the needs of any children, and
- all the circumstances of the case, other than the needs of the bankrupt.

However, under section 335A(3), where the trustee makes an application for sale or termination of matrimonial rights of occupation more than one year after the property vested in the trustee (ie, after the bankruptcy order), the court must assume that the interests of the creditors outweigh all other considerations, unless the circumstances of the case are exceptional. In practice, therefore, most trustees wait until the twelve months are up, since an order for sale is then virtually assured. It is not impossible for the court to postpone a sale in these circumstances, but very strong arguments will be needed (see 12.14).

Cohabitants

Some of the considerations of section 335A apply only to spouses or ex-spouses. Where a couple has cohabited, the courts must only take account of:

- the interests of the creditors, and
- all the circumstances of the case other than the needs of the bankrupt.

After twelve months the interests of the creditors will outweigh all other considerations.

s337 IA86 There are also similar provisions, which may allow a twelve-month breathing space, where the bankrupt has a child under 18, who is occupying the home at the time when the bankruptcy petition was presented and proceedings commenced.

12.13 Orders for sale after bankruptcy

Where the trustee in bankruptcy wishes to realise the bankrupt's assets, the following procedures must be followed:

- Where there is another party's beneficial interest involved, application for an order for sale must be made under section 14 of the Trusts of Land and Appointment of Trustees Act. For both married and cohabiting couples, the court must make such order as it thinks is just and reasonable, taking into account the factors outlined above under section 335A of the Insolvency Act

• Where a married spouse has no beneficial interest, but has rights to occupy under Family Law Act 1996, and those rights are registered as a charge, application must be made by the trustee under section 33 of the Family Law Act 1996 to terminate those rights and to be granted an order for possession as discussed above.

12.14 Exceptional circumstances warranting postponement of sale

Cases where the court finds exceptional hardship sufficient to postpone a sale of the home are rare. Case law has shown that a family becoming homeless as a result of bankruptcy is not sufficient to be considered 'exceptional circumstances' which warrant postponing the sale. It has been said that being rendered homeless was only a normal circumstance associated with bankrutpcy, even though it was 'incredibly hard luck on the innocent co-owner.'[17] In *Re Citro*,[18] (a case brought under the Bankruptcy Act 1914, which was superseded by the Insolvency Act 1986) the Court of Appeal held that, even though the sale would not provide enough to rehouse the wife and children, postponement exceeding six months would cause undue hardship to the husband's creditors. The hardship to the wife and children was not an exceptional circumstance.

There are no significant reported decisions under the current law, although the court commented in *Re Citro* that it was unlikely that the outcome would have been different if the 1986 Act had applied. There is little in the way of case law, even under the old law, to show what might justify postponement of sale in terms of 'exceptional circumstances.' The case of *Re Holliday*,[19] is considered exceptional in that the court showed sympathy and deferred sale for longer than usual. This was because:

• the husband had deliberately declared himself bankrupt in order to frustrate the wife's matrimonial claim

• the debts were considerably smaller than the equity and

• the creditors were not pressing for, nor were likely to suffer undue hardship by, waiting for payment.

s282 IA86 Where a declaration of bankruptcy has clearly been made to frustrate a spouse's claim, it may be possible to apply to annul the bankruptcy order, but only if it can also be shown that there was no justification for the order being made in the first place.[20] Following *Re Holliday*[21] it is

---

17. Lowrie (A Bankrupt), Re (1981) 3 All ER 353, Walton J (quoted in L. Ayrton, above).

18. Citro (A Bankrupt), Re (1991) 3 All ER 952.

19. Holliday (A Bankrupt), Re (1981) 3 All ER 385. This case is discussed at length in G. Howell, ibid, pp 122-3 and 209-211.

20. An example of this is F v F (1994) 24 Fam Law 253.

21. Holliday, Re, see 19 above.

clear that in cases where the other spouse really cannot pay her/his debts, there will be no basis for annulling the order, even if the primary purpose was to avoid the claims of the other spouse.

Other exceptional circumstances are difficult to predict, although possibly the adaptation of a home especially for a disabled child might weigh in the non-bankrupt partner's favour. This would probably only result in a further deferment of sale.

12.15 Effect of bankruptcy upon prior property transfers

If a couple have divorced and a property transfer order has been made transferring the whole of the property to one partner, that partner might justifiably believe that s/he would not be affected if the ex-spouse is subsequently made or becomes bankrupt. Sadly, this is not necessarily the case. In some situations, it may be possible for the trustee in bankruptcy to have a transfer of matrimonial property that has already taken place set aside. This applies where a transfer can be deemed to be a 'transaction at an undervalue,' or where it constitutes a 'preference' and takes place within certain time limits.

s339 & 340 IA86
s341 IA86

Preference

The debtor will be deemed to have given a 'preference' to someone if s/he does something which puts another person in a better position, in the event of the debtor's bankruptcy, than if the preference had not been given. The person must be a creditor, a person standing surety or a guarantor. It is also essential to show that the bankrupt had an 'intention to prefer' ie, a deliberate motive to prejudice creditors, for it to be deemed a preference. An example might be where the bankrupt repays an unsecured loan to the spouse, in preference to other debts. Transfer of the matrimonial home will therefore only constitute a 'preference' if it was transferred as financial provision where the spouse can be considered to be a creditor, and an intention to prefer can be established. A trustee is more likely to treat a transfer of the matrimonial home as a transaction at an undervalue (see below), since no intention is required to be shown.

Application for the preference to be set aside can be made, if the act was carried out within certain time limits preceding the date or presentation of the bankruptcy petition:

• Within the preceding five years, if the preference is also a 'transaction at an undervalue' (see below)

• Within two years, if preference is not an undervalue, but is given to the bankrupt's 'associate' (which includes spouse or cohabitant)

• Within six months, if not given to the bankrupt's associate.

In addition to satisfying the time limits and being shown to have the motive of improving the person's position by the preference, it must also be shown that the bankrupt was insolvent at the time of the transfer, or became insolvent as a result of the transfer. Insolvency is assumed in the case of a transfer to an 'associate' unless proved otherwise. If a spouse or partner wants to try to resist the claims of the trustee in bankruptcy, the onus would therefore be on the partner to prove that the bankrupt was not insolvent at the time the property was transferred, and not on the trustee to prove that s/he was.

The trustee can use the concept of 'preference' to have a transfer of a home under a court order set aside, even where a compensating payment is made. However, in most cases the more common procedure, as suggested above (especially where there has been a 'clean break' settlement), is for the trustee to seek to show that the transfer is a 'transaction at an undervalue.'

Transaction at an undervalue

A 'transaction at an undervalue' includes a gift or a transaction where nothing is given in return, or where the consideration given to the bankrupt in return is significantly less than the value in money or money's worth to the recipient. As with preferences, time limits and rules relating to insolvency apply. A transaction at an undervalue can be set aside if it was made within the following times preceding the presentation of the bankruptcy petition:

• At any time within the preceding five years, where the bankrupt was insolvent at the time, or was made insolvent by the transaction

• At any time within the preceding two years, regardless of whether the bankrupt was insolvent, or

• Beyond the five-year limit if and only if it can be shown that the bankrupt intended to put assets beyond the reach of claimants or potential claimants (ie, transactions defrauding creditors under section 423 IA 86).

Re Abbott (A bankrupt)[22]

In this case the husband transferred, by consent order, his interest in a property to his wife in return for her relinquishing rights to pursue a claim for maintenance. However, the Bankruptcy Act 1914 set aside transactions which were not carried out 'in good faith' and for 'no valuable consideration.' It was argued successfully that the wife's relinquishment of her right to maintenance did indeed constitute valuable consideration, and that she had acted in good faith and not in order to defraud creditors.

---

22. Abbott (A Bankrupt), Re (1982) 3 All ER 181, (1982) 126 Sol Jo 345.

> *The test under the Insolvency Act is more stringent, since it is directed not only at transfers for no consideration, but also at those for less than commercial value.*

Re Kumar (A bankrupt)[23]

The husband and wife were joint owners of the matrimonial home, worth £140,000, with a mortgage of £30,000. In June 1990, the husband transferred his interest by deed to his wife, who took over the mortgage and was registered as sole owner.

In January 1991, a decree nisi of divorce was granted to the wife and in April 1991 a 'clean break' consent order was made, in which her claim for capital provision was dismissed as a result of her husband having transferred his interest in the house to her.

In July 1991, a bankruptcy order was made against the husband, and the trustee in bankruptcy applied to have the transfer of the home set aside. The wife attempted to rely on the judgment in Re Abbott (above), which was, under the Bankruptcy Act 1914, but the court granted the trustee's application, saying that the transfer in June 1991 was 'at an undervalue' for the purposes of section 339 of the Insolvency Act. There was no consideration provided by the wife beyond her assumption of the liability of the mortgage, and the equity she gained was therefore greater than what she had given her husband. The court also felt that no divorce court would have required the husband to transfer virtually all of his capital to his wife, who had a superior earning capacity, leaving him virtually without any means to buy his own home.

In this case, the court was clearly suspicious of the couple's actions, and considered that there was an attempt to outwit the creditors. It was the first case to consider the value of the consideration given up in return for the transfer, as is now required under the Insolvency Act.

Possible precautions

- A transfer remains potentially vulnerable for the first two years. To protect the transfer between the two and five year period, it may help for the person making the transfer to swear a declaration of solvency at the time of the transfer.[24] However, it is important that this is not seen as a universal panacea, since the question of whether transfer can be set aside later is not automatically ruled out. Indeed the use of such a declaration may raise the question in the trustee in bankruptcy's mind of whether s/he should be suspicious

23. Kumar (A Bankrupt), Re (1993) 2 All ER 700.

24. See model declaration in L. Yates, 'Home Comforts: Insolvency and Property Transfers' (1992) 22 Fam Law 495.

s336 IA86

- To prove the 'commercial value' of considerations made in return for a transfer, detailed calculations of the extent of claims relinquished could be recorded in correspondence. The trustee in bankruptcy will be able to call an adviser to give evidence and supply papers.

12.16 Effect of bankruptcy where there is negative equity

Although the matrimonial home is often the bankrupt's biggest asset, it can also be one of the major liabilities. Therefore, what is the effect of bankruptcy where the bankrupt is an owner or joint owner of property which has negative equity, or where such a property was transferred to a spouse in such a way that the transaction may be liable to being set aside?

- If the bankrupt person is the sole owner, the whole property vests in the trustee in bankruptcy. If the relationship has broken down and the wife or parent is still living in the home, application has to be made to terminate any matrimonial home rights and to ask the court to order a sale (see 12.13). Where a sale will not realise any assets, but only create more debt, it seems unlikely that the court would order a sale, if the spouse or partner opposes it. Indeed, the trustee may even decline to apply for an order for sale. Instead, application may be made to the court for a charging order for the benefit of creditors, under section 313 of the Insolvency Act. The charging order is subject to the Charging Orders Act 1979, and is enforceable even after discharge of bankruptcy. However, the current practice of the Official Receiver appears to be in favour of agreeing to the buying out of the bankrupt's share (see below) rather than using charging orders which may be 'called in' (ie, repossession) at a later date. If there is a sale, the shortfall will become part of the bankruptcy debt, and therefore no separate action for the debt can usually be taken by the lender or its insurer

- A non-owner with a beneficial interest but not included on the mortgage deed is not affected by negative equity as a debt. S/he cannot be held liable for the mortgage debt, so loses out only to the extent of having lost the beneficial interest which s/he put in or would have been entitled to. Again, the trustee may decline to apply for sale in the hope of an increase in property prices; or the court may be persuaded to postpone a sale for the same reason. In a case where there are mortgage arrears, whether the court postpones a sale may also depend on the attitude of the mortgage lender

- If the property is jointly owned, an order for sale must be applied for and the situation is therefore the same as above. If the property is sold and there is a shortfall (ie, negative equity), the whole of the debt becomes part of the bankrupt's debt, since joint owners are jointly and severally liable. The other co-owner is also liable for the whole debt, and action could therefore be taken against the non-bankrupt person to recover the debt. Whichever happens, no more than 100 per cent of the debt can be recovered, ie, the whole debt cannot be recovered twice – once from each party

- Once of the most common ways of dealing helpfully with situations of negative or very small equity is for the non-bankrupt owner to see if s/he can buy out the bankrupt's interest in the property. Many transactions of this type took place during the recession of the early 1990s. Often the non-bankrupt owner has to pay only a very nominal consideration which reflects the small amount of equity. S/he will normally have to pay the Official Receiver/trustee's costs, and will have to pay for a written valuation. The main difficulty usually arises over the non-bankrupt's ability to take over and meet payments on existing mortgages, especially if the property is subject to a second mortgage that secured the bankrupt's business liabilities. For a discussion about taking over the mortgage, see Chapter 11, Section D.

C   Bankruptcy and tenancies

12.17 Effect of bankruptcy upon tenancies

s283 (3A) IA86   Most tenancies are excluded from vesting automatically in the trustee as part of a bankrupt's estate, except where the tenancy has some 'cash value.' In effect, they are excluded where the tenant cannot make a profit by charging a premium in return for assigning the tenancy. In rare cases, where a premium could be charged with no restrictions, the tenancy will vest automatically in the trustee.

Tenancies which do not automatically vest in the trustee:

- Assured tenancies or assured agricultural occupancies, where assignment is 'inhibited'

- Protected tenancies where no premium can lawfully be required as a condition of assignment

- A protected occupier under the Rent (Agriculture) Act 1976, where assignment is 'inhibited'

- A secure tenancy which cannot be assigned other than under section 91 Housing Act 1985 (ie, can only be assigned to someone qualified to succeed or under matrimonial order or mutual exchange).

Assignment is 'inhibited' where the tenancy agreement absolutely prohibits it, or states that the landlord may either charge for granting consent to an assignment or call for surrender instead of granting consent. This definition comes from section 127(5) of the Rent Act 1977. Any other type of qualified prohibition does not count as inhibited.

Vesting tenancies in the trustee

s308A IA86   If the trustee wants one of the above tenancies to vest in her/him (eg, in order to sublet it) then s/he must serve notice on the bankrupt tenant that it will be the case. This is likely to happen very rarely.

Effect of bankruptcy on the tenancy

In most cases, the rights of tenants and their partners to occupy the family homes is not affected by bankruptcy, although the ability to pay rent is obviously still highly relevant. In the rare cases where vesting in the trustee does occur, the trustee will become the tenant, and, as a result, for those tenancies where it is necessary for the tenant to occupy the accommodation to maintain the tenancy security of tenure will be lost (ie, assured and secure tenancies will become uprooted tenancies). A Rent Act protected tenancy will continue, as it is not necessary to fulfil a residence requirement, but, when the contractual tenancy ends, no statutory tenancy will arise. If the bankrupt already has a Rent Act statutory tenancy at the time of the bankruptcy, it cannot vest in the trustee, as it is a personal right to occupy. Therefore, the statutory tenancy will continue as long as the bankrupt tenant remains in occupation.

However, this does not mean a bankrupt tenant is immune to repossession. The House of Lords has upheld the granting of possession against a tenant whose lease contained a clause allowing for forfeiture in the event of the tenant's bankruptcy.[25]

12.18 Rent arrears and bankruptcy

If there are rent arrears and the tenant is made bankrupt, the arrears are a 'provable' debt (ie, on proving her/his debt, the landlord becomes a creditor sharing in the distribution of any proceeds of the bankruptcy). The debt is therefore included in the bankrupt's estate, and is normally only payable by the trustee. A tenant may have no substantial capital assets and payments to all creditors will therefore be made by the trustee out of the bankrupt's income, over and above the amount which is allowed to the bankrupt for her/his reasonable household needs.

12.19 Landlord's actions to repossess

The fact that the tenant is bankrupt, or has a petition pending, may affect the landlord's right to take possession action, although bankruptcy will not necessarily prevent a landlord from obtaining a possession order or

25. Cadogan Estates v McMahon (2000) 4 All ER 897, (2000) 3 WLR 1555 HL.

obtaining payment of any arrears. In some cases, the courts may intervene to stay actions against bankrupts and their property. In other situations the landlord will need permission from the court before action can be commenced.

Landlord seeking possession after bankruptcy order

Where a tenant goes bankrupt owing rent arrears, the arrears are a bankruptcy debt ('provable') and the landlord is prevented from taking further action, or further action to recover those arrears, except for distraint for up to 6 months' arrears (see below under 'Other action to recover the debt'). However, it appears that this does not necessarily prevent the landlord from seeking possession of the dwelling on the ground of the arrears (or another ground), provided s/he is not seeking to recover the arrears themselves.

s285(3)(a) IA86

This interpretation is based on a reading of s285(3)(a) of the Insolvency Act 1986, which says that a creditor of the bankrupt cannot have a remedy *in respect of the debt* s/he is owed. The courts have held that forfeiture of a lease was not a remedy in respect of the debt, but was a determination of the lessee's right to remain in possession of the property, because of the breach of the terms of the lease.[26] This was the case under the Bankruptcy Act 1914, but was subsequently confirmed in the case of *Razzaq v Pala*,[27] a case under the Insolvency Act 1986. The exercise of the landlord of a right to peaceably re-enter on the grounds of rent arrears, and the forfeiture of the lease on these grounds, did not constitute a remedy against the debtor in respect of the debt. The court said that it merely prevented a re-occurrence of the breach, and allowed the landlord relief from a defaulting tenant.

Although these were cases concerning leases, the same principles would appear to apply to tenancies. However, where the landlord wants to start a possession action against the bankrupt tenant after the bankruptcy order, s/he must obtain the permission of the court, and the court may attach conditions to its permission.

s285(3)(b) IA86

Applying to stay a possession action pending bankruptcy proceedings or after a bankruptcy order

s285(1) IA86

Where a bankruptcy petition has been served, or a bankruptcy order has been made, if a landlord wishes to seek possession against the bankrupt (and if applicable, a non-bankrupt joint tenant) on the basis of rent arrears or another ground, the bankruptcy court has discretion to intervene to stay the action, but it is up to the tenant to request it to do so. This will apply even if the case was started before the bankruptcy petition was served. The court in which the case is being heard also has discretion to stay the action if it is asked by the tenant

---

26. Ezekiel v Orakpo (1976) 3 All ER CA.   27. Razzaq v Pala (1997) 1 WLR 336.

s285(2) IA86 to do so and given proof of the bankruptcy. The court can allow the action or stay it, on such terms as it thinks fit.

Other action to recover the debt

s347 IA86 If the landlord wishes to pursue the debt separately from the bankruptcy proceedings by means of distraint (ie, seizure of goods), s/he has limited rights to distrain against the bankrupt's goods and effects, up to the value of a maximum of six months' arrears of rent accrued before the bankruptcy.

Summary of action for arrears once a bankruptcy order has been made

Whether the landlord can take action after a bankruptcy order depends upon whether the arrears are part of the 'provable debt' ie, owing at the time of the bankruptcy (see 12.18), or arose after the bankruptcy order.

If the landlord has a provable debt, then:

* *once the bankruptcy order has actually been, made s/he will not be able to start any action against the tenant for arrears which are a provable debt, except for distraint for up to 6 months' arrears (see below under 'other action to recover the debt')*

* *s/he may only start another action, eg, possession action, with the permission of the bankruptcy court, and the bankrupt tenant may apply for such an action to be stayed. The court has discretion to act as it sees fit.*

If the arrears arose after the bankruptcy order:

* *the landlord may start an action, but the tenant may apply to*
s285(3) IA86 *the court to use its discretion to stay the action.*

Landlords' policies

Some local authorities and registered social landlords may have specific policies when tenants become bankrupt, eg, allowing a 'fresh start.' Alternatively there may be terms written into a tenancy agreement which might affect the bankrupt's position in a negative way. Agreements and policies should therefore always be checked.

12.20 Paying current rent

Bankruptcy does not affect current liability to pay rent; nor do rent arrears accrued after the bankruptcy order count as part of the bankrupt's debt.

Where the bankrupt tenant is paying current rent, plus an amount off arrears subject to a suspended possession order, the situation is problematic and will probably depend on whether the official receiver will permit the bankrupt tenant to pay the amount ordered. If permission is not given and there is no other way to pay the amount, eg, by a partner, friend or relative, the order will be breached, and the landlord could apply for a warrant for possession.

s285(3)(b) IA86 As the action had already been started prior to the bankruptcy order, the landlord would not appear to need the court's permission (the Insolvency Act 1986 refers to permission to commence proceedings, not continue them). The only thing the bankrupt tenant can do is apply to the court to use its discretion to stay a warrant. This could possibly be allowed on the ground that the default is beyond the tenant's control, and it would not therefore be reasonable to allow the tenant to be evicted, nor would being made homeless help her/him in any attempts to pay off outstanding debts.

If the rent arrears arise after bankruptcy, the landlord may seek possession in the usual way, and it is up to the tenant to ask the court to use its discretion to stay the action. Wherever possible, an informal arrangement should be made to pay off the arrears to try to avoid possession action. If a partner has been left with the responsibility of paying rent, Housing Benefit may be claimed, and it may be possible to obtain backdated payments (see Chapter 11).

12.21 Rent arrears and joint tenancies

If the tenancy is a joint tenancy, both the bankrupt and the non-bankrupt tenant will be liable for the whole of the debt. The landlord could therefore decide to pursue the non-bankrupt joint tenant for the rent arrears. Action against the non-bankrupt tenant would not require special permission from the court, and the court could make a suspended order for payment of the arrears. The landlord could follow this line of action as well as attempting to recover arrears from the bankrupt, although s/he would not, of course, be entitled to receive payment twice.

D Effect of bankruptcy upon maintenance or lump sum orders in family proceedings

12.22 Bankruptcy and family proceedings

If there are family proceedings pending, they would usually be stayed, ie, 'put on ice,' once a bankruptcy order is made.[28] This is because all assets will vest in the trustee in bankruptcy, and thus it will be better to wait until bankruptcy is discharged and take action at that point.

---

28. Re Smith (A Bankrupt) ex parte Braintree DC (1990) 2 AC 215.

Existing orders which have been made in family proceedings cannot be added to a bankrupt's debts,[29] but neither will discharge of bankruptcy release the bankrupt from debts incurred under family proceedings. This means that the bankrupt still remains liable to pay any sums due either to a spouse or a child in terms of financial provision or assessments under the Child Support Act. Once the bankruptcy is discharged, the ex-partner should take up the proceedings or pursue any money owed.

Matrimonial claims may, however, be provable (ie, can be added into) in individual voluntary arrangements in some circumstances, and the non-bankrupt former spouse is then bound by the terms of the arrangement. This does not, however, affect future claims for maintenance.

13

Chapter 13: Domestic violence

Subjects covered in this chapter include...

What domestic violence is and whom it affects

How the government has responded to domestic violence

Responses to domestic violence

What options there are in cases of violence

What special provisions are available in cases involving immigration status

What problems arise in connection with child contact

Criminal offences

When the criminal law can be used

What powers the police have to intervene

What to expect in court

When the Protection from Harassment Act 1997 may be used

How the Crime and Disorder Act 1998 may apply

Civil actions

What legal action an individual can take

What protection is available under the Family Law Act 1996

How the courts decide who should stay in the home

What other legal actions may be available to protect children and parents

Actions in tort

Which situations fall outside domestic violence remedies

When an action for trespass or private nuisance can be brought

Social landlords' powers

How social landlords may regain possession in domestic violence cases

How social landlords may use injunctions

Domestic violence

'Domestic violence is not simply a legal problem which can be eradicated by the appropriate legal remedies. It is also a social and psychological problem which can be eliminated only by fundamental changes in society and in attitudes to women and children.'[1]

What is domestic violence?

The term domestic violence tends to mask the horror of the crimes committed often in the name of love. Domestic violence can take many forms – from physical injuries caused by slaps, punches, beatings and stabbings, right through to murder. Sexual abuse and rape within relationships frequently accompanies other physical violence. Domestic violence also takes less visually obvious forms which are nonetheless devastating. Mental cruelty can be subtle and insidious or may consist of outright bullying, insults, humiliation, degradation, taunting, pestering and harassment. Frequently, domestic violence is a combination of physical, sexual and emotional abuse.

In recent years, attempts have been made to reach a common acceptable definition of domestic violence, ranging from the simple but powerful:

'domestic violence is the use of power to assert and maintain control over another person.'[2]

to the more specific definition adopted for use in police returns:

'The term 'domestic violence' shall be understood to mean any violence between current or former partners in an intimate relationship, wherever and whenever it occurs. The violence may include physical, sexual, emotional or financial abuse.'[3]

Other definitions usefully include other domestic relationships, not merely those between intimate partners.[4]

Who perpetrates domestic violence?

- Although both men and women may commit acts of domestic violence, research has shown that in the majority of cases, men are the perpetrators,[5] with the latest Home Office research showing that 74% of incidents are against women and 26% against men.[6] In addition a high proportion of the violence against men was perpetrated not by women but by other males.

1. Law Commission Family Law, Domestic Violence and Occupation of the Family Home, Report no. 207 (London: HMSO, 1992).
2. Originally believed to have been used by the Women's Aid Federation, who now have another more complex definition.
3. Home Office definition in effect from April 1999 for use in police returns to Her Majesty's Inspectorate of Constabulary (HMIC). See also Home Office Circular HOC 19/2000 'Domestic Violence: Revised Circular to the Police' and the Home Office document 'Government Policy Around Domestic Violence.' All available at www.homeoffice.gov.uk.
4. Eg, 1993 Home Affairs Select Committee (HASC) Report on Domestic Violence refers to abuse 'within the context of a close relationship.'
5. The British Crime Survey: England and Wales. London: Home Office, 2000.
6. The 2000 British Crime Survey, Home Office Statistical Bulletin 18/00.

How many die or are injured?

- One woman is killed by her present or former partner every 3 days. In 1999, this accounted for 37% of all female homicide victims, compared to 6% of male victims.[7]

- Domestic violence accounts for almost a quarter of all violent crime[8]

- Almost one in four women have been assaulted by current or former partners[9]

- Every minute in the UK the police receive a call from the public for help for domestic violence.[10]

Statistics are commonly believed to underestimate the problem, with less than a third of all people experiencing domestic violence reporting the incident to the police.[11] Domestic violence is not restricted to any culture, age, sexual preference, body ability, class, ethnicity or creed.[12] Research has also shown that it is young women who are most at risk and that violence often starts, or escalates, with pregnancy. In a census of the refuge population in 2000, over 70% of women were 35 or under and only 8% were aged 46 or over. Almost three quarters had children under aged 10 with them, or were pregnant.[13]

13.1   Reform of the law – the Family Law Act 1996

Despite the extent and seriousness of the crime, the law has been slow to develop a suitable response to this age-old and perennial abuse. In the 1970s and 1980s a number of different pieces of legislation were enacted, and the law became complex and fragmented. In 1992 the Law Commission published a report recommending reform of the law on domestic violence, the main object being to create a single statutory code, applicable in all family courts, with coherent principles and effective remedies.[14] These proposals were enacted in Part IV of the Family Law Act 1996, which was brought into force in October 1997. The main aims of the reform were:

- the provision of protection for one member of a family against molestation or violence by another, and

- regulation of the occupation of the family home where the relationship has broken down, either temporarily or permanently.[15]

7. Criminal Statistics England & Wales 1999. London: Home Office 1999.
8. The British Crime Survey 2000 see 6 above, cites 23% of all violent crime as domestic violence.
9. Domestic Violence: a Heath Care Issue. London BMA 1998.
10. 'The Day to Count: A Snapshot of the Impact of Domestic Violence in the UK' Professor Stanko, E. 2000. Available via www.domesticviolencedata.org.
11. The British Crime Survey 2000 see 6 above.
12. 'Defining violence against women' Lloyd S. in Bewley S, Friend J and Mezey G (Eds). Violence against Women. London RCOG, 1997.
13. Women's Aid Federation England census 2000 reported in 'The provision of accommodation and support for households experiencing domestic violence in England' (Housing Report 2002), Chapter 3, para 3.5. Available at: www.housing.odpm.gov.uk/informationdomestic/index.htm.
14. Law Commission Report No. 207, see 1 above.
15. Press notice 48.95, Lord Chancellor's Department, 23.2.95.

Non-molestation orders and occupation orders

To achieve these aims, the Act replaced all previous domestic violence remedies with a single set of remedies. Orders available are non-molestation orders and occupation orders, which are designed to protect individuals from violence or unwanted pestering or molestation, and to give the courts powers to decide who should remain in the family home, and whether one party should be excluded or not. These are explained in depth in Section C of this chapter, from 13.19 onwards.

Power of arrest

The Family Law Act places on the courts stringent requirements to attach powers of arrest where there has been actual or threatened violence (see 13.40 Enforcement of Orders). Research has shown that, since the Act was introduced, power of arrest is now attached in 75% of occupation orders and 80% of non-molestation orders, compared to earlier legislation, where a power of arrest was attached in only one-third of all orders.[16]

Transfer of tenancies

The Act also gives the courts powers to order a permanent transfer of tenancies not only between divorcing husbands and wives, but also between heterosexual cohabitants and former heterosexual cohabitants, once they cease to live together as husband and wife (see 8.19). Whether this restriction of the law to men and women living together, thereby excluding lesbian and gay couples, will prove to be discriminatory in terms of human rights remains to be seen (see 2.4 for more on human rights).

13.2   Government policy response to domestic violence

In the late 1990s, the Government began work on a serious campaign to tackle violence against women. In March 2000, the Home Office launched a ten-point plan to tackle domestic violence as part of its new Multi-Agency Guidance, reminding all agencies dealing with domestic violence of the issues they should be considering (see 16.9 for details).[17] This coincided with domestic violence guidance from the Department of Health, in the form of a Resource Manual for Health Care Professionals.[18] In the previous year, the government had also produced a document on its policy on domestic violence.[19] In May 2000, this was followed by

16. 'Reducing Domestic Violence...What works? Civil Law Remedies' Crime Reduction Research series, Home Office Research, Susan Edwards, January 2000,
17. 'Multi-Agency Guidance for Addressing Domestic Violence' available free from the Home Office, Rm 157, 50 Queen Anne's Gate, London SW1H 9AT, Fax 020 7273 2568 or at www.homeoffice.gov.uk/violenceagainstwomen.
18. 'Domestic Violence: A Resource Manual for Health Care Professionals' Department of Health, 2000. Available at www.doh.gov.uk/domestic.htm or as a hard copy in a loose-leaf binder from Department of Health 020 7210 4850.
19. 'Government Policy Around Domestic Violence' Home Office 1999 available at www.homeoffice.gov.uk/cpd/cpsu/domviol98.htm or from the Home Office as above.

revised guidance to the police[20] about setting standards and influencing the attitudes and behaviour of officers.

In December 2002, the government produced a detailed and practical housing research report and summary *'The provision of accommodation and support for households experiencing domestic violence in England'*.[21] As its name suggests, this report is the result of in-depth research into the resources available to support those experiencing domestic violence, and contains detailed statistics and comment on the types of temporary accommodation provided, availability of support services, local authority rehousing and information about those who decide to stay put in their own homes. Unlike many research reports, the information has much relevance to day-to-day problems which local authorities experience in dealing with domestic violence, and also contains anecdotal comments from clients as to the standard of helpfulness and support they were offered. It is essential reading for anyone developing a domestic violence policy and/or good practice guidelines. Key points from these and other documents on good practice in dealing with domestic violence are discussed in Chapter 16, Section B.

The Government also announced funding of £7 million to develop new refuges and a further £2 million which, together with funding from Comic Relief, will be used to set up a national 24-hour helpline to help those fleeing domestic violence.

Prospective legislation

In June 2003, the Home Office published a consultation paper on changes in legislation to prevent and combat domestic violence. The proposals include anonymity for victims in court, a register of offenders convicted of domestic violence, which is available to the police and other agencies but not the public, criminal records for those who break non-molestation orders, and the provision of more safe houses and women's refuges.

A   Responses to domestic violence

Before 1997, although there were a variety of legal remedies available to offer protection to married couples and heterosexual cohabitants, there were still no specific remedies to protect partners in a lesbian or gay relationship; nor for those who were not living together as husband and wife. In the latter instances, it was necessary to find what is known as an ancillary remedy attached to other proceedings (see 13.15), or apply for an injunction to restrain assault or trespass (a common law cause of action), see Section D of this chapter, 13.45 – 13. 54. The Family Law Act improved matters from October 1997, as did the Protection from Harassment Act 1997, which came into force in June 1997, but there are still limitations.

20. HOC 19/2000 see 3 above.
21. 'The provision of accommodation and support for households experiencing domestic violence in England' (Housing Report 2002) Office of the Deputy Prime Minister, and News release 2002/0387 11 December 2002. Available at: www.housing.odpm.gov.uk/informationdomestic/index.htm.

13.3 Deciding on a course of action

It is crucial as an adviser to recognise the limitations of legal remedies. They may offer little or no real help if the offending partner is willing to flout them, or if the violence is due to drug/alcohol abuse or to mental health problems. The government's latest research showed that, for most of those surveyed, injunctions had not proved a useful means of keeping ex-partners away from their home.[22] Also, if the recipient of violence is seeking a long-term solution to the housing situation, they can offer only a breathing space. They will not affect existing rights to a financial share or to obtain a permanent transfer of the home by one of the methods explained in the earlier chapters of the book (see Chapters 3 – 9).

Many people do not want to take legal proceedings against their partners; they may just want their partners to stop being violent towards them and for the relationship to improve; or they may want to end the relationship and make a fresh start. In these instances, the availability of legal remedies can sometimes prove a disadvantage, since it may be assumed, for example by housing officers or advisers, that these should be pursued before other alternatives can be considered. The Homelessness Code of Guidance makes it clear that this should not happen in cases of domestic violence.

Homelessness Code of Guidance for Local Authorities, ODPM July 2002, paras 8.26 and 6.20.

In addition, as will be seen below, the courts' criteria for granting orders excluding one partner are governed by statute and case law. This means that even where there has been serious violence, or a family situation is intolerable, it may still not be possible to obtain an injunction.[23] This fact is often overlooked by local authority homelessness departments, who may take the line that, if an injunction is not granted, the situation cannot be serious. This is not the case. Finally, injunctions are essentially about protection in the short-term. They are normally of limited duration and do not result in a transfer of tenancy or ownership.

13.4 Options in cases of violence

A person suffering or in fear of violence from the woman or man whom s/he lives with, or has had a relationship with, needs advice on four options which, where applicable, can be pursued at the same time:

- Refuges

- Legal remedies

- Homelessness applications

- Other sources of support and advice.

---

22. See 21 above. Chapter 6, para 6.3.   23. B v B (Occupation Order) 1999 1 FLR 715 CA.

Women's Aid refuges

Refuges provide temporary accommodation for women, with or without children, who have to leave home because of domestic violence. While living in the refuge, women are given support and advice on welfare benefits, housing and legal remedies. This can provide an important breathing space for a woman who may not have decided what permanent course of action she wishes to follow. There are also some specialist refuges which cater for the needs of certain groups, for example, black women from specific ethnic groups. Unfortunately, the demand for refuge places still currently far outstrips the supply, with only one third of the recommended number of bedspaces available per year. There are 400 'safe houses' in England which sheltered 54,000 women and children in 2001. Another 35,000 contacted the Women's Aid Helpline for advice and support, and British Telecom reported a further 100,000 attempted calls had been made.[24] Information on refuges and help in finding a space can be obtained from the Women's Aid Federation.[25] At present there are no men's refuges, but help can be obtained from www.mensaid.org.

Legal remedies

These are available to both men and women, but some are limited where lesbian/gay relationships are concerned (see below). The options discussed in this chapter are:

- criminal offences
  - General police powers and offences
  - Protection from Harassment Act 1997
  - Crime and Disorder Act 1998

- civil actions
  - Family Law Act 1996
  - Protection from Harassment Act 1997 (as civil action)
  - Children Act 1989
  - Trespass or nuisance

- local authority actions
  - Injunctions under Housing Act 1996
  - Possession actions under Housing Act 1996.

Homelessness applications to the local authority

This avenue is available to men and women, including those in lesbian or gay relationships (see Chapter 14 and 15). However, a homelessness application may not be available in some immigration cases.

24. Statistics available at www.womensaid.org.uk.

25. Women's Aid Federation, PO Box 391, Bristol, BS9 7WS Tel: 0117 944 4411 for general information on refuges and the work of Women's Aid; 08457 023 468 for the National Helpline for individual cases. Email: web@womensaid.org.uk

Other sources of support and advice

There is a wide range of organisations providing general and specialist support, advice and practical help to people experiencing domestic violence, eg, Victim Support, Samaritans, Relate, welfare and housing aid and advice agencies, Women's or Gay and Lesbian helplines. Other agencies deal with specific client groups. A list of useful organisations is given in the Appendices at the end of this book.

13.5 Problems arising due to immigration status

It is important to take into account a person's immigration status before recommending a homelessness application. In some cases, the immigration status will mean that there is no right to assistance from the local authority housing department, and help from the social services authority may be limited (see Chapters 9, Section C and Chapter 14, Section E). An application could also lead to the Immigration and Nationality Department (IND) being alerted to the person's status, which could result in deportation. For more information about immigration and homelessness, see 14.10 and Chapter 15, Section B).

In addition to the legislation preventing local authorities from providing accommodation, many people from abroad are not able to have access to any welfare benefits.

Rights to remain on relationship breakdown where entry was as a spouse

Advisers should check whether the woman/man seeking advice entered the UK as a spouse, ie, to join a married partner already settled here, within the last twelve months. Both men and women entering the UK as spouses of someone settled in the country must normally complete a twelve month 'probationary period' before they can apply for indefinite leave to remain in the UK. The marriage must still subsist and the couple must intend to live permanently with each other. A similar rule now applies to unmarried partners, for whom the probationary period is twenty-four months. If the marriage/relationship breaks down before the end of the probationary period, and couples are no longer living together at the end of it, the spouse/partner from abroad no longer has any claim under the immigration rules to remain because of the marriage. They will normally have no right to remain and may be deported. In addition because s/he is subject to immigration control, which imposes conditions not to have recourse to public funds, s/he will not be eligible for homelessness assistance (see 14.10 and Chapter 15, Section B).

These rules obviously place an enormous pressure on people experiencing domestic violence: they are forced to decide whether to remain in a violent and dangerous relationship, or to flee for safety and risk being refused permission to remain, possible deportation and disgrace. However, vigorous campaigning by the Southall Black Sisters resulted in a significant concession in relation to domestic violence, which was announced by the Secretary of State for the Home Department on 16th June 1999.

> *'We have decided to introduce a concession, which will be outside the Immigration Rules, for overseas spouses who wish to remain in the United Kingdom, but who wish to leave their partner because of domestic violence before the completion of the 12 month probationary period. In order to benefit from this concession (s/he...) will need to provide objective evidence that he or she has been the victim of domestic violence... An applicant... may be granted indefinite leave to remain exceptionally outside the immigration rules.'*[26]

Once indefinite leave to remain is granted, the person will be eligible for homelessness assistance.

The concession also applies to unmarried partners who are still within the two-year probationary period required before an application for indefinite leave can be made. The domestic violence must have occurred while the marriage/relationship was still in existence, and the evidence required must be one of the following:

- An injunction, non-molestation order or other protection order (other than 'without notice,' previously 'ex parte' or interim order), or

- A relevant court conviction, or

- Full details of a relevant police caution.

Where a prosecution is pending, the applicant may be granted further periods of six months' limited leave to remain, until the outcome of the criminal prosecution is known. Where a hearing seeking an injunction of some form is pending, the decision will be delayed pending the outcome of the hearing.

13.6 Awareness of problems arising from child contact

Where children are involved, the efforts of women's refuges and housing providers to rehouse the woman in a safe place, can be undermined by the courts where the perpetrator applies for a contact order under section 8 of the Children Act 1989 (see 9.2). The courts have discretion as to whether to reveal the whereabouts of the child and in many cases, even where the woman may have been rehoused because of domestic violence, they give the address to the father applying for contact, on the grounds that the violence did not affect the child and the father has a right to know where s/he is living.

---

26. Speech by Mike O'Brien in the House of Commons on 16th June 1999. Available at www.ncadc.org.uk/letters/news15/im.html. See also more information at 'The Domestic Violence Concession' www.uk-immigration.net/news.

In April 2000, the Lord Chancellor's Department produced Good Practice Guidelines on contact with children in cases of parental violence, and these guidelines were referred to in the four Court of Appeal cases heard later in 2000, where the judge refused contact and stressed the inherent dangers and pitfalls in such cases.

---

2 FLR334

RL (Contact: Domestic Violence); Re V (Contact: Domestic Violence); Re M (Contact: Domestic Violence); Re H (Contact Domestic Violence)[27]

Dismissing four appeals against refusal of direct contact where there had been domestic violence between the parents, the Court held that when hearing a contact application in which domestic violence had been established, the court should consider the past and present conduct of both parties towards each other and towards the children, the effect on the children and on the residential parent, and the motivation of the parent seeking contact, trying to ensure that any risk of harm to the child was minimised and that the safety of the child and the residential parent was secured.

Family judges and magistrates needed to have a heightened awareness of the existence, and the effect on children, of exposure to domestic violence between their parents or other partners, and proper arrangements needed to be put in place to safeguard both from risk of further physical or emotional harm. Where allegations of domestic violence were made which might have an effect on the outcome, those allegations must be adjudicated upon, and found proved or not proved.

There should not be a presumption that on proof of domestic violence the offending parent had to surmount a prima facie barrier of no contact, but such violence was a factor in the delicate balancing exercise of discretion. The ability of the offending parent to recognise their past conduct, to be aware of the need to change and to make genuine efforts to do so would be likely to be an important consideration.

What this means in practice is that at an early stage in proceedings for residence or contact, where the woman alleges domestic violence, there is a factual hearing to determine the truth or otherwise of the allegations. If found proved, then further consideration is given to the way forward; this often means attendance by the perpetrator at a domestic violence intervention project, and acceptance of allegations before an order for contact will be made.

---

27. Re L (Contact: Domestic Violence); Re V (Contact: Domestic Violence); Re M (Contact: Domestic Violence); Re H (Contact: Domestic Violence) (2000)2 FLR 334 CA.

Since 1999 there has been a number of other cases involving domestic violence where contact has been refused, when previously it would have been granted. In *Re M (interim contact: domestic violence),*[28] the judge's initial decision to make an interim contact order because the child was too young to be affected by the parental violence, or suffer stress or torn loyalties, was overturned by the Court of Appeal: the order impacted radically on the primary carer, and she was entitled not to have the burden of contact imposed on her without a full investigation of her opposition to any form of contact. The judge had given too much weight to the age of the child and possibly insufficient to the domestic violence.

At the time of writing, the Women's Aid Federation are pressing the Government to accept the Children Act Subcommittee's recommendation that these guidelines should be introduced in the form of a Court Practice Direction. Although this would improve matters, there would still be no automatic assumption that there should not be contact in cases of domestic violence. The burden remains with the person who has been on the receiving end of the violence to show why contact is undesirable. This means there will be a court hearing revealing at least the approximate whereabouts of the person who may have fled to find a place of safety. It is unclear what can be done to prevent this, but at the very least the person who has suffered violence should be advised to urge her/his solicitor to argue against the address being revealed.

'Implacably hostile?'

It may be that housing providers and voluntary organisations could provide backup in supporting the person's request for confidentiality as being on valid grounds, since, in many cases, women are alleged to be 'making false allegations' or being 'difficult' (referred to in court terms as being 'implacably hostile'). It is important to remember the distinction between implacably hostile for frivolous reasons and implacably hostile because of allegations of domestic violence – the courts are much more aware these days, and judges are given specific training and information on domestic violence and the impact on the person who has suffered violence and her/his children. Research has been published on the significant problems of 'Domestic Violence and Child Contact.'[29]

13.7   Domestic violence and human rights

The Women's Aid Federation points out that being safe from violence is a basic human right, and is urging the government and the courts to recognise that in granting contact to violent partners, they may well be at risk of infringing this basic human right (enshrined in Articles 2 and

28. Re M (Interim Contact: Domestic Violence) (2000) 2 FLR 377 CA
29. M. Hester and L. Radford, Domestic Violence and Child Contact Arrangements in England and Denmark (University of Bristol School for Policy Studies, Joseph Rowntree Foundation, 1996); Mullender and Morley, Children, Domestic Violence and Housing (1994) and womensaid.org.uk/policy/briefings/.

3 of the European Convention on Human Rights).[30] There Is also an implied right to physical and moral integrity, ie, personal safety, within Article 8, which grants the right to respect for private, home and family life. The counter argument for the perpetrating parent who wants contact with her/his child can, of course, also be based on Article 8. Nevertheless, interference with the right under Article 8 can be permitted if it serves a legitimate aim which is necessary in a democratic society, is not discriminatory and is proportionate to the end it seeks to achieve. For example, refusing contact would be a proportionate response if it were necessary to protect the partner's rights under Articles 2 and 3. Further information on Human Rights is detailed in Chapter 2, section A.

B   Criminal offences

13.8   Crimes relating to domestic violence

Marriage does not give one spouse the right to inflict violence upon the other. In any relationship situation, married or unmarried, heterosexual, lesbian or gay, the criminal law can theoretically be used to bring proceedings against a violent partner for offences including:

OAPA 1861, CJA88, SOA56, CJPOA94 & PFHA97

* murder or manslaughter (whether actual or attempted)

* rape or indecent assault[31]

* unlawful wounding

* grievous bodily harm

* assault occasioning actual bodily harm

* aggravated assault

* common assault[32]

* intimidating a witness[33]

* harming or threatening to harm a witness[34]

* harassment and putting a person in fear of violence (see 13.12).

The Government has been consulting for some time on reforming the Offences Against the Persons Act of 1861. A new draft Offences Against the Persons Bill was produced in 1998, which aims to update the archaic provisions and replace offences such as causing or inflicting grievous bodily harm with the offences of Intentional Serious Injury or Reckless Serious Injury. A new offence of assault would also replace the common law offences of assault and battery. At the time of writing, there was no

30. See www.womensaid.org.uk/policy/briefings/ child%20contact%20dv.htm.

31. s.1(1) Sexual Offences Act 1956; offence for a man to rape a woman or another man; s.14 SOA 1956: offence for a person to make an indecent assault on a woman; s.15 SOA 1956: offence for a person to make an indecent assault on a man.

32. s.30 of the CJA 1988: offence of common assault where a person intentionally or recklessly causes another person to apprehend the immediate application to him/herself of unlawful violence.

33. S.51 CJPOA 1994.

34. See 33 above.

news as to the progress of the Bill. However, two important cases heard together by the House of Lords[35] helped to demonstrate the wide ambit of situations that the courts may be willing to consider. In one case, it was held that grievous bodily harm was held to extend to severe depression caused by the applicant's being stalked by someone with whom she had had a relationship. This involved his turning up at her home and workplace, writing threatening letters and telephoning her. In the other case, actual bodily harm was found to have been caused by a series of either obscene or silent telephone calls.

13.9 Police powers

Under the common law, a police constable may enter premises to prevent or deal with a breach of the peace, and has power to arrest to prevent a breach of the peace. Under the Police and Criminal Evidence Act 1984, a constable may also enter any premises in order to:

s17(1)(b) PACE84
- arrest someone for an arrestable offence, which includes assaults occasioning grievous or actual bodily harm or wounding

s17(1o)(e) PACE84
- in order to save life or limb or prevent serious damage to property.

A police constable may also arrest someone:

s24 PACE84
- who is suspected of having committed an arrestable offence, or is about to commit one, or for certain other specified offences, including indecent assault on a woman. (An arrestable offence is an offence which attracts a maximum sentence of five years' imprisonment or more, or where the penalty is fixed by law. A police constable may arrest in these cases without a warrant)

s25 PACE84
- where there are reasonable grounds for believing it is necessary to prevent any physical injury being caused to another, or to protect a child or other vulnerable person

s3(1) POA86
- whom s/he reasonably suspects of committing an affray. A person is guilty of an affray if s/he uses or threatens unlawful violence towards another and her/his conduct is such as to 'cause a person of reasonable firmness present at the scene to fear for his/her personal safety.'

s23(3)(b) CJA98
A person who has experienced domestic violence is often deterred from pressing charges because of fear of the perpetrator and of having to give oral evidence in court. The Home Office in its revised circular to the police reminded them of the power provided under the Criminal Justice Act 1988, which allows a written statement to be submitted in the place of oral evidence so that the abused person need not appear in court, 'where the maker of the statement does not give evidence through fear or because s/he is kept out of the way'. The circular makes the point that:

35. R v Burstow; R v Ireland (1997) 4 All ER 225; (1998) 1 FLR 105 HL.

> '*recent cases have decided that the victim does not have to prove that he or she is afraid. The proof can be from someone else, for example, a police officer. It is enough that the victim is afraid because of the original offence or has become afraid after the offence because of the possibility of having to give evidence about it.*'[36]

The Multi-Agency Guidance to the Crown Prosecution Service also states that it must consider whether it is appropriate to use an abused person's statement in this way, and that the court will have to decide whether the statement ought to be used in the interests of justice:

> '*Where the victim is the only witness to the offence it may be difficult for Crown Prosecutors to satisfy the court that justice is being served when there is no opportunity for cross-examination...The decision whether to compel a victim of domestic violence to attend court against their wishes requires great sensitivity and discretion. In many cases, compulsion will not be appropriate.*'[37]

13.10 Use of criminal law in cases of domestic violence

Whilst not discouraging a client from taking action against a perpetrator of domestic violence, it is important that advisers make the client aware of what is involved in this type of action. Awareness of what the police are meant to be doing can empower the client to insist on her/his rights:

- If someone makes a 999 emergency call because s/he or a child has been hurt, attacked or threatened by their partner or ex-partner, the police have a duty to help and investigate the complaint. The police have guidance manuals on how to proceed, and details of how the police should respond initially are given in the appendix to the revised Home Office circular to the police:[38]

  - They should not act as conciliators

  - They should not at this stage ask if the person wants to take the matter to court

  - They should not focus solely on the abused person but on the full investigation

  - The first officer at the scene should obtain as much evidence as possible in order to bring charges at a later stage. Instant photographic evidence of any injuries or damage may be appropriate

  - They should speak to each party separately, with the abused person being spoken to in a place where the perpetrator cannot overhear

  - Where an offence has occurred for which a power of arrest exists, the alleged offender should normally be arrested

36. Para 11 HOC 19/2000 ibid.
37. Paras 2b.ii9–10 Multi-Agency Guidance on Addressing Domestic Violence, Home Office March 2000 ibid.   38. HOC 19/2000 ibid.

    – If the abused person might not be safe remaining in the home, consideration should be given to finding a place of safety, eg, a refuge or relative

- The police should take a full statement from the abused person. It may be appropriate for this to be done in a neutral place, where s/he can receive any medical treatment first if necessary. A specialist Domestic Violence Officer may also be available to contact and support the person. The police should obtain family details, the history of the relationship and any other previous incidents, the actual incident, injuries incurred (physical and emotional), whether a weapon was used, whether any further threats were made after the attack, whether any children were present. The police will also speak to neighbours and any other potential witnesses

- The police can hold the abuser pending investigations for up to 24 hours (36 at weekends) before s/he has to be taken before a court, or s/he can be released on bail pending further enquiries. The abused person should be informed if the abuser has been released and the police are directed to offer support, such as panic alarms and mobile phones, regular visits to the home, or arranging emergency accommodation.

- If the abuser is charged with an offence and taken before a magistrate following her/his arrest, then the court will either remand her/him in custody or release her/him on bail. This will depend on the seriousness of the charge and other factors, as well as police recommendations. If bail is given, bail conditions can be set, which can include not going within a certain distance of the abused person or her/his house, or having to live at a certain address, for example a bail hostel, and ensuring attendance at court. If the conditions are broken, the offender can be arrested again

- It may be several weeks or months before the full case is heard. During this time, the abused person may be contacted again by the police on behalf of the Crown Prosecution Service (CPS) if they need more information. Even though the charge is likely to be for a specific incident, it is important in making any statement to the police to include any information about previous attacks or incidents where the complainant or her/his children have been hurt or threatened. If there is independent evidence (from medical or other reports, for example), the police should be told. This may not be able to be used in deciding whether the abuser is guilty of the specific offence, but it might help persuade the CPS to continue with the case, or ask for bail conditions to be set.

Appearing in court

There are often no other witnesses to any violence and an offence may be difficult to prove. There is a higher standard of proof required in criminal courts than in civil cases, as it is necessary to prove 'beyond all reasonable doubt' that an offence has been committed, whereas in civil cases the test is on 'the balance of probabilities.'

If the partner or abuser is arrested and charged, the police will pass the case to the Crown Prosecution Service, who will decide whether there is enough evidence for it to go forward. If the abuser pleads not guilty, further action will partly depend on the abused person's willingness to give evidence as a witness for the prosecution. If s/he does not wish to go to court as a witness, s/he will be asked to make a statement to say why. Even if the abused person wants to withdraw the prosecution, the CPS could insist that s/he gives evidence. It may, however, be possible for a written statement to be substituted, as explained in 13.9, and this possibility should always be considered where the spouse/partner is in fear.

The case may be heard in the Magistrates Court or the Crown Court (a higher court with a judge presiding), depending on the severity of the charge. Through the Court Liaison Officer, the local police should keep the applicant informed of the progress of the case, and s/he may be supported at court by the police Domestic Violence Officer, or a representative from Victim Support.

The applicant will only be called to court to give evidence if the abuser pleaded not guilty at a previous hearing. Once the court has heard the evidence, if the defendant is found guilty it will usually adjourn for further reports from the Probation Service, before sentencing.

What sentence is s/he likely to get?

The type or length of sentence depends on the seriousness of the offence and whether the defendant has previous convictions. It can range from a conditional discharge to a prison sentence. If the abuser is the current partner, unless a custodial sentence is given, s/he is likely to be able to return home.

Protection of injured party

Although bail conditions can be attached at a preliminary hearing until the final hearing, if the perpetrator is convicted but not committed to prison the criminal courts have no real power to protect the injured party, other than the limited powers to bind over to keep the peace or by attaching conditions to a probation order. Criminal courts cannot grant injunctions, and further civil proceedings would therefore be necessary, (but see discussion of restraining orders under the Protection from Harassment Act 1997 at 13.12).

Private prosecution

If the police decide not to prosecute, the individual can bring a private prosecution. However, no public funding for legal help is available. Where a private prosecution is brought the police have no power to keep the defendant under arrest if they have decided not to proceed themselves.

13.11 Criminal Injuries Compensation Scheme

It is now possible for a member of the same family living in the same household as the offender to make a claim under the Criminal Injuries Compensation Scheme.[39]

13.12 Protection from Harassment Act 1997 – Criminal and civil actions

The Protection from Harassment Act was promoted as the 'Stalker's Act,' but has introduced radical new powers to combat all forms of harassment in both the civil and criminal courts. In practice it is rarely used for 'stalking' offences, and is mainly being used to deal with a variety of domestic and neighbour disputes.

Although it would appear to be particularly useful for those who fall outside the provisions of the Family Law Act as non-associated persons (see 13.46), research has shown that almost half of all cases to date are those where the person making the complaint has ended an intimate relationship with the person now harassing them.[40]

Offences under the PFHA

There are two main offences in the Act, the offence of harassment, and the offence of putting people in fear of violence, sometimes referred to as 'aggravated harassment.'

- *'Harassment'* includes alarming a person or causing a person distress. Where someone pursues a course of conduct – conduct including speech – (on at least two occasions) which amounts to harassment and the person knows or ought to know that it amounts to harassment, an offence is committed

ss1-2 PFHA97
- *'Putting people in fear of violence'* where a person whose course of conduct causes another to fear (again on at least two occasions), that violence will be used against her/him, that person is guilty of an offence if that person knows or ought to know that the behaviour will cause the other to be in fear.

s4 PFHA97
As these are criminal offences, the police can prosecute (see below under 'effectiveness of the Act.'

---

39. For more information, contact Criminal Injuries Compensation Board, Blythswood House, 200 West Regent Street, Glasgow G2 4SW.
40. 'The Protection from Harassment Act 1997 – an evaluation of its use and effectiveness' Harris. J. Home

Office Research Findings No. 130 2000. Available from Communications Development Unit, Room 201, Home Office, 50 Queen Anne's Gate, London sw1H 9AT. Tel. 020 7273 2084 Fax 020 7222 0211 or at www.homeoffice.go.uk/rds/index.htm.

Tests

The tests are both subjective and objective.

- Subjectively, if the victim is vulnerable and in particular is likely to be distressed in a situation in which most people would not feel the same way, it is still an offence if the harasser knew or ought to have known that the behaviour would cause distress to that victim

- Objectively, the person 'ought to know' that it amounts to harassment or puts a person in fear of violence, if a reasonable person, who knew as much as the harasser, would expect the behaviour to cause such distress or fear.

Punishment

- The offence of harassment is a summary offence, ie, one which can be tried only in the magistrates' court, for which there is a maximum punishment of 6 months in prison and/or a fine of up to £5,000

- The offence of putting a person in fear of violence may be dealt with in either the magistrates' or the Crown Court, and carries a maximum of 5 years in prison and/or unlimited fine.

Restraining orders

s5(1) & (2) PFHA97

Where someone is sentenced for either of the offences, the court may also make a 'restraining order' to protect the victim from further harassment or behaviour which will cause a fear of violence. This can include ordering a person to stay out of a certain defined area. If this is breached, a further offence is committed, carrying a maximum of

s5(5) PFHA97

5 years' imprisonment and/or unlimited fine.

Civil injunctions under Protection from Harassment Act

s3(1) PFHA97

An individual may also apply for a civil injunction in respect of harassment and damages may be claimed. A claim may be made in respect of actual or apprehended harassment by the victim or person who may be the victim of an apprehended harassment. 'Apprehended' means a) that there has been a course of conduct which has ceased and b) the claimant can show that the perpetrator is likely to resume the harassment. Damages may be awarded for, amongst other things, any anxiety caused

s3(2) PFHA97

by the harassment and any financial loss resulting from the harassment.

s3(3) & s3(5)
s3(6) & s3(9)

Where the injunction is breached, the applicant may apply for a warrant for arrest, and the breach then constitutes a criminal offence carrying a punishment of up to 5 years' imprisonment and/or unlimited fine.

Effectiveness of the Act[41]

In 1998, 4300 actions for harassment were started by the police under s2, the lesser charge of harassment, and 1500 under the more serious

41. See 40 above.

charge of putting someone in fear of violence. Once the police have charged a suspect, the case is referred to the Crown Prosecution Service (CPS), which reviews the case and decides whether to proceed with a prosecution. 39% of harassment cases were dropped by the CPS, compared with a national average for all offences of 14%. The majority of cases were dropped on the basis of insufficient evidence, but in one-third, it was because the plaintiff did not wish to proceed. In nearly half of the cases which were dropped, the defendant agreed to be bound over.

Of the cases which proceeded to a hearing, the overall conviction rate was 84%. The most frequent sentence (43% of cases) was a conditional discharge mostly accompanied with a restraining order. Restraining orders were usually specified to run for 12 – 18 months with conditions against re-offending, eg, the offender must not contact the victim, or must keep away from the victim's home. Anecdotal evidence suggests that breaches are not always acted upon by the police.

See 13.42 for a comparison of civil actions under the Protection from Harassment Act and the Family Law Act.

13.13 Criminal – the Crime and Disorder Act 1998

Part I of the Crime and Disorder Act requires local authorities and the police to establish local partnerships to develop and implement strategies for the reduction of crime and disorder, and provides powers to prevent s1 CDA98 harassment, alarm or distress to anyone not of the same household. Other statutory and non-statutory agencies and local communities should be involved, although they have no power to bring proceedings.

In the audit of local crime problems and development of strategies required by the Act, the Government's Crime Reduction Unit has stressed the importance of addressing domestic violence.[42] Many local authority areas have developed special domestic-violence related projects funded by the Crime Reduction Unit under the Violence Against Women initiative. Others have developed 'multi-pronged' community safety policies to deal with domestic violence and racist and homophobic behaviour.

Specific powers are granted under the Act. In particular, an anti-social behaviour order (ASBO) is available on application by the police or local authority (on the civil standard of proof) to prohibit behaviour which could cause harassment, alarm or distress to anyone in a local community. The scheme relating to ASBOs was amended by the Police Reform Act 2002 which took effect from 1st April 2003, extending the power to apply for an order to include Registered Social Landlords and the British Transport Police. It also allows orders to be made to protect

42. www.crimereduction.gov.uk/domesticviolence4.htm.

people anywhere in England and Wales, and not just in the local authority district in which the application is made.

Breach of an order is an arrestable offence, with a maximum penalty, for an adult, of 5 years' imprisonment. ASBOs are mainly used to combat anti-social behaviour, as the name implies, but there is no reason in principle why they should not be used in cases of domestic violence.

There is considerable scope within the Act. Its effectiveness depends upon locally co-ordinated responses.

Key features of an Anti Social Behaviour Order (ASBO)

- The police, a local authority, a registered social landlord or the British Transport Police can apply for an order

- An order can be made against any person 10 years old or above

- An order can be made against non tenants in all tenures, i.e private tenants and owner-occupiers as well as public sector tenants; individuals or several individuals (perhaps a family); but not for behaviour within an individual family (see below)

- The order is preventative in nature

- Application is made to the Magistrates' Court acting in a civil capacity or, from 1 April 2003, application may also be made in a county court

- The minimum term of an ASBO is two years

- Breach of any order is a criminal offence with a maximum penalty of five years in prison.

The court must be satisfied that the order is necessary to protect a person or persons from further antisocial acts in the locality or anywhere in England and Wales.

The orders can be sought against anyone who has acted in a manner which 'caused or was likely to cause harassment, alarm or distress' to one or more people living in *another* household. Thus they cannot be used within an existing family context, but could be used against an ex-partner, or against people connected to the ex-partner. The statutory scheme allows for the use of professional witnesses.

C   Civil actions

In view of the shortcomings of the criminal law in relation to domestic violence, instead the decision is often made to seek a remedy in the civil courts. Local authority homelessness departments frequently advise or insist that a person in fear of violence seeks an injunction, even though it is at odds with the Code of Guidance on Homelessness (see 15.5). It is often assumed that this is a relatively straightforward solution to the problem. It has certainly not been the case in the past, nor even in more recent years. Certain points should be kept in mind:

- Injunctions are not automatically granted – the courts must have regard to a range of factors even where there has been violence[43] (see 13.28)

- Injunctions cannot provide a guarantee of protection

- Injunctions are likely to be limited in time

- Injunctions are cumbersome to enforce (the respondent is unlikely to be committed for a first breach unless it is very serious)

- Injunctions do not provide long-term solutions to disputes over property

- They are expensive to obtain, rarely costing less than £1000. Even if legal help or public funding is available, this may have to be repaid at a later date where a property or financial settlement is also reached, (see 4.40 for an explanation of what is known as the 'statutory charge'). In theory, an order for costs might be obtained against the other party, although it is not generally to be recommended, since it can provoke further aggression.

Bearing all of this in mind, however, advisers should remember how disempowering domestic violence can be and, whilst not giving clients false hopes, should try to give them encouragement to use civil remedies, if they so choose.

13.14 Definition of an injunction

An injunction is a generic or 'catch-all' term for any type of emergency legal remedy providing a written order from the court which tells a person to do, or forbids her/him from doing, one or more things. It is a civil remedy.

13.15 Obtaining an injunction

Injunctions can generally be obtained only after certain types of legal proceedings have been started. They are therefore called 'ancillary remedies.' Examples are where injunctions are granted to support to protect a legal or equitable right, for example breach of contract or tort; or where proceedings are being taken under a statute, eg, the Children Act 1989, and an injunction is also required. This means, in effect, that certain preconditions must be satisfied before the court can

---

43. B v B (Occupation Order) see footnote 23 above.

grant an injunction. The preconditions are not only related to the merits of the case in itself, but also relate to the courts' jurisdiction. This general power to grant injunctions along with other actions is sometimes referred to as the 'inherent jurisdiction' of the court, which stems both from case law and the Supreme Court Act 1981. The county court has the same power by virtue of statute. This means that the courts can grant injunctions in all cases where it appears to be just and convenient to do so.

s37 SCA81
& s3 CLSA90

13.16 Injunctions relating to domestic violence

Statutory exceptions in cases of domestic violence have been made to the rule requiring ancillary proceedings. Injunctions can therefore be applied for without any other proceedings being started. Where these domestic violence statutes do not apply, the general powers explained above in 13.15 must be relied upon.

The Family Law Act 1996 provides freestanding remedies which are available to a wide range of people, known as 'associated persons.' They are explained below. There are still some limited situations where other proceedings might have to be used because the Family Law Act 1996 does not apply. These are covered in Section D below.

ORDERS UNDER THE FAMILY LAW ACT 1996

From October 1997 the Family Law Act repealed the Domestic Violence and Matrimonial Proceedings Act 1976, the Matrimonial Homes Act 1983 and parts of the Domestic Proceedings and Magistrates' Courts Act 1978, and replaced these Acts with a wider-reaching but simpler set of remedies. Remedies under the Children Act to protect children and parents are still available, but are of lesser significance because of the scope of the new Act. These remedies and a discussion of the court's inherent jurisdiction to protect parents and children can be found in 13.43 – 13.44.

13.17 The definition of a 'cohabitant' under the Family Law Act 1996

The definition of a cohabitant is very important when looking at actions which can be taken under the Family Law Act. For the purposes of this Act, only heterosexual couples are covered by the term 'cohabitant'. Cohabitants are defined as:

s62(1)(a) FLA96

> *'a man and a woman who, although not married to each other, are living together as husband and wife.'*

This means that while lesbian or gay partners can qualify as 'associated persons' if they are sharing the same household, they cannot apply for occupation orders unless they have a pre-existing entitlement to occupy, ie, they cannot apply if they are only bare licensees in their partner's home (see 13.25 and 13.26). Since the case of *Mendoza v Ghaidan*[44], in which it was held that it was discriminatory under Article 14 of the European Convention of Human Rights to distinguish between a heterosexual and a gay or lesbian couple, the legality of such a definition must be called into doubt. See Chapter 2, Section A for a further discussion of Human Rights.

13.18 Special rules for children under 16

There is a special provision in the Act which states that a child under 16 may not apply in her/his own right for a non-molestation order or an occupation order, except with the permission of the court. The court must be satisfied that the child has sufficient understanding of the proposed application. This does not affect the right of a parent or someone with parental responsibility to apply on the child's behalf.

NON-MOLESTATION ORDERS

13.19 Non-molestation orders

These orders:

• prohibit molestation of an 'associated person'
• prohibit molestation of a 'relevant child.'

They are designed to protect individuals and forbid not only violence but also specific kinds of distressing behaviour, such as persistent telephone-calls, abusive comments and unwanted attention. They do not remove someone from the home. The court has held that molestation must include conduct which clearly harassed and affected the applicant to such a degree that the intervention of the court was justified. In *C v C*[45], the judge refused a husband a molestation order to prevent his wife from giving further information to newspaper reporters, as such an activity came nowhere near molestation as envisaged by the Family Law Act.

There is no need to prove violence, only molestation, to obtain a non-molestation order:

> *'Violence is a form of molestation, but molestation may take place without threats or use of violence and still be serious and inimical to mental or physical health.'*[46]

When orders may be made

The court may make a non-molestation order:

• on application from an associated person (with or without other family proceedings)

44. Mendoza v Ghaidan [2002] 4 All ER 1162; [2003] 1 FLR 468 CA.
45. C v C (1998) FD 1 FLR 554.
46. Davis v Johnson (1978) 1 All ER 841 CA.

- in any family proceedings, without the need for specific application, if the court considers it of benefit to any of the parties involved in the proceedings or any 'relevant' child, ie, the court may take the initiative.

s42(2) FLA96

Criteria for making non-molestation orders

In making a non-molestation order the court must have regard to all circumstances, including the need to secure the health, safety and well-being of the applicant/person concerned or any relevant child.

s42(5) FLA96

Duration of orders

Non-molestation orders may be made either for a specific period or until further order. Where an order is made during other family proceedings, it will cease to have effect if the proceedings are withdrawn or dismissed.

s42(7)-(8) FLA96

13.20 Definition of associated person

The concept of 'associated persons' is defined in section 62(3) of the Family Law Act. Any associated person may apply for a non-molestation order and does not necessarily have to have lived with the person concerned, eg, two people may have had a child together but never lived together, or they may have agreed to marry each other or be relatives and not lived together. If one party is pestering the other, a non-molestation order could be sought to prevent the unwanted behaviour.

Two people are associated where they:

- are or have been married to each other
- are or have been cohabitants (see above)
- are parties to the same family proceedings
- live or have lived in the same household (other than as employer and employee or landlord and tenant or lodger) – this means that sharers and those in lesbian and gay relationships are able to apply for non-molestation orders
- have agreed at some point to marry one another, whether or not that agreement has been terminated
- are parents of a child or people who have had parental responsibility for that child (note that they do not have to have lived together), or
- are relatives.

Agreements to marry must be evidenced either in writing or by:

1. The gift of an engagement ring from one to another, or

s44 FLA96

2. Having undergone a ceremony in the presence of witnesses.

Relatives are defined as:

'a) the father, mother, stepfather, stepmother, son, daughter, stepson, stepdaughter, grandmother, grandfather, grandson or granddaughter of that person or of that person's spouse or former spouse, or

b) the brother, sister, uncle, aunt, niece or nephew (whether of the full blood or of the half blood or by affinity) of that person or of that person's spouse or former spouse,

and includes, in relation to a person who is living or has lived with another person as husband and wife, any person who would fall within paragraph (a) or (b) above if the parties were married to each other.'

s63(1) FLA96

Where a child has been adopted, two people are associated with each other if they are in a relationship of:

- natural parent/grandparent and adopted child, or

- natural parent/grandparent and adoptive parent.

13.21 Definition of 'relevant child'

A 'relevant child' is defined as:

- any child who lives or might reasonably be expected to live with either party involved in the proceedings

- any child who is the subject of adoption or Children Act proceedings, or

s62(2) FLA96

- any other child whose interests the court considers relevant.

OCCUPATION ORDERS

13.22 Functions of occupation orders

Under the Family Law Act, the court can make two different kinds of occupation orders:

- *'Declaratory orders'*,[47] which declare, extend or confer occupation rights, and

- *'Regulatory orders'* controlling or restricting existing rights (previously referred to as ousters or exclusion orders).

These orders can therefore in principle be adapted to carry out the dual function of dealing with occupation of the home in both violent and non-violent relationship breakdown situations.

'Significant harm'

It was hoped that occupation orders would go further than the previous

---

47. Law Commission No 207, see 1 above, p. 28.

crude distinction between 'violence' and 'non-violence,' since the wording which the Act uses is that the court must consider the likelihood of 'significant harm' to any of the parties concerned. For spouses and former spouses there is a duty on the court to make an order excluding one of the parties if significant harm is likely, subject to a 'balance of harm' test (see 13.29); otherwise, the court has a power, rather than a duty, to make an order. However, there has been no noticeable change in the number of orders being granted and the courts still refer to occupation orders with an exclusion provision as 'draconian' remedies.[48] It appears that it is still unlikely that a partner will be excluded without evidence of violence, but an order was made granting occupation to an ex-husband, when the ex-wife wished to sell the home (see 4.5 *S v F*).

Effects of occupation orders

Other important points to note concerning the effect of occupation orders are that:

- orders regulating occupation of the home do not alter the parties' financial interests in the home

- an occupation order gives a non-tenant or non-owner the equivalent of matrimonial home rights whilst the order is in force. As explained in previous chapters, these include rights to pay the rent/mortgage, the right to be treated as if s/he were the tenant (thus fulfilling any residence requirement necessary to maintain the tenancy) and the right to intervene in possession proceedings.

13.23 Provisions that can be attached to occupation orders by the court

- *Occupation rent*: Where one party has been ordered to leave by virtue of an occupation order, the court may make an order obliging the person who remains to make periodical payments to her/him. This is sometimes referred to as an occupation rent, and is intended as a compensation for the loss of the right to occupy

s40(1)(b) FLA96
- *Repairs, maintenance and rent/mortgage liability*: where the court has made an occupation order (not necessarily involving exclusion), it may make an order obliging either party to repair or maintain the house or it may impose obligations regarding payment of rent, mortgage or other outgoings. For example, this could transfer an owner/tenant's liability for rent or mortgage payments and order that the other party take on that liability. However, the liability ceases when the occupation order ends (see 11.17 for problems in enforcing
s40(1)(a) FLA96
s40(3) FLA96
a transferred liability).

48. Chalmers v Johns, (1999) 1 FLR CA.

There are also powers for the court to protect property when granting occupation orders (see below).

Protecting property

A problem which frequently arises when one partner has been excluded from the home is that the excluded partner may decide to remove all the furniture or contents of the home; or the other partner may wreak vengeance on the home or the partner's belongings. In the past, it was necessary to start separate proceedings using the tort of trespass to apply for an order to prevent damage to goods (see 13.50). The Family Law Act provides that where the court has made an occupation order under sections 33, 35 or 36 it may also make an order:

s40(1)(c) FLA96

- granting either party possession or use of furniture or other contents of the home – this presumably will prevent the excluded partner from removing all the household contents

s40(1)(e) FLA96

- ordering either party to take reasonable care of any furniture or contents of the house – this is designed to prevent one partner destroying or damaging the other's belongings

s40(1)(c) FLA96

- ordering either party to take reasonable steps to keep the house and its contents secure – thus safeguarding property.

These three provisions remove the need to apply for a separate order to prevent trespass (or damage) to goods.

13.24 Eligibility for occupation orders

Occupation orders may be granted under sections 33, 35, 36, 37 or 38 of the Family Law Act. The main differences between the orders are:

- the range of people who may apply for the orders
- the criteria which the court must use when deciding whether to grant an order, and
- the length of time orders may last.

To find out who has a right to apply for which orders, it is necessary to establish three issues:

- Does the applicant have an entitlement to occupy, is s/he not entitled or is neither party entitled to occupy?
- Is the applicant a spouse, former spouse, cohabitant or former cohabitant?
- Is the respondent a spouse, former spouse, cohabitant, former cohabitant or another 'associated person' as defined by the Act (see 13.20).

13.25 Distinction between entitled and non-entitled persons

In order to decide under which provision a person can apply for an occupation order it is first necessary to know whether s/he is 'entitled' to occupy the property within the definition of the Act.

Meaning of entitled and non-entitled

s53(1)(a) FLA96

Entitled applicants are people who have an existing right to occupy the dwelling in question because they are either:

- a legal owner or joint legal owner
- someone with a 'beneficial interest' in the home (ie, a right to all or part of the proceeds of sale of the dwelling – see 5.4)
- a tenant or joint tenant
- a married non-owner with matrimonial home rights (see 4.1)
- someone with a statutory or contractual right to remain (see 5.2).

People who are not entitled applicants have none of the above rights, and therefore include:

- someone living in her/his partner's home as a bare licensee (ie, an excluded occupier (see 6.11)
- someone staying with friends or relatives as a bare licensee
- a squatter.

Applicants with no existing rights to occupy ('non-entitled')

Occupation orders are not available to all 'non-entitled' applicants, only to those who have a heterosexual relationship with the person against whom they wish to get the order, which is recognised by the Act. Those who can apply are therefore former spouses, heterosexual cohabitants, or former cohabitants who:

- have no matrimonial home rights under section 30 of the Family Law Act
- are non-owners or non-tenants
- have no beneficial interest in the property or

s35(1) & s36(1) FLA96

- have no statutory or contractual right to remain.

13.26 Lesbian/gay cohabitants

The definition of 'cohabitants' in the Act covers only heterosexual couples (see 13.17). Heterosexual cohabitants may apply for occupation orders as entitled and non-entitled applicants, but lesbian or gay cohabitants

s62(1) FLA96

may only apply for occupation orders if they have a pre-existing right to occupy, either as a joint owner or tenant or as someone who can establish a beneficial or other interest (see 5.9 onwards). See 2.4 for a discussion of possible discrimination under Article 14 of the European Convention on Human Rights which may be inherent in this provision.

13.27 Occupation orders where the applicant is entitled to occupy – section 33 orders

Where a person applying for an order is an 'entitled' person, s/he can apply for an occupation order, under section 33 of the Family Law Act 1996, against any other 'associated person,' whether or not that person is entitled (see 13.25). This therefore includes all applications from non-tenant/non-owner spouses (who have matrimonial home rights), any person with a beneficial interest, and sole or joint owners or tenants, regardless of whether the person against whom the order is directed was in a heterosexual, lesbian or gay relationship with her/him or merely shared the home with her/him. They are also available to those who may have agreed to marry but never actually did so, in respect of a property which they had lived in or intended to live in together, as long as no more than three years has elapsed since they broke off

s33(2) FLA96

the agreement.

s33(1)(b) FLA96

Orders relate only to properties which have been lived in by both persons as their home, or which were intended to be lived in as their home.

Orders available

Entitled applicants may apply for occupation orders (which may be unlimited in time or of a specific length) enforcing their rights to occupy and/or excluding an associated person or restricting that party's rights to occupy. An occupation order can contain various provisions. The

s33(4) FLA96
s33(3)(a) FLA96
s33(3)(b) FLA96

'declaratory' orders are:

• to declare that the person is entitled to occupy or has matrimonial home rights

• to enforce the applicant's right to occupy

• to allow re-entry to the home if excluded

• for married applicants, to make an order during marriage that matrimonial home rights will not be brought to an end either by the death of the spouse or by termination of the marriage, ie, that they will extend beyond divorce.

s33(3)(co FLA96

An entitled applicant may also apply for the following 'regulatory' orders:

- To regulate the occupation of the dwelling by either or both of the parties

s33(3)(f) FLA96 • To exclude the other spouse from all, or part, of the home

- To restrict or terminate the matrimonial right to occupy of a non-owner/non-tenant spouse. It is open to the court to end a non-owner or non-tenant spouse's matrimonial home rights as well as temporarily withdrawing them. An order to terminate would normally only be made together with the final settlement of the home upon
s33(3)(e) FLA96 divorce, judicial separation or nullity, to resolve an impasse

- To prohibit, suspend or restrict the other person's rights to occupy (as an owner, tenant or person with a beneficial interest). Unlike matrimonial home rights, the court has no power to terminate completely these rights, only to suspend them. Long-term solutions
s33(3)(d) FLA96 would therefore have to be sought (see Chapters 5 and 8)

s33(3)(g) FLA96 • To exclude the other party from a defined area around the home.

Duration of orders

There is no restriction on the duration of occupation orders for entitled applicants. They may be for a specific length of time or until a specific
s33(10) FLA96 event such as divorce occurs, or until further order at the court's discretion.

An application for an occupation order may not be made after the death of either party, and will end on the death of either unless the
s33(9) FLA96 court has ordered otherwise.

13.28 Criteria for occupation orders for entitled applicants under section 33

The court has power to grant an order where it considers it just and reasonable to do so, but there are specific criteria which it must consider when reaching its decision. The court must make its decision by giving regard to all the circumstances of the case, including:

- the respective housing needs and housing resources of the parties and any relevant child
- the respective financial resources of the parties
- the likely effect of any order or the effect of any order or the effect of not making an order, on the health, safety or well-being of the parties and of any relevant child

s33(6) FLA96 • the conduct of the parties.

Unlike the previous legislation, housing needs and resources are specifically mentioned. Housing resources include whether either party would qualify for rehousing under homelessness/allocations legislation (see Chapter 14); case law in the case of *B v B* (see box) has shown that the lack or otherwise of accommodation can outweigh even severe violence.

B v B[49]

After suffering substantial violence at the hands of the husband, the wife, with the parties' 2-year-old daughter, moved out of the matrimonial home, which was a council house. They were temporarily housed as homeless by the local authority in bed and breakfast accommodation. The husband remained in the house with his son from a former relationship, aged 6. The wife obtained orders from a county court under S.33 of the FLA that the husband and his child vacate the home, for transfer of the tenancy to her under Schedule 7 and for a non-molestation order. The husband appealed against the orders in relation to the home.

The Court of Appeal allowed the husband's appeal, and held that the judge's decision was plainly wrong and could not stand.

The analysis of the housing position under s.33(6) (the housing needs and housing resources of each of the parties) had been mistaken. The judge believed that the local authority was obliged under the Housing Act 1996 to rehouse the husband permanently, whereas since the husband was considered to be intentionally homeless on account of the violence, the duty under s.190(2)9(a) of that Act was only to give advice and to secure temporary accommodation, after which he would have had to fend for himself. By contrast, the authority's duty to the wife and younger child under ss.193 and 194 of the Housing Act 1996 was to provide suitable permanent accommodation.

The judge was entitled to find that the wife and younger child were likely to suffer significant harm attributable to the husband's conduct if an occupation order were not made. However, weighing the respective likelihood of harm so far as the two children were concerned, the balance came down clearly in favour of the husband's child if an occupation order were made. If he were to move, he would also have to change schools and being away from his father was an obstacle to this as an acceptable solution.

---

49. B v B (Occupation Order) see 23 above.

In effect, the basic criteria will be of secondary consideration in some situations where the court must make an order. These are where it appears to the court that the applicant or any relevant child will suffer significant harm if an order is not made. However, if the person against whom the order is to be made or any relevant child will suffer greater harm if an order is made than would be suffered by the applicant or child if the order is not made, the court should not make the order. This is known as the 'balance of harm test.' If the wife in *B v B* had still been in the matrimonial home and at risk of harm from her husband, it seems likely that she would have obtained an occupation order. In her case, she had already been found a place of safety and the interests of the respective children were the deciding factor. What if there had been no children involved? Anecdotal evidence has indicated that judges may still be unwilling to exclude someone from her/his own home if it will make s33(7) FLA96 the person homeless with no other prospect of housing resources.

13.29 Balance of harm test in making occupation orders

The Law Commission debated at length the criteria which should be used when making occupation orders. It was felt that the old criteria in the Matrimonial Homes Act 1983 (now repealed) had failed in a number of respects:

• They did not give priority to the applicant's personal protection, since it had to be balanced against hardship to the respondent. This meant that the level of protection for someone suffering from violence may not always have been adequate

• The need for allegations of blame and considerations of behaviour were contrary to the trend of reducing the need for recrimination in matrimonial law

• They gave insufficient weight to the interests of children, whose welfare was given no priority.

Definition of harm

The balance of harm test in the Family Law Act is intended to address these problems. The Act defines 'harm' in the following ways:

• For adults (ie, those over 18), harm means ill treatment or the impairment of health

• For children (under 18), harm means ill-treatment or the impairment s63 FLA96 of health and development.

'Health' includes physical or mental health; 'ill-treatment' includes non-physical forms and, in relation to a child, child abuse; and 'development' means physical, intellectual, emotional, social or behaviour development. In order to decide whether a child's health or development is impaired, the Act says that it should be compared with the health and development *'which could reasonably be expected of a* **s63(3) FLA96** *similar child.'*

In *G v G*[50] the court ruled that where, after comparing the harm that is likely to be suffered by either party and any child, it is not clear that one will suffer more than the other if the order is not made, the court has discretion to decide on the basis of the general criteria in s.33(6).

The Law Commission's report which received almost total parliamentary approval discussed the meaning of 'harm':

> *'Harm has a narrower meaning than hardship. It is defined as 'ill-treatment or impairment of physical or mental health'. In relation to children, the term will attract the definition used in section 31 of the Children Act 1989. It is likely that a respondent threatened with ouster on account of his violence would be able to establish a degree of hardship (perhaps in terms of difficulty in finding or unsuitability of alternative accommodation or problems in getting to work). But he is unlikely to suffer significant harm, whereas his wife and children who are being subjected to his violence or abuse may very easily suffer harm if he remains in the house. In this way the court will be treating violence or other forms of abuse as deserving immediate relief and will be directed to make an order where significant harm exists. However, by placing an emphasis on the need for a remedy rather than on the conduct which gave rise to that need, the criteria will not actually put a premium on allegations of violence and thus may avoid the problems which would be generated by a scheme which focuses upon it.'*[51]

It was hoped that the new criteria would be much more effective in addressing not only situations involving physical violence or abuse, but also those which encompass mental cruelty and other forms of non-physical abuse. Unfortunately, this does not appear to have been the case, as shown in the case of *Banks v Banks* and *Chalmers v Johns* (see below), in which the court reiterated the approach taken under the old legislation, ie, that ordering someone to vacate the matrimonial home is a 'draconian' remedy.

> **Chalmers v Johns**[52]
>
> *In the year prior to the couple's separation, the police had been called out four times, to deal with their assaults on each other, each of which involved minor injuries. The mother, a recovering*

alcoholic, eventually left the property and moved into temporary council accommodation. The child had regular staying contact with the father. The mother applied for an order under Part IV of the FLA 1996, orders for residence and for transfer of the tenancy. At an interim hearing, the judge, although she pointed out that this was not in ordinary terms a domestic violence case, made an interim occupation order under section 33 FLA 1996, in favour of the mother on the basis that the mother and child were likely to suffer significant harm attributable to the father's conduct if the order were not made. The father appealed successfully.

It was held that under section 33, the court's first consideration was whether the evidence established that the applicant or any relevant child was likely to suffer significant harm attributable to the conduct of the respondent if an order was not made. If the answer was yes, then the court had to make the order unless, balancing one against the other, the harm to the respondent or the child was likely to be as great. If, however, the answer was no, then the court had discretion. Neither the mother nor the child was likely to suffer significant harm attributable to the conduct of the father if the order was not made, and the matter was, therefore, one for discretion.

The fact that the matter was due for final hearing very shortly weighed against making such an order at an interlocutory hearing. The appeal was allowed, with comment made that occupation order applications were to be determined at the principal hearing.

An order to vacate the matrimonial home is a draconian one and should be restricted to exceptional cases under the 1996 Act, as was recognised in previous case law under the DVMPA 1976. The facts of the case came nowhere near that category. The disharmony between the parties would have been perfectly capable of control by injunctive order. In addition, the parties were encouraged to take advantage of mediation facilities to resolve their dispute.

Banks v Banks[53]

A 75-year-old husband sought non-molestation and occupation orders against his 79-year-old wife who suffered from manic depression and dementia. The husband was a frail old man, had impaired mobility and could no longer tolerate his wife's condition, and did not want to live with her anymore. The husband's GP thought that the husband's health was suffering from the strain of living in these conditions. The Judge found that although the wife

continued overleaf

---

53. Banks v Banks (1999) 1 FLR 726.

> *could be both physically and verbally aggressive, her behaviour did not significantly threaten his health. Conducting the balance of harm test, the judge found that the harm to the wife if the order was made would be significantly greater than the harm to the husband if the order were not made. Applying Wookey v Wookey,[54] the judge found that a non-molestation order would serve no useful purpose as the wife would not be capable of understanding it.*

13.30 Applications for occupation orders by non-entitled applicants

Where the person who wishes to apply for an occupation order is not within the list of those entitled to occupy, then the type of order that s/he can apply for will depend upon:

- whether the person against whom s/he wishes to obtain the order is her/his spouse, former spouse, a cohabitant or a former cohabitant, and

- whether the person against whom s/he wishes to obtain the order is 'entitled' to occupy the property.

Former spouses

Where the non-entitled person applying is a former spouse and the former spouse against whom s/he is applying for the order is entitled to occupy, the application should be under section 35 of the Family Law Act (see 13.31). (NB. Spouses will never fall into this category, because if one is entitled to occupy then the other will have matrimonial home rights, and so applications will nearly always be made under section 33).

Former heterosexual cohabitants

Where the non-entitled person applying is a heterosexual cohabitant or former cohabitant and the cohabitant or former cohabitant against whom s/he is applying for the order is entitled to occupy, then the application should be under section 36 of the Family Law Act (see 13.33).

Neither spouse or former spouse is entitled to occupy

Where the non-entitled person applying is a spouse or a former spouse and the spouse or former spouse against whom s/he is applying for the order is not entitled to occupy (ie, neither is entitled), then the application should be under section 37 of the Family Law Act (see 13.35).

Neither heterosexual cohabitant or former heterosexual cohabitant is entitled to occupy

Where the non-entitled person applying is a cohabitant or former cohabitant and the cohabitant or former cohabitant against whom s/he

54. Wookey v Wookey (1991) 3 All ER 365.

is applying for the order is not entitled to occupy (ie, neither is entitled) then the application should be under section 38 of the Family Law Act (see 13.36).

13.31 Occupation orders for former spouses with no entitlement to occupy – section 35 orders

Non-entitled former spouses may apply for occupation orders under section 35 of the Family Law Act where the other spouse is entitled to occupy because of ownership, a tenancy, beneficial interest or contractual or statutory right to remain in the home. The orders grant rights to occupy, or restrict/exclude the former spouse. The maximum length of an order is initially six months, renewable thereafter. Orders may relate only to a dwelling which is, was or was intended to be the matrimonial home of the applicant and the former spouse.

s35(1)(c) FLA96

Orders available

Unlike an owner, tenant or married partner (entitled applicants), non-owner and non-tenant former spouses (non-entitled applicants) do not have a legal right to occupy unless they are successful in obtaining an occupation order or had their occupation rights extended before the end of the marriage.

If an order is made, it must contain one of the following declaratory provisions:

s35(3) FLA96

• That the applicant has the right not to be evicted or excluded from the house or any part of it for the duration of the order and prohibiting the other former spouse from evicting or excluding the applicant, or

• If the applicant is not in occupation, the right to enter and remain in occupation for the duration of the order and requiring the other former spouse to allow this.

s35(4) FLA96

In addition, the court may attach further regulatory provisions to the order as for entitled applicants:

s34(4) FLA96

• Regulating the occupation of the dwelling by either or both parties

• Prohibiting or suspending the exercise by the other former spouse of her/his right to occupy the dwelling

• Requiring the other former spouse to leave all or part of the dwelling

• Excluding the former spouse from a defined area around the dwelling.

The court may also attach the same provisions as listed in 13.23 above (ie, occupation rent, liabilities etc).

The main difference between orders made under section 35 of the Act and those made under section 33 for entitled applicants is in the criteria which the court must use (see below).

13.32 Criteria for occupation orders for non-entitled former spouses

Whilst the same basic criteria apply as for entitled applicants (see 13.28), there are additional criteria for former spouses. A distinction must be drawn between declaratory orders and regulatory orders:

Declaratory orders

When deciding whether to make a declaratory order granting the right to occupy and not be excluded without a court order, the court must, in addition to the criteria for entitled applicants (ie, all the circumstances including housing needs and resources, financial resources, the likely effect of an order on the health, safety or well-being of all parties
s35(6)(a)-(d) FLA96   concerned and the conduct of the parties), also consider the following:

• The length of time since the parties ceased to live together

• The length of time since the marriage was dissolved or annulled

• Any other proceedings pending, eg, for a property adjustment order,
s35(6)(e)-(g) FLA96   Children Act transfer or to establish a legal/beneficial interest.

Regulatory orders

s35(6)(a)-(e) FLA96   Where the court has to decide whether to include a provision restricting or excluding the other partner, the matter must be considered separately, and is based on the same criteria as for entitled applicants (all the circumstances including housing needs and resources, financial resources, the likely effect of an order on the health, safety or well-being of all parties concerned and the conduct of the parties) and the length of time since the parties lived together. When deciding whether to attach a regulatory provision to the order, the court must also consider whether there is any risk of significant harm to the applicant or children. If so, it must include a restriction or exclusion provision, unless the balance of harm suffered by the other party or any children is likely to
s35(8) FLA96   be as great or greater. Balance of harm is explained above (13.29).

The object of the two-tier criteria was explained in the Law Commission report:

> 'We consider this procedure is desirable to ensure that the qualifying criteria for the grant of occupation rights to non-entitled applicants do not obscure the merits of the applicant's case for the grant of a regulatory order in a situation of overwhelming need. There may, for example, be cases in which the applicant's case for

an occupation rights order is not particularly strong (perhaps because she has lived with the respondent only for a matter of weeks), but in which her need is so great that it would nevertheless be just for her application to be granted (perhaps because she is ill, has the respondent's baby to care for and nowhere else to go).'[55]

Duration and effect of orders

Under section 35, orders can be made for not longer than six months, but may be extended on one or more occasions for further specified periods of not more than six months.

s35(10) FLA96

An application for an occupation order may not be made after the death of either party and will end on the death of either.

s35(9) FLA96

Occupation order keeps tenancy 'alive'

The Law Commission's intention was to give non-entitled applicants a chance to apply for a Family Law Act or Children Act transfer of property (see 8.18 – 8.19 and Chapter 9) or to 'keep alive' a tenancy whilst a decision was being made on its transfer.[56] To make this possible, the Act also provides that whilst the occupation order is in force the person given the right to occupy has all the same rights as those given to a non-owning spouse in relation to the home, ie, the matrimonial home rights to pay rent/mortgage, occupy as if s/he is the spouse, and to intervene in possession proceedings (see 4.2 and 7.4).

s35(13) FLA96

13.33 Occupation orders for cohabitant and former cohabitants with no entitlement to occupy – section 36 orders

Non-entitled cohabitants and former cohabitants may apply for occupation orders under section 36 of the Family Law Act which states that the other (former) cohabitant is entitled to occupy because of ownership, a tenancy, beneficial interest or contractual or statutory right to remain in the home. The order grants rights to occupy or restrict/exclude the (former) cohabitant. The maximum length of an order is initially six months, renewable once only, ie, an overall maximum of twelve months. Orders may relate only to a dwelling which the applicant and the (former) cohabitant live together in or intended to live together in.

s36(1)(c) FLA96

Orders available

Unlike an owner, tenant or married partner (entitled applicants), non-owner and non-tenant (former) cohabitants (non-entitled applicants) do not have a legal right to occupy unless they are successful in obtaining an occupation order.

If an order is made, it must contain one of the following declaratory provisions:

s36(3) FLA96

---

55. Law Commission No 207, see 1 above, para 4.18.   56. Law Commission No 207, ibid, para 4.17.

- That the applicant has the right not be evicted or excluded from the house or any part of it for the duration of the order, and prohibiting the other (former) cohabitant from evicting or excluding the applicant, or

- If the applicant is not in occupation, the right to enter and remain in occupation for the duration of the order, and requiring the other (former) cohabitant to allow this.

s36(4) FLA96

In addition, the court may attach further regulatory provision to the orders, as for entitled applicants:

s36(4) FLA96

- Regulating the occupation of the dwelling by either or both the parties

- Prohibiting or suspending the exercise by the other (former) cohabitant spouse of her/his right to occupy the dwelling

- Excluding the (former) cohabitant from a defined area around the dwelling.

The court may also attach the same provisions as listed in 13.23 above (ie, occupation rent, liabilities etc).

The main difference between orders made under section 36 of the Act and those made under section 33 for entitled applicants, is in the criteria which the court must use (see below).

13.34 Criteria for occupation orders for non-entitled cohabitants and former cohabitants

Whilst the same basic criteria apply as for entitled applicants, there are additional criteria for (former) cohabitants. A distinction must be drawn between declaratory orders and regulatory orders.

Declaratory orders

When deciding whether to make a declaratory order granting the right to occupy and not be excluded without a court order, the court must, in addition to the section 33 criteria (ie, taking into account all the circumstances including housing needs and resources, financial resources, the likely effect of an order on the health, safety or well-being of all parties concerned and conduct of the parties) also consider the following:

s36(6)(a)-(d) FLA96

- The nature of the parties' relationship

- The length of time during which they lived together as husband and wife

- Whether there are any children of both parties or for whom both parties have parental responsibility

- The length of time since the parties ceased to live together

- Any other proceedings pending under the Children Act or to establish a legal/beneficial interest.

s36(6)(e)-(i) FLA96

When considering the nature of the parties' relationship, the court must have regard to the 'fact that they have not given each other the commitment involved in marriage.'

s41 FLA96

Regulatory orders

Where the court has to decide whether to attach a provision restricting or excluding the other partner, the matter must be considered separately and is based on the same criteria as for entitled applicants (taking into account all the circumstances, including housing needs and resources, financial resources, the likely effect of an order on the health, safety or well-being of all parties concerned and the conduct of the parties). When deciding whether to attach a regulatory provision, the court must also consider whether there is any risk of significant harm to the applicant or children and whether the balance of harm suffered by the other party or any children is likely to be as great or greater. It must take this into account when deciding whether to include the provision in the order, but is not bound to make an order. The balance of harm test is explained at 13.29.

s36(6)(a)-(d) FLA96
s36(7) & (8) FLA96

Duration and effect of orders

Under section 36 orders can be made for not longer than six months, but may be extended on one occasion only, for a further period of not more than six months.

s36(10) FLA96

An application for an occupation order may not be made after the death of either party, and will end on the death of either.

s36(9) FLA96

Occupation order keeps tenancy 'alive'

As for section 35 (orders for former spouses), the Act also provides that whilst the occupation order under section 36 is in force, the person given the right to occupy has all the same rights as those given to a non-owning spouse in relation to the home, ie, the matrimonial home rights to pay rent/mortgage, occupy as if s/he were the spouse and intervene in possession proceedings (see 4.2 and 7.4).

s36(13) FLA96

13.35 Occupation orders where neither spouse/former spouse is entitled to occupy – section 37 orders

Orders under section 37 can be applied for where neither spouse/former spouse has a legal right to occupy. Examples are squats, couples living at home with parents or relatives, or other situations where both partners are bare licensees. It applies where neither party:

- is an owner
- has a beneficial interest in the property
- is a tenant
- has a contractual or statutory right to remain.

If the (former) spouses are living in the home or have lived in the home as a married couple, one can apply for an occupation order under

s37(3)(a) FLA96 section 37 against the other spouse to:

- require the other (former) spouse to allow her/him to enter and remain in the home

- regulate the occupation of the home by either or both of the parties

- require the other (former) spouse to leave all or part of the dwelling

- exclude the other (former) spouse from a defined area.

The court's criteria for making occupation orders where neither applicant is entitled are the same as for entitled applicants (ie, all the circumstances including housing needs and resources, financial resources, the likely effect of an order on the health, safety or well-being of all the parties concerned, conduct of the parties and the balance of harm test (see 13.29). The court is bound to make an order where one party is likely to suffer greater harm that the other. Orders are for a maximum of six months, which may be extended on one or more occasions, for further specified periods of not more than six months. Obviously, the lessor/owner of the property

s38(4) FLA96
s37(5) FLA96 will still be able to evict both parties using the normal procedures.

13.36 Occupation orders where neither cohabitant or former cohabitant is entitled to occupy – section 38 orders

Orders under section 38 can be applied for where neither cohabitant nor former cohabitant has a legal right to occupy (as for section 37 orders above). The same orders can be applied for as under section 37 above.

The court's considerations for making occupation orders where neither (former) cohabitant is entitled are the same as for entitled applicants (ie, all the circumstances including housing needs and resources, financial resources, the likely effect of an order on the health, safety or well-being of all the parties concerned and the conduct of the parties) and the likelihood of significant harm and the balance of that harm (see 13.29). The court is not bound to make an order. Orders are for a maximum of six months, and may be extended once only for a further specified period of not more than six months. Obviously, the lessor/owner of the property will still be able to evict both parties using the

s38(4) FLA96
s37(5) FLA96 normal procedures.

NON-MOLESTATION AND OCCUPATION ORDERS – PROCEDURE FOR APPLYING

13.37 The scope of the court's jurisdiction under the Family Law Act

The courts now have discretion to help a much wider group of applicants with the two types of order which are created by the Family Law Act. The possible types of orders and to whom they are available is set out in the table in 13.39.

13.38 Courts which may be used

Proceedings may be heard in any court which has jurisdiction in Family Proceedings – there is no longer any distinction between county or magistrates' court in terms of the orders which may be made. Notice of two days must normally be given to the other person, but in certain circumstances, a 'without notice' order (previously an 'ex parte' order) may be granted, ie, without notice of the hearing being served on the person.

The applicant will have to submit evidence on affidavit (ie, a sworn statement of the facts) and the court will require a full hearing, usually within a week, although this can vary depending on court schedules. S/he will have to attend court for the hearing of the application, but oral evidence will not usually be required unless the application is contested.

13.39 Emergency orders – 'without notice'

The court may make a non-molestation or occupation order without notice of the proceedings having been given to the respondent if it considers it just and convenient to do so. These were previously known as ex parte orders, but are now simply called 'without notice orders.' It must also have regard to all the circumstances including:

• any risk of significant harm to the applicant or child if an order is not made immediately

• whether the applicant might be prevented or deterred from making an application if the order is not made immediately, eg, the partner may intimidate the would-be applicant so that s/he withdraws the application

• whether there is reason to believe the respondent is deliberately evading service of notice and the applicant could be seriously prejudiced by the delay. If a 'without notice' order is made, the respondent must be notified that the hearing took place and be given the opportunity to make representations at a full hearing which should be held as soon as is 'just and convenient' according to court rules. Without notice orders do not become effective until the respondent has been served with a copy.

s45(3) FLA96

Scope of jurisdiction under the Family Law Act

In this table, 'cohabiting' includes people who formally cohabited, even if they no longer do so.

Relationship and status under Family Law Act	Non-molestation orders	Occupation orders
Married owners/tenants (entitled)	Yes	Under s.33
Married non-owners/non-tenants (entitled)	Yes	Under s.33
Former spouse owners/tenants (entitled)	Yes	Under s.33
Heterosexual cohabiting owners/tenants (entitled)	Yes	Under s.33
Heterosexual former spouse non-owners/non-tenants (non-entitled)	Yes	Under s.35
Heterosexual cohabiting non-owners/non-tenants (non-entitled)	Yes	Under s.36
Heterosexual former spouses – neither is owner or tenant (non-entitled)	Yes	Under s.37
Heterosexual cohabitants – neither is owner or tenant (non-entitled)	Yes	Under s.38
Lesbian/gay cohabiting owner/tenants (entitled)	Yes	Under s.33
Lesbian/gay cohabiting non-owners/non-tenants (associated persons)	Yes	No
Lesbian/gay cohabiting – neither is owner or tenant (associated persons)	Yes	No
Lesbian/gay partners – never lived together	No	No
Heterosexual partners agreed to marry each other – never lived together but applicant has joint or sole tenancy/ownership or beneficial interest in property they intended to live in (associated entitled persons)	Yes	Under s.33
Heterosexual partners agreed to marry each other – never lived together and applicant is not joint or sole tenant and does not have beneficial interest in property they intended to live in (associated non-entitled person)	Yes	No
Heterosexual partners – never lived together and no children	No	No
Parents of child – never lived together (associated persons)	Yes	No
Relatives*/sharers – owners/tenants (entitled)	Yes	Under s.33
Relatives*/sharers – non-owners/tenants (associated persons)	Yes	No
Other related people – never lived together (associated persons)	Yes	No

indicates relatives who share or who have shared or intended to share a home together.

13.40 Enforcement of orders – power of arrest

s47(2) FLA96 Where a non-molestation or occupation order has been made and it appears to the court that violence has been used or threatened against the applicant or child, then the court must attach a power of arrest unless it is satisfied that the applicant or child will be adequately protected without it. If the order is without notice, attaching a power of arrest is at the court's discretion, dependent upon whether there is a s47(3) FLA96 risk of significant harm.

If power of arrest is granted, a police officer may arrest without warrant if an order is breached. The offender must be brought before the court within 24 hours.

If there is no power of arrest and an injunction is breached, an application for committal to prison for contempt may be made, by way of service of summons by court officials. If contempt of court is found it is punishable by fine or imprisonment. However, courts will not generally order committal on a first breach, unless it is very serious. Orders are more likely to be suspended conditionally.

The Family Law Act has extended the powers, previously available only in the magistrates' courts, which allow an applicant to apply for a warrant for arrest for breach of a non-molestation or occupation order. This may be useful where the respondent has 'gone to ground' and is avoiding service of papers, or where service of a summons could exacerbate violence. The application for a warrant for arrest must be sworn on oath, and a warrant must only be issued where there are reasonable grounds s47(9) FLA96 for believing that the respondent has not complied with the order.

13.41 Protection of children – application by social services

Non-molestation orders and occupation orders can be sought to protect a child under the Family Law Act, as explained in the sections above.

s52 & Sch 6 FLA96 The Family Law Act also amends sections 38, 39, 44 and 45 of the Children Act so that the courts have power to include an exclusion requirement in an application from a social services department for an interim care order or an emergency protection order, eg, an abuser can be ordered to leave the home, rather than the child having to be removed to a place a safety.

13.42 Which proceedings to choose – Protection from Harassment Act or Family Law Act?

It seems that in many cases someone experiencing domestic violence may choose either Act to proceed under (see 13.12 for an explanation of both criminal and civil actions under the Protection from Harassment Act 1997). Where such a choice is available, there are pros and cons to be weighed up.

Enforcement of civil injunctions is weaker under the Protection from Harassment Act than the Family Law Act in the following ways:

- Warrants for breach can be issued in the county but not magistrates' courts, in the area where either party lives or works (FLA can be in any court)

- Where a warrant for arrest is issued, the defendant must be brought before the court immediately (no 24 hour or weekend allowance)

- There is no power to remand defendant pending an adjourned hearing, as in FLA

- If the hearing is ineffective, the warrant abates – fresh proceedings are needed; under the FLA, the applicant can rely on the original application.

However, the PFHA is less form-bound, administratively simpler and probably less expensive than proceedings under the FLA. There have, however, been some reports by solicitors that it can be harder to obtain public funding from the Legal Services Commission when using the PFHA than when applying under the Family Law Act.

ADDITIONAL CIVIL REMEDIES PROTECTING CHILDREN AND PARENTS

Remedies are also available under the Children Act and under the court's inherent jurisdiction. However, the provisions of the Family Law Act will normally be used in preference. Nevertheless, if the parties are already involved in Children Act proceedings, as in cases where residence/contact is disputed, the Children Act would probably be used to save having to start another set of proceedings. Alternatively, the Children Act might be used where an injunction is needed and residence or contact also needs to be settled.

13.43 Injunctions available to prevent violence to children and parents under the Children Act 1989

Non-molestation orders

It is possible to obtain an injunction to prevent molestation to a child and also to a parent when applying for an order under the Children Act 1989.

Ouster orders

There has been some confusion over the inherent power of the court to grant injunctions. In *Wilde v Wilde*[57], the Court of Appeal held that the court had jurisdiction to intervene to protect the interest of children, and could therefore exclude someone, no matter what the proceedings, if it could be shown to be in the child's interests. It had been suggested that it might be possible to use orders under the Children Act in the same way, effectively to exclude a partner from the home.[58]

However, more recent cases appear to contradict this. In *Re F*[59], the court held that, in cases where no violence was involved, the court had no jurisdiction to oust a joint tenant in order to provide a home for the children and their mother. This followed the judgement in *Ainsbury v Millington*[60], where it was held that, whilst the child's welfare is paramount under the law relating to children, following *Richards v Richards*[61] the child's welfare is not paramount in an application for an exclusion order. The applicant therefore had to show a legal right on which she could rely: as a joint tenant she had an equal right to occupy, but not a right to exclude the other joint tenant, her partner.

Re F (Minors)[62]

A cohabiting couple were joint housing association tenants. After the relationship broke down, the mother left taking the children to live with her parents. The man remained in the home. The woman applied to live in the house in the absence of the father, arguing that the order could be granted by way of a specific issues order under section 8 of the Children Act (see 9.2), because of the importance of the welfare of the children.

The court observed that there was no violence and even though the children were in unsatisfactory accommodation, refused the ouster. It was held that neither the specific issues order provisions of the Children Act, nor the inherent jurisdiction of the court to grant injunctions enabled an order to be made ousting the father from the house of which he was a joint tenant. The woman's only remedy was to apply for a transfer of tenancy under the Children Act, for the benefit of the children.

The case law[63] appears to illustrate two main principles:

- That the courts do not accept that the Children Act principle of the paramountcy of the child's welfare applies in ouster cases. The test in *Richards v Richards* of considering all factors of the case is not

57. Wilde v Wilde (1988) 2 FLR 83.
58. See M. Parry, The Law relating to Cohabitation, third edition (Sweet and Maxwell, 1993) pp.176–9.
59. Re F (Minors) (Parental Home: Ouster) (1994) 1 FLR 246 CA.
60. Ainsbury v Millington (1986) 1 All ER 73.
61. Richards v Richards (1983) 12 HLR 68; (1984) 1 AC 174 HL.
62. Re F, see 60 above.
63. Gibson v Austin (1992) 2 FLR 437 CA; Ainsbury v Millington (1986) 1 All ER 73.

overruled by the Children Act. The main thrust of the *Richards* case was to curtail the possibility of relying on an inherent jurisdiction of the court when there was already an express provision to deal with a particular situation.

• That the court has inherent jurisdiction to grant an ouster of a non-owner or non-tenant where the tenancy or ownership is in a sole name, but not when it is in joint names.

This means that the Family Law Act should be used wherever it can be applied, rather than relying on the court's inherent jurisdiction.

13.44 Injunctions to protect a child's parent

Non-molestation orders

It has been suggested that the court has the power to grant an injunction forbidding molestation of a child, or the person who has care of the child, in any family proceedings[64] by any party to the proceedings. An application for such an order must be made by a party to the proceedings who has parental responsibility for, or actual care of, a child who is the subject of the proceedings. Orders would be made under the powers of the High Court under section 37(1) of the Supreme Courts Act 1981, available in a county court through s3 of the Courts and Legal Services Act 1990.[65]

In the case of *Webb v Webb*,[66] the Court of Appeal held that there is jurisdiction to grant a non-molestation injunction to protect a former spouse after decree absolute, again under the inherent jurisdiction of the High Court.

There is also jurisdiction to grant a non-molestation order against a former cohabitant to protect the applicant and/or child, in support of an application under section 8 of the Children Act 1989, ie, residence orders, contact orders, prohibited steps orders, specific issue orders, if it is necessary for the child's well being.

S v C[67]

The unmarried mother of a two-year-old child was assaulted by the child's paternal grandmother, who also threatened to remove the child. The mother successfully obtained a prohibited steps order under the Children Act to prevent the removal of the child, with an attached non-molestation order to protect herself. The proceedings took place in the county court, since injunctions are not available in the family proceedings court.

---

64. See s10 Children Act 1989 for a definition of 'family proceedings.'
65. Judge N. Fricker, Injunctive Orders Relating to Children (1993) Fam Law 141.
66. Webb v Webb (1986) 1 FLR 541.
67. S v C (1992) Legal Action, March 1992.

D   Actions in tort

If none of the above remedies is applicable, it may be possible to bring an action in tort, to which an application for an injunction can be attached. The High Court has a general jurisdiction to grant an injunction where it appears just and convenient to do so on whatever grounds or conditions the court sees fit, and the county court has a similar power by virtue of statute.

s37(1) SCA81
& s3 CLSA90

However, such an injunction is 'not a remedy in itself and can only be granted in support of a legal or equitable right.'[68] Therefore, it will always be necessary to apply for such an injunction along with other proceedings, usually in tort, or possibly contract, eg, where an occupier has a tenancy or licence and where the landlord or licensor is the abuser.

s37 SCA81
& s38 CCA84

13.45   What is a tort?

Broadly, a tort is the infringement of, or harm suffered by violation of, a legal right of the injured party, ie, the commission of a civil wrong. An action could be both a crime and civil wrong (tort).

• In criminal proceedings, a prosecutor prosecutes a defendant in the criminal courts. The outcome may be a custodial or non-custodial sentence and/or fine

• In civil proceedings, a plaintiff sues or brings an action against a defendant in the civil courts. The outcome may be damages and/or an injunction.

> **Example**
>
> *If Carl is hospitalised by violence from Phil, his partner with whom he is no longer living, the police may decide to prosecute Phil for the criminal offence of grievous bodily harm or wounding, as the case may be. However, if Carl wants to keep Phil out of the house, he will have to bring a separate civil action to obtain an injunction against him. To do this he has to show that a legal right of his has been infringed, for example, that Phil has trespassed on his property. Carl could also sue Phil for the tort of assault and claim damages. In legal terminology, Phil's act is 'tortious.'*

See 13.49 – 13.51 for explanations of the torts of trespass and private nuisance.

---

68. M. Parry, *The Law relating to Cohabitation*, third edition (Sweet and Maxwell, 1993) p.173.

13.46 Situations outside the scope of domestic violence remedies

The relevance of these remedies since October 1997 is now limited. Although they remain available in the situations outlined in this section, in most cases the alternative Family Law Act 1996 or Protection from Harassment Act 1997 remedies are more appropriate, easier to obtain and also stronger. The cases to which Family Law Act remedies do not apply are set out below.

People who cannot apply for either non-molestation orders or occupation orders under the Family Law Act

• *Heterosexual or lesbian/gay couples who have never lived together.* It is quite common for people who have had a relationship without living together to harass or molest each other. The Law Commission's original draft of the Act proposed to offer protection to people who had had a sexual relationship with each other (whether or not involving sexual intercourse), but this was removed by parliament because of the difficulties of establishing that the relationship had existed. If harassment can be shown, the Protection from Harassment Act is now most likely to be used. Nevertheless, the civil actions of trespass or nuisance to gain protection (see below) or criminal action for assault (see 13.8) remain available

• *Anyone else without the nexus established by being an 'associated person'* (see 13.20). This means, for example, that neighbours, friends, acquaintances or strangers would not be covered. They too could take action under the Protection from Harassment Act or for trespass or nuisance.

People who cannot apply for occupation orders under the Family Law Act

• *Lesbian or gay cohabitants who are merely their partner's licensees.* They cannot therefore gain a right to occupy if the partner wants them out (although see 5.4 onwards), nor can they exclude the owner/tenant partner. Since they are the ones who become trespassers, the law on trespass clearly cannot help them, nor can the PFHA give rights to occupy

• *Lesbian or gay partners where neither is an owner or tenant nor has any other statutory or contractual entitlement to remain.* If they were staying with friends or relatives or in a squat, neither would have any right to apply to exclude the other. In cases of violence, homelessness would be the likely result.

• *Relatives or sharers who are licensees.* These could include, for example, older relatives living with sons or daughters or children or stepchildren. If they are told to leave, neither the Family Law Act nor the Protection from Harassment Act can offer them any protection, nor can they exclude the owner/tenant, although a parent or social services may be able to apply to protect a child (see 13.41). It is possible that an action for trespass to the person might offer some personal protection if they are being threatened. They can, of course, also apply for non-molestation orders against any associated person

- *Relatives or parents of children who have never lived together.* This group cannot apply for occupation orders to keep someone away from the home. They may be able to take an action for trespass or nuisance to keep an unwanted visitor away (see below), or seek an injunction under the Protection from Harassment Act to keep the visitor at a distance. If the abused person is an owner or tenant, s/he may be able to bring an action for private nuisance. Parents may also apply for a long-term transfer of property from one parent to the other for the benefit of the child, under the provisions of the Children Act (see Chapter 9).

13.47 Injunctions against minors

It is not unusual for parents to suffer violence from sons or daughters within the family home. Under the Family Law Act, both non-molestation and occupation orders are available to relatives or other associated persons. An action in tort such as assault or battery may still also be sought.

13.48 Injunctions against third parties

If the third party is sharing a household with the would-be applicant, they will be associated persons and the Family Law Act orders may be available. Otherwise, the position will depend on the status of the third party and the person trying to exclude her/him.

- An owner or tenant could evict a third party who is an excluded licensee without legal proceedings (provided physical force is not used)

- Whether a joint owner or joint tenant could exclude the third party against the wishes of the other joint owner/tenant will depend on the individual case. Alternatively, an action for private nuisance might be possible.

13.49 Torts of trespass affecting a person

- *Assault*: an assault is any act which attempts or offers to apply unlawful force to another person. It applies when a person is put in immediate fear of a 'battery' (see below). It does not call for violence or physical contact itself. Threats of physical force accompanied by an act, ie, if a person does not leave the premises, have been held to be an assault. A threat to use force some time in the future does not constitute an assault, unless it is an active threat to use force if the person does not immediately perform some act. There must be some active conduct to constitute an assault, eg, brandishing a weapon – verbal threats alone will not suffice

• *Battery*: intentionally bringing any material object into contact with another's person is sufficient to constitute a battery. Throwing water over somone[69] or putting an arm out to prevent someone from leaving the room can give rise to an action for battery

• *False imprisonment*: this is inflicting unlawful bodily restraint without lawful justification. If a person refuses to allow her/his partner out of the house and physically blocks all exits, this would amount to unlawful imprisonment.

Defences

There are certain defences to actions for trespass to the person, the most relevant in relationship breakdown being:

• *self-defence*: this can include protection of another or of property, but in the latter case, no more than reasonable force must be used

• parental or similar authority.

Prosecution in a magistrates' court

Assault and battery is a crime as well as a civil wrong, although the definition of assault and battery as a crime is different from the definition given in tort. To sustain an action for trespass to the person, it is necessary to prove intention or negligence, though not necessarily damage.

13.50 Torts affecting property

Trespass to land

This involves interference with the possession of land. This can take many forms but must be direct. It includes:

• unauthorised entry onto land or into a house

• placing things on the land, such as dead animals or other unpleasant objects in an ex-partner's garden

• staying after permission to remain has been withdrawn – a licensee who has been told to leave but refuses to go becomes a trespasser

• abusing the purpose for which the person was originally allowed in.

---

69. Pursell v Horn (1938) 8 A&E 602.

Wrongful interference with goods

- *Trespass to goods*: to prove this it is necessary to show that there has been a direct interference with goods, such as throwing an object at belongings or moving things. Damage to belongings in an argument or fight would constitute trespass to goods

- *Conversion (detaining goods)*: if one partner refuses to return belongings or will not let the other party have them back, thus denying her/his right to them, this would constitute wrongful interference by conversion. So also would selling them, destroying them or throwing them away.

13.51 Tort of private nuisance

Private nuisance is 'an unlawful interference with a (person's) use of her/his property or with (that person's) health, comfort or convenience... It is a wrongful act causing material injury to property or sensible personal discomfort.'[70]

The tort of private nuisance was developed originally to protect private property or rights of property, in relation to the use or enjoyment of land. Until the Protection from Harassment Act, English law never recognised molestation or harassment as torts as such. Nevertheless harassment, eg, by unwanted telephone calls to a legal owner of property, could be held to constitute the tort of private nuisance and an injunction sought to restrain them.[71]

13.52 Types of injunctions which can be claimed

Orders restraining a person from harassing, assaulting or otherwise interfering with the applicant and children could be sought in tort actions (ie, non-molestation type orders). It is unlikely that an injunction ordering someone out of a property could be obtained unless it were attached to an action relating to land through trespass or nuisance. The applicant would need to have an existing proprietary right in the property, such as ownership, a tenancy or matrimonial right of occupation, in order to take such an action, and therefore this would not help a lesbian/ gay cohabiting licensee who wants an owner/tenant partner to leave.

13.53 Enforcement of injunctions

The court has no jurisdiction to grant a power of arrest with these injunctions, and they are therefore weaker than the specific domestic violence remedies. Enforcement of the injunctions would be by proceedings for committal resulting in a fine or imprisonment, which may, of course, be suspended (see 13.40).

---

70. K. Smith and D. Keenan, English Law (Pitman, 1983) p. 356.

71. Motherwell v Motherwell (1976) 73 DLR (3rd) 62, Alberta Supreme Court.

13.54 Inherent jurisdiction of the court – protecting rights in land

Where there has not been any unlawful act, ie, an act which constitutes a civil wrong, but there is an issue regarding protecting rights in land, the High Court has what is known as an inherent jurisdiction (given to the county court by statute) to protect those rights by granting injunctions. Where property is owned or rented jointly, the courts will not normally be able to intervene, but a sole tenant or sole owner may be able to make use of these powers. There would need to be a cause of action, such as to protect or declare rights in land.

s37(1) SCA81 & s3 CLSA90

E   Social landlords' powers

In some cases, none of the above measures may be appropriate: the police may have declined to act, the person may be too afraid to pursue an action or not be able to afford court proceedings. Since the Housing Act 1996 came into force, local authorities and registered social landlords have powers to intervene which may help someone at risk of further violence.

13.55 Social landlords' powers to gain possession in cases of domestic violence

The Housing Act 1996 gave powers to social landlords, ie, local authorities and registered social landlords, to seek possession against perpetrators of domestic violence. Social landlords may choose to follow this procedure as a management tool, where, for example, they have rehoused the person fleeing violence and her/his children, and the perpetrator remains alone, perhaps in a 3-bedroomed house. Taking such action is a policy decision, and authorities need to carefully consider the implications of such actions. Research by the government published in December 2002[72] showed that only 5% of local authorities had used this provision, although almost half highlight the risk of eviction to those who are perpetrators of domestic violence in the information they provide to tenants (see 16.24 for a further discussion on steps social landlords might take).

Possession proceedings for secure and assured tenancies

Secure tenancies – Domestic violence ground

The Housing Act 1985 and the Housing Act 1988 lay down grounds which a landlord must prove in order to be granted possession.[73] The Housing Act 1996 added a domestic violence possession ground to these grounds.[74] The ground applies where the dwelling is occupied by a married couple or a couple living together as husband and wife, whether or not there are other people living there as well.

---

72. Chapter 4, para 4.3 'The provision of accommodation and support for households experiencing domestic violence in England (Housing Report 2002)' see 21 above.

73. Schedule 2 of the Housing Act 1985 for secure tenancies and Schedule 2 of the Housing Act 1988 for assured tenancies.

74. Ground 2A is added to schedule 2 of the Housing Act 1985 by section 145 of the Housing Act 1996.

Conditions for seeking possession

The conditions for seeking possession are that:

- one or both of the partners is a tenant, ie, it is a sole or joint tenancy

- one partner has left because of violence or threats of violence by the other towards her/himself or another member of her/his family who was also living with her/him immediately before s/he left, and

- the court is satisfied that the partner who has left is unlikely to return

- if the 'domestic violence' ground is being used, and the partner who has left is not a tenant, ie, the tenancy is in the perpetrator's sole name, the landlord must serve a copy of the notice on the partner who has left, or take all reasonable steps to do so. If this has not been done, the court will not entertain proceedings.

s83A(3) & (4) HA85

The court has discretion to decide whether it is reasonable to grant possession, and clearly will need to be convinced on the balance of probabilities that the violence has not only occurred but also that it was the real and overriding cause of the departure of the partner (see *Camden v Mallett* in box).

Camden LBC v Mallett[75]

Where possession was sought from a tenant using the 'domestic violence' possession ground, it was not sufficient that her/his alleged violence or threats of violence was merely one of a range of causes of equal significance in the departure from the property of the partner. For the ground to be made out it had to be established that the alleged violence or threat of violence was the dominant, principle and real cause of the departure.

Assured tenancies – Domestic violence ground

A domestic violence ground was added to the Housing Act 1988[76] which is the same as for secure tenants (see above), but it can only be used by registered social landlords or charitable housing trusts, ie, it is not available to private landlords letting on assured tenancies.

13.56 Local authority powers to obtain injunctions

s152 HA96 The Housing Act 1996 also gives power to the High Court or county court to grant injunctions in response to an application by a local authority (but not registered social landlords) to prohibit certain types of behaviour by any person, not just local authority tenants, towards people living in:

---

75. Camden LBC v Mallet, (2000) LTL 17/3/2000 Extempore CA, unreported elsewhere.

76. Ground 14A is added to Schedule 2 by section 149 of the Housing Act 1996.

- secure or introductory local authority tenancies
- accommodation provided by the authority for homeless people.

Injunctions can forbid the person to:

- cause or threaten to cause a nuisance or annoyance or behave in such a way as is likely to cause a nuisance or annoyance
- use or threaten to use the premises for immoral or illegal purposes
- enter a tenant's home or be in its locality.

However, injunctions will only be granted where the court is satisfied that:

- the person against whom the injunction is sought has used or threatened violence against the tenant or a member of the tenant's household, or a tenant's visitor

and

- that there is a significant risk of harm to that person if the injunction is not granted.

The court may also attach a power of arrest to any injunction it makes under this section.

This power can be used in cases where tenants, or their families, are being violently harassed or threatened by persons not even living on the same estate, but who may be coming into the area to cause trouble. Although it is most commonly used in cases of anti-social behaviour, some authorities have used it as part of an overall strategy of community safety to combat domestic violence.

Power to apply for power of arrest for breach of injunctions against anti-social behaviour

Registered social landlords, or charitable housing trusts (but not private landlords), as well as local authorities, can apply for power of arrest to be attached to an injunction being granted in relation to a breach or s153 HA96 anticipated breach of certain terms of the tenancy.

The injunction must be against the tenant or a joint tenant of an assured or secure tenancy or accommodation which is provided under homelessness duties. The breach or anticipated breach of tenancy conditions must relate either to the tenant:

- behaving in such a way as to cause or be likely to cause nuisance or annoyance (or threats of behaviour likely to cause a nuisance) to a person residing, visiting or otherwise engaged in a lawful activity in the locality

- using the premises for illegal or immoral purposes, or
- allowing someone else living in or visiting the premises to behave in either of the above ways.

The court must also be satisfied that violence or threats of violence have been used against a person residing, visiting or otherwise engaging in a lawful activity in the locality, and that there is a significant risk of harm if the power of arrest is not attached.

This power can only be used against tenants or joint tenants and not against other persons.

Chapter 14: The legal framework of homelessness and allocations

Subjects covered in this chapter include...

The law on homelessness

What the difference is between applying as homeless and being considered under the allocation scheme

Local authority procedure and duties

How housing authorities must investigate a homeless person's situation

What housing authorities must establish under the law

What duties housing authorities have towards homeless people

What procedures housing authorities should follow

Enforcing homelessness duties

How to challenge a housing authority's decision

Allocations

What procedures the housing authority must follow in allocating its permanent housing stock

Social Services' duties

What duties social services have under community care legislation towards people over 18 with special needs

The legal framework of homelessness and allocations

When a relationship breaks down, many partners want to remain in the family home to avoid disruption not only for themselves, but predominantly for their children. Advisers therefore need to have a good working knowledge of the rights outlined in earlier chapters. However, a significant number of those who seek advice upon relationship breakdown, particularly where domestic violence has taken place, may either be unable to remain in the home for safety reasons, or find it hard to remain because of the associations which the home holds for them. In other cases, the home may have been sold and there may not be sufficient money to rehouse either or both partners. Whatever the reason, many people have to turn to the local authority for help.

*Where immediate help is needed, the homelessness legislation may offer assistance in the form of temporary or long-term accommodation, or advice and assistance in finding accommodation. Almost a quarter of all homelessness applications are as a result of relationship breakdown and seven out of ten of those involve domestic violence.[1] If a person is not eligible for help under the homelessness legislation, advisers should be aware of social services' powers and duties under the Children Act 1989 towards those with children in need (see Chapter 9, Section C). In the case of asylum seekers and destitute people **with a special need** and no other means, assistance may also be available under Community Care legislation, in particular the National Assistance Act 1948, as well as from the National Asylum Support Service (NASS) (see 14.10 and Section E).*

Changes in homelessness legislation in 2002

The Homelessness Act 2002 and accompanying Statutory Instrument on Priority Need[2] amended the Housing Act 1996, with most provisions coming into force from 31 July 2002. It brought welcome changes to the homelessness legislation by:

- requiring local authorities to take a more strategic approach to review existing provisions and develop policies to prevent homelessness

- strengthening the 'safety net' by ensuring that accommodation must normally be provided until a settled housing solution is found (instead of for a minimum of two years, as previously)

- extending the definition of those who are homeless beyond those experiencing domestic violence to people who are experiencing violence or threats of violence from any person

1.   www.odpm.gov.uk/policybriefing/pdf/statistics.pdf.

2.   The Homelessness (Priority Need for Accommodation/England) Order 2002 SI No. 2051.

- extending the definition of those who are in priority need. This
includes, in particular, someone who is vulnerable as a result of
having to leave her/his home because of violence

- allowing authorities greater discretion to provide accommodation,
even for those who are not in priority need

- allowing greater flexibility to local authorities in their allocation
schemes, to offer greater choice to applicants.

Despite these changes brought in by the Homelessness Act 2002, local
authorities may still only allocate permanent housing stock, or nominate to a
Registered Social Landlord (RSL) for an assured tenancy, through their
allocation schemes (Part 6 of the Housing Act 1996). Homelessness is still
therefore the main route for immediate assistance, although housing
authorities must give 'reasonable preference' to people who are homeless
s167(2)(a)   when deciding on priorities for allocating their permanent housing stock.
& (b) HA96

Relationship breakdown in itself, where violence is not involved, does not
automatically qualify a person as being statutorily homeless, even where
the situation in the family home is strained. In many cases, those whose
relationships have broken down will find themselves being considered solely
under the council's allocation scheme, which, although it may in some cases
lead to a permanent solution in the long term, is unlikely to meet immediate
needs. Clients may therefore need help in finding alternative temporary
accommodation in the private sector, or support in making a case for
more immediate assistance from the housing authority through the
homelessness route.

This chapter looks at the basic framework of the homelessness and allocations
legislation and the local authority duties which accompany it. The next
chapter looks at common problems which arise from interpretation of the
homelessness legislation.

14.1   Homelessness legislation

Homelessness legislation as we know it today first came into being in
the Housing (Homeless Persons) Act 1977. This was the first legislation
to lay absolute duties on local housing authorities to provide
accommodation for certain homeless people in certain circumstances.

The Housing (Homeless Persons) Act 1977 was consolidated and
amended in Part 3 of the Housing Act 1985, but was subsequently
superseded by Part 7 of the Housing Act 1996, which in its turn was
significantly amended by the Homelessness Act 2002. References to

'the Act' in the rest of this chapter refer to the 1996 Act as amended by the Homelessness Act 2002, unless stated otherwise.

For those people whose applications were being considered on July 31 2002, the amended legislation applies.

14.2 The allocations legislation

Under the original Housing Act 1996, local authorities were required to operate a housing register and give reasonable preference in allocating properties to certain groups of people. The Homelessness Act 2002 amended the legislation to abolish the absolute requirement to maintain a housing register, in order to allow local authorities to operate 'choice-based lettings schemes.' Although greater discretion is now allowed to local authorities, the categories of people who are owed 'reasonable preference' are maintained, but amended. See section D for further information on allocation schemes.

14.3 The difference between homelessness applications and the allocation scheme.

There is a crucial difference between being dealt with under the homelessness legislation and being considered under the council's housing allocation scheme.

Homelessness legislation: Under the homelessness legislation, local housing authorities are under a variety of statutory duties, ie, there are things which they must do immediately for the homeless person once there is reason to believe that s/he may be homeless, eligible for assistance and in priority need within the definition of the Act (see 14.16). These duties continue until such time as a permanent housing solution is found or one of a number of other situations arises (see 14.18). The Act also prevents local authorities from giving secure council tenancies to homeless people unless they are eligible under the allocation scheme.

Housing allocation schemes: Since January 31 2003, authorities may make an allocation of a secure or introductory tenancy, or a nomination to an assured tenancy, to anyone who is eligible for allocation. The only people who are statutorily excluded from eligibility are certain categories of people from abroad and those whom the authority have decided to treat as ineligible because of 'unacceptable behaviour' (see 14.37).

Even if people are eligible for allocation, this is no guarantee of rehousing in the immediate future or even in the long-term. Local authorities still have wide discretion about how they frame their allocations schemes, and although they are required to give preference to homeless people, that preference can be overridden if the applicant's, or a member of the applicant's family's, behaviour is deemed, once again, to be 'unacceptable.' As the allocation scheme is the sole access route to most permanent social housing, the importance of becoming familiar with the allocation provisions and the local authority's policy cannot be stressed too much.

It is important to check from the outset that cases where immediate assistance is required are being dealt with under the homelessness provisions, and that, in addition, applicants are being considered under the allocation scheme in order to be considered for permanent accommodation. In the past it was quite common for people who needed immediate assistance to be deterred from making further enquiries, because they were given the impression that they could only be considered for a transfer or allocation, and it could be several years before they would be rehoused. This was particularly the case for people whose relationships had broken down, but who had not actually had to leave their current accommodation. Advisers must be clear about both short- and long-term rights to assistance in order to give the best advice.

14.4 Impact of immigration status on rights to assistance and rehousing

The Housing Act 1996 restricts the rights to assistance from the local authority of those who are deemed to be 'people from abroad.' In many cases, people from this group are not eligible for assistance under the homelessness legislation, and cannot be considered under the allocation scheme. For more details on who can and who cannot be given assistance, see 14.7 – 14.10.

A   The law on homelessness

14.5 What must a local authority establish?

When dealing with an application for help with accommodation, where there is reason to believe that the applicant may be homeless or threatened with homelessness, the local authority is under a legal duty to make enquiries. Those enquiries must establish:

• whether the applicant is homeless or threatened with homelessness
• whether the applicant is eligible for assistance
• whether the applicant is in priority need
• whether the applicant is intentionally homeless
• whether the applicant has a local connection
  (This last enquiry is discretionary for the local authority).

14.6   Definition of homelessness

s175(1) HA96   A person is homeless if s/he has no accommodation available in the United Kingdom or elsewhere which s/he has a lawful right to occupy.

A person is treated as having no accommodation available where the following apply:

s176 HA96   • S/he has no accommodation which the whole family can occupy (see Chapter 15 Section A, 15.3)

s175(1)(a) HA96   • S/he has no right to occupy by virtue of a legal interest or court order (eg, owner, contractual tenant, occupation order)

s175(1)(b) HA96   • S/he has no express or implied licence to occupy (eg, living with family, short-life occupant, etc.)

s175(1)(c) HA96   • S/he has no statutory or legal right to remain (eg, statutory tenant, or matrimonial home rights, or protection under the Protection from Eviction Act 1977)

Reasonable to continue to occupy

s175(3) HA96   A person should not be treated as having accommodation unless it is accommodation which it would be reasonable for him/her to continue to occupy. It may be possible to argue that this is affected by physical conditions, unsuitability, lack of affordability, non-violent harassment from non-associated persons or relationship breakdown.

Violence

The Act also specifically states that it is not reasonable to continue to occupy accommodation if it is probable that continued occupation will lead to violence or threats of violence that are likely to be carried out
s177(1) HA96   from an 'associated person,' or from any other person. This can therefore include violence from, for example, people connected with a spouse or partner, or from neighbours, acquaintances or even strangers. Violence from both within and outside the home falls within the definition of homelessness. The definition of an associated person is almost the same as that used in the Family Law Act 1996 (see 13.20), except that it does not exclude employer/ees, tenants, lodgers and boarders, and does not specifically include parties to the same family
s178 HA96   proceedings (unless they fall into another category).

Local authorities may have regard to the general circumstances prevailing in the local area in relation to housing when deciding whether it would be reasonable for a person to continue to occupy the accommodation, but not where there has already clearly been violence
s177(2) HA96   or threats of violence[3] (see 15.5 – 15.6).

3.   Bond v Leicester CC (2001)EWCA Civ 1544: HLR 6 CA.

A person is also homeless if s/he has accommodation but:

- cannot secure entry to it (eg, illegal eviction)

- it is a moveable structure and there is no place where s/he is entitled or permitted to put it and live in it

A person is threatened with homelessness if it is likely that s/he will become homeless within 28 days.

s175(4) HA96

14.7   Eligibility for assistance

In order to qualify for help under the homelessness legislation, an applicant must be eligible for assistance. This is defined in the Act and in regulations which have been issued.[4] The tests for eligibility are based upon immigration status and whether an applicant is entitled to claim social security benefits. Eligibility is a complex area and readers are referred to other publications for a more in-depth explanation (see Chapter 15, Section B for a further discussion and case law).[5] A broad outline is given below.

The Housing Act 1996[6] defines the groups of people who are not eligible for assistance under the homelessness legislation. These are:

- 'persons subject to immigration control', unless they fall within a class of persons prescribed by regulations by the Secretary of State as being eligible for assistance[7]

- anyone who is excluded from entitlement to housing benefit under the Immigration and Asylum Act 1999[8]

- other 'persons from abroad' where the Secretary of State has made regulations that they are not eligible for assistance.[9]

To simplify, there are broadly three groups of people to be considered when assessing for eligibility for homelessness assistance:

- Those subject to immigration control who are in the permitted groups, some of whom also have to pass the habitual residence test

- Those not subject to immigration control, eg, British citizens; but some of these nevertheless may have to pass the habitual residence test, unless they are exempt

- Asylum-seekers, the majority of whom are now the responsibility of the National Asylum Support Service.

In deciding whether an applicant is homeless or in priority need, a non-eligible person must be disregarded, eg. a non-eligible child cannot confer priority need on its parents (see 15.15).

4. The Homelessness (England) Regulations (2000) SI 2000 (No. 701).
5. Shelter Factsheet C3.1 'Eligibility for Assistance'; Chapter 4, Homelessness and Allocations, Arden and Hunter, 6th Edition, Legal Action Group 2002; JCWI Immigration, Nationality and Refugee Law Handbook

2002 (Joint Council for the Welfare of Immigrants).
6. s185 Housing Act 1996.
7. s185(2) HA 1996.
8. s115 Immigration and Asylum Act 1999, s.185(2A) HA 1996.
9. reg 3 The Homelessness (England) Regulations 2000 (SI 2000 No. 701).

14.8 People subject to immigration control

A 'person subject to immigration control' means a person who, under the Immigration Act 1971, requires permission to enter or remain in the UK, whether that permission has been given or not. The Homelessness Code of Guidance states that, for homelessness purposes, unless a person is a national of a country within the European Economic Area (EEA), s/he will be a person subject to immigration control.

para 5.6 HCOG02

People subject to immigration control who are eligible for assistance (other than asylum-seekers)

The following groups of people who are subject to immigration control are eligible for assistance:

- A person granted refugee status in the UK is eligible for assistance. Refugee status is granted as a result of having a request for asylum accepted

- A person granted exceptional leave to remain in the UK without conditions requiring her/him to maintain and accommodate her/himself and any dependants without recourse to public funds is eligible for assistance.

Exceptional leave to remain can be granted at the discretion of the Home Office, and may, for example, be granted to people who have had to leave a relationship because of domestic violence (see 13.5).

- A person with indefinite leave to remain (permanent stay, or settled status), who is habitually resident in the Common Travel Area (ie, the UK, Republic of Ireland, Channel Islands and the Isle of Man), other than a person who has been given leave on the basis of a sponsorship undertaking, and who has been resident for less than five years (unless the sponsor has died), is eligible for assistance

- A person who left Montserrat after 1st November 1995 because of the effect of the volcanic eruption is eligible for assistance

- A person who is habitually resident in the Common Travel Area *and who is* lawfully present in the country (asylum seekers are not deemed to be lawfully present in the country, since they are normally given temporary admission only and do not have permission to enter or remain) and who is:

para 5.8 HCOG02

    – a national of a state which has ratified the European Convention on Social and Medical Assistance, or the European Social Charter, and who is lawfully present in the United Kingdom. This category includes all the member states in the European Union (except Austria and Finland), and also includes nationals of Cyprus, the Czech Republic, Hungary, Iceland, Latvia, Liechtenstein, Malta, Norway, Poland, Slovakia, and Turkey)

Annex 17 HCOG02

or

– a person who was owed a homelessness duty under the 1985 or 1996 Act before 3rd April 2000, and is a national of a state which is *a signatory* of the above (ECSMA or ESC). These are Croatia, Estonia, Macedonia, Romania, Slovenia, Switzerland and Ukraine, is eligible for assistance.

Most of these states are within the European Economic Area, and their nationals are not treated as people subject to immigration control; therefore, they will be eligible, unless they fail the habitual residence test or are required to leave the UK by the Home Secretary. Non-EEA states which are signatories are Turkey, Malta, Poland, Slovakia, Cyprus, the Czech Republic and Hungary

- A person who is on an income-based Jobseeker's Allowance or in receipt of Income Support is eligible for assistance, unless:

– s/he has limited permission to enter or remain in the UK, and

– s/he is temporarily without funds because payments from abroad have been disrupted.[10]

14.9 People not subject to immigration control

Persons from abroad and returning British citizens

Most other people from abroad (ie, those who are not subject to immigration control which includes most EEA nationals, which in turn includes British citizens) will not be eligible for homelessness assistance unless they are habitually resident in the Common Travel Area (ie, the UK, Republic of Ireland, Channel Islands and the Isle of Man). Certain exceptions to this rule are listed below.

People who are exempt from the habitual residence test

The following groups of people who are not subject to immigration control are exempt from the habitual residence test:

- A worker for the purposes of EEC law[11]

- A person with a right to reside in the UK in accordance with EEC law[12]

- Someone who left Monserrat after 1st November 1995 because of the effect of the volcanic eruption

- Someone who is on an income-based Jobseeker's Allowance or in receipt of Income Support.[13]

People who must pass the habitual residence test

The test of habitual residence, which is also a condition of entitlement to Income Support/Jobseeker's Allowance, Housing Benefit and certain other benefits, applies to all applicants, including British citizens and

---

10. Reg 3(1)(i) Class I, The Homelessness (England) Regulations 2000 (SI 2000 No.701).
11. Council Regulation (EEC) No.1612/68 or (EEC) No.1251/70.
12. Council Directive No.68/360/EEC or No. 73/148/EEC.
13. Reg 4 The Homelessness (England) Regulations 2000 (SI 2000 No.701).

nationals of the EU, unless they fall within an exempted group as above. The authority must be satisfied that the applicant is not habitually resident: the burden of proof is not on the applicant.

Annex 22 and para 5.13 HCOG02

The Homelessness Code of Guidance states that, for this class of applicants, it is normally only necessary to investigate habitual residence if the applicant has entered the UK in the last two years. This follows Housing Benefit and Council Tax Guidance.[14]

Annex 22 p.134 HCOG02

The Code of Guidance also states that if an applicant who was previously habitually resident in the UK has returned to the UK to resume her/his former period of habitual residence, s/he is immediately habitually resident. The Code gives a list of questions which authorities should consider when deciding whether the applicant is actually resuming the former period of residence, including when and why the applicant left the UK, how long they intended to be abroad, why they have returned and what links they have kept with the UK.

Habitual residence test

Annex 22 HCOG02

'Habitual residence' is not defined in any legislation. The words must be given their ordinary and natural meaning. Whether a person is habitually resident must be decided according to all the circumstances in each case. The Homelessness Code of Guidance says that it is important to consider the applicant's stated reasons and intentions for coming to the UK, and if s/he states s/he intends to live in the UK and not return to the country s/he came from, the intention must be consistent with her/his actions.

In UK law, the concept of habitual residence has sometimes been given the same meaning as 'ordinary residence' which features in other legislation. In one case, the House of Lords found that 'habitually' required that the residence should be adopted voluntarily and for a settled purpose. A settled purpose could be for a limited period; there is no need for the person to wish to stay indefinitely. The reasons for the person's presence in the UK could include education, employment, family matters, health or merely 'love of the place.'[15]

14.10 Eligibility for assistance and asylum seekers

Whether an asylum seeker is eligible for assistance depends upon her/his current status and when s/he applied for asylum. Since April 2000, asylum-seekers are no longer normally the responsibility of housing authorities, but are meant to be dealt with by the National Asylum Support Service (NASS), which has power to disperse asylum-seekers anywhere in the country, leaving them virtually no choice as to where they go. Although the long-term aim is for NASS to deal with all

---

14. HB/CTB circular A22/2000. 15. Shah v Barnet LBC (1983) 2 AC 309; (1983) 1 All ER 226.

asylum-seekers, some asylum-seekers are still being assisted by local authorities' social services departments under 'interim' responsibilities, which are set to continue until at least April 2004, because of the difficulty experienced by NASS in obtaining sufficient accommodation.

The Nationality, Immigration and Asylum Act 2002, which received Royal Assent on 8th November 2002, amended the scheme for provision of support and accommodation with the aim of setting up special accommodation centres. The first centres are to be established on a trial basis, and to start with will run alongside the NASS and local authority asylum support schemes. Although originally scheduled to open some time in 2003, at the time of writing the date was expected to be later, due to difficulties encountered in establishing centres.

Late claims: refusal of support

s55 NIAA 02   The Nationality, Immigration and Asylum Act 2002 also allows the National Asylum Support Service (NASS) to refuse support to an asylum seeker if it is not satisfied that the asylum claim was made as soon as reasonably practicable after the person's arrival in the United Kingdom.

The section does not apply to families with children, those with special needs, those claiming asylum in the country following a significant change in circumstances in their country of origin (provided they make their asylum claim at the earliest possible opportunity following that change of circumstances) and those who can show they would otherwise suffer treatment contrary to Article 3 of the European Convention on Human Rights. Anyone else may be left destitute. This section came into effect on 8 January 2003. Initially, many asylum seekers were refused support, and injunctions were successfully obtained ordering provision of accommodation on an emergency basis. The Court of Appeal held that a proper investigation of each case is necessary to avoid breaching an applicant's human rights, and that accommodation must be provided whilst those investigations are being carried out. However, the court did not rule that the provision was unlawful in itself and therefore it would seem that an asylum seeker could still be left destitute, if s/he does not have any special needs. At the time of writing, it was unclear what impact this decision would ultimately have upon this section of the Act.

Asylum seekers who are eligible for assistance

The following are the only asylum-seekers who can be eligible for homelessness assistance:

- A person who is an asylum-seeker who made a claim for asylum before 3rd April 2000:
  - Which is recorded as made on arrival (other than re-entry) in the UK from outside the Common Travel Area, and

- Which is not recorded as decided (other than on appeal) or abandoned

- A person who is an asylum-seeker who made a claim for asylum before 3rd April 2000 and:

  - Was in Great Britain when it was declared that her/his country was subject to such a fundamental change in circumstances that the Secretary of State would not normally order the return of the person (upheaval country)

  - Asylum claim was made within 3 months of the declaration, and

  - The claim has not been decided (other than on appeal) or abandoned

- A person who is an asylum-seeker who:

  - Claimed asylum before 4th February 1996, and

  - Was entitled on 4th February 1996 to Housing Benefit as a person from abroad

  and

  - The claim has not been decided or abandoned or it has been decided and an appeal was pending on 5th February 1996 or was made within specified time limits.

Broadly, only those asylum-seekers who claimed asylum immediately upon arrival in the country before April 2000, whose claims have not been abandoned or decided, or which are being appealed, remain the responsibility of the housing authority, and the housing authority is also entitled to disperse those asylum-seekers to other authorities within agreed areas, and need have no regard to local connection.

No accommodation however temporary

s186 HA96

s186(1) HA96

s175(3) HA96

The situation is further complicated by provisions in the Housing Act 1996, which put further restrictions on eligibility of asylum-seekers. Any asylum-seeker who could be eligible for assistance under section 185 will not be eligible for assistance if s/he has any accommodation available to her/him in the UK, no matter how temporary. The accommodation must be reasonable to continue to occupy.

Summary of position of asylum-seekers

The position of asylum-seekers can be summarised as follows:

- Anyone who has been accepted as a refugee will be eligible

- Anyone who has applied for asylum on entering the country before 3rd April 2000 (port of entry applicants) will be eligible if they have no other accommodation available in the UK, no matter how temporary, but they may be sent to another area regardless of local connection

- Anyone who has applied for assistance after entering the country on or after 4 February 1996 (in-country applicants) will not normally be eligible for assistance, and will be the responsibility of NASS. However, if s/he did not apply as soon as reasonably practicable, NASS may refuse to provide any support whatsoever
- Asylum-seekers after 3rd April 2000 may still obtain help from the local authority's' social services department if they have special needs (see 14.43 and 15.15 below).

14.11   Definition of priority need

The definition differs depending upon whether the application is made under English or Welsh law.

PRIORITY NEED IN ENGLAND

The Act (extended by Statutory Instrument from 31st July 2002[16]) defines five categories of people who *must* be accepted as in priority need. They are:

Any person who is:

- A pregnant woman, or a person with whom a pregnant woman resides or might reasonably be expected to reside
- A person with whom dependent children reside or might reasonably be expected to reside
- All 16 and 17-year-olds, except 'relevant children,' who are owed an accommodation duty by social services under the Children (Leaving Care) Act 2000 (see 9.11) or as 'children in need' under section 20 of the Children Act 1989[17]
- 18 – 20-year-olds (other than 'relevant students'), who at any time whilst 16 or 17 were, but are no longer, looked after, accommodated or fostered[18]
- Any person who has lost her/his accommodation as a result of an emergency such as flood, fire or other disaster.

The Act also defines the following groups who will be accepted as in priority need, provided that the authority is satisfied that they are vulnerable:

Any person who is vulnerable as a result of:

- Old age, mental illness or handicap, physical disability or other special reason, or someone who lives with one of these categories of vulnerable person

---

16. The Homelessness (Priority Need for Accommodation) (England) Order 2002 SI No. 2051.

17. Para 3, ibid.
18. Para 4, ibid.

- Having been looked after, accommodated or fostered and is aged 21 or over (other than 'relevant students')

- Having been a member of her Majesty's regular naval, military or air forces

- Having served a custodial sentence, been committed for contempt of court or similar offence, or been remanded in custody

- Having had to leave accommodation because of violence or threats of violence from another person which are likely to be carried out.

The categories have been further clarified by case law (see Chapter 15, Section C) and by the Code of Guidance.

Ch8 HCOG02

Interim accommodation for those who may be in priority need

Where someone falls into one of the specified categories, it is suggested that this gives rise to a reason to believe that the person may be in priority need, and that therefore interim accommodation should be provided by the authority whilst it is making its inquiries. The Homelessness Code of Guidance supports this interpretation. Whatever the outcome, authorities have to give clear reasons in their written decisions as to why people who appear to fall into the categories are not being accepted as vulnerable.

s188 HA96
para 8.3 HCOG02

For a further discussion of vulnerability, see 15.21 – 15.23.

PRIORITY NEED IN WALES

The amendments made to the priority need categories in Wales are more generous.[19] In Wales, the following groups are automatically in priority need:

A person who is:

- A pregnant woman, or a person with whom a pregnant woman resides or might reasonably be expected to reside

- A person with whom dependent children reside or might reasonably be expected to reside

- Anyone who is 16 or 17

- Careleavers or people who are at particular risk of sexual or financial exploitation aged 18 – 20

- A person fleeing domestic violence (does not also have to satisfy the vulnerability test)

- Those homeless after leaving the armed forces (also does not have to satisfy the vulnerability test)

19. Homeless Persons (Priority Need) (Wales) Order 2001, SI 2001, No. 607 (w30).

- A former prisoner (defined as anyone detained in lawful custody as required by the court) who has been homeless since leaving custody, and who has a local connection with the area (does not also have to satisfy the vulnerability test)

- Any person who has lost her/his accommodation as a result of an emergency, such as flood, fire or other disaster.

In Wales, also:

- Any person who is vulnerable as a result ofOld age, mental illness or disability, physical disability or other special reason, or someone who lives with one of these categories of vulnerable person.

14.12 Definition of intentional homelessness

There are two ways in which someone can become homeless intentionally:

s191(1) HA96

s191(2) HA96

- A person becomes homeless intentionally if s/he deliberately does or fails to do anything, and as a result s/he ceases to occupy accommodation which was available for her/his occupation and which it would have been reasonable for her/him to continue to occupy. Where a person was acting in good faith but was unaware of a relevant fact and as a result lost the accommodation, this is not treated as deliberate

s191(3) HA96

- A person is also intentionally homeless if s/he enters into an arrangement under which s/he is required to leave accommodation which it would have been reasonable to continue to occupy, and the purpose of the arrangement is to enable her/him to become entitled to assistance under the homelessness legislation. If there is any other good reason why s/he is homeless, then this will not apply.

For further explanation and comment see Chapter 15, Section D.

14.13 Definition of local connection

A person has a local connection in a district if:

- s/he is or was in the past normally resident in that district and that residence is or was of her/his own choice

- s/he is employed in that district

- s/he has family associations there

or

s199(1) HA96

- there are special circumstances.

A person is not considered to be employed in a district if s/he is serving in the regular armed forces of the Crown, nor is residence considered of a person's own choice if s/he becomes resident as a result of serving in the armed forces or due to imprisonment.

s199(2) & (3) HA96

The Act itself says nothing about length of residence, family associations or other types of accommodation. The Local Government Association has, however, produced 'Guidelines for Local Authorities on Procedures for Referral (2001),[20] which sets out what would usually be sufficient to constitute a local connection.

Conditions for local connection referral

Once the local authority has established eligibility, homelessness, priority need, and that the applicant is not intentionally homeless, it can refer the applicant to another authority, provided that:

s198(2) HA96

- neither the applicant nor anyone who might reasonably be expected to live with her/him has a local connection with the area applied to, but

- they do have a local connection in the area to which they are to be referred, and

- there is no risk of domestic or any other violence to any of the household in that area.

A person may not therefore be referred to an area where s/he or anyone who might reasonably be expected to live with her/him has suffered violence of any kind from any person, and it is probable that returning to that area would lead to further violence of a similar kind. This extension of the definition to include violence other than domestic violence was added by the Homelessness Act 2002.

s198(2A) HA96

- 'Violence' is defined as: violence from another person, or

- Threats of violence from another person which are likely to be carried out

and

s198(3) HA96

- Violence is 'domestic violence' if it is from a person who is associated with the victim (see also 15.31).

Referral where applicant placed in area under homelessness duty

The local authority can also refer an applicant back to an authority which placed the applicant in its district in discharge of a previous homelessness duty, ie:

20. Guidelines for Local Authorities on Procedures for Referral [2001], Local Government Association available at http://www.lga.gov.uk.

s198(4) HA96

• Authority (A) may refer an applicant back to Authority (B) to which s/he previously applied, and which placed her/him in the current authority's area (A), when the previous application was within the last five years.

No safe connection anywhere

para 15.12
HCOG02

If an applicant has no local connection, or no safe local connection, anywhere, the authority to which s/he has applied must accept responsibility.

Date for establishing local connection

The date for deciding whether someone has a local connection with the area is the date on which the authority reaches its decision, and if there is a review, that means the date of the review decision. It is not the date of homelessness or date of application, and time spent in temporary accommodation in an area whilst a decision is being reached should count towards establishing a local connection.[21] National Asylum Support Service accommodation does not however establish a local connection (see 15 31).

B   Local authority procedures and duties

In the course of making inquiries about an applicant, the local authority is legally obliged to do certain things. These are the local authority's statutory duties, and, if a local authority does not comply with them, it may be possible to get a court order insisting they are carried out (see Section C below).

14.14 Duty to carry out homelessness reviews and strategies

ss1-4 HA 2002

para 1.13-1.14 &
1.17 HCOG02

The Homelessness Act 2002 imposed a duty on local authorities to carry out homelessness reviews and devise homelessness strategies. These should take into account factors such as the incidence of relationship breakdown and domestic violence in the area, and the resources available to people when such events occur. See 16.17 for further details on reviews and strategies.

14.15 General duty to give advice

s179 HA96

Local authorities have a general duty to give advice and information, free of charge, about homelessness and the prevention of homelessness, to any person in their district. This is irrespective of whether s/he is homeless, eligible for assistance or in priority need, etc.

14.16 Duties while establishing homelessness or priority need

Local authorities' duties arise at different stages of a homelessness inquiry. They are as follows:

---

21. Mohammed v LB Hammersmith and Fulham [2001] UKHL57: [2002] HLR7, HL.

Making inquiries

s183 HA96

If a person applies to a local housing authority for accommodation or help in obtaining accommodation, and the authority has reason to believe that the person may be homeless or threatened with homelessness, this will trigger the local authority's duty to make inquiries. It is not necessary to make a formal application as homeless. Local authorities will be under a duty to inquire as to whether:

• the applicant is eligible for assistance, and, if so

s184(1) HA96

• whether it is under any duty to assist, and what that duty will be.

Interim accommodation during inquiries

s188 HA96
s206 HA96

If the authority has reason to believe that an applicant may be eligible for assistance, homeless and may have a priority need, it must secure accommodation for that person whilst it makes further inquiries, irrespective of any issue of local connection. The accommodation must be 'suitable.'

Power to provide accommodation where no priority need

s192(3) HA96

The Homelessness Act 2002 gave local authorities a new power to provide accommodation to non-priority homeless people who are not intentionally homeless. This is particularly aimed at areas of low demand, and where local authorities have excess housing stock. Whilst many authorities had already made their stock available to non-priority homeless people in areas of low demand, the practice was variable and this amendment strengthens the 1996 Act, which previously only required local authorities to provide advice and assistance. Now the authority needs to consider in each case whether to exercise its discretion and the Act also implies that the issue of intentionality needs to be addressed, even when there is no priority need, in order for the local authority to decide whether to exercise this power.

Advice and assistance where no priority need

s192(2) HA96
inserted by
Schedule 1
paras 9-12 HA
2002

If it is established that the applicant is not in priority need, the authority must provide her/him with advice and assistance to help secure accommodation and prevent the loss of any existing accommodation. This applies regardless of whether the applicant is intentionally homeless or not. This is a stronger duty than the general advice and information duty (see 14.15), as local authorities are obliged to give assistance. The phrase 'appropriate in the circumstances' was removed in 2002, making it a categoric duty to provide advice and assistance.

In addition, the local authority is required to assess the applicant's needs before advice and assistance is provided. This means that advice must

be 'applicant-specific.' The advice and assistance must include
information about the likely availability in the district of types of
accommodation appropriate to the applicant's needs, including where
it is and how the applicant can access it.

s190(3) S192(4)
S195(5) HA96,

The Homelessness Code of Guidance states that the assessment of the
applicant's needs may need to range wider than the inquiries into
homelessness, and should identify any factors which may make it
difficult for the applicant to secure accommodation for him or herself,
for example, poverty, outstanding debt, health problems, disabilities
and whether English is a first language or not.

para 9.22
HCOG02

Notification

If a local authority completes its inquiries at this stage because it has
decided that the applicant is not homeless, not eligible, or is not in
priority need, the authority must notify the applicant of its decision in
writing and give reasons for it. It must also inform the applicant of
her/his right to review of the decision.

s184(3) HA96

14.17 Duties where homeless, not eligible, or intentionally homeless, and with children under 18

Co-operation in cases involving children

The Homelessness Act 2002 imposed a new duty on a local housing
authority where:

s213A HA96

• the applicant is someone with whom a person under age 18
normally resides, and

• it has reason to believe that the applicant –

 – may be ineligible for assistance

 – may be homeless and may be homeless intentionally or

 – may be threatened with homelessness intentionally.

Once there is reason to believe the above, the applicant should be:

• invited to consent to the referral of the essential facts of her/his
case to the local social services authority, and

• if the applicant gives consent, the social services authority should
be made aware of the facts, and of the subsequent decision of the
housing authority.

The same duty applies if the housing authority and the social services
authority are one and the same authority (a 'unitary authority').

s213A(3) HA96

Once the social services authority is aware of the facts, if they request the housing authority to provide them with advice and assistance in carrying out their functions under Part 3 of the Children Act 1989, the local authority is under a duty to provide such advice and assistance as is reasonable in the circumstances. This does not prejudice the pre-existing provisions on co-operation under s.27 of the Children Act 1989 (see 9.10).

Homeless, not eligible and no children under 18

s184 HA96

The only duties which arise if someone who has no children is found not to be eligible, eg, does not pass the habitual residence test, are to notify the applicant of the decision and her/his right to review, and the general duty to give advice under s.179. If the applicant is elderly or has some kind of special need, s/he may be able to obtain assistance from social services under s.21 of the National Assistance Act 1948 (see Section E, 14.42 onwards).

14.18 Duties where homeless eligible and in priority need

s188 HA96

If the applicant is found to be in priority need as well as homeless and eligible, the authority should then consider whether the applicant is intentionally homeless. Temporary accommodation should continue to be provided during these inquiries.

s184(2) HA96

If a person is homeless, eligible, in priority need and not intentionally homeless, the authority may, if it wishes, consider whether s/he has a local connection.

Notification of finding intentional homelessness

s184(3) HA96

Where a local authority completes its inquiries with a finding of intentional homelessness, the authority must notify the applicant in writing of its decision, giving reasons. It must also inform the applicant of her/his right to review.

Accommodation duty after a finding of intentional homelessness

s190(2) & 190(3) HA96
s206 HA96

If the person is homeless, eligible, in priority need, but intentionally homeless, the authority must secure accommodation, or secure that the applicant is provided with accommodation, for long enough to give her/him a reasonable opportunity of securing her/his own accommodation and give her/him advice and assistance in her/his attempts to secure accommodation. The accommodation provided must be suitable.

In addition, the local authority is required to assess the applicant's needs before advice and assistance is provided. This means that advice must be 'applicant-specific.' The advice and assistance must include information about the likely availability in the district of types of accommodation appropriate to the applicant's needs, including where

s190(4) &
s190(5) HA96

it is and how the applicant can access it. This duty is the same as the duty owed to those who are not in priority need (see 14.16 above). For intentionally homeless households, an assessment will be necessary to see exactly how they will secure accommodation, and may also affect the length of time for which it is reasonable for the local authority to provide accommodation.

At this stage, the authority may also have made investigations regarding local connection. Note that if a person is deemed intentionally homeless, s/he cannot be referred on. The duty to provide accommodation for a reasonable time rests with the original investigating authority.

Accommodation pending local connection referral where not intentionally homeless

s200(1) HA96

s206(1) HA96

If the authority (the first authority) notifies another authority (the second authority) of an application under the local connection grounds, the first authority must provide accommodation until the referral procedure is complete. The accommodation must be suitable.

s200(2) &
S202(1)(c)HA96

When a local authority has notified another authority or intends to do so, it must notify the applicant of this decision and the reason for it, and inform the applicant that s/he has a right to request a review of the decision.

s200(4) HA96 &
s193 HA96

s200(3) HA96 &
s193 HA96

If it has been established that there is a local connection with the second authority, then that authority is subject to the main ongoing housing duty. If it is decided that the conditions for making a referral are not met, for example, if the person would be at risk of violence, then the first authority is subject to the ongoing housing duty.

s200(2) HA96

The first authority must notify the applicant as to which authority has the duty to secure accommodation and the reasons for the decision. It must also notify the applicant of her/his right to a review of the decision.

Accommodation duty where not intentionally homeless and no local connection referral pending

s193(2) HA96

s206 HA96

s193(3) HA96

If an authority is satisfied that an applicant is homeless, eligible for assistance, in priority need, not intentionally homeless and is not making a local connection referral to another authority, or the referral process has been completed, it must ensure that accommodation becomes available for her/his occupation. This is usually referred to as the 'main housing duty.' The accommodation must be suitable. The duty to secure accommodation is not time-limited, but will end in certain specified circumstances.

Circumstances in which the main housing duty ends

The main housing duty will end if the applicant:

s193(5) HA96

para 9.8 HCOG02

- refuses an offer of accommodation which the authority is satisfied is suitable, having been informed of the possible consequences of refusal, and the authority notifies her/him that it considers that it has discharged its duty. The Code of Guidance makes it clear that this section refers to offers of temporary accommodation

s193(6)(a) HA96

- ceases to be eligible for assistance

s193(6)(b) HA96

- becomes homeless intentionally from the accommodation provided

s193(6)(c) HA96

- accepts an offer under the allocation provisions

s193(6)(cc) HA96

- accepts an offer of an assured tenancy (but not an assured shorthold tenancy unless it is a 'qualifying offer' – see below) from a private landlord (including RSLs)

s193(6)(d) HA96

- stops living in the accommodation voluntarily

s193(7) HA96

- unreasonably refuses an offer which states that it is a final offer under the allocations provisions, having been informed of the possible consequences, and the right to request a review of the suitability of the accommodation, provided the authority is satisfied that it was suitable, and had notified the applicant that the duty had ceased within 21 days of the refusal.

Qualifying offers of assured shorthold tenancies

The Homelessness Act 2002 also added a section regarding offers of assured shorthold tenancies, which may be refused as a discharge of the main housing duty, without affecting the authority's ongoing duty to provide accommodation. The duty will only end if the applicant specifically accepts an assured shorthold which is a 'qualifying offer.' A qualifying offer is one which:

- has been arranged by the authority with a private landlord with the aim of ending the duty, and

- is for a fixed term, and

- is accompanied by a written statement of the tenancy terms which also explains in ordinary language that

  – the applicant is not obliged to accept the offer, but

  – if s/he does accept, the authority's duties will end, and

ss193(7B-E) HA96

- the applicant has signed a statement saying that s/he has understood the written statement.

Fresh applications

s193(9) HA96

If the duty ceases for any of the above reasons, the applicant may still make a fresh application to the authority for accommodation or help in obtaining accommodation.

Notification on completion of inquiries

s184 HA96

On completing its inquiries and deciding upon its duties, a local authority must notify the applicant of its decision and what duty it considers it has and, if the decision is against the interests of the applicant, the authority must give reasons. The notification must also inform the applicant of her/his right to a review.

14.19 Discharge of accommodation duty

Ways of securing accommodation

s206 HA96 para
11.2 HCOG02

Where an authority has reached a decision and has to ensure that accommodation is available for the applicant, whether for a limited or ongoing period of time, it may do so in one of three ways:

• Making available its own suitable accommodation

• Securing that the applicant obtains suitable accommodation from some other person, or

• By giving such advice and assistance as will ensure that s/he obtains suitable accommodation from some other person.

para4 Sch 1
HA85 & para3
Sch 17 HA96

If the authority uses its own housing stock to discharge its duty, such an arrangement cannot be a secure tenancy, unless it is subsequently allocated to the applicant under the allocation provisions.

Discharge of interim duties to accommodate

s209 HA96

If the authority discharges an interim duty (ie, accommodation pending inquiries, after a decision that someone is in priority need but intentionally homeless, or whilst making a local connection referral) by making a nomination to a private or registered social landlord, this cannot be an assured or assured shorthold tenancy for up to twelve months from the date the authority notified the applicant of a final decision on her/his application or appeal of a decision, unless the landlord notifies the tenant that it will be an assured or assured shorthold tenancy.

Location of accommodation

The authority should, as far as possible, place applicants in accommodation within its area, except where the applicant would be at risk of violence in the district and needs to be accommodated away

11.13 HCOG02

s208 HA96

from the perpetrator. If it has to place the applicant in another district, it must notify the other district in writing within 14 days of the placement, giving details of the household and the duty under which the placement was made.

paras 11.15-11.16,
12.9-12.10
HCOG02

Where an applicant has special support needs, such as for medical services or special schools, s/he should be given priority for accommodation within the authority's own district.

Suitability of accommodation

s210 HA96

In determining whether accommodation is suitable, authorities must have regard to legal provisions relating to slum clearance, overcrowding and houses in multiple occupation. For more information about how the courts have viewed suitability, see 15.36. Regulations have also been issued which state that local authorities should also take into account the affordability of the accommodation.[22] The Homelessness Code of Guidance states that 'the question of whether accommodation is suitable requires an assessment of all the qualities of the accommodation in the light of the needs and requirements of the homeless person and his or her family.' The authority must also consider medical and physical needs and other social considerations,

para 12.3-4 HCOG02

as well as the risk of violence or harassment.

Charging for accommodation

When providing accommodation under an interim or main duty, authorities may require a person to:

• pay reasonable charges for accommodation secured by them, or

• pay a reasonable amount, as decided by the local authority, to cover costs paid by the authority for accommodation made available

s206(2) HA96

by another person.

14.20 Protection of property

s211 HA96

Where the authority is subject to either an interim or main housing duty, it must take reasonable steps to prevent loss or damage to personal property of an applicant where:

• there is danger of loss of or damage to the property by reason of the applicant's inability to protect it or deal with it, and

• no other suitable arrangements have been or are being made.

Even if it is not subject to a housing duty, an authority can take any steps it considers reasonable (eg, for non-priority homeless people). The authority may, however, impose conditions in the form of

22. Homelessness (Suitability of Accommodation) Order 1996, SI 1996 No.3204. HCOG 12.7-12.8.

reasonable charges for the action taken. In connection with these duties, authorities have powers of entry and disposal of the property if they lose contact with the applicant.

s212 HA96

Homelessness procedure and local authority duties

1. Person applies to local authority for help with accommodation and there is reason to believe s/he may be homeless.

s184 HA96

2. Local authority must make appropriate enquiries.

s188 HA96

3. If reason to believe person is homeless, eligible for assistance, and s/he may have priority need, then the local authority must secure temporary accommodation, pending enquires.

s184 HA96
s179 HA96
s213A HA96

4. If not eligible for assistance, no further duty other than notification and general advice, unless children under 18, in which case, referral procedure to social services applies.

s190(3-5) HA96
s192(3) HA96

5. If eligible but no priority need, the local authority must provide advice and assistance. If also unintentionally homeless, has power to provide accommodation.

s191 HA96

6. If eligible, homeless and priority need, the local authority must decide whether or not applicant is intentionally homeless.

s190(1) & (2) HA96
s193-5 HA96
s213A HA96

7. If applicant is intentionally homeless, the local authority must still secure accommodation for a reasonable period of time, provide advice and assistance, and, if children under 18, referral procedure to social services applies.

s198 HA96

8. If homeless, eligible for assistance, priority need and not intentionally homeless, but no local connection, the local authority may refer to another safe authority where there is a local connection.

s193(2) HA96

9. If homeless, eligible for assistance, priority need, unintentionally homeless and local connection, the authority must secure that suitable accommodation becomes available.

s184(3)-(6) HA96

10. When enquires complete, the local authority must notify applicant in writing of decision and right to request a review of that decision.

C   Enforcing homelessness duties

Once the applicant, who may be homeless or threatened with homelessness, has approached a local authority, then the above duties fall upon it. Unfortunately, in practice local authorities may fail to carry these duties out. Alternatively, the applicant may be unhappy with the authority's decision or the way in which it has carried it out. If the local authority cannot be persuaded to change its mind, it may be possible to challenge the decision in a number of ways, including through the courts.

14.21 Statutory homelessness reviews

Homeless applicants have a right to:

s202 HA96

- request a statutory review of most elements of a homelessness decision (see 14.25), and then

s204 HA96

- appeal against the review decision in the county court (see 14.27).

An appeal against a decision of the county court must be brought in the Court of Appeal, if permission is granted. A further appeal may be allowed to the House of Lords, if the case involves a matter of principle of sufficient importance.

14.22 Other methods of challenging decisions

- If there is no statutory right to a review of the decision, then an application for judicial review may be appropriate (14.30 – 14.32)

- A complaint could be made to the local government ombudsman

- It may be possible to claim damages in respect of a breach of human rights, as in the case of *R(Bernard) v Enfield LBC*,[23] a community care case.

These actions are explained below, with a comparison of the different courses of action and their different applications.

14.23 The adviser's role

An adviser should not necessarily refer clients for legal action automatically if the situation is not totally straightforward. At the first interview, the adviser should obtain the client's written authority to request a copy of her/his file from the local authority. Subsequent discussion and negotiations with the local authority, highlighting the legal issues involved and any relevant case law, may result in a satisfactory solution. However, advisers must also ensure, when negotiating, that they are aware of the time limits for taking different types of action, and do not lose the opportunity for requesting a review or taking further legal action. Negotiations can continue whilst a legal case is being prepared, in the hope that the council may retract. If they do not, the client will not have wasted precious time.

---

23. Bernard v Enfield LBC [2002] EWHC 2282 (Admin).

Time limits

s202(3) HA96
- A request for a review normally has to be made within *21 days* of the authority's written decision

s204(2) HA96
- An appeal to the county court normally has to be made within *21 days* of the authority's review decision, or the date when the applicant should have been notified of the decision

CPR 54.5
- An application for judicial review normally has to be made within *3 months* of the decision or action complained of. This period may not be extended by agreement between the parties concerned.

14.24 Checking homelessness decisions

Reviews and appeals take up valuable time and resources. In practice, an advisor should obtain the applicant's file from the housing authority, take instructions from the applicant and make as many salient points as possible (see Appendix A4).

Steps which advisers may wish to take to prepare themselves for negotiations, reviews or subsequent court challenges are suggested below. This is not an exhaustive list and is suggested for guidance only:

- Check whether full and clear reasons for the decision have been given. Failure to give adequate reasons is a common ground for decisions being quashed by the courts[24]

- Check whether the authority has considered all the circumstances and made sufficient inquiries

- Compile all the information relevant to the case in order to identify the key points in dispute (if any have been raised by the applicant)

- Check what the legislation says and whether it has been accurately applied and interpreted

- Check the duties owed and whether they have been complied with

- Check any relevant information in the Code of Guidance and whether the authority can clearly show it has had regard to it

- Consult case law, since there may have already been challenges to local authority interpretation on similar points (much of the case law established under Part 3 of the Housing Act 1985 will still be relevant to challenges under the 1996 Act).

14.25 Decisions which carry a right to a review

s202 HA96
Not all aspects of the homelessness procedure carry the statutory right to request a review.

---

24. R v Newham LBC ex parte Qureshi (1997) 18 September QBD; Legal Action March 1998; R v Wandsworth LBC ex parte Dodia (1998) 30 HLR 562 QBD.

What can be reviewed?

Applicants have the statutory right to request a review by the authority of any decision as to:

• eligibility for assistance

• what duty is owed to those who are:

– non-priority need

– intentionally homeless

– unintentionally homeless and in priority need or

– threatened with homelessness intentionally or otherwise

• the making of a local connection referral

• whether conditions for referral are met

• duty to those who are referred

• suitability of accommodation offered as discharge of any of the homelessness duties (except the provision of interim accommodation whilst making enquiries or pending a referral) or under Part 6 as a final offer.

What is not subject to the right to review?

• The suitability of interim accommodation

• The decision not to provide accommodation pending a review

• Decisions about protection of property

s202 HA96

• Any other decision not listed in s202 HA 96, for example, a refusal to entertain an application or issue a decision.

These must be challenged by way of judicial review in the High Court. See also 14.30 below, 'When to use judicial review,' for other instances where judicial review may be appropriate.

s204A HA96

The Homelessness Act 2002 granted a right to appeal to the county court against a decision not to accommodate pending a county court appeal, but it is very difficult to win such cases.

14.26 Local authority homelessness reviews – procedure

Some authorities imply to applicants that they must have reasons or grounds for seeking a review, but it is not necessary for the applicant to put forward any grounds, specific objections or counter-arguments for review, although s/he is of course free to do so, and should raise all the issues that s/he could properly be expected to raise at the review stage. Advisers should put forward full arguments as soon as possible. If a homeless applicant requests a review of a decision relating to her/his homelessness application, the authority must look at the whole issue and its own actions and decisions again.

Regulations set out how local authorities must undertake reviews:[25]

s184(5) HA96
s202(3) HA96

- A request for a review must normally be made within 21 days of the date of notification of the decision. The right to request such a review must be included in the decision letter. The local authority has the power to extend this time limit if it so wishes. If the authority will not review its own decision, it may be open to challenge by way of judicial review

- The applicant may wish to ask for a copy of the information held by the local authority on her/his case, known as a 'Subject Access Request,' and this must be provided[26] (s.7 of the Data Protection Act 1998). However, the authority has 40 days in which to do so, and may charge a £10 fee

- Once the local authority has received a request for a review, it must notify the applicant that s/he or her/his representatives may make written representations and explain the procedure for the review. A reasonable time must be allowed for representations to be made

- The authority must take into account all matters raised by the applicant up to the time of review, even if they were not mentioned in the original application[27]

- The review must be carried out by a senior officer who was not involved in the original homelessness decision. However, the taker of the decision is not prevented from assisting the reviewer with routine matters in the conduct of the review[28]

- The authority can then carry out the review and notify its decision to the applicant.

Notification of review decision

para 13.12 HCOG02

The local authority must notify the applicant of its decision on review within eight weeks of the original request for a review being made, ten weeks where the decision was made jointly by two housing authorities about whether the conditions for referral are met, or up to twelve weeks if the review relates to arbitration on local connection.

25. Allocation of Housing and Homelessness (Review Procedures) Regulations 1999 SI No. 71.
26. see www.dataprotection.gov.uk/dpr/dpdoc.nsf for useful information on 'Compliance Advice' in relation to the Data Protection Act 1998.
27. Mohammed v LB Hammersmith and Fulham, see 29 above.
28. Butler v Fareham BC 15 November 2000 CA Legal Action May 2001 Case No: B2/00/2492.

Oral hearing

In some cases where the decision on review is negative, the applicant will also have the opportunity to make further oral representations before the authority makes its final decision. This will apply where the authority finds that there has been an irregularity with the original decision, but does not immediately decide to reverse the decision. The Homelessness Code of Guidance suggests that an irregularity will include:

para 13.10-13.11
HCOG02

• failure to take into account relevant considerations

• ignoring relevant considerations

• failure to base a decision on the facts

• bad faith or dishonesty

• mistake of law

• decisions which run contrary to the policy of the 1996 Act

• decisions which are 'Wednesbury unreasonable' (see 14. 28).

14.27 Right of appeal to the county court on a point of law

s204 HA96

If the applicant is either dissatisfied with the review decision, or the local authority have failed to notify her/him of the decision within the prescribed time limit, then the applicant can appeal to the county court on any point of law arising from the original, or the review, decision.

County court's powers

The county court then has power to make an order confirming, quashing or varying the decision as it thinks fit: for example, it could vary a decision from non-priority need to priority need,[29] or from intentional to non-intentional homelessness.[30]

Breadth of Jurisdiction of the County Court

In *Begum (Nipa) v Tower Hamlets London Borough Council*,[31] it was established that an appeal on a point of law included not only matters of legal interpretation, but also the full range of issues which would otherwise be the subject of an application to the High Court for judicial review, such as procedural error and questions of power, irrationality and adequacy or inadequacy of reasons (see 14.28).

There is no jurisdiction for the county court to consider appeals on disputes of fact, eg, whether in fact someone is or is not in fear of violence. The only way this could be challenged would be if it could be shown, for example, that the authority had not investigated properly or had reached a conclusion which no reasonable authority could reach.

29. Woodrow v Lewisham LBC (2000) Woolwich County Court 2 August, Legal Action November 2000.
30. Bond v Leicester CC, see 3 above.
31. Begum (Nipa) v Tower Hamlets LBC (1999) 32 HLR 445 CA.

Despite this shortcoming, the courts have held that the statutory review process does not amount to a breach of an individual's human rights under Article 6 of the Convention (right to a fair trial and an independent and impartial hearing). The decision was upheld by the House of Lords in the case of *Tower Hamlets LBC v Begum* (see box).

Review procedure and human rights
Tower Hamlets LBC v Begum[32]

The House of Lords held that a statutory review under s.202 of the Housing Act 1996 was an appropriate means of reconsidering issues of fact and discretion and that the requirement of fairness under Article 6 of the European Convention on Human Rights was satisfied by the procedures laid down in the review regulations.[33] *The discretion allowed the local authority within the legislation, together with the overseeing role of the county court, to assess the process by which the local authority reached its decision, together gave a right of access to a court of 'full jurisdiction' for Article 6 purposes. This was held to be so despite the fact that an appeal to the county court is limited to a point of law and the decision may involve issues of fact. It was enough if the court had 'jurisdiction to deal with the case as the nature of the decision requires.'*

This overrules the Court of Appeal's earlier judgment in Adan v Newham LBC[34] *in which it was suggested that where dispute is about facts or something not subject to judicial review/point of law, a local authority would have to exercise its contracting out functions in order to reach the degree of impartiality required to satisfy Article 6.*

Time limits for bringing an appeal in the county court

The appeal must normally be made within 21 days of the date the applicant was, or should have been, notified of the decision. However, under the provisions of the Homelessness Act 2002, the county court has the discretion to extend the time limit, but only where it is satisfied there was good reason for the delay. Advisers should therefore work on the basis that the deadline is 21 days, and not rely on the favourable exercise of the court's discretion.

s204(2) &
204(2A) HA96

14.28 Principles of administrative law

Although challenge of homelessness decisions is no longer normally by way of judicial review, the principles which the county court and Court

---

32. Tower Hamlets LBC v Begum [2002] HLR 29, CA;
    [2001] EWCA Civ 239.
33. Allocation of Housing and Homelessness
    (Review Procedures) see 36 above.

34. Adan v Newham LBC and Secretary of State for
    Transport Local Government and the Regions [2001]
    EWCA Civ 1916; [2002] HLR 28 CA.

of Appeal will consider include the full range of issues which would give rise to judicial review, and therefore an understanding of the process is essential.

Clearly, a public administrative body such as a local authority may only do what it has been given statutory power to do, and it must fulfil its statutory duties. Even if the authority has acted within its powers and carried out its duties, it may be possible to argue that it has not carried them out properly, or with the correct procedures, and so is not acting within the agreed principles of administrative law.

The principles of administrative law apply to all actions of all public bodies. They were encapsulated in the case of *Associated Provincial Picture Houses v Wednesbury Corporation,*[35] and can be summarised as follows:

- *Decision-making cannot be delegated*: it is the authority with the decision-making power which must make the decision. It cannot avoid its duties by adopting the decision of another body, eg, a council cannot say someone is intentionally homeless because another authority has made that decision, nor can it rely on a medical officer's opinion about priority need. It must make the decision for itself, unless it has statutory authority to contract it out

- *Decision makers must be properly authorised*: decisions must be made by full council, unless it has, as it is allowed to do, delegated the power to a subcommittee or officer of the authority. A single councillor cannot be given delegated power to do anything

- *An authority must have understood and applied the law correctly*: eg, saying that someone is not homeless where s/he is forced to live separately from her/his partner because of lack of accommodation is a misunderstanding of the law

- *The facts which form the basis of the decision must be correct and must provide a basis for the decision*

- *An authority must take into account all relevant matters before reaching a decision*: eg, why rent arrears accrued

- *An authority must disregard all irrelevant matters when making a decision*: eg, prejudice because of race, sex or previous knowledge of the applicant

- *An authority must act so as to promote and not to frustrate the policy and objects of the statute under which the decision is made*

- *The authority must not act in bad faith or dishonestly*

---

35. Associated Provincial Picture Houses v Wednesbury Corporation (1947) 2 All ER 680.

- *The decision must be reached fairly in accordance with natural justice*: eg, an applicant must have a chance to answer allegations which may affect her/his case

- *The authority must reach a decision after considering each case on its individual merits*: it must not restrict (or fetter) the use of its discretion by adopting a uniform, predetermined, policy to cover all cases in a particular class, ie, a 'blanket policy'

- *Any statutory procedural requirements must be followed*: eg, failure to give proper reasons in a written homelessness notification is challengeable

- *The decision must not be one to which no reasonable authority would come*: the court will not intervene lightly and it has been said that the decision must be so unreasonable as to be absurd.[36]

'Wednesbury' reasonableness

Acting 'reasonably' is a key principle for local authorities. Because of the case in which the above principles were clarified, the courts may refer to an authority's actions as *'reasonable in the Wednesbury sense'* or *'Wednesbury unreasonable.'* It is important to recognise that the court will not necessarily intervene simply because it disagrees with the local authority's decision:

'...The decision of the local authority... must be proved to be unreasonable in the sense that the court considers it to be a decision that no reasonable body could have come to. It is not what the court considers unreasonable, which is a different thing altogether.'[37]

The question of how far the courts should go in investigating the motives and merits of an authority's action and how far they should interfere with local authority discretion was considered in relation to a very important homelessness case in the House of Lords in 1986, *R v LB Hillingdon ex parte Puhlhofer.*[38]

'The grounds upon which the courts will review the exercise of an administrative discretion is abuse of power – eg. bad faith, a mistake in construing the limits of the power, a procedural irregularity or unreasonableness in the 'Wednesbury' sense – unreasonableness verging on an absurdity... Where the existence or non-existence of a fact is left to the judgement and discretion of a public body and that fact involves a broad spectrum ranging from the obvious to the debatable to the just conceivable, it is the duty of the court to leave the decision of that fact to the public body to whom Parliament has entrusted the decision-making power, save in a case where it is obvious that the public body, consciously or unconsciously, are acting perversely.'

36. R v LB Hillingdon ex parte Puhlhofer (1986)
      18 HLR 158 HL.

37. See 35 above.
38. See 36 above.

14.29 Breach of statutory duty

In the past, it was thought that immediate action could be taken in the county court to force the council to carry out its homelessness duties towards an individual and damages sought for failure to carry out the duty. This is no longer the case.[39] Orders to comply with duties must usually be obtained either through the right of appeal to the county court or by way of judicial review.

14.30 Taking action to challenge a decision

In homelessness cases the choice of action will depend upon what grounds are the basis for challenging the decision and whether the applicant needs accommodation whilst the review or appeal is being heard (see 14.31 for a summary of action to enforce provision of interim accommodation).

In general, where the statutory review and appeal procedure applies, permission will not normally be given for judicial review proceedings.

Getting the local authority to review its decision

Under the Housing Act 1996, homeless people have a right to request a review of a local authority's decision, if it is one of the circumstances set out at 14.25. If a review is available, then this should normally be the first remedy which the applicant pursues. However, if the applicant needs to be rehoused during the review and the local authority decide not to provide or continue to provide accommodation, then the applicant may instead be able to get permission for a judicial review which would allow her/him to get an emergency injunction ordering the authority to house the household pending the hearing.

Appealing to the county court

Appeal to the county court is only available after a local authority review. It can be used if the applicant is dissatisfied with the review decision, or if the authority fails to notify the applicant of its decision within the time limit and if there is a point of law issue. As explained above (14.28) a point of law includes the issues which would have been considered by way of judicial review. Where this remedy applies it must be used instead of judicial review proceedings.

s204A HA96 Local authorities have a power and not a duty to house applicants pending the hearing. The county court has power to grant an emergency injunction ordering the authority to house the applicant in the interim period, but only if it is satisfied that the applicant's ability to pursue the appeal would be 'substantially prejudiced' if accommodation is not provided.

---

39. O'Rourke v Camden LBC (1998) AC 188.

When to use judicial review

Judicial review can only usually be applied for if all other legal remedies have been exhausted, or if it is the only way of getting the remedy required. It is first necessary to get permission from the court to make an application. Application must be made in the Administrative Court (see 14.32) within 3 months of the decision which is being challenged. An application would normally be refused if it is considered that there is another remedy available, or that there is no case to answer. When applying for permission for judicial review, it is also possible to get an injunction from the court ordering that the council should accommodate the applicant in the interim.

In homelessness cases, therefore, judicial review will normally only be appropriate if the matter being questioned is outside the scope of the local authority review, or an injunction is needed to provide temporary housing whilst awaiting the appeal hearing in the county court. Other authors have suggested the following examples of additional situations where judicial review proceedings might be allowed:[40]

- Where a decision letter is so unsatisfactory and the authority refuses to correct any deficiency, that any internal review would be unfair to the applicant
- Where the challenge is to the legality of the policy
- Where there is an important matter of law
- In exceptional circumstances.

Also:
- Discharge of property duties
- Failure to entertain an application
- Failure to issue a decision letter at all.

There may be other circumstances in which judicial review will remain available but which have not yet been considered by the courts.[41]

14.31 Action to obtain interim accommodation

Advisers need to be able to distinguish the following:

Local authority refusal to provide accommodation at initial presentation stage

An authority is under a duty to provide interim accommodation whilst it makes inquiries, (ie, before it reaches a decision) if there is reason to believe the person may be homeless, eligible for assistance and in

s188 HA96   priority need.

---

40. see 'Homelessness and Allocations' Arden A and
   Hunter C, sixth edition, 2002 Legal Action Group, page 78. 41. ibid. page 79.

For example, if the applicant is fleeing violence but has no dependent children, the authority will need to consider whether s/he is vulnerable and should provide accommodation until the decision is reached.

If the authority refuses to provide interim accommodation at this stage, the remedy is to apply for an injunction within judicial review proceedings to enforce provision.

Local authority refusal to provide accommodation at review stage

Since the decision to provide accommodation at review stage is at the local authority's discretion, the remedy is to apply for an injunction within judicial review proceedings, which would need to argue that the authority had either failed to consider exercising that discretion, or acted unreasonably or incorrectly in the way the discretion had been exercised. The courts will not interfere lightly with the local authority's discretion, and exceptional circumstances need to be shown.[42]

Local authority refusal to provide accommodation at appeal to county court stage

The remedy is to apply for an injunction within the proceedings for the appeal to the county court. The court may only grant such an order if it is satisfied that a failure to provide accommodation pending the appeal would substantially prejudice the applicant's ability to pursue the main appeal.

s204A(6)(a)
HA96

Local authority refusal to provide accommodation pending appeal from the county court to the Court of Appeal

Application for an injunction would be made to the Court of Appeal as part of the appeal proceedings.

14.32 Judicial review proceedings

It is not easy to obtain a hearing for judicial review of a local authority decision. In the case of *Cowl and Others v Plymouth City Council*,[43] the court stressed the paramount importance of avoiding applications for judicial review wherever possible. All other avenues, such as complaints procedures and/or some other form of alternative dispute resolution should be explored. It was held that the courts should not permit, except for good reason, proceedings for judicial review to proceed, if a significant part of the issues could be resolved outside the litigation process.

If judicial review is the appropriate action, the public body can be challenged in the Administrative Court (formerly the Queen's Bench Division of the High Court) by way of judicial review. Appeals would go

---

42. R v Camden LBC ex parte Mohammed (1998) 30 HLR
     315 QBD; R v Hammersmith and Fulham LBC ex parte
     Fleck (1997) 30 HLR 679 QBD; R v Brighton and Hove   43. Cowl and Others v Plymouth City Council; [2001] EWCA
     Council ex parte Nacion (1999) 31 HLR 1095 CA.   Civ 1935 CA.

to the Court of Appeal and House of Lords, although these are only likely to be given permission to be heard in fairly limited circumstances.

Court Orders

If the court finds in favour of the applicant during the process of judicial review, it will normally make an order quashing the local authority's action or decision, ie, a quashing order, previously known as 'certiorari.' This returns everything to square one and the authority must start all over again. If a homelessness decision is quashed as a result of a judicial review, or by the county court or Court of Appeal, there is nothing to prevent the same homelessness decision being made in the same case provided that it is done lawfully.

In some exceptional circumstances, where the court considers there is a duty on the authority to act in a certain way, eg, to provide accommodation whilst a hearing for judicial review is pending, it may also make a mandatory order (previously an order for 'mandamus'). This is an order telling the authority it must do something, unlike a quashing order, where the courts are simply saying either: 'you cannot do this' or, 'you have not done this right – go back and do it again.' The court can also make a prohibiting order, and make a declaration.

14.33 Ombudsman

In some cases, there may not be grounds for an appeal or a judicial review, but the client may still feel the council have acted unjustly, incompetently, ineptly or unfairly, eg, by failing to deal with an application properly, causing unnecessary delays, repeatedly losing papers, discriminating against a person or acting arbitrarily. In all these cases a complaint to the Ombudsman may be appropriate, even after the council have finally done what they should have done much earlier.

Complaint against Lambeth LBC[44]

Maladministration was found in a case where the Ombudsman found an unreasonable delay of 14 months to rehouse a homeless family with a child with cerebral palsy. This was caused by a lack of prompt and proper liaison over the type of accommodation she needed. The Ombudsman recommended that the council should pay £1,000 to recognise the injustice.

In many cases,[45] the Ombudsman has recommended damages for the complaint and changes in policies or procedures on the council's part.

The procedure for complaining to the Ombudsman is explained below.

44. Complaint against Lambeth LBC: Omb 92/A/1293.
45. For example, Complaint against Bristol CC: Omb 94/B/0334, where there had been an unreasonable delay in a homelessness referral, the complainants were awarded £1,500 and a further £250 for time and trouble, plus £100 to an organisation who had acted as advocate. See also Complaint against LB Hackney: Omb 92/A/1540 where the complainant was awarded £1,450 for injustice relating to standards of temporary accommodation and the authority was told to review its pre-allocation policy.

14.34 Maladministration

Maladministration can cover a wide variety of actions or non-actions; hence its scope is much broader than that of judicial review. Allegations of maladministration can be based on instances of:

- bias, arbitrariness or treating the applicant unfairly
- inattention, neglect or unnecessary delay
- incompetence or ineptitude, eg, giving the applicant wrong information
- turpitude, eg, dishonesty, corruption, breaking promises
- perversity, not following its own rules or the law, or not making a decision in the correct way.

In order to complain to the Ombudsman:

- The complainant must have suffered an injustice (see below) arising from a specific act or omission of the local authority
- The complaint must be specific, ie, it cannot be about an authority's policies in general
- It cannot normally be about something that the complainant knew about more than twelve months before contacting the Ombudsman or complaining to a councillor
- It should not be about something that could more appropriately be dealt with by the courts, an appeal tribunal or a Minister, unless there are good reasons why the applicant could not be expected to do so eg, costs of litigation are disproportionate.

The Ombudsman cannot question what a council has done just because someone does not agree with the council. If any decision, action or inaction resulted in injustice to the complainant a complaint can be made. Injustice includes:

- financial loss
- being deprived of an opportunity to object or appeal
- being deprived of an amenity, service or benefit you were entitled to or there was delay before you got it, eg, housing
- causing concern, distress, confusion, inconvenience or uncertainty.

14.35 Ombudsman complaint procedure

The complainant must first complain directly to the council concerned, either through the relevant department or the Chief Executive. If the issue is not resolved, s/he can then send the complaint directly to the Local Government Ombudsman. A complaint form is available,[46] or the applicant can simply send a letter to the Local Government Ombudsman.

46. From www.lgo.org.uk/pdf/howcompcouncil.pdf.

S/he could also ask a councillor to look into the matter, but this is no longer essential. If the Ombudsman considers the complaint is one that can be investigated:

• an investigator will contact the council for their comments

• the Ombudsman's office can examine files and interview anyone concerned with the complaint

• a report will be issued with the findings.

The process can be lengthy – usually some months at least, and, in a few cases, possibly as long as one or two years.

If maladministration and injustice have been found, the authority should say what it intends to do about it. Often the Ombudsman will recommend a course of action, which can include financial compensation. The Ombudsman cannot force a council to act if it decides not to, but can arrange for a statement to be published in a local newspaper about the council's refusal.

D Allocations

The Homelessness Act 2002 made some significant changes to allocations under Part 6 of the 1996 Act. They follow through the Government's commitments to extend choice in social housing and reform allocations schemes.

Homelessness Act 2002 changes

The 2002 Act:

• brings into the allocations framework tenants who are waiting for transfer. This will mean that tenants waiting for transfer will be considered alongside new applicants, unless the transfer is initiated
s159(5) HA96   by the local authority (see 14.36)

• abolishes the requirement of the local authority to maintain a housing register and sets out eligibility criteria that a person must
s160A HA96   meet to be considered for housing (see 14.37)

• abolishes restrictions except in limited circumstances (see 14.37 – 14.38)

• introduces a right to apply for housing, and requires that the local authority provides advice and information to enable people to make
s166 HA96   an application

• requires local authorities to have an allocations scheme, and to publish a statement describing how choice will be offered
s167 & s168 HA96   to applicants.

Under Part 6 of the Housing Act 1996, a local authority may, in most cases, only allocate its housing stock through its allocation scheme. Advisers must be aware what rights a client may have to be considered for allocation and ultimately to be rehoused. This section sets out the law as it applies since 31st January 2003, when the amendments to Part 6 were implemented.

14.36 What is an allocation?

The rules on allocations apply only to situations set out in the Act. For these purposes, an allocation will be:

- selecting secure or introductory tenants for the authority's own stock

- nominating a new secure or introductory tenant to another organisation

- nominating a new assured tenant to a registered social landlord (eg, a housing association)

- granting a transfer to an existing secure or introductory tenant at the tenant's request.

Transfers

The provisions *do not* apply to allocations to existing secure or introductory council tenants, unless they are as a result of a transfer application made by the tenant. Transfers were brought into the allocation scheme by the Homelessness Act 2002, and this could have important implications for people whose relationships have broken down. If they apply for a transfer, they will have to qualify within the reasonable preference categories and the general provisions of the allocation scheme (see 14.38). However, the authority does not have to s159(5) HA96 operate the allocation scheme rules if it initiates the transfer itself. This therefore seems to leave the way open for special policies, such as 'management transfers,' to be implemented by a local authority where a relationship breakdown is involved.

Joint tenancies

Granting a joint tenancy where one of the tenants is already an existing s159(5) & tenant (provided that the other person is not excluded from being s160A (1)(c) HA96 eligible for allocation) does not count as an allocation.

Assignments, succession and court orders

Assignments, successions and vesting of the tenancy in family proceedings on relationship breakdown are not subject to the s160 HA96 allocation provisions.

14.37 Who allocations can be made to

General exclusions of certain groups of people, eg, those in rent arrears, are no longer permitted, but allocations can only be made to people who are 'eligible.' Broadly, ineligible people are people subject to immigration control or persons from abroad.

The authority may also decide that any individual applicant (but not a general class of applicant) shall be treated as ineligible on the grounds of 'unacceptable behaviour' (see below). Anyone else must be

s160A(2) HA96   considered eligible for allocation.

Ineligible persons:

s115 IAA99

s160A(1)(a) &
(3-5) HA96

• Persons from abroad, unless they are in the groups permitted by regulations,[47] and anyone excluded from housing benefit as a result of the Immigration and Asylum Act 1999. Regulations may prescribe who cannot be an eligible person

• An authority may treat someone as ineligible if they are satisfied that

– the applicant or member of her/his household has been guilty of unacceptable behaviour serious enough to make her/him ineligible and the authority consider her/him unsuitable to be a tenant as a result of that behaviour.

Pt 1 Sch 2 HA85

This is defined as behaviour which would, if the applicant had been a secure tenant of the housing authority at that time, entitle the authority to a possession order under any of the discretionary grounds in the Housing Act 1985, (other than ground 8, which relates to rehousing during temporary works). These are grounds where the tenant has broken some tenancy condition, committed nuisance or domestic violence, etc.

Although the Act refers only to a 'possession order,' the housing minister during the Act's passage through parliament made it clear that only an outright possession order would meet the test. The Code of Guidance on Allocation of Accommodation states that the housing authority would need to be satisfied that, if a possession order were granted, it would not be suspended by the court.[48] It also refers specifically to situations which might arise when a relationship breaks down:

para 4.11(ii)
ACOG02

'Behaviour such as accrual of rent arrears which have resulted from factors outside the applicant's control – for example, liability for a partner's debts, where the applicant was not in control of the household's finances or was unaware that arrears were accruing – should not be considered serious enough to make the person unsuitable to be a tenant.'

47. The Allocation of Housing (England) Regulations 2002 SI 2002 No.3264.

48. Para 4.11 ii) Allocation of Accommodation, Code of Guidance for Local Authorities, available at www.housing.odpm.gov.uk/local/allocation/pdf/accomm.pdf.

14.38 The allocation scheme and 'reasonable preference'

A local authority must allocate accommodation to people via an allocation scheme which determines the priorities and procedures for allocations. It is up to the local authority to decide upon priorities, but it must give reasonable preference to certain groups. The groups to whom "reasonable preference" must be given are:

s167(2) HA96

- homeless people (whether or not they have made a homelessness application)

- homeless people who are intentionally homeless, but in priority need

- unintentionally homeless people in priority need

- people who are threatened with homelessness unintentionally and are in priority need

- people who are non-priority need and unintentionally homeless, but who have had accommodation secured by the authority

- people in insanitary, overcrowded or otherwise unsatisfactory conditions, people who need to move on medical or welfare grounds, and

- those who would suffer hardship unless they are moved to a particular locality.

Determining priorities

A scheme may contain provision for determining priorities within the above categories, and the factors which the scheme may allow to be taken into account include:

- the financial resources available to a person to meet her/his housing costs

- any behaviour of a person or member of the household which affects the suitability to be a tenant

s167 (2A) HA96

- any local connection with the authority's district.

Removing preference

However, the Act also states that preference does not have to be given to people in the above categories, if the authority is satisfied that:

- s/he or a member of her/his household has been guilty of unacceptable behaviour serious enough to make her/him unsuitable to be a tenant, and

s167 (2B-2C) HA96

- in the circumstances at the time the case is considered, s/he deserves not to be treated as a member of a group of people who are to be given preference under the above categories.

Allocations Code of Guidance

paras 5.10-5.12
ACOG02

The Government's Code of Guidance on Allocation of Accommodation discusses how authorities may give priority to those in the most urgent housing need. It also states that people to whom authorities should consider giving additional preference include those owed a homelessness duty '*as a result of violence or threats of violence which are likely to be carried out and who as a result require urgent rehousing*'. This will

para 5.18 ACOG02

include '*victims of domestic violence.*'

14.39 Local authority policies

para 5.23-5.25
ACOG02

In order to advise about allocations, it is necessary to get information about the allocation scheme and how the authority uses its discretion to decide on who should be given priority. Local authorities must provide free advice and information to everyone in their district about the right to make an application for allocation of housing accommodation and, if a person is likely to have difficulty in making an application without

s166(1) HA96

help, they must also provide that help free of charge. All applications must be considered.

s168 HA96

Local authorities must also provide a free summary of the allocation scheme to anyone who asks for one, and keep a copy of the full scheme available for inspection at the authority's main office, and make copies available (at a reasonable fee) on request. It must also ensure that applicants are informed of their rights to be notified about decisions in

para 6.13 ACOG02

relation to their applications.

para 5.25 ACOG02

Generally speaking, local authority policies should not be so rigid that they cannot take account of the special circumstances of an individual case. Local authorities must maintain sufficient discretion in their policies in order to avoid the policies being unlawful (ie, they must not fetter their discretion).

14.40 Challenging decisions about allocations

There are two ways of challenging allocations decisions:

Asking for a review of the decision

para 5.58 ACOG02

s167(4A)(c) HA96

An applicant has a right to be informed about any decision on her/his case and the facts that have been or are likely to be taken into account in considering whether to make an allocation to her/him. If an authority decides that a person is ineligible for allocation or should not be given reasonable preference because of unacceptable behaviour, the applicant has the right to request the authority to

s167(4A)(d) HA96

review its decision.

Judicial review

If a local authority's decision making process is flawed, it may also be possible to seek judicial review. Judicial reviews may be available in the circumstances set out at 14.29 – 14.31. However, see the comments in 14.32 about the reluctance of the courts to entertain judicial review proceedings, unless no other course of action is available to the applicant. If the applicant is entitled to ask for a review of the authority's decision, s/he must therefore always do this first, before judicial review proceedings can be considered.

Some of the more common grounds for judicial review that are likely to be available are:

- unlawful policies where the local authority has fettered its discretion to look at individual circumstances (ie, operates 'blanket' policies)

- failures to follow the statutory framework.

Certain local authority allocation schemes have been challenged by way of judicial review and found unlawful.[49]

E   Social services' duties

14.41 Social services' duties to 'children in need'

There are discussed in section 9.7 onward. Where an applicant is homeless and has children living with her/him, then it may also be possible to get assistance from the social services department, as the child will normally be 'in need' in these circumstances. This may be of particular assistance where a decision of intentional homelessness or ineligibility has been made. There is, however, no case law about what sort of accommodation or assistance will be offered in these situations, but advisers could suggest to social services that they could at least provide a deposit for the family to secure accommodation in the private rented sector. The duty towards children in need is a totally separate duty from the duty under homelessness legislation, and if accommodation is provided, there are no conditions as to whether it should be temporary or permanent or even suitable. However, the assistance offered must be such that the child is no longer in need otherwise the duty on social services remains.

14.42 Social services' duties under community care legislation

When a relationship breaks down and a person has no children, it may be difficult to obtain accommodation through any of the usual routes (homelessness, allocations, Local Government Act or Children Act

---

49. Lambeth LBC v A, Lambeth LBC v Lindsay [2002] EWCA Civ 1084 HLR 57 CA; R v Islington LBC ex parte Reilley and Mannix (1998) 31 HLR 651 QBD.

where there are children involved). If someone has any kind of special need, eg, is elderly, has a mental or physical illness or disability, community care legislation may be of assistance. Research has shown that a high proportion of male rough-sleepers are homeless as a result of relationship breakdown. They may have alcohol, drug, or mental health problems. Requesting a community care assessment may be a step towards obtaining help with accommodation.

Although this will not necessarily result in rehousing, it may be that social services will be obliged to give support or assistance in order to help the person live in her/his own accommodation.

Community care assessments

s47 NHSCCA 1990
The National Health Service and Community Care Act 1990 (NHS CCA) made it a duty of local authorities to assess people's needs for social care and support. People who 'appear to need community care services' are entitled to an assessment. However, the community care services themselves arise under a number of other Acts, making local authorities subject to duties and providing them with powers.

Community care legislation

s46(3) NHSCCA 1990
The NHS CCA defines 'community care services' as services which local authorities may provide or arrange to be provided under the following provisions:

- National Assistance Act 1948, Part III
- Health Services and Public Health Act 1968
- National Health Services Act 1977
- Mental Health Act 1983.

14.43 Duty to provide accommodation as a community care service

s21 NAA 1948
Under the National Assistance Act 1948, a local authority must make arrangements for providing:

> 'residential accommodation for persons aged 18 years or over who by reason of age, illness, disability or any other circumstances are in need of care and attention which is not otherwise available to them
>
> and
>
> residential accommodation for expectant and nursing mothers who are in need of care and attention which is not otherwise available to them.'

A person does not have to be homeless to be entitled to accommodation under the National Assistance Act 1948, but case law has established that section 21 is a 'safety net of last resort'. *Overcrowding and housing conditions alone cannot trigger the duty to provide accommodation, nor does a need for better housing trigger the duty. It must be shown that there is an 'urgent' need which is not otherwise being addressed.*[50]

R v Newham LBC ex parte Patrick[51]

Where an authority failed to carry out an assessment of the needs of an applicant with mental health problems, but merely offered a hostel place, it was insufficient to comply with the duty to assess and to provide such accommodation as is required to meet the applicant's needs.

The applicant had been declared intentionally homeless. She had been sleeping rough for over three weeks after the interim accommodation offered to her under the homelessness legislation ended. She came to the attention of the council again, who offered her a place in a hostel for people with mental health problems. She refused it. Ten days later, a certificate of mental incapacity was granted. Her solicitors asked the council to arrange accommodation. It declined.

An application was made for judicial review and an interim injunction to accommodate. The council argued that the offer of the hostel place discharged any duty owed under s21 NAA 1948.

The judge allowed the application. The council had:

- *failed to carry out any assessment of needs under s.47 NHS CCA 1990, and*

- *they could not rely on her refusal of the hostel, since they had failed to ensure that it had explained the offer and the consequences of refusal to the point of comprehension.*

He granted an order requiring the council to conduct a s.47 assessment and provide NAA 48 Part III accommodation 'forthwith.'

However, there is a restriction placed on the assistance available to people from abroad. (see below).

Non-eligible asylum-seekers and persons subject to immigration control from 6 December 1999

With effect from 6 December 1999, all asylum-seekers and other people subject to immigration control are not eligible for help, on grounds of destitution only, under:

s116 IAA99

- s.21 National Assistance Act 1948

---

50. R (Wahid) v Tower Hamlets LBC [2002] EWCA Civ 287 CA.

51. R v Newham LBC ex parte Patrick [2001] 4 CCLR 48.

s117(1) IAA99

- s.45 Health Services and Public Health Act 1968 (protection by local authorities of welfare of old people)

s117(2) IAA99

- paragraph 2, Schedule 8, National Health Service Act 1977 (arrangements by local authorities for prevention of illness and for care and after-care).

Nevertheless, people with special needs are still eligible for help from social services (see 15.15 for case law on this issue).

Duty to provide other facilities

s29 NAA48 & s2 CSDPAct70

There is also a duty to provide other facilities under the National Assistance Act or the Chronically Sick and Disabled Persons Act 1970.

These are duties to a person 'ordinarily resident' in the area of the local authority to make arrangements to provide certain services to that person, if those services are necessary to meet that person's needs.

The duty applies to individuals '*18 years or over who are blind, deaf or dumb, or who suffer from mental disorder of any description, and other persons aged 18 or over who are substantially permanently handicapped by illness, injury or congenital deformity.*'

Interim accommodation pending community care assessment

If someone appears to have an urgent need for accommodation, and it may take some time for a community care assessment to be carried out, social services have power to provide accommodation pending the assessment.

s47(5) NHSCCA90

Steps which an adviser could take to obtain accommodation urgently:

1. Contact social services and state that you are requesting an assessment of the client's need for accommodation as a community care service as required under s.47 of the NHSCCA 1990 (National Health Service and Community Care Act 1990).

2. State the reason why you are requesting such an assessment, couched in the terms of s21 NAA 1948, eg, that because of the mental health problems/drug and alcohol-related problems, (specify) the client is a person in urgent need of care and attention, which is not otherwise available to that person, as defined in s21 NAA 1948 (National Assistance Act 1948).

3. If there is an urgent need for accommodation, request that they exercise their powers under s.47(5) of the NHSCCA 1990 to temporarily provide or arrange provision of accommodation as a community care service prior to the assessment of her/his needs, because the condition of the person is such that s/he requires such a service as a matter of urgency.

14.44 Challenging social services decisions relating to the Children Act and community care

Where a local authority's social services department fails to assess an applicant's needs, or provide services, either under the Children Act 1989 or the community care legislation, the ultimate remedy will be to seek permission for judicial review proceedings (as explained in 14.30), and possibly apply for an injunction within those proceedings to enforce an assessment or provision of accommodation. However, advisers should be aware of the court's extreme reluctance to entertain judicial review proceedings where it appears that the problems could be solved by other means (see 14.32). Communication and negotiations with the authority's department should therefore be thorough, whilst bearing in mind the strict three month time limit, commencing from the date of the action or decision complained of, for applying for judicial review proceedings (see 14.23).

15

Chapter 15: Homelessness and relationship breakdown

Subjects covered in this chapter include...

Homelessness investigations and decisions
– common problems with relationship breakdown

Homelessness

The impact of case law and government guidance

How and when local authorities should make inquiries
into homelessness

Eligibility for assistance

When a person is homeless within the Act

How violence makes it unreasonable to remain
in accommodation

Priority need

What help is available for people not eligible for assistance

Priority need

Intentional homelessness

When someone can be declared to have made her/himself
intentionally homeless

Local connection

How local connection should be investigated

Discharge of duty

How the local authority must carry out its duties

Homelessness and relationship breakdown

The legal framework and basic principles of the homelessness legislation were explained in the preceding chapter. This chapter examines case law under both Part 7 of the 1996 Housing Act and Part III of the 1985 Housing Act, since the body of case law under the 1985 Act is still relevant in interpreting the current legislation. Case law is built up from **precedents***. A precedent is a previous decision of a court which may, in certain circumstances, be binding on another court in deciding a similar case. It also examines interpretation and guidance offered by the Government's Homelessness Code of Guidance[1] (see 15.1 below).*

This chapter refers to some county court decisions based on appeals under the 1996 Act. County court decisions are **not binding** *on other courts and serious points of law need to be affirmed by the Court of Appeal before they can be relied on as authoritative. County Court decisions cannot be quoted as precedents in court, but give useful guidance.*

Surprisingly little homelessness case law relates directly to cases involving relationship breakdown or domestic violence, although the important case of Bond v Leicester CC[2] is a significant development in case law on domestic violence (see 15.6). This may be because those undergoing personal trauma and domestic upheaval are unwilling to go through the distress and delay of taking court action. However, other homelessness cases involve principles, which can be directly applied to such situations, and awareness of them may be sufficient to lead a local authority to review a decision favourably, rather than risk the time and expense of further court action.

This chapter examines the common problem areas that are encountered when applying as homeless on relationship breakdown. It looks at what the courts have had to say on these issues and refers to relevant case law, as well as the recommendations of the Government's Homelessness Code of Guidance. It also examines possible problems which may be encountered under the legislation. It is hoped that this examination of case law will encourage advisers and local authorities to take a closer look at the decisions being made when homelessness results from relationship breakdown, and to recognise when the decisions may be open to review or appeal.

The chapter broadly follows the five areas of homelessness investigation, ie, homelessness, eligibility, priority need, intentional homelessness and local connection, and also the discharge of duties, highlighting issues which can be particularly problematic in relationship breakdown.

References in this chapter to 'the Act' refer to Part 7 of the Housing Act 1996 as amended by the Homelessness Act 2002. Most of the homelessness provisions of the Homelessness Act came into force on 31 July 2002, with others coming into force by October 2002.The allocation provisions came into force on 31 January 2003. References to the code of guidance relate to the Homelessness Code of Guidance issued in July 2002, which took effect with the Homelessness Act provisions from 31 July 2002.

---

1. Homelessness Code of Guidance for Local Authorities,
    ODPM and Department of Health July 2002.　　　2.　Bond v Leicester CC [2001] EWCA Civ 1544; HLR 6 CA.

15.1 The Code of Guidance

s182 HA96

The Government provides a 'Homelessness Code of Guidance'[3] to the Act, to which local authorities must have regard. It does not in itself have statutory force, but a number of cases have been quashed by the courts because of local authorities' failure to have proper regard to the Code or having regard to the wrong edition.[4] It is therefore important to be familiar with the issues raised in the Code and references are made where appropriate. The National Assembly for Wales publishes its own Code of Guidance for allocations and homelessness, which became available in March 2003.[5] Advisers and local authorities can ensure that they are referring to the most recent version of the code by contacting the relevant government department or its website.[6]

15.2 Making enquiries

para 3.12 HCOG02

s184 HA96

Many local authority decisions are overturned by the courts because the enquiry process itself was carried out inadequately or incorrectly. The courts have repeatedly stressed that it is not for the applicant to prove her/his case, but for the authority to make proper enquiries. The Homelessness Code of Guidance confirms this. The notification of decision letter should therefore always be checked to see whether the authority has taken all the relevant matters into account and proceeded correctly, following the principles of administrative law.

> ### Hawa Abdullah Ali v Newham LBC[7]
>
> *The tenant fled her home, alleging numerous incidents of harassment. The council held that she was not homeless as it was reasonable for her to continue to occupy her home. The reviewer said he had received no evidence from the police or Victim Support. In fact the applicant had reported the incidents, which had in turn been reported to the council. The judge quashed the decision on the basis that it was not for the applicant to prove her homelessness or bring forward the evidence in support of her assertions. If the council felt the views of the police and others were relevant, it should have made inquiries of them.*

The Code of Guidance stresses that where there is any violence, or threats of violence, which are likely to be carried out, it follows that it is not reasonable for a person to continue to occupy accommodation.

3. Homelessness Code of Guidance, see 1 above.
4. R v Newham LBC ex parte Bones (1992) 25 HLR 357 QBD; R v Tower Hamlets LBC ex parte Mouna Mahmood (1992) Legal Action 12 QBD; R v Shrewsbury and Atcham BC ex parte Griffiths (1993) 25 HLR 613, QBD; R v Brent LBC ex parte Macwan (1993) 26 HLR CA; R v Tower Hamlets LBC ex parte Hoque (1993) TLR 20.7.93.
5. see www.housing. wales.gov.uk/pdf.asp?a=j9. consultationpapers/accommodation-e.rtf.
6. www.homelessness.odpm.gov.uk/homelessness/pubs /code/index.htm.
7. Hawa Abdullah Ali v Newham LBC Bow CC (2000) 11 July (Legal Action Nov. 2000).

It goes on to say that:

'Inquiries into cases where violence is alleged will need careful handling. It is essential that inquiries do not provoke further violence. It is not advisable for the housing authority to approach the alleged perpetrator, since this could generate further violence, and may delay the assessment.'

para 3.14 HCOG02

The Code further suggests people whom the authority may wish to contact for information, but it should always be remembered that it is not legally necessary to have proof of violence having taken place (see 15.7). Interviewing should be carried out sensitively, by people trained for the job:

'Housing authorities may, however, wish to seek information from friends and relatives of the applicant, social services and the police, as appropriate. In cases involving domestic violence, the applicant may be in considerable distress, and for inquiries to be effective, an officer of the same sex as the applicant, trained in dealing with circumstances of this kind, should conduct the interview.'

para 3.14 HCOG02

R v Southwark LBC ex parte Solomon[8]

The applicant turned down an offer because her former violent partner visited friends in the area. The council refused the appeal on the basis that it only took into account the violent ex-partner's visits to an immediate family member.

The court held that the council had not sought adequate information, and quashed the decision ordering the council to reconsider the matter.

A   Homelessness

One of the most common problems facing people whose relationships have broken down and who are seeking help from the local authority is being accepted as homeless in the first place. This is because a person who has a legal right to remain in the property will not normally be treated as homeless. Such a right could arise from:

- being a tenant/owner or joint tenant/owner

- having permission to be there, eg, being a partner's licensee

- having statutory rights to remain, eg, matrimonial home rights either from marriage or granted as a result of obtaining an occupation order under the Family Law Act.

8.   R v Southwark LBC ex parte Solomon (1994) 26 HLR 693 QBD.

It is possible to have a right to remain but still be homeless within the legal definition of the Act. This might happen where:

s176 HA96

• the accommodation is available to the applicant but not to other members of her/his household or people who might reasonably be expected to reside with the applicant (ie, split households), or

s175(2)(a) HA96

• the person is unable to get into the property, for example, the other partner has locked her/him out, or

s175(3) HA96

• it is not reasonable to continue to occupy the accommodation, or

s177 HA96

• it is probable that continued occupation will lead to domestic violence from an 'associated person' or violence from any person (see 14.6) against the applicant, a member of her/his household or someone who could reasonably be expected to live with her/him. If such a probability exists, it will not be reasonable for the applicant to continue to occupy the accommodation. It is not necessary for violence to have taken place, only that there is the probability of violence or threats which are likely to be acted upon.

15.3 Split households

A person is regarded as being homeless, even though s/he may have a clear right of occupation, if the accommodation cannot also be occupied by any other person:

• who normally resides with her/him as a member of her/his family, or

s176 HA96

• who might reasonably be expected to reside with her/him.

A distinction must be made between the two parts of the definition. The decision as to whether it is *reasonable* for someone to reside with the applicant only comes into play if that person does not normally reside with the applicant, or is not residing with her/him as a member of the family.

People normally residing with the applicant as a member of the family

para 6.3 HCOG02

The Code of Guidance says that *'as a member of his family'* includes those with *'close blood or marital relationships and cohabiting partners.'* So if they are established members of the household, accommodation must be provided for them as well. Although not specifically mentioned, same sex partners appear to be included.

If someone normally resides with the applicant as a member of the family, it is not open to the local authority to say that it is not reasonable for them to live together. The general approach should be that family members who normally live with the homeless person, but who are unable to do so for no other reason than that there is no accommodation they can occupy together, should be included in the assessment, and they should not be separated.[9]

When dealing with a family that has separated, the Code states that authorities need to decide which members of the family normally reside, or might be expected to reside, with the applicant. The Code reminds authorities that residence orders may not always have been made, and para 6.4 HCOG02 it may simply be a matter of agreement between the parents.

R v LB Newham ex parte Khan and Hussain[10]

The family consisted of sisters, their husbands and children and their mother. They were made homeless from an assured shorthold tenancy. The local authority maintained the sisters and their respective families should be treated separately, despite their request to be housed together.

The court held that as they were all normally residing together, accommodation secured for them had to be suitable for everyone.

People who might reasonably be expected to live together

Another common problem is where an applicant forms a new relationship and wants the new partner to be included as a member of her/his household, even though they have never lived together before.

Where people are either:

• not members of the family but are living with the applicant, or

• have never lived together

they do not satisfy the 'normal residence' criterion. In this case, the authority must consider whether it would be reasonable to expect them to reside together. The Code gives examples of such people as housekeepers, or companions, or foster children. Of course, others may be included and each case should be judged on its merits. The Code also says that this group should include those members of the family who were not living as part of the household at the time of the application, but who nonetheless para 6.3 HCOG02 might reasonably be expected to form part of it.

In one case,[11] the court held that where a single man applied for accommodation for himself and a carer, with whom he had lived for several years, the test was not whether the applicant was so disabled that he *needed* a live-in carer, but rather whether it *would be reasonable* for the friend to live with him.

9. R v Newham LBC ex parte Khan and Hussain [2001]
    33 HLR 29 QBD; R v Ealing LBC ex parte Surdonja (1998)
    Times 28. October QBD Legal Action December 1998.
10. See 9 above.
11. R v Hackney LBC ex parte Tonnicodi (1998)
    30 HLR 916 QBD.

> ### RB Kensington and Chelsea and Westminster CC Referee's determination[12]
>
> *In this case which was an arbitration on local connection, the referee decided that the onus was on the two parties to prove that there was a genuine and established relationship. If it could be established that there was a real and genuine intention to reside together as a couple and there was nothing, other than the lack of accommodation, to prevent this from happening, there should normally be a duty to secure accommodation for them.*
>
> ### R v Peterborough ex parte Carr [13]
>
> *The local authority had found Ms Carr intentionally homeless after she had given up her accommodation with her sister when her sister's (non-resident) boyfriend attacked and injured her (non-resident) boyfriend. The authority said that the issue of her boyfriend was irrelevant to the issue of intentionality, since he was not a person who normally resided with her. The court held that the applicant's boyfriend, by whom she was pregnant, was someone with whom she might reasonably be expected to live, even though she had never lived with him. The local authority had failed to consider intentionality in conjunction with whether the boyfriend was someone who could reasonably be expected to reside with her. As a result it had come to the wrong decision.*

15.4 Homeless in a refuge

Women who seek shelter in a refuge are sometimes only considered for allocations under Part 6 of the Housing Act 1996 and not treated as homeless. This was stated to be a misinterpretation of the law in the well-known case of *R v Ealing LBC ex parte Sidhu*,[14] where it was clearly held that a woman remains homeless whilst she is in a refuge.

In reaching this decision in the case of Sidhu, it was said:

> 'It was important that refuges be seen as temporary crisis accommodation and that women living in refuges were still homeless... If... not... it would be necessary for voluntary organisations to issue immediate 28 days' notice when women came in, so that they would be under threat of homelessness. This would be totally undesirable and would simply add stress to stress. If (it)... took women out of the 'homeless' category, then the Act was being watered down, and its protections would be removed from a whole class of persons that it was set up to help, and for whom it was extremely important.'

12. Kensington and Chelsea RBC and Westminster CC Referee's determination 2.1.89.

13. R v Peterborough ex parte Carr (1990) 22 HLR 206 CA.
14. R v Ealing LBC ex parte Sidhu (1982) 2 HLR 45 QBD.

15.5 Violence or threats of violence

The definition of homelessness caused by violence was widened by the 1996 Act and further widened by the Homelessness Act 2002, and it is important that there is no confusion amongst advisers and local authorities about its scope (see 14.6). There is no requirement that the violence should be from within the home. The Act now also includes both domestic violence from an 'associated person' and violence from other persons. This includes non-associated persons such as couples, whether heterosexual or lesbian or gay, who have never lived together.

Violence can be against the applicant, a member of the applicant's household, or anyone who might reasonably be expected to live with the applicant.

Situations of violence from non-associated persons are now in line with the provisions on domestic violence. This means that if someone is afraid an ex-partner's friends might be a violent threat to her/him, the authority must now ask whether it is *probable*, regardless of the access to legal remedies, that continued occupation would lead to violence, or threats of violence which are likely to be carried out.

The Code of Guidance states that authorities may wish to inform applicants of their legal options, but should recognise that injunctions will not always be effective in deterring perpetrators from carrying out further violence, and that applicants should not automatically be expected to return home on the strength of an injunction. The Code also suggests that housing authorities should consider improving the security of the applicant's home if s/he wishes to stay there. The authority should also consider the scope for evicting the perpetrator to allow the applicant to remain in the home.

para 6.21 COG02

> *'However, where there would be a probability of violence if the applicant continued to occupy his or her present accommodation, the housing authority must treat the applicant as homeless, and should not expect him or her to return to the accommodation.'*

para 8.26 COG02

The Code says that authorities should only take into account the probability of violence, and not actions which the applicant could take (such as injunctions), but which s/he does not intend to take. This is based on the clarification of the legislation that has been provided by case law. This is explained in the next section.

15.6 Whether there is a probability of violence

s177(1) HA96

It is not reasonable to continue to occupy accommodation if it is probable that this will lead to domestic violence or other violence directed against the applicant, or someone who lives with or might reasonably be expected to live with the applicant.

The court has held that the words probable and likely carry separate and different meanings:

• 'Probable' means 'more likely than not'

• 'Likely' includes a real or serious possibility.[15]

s177(1) HA96

Provided that it is *probable* that continued occupation will lead to a further *risk of violence*, it will not be reasonable for the applicant to remain in the accommodation. A random act of violence near the home, which was unlikely to be repeated, might not therefore mean that the applicant would qualify under this section, although if s/he was traumatised by remaining in the area, eg, where a rape had occurred, it might be deemed that it was not reasonable for her/him to continue to occupy under the general test.

s175(3) HA96

The 'Probability Test'

The test in relation to domestic or other violence is different from the general test of reasonableness found in s.175 of the Housing Act 1996. Many authorities have in the past confused this part of the definition on homelessness with section 175, which relates to whether it is reasonable to continue to occupy in general terms. Section 177 lays down that it is not a question of whether it is reasonable or not to remain when there is violence. *The only test in violence cases is that of 'probability' – whether further occupation will probably lead to violence or threats of violence which are likely to be carried out, and the authority 'cannot take other matters into account.'*[16]

The important case of *Bond v Leicester CC*[17] has clarified that where domestic violence is concerned, (and therefore under the amended legislation, any violence) it is not open to the authority to apply s.177(2), which allows the housing authority to have regard to general circumstances, such as overcrowding in the district, or other measures the applicant might take, such as using legal remedies to abate nuisance or other problems, when deciding whether it is reasonable to occupy. Those considerations are only relevant where the authority is deciding in general terms whether it is reasonable for a person to remain or not. Although this was a case about intentional homelessness, similar arguments apply in relation to assessments of whether the applicant is homeless or not.

s175 HA96

> #### Bond v Leicester CC[18]
>
> *In Bond, the County Court, in the first instance, had held that it would have been reasonable for Ms Bond to return to her former accommodation by taking legal proceedings to evict her violent*

15. Bond v Leicester CC [2001] EWCA Civ 1544, [2002] HLR 6 CA.

16. Bond v Leicester CC see 19.
17. Bond v Leicester CC ibid.
18. Bond v Leicester CC ibid.

partner. The Court of Appeal overturned this decision. It is not a question of whether it is reasonable or not to remain when there is violence, but simply whether it is probable that further occupation will lead to violence or threats of violence that are likely to be carried out.

The judge also gave useful clarification to the meaning of 'threats which are likely to be carried out.'

'The definition of violence in section 177(1) of the 1996 Act included 'threats of violence, which are likely to be carried out.' 'Likely' was different from 'probable', which meant 'more likely than not.' 'Likely' included a real or serious possibility. Such behaviour (as the applicant's partner had shown) might readily be held to constitute a threat of further violence which was likely to be carried out by a person who had not only done it before but shown a readiness to use it as a response to exclusion from home.'

In exploring the Act and the Code of Guidance, the judge said that 'the mere availability of such remedies (ie, injunctions) does not answer the probability question.'

The judge also said that once violence had begun, it was likely to be repeated, often with escalating severity. It induced a sense of shame and of powerlessness in the victims, who often blamed themselves and found it impossible to escape. There were various legal and practical remedies available, but it was by no means easy for many victims to invoke them. However hard the family courts tried, they were often ineffective. Escape might well be the only practical answer. The victim was the one who knew the perpetrator best and was likely to be best able to judge this. It was not, after all, a decision to be taken lightly by a young mother of two young children.

When the applicant repeatedly has contact with a violent partner, it is tempting for the local authority to say that it cannot therefore be unreasonable for her/him to continue to occupy the dwelling s/he is in, or, if s/he leaves that s/he has made her/himself intentionally homeless. Lady Justice Hale held otherwise:

'Neither the continuation of a woman with two young children to have contact with her violent male partner, nor her failure to take criminal or civil proceedings against him, was relevant to the decision of the local housing authority whether to refuse housing under s193 of the Housing Act 1996, on the ground of intentional homelessness. Where there was a 'probability'

continued overleaf

> *of domestic violence within the meaning of section 171(1) of the Housing Act 1996, as opposed to actual violence from the partner, the applicant's departure from her former home did not make her intentionally homeless.'*
>
> *The judge went on to stress that until recently the courts have done their utmost to insist that the parent with the children allows the other parent contact with them, despite risk of violence. It would therefore be wrong to penalise a mother for resuming contact with the father.*

15.7 No requirement for proof of violence

Those who have experienced domestic violence are frequently required by local authorities to somehow prove that the violence has occurred. From the wording of section 177 of the Act (see 14.6 and 15.6 above), and from the Code of Guidance, it is clear that it is not even necessary for violence to have taken place, but there must be a *probability* of violence or threats which are likely to be carried out.

para 6.18 HCOG02

It is sometimes implied that violence poses a special problem for an authority in deciding whether what the applicant tells them is true. However, as with many other types of statements by applicants about their past lives, a local authority simply cannot always know for sure whether the statement is true or not. Case law has established that local authorities are not required to make CID-type enquiries and establish facts 'beyond reasonable doubt.'[19] The Code confirms this stating that authorities need to make inquiries but *'should not necessarily expect evidence of violence as such from the applicant. And an assessment of the likelihood of a threat of violence being carried out should not be based solely on whether there has been actual violence in the past.'* The Code also reminds authorities that inquiries where violence is alleged need careful handling, and it is essential that inquiries do not provoke further violence.

para 6.18 HCOG02

> *'It is not advisable for the housing authority to approach the alleged perpetrator, since this could generate further violence, and may delay the assessment. Housing authorities may, however, wish to seek information from friends and relatives of the applicant, social services and the police, as appropriate.'*

para 3.14 HCOG02

In addition, the Code of Guidance emphasises that *'the obligation to make enquiries... rests with the housing authority, and it is not for applicants to 'prove their case'... inquiries... should be carried*

19. Lally v RB Kensington and Chelsea (1980) Times 26 March; Lazare v Slough DC (1981) LAG Bulletin 66.

out as quickly as possible. Inquiries must be sufficiently thorough
to establish the facts, and applicants should always be given the
para 3.14 HCOG02 *opportunity to explain their circumstances fully.'* Where it is not
possible to be sure of the truth, the benefit of the doubt should be
given to the applicant.[20]

The Act states that if an applicant 'knowingly or recklessly' makes a
false statement with the intention of making the authority believe
that s/he is homeless, then s/he commits a criminal offence and may
s214 HA96 be fined. If the authority has no reason to believe there has been such
a wilful false statement, then the applicant's statement should be
accepted.

15.8 Whether it is reasonable to continue to occupy accommodation when there is no violence

The question of whether it is reasonable to continue to occupy is of
the utmost importance in relationship breakdown situations, since the
whole of the case may hinge upon whether it is reasonable to expect
someone to remain in the matrimonial/family home, given the state
of the relationship.

In deciding whether it is reasonable for someone to continue to occupy
a home, a local authority must consider a variety of factors, and should
not just turn away applicants where there is no actual physical violence
or threats.

A person must not be treated as having accommodation unless it is
accommodation which it is reasonable for her/him to continue to
occupy. This is laid down by section 175(3) of the Act. The Act also
says that in deciding whether it is reasonable for someone to remain,
the authority can have regard to the general housing circumstances in
the area, eg, the relative levels of fitness or overcrowding in the area,
s177(2) HA96 and the pressure or demand for housing in the area.

Cases where there is no violence

It is clear from case law that even where there is no actual physical
violence or threats, it can still be unreasonable for someone to remain
in accommodation. In one case the Court of Appeal found that simply
watching and remaining around someone's home so as to create a siege
environment was quite sufficient to render life intolerable, even though
nothing took place in the premises themselves.[21] The Home Office, police,
Department of Health and many other organisations involved with
dealing with domestic violence, now acknowledge the complexity of
domestic violence and the fact that it does not always need to include

20. R v Thurrock BC ex parte Williams (1981) 1 HLR 128 QBD.

21. Hammell v Kensington and Chelsea RBC (1988) 20 HLR 666 CA; (1989) 1 All ER 1202.

obvious physical violence.[22] See also Chapter 13 for a full discussion on domestic violence, including mental cruelty.

In addition, the stress and strain of living with someone after a relationship has broken down may in certain cases mean that it could be unreasonable for someone to continue to occupy the home.

Affordability

Where one partner has left the home, the other may also find the home too expensive to maintain. Housing authorities must consider whether accommodation is affordable when deciding whether it is reasonable for someone to remain in the home.[23] The Secretary of State in the Code of Guidance recommends that *'housing authorities regard accommodation as not being affordable if the applicant would be left with a residual income which would be significantly less than the level of Income Support or income-based Jobseeker's Allowance that is applicable to the applicant, or would be applicable if he or she was entitled to claim such benefit'*. Case law has also supported this approach.[24]

para 6.15 HCOG02

para 12.8 HCOG02

15.9 Reasonable to continue to occupy accommodation – physical conditions

Those whose relationships have broken down frequently find themselves in inadequate or substandard accommodation. Housing standards and the degree of overcrowding are something that the courts have stated must be considered in relation to whether it is reasonable to occupy somewhere. Factors the court should consider are overcrowding (whether statutory or non-statutory), medical need and other related matters.[25]

> ### R v Medina ex parte Dee[26]
>
> *In this case the judge held that the council was wrong to consider that a woman was not homeless after it had declared her property was fit for human habitation. The applicant lived in a prefabricated beach bungalow and refused to move back in after the birth of her baby, having been advised by her GP and health visitor that it was not suitable for a new born child. The judge held that the council should have considered the physical condition of the property and whether it was suitable for Ms Dee and her baby. Although it was found to be fit for human habitation, it was not reasonable for a new mother to override the decisions of medical advisers and return to the property.*

22. 'Multi-Agency Guidance for Addressing Domestic Violence' available free from the Home Office at www.homeoffice.gov.uk/violenceagainstwomen; 'Domestic Violence: A Resource Manual for Health Care Professionals' Department of Health, 2000. Available at www.doh.gov.uk/domestic.htm. See also Home Office Circular HOC 19/2000 'Domestic Violence: Revised Circular to the Police' and the Home Office document 'Government Policy Around Domestic Violence'. All available at www.homeoffice.gov.uk.
23. Homelessness (Suitability of Accommodation) Order 1996 (SI 1996 No.3204).
24. R v Hillingdon LBC ex parte Tinn (1988) 20 HLR 305 QBD.
25. R v Westminster CC ex parte Alouat (1989) 21 HLR 477 QBD.
26. R v Medina ex parte Dee (1992) 24 HLR 562 QBD.

15.10 Being asked to leave by partner

Many cohabitants have no right to remain in their partner's homes except with their partner's permission. When they are asked to leave, councils frequently state that they must seek legal remedies to remain as long as possible. However, in most cases they are excluded occupiers and have no statutory right to protection from eviction without a court order (see 6.11).

Advisers should check the cohabitant's status and rights to occupy (see 5.3 and following sections and 8.4). If s/he is an excluded licensee, once permission to remain and reasonable notice has expired, the cohabitant is a trespasser with no legal right to remain, and therefore statutorily homeless within the definition of the Act. Case law has established in relation to intentional homelessness that if someone is asked to leave and they have no legal right to remain, it cannot be reasonable to expect them to remain in contravention of the law.[27] The same cases can be used to apply to the definition of homelessness and reasonableness to remain.

Although non-owner/tenant cohabitants may have the right to apply for an occupation order granting them short-term rights to occupy (see Chapter 13, Section C), it is important that local authorities do not treat this as an automatic right. Where there is no risk of significant harm greater to one party than the other, the court has discretion in deciding whether to make an order. Case law has shown[28] that even the acknowledged fact of severe violence is not in itself always enough to guarantee the granting of an occupation order (see 13.28). In 'non-violent' relationship breakdown cases, it is therefore unlikely that the courts will readily exclude an owner or tenant, even if they are prepared to grant an order giving a right to the non-owner/tenant to remain in occupation. Local authorities must therefore still ask whether, if a cohabitant is able to obtain an occupation order, it is reasonable to expect her/him to continue to occupy and share a home where s/he has no legal interest and has been asked to leave by her/his ex-partner. In addition, occupation orders are not long-term solutions, and can only last for a maximum of twelve months for non-owner/non-tenant cohabitants.

15.11 Duty to secure temporary accommodation pending enquiries into reasonableness to occupy

If a person whose relationship has broken down approaches a local authority for help as homeless, on the basis that the situation is so bad that it is not reasonable to remain, then there is reason to believe that the person may be homeless. If s/he may also be in priority need, then the

27. R v Hammersmith and Fulham LBC ex parte O'Sullivan (1991) EGCS 110 QBD; R v. Portsmouth CC ex parte Knight (1984) 10 HLR 115 QBD; R v. Surrey Heath BC ex parte Li (1984) 16 HLR 79 QBD.   28. B v B (1999) 31 HLR 1059.

s188 HA96   authority must offer interim accommodation. Case law has indicated that the council is under a duty to provide interim accommodation in such cases, no matter how onerous it might seem.[29] This means that local authorities should secure accommodation whilst they make inquiries into the situation and assess what duty if any is owed to the applicant.

15.12   No need for formal homelessness application

A person may not be aware that s/he can apply as homeless, for example, where s/he has accommodation but it is not reasonable for her/him to continue to occupy. S/he may as a result apply for housing under the allocation scheme. It has been held that there is no need for the would-be applicant to mention homelessness. The Act says that where someone applies for accommodation or help with obtaining accommodation, and the local authority has reason to believe s/he may be homeless or threatened with homelessness, the authority is

s184 HA96   under a duty to make inquiries. If someone approaches the authority for help and there is reason to think that it might not be reasonable for someone to continue to occupy, the burden is on the authority to investigate the possible homelessness, not for the applicant to request specifically to be considered as homeless. In the case of *R v Islington LBC ex parte B* (see box), the court held that the council was obliged to make enquiries, unless the applicant, having been informed of her rights, specifically requested otherwise.

R v Islington LBC ex parte B[30]

The applicant, a secure tenant of 20 years, was a prime prosecution witness in a murder trial, and received threats and was subject to intimidation and abuse from neighbours associated with the defendant. She applied to the council for alternative accommodation. The council agreed she should be moved, but treated it as a management transfer. She applied for judicial review because of failure to treat her application as one under homelessness provisions.

The judge stated that the council had misconstrued its responsibilities. Once the conditions sufficient to trigger a duty to inquire were satisfied (as in this case, it was plainly not reasonable to expect her to continue to occupy her accommodation), the council was bound to proceed under homelessness legislation, unless the tenant expressly indicated that s/he did not want such consideration. However, her application for damages failed, because the judge held that on these facts there was no prejudice to the applicant by the manner in which she was treated.

---

29. R v LB Haringey ex parte Ulger (1992) December Legal Action QBD. Leave to take the case was granted but the full case was not heard, as the local authority then provided accommodation. The implication was that there was clearly a duty.

30. R v Islington LBC ex parte B (1998) 30 HLR 706 QBD.

In another case, where a council tenant asked for urgent rehousing after suffering serious domestic violence, and the authority failed to treat her case as a homelessness application, the Ombudsman made a finding of maladministration against the London Borough of Tower Hamlets.[31]

R v Northavon DC ex parte Palmer[32]

Mrs Palmer applied for housing when the family were squatting in a council property. They were told that the waiting list was very long. The local authority denied that it had any duty to enquire into homelessness because:

- *the applicants had not applied as 'homeless' and/or*
- *there was no material in the application which should have satisfied it that the applicants were homeless.*

The court subsequently held that at the point when the applicants applied for housing, the local authority should have concluded that:

- *the application for housing was a homelessness application*
- *there was reason to believe they might be homeless, and*
- *the authority was therefore under a duty to make enquiries into homelessness.*

B   Eligibility for assistance

Eligibility for assistance is concerned with immigration status (see 14.7 – 14.10). When investigating into eligibility for assistance, it is essential that local authorities do not discriminate on the basis of racial or ethnic origin or language.

15.13 Investigations into eligibility

Under section 71 of the Race Relations Act 1976, local authorities are under a duty to:

> *'make appropriate arrangements with a view to securing that their various functions are carried out with due regard to the need:*
>
> *a) to eliminate unlawful racial discrimination, and*
>
> *b) to promote equality of opportunity and good relations between people of different racial groups.'*

---

31. London Borough of Tower Hamlets (Investigation 91/A/2474) (1992) 18 November.

32. R v. Northavon DC ex parte Palmer (1994) 26 HLR 572 QBD.

In order to avoid breaching this duty, the authority must ensure that the same questions are asked of every applicant, regardless of race, nationality or ethnic or national origins.

Liaison with the Immigration and Nationality Department

s187 HA96 Under the Housing Act 1996, the Immigration and Nationality Department (IND) have a duty to assist authorities in making decisions about eligibility, by providing information about the applicant's status. It is good practice to inform applicants about the possibility of this when they make their application.

Accommodation during inquiries

s188 HA96 It is clear from the Housing Act 1996 that whilst investigations are made into eligibility, interim accommodation must be provided where there is also apparent homelessness and priority need. As housing officers are unlikely to be experts in immigration law, it is likely that in most cases the authority will have to confirm its findings with the IND, and so accommodation must be provided until status is confirmed.

15.14 Limited one-year stay for spouses

In relationship breakdown cases, it is important to check whether the woman/man seeking advice entered the UK as a spouse, ie, to join a married partner already settled here, and whether this was within the last year. Such people will normally be subject to immigration control, with the condition that they must not have recourse to public funds. This means that they will not be eligible for homelessness assistance in their own right.

A special concession may apply if the person concerned is experiencing domestic violence; this is explained in 13.5. Expert immigration advice will be necessary to assist with an application for such a concession.

This concession will not necessarily help those ineligible people whose relationships have broken down for reasons other than outright physical violence, or who have been too afraid to take action against the perpetrator. They will have to try to find some other way of fitting into the immigration rules, such as arguing strong compassionate grounds, but this would again require expert advice from experienced immigration advisers.

15.15 Advice to non-eligible groups

Even where a person is not eligible for assistance s/he is entitled to advice and information about homelessness and the prevention of
s179 HA96 homelessness. Local authorities and advisers should ensure that applicants are aware of the possibility of applying under the

homelessness legislation in the future, should their immigration status change (eg, if the habitual residence test is likely to be satisfied in the future, a sponsored applicant will have been in the country for more than five years or a favourable decision is made on an asylum case).

If the applicant has children, s/he may request assistance from social services under s.17 of the Children Act 1989 (see below, and Ch 9 for details of case law developments and limitations on the help that may be provided). People with special needs, such as people who are elderly, disabled, or who are physically or mentally ill, may also be able to obtain assistance from social services under the National Assistance Act 1948 (see 14.41 – 14.44). However, there appears to be no source of help for those without children or any special need, since the National Assistance Act 1948 cannot be used on the grounds of destitution alone by non-eligible asylum-seekers and people subject to immigration control (see below).

Help for those who have children

The amended Housing Act 1996 imposes a duty on housing authorities to refer families with children under 18 who are potentially ineligible to social services departments, after seeking the household's consent. Once the social services authority is aware of the facts, if it requests the housing authority to provide them with advice and assistance in carrying out their functions under Part III of the Children Act 1989, the local authority is under a duty to provide such advice and assistance as is reasonable in the circumstances. This does not prejudice the pre-existing provisions on co-operation under s.27 of the Children Act 1989 (see 9.10).

Help for the destitute

Under the provisions of the Immigration and Asylum Act 1999, which came into force on 3rd April 2000, most people subject to immigration control are now excluded from benefits, and also from obtaining assistance under the National Assistance Act 1948, if their need for care and attention has arisen solely:

a) because s/he is destitute, or

b) because of the physical effects of being destitute.

People in this position should be referred for specialist immigration and/or legal advice. See also 14.10 for details of the position for asylum-seekers who make late claims for asylum and may be refused support from NASS.

s55 NIAA02

However, if s/he has special needs, social services will still be under a responsibility to provide assistance. In one case (see R (*Khan*) v *Oxfordshire CC* in box), where the local authority said it had no duty to an ineligible woman who was fleeing domestic violence, since her situation was one of just destitution, and not other special needs, the court held that domestic violence *may* give rise to a community care need which is other than destitution.

Social Services are responsible for asylum seekers with special needs

R (Westminster CC) v National Asylum Support Service[33]

The Court of Appeal confirmed that local authorities remained liable to provide care services to destitute asylum-seekers whose need for care and attention arose from reasons other than simply their status as asylum-seekers. Accordingly, disabled people, those who are vulnerable, and elderly people were still to be provided with support by local authorities.

Illegality should not lead to the denial of support in the last resort

R v Wandsworth LBC ex parte O; Bhikha v Leicester City Council[34]

Even though the applicants were in the country unlawfully, the Court of Appeal held that s.21 NAA offered the very last possibility of relief, and not even illegality should lead to the denial of support. It is not sufficient to be destitute, however, the applicant must be in need of care and attention because s/he is sick or disabled, or because of age.

Domestic violence could amount to a care need under NAA 1948

R (Khan) v Oxfordshire CC[35]

The applicant's marriage broke down as a result of domestic violence. She was not eligible for assistance because of her immigration status.

After assessing her needs under s. 47 NHSCCA 1990, the authority concluded that she did not have any physical or mental problems, and therefore did not qualify for community care services, including housing under s.21 NAA 48. If she feared violence, she could call the police or obtain an injunction. Any other need was from destitution, which was debarred under the NAA.

The court allowed her claim for judicial review. The judge said that authorities had to be particularly astute to the potential vulnerability of battered women. The authority had failed to

---

33. R (Westminster CC) v National Asylum Support Service [2001] EWCA 4 CLLR 143.

34. R v Wandsworth LBC ex parte O; Bhikha v Leicester City Council (2000) LWLR 1539 CA.

35. R (Khan) v Oxfordshire CC [2002] All ER 901 CA.

> *approach the question correctly, and had not asked whether the need would arise solely from destitution rather than the experience of domestic violence. However, payment could not be made under s.2 LGA 2000.*

Eligible and ineligible members of the household

In deciding whether an applicant is homeless or threatened with homelessness, or in priority need, a non-eligible person must be disregarded, eg, a non-eligible child cannot confer priority need on its parents.

However, if the applicant is accepted as eligible, accommodation must also be provided for non-eligible members of the household if they normally reside with the applicant, or it is reasonable to expect them to reside with her/him.

Equally, although a non-eligible member of a family may not qualify on the housing register in his/her own right, his/her needs must be taken into account when assessing the application.

> **R (Kimvono) v Tower Hamlets LBC (2000) 33 HLR 889 QBD**[36]
>
> *The applicant was on the housing register. The scheme provided that for a family of K's size, 3-bed accommodation would be offered. One of his children was waiting for indefinite leave to remain. The council decided that she was not a qualifying person (s.161), and therefore they would only offer 2-bed accommodation.*
>
> *The court quashed the decision. Section 161 (of the unamended HA96) was only concerned with whether the applicant, and not a member of his household, was a qualifying person. Furthermore, the council could not ignore the child's needs, as an allocation scheme required preference to be given to families with children.*

C   Priority need

A definition of priority need is given at 14.11. Where there is reason to believe a person may be in priority need, there is a duty to provide interim accommodation pending further inquiries (see 14.16).

15.16 Reasons for a decision about priority need

Standards of investigation into the possible priority of those without children are not always what they should be. The decision letter should state clearly what factors have been considered.

---

36. R (Kimvono) v Tower Hamlets LBC (2000) 33 HLR 889 QBD.

In one case,[37] it was held that the mere recital of the four possible routes to priority need was a failure to comply with the duty to give proper reasons for a decision.

15.17 Dependent children – no need for custody/residence orders

Before the Children Act 1989 came into force in October 1991, it was not uncommon for local authorities to insist on custody orders as proof that a child was dependent upon a parent.

Under the Children Act, the law changed, and instead of routinely making custody orders upon divorce, the court must not now make a residence order, unless it can be shown to be positively in the interests of the welfare of the child. This means that if the parents come to an agreement, the court will not normally intervene (see 9.2). Local authorities should not, therefore, insist upon an order where the child is living with a parent. This was made clear in the early 1980s in the *Sidhu* case (see box), even before the Children Act 1989 came into force. This case remains good law, and deserves to be given more frequent attention, as it is an important precedent in the context of relationship breakdown.

R v Ealing LBC ex parte Sidhu[38]

Mrs Sidhu obtained interim custody, care and control of her two children whilst in a women's refuge. The council said they could not make a decision on priority need until she was legally separated and had full custody of the children:

'Her husband could make a counter claim and obtain custody himself, at which point Mrs Sidhu would no longer have any priority under the Act.'

They argued that not only must an authority be satisfied that there are dependent children living with the applicant, but also that there is no suggestion that that situation might not continue in the future. The judge, however, could not see a single word in the Act which justified that interpretation. Inquiries should be made with 'due diligence and speed.'

'Once they knew that the applicant and her children, having been forced by violence to leave, had been admitted into refuge accommodation, they ought to have been satisfied ... that the applicant was homeless.'

Then, knowing that she had two children living with her, they should have been satisfied that she had a priority need. The

---

37. R v Islington LBC ex parte Trail (1993)
Times 27th May QBD.   38. R v Ealing LBC ex parte Sidhu, (1982) 2 HLR 45.

> judge was asked to rule on whether a custody order was ever an appropriate test to apply before a separated spouse could be accepted as homeless and in priority need.
>
> 'Not only is there not the faintest suggestion that a final custody order is anything which the local authority are entitled to take into account under the Act ... but quite apart from that, it seems to me that it is a wholly inappropriate test.'
>
> He pointed out that custody frequently has nothing to do with dependence and residence. Quite often, one partner was given custody, while the other had care and control. If the latter had the children living with her/him and dependent upon her/him, s/he would come within the Act. Indeed, a local authority could have care and control under a care order, but were entitled to allow the children to live with a parent who, in that case, would also fall within the Act.

More recently, the courts clarified that if someone has been accepted as in priority need but subsequently loses the right to have her/his child live with her/him, the decision cannot be reversed (see case of *Sadiq* below).

> **R v Brent LBC ex parte Sadiq**[39]
>
> The council accepted that the applicant was in priority need on the basis that he had a dependent child, but did not secure accommodation for him and his son. A few weeks later, in family proceedings, the child was ordered to reside with the mother. The council decided that the change in circumstances meant that the housing duty was no longer owed. It informed him it was unable to provide further assistance, because he no longer had a priority need.
>
> The court quashed the decision. s.193 set out a complete code as to when and how the duty might end prematurely. It did not include 'loss' of priority need.

15.18 Residence of child split between parents

Shared residence, where a child spends a proportion of her/his time with each parent, is becoming increasingly common. Before the Children Act came into force, joint custody was frowned upon by the courts as being

---

39. R v Brent LBC ex parte Sadiq (2000) 33 HLR 47 QBD.

upsetting for the child. Now, if parents make sharing arrangements, the court will not intervene unless it is necessary for the child's welfare.

Local authorities therefore have the difficult task of deciding whether one or both parents are in priority need.

Case law has established that the key issues are not how long a child spends with a person, but whether:

• the child is dependent on the person, and

• the child is residing with rather than visiting the person.

The Code of Guidance states that, for there to be deemed to be residence, the child must be actually residing with the applicant with some degree of permanence or regularity, (or there must be a reasonable expectation of this happening), rather than a temporary arrangement where the children are merely staying with the applicant for a limited period. The Code also makes the following points:

para 8.6 HCOG02

• The Code states that residence does not have to be full-time, and can be divided between parents

• If the child is not currently residing with the applicant, it is open to the authority to decide whether it is reasonable for her/him to do so, regardless of any agreement made between the parents, or even a joint residence order[40]

para 8.10 HCOG02

• However, the Code also reminds housing authorities that where parents separate, it will often be in the best interests of the child to maintain a relationship with both parents

para 8.10 HCOG02

• Each case must be considered individually.

In some cases, a local authority may try to argue that if a parent has not normally had the care of children, then it is not reasonable for her/him to do so once homelessness occurs. It is not open to the authority to decide this if the children are actually with the parent at the time of the homelessness application, ie, they cannot undermine the status quo.[41]

In *R v Oxford CC ex parte Doyle*,[42] despite the fact that Mr Doyle had a joint residence order stating that the children should stay with each parent for half the week, the authority was entitled to decide the arrangement would be unworkable and it was not reasonable for them to reside with him. In contrast, in another case where the applicant's five children spent some time of each week with the applicant, the court held the authority could not argue that the female partner had 'greater residence responsibility' – the test was whether the dependent children actually resided with the applicant, and if they did, then he would be in priority need.[43]

40. R v Oxford CC ex parte Doyle (1998) 30 IILR 506 QDD.
41. Re. Islam (1982) 1 HLR 107 HL (also known as R v Hillingdon LBC ex parte Islam); R v Lambeth LBC ex parte Bodurin (1992) 24 HLR 647 QBD.
42. R v Oxford CC ex parte Doyle, see 40 above.
43. R v Leeds CC ex parte Collier (1998) 13 LTL 13.02.98 (unreported elsewhere) QBD.

> ### R v Lambeth LBC ex parte Vagliviello[44]
>
> *The court held that where the Act refers to 'dependent children residing with' an applicant, it requires two aspects to be established before priority need is proved:*
>
> *i) the child must be dependent, and*
>
> *ii) the child must be residing.*
>
> *The Act does not say that the child should be:*
>
> *• wholly and exclusively dependent upon the person, nor*
>
> *• wholly and exclusively residing with the person.*
>
> *In this case, the child was with the father three and a half days a week. This had not been formalised in a custody order. The local authority based its decision, that he was not in priority need, upon the fact that:*
>
> *'Your child has to be in your full-time custody and (residing) with you permanently.'*
>
> *The decision was quashed on the basis that the council had applied a test which was both too strict and, in fact, the wrong test. Evidence that all social security claims were in the mother's name did not affect the decision.*

Some local authorities have taken the approach that, unless a child is resident with a parent for at least half the time s/he is not in priority need. This was partly as a result of the *Vagliviello* case (see above), even though the court had quite clearly placed no weight upon the length of time the child lived with the father. The important issue was whether the child was dependent upon the father, and whether he was 'residing' with him, rather than 'visiting' him.

A further case, *R v Kingswood BC ex parte Smith-Morse,*[45] clarified that an authority is not entitled to make a judgement on priority need based upon whether the residence is the child's main residence. The Act states that a person with whom dependent children reside or might reasonably be expected to reside has priority need.

The local authority was not entitled to compare the time the child spent with his father with the so-called 'main' residence with the mother. The judge said:

> *'...to insert the word 'main' as a qualification to 'residence' seems only to confuse what was absolutely clear in the legislation, that the local authority had to find whether the applicant's son resided with his father, the applicant.'*

44. R v Lambeth LBC ex parte Vagliviello (1990) 22 HLR 392 CA.

45. R v Kingswood BC ex parte Smith-Morse (1994) The Times 8 December.

> '*In my judgement, the qualification in fact was not merely unhelpful... but was in fact misapplying the law, because it suggested that what the local authority was doing was making a comparison between the dependent child's pattern of life with his mother... whereas the statute requires that the focus should be on the question of residence of the child with the applicant.*'

In addition, the court held that the local authority has a dual function of deciding not only whether dependent children reside with a person now, but also whether they might reasonably be expected to reside with that person in the future (see 16.26).

15.19　Meaning of dependent child

For an applicant to be in priority need it is necessary that the child is dependent at least in part on the applicant.[46] In a case where a child was on a Youth Training Scheme, the court held that he was not dependent on his parents, since Parliament intended to limit the definition of dependency to financial support and nothing more.[47] This does not necessarily mean that a child is not dependent on someone who is not the recipient of child benefit, since there may be other ways a parent provides for a child's material needs. However an award of child benefit is obviously helpful evidence.

The Court of Appeal has also held that a married 17-year-old could not be both the wife and the 'dependent child' of her husband.[48] However, since the amendments made to the priority need categories by statutory instrument,[49] all 16 and 17-year-olds who are not the responsibility of social services are automatically in priority need in their own right, so the outcome of the above case would now be different – the 17-year-old wife would be in priority need and accommodation would have to be arranged for both her and her husband, as someone who normally lives with her as a member of her family.

15.20　Whether a child is under a parent's care

Where a child is temporarily separated from the parent, the parent should still be considered in priority need, as in the case of *Crawley BC v B*,[50] in which the council, upon an appeal being made to the county court, reversed its decision of non-priority need where the children had been placed with foster carers but the court had ordered that steps be taken to reunite the children with the applicant and her partner.

15.21　Meaning of vulnerability

If there are no dependent children, and the applicant is over 18 and has no history of being in care, it will be necessary to show that s/he is

---

46. R v Westminster CC ex parte Bishop (1996) 29 HLR 546 QBD.
47. R v Kensington and Chelsea RBC ex parte Amarfio (1995) 27 HLR 543 CA.
48. Hackney LBC v Ekinci [2001] EWCA Civ 776 [2002] HLR 2 CA.
49. Para 3, Homelessness (Priority Need for Accommodation)(England) Order 2002 SI 2002 No.2051.
50. Crawley BC v B 22 February (2000) 32 HLR 636 CA.

vulnerable in some way in order to qualify as being in priority need under the Act. This is a difficult area, and it is therefore important to be aware of what the courts have said on this matter.

The definition of vulnerability has been established through case law. A person is vulnerable where s/he is:

> *'less able to fend for (her/him)self so that injury or detriment will result when a less vulnerable man (or woman) will be able to cope without harmful effects.'*[51]

para 8.13 HCOG02

This definition has been adopted in the Code of Guidance. Other cases have also confirmed it.[52]

In assessing vulnerability, it has to be established:

• whether there is vulnerability, and

s189(c) HA96

• whether the vulnerability is attributable to any of the factors set out in the Act, ie, old age, mental illness or handicap, physical disability or other special reason, or the extended English statutory instrument, ie, institutional backgrounds, or fleeing violence or threats of violence.[53] Vulnerability may arise from one of the categories specified in the section, or from a combination of causes.[54]

The court has made clear that vulnerability involves:

• not only the issue of whether applicants can find *and* keep accommodation

• but also whether they are less able to fend for themselves in coping with the state of homelessness generally.[55]

The decision involves considering both aspects, eg, someone suffering from severe asthma or bronchitis might not have any greater difficulty than anyone else in finding and keeping accommodation, but would be likely to come to greater harm if s/he were literally homeless.

The test of vulnerability is therefore basically a comparative test.

In cases of violence where there is no other priority need, it is therefore necessary to show why a person who has experienced violence is 'less able to fend for (her/him)self'.

15.22 Vulnerable as a result of violence

Regulations in Wales and England on priority need have resulted in changes to the categories of people who should be considered in priority need (see 14.11 for details).[56]

51. R v Waveney DC ex parte Bowers (1982) 4 HLR 118.
52. R v Bath CC ex parte Sangermano (1984) 17 HLR 94 QBD; Kelly and Mallon v Monklands DC (1986) SLT 165, Court of Session OH.
53. The Homelessness (Priority need for Accommodation) (England) Order 2002.
54. R v Bath CC ex parte Sangernamo (1984) 17 HLR 94 QBD.
55. R v Camden LBC ex parte Pereira (1998) 30 HLR 317 CA.
56. Homelessness (Priority Need for Accommodation) England Order 2002, SI 2002 No. 2051 and Homeless Persons (Priority Need)(Wales) Order 2001 SI 2001 No. 607 (W30).

The English amendments extend the reasons which may give rise to a finding of vulnerability. People may now be vulnerable as a result of leaving accommodation because of violence or threats of violence from any other person which are likely to be carried out. In Wales a person in the same position is automatically considered to be in priority need and does not also have to pass the 'vulnerability test.'

The Code of Guidance states that in deciding whether someone is vulnerable as a result of leaving because of violence, the local authority may wish to take into account:

para 8.27 HCOG02

- the nature of the violence. The Code indicates that a single significant incident may have been the cause of someone leaving, or it may be the cumulative effect of a number of incidents over a period of time

- the impact and likely effects of the violence on the applicant's physical and mental health and wellbeing

- whether the applicant has any existing support networks, particularly by way of family or friends).

Other arguments that could be used to support that the applicant is vulnerable are suggested below. These are not based on specific case law, but could lend weight to the argument that someone is less able to fend for her/himself without coming to harm than a less vulnerable person:

- The violence, or fear of it, has so disturbed the person that s/he needs additional support in finding accommodation

- S/he may be pursued by the violent person, so that s/he is unable to stay with friends or relatives, as another homeless person might

- Accommodation in the private sector might not be sufficiently secure

- The applicant may have had to give up employment to move, and may have insufficient income to find accommodation. In addition, s/he may not be able to call on referees to help obtain accommodation for fear of her/his whereabouts becoming known

- If s/he has moved to another district, s/he may also be less able to fend for her/himself than the average person, who would have a network of support in the area s/he came from.

The key point is showing how and why the person at risk of violence is in a worse position than another in being able to cope with the state of homelessness in general, and especially in finding and keeping accommodation.[57]

---

57. See 55 above.

> ### Re Susan Wilson[58]
>
> *Ms Wilson applied as homeless in September 1991, having been asked to leave the hostel where she had been staying. She had lived at various addresses between the end of January and September, having been thrown out of her parents' house. In February 1991 she had been subjected to a sexual attack, and in March 1991 she had an ectopic pregnancy. At the time of her application, Ms W was 18 years old. The council found that Ms W was homeless but was not vulnerable, and as such she could not be considered to be in priority need. Ms W sought judicial review of the decision and her application was allowed.*
>
> *The homeless persons officer concerned had applied the wrong test during his enquiries. He had considered whether the applicant would be at 'great risk' without an offer of accommodation from the council. Instead he should have applied a comparative test, and asked whether the applicant was at greater risk of harm and less able to cope with homelessness, than the 'average' homeless person. The comparative test to be applied followed the case of Kelly v Monklands DC.[59] Had the correct test been applied, it would have emerged that the applicant was less able to fend for herself than someone without her specific problems. The judge ordered the council to provide temporary accommodation for the applicant immediately.*

15.23 Making the decision on vulnerability

Some local authorities rely heavily upon medical reports to decide upon vulnerability. This may amount to a breach of administrative law challengeable by judicial review: any suggestion that the decision has been made by a medical officer rather than the housing officers, eg, statements such as 'the community health physician has decided that you are not vulnerable,' would immediately be open to challenge.

In *R v Lambeth LBC ex parte Carroll*,[60] the court stressed that the decision on vulnerability is for the authority to make – it cannot be delegated. They must take into account opinions other than medical opinions, especially those with experience of housing or social welfare.[61]

D   Intentional homelessness

The definition of intentional homelessness is given at 14.12.

When assessing intentional homelessness, the authority should consider the following points:

s191 HA96

58. Re. Susan Wilson (1992) Court of Session 28 February.
59. See 52 above.
60. R v Lambeth LBC ex parte Carroll (1987) 20 HLR 142 QBD.
61. See also R v Wycombe DC ex parte Hazeltine (1993) 25 HLR 313 CA; and R v Reigate and Banstead BC ex parte Di Domenico (1987) 20 HLR 153 QBD.

- Was the act which led to homelessness a deliberate act?

- Was the act carried out in good faith and whilst unaware of a relevant matter?

- Did the act relied upon cause the present homelessness?

- Was the accommodation which was lost available for not only the applicant, but also whoever could reasonably be expected to live with her/him?

- Even if a deliberate act caused the loss of accommodation, would it have been reasonable to continue to occupy that accommodation?

In addition, an authority should consider whether the eviction/loss of accommodation was contrived.

15.24 Deliberate acts

When there is violence, a person may often have to leave a tenancy and rent arrears may accrue. Whether this amounts to intentional homelessness depends upon the actual cause of the homelessness: the violence or the arrears.[62]

15.25 Act or omission must have caused the present homelessness

The cause of the homelessness can be difficult to pinpoint. However, if an act or omission which could lead to a finding of intentional homelessness is taken by a couple and subsequently the relationship breaks down, there may be a change of circumstances resulting in a break in the chain of causation of homelessness. The cause of the present homelessness would therefore be the relationship breakdown, and not the previous act.

> ### *R v Basingstoke and Deane DC ex parte Bassett*[63]
>
> *A couple gave up a council tenancy to go to Canada. This did not work out and the family were deported and went to stay with the husband's sister. The marriage broke down and the wife left – it was held that the homelessness was caused by the breakdown of the marriage, not the surrender of the council tenancy.*

15.26 Acts or omissions by other members of the household

The principle of 'acquiescence' – whether a partner is party to conduct which leads to a finding of intentional homelessness – is an extremely important one in the context of relationship breakdown. Each applicant

---

62. R v Newham LBC ex parte Campbell (1993) 26 HLR 183 QBD.

63. R v Basingstoke and Deane DC ex parte Bassett (1983) 10 HLR 125 QBD.

is entitled to be considered separately and if one partner is found to be intentionally homeless, then the other may be able to apply and, if found unintentionally homeless, be housed together with the intentionally homeless partner. A couple do not have to be living separately to be considered in this way.

There have been a number of cases on this point but the first to give a ruling was *R v North Devon DC ex parte Lewis*.[64] An authority is usually entitled to consider a family as a unit; however, in cases where there is a reason to consider that one family member did not have a part in a particular action, the authority must consider the other person's actions separately. This is important, because if the person did not acquiesce to a particular action s/he cannot be declared intentionally homeless because of it. The judge's comments are quoted at some length:

> '*In my view, the fact that the Act requires consideration of the family unit as a whole indicates that it would be perfectly proper in the ordinary case for the housing authority to look at the family as a whole and assume, in the absence of material which indicates to the contrary, where the conduct of one member of that family was such that he should be regarded as having become homeless intentionally, that was conduct to which the other members of the family were a party...*
>
> '*If, however, at the end of the day because of material put before the housing authority by the wife, the housing authority are not satisfied that she was a party to the decision, they would have to regard her as not having become homeless intentionally. In argument the housing authority drew my attention to the difficulties which could arise in cases where the husband spent the rent on drink. If the wife acquiesced to his doing this then it seems to me it would be proper to regard her, as well as him, as having become homeless intentionally. If, on the other hand, she had done what she could to prevent the husband from spending his money on drink instead of rent then she had not failed to do anything (the likely result of which would be that she would be forced to leave the accommodation) and it would not be right to regard her as having become homeless intentionally.*'

Cases where partners have been found not to be intentionally homeless include:

- the wife of an alcoholic who spent the rent money on alcohol[65]

- the husband of a wife who had surrendered a tenancy against his wishes, even though they were subsequently reconciled[66]

- a wife who had a genuine belief in what her husband told her[67]

64. R v North Devon DC ex parte Lewis (1981) 1 WLR 328 QBD.
65. R v West Dorset DC ex parte Phillips (1985) 17 HLR 336 QBD.
66. R v Penwith DC ex parte Trevena (1984) 17 HLR 526 QBD.
67. R v Mole Valley DC ex parte Burton (1988) 20 HLR 479 QBD.

- a wife who only discovered arrears after they were so great they could not be cleared[68]

- a wife who was left with the responsibility of rent arrears accrued by her husband.[69]

However, in another case, even though the wife said she had lied to her husband about arrears, which had spanned six years and a separation, it was held the council was entitled to decide that the husband was either '*lying or had been deliberately reckless*' in shutting his eyes to the problem, when their financial difficulties were long-standing. The court felt the council had made adequate enquiries and their decision was not so absurd that it could not stand.[70] In another case, an authority was held to be justified in finding acquiescence where a woman clearly told her husband that she did not want to leave the accommodation, but agreed to go because he said that she must if she wanted their relationship to continue.[71]

15.27 Unaware of a relevant fact/acting in good faith

s191(2) HA96 Even if an act can be considered to be deliberate, the legislation provides a concession: an act should not be deemed deliberate for the purposes of intentional homelessness if the applicant is unaware of a relevant fact *and* has acted in good faith. Sometimes this overlaps with the issue of acquiescence described above. The courts have clarified that in deciding whether someone was unaware of a relevant fact the authority must ask three questions:

- Was the fact relied on a relevant one?

- Was the applicant unaware of the fact?

- Was the applicant, in deciding to give up the former accommodation in ignorance of that fact, acting in good faith?[72]

15.28 Must have ceased to occupy accommodation

A person cannot be held intentionally homeless for refusing an offer of accommodation, since s/he will never have occupied it in the first place, and therefore cannot have 'ceased to occupy it' (but the council may have discharged its duty by making a reasonable offer).[73]

15.29 Accommodation must have been available to the applicant and his or her family

After a relationship breaks down, a person may be forced into very unsuitable accommodation, which may not be big enough for the children as well. If someone gives up such accommodation, such as

68. R v East Northamptonshire DC ex parte Spruce (1988) 20 HLR 508 QBD.
69. R v Thanet DC ex parte Groves (1988) 22 HLR 223 QBD.
70. R v LB Ealing ex parte Salmons (1990) 23 HLR 272 QBD.
71. R v London Borough of Tower Hamlets ex parte Khatun (1993) 27 HLR 344 CA.

72. R v Wandsworth LBC ex parte Rose (1984) 11 HLR 107 QBD; R v Mole Valley DC ex parte Burton, see 67 above. R v Barnet LBC ex parte Rughooputh (1993) 25 HLR 607; R v Westminster CC ex parte Ali and Bibi (1992) 25 HLR 109 QBD.
73. R v Westminster CC ex parte Chambers (1982) 6 HLR 24 QBD.

a parent's home or a very small room, which the rest of her/his family could not live in with her/him, s/he could not be intentionally homeless, since the accommodation was never available to the whole family in the first place.[74]

15.30 It must have been reasonable to continue to occupy that accommodation

The case law at 15.8 onwards addresses the principle of when it is reasonable to continue to occupy accommodation, and can also be applied to intentional homelessness, eg, violence from inside and/or outside the home and/or physical conditions, may make it no longer reasonable to continue to occupy accommodation. Physical or mental abuse or harassment are also relevant factors which a local authority should consider when deciding whether it would have been reasonable for someone to continue to occupy the home. In cases where applicants have left accommodation, alleging sexual harassment from within the home[75] or sexually abusive intimidation from outside the home,[76] findings of intentional homelessness have been quashed by the courts. In both cases, the local authorities had failed to investigate properly and in the latter, the local authority had wrongly held that it was up to the applicant to prove that the incidents had occurred and been reported.

Domestic violence

It is not uncommon for women, in particular, to be told that failure to exercise a legal right will render them intentionally homeless. Section 177(1) of the Housing Act 1996 states that *'it is not reasonable for a person to continue to occupy accommodation if it is probable that this will lead to violence or threats of violence against (her/)him'*. Therefore, if someone leaves accommodation in these circumstances s/he should not be held intentionally homeless. The same arguments about the probability of domestic violence apply as under the test for homelessness, and the court's judgment in the case of *Bond v Leicester CC* held that the authority was wrong to find Mrs Bond intentionally homeless for simply not availing herself of legal protection from the police, or by means of an injunction, (see 15. 6 above). Where there is repeated violence, a person may end up applying more than once to a local authority. The same principles must be followed every time.

para 7.12(d)
HCOG02

In *R v Tynedale DC ex parte McCabe*,[77] a woman rehoused because she was threatened with violence was found by her husband and threatened again. She moved from there to her mother's and applied as homeless. She was told that if she abandoned her tenancy she would be intentionally homeless and she should therefore return. She declined to do so.

---

74. See 41 above.
75. R v Northampton ex parte Clarkson (1992) 24 HLR 529 QBD.
76. R v Barnet LBC ex parte Babalola (1995) 28 HLR 196 QBD.
77. R v Tynedale DC ex parte McCabe (1991) 24 HLR 384 QBD.

The judge held that the council had failed to make sufficient enquiries as to whether it had been reasonable for her to continue to occupy the property;

> 'Her assertion is that she was brutally treated by (her husband); so much so that she was quite unable to tolerate it and therefore to remain in a home which they at one time had shared. The respondents, so it seems to me, have not up to the present investigated the reasons why the applicant left her first home and why of course she is no longer able to return to it. Those inquiries at least need to be undertaken to a far greater extent than they have been, if they have been enquired into at all by the respondents.'

Agreeing to sell the home on relationship breakdown

When a relationship breaks down, there may be considerable pressure to agree to a sale of the matrimonial home for financial reasons. Regulations[78] have been issued which make it clear that authorities must consider affordability when deciding whether it is reasonable to continue to occupy accommodation (see 15.8). The case of *Tinn* (see below) suggests that it is not reasonable to continue to occupy accommodation which is not affordable.

R v Hillingdon LBC ex parte Tinn[79]

The court expressed the view (although obiter) that it would not be reasonable to continue to occupy accommodation which the person could no longer afford without depriving her/himself of the basic necessities of life, eg, food, clothing, heating and transport.

E   Local connection

15.31   Conditions for local connection referral

s198(2) & (2A)HA96

The Act states that it is a condition for referral that a person may not be referred back to a district where s/he or anyone who might reasonably live with her/him will be at risk of violence (see 14.13 for the full definition).

s198(1) HA96

A local authority may only make a referral where the conditions for referral are satisfied. This means that if a person has no connection except with an area where there is a risk of violence, then the authority which s/he approaches must take responsibility for housing under the homelessness legislation.

The onus to confirm there is no risk of violence rests clearly upon the local authority. In the case of *R v Greenwich LBC ex parte Patterson,*[80] the court

---

78. Homelessness (Suitability of Accommodation) Order 1996 SI 1996 No. 3204.
79. R v Hillingdon ex parte Tinn (1988) 20 HLR 305 QBD.
80. R v Greenwich LBC ex parte Patterson (1993) 23 Fam Law 555 CA.

held that the duty of the local authority is to make relevant enquiries before reaching a decision, including establishing whether there is a risk of violence. This could even be done by just asking the applicant. *There is no duty on the applicant to volunteer the information.*

In this case, when the woman applied as homeless she made no reference to a risk of violence from a former boyfriend in Birmingham. Neither was she asked whether there was such a risk. All the other conditions being satisfied, the council made a local connection referral.

The Court of Appeal held that before the council could be satisfied that there was no risk of violence, they had to make enquiries to establish that fact. They had not done so, and the decision was quashed.

Date for establishing local connection

The House of Lords has clarified that the date for establishing a local connection is the date of the local authority's final decision, ie, the decision, or review decision if a review is held. In the same case, it confirmed that periods spent in temporary accommodation should also contribute to periods of residence for local connection purposes.

> **Ealing LBC v Surdonja; Mohammed v LB Hammersmith and Fulham**[81]
>
> *The correct date for determining whether an applicant has a local connection is not the date s/he becomes homeless, nor the date s/he applies to an authority, but rather the date on which the issue is decided by the council. If the applicant seeks a review of that decision, the material date becomes the date the review is determined.*
>
> - *For the purpose of establishing local connection by residence, the council must not ignore the period the applicant has spent in interim accommodation waiting for the initial or review decision*
>
> - *For the purpose of local connection by family association or special circumstances, the court said that they are undefined by Parliament and 'to be judged as a matter of fact and degree in every case. For instance the actual closeness of the family association may count for more than the precise degree of consanguinity'*
>
> - *The scope of the review procedure under s.202 must be wide enough to consider all the up-to-date facts with all others as a whole, to see whether a local connection has been established.*

81. Mohammed v LB Hammersmith and Fulham [2002] HLR7, HL.

National Asylum Support Service accommodation is not accommodation 'of own choice'

The Court of Appeal has held[82] that residence in accommodation in an area in which an asylum-seeker is placed by the National Asylum Support Service (NASS) can never be regarded as residence of that person's own choice. It does not therefore give rise to a local connection with that area. It is therefore open to an ex-asylum-seeker who has become eligible for assistance to either:

- apply to the area in which s/he has been placed, if s/he wishes to remain there, provided there are no grounds for local connection elsewhere, or

- apply to the area of her/his choice.

F   Discharge of duty

The previous chapter lists the duties of a local authority under homelessness legislation, and readers are referred to Section B for details. This section looks at some of the main issues about the way in which local authorities carry out those duties which have given rise to challenge in the courts.

15.32 Speed and nature of enquiries

When relationships break down, it is still the norm for women to remain the carers of children. Their incomes are reduced and they may be unable to work because of child-care commitments. Many become dependent upon the local authority for housing, and therefore are particularly disadvantaged. They may feel they are not in a position to argue about the way they have been treated or the accommodation they have been offered. Two key principles involving the speed and style in which homelessness duties must be discharged have been established by case law:

- Enquiries must be carried out with due speed and diligence and not delayed unnecessarily[83]

- If enquiries result in uncertainty, the benefit of the doubt should be given to the applicant.[84]

para 3.18 HCOG02   In addition, the Code of Guidance suggests that inquiries should be completed and the applicant notified within thirty-three working days. It also states that applicants should be kept informed of the progress of their application and the time scales involved, and given a realistic
para 3.8 HCOG02   expectation of the housing assistance they may be entitled to.

---

82. Al-Ameri and RB Kensington and Chelsea, and Osmani v Harrow LBC [2003] EWCA Civ 235 [2003] 2 All ER 1 CA.

83. R v Ealing LBC ex parte Sidhu (see 38 above).

84. R v Thurrock BC ex parte Williams (see 20 above).

15.33 Adequate inquiries

The depth of inquiries and sensitivity shown by the local authority have been held by the courts to be matters of importance. Failure to inquire into the full reasons why someone left a family home is an example of inadequate inquiries. Equally the court has said that an authority must make 'necessary but not exhaustive inquiries, conducting them with humanity and care.'[85]

15.34 Adequacy of decision letter

When dealing with homelessness cases, it is crucial to insist on a notification letter being issued. This is particularly relevant in relationship breakdown cases, because it is sometimes unclear whether, for example, an authority is treating someone as homeless or as an applicant for an allocation. If there is a decision letter, then obviously it follows that the authority has accepted the person as a homeless applicant. The letter should make clear the areas which the council has considered, and if it is not accepting the applicant, it should give full, clear reasons as to why not.

The courts have held that the notification letter is there to enable an applicant to see the reasons for a decision and to challenge those reasons if they are inadequate.[86]

15.35 Having regard to the Code of Guidance

The Code of Guidance says many things of importance for those who have experienced a relationship breakdown, especially where there has been domestic violence (see 16.22). Unfortunately, it is often felt that because the Code is not law, but guidance, authorities can afford to disregard it. Case law covering the Housing Act 1985 has shown that this is not so, and cases have been quashed because of a failure to have regard to the code of guidance.[87] In addition, much of the Code is in fact derived from case law and therefore must be followed.

15.36 Suitability of offers

When a relationship has broken down, one-parent families are frequently offered accommodation which they feel is unsuitable, perhaps in an area which they consider is rough and which may have an adverse effect on a child's upbringing. Advisers should be alert to decisions which are alleging that the accommodation is suitable in general. Case law has established that accommodation must be suitable for the applicant in question, and take her/his circumstances into account.[88]

Other cases have established that, when deciding whether an offer is suitable, local authorities must also consider:

85. R v Ealing LBC ex parte Chanter, Legal Action December 1992 QBD; and R v Dacorum BC ex parte Brown and Another (1989) 21 HLR 405 QBD, where there had been insufficient garnering of material in a ten minute interview to decide whether an action was wilful or the result of emotional stress.

86. R v Northampton BC ex parte Carpenter (1992) 25 HLR 349 QBD.

87. See for example R v Shrewsbury and Atcham BC ex parte Griffiths (1993) 25 HLR 613 QBD.

88. R v Brent LBC ex parte Omar (1991) 23 HLR 446 .

- racial harassment[89]

- social and medical factors.[90]

In some cases, evidence which affects the suitability of an offer only comes to light after the offer has been made, eg, where the accommodation is near someone who has abused the applicant.[91] The court has held if a local authority alleges that what is being said is untrue, it is a failure in procedural fairness not to give the applicant an opportunity to deal with its concerns. Also, if an authority refuses to consider new information it is acting irrationally.

Challenging decisions on suitability

Decisions on suitability of offers after a person has been accepted as owed the main housing duty may be challenged by way of review and appeal in the county court. The suitability of accommodation which is offered pending inquiries must be challenged by way of judicial review. (see Chapter 14, Section C for detailed information on challenging decisions). An applicant is entitled to accept an offer and yet still

s202(1A) HA96   request a review of the decision. This is generally the safest course of action, as the authority is not obliged to make another offer if the review goes against the applicant. Some authorities may be prepared to keep an offer open pending review.

89. R v Tower Hamlets LBC ex parte Subhan (Abdul)
     (1992) 24 HLR 541 QBD.
90. R v Lewisham LBC ex parte Dolan (1992) 25 HLR   91. R v Hackney LBC ex parte Decordova (1994)
     68 QBD.   27 HLR 108 QBD.

Chapter 16: Good practice

Subjects covered in this chapter include...

The role of the advice worker in relationship breakdown cases

What good advice-giving entails

What needs to be considered when interviewing

Housing Management issues

What guidelines and policies the Government has laid down

What a domestic violence policy should include

What policies housing providers should consider in dealing with allocations and transfers when a relationship breaks down

What issues relate to lesbian and gay partners

How agencies should liaise and develop awareness of resources

Good Practice

Despite the frequency of relationship breakdown, relatively few organisations that deal with housing issues have comprehensive policies covering the wide range of problems to which it can give rise, although an ever-increasing number have developed guidelines or policies relating to domestic violence. This chapter does not aim to provide a model policy for all organisations, but it does attempt to highlight the issues which need to be considered in devising appropriate policies.

16.1 Good practice policies and guidelines

Organisations should develop policies or guidelines for dealing with relationship breakdown cases. Such policies help both the client and the organisation in the following ways:

- They mean a better thought-out response to clients at a time of emotional stress. They ensure consistency of approach, regardless of which staff member a person sees, and regardless of individual staff feelings on the subject. Hopefully, they will result in better resources in terms of advice, information and provision of emergency and long-term accommodation

- They lead to a more efficient use of staff time: staff should be clear about the organisation's policy, so that they do not constantly need to make *ad hoc* decisions. This does not mean that policies should be rigid, but rather that there is a clear framework for responding to problems

- Work will be less stressful for staff if they know that issues have been properly considered, where appropriate at a senior policy-making level, and that there is support for them on a day-to-day basis

- Provision of staff training and necessary resources will also help to relieve stress and pressure on staff.

16.2 Organisations which need good practice guidelines

Good practice is often seen solely as an issue for housing providers, eg, local authorities and registered social landlords, but all organisations who come into contact with people whose relationships have broken down, or who have experienced domestic violence, should have good practice guidelines. What those guidelines will cover may vary depending upon the primary role of the organisation, but some issues are common to all (a list of agencies likely to be involved is given at 1.9).

16.3   Factors which need to be considered in developing policies and good practice

A relationship breakdown policy must give special recognition to the problems surrounding domestic violence, but a 'domestic violence policy' is only part of the picture. Some matters will relate to all relevant agencies and organisations, such as developing advice and interviewing skills, and raising awareness of domestic violence and relationship breakdown issues both inside and outside the organisation.

Additional areas for good practice and policy guidelines may vary, depending upon whether the organisation has a mainly advisory role, whether it is voluntary or statutory, and whether its chief function is as a housing provider:

- Advisory agencies need to be aware of specific problem areas and how advice may prevent further difficulties

- Housing providers need to address the housing management implications of relationship breakdown.

A   The role of the advice worker in relationship breakdown cases

Someone experiencing relationship breakdown is having her/his world turned upside down. Emotional trauma exacerbates practical difficulties. Known landmarks have gone; security and stability are threatened. The person seeking advice may never have encountered the 'system' before: the maze of welfare benefits, Department for Work and Pensions' procedures, advice centres, housing departments, homelessness hostels, refuges, solicitors and social workers. There may be language difficulties, problems arising from immigration status, problems specific to those from ethnic minority cultures, or to those with certain religious beliefs.

In many cases, the person will not have had her/his position fully explained. Use of jargon can be very alienating and may add to a general feeling of disempowerment.

Traditionally, many advice workers see their role as giving information or providing practical assistance. However, there are a number of necessary steps before this can be done. A client experiencing relationship breakdown is likely to be under emotional stress and subject to a whole range of uncertainties. Decisions need to be made. One of the most helpful things an adviser can do is to enable the client to clarify and prioritise the issues facing her/him. Being able to advise on options, demystify procedures and explain the implications of different courses of action are all crucial skills for the advice worker.

This section aims to provide a reminder and useful checklist for the adviser of things to remember and steps to follow when interviewing someone whose relationship has broken down. It does not aim to be a comprehensive guide to interviewing and advice skills: such works are available elsewhere, and it is hoped that readers will find encouragement here to read further and undertake appropriate training.

16.4 The principles of good advice-giving

Before even considering specific advice-giving, it is important that agencies review the underlying principles on which they base their advice-giving. A good advice service should be:

- confidential

- free

- independent

- impartial.

In addition, it should have policies covering:

- equal opportunities

- service delivery

- referrals to other organisations.

16.5 Confidential

All advice-giving organisations should have a statement on their principle of confidentiality. The basics of confidentiality are that unless the client has given her/his consent:

- the content of any dealings or conversations should not be told or passed on to anyone else

- the records of conversations or dealings will also not be passed on.

In an advice-giving situation they may need to go further. The very fact of the client having been in contact with the agency should not be revealed without the client's consent. In cases involving domestic violence, this is of particular significance. Special difficulty in preserving confidentiality may be encountered in connection with the service of court papers and arrangements for child contact (see 13.6).

In some cases advisers may be under a legal obligation to provide certain information to third parties, for example, when summonsed to a court hearing. Advisers need to be aware of this and alert their clients if it is a possibility.

16.6   Free

The service provided to clients should be provided free, regardless of whether the client can afford to pay, or whether a case takes up a lot of staff time. The fact that a service is free does not mean that it is inferior: it indicates that it is available to all and that the agency has no financial interest in the speed at which the case progresses.

Organisations which operate community legal service franchises that give advice under the legal help scheme on housing and welfare benefits are still, in effect, providing the service free to clients. However, the statutory charge applies to legal help family cases, and so the client may have to contribute to the costs of legal help, and they should always be advised of this possibility. Thought needs to be given to the extent to which the service can be offered to clients who do not qualify for legal help.

16.7   Independent

The client needs to feel assured that advice is given in her/his best interest, and not in the best interests of the advice organisation, agency or funders. This can be difficult where the advice-giving agency is within another organisation, such as a local authority, which may have conflicting interests. For example:

• Local authority housing advice centres required to advise on the authority's homelessness service

• Local authority money advice centres where the local authority has the recovery of rent arrears as a priority.

However, it is possible for local authority advice centres to operate with a relative degree of independence, and good authorities will respect this.

16.8   Impartial

An adviser must first of all recognise that the starting point should be one of partiality to the client, ie, a 'client-centred' approach. Impartiality in an advice setting requires the adviser not to be:

• biased

• judgemental, or

• influenced by her/his own or other people's opinions, attitudes or beliefs.

This means advisers should try to remain objective. Even if strong political or religious beliefs are held, this should not influence the way an adviser works with her/his clients. Someone with differing beliefs should not be treated differently or be given less help. Equally, if an adviser does not approve of someone's behaviour, this should not affect the quality of the advice given, for example, where someone is an alcoholic, has been violent or abusive in a relationship, has had an incestuous relationship, or has committed adultery.

Some organisations may decide that they can only give advice to certain groups and, for example, will not give advice to a perpetrator of violence. If this is the case, it should be made clear to the client, and alternative sources of advice could be suggested. Advisers should beware of giving less wide ranging advice in these circumstances without making the position clear to the client and giving her/him the opportunity to go elsewhere.

Difficulties can, of course, arise when someone makes, for example, racist comments. This is why it is important for all organisations to have an active equal opportunities policy. It is not uncommon for organisations to have policies of not giving advice in these cases.

16.9   Equal Opportunities policy

An organisation should have policies on discrimination. It is important to monitor how well the service attracts and deals with enquiries from different groups, and to look at ways of improving the service to those groups who may be under-represented, such as:

• women

• lesbians and gay men

• people with disabilities

• black and ethnic minorities.

16.10   Service delivery

The advice process should always be client centred. It is not what the adviser thinks is best, but what the client wants that is important. Nevertheless, it is also important that advisers do not raise unrealistic expectations of what may be achieved. Advisers should respond in a positive way that will help the client to:

• explore the problem

• explore possible outcomes

• explore the realistically available options

• prioritise

• decide on a course of action.

In doing this, advisers will obviously need to be sensitive to the emotionally fraught situation that clients are in, and may need to help to build their confidence to follow the most appropriate course of action. It may also be appropriate to build up contacts with counselling organisations to help clients deal with these issues.

16.11 Referral

There is a professional and ethical responsibility, both to the adviser and the client, to refer a case to another professional if there is a reason to do so.

Criteria for referral

Advisers should ask themselves:

- *'if I offer this person advice, will the person or anyone else (including the adviser) suffer in any way?'* (eg, the client might miss a possible reconciliation, risk violence, lose her/his home, miss an opportunity to be rehoused, or the adviser might get too involved in emotional problems), and

- *'do I have the skills, training and support necessary to advise this person?'*

Answering these questions may not be easy. The situation might be complicated if clients are in a crisis situation. Advisers should use their personal judgement responsibly and in consultation with their support system.

Referral is clearly indicated in some circumstances:

- When a client has received a divorce petition or court summons – representation will almost always be needed and a client should be advised to seek additional legal support from a solicitor

- Where the advice organisation is already acting for another party involved in the same situation, the new client should be referred elsewhere if to do otherwise would create a conflict of interest. Organisations should have clear policy guidelines to identify and deal with conflicts of interest. It is important, wherever possible, not to breach confidentiality in this situation by letting it be known that the other party has been in contact, although in some cases the second party may understand this implicitly

- There may be other situations in which individual organisations may agree that referral is appropriate, and advisers should know and operate within these guidelines. It is important to be clear about the resources available in the area, and to check on their appropriateness for various clients in terms of accessibility, both financially and physically, and to groups such as lesbians, gay men and ethnic minorities.

THE INTERVIEW

16.12 Obtaining information

The approach and style of interviewing when concerned with a relationship breakdown problem needs particular sensitivity. The client may be embarrassed, or emotionally distressed by the personal nature of her/his problems, which could include rape or sexual abuse, as well as other forms of physical violence. Such experiences are not readily revealed to a stranger, yet they are very relevant when advising on housing options, for example, when deciding whether, under the homeless legislation, it is reasonable to expect the person to continue to occupy the accommodation in which s/he lives (see 15.5 – 15.8).

Same-sex interviewers and staff training

Organisations should endeavour to give women the option of being interviewed by a female adviser. There may be times when a woman is not available; if so, a male interviewer should offer to deal with any emergency issues, whilst making it clear that the client could see a woman at a later stage. It is necessary to be proactive in this respect, since a natural response to a male interviewer may be a wish not to offend by asking to see someone else. It will be necessary to establish a good relationship with the client, assuring her/him of the confidentiality of the interview, so that s/he feels able to be open, yet is assured that s/he is in control of the outcome.

The Homelessness Code of Guidance recommends that same sex interviewers should be available in cases of violence, or threats of violence, and states that *'someone trained in dealing with circumstances of this kind'* should conduct the interview. This advice is appropriate not only for local authorities, but for all organisations which deal with situations involving violence or abuse. Although many organisations now offer same sex interviewers, there may not have been adequate consideration given to the needs of a staff member, usually female, who is having to deal with a disproportionate number of distressing and traumatic cases. It is suggested that special training and support are not merely preferable, but essential.

- All staff should undergo domestic violence awareness training

- Staff should have training on tenancy matters affected by relationship breakdown, eg, assignments, dealing with joint tenancies, and the effects of notice to quit on joint tenancies. If the organisation has relevant policies on such matters, staff should be given training in them and any updates in policy should also be the subject of training. Policies are of no value if the staff do not know they exist or how to implement them

- Specialist training in counselling skills and dealing with situations involving abuse should be provided for those dealing with domestic violence on a regular basis

- Steps should be taken to see that there is a rota system, to relieve staff pressure and spread the interviewing load in cases of domestic violence

- Counselling and support should be available for staff regularly dealing with domestic violence.

Interpreters

The ability to speak a particular language does not necessarily qualify someone to interpret. In domestic violence cases in particular, it is important to ensure that the person translating is not biased in any way, and has the ability to express the full meaning of the client.

Specifically trained interpreters should be available to translate in domestic violence cases. Such people need to be chosen with care. In some ethnic minority cultures, it is considered unacceptable for a woman to complain about her husband, regardless of the way she has been treated. A male translator of the same culture may severely inhibit a woman from explaining her situation.

16.13 Awareness Issues

The need for awareness training on domestic violence and relationship breakdown has been referred to above. This is a crucial issue and far more complex than is commonly realised. Good awareness training will highlight and, if appropriate, challenge individuals' attitudes and assumptions which are often unconsciously held. It should also aim to dispel myths and stereotypes. It is beyond the scope of this book to cover all the matters which should be addressed, and readers should identify appropriate training within their area. Some useful contacts for training are given in the appendices.

Even if a full training programme is not immediately possible, organisations should ensure that certain fundamental questions are addressed.

How should domestic violence be defined?

This is a fundamental question. The definition which the organisation adopts shapes the attitudes and responses of its workers. The following might be considered:

> *'Domestic violence is about the use of power to assert and maintain control over another person.'*

In addition to actual physical violence, domestic violence may include:

- threats of violence

- sexual violence

- bullying

- violence/threats to children

- humiliation/degradation/constant undermining

- deprivation of money and food

- confinement in the home/control over when the other person goes out and who s/he sees

- prevention from working/studying.

The phrase often used to cover these forms of abuse is 'mental cruelty.'

In the case of mental cruelty, help may not have been sought from a doctor, solicitor, social worker or the police. Corroborative evidence may not therefore be available (see 16.21). In the same way, threats of physical violence may not have been reported or may not have been taken seriously. The organisation needs to consider seriously what types of behaviour it is reasonable to expect a human being to put up with.

All too often, responses to domestic violence are not based on a genuine response to the problem, but stem from an awareness of limited resources in terms of available alternative accommodation. This is an unacceptable approach when life, health and sanity may be at risk.

16.14 Environmental factors

Privacy: It is crucial to be able to interview in private. No-one is going to want to reveal intimate, and perhaps distressing details of her/his personal life in public. In addition, thought should be given to waiting areas. How long a person is likely to have to wait and whether they can be seen, for example, from the street, may affect their willingness to seek advice.

Body language: 'Body language' covers all sorts of non-verbal signals or gestures, which we all give out, often unconsciously. It can also include the tone of voice and the manner in which we speak. Full attention and eye contact should be maintained if this is culturally appropriate. Even where the details the client is giving are embarrassing or shocking, the adviser should not let this show.

Atmosphere: Interview and waiting rooms can be very forbidding. A bare room with no windows, an empty table and two chairs can make going for an interview seem like an interrogation. Whilst advisers may not have much control over the premises, it is important to consider ways in which the interviewing space could be made more 'user friendly,' for example, easy chairs with cushions, less harsh lighting, plants and tissues.

More importantly, the attitude and approach to the client is a crucial part of the atmosphere. A friendly and helpful introduction sets the tone for the interview. This atmosphere is built on by the careful use of interviewing skills.

16.15 Interviewing skills

Asking questions

Questioning is essential in establishing the true extent and nature of the problem. In order to allow the client to explain the situation fully and to ensure that all the necessary information is gathered, it is best to use 'open' questions where no particular information is sought, eg,

> 'Would you like to tell me a bit more about what has been happening?'

Follow up later with 'closed' questions to clarify issues, or information. These require yes or no, or a specific response, eg,

> 'So, you have been living with Jim for three years and he owned the house before you moved in?'

Starting with very practical information may make a client feel that s/he cannot explain fully the nature of the problem. Whilst the advice worker is not expected to be a marriage guidance counsellor, the emotional aspects of the situation cannot be entirely separated from the practical needs of the client. For example, severe mental cruelty may render a person homeless within the legal definition of the word, in that someone is homeless if it is not reasonable to expect her/him to continue to occupy the accommodation in which s/he is living (see 14.6).

Beware of hypothetical, or leading questions, which may be loaded with an expected answer:

- 'If you have to stay in the refuge for six months, how do you think you would feel?'

- 'Wouldn't you rather be housed under the allocation scheme and have a choice of where you go, rather than have to go into a homeless hostel?'

Active listening

In interviewing, listening is often referred to as 'active listening.' Active listening involves more than just hearing the gist of what someone is saying to you. It involves giving attention and being seen to give it. Remember:

- wait for the person to finish and don't interrupt her/him
- avoid relating similar incidents which happened to you
- don't give directive advice, eg, 'If I were you...' – the adviser is there to show clients the options and help them to make their own decisions
- don't plan the response whilst the person is talking
- don't try to make everything better
- don't judge
- do give appropriate eye contact
- do give total and clear attention
- do be receptive.

Remember, an adviser is there to listen to the client, not the other way round!

This may involve:

- paying attention to both verbal and non-verbal clues
- evaluating what is being said – is the content consistent with the tone, for example, or does the person really want to say more?
- encouraging the person to speak by giving non-verbal encouragement, and by allowing for some silence, however uncomfortable this may seem.

Some of the important things to concentrate on when listening are set out below. Training in counselling skills will help develop these skills and make interviewing practice more sensitive. This should be considered seriously, even by those advisers who do not see counselling as a central part of their jobs.

Clarifying
This involves checking with the person that you have understood correctly what s/he has said: eg,

> *'Just a moment, I want to check that I have this right, do you mean...? 'Is this the problem as you see it now?'*

Paraphrasing
This is a way of demonstrating to the client that you have heard the content of what s/he is saying and ensures that the client is really sure about what s/he wants:

Client: *'After the way she treated me, I never want to have anything to do with her again.'*

Adviser: *'So you are saying that you feel you could not possibly return to that house?'*

or

Client: *'I daren't do anything legal – he'd go berserk.'*

Adviser: *'You have definitely decided that you do not want to go to a solicitor in case it angers your partner more?'*

Reflecting

This can be used to mirror back to the client what s/he has just said. It is particularly useful for reflecting feelings and can help in defusing a potentially aggressive/defensive situation.

Client: *'I don't know why I'm telling you all this. You must think I'm an emotional wreck.'*

Adviser: *'I can see you're very upset about the situation.'*

Summarising

A combination of paraphrase and reflection to summarise the main elements of what the client has said.

16.16   Developing an appropriate response

The following points apply to all good interviewing and advice giving, but are worth reiterating because of their particular importance in cases of domestic violence, when the person is likely to be confused, disempowered and suffering a low sense of self-esteem.

- Make the interviewing situation feel safe and confidential
- Ensure the client's immediate safety
- Take a non-judgemental and believing approach
- Be open and approachable and listen actively
- Be sensitive to the client's immediate needs when interviewing
- Ask the client what s/he wants
- Explore options which deal with the presenting problem without assuming what s/he wants
- Empower her/him by enabling her/him to reach her/his own decision
- Take account of and respect the different cultural and religious realities and situations for different groups
- Provide clear and accurate advice and information, preferably in a written form which can be taken away and read later

- Offer time and ongoing support and enable her/him to come back

- Don't patronise, pressurise, make assumptions or take over.

It is necessary to recognise the practical problems that stem from relationship breakdown, which focus around accommodation, finance and children's schooling and other needs. There will also be underlying emotional problems: these can cover a wide and often conflicting range of emotions, such as:

- guilt

- shame

- fear

- love

- dependence

- responsibility

- confusion

- pressure of children's needs

- disbelief (self and others)

- cultural and religious factors.

A person may want to stop the violence s/he is experiencing, but nevertheless want to continue the relationship. Good practice responses from organisations should recognise emotional needs and address her/his safety.

There may also be special difficulties faced by people in rural, isolated or close-knit communities, both in practical terms (eg, getting access to resources, getting away from the situation) and because of the attitudes and involvement of others. These should be acknowledged and respected.

B   Housing management issues

Relationship breakdown gives rise to many problems involving housing management, and these need to be recognised and addressed. Good practice issues relating to homelessness are also covered in Chapter 15.

This section is broken down into four broad policy areas:

- Government guidelines and policies

- Domestic violence policy

- Housing management – lettings/transfer policy on relationship breakdown

- Resources and liaison with other agencies.

GOVERNMENT GUIDELINES AND POLICIES

This section looks at Homelessness Reviews and Strategies, provision of advisory services, and Home Office Multi-Agency Guidance on dealing with domestic violence.

In December 2002 the government also produced a detailed and practical research report and summary entitled '*The provision of accommodation and support for households experiencing domestic violence in England.*'[1] This is essential reading for housing organisations concerned with developing good practice guidelines since it investigates the following issues, indicating which practices and policies have been adopted by local authorities and other organisations, giving statistics and evaluations of the experiences of both the providers and the service users:

- *Steps to seeking help* – available resources and how effectively contact is made with them; the type of advice respondents receive; service users experience of local authorities; accommodation options

- *Homelessness and temporary accommodation* – information about the numbers and type of people accepted as homeless as a result of domestic violence and the types of temporary accommodation provided; a critique of common problems encountered by local authorities

- *Being rehoused* – research results on specific domestic violence allocation policies adopted by local authorities; problems in providing permanent accommodation; policies towards perpetrators of violence

- *Support services* – services available and problems of accessing support

- *Staying put* – problems identified where people stay put; initiatives to improve safety and security; users' evaluation of use of injunctions.

In December 2002, the government also announced funding of £7 million to extend refuge provision and a further £2 million to establish a national 24-hour helpline.

16.17 Homelessness reviews and strategies

The Homelessness Act 2002 requires housing authorities to carry out a review, and to formulate and publish a homelessness strategy based on the results of the review, within twelve months from 31st July 2002. A further

---

1. The Provision of Accommodation and Support for Households Experiencing Domestic Violence in England (Housing Report 2002) Office of the Deputy Prime Minister, and News release 2002/0387 11 December 2002. Available at: www.housing.odpm.gov.uk/informationdomestic/index.htm.

s1 HA02 & paras
1.1-1.3 HCOG02 review needs to be carried out and a new strategy has to be formulated and published at least every five years afterwards. Social services must be involved, along with a wide range of other agencies, and are required to take the strategy into account when carrying out their own duties.

Reviews

The review has to assess the levels and likely levels of homelessness in the local district and also review what is being done to:

- help prevent homelessness

- find accommodation for those who become homeless, and

s2(1) HA02
& para 1.9-1.10
HCOG02 • provide support for homeless and potentially homeless people.

para 1.17 HCOG02 Since relationship breakdown is a key factor in almost a quarter of all cases of homelessness, it is clearly important that authorities address the issue when developing their homelessness strategies. The Homelessness Code of Guidance acknowledges relationship breakdown as a cause of many cases of homelessness. The need for larger numbers of smaller units of accommodation is one obvious consequence of relationship breakdown. Surveys have shown that a high percentage of homeless men sleeping rough have lost their homes as a result of relationship breakdown.[2] The majority of single parents are dependent upon benefit[3] and so affordable social housing is likely to be their only realistic option for obtaining a settled home. Relationship breakdown also means that often two new households are formed instead of one. The Code of Guidance says that housing authorities must make themselves aware of the local population and demographic para 1.16 HCOG02 trends and the rate of new household formation in the district.

The Code of Guidance also suggests that, in compiling information on levels of homelessness, authorities may be able to draw on a number of sources of pre-existing records, including records available from para 1.13 HCOG02 hostels and refuges. It also states that people exposed to domestic or para 1.14 HCOG02 other violence are more likely to be at risk of homelessness than others.

In assessing available resources, the authority will need to be aware of the number of refuge and hostel spaces available and any development para 1.22 HCOG02 programmes being considered.

Strategies

Once the authority has a clear picture of the problems and resources in its area, it must develop an appropriate strategy to deal with them. Different responses may be needed to cater both for emergencies, such as more emergency accommodation including refuge spaces for people experiencing violence, and for longer-term needs, eg, working with RSLs to develop more affordable homes of appropriate size. The Code

3. Over half of all lone parents were receiving Income Support in February 2001, and over one third were in receipt of Working Families Tax Credit. Figures from National Council for One Parent Families available at www.ncopf.org.uk.

2. See www.mungos.org.facts.shtml and www.crisis.org.uk.

paras 1.27-1.61
HCOG02 of Guidance gives useful guidelines on the development of a strategy, including the need to consult with other agencies. Authorities will also find practical ideas and good practice examples in the DTLR's (now ODPM) handbook "*Homelessness Strategies: A Good Practice Handbook.*"⁴

16.18   Provision of advisory services

s.179 HA96

para 2.2 HCOG02

Housing authorities are under a duty to ensure that free advice and information about homelessness and preventing it is available to anyone in their district. This advice duty clearly ties in with delivering an effective homelessness strategy, and the Code of Guidance once again identifies relationship breakdown as one of the key causes of homelessness. This means that it is essential that housing authorities either provide sufficient training for their own staff to give high quality advice on relationship breakdown, or ensure that such advice is provided by specific arrangement with other agencies.

16.19   Home Office 'Multi-agency guidance for addressing domestic violence'

In April 2000, the Home Office launched a 10-point plan to address domestic violence, calling for a multi-agency response to tackling the problem as part of its *'Living without Fear'* campaign⁵ to prevent and reduce domestic violence. This multi-agency guidance⁶ gives specific guidance to individual agencies within the criminal justice system (ie, the courts and Court Service, Crown Prosecution Service, the police and the probation service), local government departments (ie, education, youth and leisure services, housing and social services), and the Health Service Guidance to the police and Crown Prosecution Service is discussed further at 13.9.

s17 CDA98 Authorities are reminded that, under the Crime and Disorder Act 1998, they are required to have partnerships with the police and other agencies to reduce crime in their areas. Since domestic violence accounts for almost a third of all violent crime, the guidance states that authorities must not overlook the need to take action against domestic violence and to help its survivors.

The guidance states quite clearly that *"every authority should publish a clear policy on domestic violence, which is understood and complied with by all its staff."* The policy should:

• cover the detail of good practice expected from council staff

• promote good practice in individual departments of the authority

---

4. "Homelessness Strategies A Good Practice Handbook" DTLR,(now ODPM) February 2002, available from Office of the Deputy Prime Minister, Eland House, Bressenden Place, London SW1E 5DU Tel: 020 7944 3000 or www.homelessness.odpm.gov.uk/homelessness/ pubs/handbook/.

5. Living without Fear – an Integrated Approach to Tackling Violence against Women (1999), published jointly by the Home Office and the Women's Unit (now Women and Equality Unit), available at www.asylumsupport.info/ publications/cabinetoffice/withoutfear.pdf.

6. Multi-Agency Guidance for Addressing Domestic Violence, Home Office. Tel: 0870 000 1585 Fax 020 7273 2065 www.homeoffice.gov.uk/docs/mag.html.

- provide a framework of co-ordinated and measurable responses to domestic violence by all key departments, including social services, education, housing, and youth and leisure services
- include a clear emphasis on effective monitoring and evaluation, and ensure that staff receive appropriate training.

The guidance to housing departments specifically states that housing officers should have a detailed knowledge of housing legislation and statutory guidance, and how this applies to people fleeing domestic violence. A knowledge of what information and help is available to domestic violence survivors is also essential. In addition, the guidance lists a number of points that emphasise the need to interpret correctly the homelessness legislation, as well as suggesting certain courses of action that authorities should consider:

- psychological abuse must be recognised as leading potentially to statutory homelessness, where it would not be reasonable for someone to continue to live at home
- authorities must be sure that they obey the law by not referring homeless applicants back to an area where they would be at risk of domestic violence
- women fleeing domestic violence may be vulnerable and therefore in priority need
- failure to return home under the protection of court orders should not give rise to the decision that the person is intentionally homeless, on the basis that it is safe for them to return
- positive consideration should be given to accepting the referral of homelessness cases from other authorities where the applicant needs to move away from their home area to escape domestic violence
- eviction action should be taken against local authority tenants whose partner has fled their home because of domestic violence perpetrated by the tenant
- sympathetic treatment should be given to victims of domestic violence, for example where there are rent arrears or a need to fit new locks.

DOMESTIC VIOLENCE POLICY

All of the points discussed in Section A above with regard to advice, interviewing and awareness issues are relevant to housing providers. Some areas require particular attention, and the matters raised by government guidance outlined above in 16.19 must be taken into account.

16.20 Confidentiality guidelines

para 3.14 HCOG02

In cases where safety is concerned, confidentiality is crucial. The code of guidance states *'Inquiries of the perpetrators of violence should not be made.'* Corroboration should never be sought from the perpetrator. This may seem obvious, but some authorities still seek the views of the allegedly violent partner.

The fact that the person has even applied as homeless should in no way be revealed without the applicant's permission. If it is necessary to contact third parties, special care should be taken to indicate that the enquiries are of a strictly confidential nature. Information should only be given over the telephone in exceptional circumstances, after checking the identity of the caller and ensuring that no unauthorised third parties can overhear confidential information.

paras 6.20 & 7.12(d) HCOG02

Authorities should not insist that the applicant applies for an injunction. Those who still do, despite the Code of Guidance's recommendations, should remember that the court papers will often serve to tell the perpetrator the area in which the applicant is living, even if the specific address is omitted. Similar problems will arise if a residence order is insisted upon. There is also clear case law that such orders should not be required (see 15.17). For comment on problems of confidentiality arising from child contact see 13.6.

- A special policy on confidentiality, over and above normal procedures, should be developed and observed in all cases of domestic violence.

16.21 Corroborative evidence of violence

If corroborative evidence, eg, from doctors, police, social workers etc., is available and if the applicant has given permission for them to be contacted, such procedure is acceptable and may help the authority deal with the case more sensitively. In many cases, such evidence is not available: much domestic violence takes place behind closed doors. The person on the receiving end frequently experiences guilt and shame, not to mention fear, which may inhibit confidences to third parties.

s177 HA96

It should also be remembered that threats of violence which are likely to be carried out are sufficient to make a person legally homeless.

- Authorities should take a 'client-centred' approach, ie, the applicant should always be believed in cases of domestic violence, unless there is clear evidence to suggest the contrary.[7]

As part of a homelessness application, the applicant signs a statement acknowledging that knowingly giving false information is an offence. If

---

7. R v Thurrock BC ex parte Williams (1981) 1 HLR 128 QBD.

the authority refuses to believe an applicant, it is in fact alleging that false information has been given. It should therefore be able to show good cause for such an allegation (see 15.7).

s214 HA96

16.22 No insistence on injunctions

Some local authorities may insist that applicants take legal action, either to protect their legal rights in the home or, in effect, to 'prove' that the violence is genuine (see 15.5 – 15.7). The Code of Guidance states:

> 'Authorities may wish to inform applicants of the option of seeking an injunction. However, housing authorities should recognise that injunctions ordering persons not to molest, or enter the home of, the applicant will not always be effective in deterring perpetrators from carrying out further violence or incursions. Applicants should not automatically be expected to return home on the strength of an injunction.'

para 6.20 HCOG02

16.23 Priority to cases involving domestic violence

In cases involving domestic violence, there should be an immediate response to ensure the safety of the applicant whilst any further inquiries are being made. Authorities should not simply treat an applicant who is their tenant as if s/he is applying for a transfer, but should consider her/him as homeless.

- If someone is placed in temporary accommodation or a refuge, the ability of the applicant to cope in that situation must be considered. The effect of the applicant's experiences should be given special consideration in deciding on longer-term rehousing

- The Code of Guidance on allocations also says that authorities should consider giving additional preference in their allocation schemes to people with urgent housing needs, and these specifically include people owed a homelessness duty as a result of domestic or other violence.

para 5.13 ACOG02

16.24 Steps to protect someone at risk of domestic violence

The organisation should examine what policies it should adopt to deal with cases of domestic violence, ie, should it have policies which clearly state its opposition to domestic violence in the same way as for racial harassment.

Other steps which could be considered are:

- making a public statement that action will be taken against perpetrators of domestic violence, again in a similar way to racial harassment or other nuisance or harassment cases. This could involve use of the McGrady procedure to end a joint tenancy (see 6.34), resulting in eviction of the perpetrator and re-grant to the other partner. However, there are problems attached to using this procedure (see 16.28), and housing providers should consider these carefully. The outcome of the case of *Harrow LBC v Qazi* in the House of Lords will also be crucial in determining whether the use of the McGrady procedure involves a breach of an individual's human rights (ie, Article 8 right to respect for home) (see 2.4 and 7.42).

- in the case of a sole tenancy in the non-violent partner's name or a joint tenancy, landlords could offer rehousing to her/him alone if s/he gives notice to quit to end the tenancy, thus excluding the perpetrator

Ground 2A Sch 1
HA85

- the authority could use the ground for possession that the remaining partner has been violent or threatened violence and the partner who has left is unlikely to return. The court has held that the violence must be the immediate, effective cause of the partner's leaving and not just one of a number of factors[8] (see 13.55 for more information on the use of this power).

MANAGEMENT – LETTINGS, TRANSFER AND HOMELESSNESS POLICIES

There are a number of options open to housing providers; in deciding which to adopt, various factors need to be considered.

16.25 Rehousing prior to matrimonial/family settlement

This reduces stress for the family and limits damaging effects on children, as well as being in the interests of good management. Some organisations have in the past had a policy allowing the offer of a small, eg, one-bed roomed, unit to be made to a party to a relationship breakdown who will not be caring for the children. Under the allocation provisions of the Housing Act 1996 (see Chapter 14, Section D, 14.36 – 14.40) this needs to be done within the framework of the allocation scheme. Although initially this may seem costly in terms of resources, it can prove to be efficient management. It may prevent the situation from developing into a violent one, which would necessitate the provision of costly temporary accommodation, as well as adding to the personal cost to the applicant. It may also prevent the carer and children having to be rehoused in a family unit, whilst the single person is left in a two or three-bed roomed house.

Where both partners are going to share residential care of the children, it is necessary to provide appropriate sized accommodation. If a person is accepted as in priority need, the homelessness legislation lays down that accommodation must be provided both for the applicant and *'any other person who normally resides with him/her as a member of the*

---

8. Camden LBC v Mallett [2001] 33 HLR 20 CA.

s176 HA96 *family, or who might reasonably be expected to reside with her/him.'* In practice, many local authorities offer smaller accommodation if the children are not living with a parent full-time, but it should be recognised that there is no legal justification for this once the applicant has been accepted as in priority need. It is largely a thorny issue because of limited resources, and housing providers need to consider their policies carefully, see also the next section, 16.26.

Early rehousing can also help to avoid the tenant having to pay compensation if the tenancy is transferred by the court (see 7.49).

Organisations should beware of trying to remove one tenant's name from a joint tenancy or of 'transferring' a sole tenancy, and be clear about whether a new tenancy is being created or not (see 6.15).

16.26 Rehousing partners without full-time care of child

Since the enactment of the Children Act 1989, arrangements for shared residence by children no longer have to be ratified by the court. Nevertheless, some housing providers may try to insist on residence orders before they accept someone as in priority need as homeless (see 15.17 – 15.20). The courts do not appear to be willing to entertain applications where the sole purpose is to provide evidence of priority need for the housing organisation. It should also be realised that if, for example, a woman who has been forced to leave the home applies for a residence order, the partner who has remained in the home may try to exploit the stability of his situation and the availability of the home, as grounds for arguing against the residence order. It could also mean that the woman's whereabouts are revealed to her/his partner.

Authorities have to decide whether a partner with contact or part-time residence should be rehoused (see 15.18). The following are some of the points which may be considered:

- Is the child genuinely dependent during the time s/he will be with the applicant?
- Is s/he genuinely residing with the applicant or merely visiting?
- Will the child need to do homework or have toys and belongings in the second home?
- Will regular meals need to be provided?
- What alternatives are there for the child, if the parent cannot provide care?
- Do social services consider the child to be in need and do they feel it appropriate that the child should be able to spend time with the parent in question?

- If the child has not already lived with the applicant, case law has made it clear that the authority must consider the future and whether the child might reasonably be expected to reside with the applicant in the future[9]

This is not intended to be a comprehensive checklist, nor would there have to be a positive response to all the above points: liaison with social services may be appropriate to help decide what is in the best interests of the child.

16.27 Insistence on legal rights – occupation orders and transfer of tenancies

In cases which do not involve physical violence, housing providers may suggest that, where available, the parties involved should seek exclusion/occupation orders to allow the court to decide who should live in the home, at least in the short term. It should be remembered that occupation orders are twofold:

- They can grant a right to a non-tenant to occupy the home together with the tenant, ie, enable her/him to stay, or

- They can grant a right to occupy and also exclude the other partner.

It is important that authorities do not consider that occupation orders are an automatic right and a solution to all situations. The court is obliged to make an exclusionary order only in the case of entitled applicants or former spouses, where it is satisfied that there is a greater risk of significant harm to the applicant than there will be to the other party if the order is made (see 13.29). In other cases, the court has wide discretion and must consider the health, safety and well-being of all parties concerned. In *G v G (Occupation Order: Conduct)*,[10] the court ruled that where, after comparing the harm that is likely to be suffered by either party and any child, it is not clear that one will suffer more than the other if the order is not made, then the court has discretion to decide on the basis of the general criteria in s.33 (6).

Government research published in December 2002[11] showed that only one local authority of the 280 surveyed insisted on an injunction or occupation order before the person could be transferred or accepted as homeless. The report stresses that this practice is contrary to the Code of Guidance. Most respondents to the survey had found that injunctions were not a useful means of keeping ex-partners away from the home.

In addition, an occupation order cannot terminate a tenancy – it can merely suspend the right of the tenant or one joint tenant to occupy. It seems unlikely, in cases which do not involve violence, that the

---

9. R v Kingswood DC ex parte Smith-Morse (1994) The Times, 8 December CA (1995) 2 FLR 137 QBD.
10. G v G (Occupation Order: Conduct) (2000) 2 FLR 36 CA.
11. Chapter 6, para 6.3 'The Provision of Accommodation and Support for Households Experiencing Domestic Violence in England (see footnote 1).

courts will readily exclude an owner or tenant, even if they are prepared to grant an order giving a right to the non-owner/tenant to remain in occupation, especially where the other party would be entitled to homelessness assistance.

Local authorities must ask whether, even if a cohabitant is able to apply for an occupation order, it is reasonable to expect her/him to continue to occupy and share a home where s/he has no legal interest, and has been asked to leave by her/his ex-partner.

Although heterosexual cohabitants may apply for a court order to transfer the tenancy after cohabitation ceases, the court has discretion and may also order payment of compensation from the tenant who gets the tenancy to the person who has lost the tenancy. Court proceedings are, in many cases, time-consuming and cumbersome, and the outcome is not guaranteed. Relationship breakdowns often require a more immediate response, which may be available as a result of local authorities' established good practice.

16.28 Encouraging termination of the tenancy

It has become fairly common for housing providers to encourage tenants whose relationships have broken down to give notice to quit, so that the partner can be evicted and the other person rehoused or regranted the tenancy (see 6.34). This is often called the *McGrady* procedure. Government research published in December 2002[12] revealed that over 70% of local authorities inform their tenants who are experiencing domestic violence of the possibility of issuing a unilateral notice to quit. In 1998/9 103 such unilateral notices to quit were served by joint tenants as a result of domestic violence. At the time of writing, the lawfulness of this policy was under question on human rights grounds, and a ruling from the House of Lords was awaited. The human rights issue is explained at 7.42.

If it is decided that the *McGrady* procedure is unjustified in human rights terms, clearly other methods of dealing with a tenancy will have to be used. Possibilities are court transfers of tenancies (see Chapter 7, Section F, 7.43 – 7.56 and Chapter 8, Section D, 8.18 – 8.19), or assignment of tenancies (see 6.13 – 6.24). Alternatively, registered social landlords and local authorities may use the grounds introduced by the Housing Act 1996 to evict perpetrators where the partner has left, but should bear in mind that the partner may have to give evidence (see 13.55 and 16.24).

Case 2A Sch 2 HA85, case 14A Sch 2 HA88

If it is deemed lawful to continue using the *McGrady* procedure, the following are points for housing providers to consider:

12. See footnote 1, Chapter 4, para 4.3.

- It has been suggested in the past that unilateral termination of a joint tenancy against the other joint tenant's wishes may give rise to a breach of trust on the part of the tenant giving notice. This has been held not to be the case (see 6.34).

- A local authority was found guilty of maladministration by the Ombudsman when it sanctioned the use of the *McGrady* procedure effectively to evict a joint tenant who had left to stay with his relatives when his relationship broke down. Once the other joint tenant's notice to quit expired, she was granted a new sole tenancy. She then very rapidly obtained consent for a mutual exchange. The man had no knowledge of what had happened until the removal vans went to move his possessions out of the house. The Ombudsman found that the officers had broken the council's procedures, which required them to contact and interview the other joint tenant. The Ombudsman recommended that he be rehoused immediately and granted compensation, even though he was not in priority need[13]

- If notice to quit is being considered when divorce proceedings are pending, section 37 of the Matrimonial Causes Act 1973 permits the court to grant an injunction to prevent a notice to quit (see 7.42).

If a couple are divorcing, or if proceedings are pending under the Children Act, it may be possible to obtain an injunction preventing service of notice. The case of *Bater v Greenwich LBC*[14] (see 7.42) established that injunctions, which effectively prevent a notice to quit from taking effect, can be obtained in other family proceedings. An occupation order under the Family law Act 1996 declaring or granting rights to occupy does not in itself prevent service of a notice to quit.

16.29 Lesbian and gay couples

Housing providers need to consider having special guidelines for those in lesbian or gay relationships. This is because lesbian and gay couples do not have the same legal avenues open to them to resolve disputes over tenancies:

- There can be no transfer of tenancy under family/matrimonial law

- There can be no transfer of tenancy when cohabitation ceases

- There can normally be no transfer of tenancy under the Children Act

- There can be no voluntary assignment of joint secure tenancies except following a matrimonial or Children Act order (see 6.18) as ruled in the case of *Burton v Camden*[15]

- Assignment of assured tenancies requires the express permission of the landlord.

13. Complaint against Hackney LBC: Omb 88/A/979.
14. Bater v Greenwich LBC (1999) EGCS 111; 4 All ER 944 CA   15. Burton v Camden LBC (2000) 1 All ER 943 HL.

However, since the case of *Mendoza v Ghaidan*[16] it would appear that it is now possible for a sole secure tenancy to be assigned from one lesbian or gay partner to the other (see 6.17).

The Code of Guidance on allocation of accommodation says that housing authorities should normally grant joint tenancies to partners, including lesbian and gay couples and, it should consider granting new tenancies on death of a sole tenant, where the survivor has been living with the tenant for the year before the tenant's death. This could be a tenancy of the same property or in other suitable alternative accommodation. Local authorities should consider extending this to the analogous situation on relationship breakdown, and frame their allocation policies to allow the grant of new tenancies to remaining non-tenants or joint para 3.8 ACOG02 tenants on relationship breakdown.

Secure local authority tenancies

Joint tenancies

If a lesbian/gay relationship breaks up and the secure tenancy is a joint tenancy, the only way for a partner to end liability on the tenancy is to give notice to quit (ie, it is not possible to give up 'half a joint tenancy,' see 6.34). This is because assignment of a joint secure tenancy is not possible without a court order (see 6.18).

As a short-term measure, under the Family Law Act 1996, any joint tenant can apply for an occupation order and at the same time ask the court to make an order transferring the liabilities and outgoings to the other tenant (see 13.23). However, the court has discretion as to whether to make an occupation order: its criteria must be the health, safety and well-being of all concerned. An occupation order does not end or transfer the joint tenancy, and the departing partner may want to end the involvement, eg, s/he may not be eligible for other tenancies if s/he still has a joint tenancy. S/he may still therefore decide to serve notice to quit.

However, a valid notice to quit will end the whole tenancy: the local authority needs to decide whether, in such cases, it will be prepared to re-grant the tenancy to the remaining partner. A re-grant of a sole tenancy of the same property to an existing joint tenant now falls within the restrictions of the allocation provisions of the Housing Act 1996, if it is treated as a transfer request by the tenant. However, where it is at the local authority's instigation, it is a matter for local discretion (see 14.36). This may leave room for local authorities to adopt special policies in cases of relationship breakdown.

The authority also needs to consider whether joint tenancies should always be offered or whether those about to take on a joint tenancy

---

16. Mendoza v Ghaidan [2002] 4 All ER 1162; [2003] 1 FLR 468, CA.

should be advised of the effect of notice to quit (although this must be contrasted with the advantages for same-sex couples in having a joint tenancy, which gives a right of survivorship if one tenant dies).

Sole tenancies

Provided that the judgement in *Mendoza v Ghaidan* is upheld in the House of Lords, a sole secure lesbian or gay partner may assign the tenancy if the twelve month residence rule is satisfied (see 6.17 for details). However, a same-sex, non-tenant cohabitant has no right to apply for an occupation order or transfer of tenancy under the Family Law Act 1996. S/he will therefore become homeless if the tenant wants her/him to leave. Local authorities should consider what policies they should have towards the homeless partner in such cases.

As explained above, guidance issued by the ODPM suggests that a new tenancy should be granted to a remaining non-tenant partner on death. The same policy could be adopted on relationship breakdown, but must be within the framework of the allocation scheme.

Registered social landlord tenancies

If the tenancy is a joint secure tenancy, assignment is not permitted. The considerations for both joint and sole tenancies are the same as for local authorities (see above), although if a new tenancy is granted after a notice to quit ending a joint tenancy, it can only be a secure tenancy if it is granted immediately upon the expiry of the notice on the previous tenancy. This is because, to remain secure, it must be granted to someone who, immediately before it was entered into, was a secure tenant. If there is a time lapse between the termination of the old tenancy and the grant of a new one, the new tenancy will be assured s35(4)(d) HA88 and not secure. RSLs should act promptly in granting new tenancies, to prevent this reduction in security.

If the tenancy is assured, there is nothing to prevent the RSL from allowing contractual rights to assignment between lesbian and gay couples.

16.30 Arrears on relationship breakdown

Arrears frequently accompany relationship breakdown. If there has been a transfer of tenancy under matrimonial/family law, the court has power to make an order deciding who should be liable for arrears see 7.52 – 7.53). If such an order has not been made, the organisation needs to be clear about how arrears should be dealt with.

Joint tenancies

If the tenancy is a joint tenancy, either or both tenants could legally be held liable for all the arrears. In practice, one partner may have had little control over family finances, and so may have been unable to pay the rent. In such cases, it is hoped that landlord organisations will take a sympathetic approach, agreeing to accept current payment of rent and, if possible, pursuing the outgoing tenant for arrears. If this is not possible, small weekly payments of arrears may be negotiated. The authority should also consider using its discretion, in certain cases, to waive payment of arrears.

Sole tenancies

Where the tenancy was a sole tenancy and where voluntary assignment has taken place, the outgoing tenant will be liable for arrears accrued up to the date of assignment (see 6.26 – 6.27).

Problems may arise where the sole tenant has left, leaving a non-tenant cohabitant in the property. In such cases, a same-sex cohabitant is at the mercy of the landlord, since there is no legal right to a tenancy transfer. Heterosexual, non-tenant cohabitants may apply for a transfer of tenancy through the court, but if legal proceedings are not being taken, the same problems could apply. In these cases, the landlord body may try to suggest that the cohabitant must accept liability for arrears in order not to be evicted. It should be stressed that making the grant of a tenancy conditional upon paying a former tenant's arrears has been held by the ombudsman to be an illegal premium (see 11.30).

16.31 Landlord's role in assignment

A landlord cannot prevent an assignment of an assured or a secure tenancy where it falls within one of the permitted groups (see 6.17 and following pages). If it is carried out properly by deed, the tenancy will have been assigned, but if there is a prohibition against assignment in the tenancy agreement, such an assignment may be a breach of tenancy conditions and, if so, will give rise to a ground for possession. Breach of tenancy conditions is always a discretionary ground, and the court will therefore have to decide whether it thinks that it is reasonable to grant possession because the tenancy has been assigned. In cases of relationship breakdown, it is suggested that housing providers should not oppose assignment.

16.32 Priority for transfers in relationship breakdown cases

Organisations should have a policy on the degree of priority to be awarded in deciding on transfers when a relationship has broken down. The degree of priority will be affected by factors such as:

• domestic violence or mental cruelty

- bad or disturbing associations or harassment of the applicant or children in the present home

- suitability of the present home, in terms of size, cost, ease of upkeep, etc.

Similar factors should be considered when dealing with housing applications from owner-occupiers whose relationships have broken down. Local authorities should also be alert to their duties under the homelessness legalisation. Applicants for transfers in these circumstances are also likely to be homeless, as it is not reasonable for them to continue to occupy the accommodation (see 14.6).

16.33 Mobility schemes

In some cases, the person whose relationship has broken down may wish to make a fresh start in a new area. Organisations should consider how mobility schemes and reciprocal arrangements could best be used to help in these situations.

RESOURCES AND LIAISON WITH OTHER AGENCIES

16.34 Inter-agency contact

In addition to providing information, organisations should try to maintain links with other agencies. Regular contact helps to maintain awareness of resources available in the area, and means that inappropriate time-wasting referrals are not made. Often agencies will be working together to provide short- and long-term solutions to a problem, and liaison will be essential.

16.35 Legal knowledge

Organisations need to decide what level of legal knowledge staff should be able to offer. Handbooks of this kind as well as other textbooks and journals may be helpful for staff.[17] However, it is important that detailed legal advice is not given unless the adviser is certain of its accuracy.

Equally, it should be recognised that legal advice may not always be appropriate, eg, where it will exacerbate a situation; and care should be taken in suggesting that legal remedies such as injunctions (see Chapter 13) are readily available, when in reality that may be difficult to obtain.

---

17. See also 'Relationship Breakdown – A Guide for Social Landlords' DETR, (now ODPM) May 1999 and see further reading at the end of this book.

A

A1 Court jurisdiction

Relationship breakdown usually involves many complicated issues including divorce or judicial separation, domestic violence, homelessness, property law, and landlord and tenant law. Financial issues such as maintenance, bankruptcy, property adjustment and transfer are also often a feature of such cases.

The court system in England and Wales is complex with different courts having jurisdiction over different issues.

- Statutory homelessness appeals are heard in the county court. However, a number of homelessness related issues remain within the jurisdiction of the Administrative Court, which is a division of the High Court. Notably, these include judicial review claims against a decision of a local authority not to provide accommodation pending a statutory review under section 202 Housing Act 1996 (see 14.30 for other situations where judicial review may be appropriate)

- Most issues in divorce or judicial separation, including formally ending the relationship itself, domestic violence, maintenance and property related issues will be dealt with in the county court. However, cases involving large financial claims or issues of particular complexity may be heard in the High Court. Additionally, the Family Proceedings Court, a separate part of the magistrates' court, has jurisdiction over some of these issues and may, in appropriate circumstances, provide an alternative forum

- Most Children Act cases, including orders for financial provision, will be heard within the county court although the Family Proceedings Court (and, in exceptional cases, the High Court) can hear cases.

When dealing with child support and maintenance, the Child Support Agency, which is run by the Department of Work and Pensions, is now responsible for assessing, collecting and enforcing child maintenance cases. The Child Support Act 1991, from which the agency derives its powers, came into force in April 1993. Even where existing court arrangements are in force, the Child Support Agency may, in many cases, impose a maintenance formula on family members (see Chapter 10).

The Charter for Court Users issued by the Court Service offers a number of guides to how the different courts operate and other useful information. It is available from local courts or directly from Court Service by phoning their Customer service unit on 020 7210 2266. Alternatively, the guides may be downloaded from the Court Service website – www.courtservice.gov.uk.

A1.1 County Court

The county court will usually deal with most issues relating to relationship breakdown cases. Divorce itself, judicial separation, deciding where the children of the relationship will reside and contact arrangements can all be dealt with in the county court. Additionally, where there is domestic violence, the court has powers to vary rights of occupation and to restrain behaviour so as to protect individuals and their families and keep them in their homes. The county court derives its powers from a number of statutory sources, in particular, the Family Law Act 1996, the Matrimonial Causes Act 1973 and the Children Act 1989. The provisions of these Acts are examined in more detail earlier in this book. In addition, appeals against homelessness review decisions are heard in the county court.

County courts can usually be found in most large towns and localities numbering about 300 throughout England and Wales. Two types of judges sit in county courts – circuit judges and district judges. Most of the issues involved in relationship breakdown cases, such as formal divorce or judicial separation, obtaining an injunction to stop or prevent violence and protecting someone's position in the home, may be dealt with by either type of judge. However, not every county court has jurisdiction to deal with these particular matters such cases being heard in designated divorce county courts and family hearing centres. Where divorce or other relationship breakdown issues are contested these will be heard at a family hearing centre, which may not be the local county court but another specially designated county court in the vicinity.

The court will have a court manager who is responsible for the day to day administration of the court and to whom correspondence should always be addressed. The court office will contain staff who should be familiar with the forms and procedures used in relationship breakdown cases. Although the court staff cannot give advice about particular cases they will usually help with the completion of court forms and give general advice about court fees and procedures. Some county courts also have advice desks staffed by representatives from local advice agencies such as law centres and citizens advice bureaux. These will often be a good source of advice.

Court fees

In the county court, relationship breakdown fees are payable when proceedings are commenced or issued except where the claimant is entitled to an exemption or qualify for a remission. Exemptions apply where the claimant is in receipt of Income Support or income-based Job Seekers Allowance. A person may also be exempt where they receive Working Tax Credit or Child Tax Credit (which replaced Working Families' Tax Credit and Disabled Person's Tax Credit from April 2003) though this may depend on the level of Credit they receive, the type of case and whether or not they are being assisted under the Legal Help scheme.

In addition, a claimant may be entitled to a full or partial remission of the fees where the court considers that they would suffer financial hardship if they had to pay them.

Fees are payable where a claimant is in receipt of Legal Representation (full public funding) but these will generally be paid on behalf of the client and claimed back from the Community Legal Service fund.

Additional fees may be payable at various stages of the court proceedings.

Forms

There are many different forms used in relationship breakdown cases. These are obtainable from law stationers, county courts or from the court service website (see above). The forms vary depending on the type of claim or application being made to the court. Divorce petitions, applications for occupation orders and injunctions are examples of types of cases where particular specialist forms must be used though other types of cases will involve using the more general court forms.

Getting advice on county court procedure

In general, if a solicitor or an advice agency is not readily available, a telephone call to the local county court will usually elicit general guidance as to the procedures available and the appropriate court fees (if these are payable).

A1.2 Family Proceedings Court

Family Proceedings Courts form a separate part of the magistrates' court and deal with civil matters relating to children and families, but not divorce cases. Magistrates sitting in the Family Proceedings Court are drawn from a family panel composed of specially trained justices and District Judges. Court procedure tends to be less formal than in the criminal magistrates' court; the usual court rooms are not used and the public is not allowed in.

Since the implementation of the Family Law Act 1996 in October 1997, Family Proceedings Courts, the county courts and the High Court all have jurisdiction with regard to applications for occupation and non-molestation orders. The nature and scope of such orders is now the same regardless of the court in which the application was made, in accordance with the overall intention of the Act to provide a uniform approach to these matters. However, the magistrates' court can decline to hear cases which it considers would be more conveniently heard in another court and cannot make orders where it is necessary to decide disputed issues about beneficial interests or other rights of occupation.

The Family Proceedings Court can also make orders for the maintenance of a spouse and for a child of the family. The court staff in a magistrates' court will usually be able to help with court fees and the appropriate forms.

A1.3 The High Court

Although the High Court can deal with some cases involving maintenance and other issues on relationship breakdown, this will be extremely rare. The High

Court is, however, the court which must be used in judicial review cases, eg, Children Act and community care cases where a decision of a public body is to be challenged and all other avenues of review/appeal have been exhausted. The Administrative Court (part of the High Court) can quash a decision and require the local authority to make a fresh decision or require the local authority to take a specified act or prevent it from taking a specified act. This may result because the authority has misunderstood the law, has not acted fairly or because it has taken into account irrelevant matters or left out relevant ones in reaching the particular decision (see 14.28). Specialist legal advice (which may be obtained from solicitors or advisers) will usually be needed before an application to the High Court is made.

Applications for judicial review cases are in two stages. The first or 'permission' stage involves a High Court judge looking at the papers or hearing the applicant's case in order to decide whether the applicant should be permitted to progress to a full hearing. This may be as much as a year or 18 months later. In emergencies the judge has power to grant injunctions which can, for example, order that interim accommodation be provided pending a full hearing.

A High Court application for judicial review is an expensive step (the costs for each side at the leave stage will usually be between £1,000 and £2,000 with these figures more than doubling by the time of the full hearing). For these reasons, nearly all applications are made by applicants who have applied for and been granted legal representation. The court fees in judicial review are relatively modest – £30 is the fee when an application is lodged with a further £180 payable if permission is granted. It is the lawyer's costs that make the procedure very expensive.

A1.4 Children Act 1989

The Children Act 1989, which enables orders to be made for the protection of children and for financial provision for the benefit of a child (although see Chapter 10 regarding the effect of the Child Support Act), has resulted in the assimilation (so far as this is practicable) of the procedures in the three courts which deal with the welfare of children; the High Court, county court and the Family Proceedings Court. The county court will be the usual venue for hearing these issues. Where the Family Proceedings Court is used the justice's clerk may, in some cases, allocate the case to a different court usually transferring it to the county court (or, rarely, to the High Court).

A2 Getting an occupation/non-molestation order

The injunctions and orders which are available in cases of domestic violence are covered in Chapter 13. This appendix concentrates on the procedure to apply for an occupation or non-molestation order in operation since October 1997.

As indicated earlier (see A1.2) the Family Law Act 1996 implemented a more uniform approach with regard to the jurisdiction of the courts to deal with applications for occupation and non-molestation orders. However, the county court remains the most usual venue for making these types of orders. Circuit judges or district judges may make different types of occupation and non-molestation orders to achieve different aims. A non-molestation order will generally be used to protect a party by restraining the aggressive or violent behaviour of another party. Occupation orders can vary the rights of occupation of the parties involved, whether tenant or owner-occupier, which may involve the ousting of one party from the property altogether. Due to the nature of such cases, these orders may be made very quickly and, in emergencies, without informing the other party that an application is being made. Often, it will be wisest not to inform the other of the application where to do so may increase the risk of violence to the applicant. It is important to appreciate that non-molestation and occupation orders may be granted to deal with a short-term crisis or longer-term affairs. Applications may also be made on a freestanding basis, that is, before the issue of any other proceedings. However, substantive proceedings will often be issued subsequently, for example, where a divorce is sought, a claim for damages made or a claim is made for the transfer of the property from one party to another.

Procedure in the County Court

An application for a molestation/occupation order is made by completion of a Form FL401, which is then filed at court. The form requires information including details about the applicant and the respondent, the property in relation to which an occupation order is sought (if applicable) and the nature of the order sought. The application form should be signed by the applicant and dated. If the applicant may be at risk by disclosing their current address they should indicate this on Form FL401 and complete a separate Confidential Address Form C8.

In support of the application, a statement should be prepared, setting out the evidence the applicant wishes to submit in support of the application. The statement must be signed by the applicant and sworn (or affirmed) by her/him to be true. The statement will be filed at court with the application form. Accompanying the application and statement should be a certificate of Legal Representation (if one has been granted) and any fees payable.

Unless the circumstances are such that it is appropriate to make an application without notice to the other party (see below), the application form, the supporting statement, a notice of proceedings and guidance notes (Form FL402) should be personally served on the other party (the respondent) not less than two days before the date of the hearing. After service has been effected the applicant should file a statement of service at court (FL415). Where an applicant is not represented s/he may ask the court to carry out service. In appropriate cases, however, the court may allow a shorter notice period where necessary.

Where an application is being made for an occupation order under sections 33, 35 or 36 of the Family Law Act 1996 (see Chapter 13, Section C) a copy of the application must be served by the applicant by first class post on the mortgage lender or landlord (as the case may be) of the property in question.

If an order is made the court will prepare a copy for sealing. The applicant must personally serve a sealed copy on the respondent. Again. where an applicant is not represented s/he may ask the court to carry out service. A power of arrest may be attached to one or more of the terms of the non-molestation or occupation order. The relevant provisions to which the power of arrest is attached should be set out on a separate order (Form FL406) and served with the main order.

Undertakings

It is fairly common for a respondent to give an 'undertaking' (or promise) to the court instead of that person being subject to a non-molestation or occupation order. This practice now has a statutory basis in Section 46 Family Law Act 1996. However, the ability of the court to allow undertakings to be given is restricted. An undertaking may not be given unless the court is satisfied that it has the power to make an occupation or non-molestation order or both. An undertaking is enforceable as though it were an order of the court. Importantly, however, a power of arrest may not be attached to an undertaking and the court may not accept an undertaking where it takes the view that grounds are made out for attaching a power of arrest. So, if a power of arrest is appropriate an order should be made rather than an undertaking.

Urgent cases

As referred to earlier, applications may be made without giving notice to the respondent, for example, where the applicant may be at risk if notice is given, or the applicant otherwise needs an immediate remedy. These can be obtained very quickly. In such cases, the same application form is used but the statement filed in support must include reasons why notice has not been given. Non-molestation and occupation orders made in this way will usually be temporary and short-term only, in recognition of the fact that the respondent did not have the opportunity to make representations at the initial hearing. The orders will be made until the 'return day' when a second hearing will be made. At this second hearing it is usual for both parties to be legally represented and for the judge to consider whether the temporary order(s) should be extended. Non-molestation orders will usually be made for such time as the judge considers will resolve the prevailing crisis and will not be open-ended. The maximum duration of an occupation order will depend on which particular section of the Family Law Act 1996 the order is made under, parties and their existing rights of occupation (See Chapter 13, Section C)

Once an order is made, a sealed copy of the order must be accompanied by a copy of the application and the statement and served on the respondent. If the applicant acted in person then the court must carry out service if requested by the applicant to do so. An order made without notice is only effective once it has been served on the respondent.

Injunctions in the Family Proceeding Court

The procedure for obtaining a non-molestation or occupation order is essentially the same as described above for the county court. There are minor variations. The application on Form FL401, supported by a statement, must be signed and declared to be true or, with the permission of the court, by oral evidence. If an application is made on notice, the respondent must be given two business days' notice unless this is shortened by the justices' clerk.

Injunctions by landlords

In some relationship breakdown cases where one or both of the parties are tenants, an injunction may be obtained by a landlord to restrain a breach of the tenancy. For example, where violence is threatened or takes place, there may often be a breach of a term of the tenancy. In these circumstances the county court only has a limited power to refuse an order where it is sought by a landlord: *Doherty v Allman* (1878); *Sutton Housing Trust v Lawrence* (1987) 19 HLR 520 CA. Injunctions area also available to restrain nuisance or trespass where a landlord seeks to restrain behaviour by a tenant or a third party: *Patel v W H Smith (Eziot) Limited* (1987) 2 All ER 569. The procedure to be adopted for injunctions of this nature is contained in Parts 23 and 25 of the Civil Procedure Rules 1998. Form N16A is the general form of application to be used and this must be supported by a witness statement in support, verified by a statement of truth.

Local authority and registered social landlords

See 13.56 for details of specific powers available to local authorities to apply for an injunction to prevent nuisance and annoyance to any person residing in, visiting or engaging in any lawful activity in or in the locality of certain properties it owns. The same section also explains how a registered social landlord or local authority which applies for an injunction against one of its tenants for a breach of certain terms of the tenancy can apply for power of arrest to be attached.

The cost of an injunction

Clients on low incomes may be able to get legal representation to get an injunction but where this is not available, getting an injunction may cost anything from £500 to £1,500.

Occupation orders under the Family Law Act

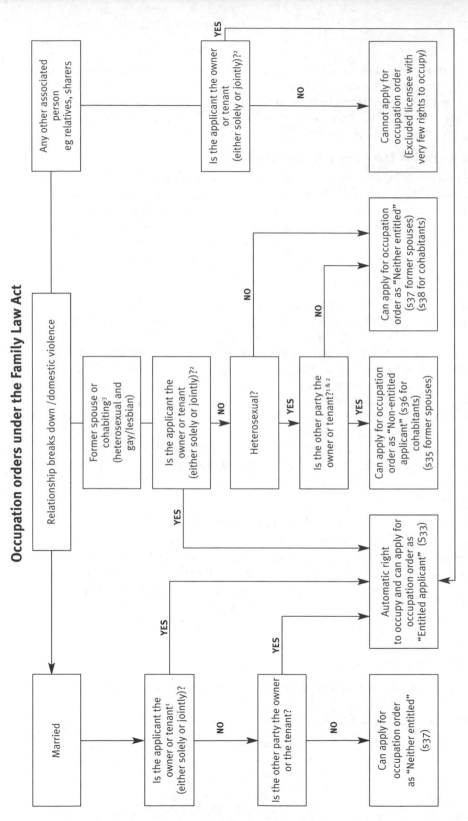

Note: 1 Or does s/he have a legal, contractual or statutory right to remain.

o If the client has an established beneficial interest then s/he should be treated as if s/he is an owner / tenant. If the client may have a beneficial interest but this has not been established then s/he should be treated as a non-owner.

3 Cohabitant includes former cohabitants.

A3 Public Funding

A: Community Legal Service

On 1 April 2000, the public funding scheme in England and Wales underwent a complete overhaul as the provisions contained in the Access to Justice Act 1999 were implemented. The legal aid system was replaced by the Community Legal Service aimed at bringing together the work of various different types of providers of legal assistance such as solicitors, law centres and advice agencies (eg, Shelter, Citizens Advice). The Legal Services Commission replaced the Legal Aid Board as the body responsible for administering the scheme.

All court proceedings are expensive. In relationship breakdown cases proceedings will usually only be affordable if the person contemplating the court action can benefit from the CLS scheme, or s/he otherwise has access to considerable resources. The hourly charging rates applied by solicitors will vary from firm to firm and from region to region and they will depend on the type of 'fee earner' handling the work. However, the lowest rates that will apply where a clerk deals with routine aspects of a case will rarely be lower than £60 per hour with higher rates applying where solicitors carry out work. Partners in firms will often charge well in excess of £100 per hour in private cases. Where CLS work is undertaken by solicitors, lower rates will apply. These are prescribed by regulations and updated on an annual basis.

Basic structure of Community Legal Service scheme

There are a number of levels of service now available under the CLS scheme. For the purposes of this publication, an outline only is given of the Legal Help and Legal Representation (including Emergency Representation) schemes. However, practitioners should refer to the Funding Code (see below) and the current regulations governing the scope and levels of funding available. Both schemes are subject to a financial eligibility test dealt with briefly below in the section on 'means testing.'

1. *Legal Help*: this scheme essentially replaced the Legal Advice and Assistance Scheme ('green form scheme'). Generally, it enables help to be given before representation is required, and does not cover the issue and conduct of court proceedings. In order to provide Legal Help, a firm or agency must have entered into a general civil contract with the Legal Services Commission in the category of work involved. The scheme enables an advisor to undertake a maximum of two hours' work on behalf of a client though this may be extended by a solicitor in exercise of devolved powers. Guidance on the exercise of these powers is contained in the Commission's Franchise Manual. Financial eligibility is determined by an assessment of a client's income and capital (see section on 'means testing' below).

2. *Legal representation*: this scheme covers representation in court proceedings and replaced both the civil legal aid and assistance by way of representation (ABWOR) in civil cases. Legal Representation would be appropriate where, for example, a non-molestation or occupation order under the Family Law Act 1996 is required. Emergency Representation is available where a certificate should be granted as a matter of urgency and it is in the interests of justice. The Funding Code contains very detailed guidance for assessing the merits and scope of Legal Representation certificates. Other schemes exist for family law matters, (ie, Approved Family Help and Family Mediation), but the details of these are outside the scope of this publication. See Chapter 2, Section B for general information on family mediation.

The Funding Code

The Funding Code provides detailed guidance on the 'levels of service' available and the criteria under which decisions are made as to whether to fund or continue to fund legal services. It is essential that practitioners consult the relevant section of the code for the appropriate type of work being undertaken.

Means Testing

Eligibility for public funding requires the completion of detailed forms including details of an applicant's 'disposable income' and capital. Limits are set annually by the Legal Services Commission in relation to both income and capital. Legal Representation may be granted completely free or on the basis of a contribution from the applicant. Once the limits are exceeded, however, the client will be ineligible.

Franchising

The introduction of exclusive contracts now means that only those firms with a contract can undertake particular types of work. In return for certain quality standards, franchise holders have been delegated powers, which include the grant of emergency legal representation certificates, previously exercised by the Legal Aid Board.

The statutory charge

The system of public funding may be looked upon as more akin to a loan of resources by the state than as a grant. The statutory charge, now applied under section 10(7) of the Access to Justice Act 1999, means that where money or property is recovered or preserved in the proceedings this must be used to pay her/his legal expenses. Only the balance (if any) is passed on to the client.

Under the Legal Help scheme the charge can be waived on the ground that if it is applied the client will suffer grave hardship, grave distress or where there might be difficulty enforcing the statutory charge due to the nature of the property recovered or preserved. Repayment will not be required if the applicant loses the case, or if all the solicitor's costs are paid by the losing side (although this will be rare).

There are also a number of exceptions. For example, the charge will not be applied to periodical payments paid to a spouse, former spouse or child, nor to the first £3000 of any money or property recovered or preserved in proceedings under the Matrimonial Causes Act 1973, a property adjustment order, or a lump sum order made under the Children Act 1999.

The charge may also be postponed or deferred in certain circumstances such as when the property is the home of the client or her/his dependants. A charge will be registered against the property instead. Simple interest will then accrue in respect of the amount charged against the property. In these cases, payment of the charge will be made when the property is sold or the legally funded person can make other arrangements to pay the amount due.

Financial eligibility rules

These rules are complex and usually change annually. At the time of writing the current rules are available in the April 2003 edition of Legal Action magazine.

A4   Negotiating on homelessness and using case law

Chapter 14 looks at methods of enforcing the homelessness legislation and challenging local authority decisions and Chapter 15 looks at case law decisions based on the legal principles of administrative law. Legal methods are costly and time-consuming and, even if successful, may not necessarily produce the end result of housing the applicant. Local authorities may find that they end up paying large sums to keep people in temporary accommodation such as bed and breakfast pending the outcome of a hearing. If at all possible, both advisers and local authorities should be sufficiently well-versed in both the principles of the legislation and the application of case law to know whether the case is one which can realistically be challenged in law. Acknowledging this can save a lot of time, effort and trauma.

For a case to succeed in judicial review proceedings it is necessary to show a breach of administrative law (see 14.28), or a point of law, if appealing to the county court (see 14.27). This means advisers must check the way the local authority has dealt with the case in question, e.g. whether it has taken all the relevant facts into account, whether it gave the applicant a fair hearing etc. In addition, when dealing with a particular case of homelessness, it is important to try to extract from the surrounding mass of personal details the exact principle at issue. For example, the home may have been lost as a result of various problems which involve rent arrears, alcoholism, and disputes between the partners. Key questions in such a case could be:

• What was the dominant cause of the homelessness?

• Who was responsible for it?

• Was the other partner a party to the actions?

Once questions such as these are isolated, it is possible to refer to case law which has given rulings, for example, on the cause of homelessness and 'acquiescence' of one partner to the other's actions (see Chapter 15).

Even if the personal details are not the same as the reported case, the decision will still be relevant if it can be shown to hinge upon the same principle as the one in question. Where an adviser is acting as an advocate for the applicant and preliminary discussions have failed to change a decision the adviser should:

• Write to the local authority spelling out the legal principle which is to be challenged, e.g. a blanket policy is being operated, or all the relevant facts have not been taken into account. (see 14.28 for an explanation of what constitute breaches of administrative law). Do not rely on emotive arguments about the applicant's circumstances

• Support the argument by reference to case law if a decision has been made on a similar principle to the one in hand. This could include case law where an adverse decision has been made, because it may be possible for an adviser to demonstrate that whilst the same principle of law applies, the circumstances of their client's case differs sufficiently from the case law to warrant a different decision being made.

However, advisers must also bear in mind that the normal time limit for requesting a formal review of the decision is 21 days and so it will usually be appropriate to include a request for a review of the decision if the authority is not prepared to accept the arguments presented. (see 14.26 for details of review procedure).

If the arguments are not successful, they can nevertheless form the basis of the review and any subsequent appeal to the county court. If the decision is not one which carries a right to review it may be necessary to apply for judicial review (see 14.30). The questions above will help to provide the groundwork for the review.

All telephone conversations, interviews or correspondence should be carefully recorded, signed and dated and kept with the applicant's papers. Accurate and unbiased record-keeping is essential if a case finally comes to court.

Similar points hold good for the local authority:

• It should be aware of the principles upon which it has based its decision

• It should be aware of relevant case law and how it relates to the case in hand

• It should keep accurate and unbiased records of all conversations and investigations.

See also 14.24 for a suggested checklist of steps to take in checking homelessness decisions.

Useful Organisations

Advice UK (Federation of
Independent Advice Centres)
12th Floor
New London Bridge House
25 London Bridge St
London
SE1 9ST
Tel 020 7407 4070
www.adviceuk.org.uk

Building Societies Association
3 Savile Row
London
W1S 3PB
Tel 020 7437 0655
www.bsa.org.uk

Child Poverty Action Group
94 White Lion Street
London
N1 9PF
Tel 020 7837 7979
www.cpag.org.uk

Children's Legal Centre
University of Essex
Wivenhoe Park
Colchester
Essex
Co4 3SQ
Tel 01206 873820
www.childrenslegalcentre.com

**Commission for Local Administration
in England** (Local Government
Ombudsman)
Millbank Tower
Millbank
London
SW1P 4QP
Tel 0845 602 1983
www.lso.org.uk

Commission for Racial Equality
Head Office
St Dunstan's House
201-211 Borough High Street
London
SE1 1GZ
Tel 020 7939 0000
www.cre.gov.uk

Council of Mortgage Lenders
3 Savile Row
London
W1S 3PB
Tel 020 7437 0075
www.cml.org.uk

DEFRA (Department of Environment,
Food and Rural Affairs)
Ergon House
17 Smith Square
London
SW1P 3JR
Tel 08459 33 55 77
www.defra.gov.uk

Disability Alliance
Universal House
88-94 Wentworth Street
London E1 7SA
Tel 020 7247 8776
www.disabilityalliance.org

Equal Opportunities Commission
Arndale House
Arndale Centre
Manchester
M4 3EQ
Tel 0845 601 5901
www.eoc.org.uk

Family Rights Group
The Print House
18 Ashwin Street
London
E8 3DL
Tel 020 7923 2628
www.frg.org.uk

**Federation of Black Housing
Organisations**
1 King Edwards Road
London
E9 7SF
Tel 020 8533 7053
www.fbho.org.uk

Gingerbread
7 Sovereign Close
Sovereign Court
London E1W 3HW
Tel 020 7488 9300
www.gingerbread.org.uk

**Home Office
Public Enquiry Team**
Room 856
50, Queen Anne's Gate
London
SW1H 9AT
Tel 0870 000 1585
www.homeoffice.gov.uk

Housing Corporation
Maple House
149 Tottenham Court Road
London
W1T 7BN
Tel 020 7393 2000
www.housingcorp.gov.uk

**Housing Directorate
National Assembly for Wales**
Cathays Park
Cardiff
CF10 3NQ
www.cymru.gov.uk/subihousing

Immigration Advisory Service
3rd Floor, County House
190 Great Dover Street
London
SE1 4YB
Tel 020 7357 7511
www.iasuk.org

**Independent Hosing Ombudsman
Norman House**
105-109 The Strand
London
WC2R 0AA
Tel 020 7836 36 30
www.ihos.org.uk

**Joint Council for the Welfare
of Immigrants**
115 Old Street
London
EC1V 9RT
Tel 020 7251 8708
www.jcwi.org.uk

Law Society
113 Chancery Lane
London
WC2A 1PL
Tel 0207 242 1222
www.lawsoc.org.uk

Law Centres' Federation
The Law Centres Federation
Duchess House
18-19 Warren Street
London
W1T 5LR
Tel 020 7387 8570
www.lawcentres.org.uk

Legal Services Commission
(Legal Aid)
85 Gray's Inn Road
London
WC1X 8TX
Tel 020 7759 0000
www.legalservices.gov.uk

Lesbian and Gay Switchboard
PO Box 7324
London N1 9QS
Tel 020 7837 7324
www.llgs.org.uk

Lord Chancellor's Department
Selborne House
54-60 Victoria Street
London
SW1E 6QW
Tel 020 7210 8500
www.lcd.gov.uk

Men's Aid
Website and email only
Email in first instance to
admin@mensaid.org
www.mensaid.org

NACAB (National Association of
Citizens Advice Bureaux)
Myddleton House
115-123 Pentonville Road
London
N1 9LZ
Tel
www.nacab.org.uk

National Child Protection Helpline
(run by the NSPCC)
PO Box 18222
London
EC2A 3RA
Freephone 0808 800 5000
Textphone 0800 056 0566
www.nspcc.org.uk

Also runs multi-lingual Asian child
Protection Helpline 0800 096 7719

National Debtline
The Arch
48 - 52 Floodgate Street
Birmingham
B5 5SL
Tel 0808 808 4000
www.nationaldebtline.co.uk

**National Council for One
Parent Families**
255 Kentish Town Road
London
NW5 2LX
Tel 020 7428 5400
www.ncopf.org.uk

National Family Mediation
Star House
104-108 Grafton Road
London
NW5 4BD
020 7486 8809
www.nfm.u-net.com

National Housing Federation
175 Gray's Inn Road
London
WC1X 8UP
Tel 020 7278 6571
www.housing.org.uk

OYEZ Stationery Ltd
(Suppliers of legal stationery)
144-146 Fetter Lane
London
EC4 1BT
Tel 020 7405 2847
www.formslink.co.uk

Refugee Council (and Refugee
Advisors Support Unit)
3 Bondway
London SW8 1SJ
Tel 020 7820 3000
www.refugeecouncil.org.uk

Samaritans
The Upper Mill
Kingston Rd
Ewell
Surrey KT17 2 AF
National helpline: 08457 90 90 90
Admin: 020 8394 8300
www.samaritans.org.uk

Refugee Legal Centre
153-157 Commercial Road
London
E1 2DA
Tel 020 7780 3200
www.refugee-legal-centre.org.uk

Relate (National Marriage Guidance)
Herbert Gray College
Little Church Street
Rugby
Warwickshire
CV21 3AP
Tel 0845 456 1310 or 01788 573241
www.relate.org.uk

Rights of Women
52-54 Featherstone Street
London
EC1Y 8RT
Tel 020 7251 6577
www.rightsofwomen.org.uk

Shelter
88 Old Street
London
Tel 020 7505 2000
www.shelter.org.uk

Shelter Cymru
25 Walter Road
Swansea
SA1 5NN
Tel 01792 469400
www.sheltercymru.org.uk

Shelter Scotland
4th Floor, Scotiabank House
6 South Charlotte Street
Edinburgh
EH2 4AW
Tel 0131 473 7170
www.shelterscotland.org.uk

Rights of Women
52-54 Featherstone Street
London EC1Y 8RT
Helpline 020 7251 6577
Tues – Thurs 2-4, Fridays 12 – 2
Admin: 020 7251 6575/6
www.rightsofwomen.org.uk

Survivors of Lesbian Abuse (SOLA)
West Hampstead Women's Centre
55 Hemstal Road,
London NW6 2AD
020 7328 7389
email: solalondon@hotmail.com

Welsh Women's Aid
National Office
38/48 Crwys Road
Cardiff
CF24 4NN
Wales
Tel 029 2039 0874

Women's Aid Federation England
PO Box 391
Bristol
BS99 7WS
Tel 08457 023 468 or 0117 944 4411
www.womensaid.org.uk

Victim Support
PO Box 11431
London SW9 62H
Tel; 0845 30 30 900
www.victimsupport.org.uk

Further reading

Children Act Manual
J. Masson and M. Morris
Sweet and Maxwell 2003

Child Support Handbook
J. McDowell
Eleventh edition;
Child Poverty Action Group 2003

Claims to the Possession of Land
Bryan McGuire
Etal; Tolley 2000

Community Care
L. Clements
Third edition; 2003

Debt Advice Handbook
M. Wolfe
Fifth edition;
Child Poverty Action Group 2002

English Law
K. Smith and D. Keenan
Pitman 1983

**Evans and Smith: The Law
of Landlord and Tenant**
P. F. Smith
Butterworths 2002

Family Breakdown and Insolvency
G. Howell
Butterworths 1993

Family Law
D Bloy
Blackstone Press 1989

**Family Law Domestic Violence and
Occupation of the Family Home**
Law Commission
Report No. 207; HMSO

Family Emergency Procedures
N. Wyld and N. Carlton
Second edition;
Legal Action Group 1998

A Guide to the Housing Act 1996
J. Driscoll
Butterworths 1996

**Guide to Housing Benefit and
Council Tax Benefit 2003/04**
J. Zebedee, M. Ward and S. Lister
Twenty-six edition;
Shelter/CIH 2003

**Homelessness: A Good Practice
Guide**
L. Moroney with J. Goodwin
Shelter 1993

Housing Association Law
A. Alder and C.R. Handy
Second edition;
Sweet and Maxwell 1991

**Immigration, Nationality and
Refugee Law Handbook**
D. Seddon
JCWI 2002

Individual Voluntary Arrangements
S. Lawson
Third edition;
Jordans 1999

Legal Aid Handbook 1998/99
Sweet and Maxwell 1998

Land Law
K. Green and J. Cursley
Fourth edition;
Macmillan 2001

The Law Relating to Cohabitation
M.L. Parry
Third edition;
Sweet and Maxwell 1993

Manual of Housing Law
A. Arden and C. Hunter
Seventh edition;
Sweet and Maxwell 2002

Personal Insolvency: Law and Practice
Berry, Bailey and Schaw-Miller
Butterworths 2001

A Practical Approach to Family Law
J. Black, J. Bridge and T. Bond
Blackstone Press 2000

Property Distribution on Divorce
K.H.P. Wilkinson and M. de Haas
Third edition; Longman 1989

Quiet Enjoyment
A. Arden, QC, D. Carter
and A. Dymond
Sixth edition;
Legal Action Group 2002

Residential Security
J. E. Martin
Sweet and Maxwell 1995

Welfare Benefits and Tax Credits Handbook
Carolyn George
Child Poverty Action Group 2003